THE
EUROPEAN UNION
AND THE
MEMBER STATES

THE
EUROPEAN UNION
AND THE
MEMBER STATES

THIRD EDITION

EDITED BY
ELEANOR E. ZEFF
ELLEN B. PIRRO

LYNNE
RIENNER
PUBLISHERS

BOULDER
LONDON

Published in the United States of America in 2015 by
Lynne Rienner Publishers, Inc.
1800 30th Street, Boulder, Colorado 80301
www.rienner.com

and in the United Kingdom by
Lynne Rienner Publishers, Inc.
3 Henrietta Street, Covent Garden, London WC2E 8LU

Library of Congress Cataloging-in-Publication Data
A Cataloging-in-Publication Record for this book
is available from the Library of Congress.
ISBN: 978-1-62637-256-6

British Cataloguing in Publication Data
A Cataloguing in Publication record for this book
is available from the British Library.

Printed and bound in the United States of America

The paper used in this publication meets the requirements
of the American National Standard for Permanence of
Paper for Printed Library Materials Z39.48-1992.

∞

5 4 3 2 1

*To the future of the EU and
to those young people who may interact
with it in coming years,
including:*

*Nicolas and Alexander Zeff
Louisa, Tessa, and Priscilla Cohen
Xavier and Jennia Wilson
Chance Cleveland*

Contents

Preface

IN 2001 THE FIRST EDITION OF THIS BOOK PIONEERED A NEW WAY of looking at the European Union, a bottom-up approach that focused on how the member states related to and cooperated with the EU's supranational structure. After the EU faced its first major challenge, absorbing ten new member states, we published the second edition of the book in 2006 to consider if any changes were occurring in the way the member states were relating to the EU, again focusing on the member states' views. Now the EU faces other major challenges, or rather a set of challenges. There is of course the financial "meltdown" of the recent recession and the subsequent need to bail out a number of countries, especially Greece. Pulling out of this downturn is an ongoing effort. At the same time, the EU has been confronting a resurgent threat from Russia on its eastern borders, rapidly increasing numbers of immigrants, and the extent of Euro-skepticism within most member states. This third edition addresses the evolving relationships between the EU and its member states as they confront these new issues.

Once again we have collected a group of knowledgeable authors, both returnees and those new to the project, who are able to delineate the nature of the relationship between each European Union nation and the EU itself, examining the strength of the ties, the responses to financial and security difficulties, and the planning for the future. Our authors come from a number of countries, bringing a wealth of knowledge and experience and a wide perspective to the task of exploring where the European Union is heading. We also provide a history of EU theorizing and propose a reconsideration of confederalism as a way forward to explain the relationships between the member states and the EU. The resulting volume represents another step toward a better understanding of the nature of the union that binds the EU and the member states.

We would like to thank some special people who have helped immensely with the preparation of this latest volume. First, we would like to thank Matthew Herman for his work on the bibliography. Second, there are a number of people who helped with the manuscript, including: Laura Poole, Steve Barr, and Alejandra Wilcox. We especially want to thank our editor and publisher, Lynne Rienner, for supporting our work through all three volumes. To our families, especially Bob Zeff and Chris and Clay Cleveland, we appreciate your ongoing support. To all we say, "Thank you."

—Eleanor E. Zeff and Ellen B. Pirro

THE
EUROPEAN UNION
AND THE
MEMBER STATES

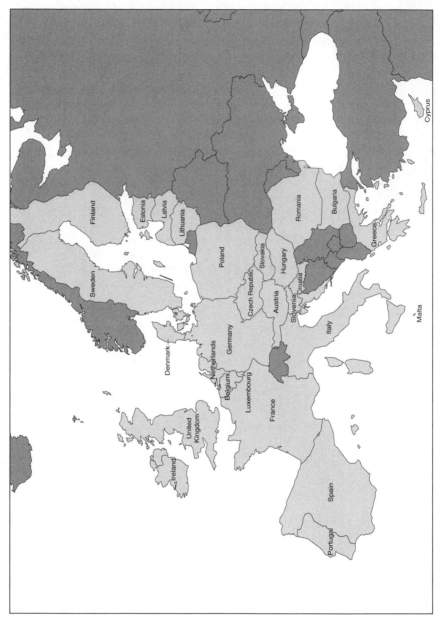

The European Union, 2015

1

Introduction

Eleanor E. Zeff and Ellen B. Pirro

THE EUROPEAN UNION IS CONSTANTLY CHANGING: UPDATING INSTI-
tutions and regulations, expanding with new members, and often defying
scholars as they attempt to explain it. The focus of this book is on the relationships between the EU and its member states, an essential key to understanding how the EU operates. This book is now in its third edition and has
observed the changes to the EU and the member states from 1998 to 2014.
This initial chapter reviews the evolution of the EU as it has grown toward
"Ever Closer Union."[1]

Facing Crises

Since its creation, the EU has experienced a number of crises. Current major
crises include the aftermath of the 2008 economic crisis in Europe, the potential upheaval caused by the Greek financial difficulties, and the ongoing
problems in Ukraine with its implications for Europe's energy future and relations with Russia. These issues have proven so difficult that some people
have gone so far as to question the fundamental viability of the Union. Relationships between the EU and its member states have become topics of
great interest, as have the theoretical notions of confederation and federalism to explain recent EU developments.

The European Union has been around since 1958 (see Table 1.1), and
remains unique among political and international institutions. On one hand,
it received the Nobel Peace Prize in 2012 for its success in keeping peace in
Europe. On the other hand, in 2008, it experienced economic and financial
crises, with significant sovereign debt problems in several member states
(Greece, Portugal, Spain, etc.) as well as other Eurozone and financial complications. Currently, it is fighting to recover. Similarly, Ukraine's attempts

Table 1.1 The Ever Wider Union

Original Member States (1958)	First Enlargement (1973)	Second Enlargement (1981)	Third Enlargement (1986)	Fourth Enlargement (1995)	Fifth Enlargement (2004)	Most Recent Enlargements
Belgium	Britain	Greece	Spain	Austria	Czech Rep.	Romania(2007)
France	Denmark		Portugal	Finland	Cyprus	Bulgaria(2007)
Germany	Ireland			Sweden	Hungary	Croatia (2013)
Italy					Estonia	
Luxembourg					Latvia	
Netherlands					Lithuania	
					Malta	
					Poland	
					Slovakia	
					Slovenia	

to move closer to Europe provoked Russia to annex the Crimea and resulted in ongoing fighting in eastern Ukraine and Ukrainian government bailouts. Russian military thrusts in the area, by air and land, and threats to Europe's supplies of oil and natural gas have put the EU in potential peril. Other foreign affairs crises are also dangers to the EU as a supranational entity as well as several of its individual member states. Today, the ISIS (Islamic State of Iraq and Syria) crisis in the Middle East threatens European nations as diverse as Sweden and Italy. The Muslim inflow into Europe, much of it illegal, has had major effects on most EU member states. Citizens who leave to fight for Islamic jihad may return to terrorize European states and add more impediments to economic growth and states' abilities to recover from economic and other crises.

A Bottom-up Approach

How the EU responds to and directs its members sheds light on its operations and future potential. As new states join, the relationships between states change, as do relations between the states and the EU institutions. Some events have strengthened the EU, whereas the recent crises demonstrated weaknesses and led to fears of abandonment of the euro and a restructuring of the EU. Despite crises throughout much of Europe, additional states are still applying to join, and no state has withdrawn, either from the EU or from the Eurozone, once becoming a member. However, Euro-skepticism has increased in many member states and emerged in new ones, and scholars are daring to ask if the EU, and especially the euro, will be viable in the future.

This third edition of the *EU and the Member States* takes a bottom-up approach (as did the previous editions), to explain how the EU functions. Taken together, the three editions constitute an excellent overview of the changing relations of the member states and the EU institutions over a more than fifteen-year period. Each volume stands alone and gives a slice of the picture for a particular period of time. This current volume focuses on the period between 2007 and 2014, when Europe has faced a number of crises but has continued to grow and expand its mandates over its members. A major premise is that we cannot understand the EU unless we also know what is happening at the state and regional levels of governance.

Development of a Union of European States
The Early Post–World War II Years
Researchers have long suggested that a united Europe would put an end to centuries of war. Even as early as 1946, Winston Churchill called for a "United States of Europe,"[2] and by the early 1950s, Jean Monnet began to push for the development of greater unity among the states in Europe, reached gradually and achieved incrementally.[3] The implementation of the Marshall Plan encouraged European states to work together for mutual benefits, and the beginning of the Cold War further increased pressures for joint efforts. The old League of Nations and the new United Nations served as models for functional unions as well as examples for problems that arise when individual states work together in international organizations.[4] By the late 1940s, many Europeans were thinking about new methods of integration. Encouraged by US advisers, Europeans established the Organisation for European Economic Co-operation (OEEC) in 1947 to facilitate cooperation among states and meet the prerequisites to receive Marshall aid. In 1948, the Council of Europe opened another attempt at European integration. Decisionmaking in these two organizations remained intergovernmental following a more "unionist" rather than federalist pattern. Monnet and others recognized that relations between Germany and France had to be normalized and cooperative before any meaningful union could develop. By 1958, it became obvious that the OEEC had failed to further unite Europe as had been hoped, but efforts at integration continued with the Organisation for Economic Co-operation and Development (OECD), started in Paris in 1948.[5]

The Coal and Steel Community and the Treaties of Rome: A Different Kind of Union
The Schuman Declaration of 1950 laid out an innovative plan for Franco-German pooling of coal and steel production managed by a joint high authority. Other states willing to pool their resources for mutual benefits and relinquish state control over this industry could also join. The declaration set the stage for further economic cooperation in other functional areas. By 1952, six states had signed the Treaty of Paris and created the European Coal and Steel Community (ECSC). The treaty stated rules for the six member states—

France, Germany, Italy, the Netherlands, Belgium, and Luxembourg—to follow that changed the way states in Europe interacted. The six states were willing to collaborate and give up sovereignty over decisionmaking for The Coal and Steel Community (this is the proper name of this organization) because they saw that earlier attempts at integration, such as the OEEC, were not effectively bringing Europe together. To promote the public's well-being and their states' economic development, they gambled on a different approach to European integration.

In 1958, these nations ratified the Treaty of Rome and joined together to form the European Community (EC), a combination of the ECSC, Euratom, and the European Economic Community, with cooperation emphasized over intergovernmental decisions. Britain declined to join because it still had commonwealth responsibilities and was wary of losing sovereignty. At the time, its relations with France were strained, and cooperation would have been difficult. The original six members had time to learn to work together before any new members joined in 1973. Achieving closer union was not always easy or even assured. Some strain among the original members and between the members and the EC became apparent during the "empty chair crisis" when Charles de Gaulle was absent, and a joint decision was made in the Luxembourg Compromise to return to a mostly unanimous voting system.

Adding New Members and Continuing Efforts to Deepen European Integration

In 1973, in the post–de Gaulle era in France, three new states were finally able to join in the first enlargement. These new member states were the UK, Ireland, and Denmark, often known as the reluctant member states because their relations with the European Union are often strained. The UK remains skeptical of the EU, desiring a looser, less deep union that does not take away its sovereignty and threatening to call a national referendum to withdraw.[6] Denmark voted "no" in its referendum on the 1992 Treaty of European Union (TEU or Maastricht Treaty), and it later voted against joining the Eurozone. Eric Einhorn and Jessica Erfer called Denmark a "hotbed of Euro-skepticism" and a "pragmatic skeptic."[7] Ireland's economy was so tied to Britain that its membership was an economic necessity, but entry into the EU has allowed Ireland to shift its balance of trade from the UK to the EU. Neither Denmark nor the UK uses the euro, but Ireland does and was able to draw on EU resources when its banks went into crisis after the recession of 2008.

The second enlargement occurred in 1981 with the entry of Greece. Originally Greece, Portugal, and Spain began negotiations together as the southern tier countries, but agricultural talks between Spain and France proved difficult, so Greece acceded first, with Spain and Portugal admitted in 1986. Membership for Greece was generally positive in the early years, despite the fact that its economy was highly affected, and its industries had to compete internationally without protection.[8] Spain and Portugal had a harder time acceding to the Union. Both countries had just ended authoritarian governments, and had to prove their democratic credentials, so joining took over ten years.[9] The two countries had to agree to a ten-year waiting period for full entry into the common market. All three new member states were significantly less wealthy than the earlier members, except Ireland, so their incorporation into the EC was stressful and changed the relationships among the member states. The budget faced multiple readjustments, especially in the agricultural sector. With twelve members, unanimous decisions became more difficult to achieve, and it became evident the EC institutions needed reorganization.

In 1986, the member states negotiated and signed the Single European Act (SEA). The act set a January 1, 1993, deadline to better harmonize national production standards and ease decisionmaking by allowing qualified majority voting (QMV). This ruling helped the EC pass more legislation that was beneficial to the member states. The TEU was ratified in 1993, and the EC became the European Union (EU), facilitating freer trade and movement of goods and services when trade barriers between and among states were removed. With the TEU came the new "three-pillar" system, an attempt to clarify the areas of integration among the member states and the EU institutions. Within a few years the Treaty of Amsterdam was signed, opening up more areas of potential cooperation among the member states, such as immigration, visas, refugees, and more judicial issues. After this intense period of rapid integration, some states began to pull back, request "opt outs" for various areas of legislation, or manifest other types of protests. In 2001, Ireland refused to ratify the Treaty of Nice until its policy of neutrality was reconfirmed. These various special considerations and opt outs allowed states to have differing levels of cooperation with the EU institutions and regulations.

In the 1990s, negotiations began for the entry of three more member states, and Austria, Sweden, and Finland gained entry into the EU in 1995, bringing membership to a total of fifteen states. Sweden was a somewhat reluctant candidate as it had very strong environmental protections and other welfare benefits that would have to be lowered to keep their industries competitive with other member states. Austria also had environmental problems and feared its delicate Alpine environment would be endangered because of the increased traffic through the Alps. Finland was very pro-Europe at the time and happy to join, even though changes would be necessary to the executive power distribution between its president and prime minister. Austria and Finland both accepted the euro in 2002, but Sweden did not.

Developments in the Twenty-First Century:
New Members, the Lisbon Treaty, the Euro, and Crises
The great EU expansion occurred in 2004 with eight former Soviet states: the Czech Republic, Hungary, Slovakia, Slovenia, Latvia, Lithuania, Esto-

nia, and Poland joined along with Malta and Cyprus. Up to the last moment, it had been unclear whether Cyprus could accede into the EU because it is a divided island, with the majority of territory in Greek Cypriot hands and some of the island under Turkish Cypriot control. Greece pushed hard for its entry, and it met the other requirements of democratic governance (in the Greek part) and a capitalist economy.

The addition of the postcommunist and island member states, all with different backgrounds from the earlier members, changed the dynamics of relations among the EU member states and between the EU and the states. These changing relations demonstrated a need for restructuring to streamline and democratize as well as harmonize relations among the member states. The European Council and the heads of government agreed to a new constitutional treaty by the end of 2004, but it was impossible to get the required unanimous agreement from the member states. France and the Netherlands feared the treaty would further erode their sovereignty, and both states voted in referenda against ratification in 2005. Bulgaria and Romania joined the EU in 2007 and a revised "reform treaty" began its rounds, modifying the aims of closer union, but proposing reforms to streamline the EU's operations and the relations among the states. These reforms included eliminating the three-pillar system, strengthening the European Parliament to improve its democratic image, and establishing a presidency and a more unified structure to represent it internationally.

The Lisbon Treaty faced considerable controversy before ratification. The Czech Republic worried about the effect the treaty would have on its relations with Germany and was allowed to opt out. The Irish voted "no" in 2008, and the French had only a "petit oui" vote. Despite continuing opposition, all the states ultimately ratified the treaty, and it went into force in 2009. Although the EU sought closer integration, the individual member states were still able to keep a lot of sovereignty. The Lisbon Treaty made several major changes to the EU, namely, giving the European Parliament more power and creating an EU presidency and a new department for foreign affairs, all with the idea of increasing EU integration, streamlining its decisionmaking and the relations among its member states, and creating more integrative "European" policies.[10]

By 2002, the euro[11] as a currency became official, even though only twelve of the fifteen member states joined the Eurozone at that time, and accession negotiations were ongoing with several states and especially intense with the ten candidate states about to join the EU in 2004. Eighteen of the current twenty-eight member states, most recently Latvia, had adopted the euro as their currency by 2015. Between 2008 and 2015, a number of financial crises led to government changes and riots in Greece, Ireland, Portugal, Spain, and other EU member states that called into question the viability of the euro as well as the relations of several EU member states. The profound worldwide economic slowdown, which began in 2007, led to recession throughout the EU, with some countries experiencing deeper problems than others. A slow, very gradual recovery began around 2012 and continued into 2013. However, for a variety of reasons, at the end of 2014, some EU member states had once more slipped into recession.

The ongoing and serious problem of unemployment in the EU increased, for persons aged fifteen to sixty-four, in most of the member states (except Germany) and peaked in 2008, according to a EU Labor Force survey.[12] This decrease, of 1.7 percentage points, during the global financial crisis was halted in 2011 when there was a small increase in the EU-27 employment rate, to 64.3 percent.[13]

Economic and euro crises in Greece, Portugal, and Ireland not only caused changes to sitting governments but also led to economic restructuring and considerable downsizing in many of the member states. While the EU sought to reform its banking and finance structure in light of the global financial crisis, in other areas the Union continued to grow and develop. The EU has worked with the states of the former Yugoslavia to stabilize their situations. Similarly, the first foreign secretary, Lady Catherine Ashton, chaired the Iranian nuclear talks and the Syrian peace talks, and EU leaders have been instrumental as mediators in a number of potential and actual conflict situations, notably Georgia and Ukraine. In 2012, the EU received the Nobel Peace Prize for its record of promoting peace in Europe for over sixty years. Croatia entered the EU in 2013, and there are other states still hoping to enter, notably Serbia, Bosnia and Herzegovina, Montenegro, and Kosovo. It appears that the EU has the potential to continue integrating Europe.

Theoretical Explanations for the European Union over the Years

Functionalism

As the EU has evolved, so have a series of explanations for its continued existence and successes. The addition of each new member state leads to changes in the relationships among the member states and between the states and the EU institutions. Each new accession necessitates a reevaluation of past theory and the development of new theoretical explanations for European integration.

In its early days, functionalism was the preferred explanation for how Europe would integrate its member states.[14] Indeed, there is evidence that Robert Schuman, credited as the father of the EU, championed the idea that starting small would lead to spillover into other areas and inevitably to European integration. Beginning with the coal and steel industries, cooperation in one functional area would move to other industries, including whole areas of commerce and trade with the ultimate result of spillover into political areas, leading to one Europe. As the European experiment grew, functionalism developed into neofunctionalism. All the variations of functionalism see the nation-state continuing to play a major role in any integrated model. However, the neofunctionalists see the growth of the European Commission as changing the basic nature of the relationship between states and the EU. Member states are inevitably drawn into more common activities, as bureaucrats take the basic common functions and nurture them into growth and development. The ultimate result, say the neofunctionalists, is that it becomes ever easier for member states to assign functions to the EU and give up more of their own sovereignty. The ultimate objective is to spill over from the economic sphere into the political one, but functionalists concede this is a long process.[15]

Intergovernmentalism

Andrew Moravcsik[16] takes the international relations theory of realism and applies it to European integration. His volume, *A Choice for Europe*, develops the theory of intergovernmentalism, a new approach to the integration of European states. This theoretical approach arrives on the scene after the accession of Great Britain, Denmark, and Ireland. These three countries each have many concerns about joining the EU and losing sovereignty. Their accession was dictated by economic imperative—the need for European trade—rather than a desire to be a part of an integrated Europe. To this day, these states continue to express their reluctance to agree to new EU integrative policies and give up any more sovereignty. Britain is actively seeking renegotiation of its relationship with the EU, and Denmark ranks as one of the highest in Euro-skepticism.

For Moravcsik, nation-states are the most important and central units. He believed that the EU was nothing more than a group of states coming together for rational purposes—the growth of trade and economic development. The success of the single market and high levels of intra-European trade seemed to bear out his theories. The relationship between the EU and its member states should only be what each state chose to do in common, not a supranational unit moving toward complete integration. The goal of the member states was domestic well-being and cooperation in trade, finance, transport, and other economic zones, not a union of states.

Intergovernmentalism in Europe means that the member states develop their goals internally, from decisions taken at the national political level, in policies derived from negotiated outcomes of domestic coalitions. These national leaders take their policy goals to the supranational, the EU level, where they try to achieve as many of them as possible, although they invariably have to compromise. Each nation tries to maximize its gains. Naturally the larger, more advanced nations tend to gain more and the smaller, less developed countries get less. The EU provides payoffs for cooperation, even for the smallest members, with benefits such as structural funds—

money set aside for development. Moravcsik says that in the absence of high levels of trust among the member states, EU institutions were created to be sure all states kept their bargains.[17]

It was natural that intergovernmentalism would lead to several variations, some of which go beyond its basic premises. A number of these have been widely used in recent decades. One of them, institutionalism, suggests that the creation of one institution after another to handle each new area of growth would lead to a whole that was more than the sum of its parts.[18] Moravscik's idea was that institutions would occasionally be created to monitor compliance with agreements among the states. The institutionalists go beyond this in two ways. First, institutions multiplied to handle the new policy areas coming under EU governance. Second, these institutions make regulations, which are binding on the member states. These regulations help keep the states in order and facilitate monitoring the institutions.

Another variation, rational choice, is based on national behaviors in the supranational negotiations, which are considered to be totally self-serving and devoid of common purpose.[19] For the rational choice theorists, nation-states are calculating, totally rational units, which try to maximize gains in any and every international gathering. Cooperation is minimal and occurs only when it doesn't cost the state too much and there is something significant to be gained. Rational choice has become very popular because it easily lends itself to the analysis of cause and effect sequences in state behaviors.

Multilevel Governance

Multilevel governance, a newer perspective, emerged from the heavy criticism that intergovernmentalism received.[20] This theoretical perspective suggests that the EU operates within a series of levels—local, regional, national, and supranational—which interact and produce outcomes with differing impacts at different levels. One major question for research is what level handles what questions? Some suggest that nations no longer handle the tough issues but leave them to the European Union. Others believe that the EU wants to resolve issues at the lowest levels of government in a process known as subsidiarity. There has been a concerted effort by the European Commission to bypass the national level and deal directly with the regions, especially when dealing with development issues and allotting the structural funds, which are intended to help the most backward of regions catch up with the more advanced regions.

The national level is one "analytic stage"[21] at which the various activities of the EU member states can be analyzed. It is only one of several such stages and by no means the most important. There are multiple different combinations, considering that there are a number of different stages, each with a number of units that can interact with the EU institutions and each other. These interactions become dense networks. Thus, a member state not only interacts with the supranational EU level and other national levels but also with the subnational entities, regions, and even lesser units. The nation-state is still very important in this perspective. The question for the state and the other analytic units is how to distribute and share the authority and responsibilities for governance activities with the EU. States negotiate outcomes with the EU, and accountability is a major issue. The EU does not possess enforcement mechanisms. Nor does it have the power to demand funding or tax its members, leaving member states in a powerful position vis-à-vis the EU institutions. There is the suggestion that competition occurs at the state level, and cooperation happens when the EU gets involved.

Other Theoretical Perspectives

Social constructivism has held sway in contemporary international relations and been applied by several scholars to explain the European Union's integration. Notably, the work of Thomas Risse, derived from this perspective, focuses on the "Europeanization" of EU citizens and the development of a EU identity.[22] We note that social constructivism takes elements of the prior theories discussed and utilizes them in its discussion. One type of social constructive theorizing is discourse analysis. Discursive theorists such as Vivian Schmidt and Ole Waever use discourse analysis to examine some of the major questions of EU policy.[23] There is a general feeling that discourse analysis is more methodology than theory. Social constructivism today is regarded as more of an approach than a fully developed theory.

Federalism and Feminist Theories

EU theorizing also includes federalism, which referred in the early years of European integration to a kind of "United States of Europe" with power distributed between the European and nation-state levels and institutions, but where the "union" had sovereignty over important areas such as defense, foreign policy, and fiscal and monetary affairs.[24] A federal explanation did not take hold in the early years of the EU, but has recently been used to frame discussions about relations between the EU and its institutions and the member states, as well as to compare the EU with other federal unions.[25]

Finally, there are the feminists, who feel that discussion of the EU needs to take a women's perspective into account, especially in the development of the EU's institutions.[26] It is seen as particularly appropriate for the discussion of the EU because of its emphasis on cooperation, a major feminist approach. Yet gender theorists, including feminists, seem to offer more of a perspective and not a fully developed theory for European integration.[27]

Confederalism

What about a confederal model for Europe? John McCormick notes that the European Union is frequently described as a confederation in all but name.[28] A confederal model or a confederation is a "union of states in which each member state retains some independent control over internal and external affairs. A federation, in contrast, is a union of states in which external affairs are controlled by a unified, central government."[29] Both federations and confederations are unions that are based on treaties (*foedus* = treaty) between states, and "the union established by the foedus or treaty is represented not simply by a single person, but by some form of assembly, congress, diet or council of the states that create the union."[30]

Many dismiss confederations as too loosely structured to effectively bind states together under a common governance that can solve political problems and meet political demands. Researchers, such as Frederick Lister, who described a confederation as a union of states, found very little written about confederalism,[31] and McCormick cites a lack of confederal models compared with federal models to use for comparison.[32] Yet there have been some forms of confederation in the past; the US confederation was one example,[33] but also the Swiss and Dutch confederations,[34] which both lasted for several centuries, demonstrating that confederations can provide solutions to bringing states together, while also offering models for comparison.[35]

Another problem with confederations is that the relationships among the states differ considerably, making them hard to analyze, recognize, or even distinguish from some forms of federations. In addition, the relationship between the member states and the central government, and the distribution of powers among the member states, vary greatly. Confederations may operate like intergovernmental organizations, and even allow states to secede from them. Because there is no set pattern of joint action that confederations follow, comparisons and modeling are more difficult for researchers and other confederations to do. However, the looseness of the model allows wide variations among the members, and provides states greater flexibility to join and cooperate together, an advantage that many European states may find attractive.

Recently, EU specialists have begun to rethink the possibilities of confederalism, especially in relation to the development of the European Union.[36] In his book *Unions of States: The Theory and Practice of Confederation*, Murray Forsyth adopted a historical approach to the study of confederalism and noted from these studies that it offered an opportunity for diverse states to integrate and coexist peacefully.[37] Since peace was a priority for European states and citizens in the 1950s, this form of governance was appealing, especially if achieved with a minimum loss of sovereignty for the member states.

What is a confederation? Is a confederation just a loose form of federation, and do confederations eventually turn into federal governments? Perhaps, instead, confederations should be studied as distinct forms of governance on their own. We could then consider the possibility that the EU is more of a confederation than a federation, and that its end goal could be confederation, rather than supposing that the EU should ultimately become a federation. These considerations reveal a different kind of understanding about the EU and its relations with and among its member states.

Various ideas exist about what would allow a confederation to work, and these ideas suggest the necessity for some interest of primary importance to all the members, such as defending against a common enemy or promoting a common cause, such as freer trade or economic growth through interdependent actions. The presence of a common interest is a key for the unity of any confederation, but the success of a confederation, especially one that can accommodate heterogeneity and initiate integration, also depends on the members' "will to confederate," tolerance of different views, and desire to cooperate. McCormick's definition, which takes into account earlier explanations, is that a confederation is "an administrative system in which independent states come together for reasons of security, efficiency, or mutual convenience, retaining the powers that they consider best reserved to themselves, and working together through joint institutions on matters best dealt with together such as foreign, trade and security policy."[38] In a confederal governance model, the citizens relate to the central government via their individual states, rather than directly to the joint government.[39] This definition seems to fit the creation and functioning of the European Union and how it relates to its member states.

States must be willing to join such a confederation. They are more likely to do so when they realize they have interests in common with other possible members and that there are considerable benefits to be gained. Such common interests could be defensive needs against a common enemy or economic interdependency. The presence of the common interest, stressed by the authors writing in this volume, is vital for the unity of the confederation. To the extent that confederalism can accommodate heterogeneity in peace and initiate integration, it relies much on the will to confederate, a will shared by all ethnic groups and their politicians. The will to confederate means the attitude of tolerance, the willingness to cooperate, and a desire for peace.

The Views of the Member States

Chapters 1 and 2 ask several questions: what is the relationship of each member state to the EU, and what does the EU do for each state? How has the financial crisis affected each member state, and what are their positions about the ongoing economic problems? How have foreign crises, specifically the problems with Russia, affected the member states and what are the prospects for tackling foreign affairs crises in the future? What is the level of support for the EU in the member state, and how has the growth of Euroskepticism manifested itself? What institutional form will the EU adopt in the future? Will it ever arrive at a full federation, or will it remain as a multilevel governance or functional institution or evolve into a more formal confederation? Although we may not be able to arrive at concrete answers to these questions, it is important to ask them.

Chapter 3 describes Germany as the pivot on which much of the EU depends. It is seen as the strength of Europe with its massive economy, which has withstood the economic crisis and regained its industrial might. Yet Germany has weaknesses, although not as major as those pointed out in Chapter 4 on France, which has failed to take advantage of reform possibilities and now finds itself in difficulties. Ireland (Chapter 8) has managed to emerge from the fiscal crisis and repaid the EU, but as Richard B. Finnegan points out, it needs to stimulate economic growth. This is unlike Spain and Portugal, which remain on the edges of economic difficulties and poor prospects for growth as seen in Chapter 11. Chapters 9, 13, and 14 indicate that the Scandinavian nations of Denmark, Sweden, and Finland are emerging from the economic slowdown. But they face growing Euro-skepticism and new political parties and interests, as is happening also in Austria. Yet as Chapter 12 indicates, there is currently no serious discussion of a major change of policy toward European integration in Austria, and the country remains committed to the euro and the EU.

Eastern Europe was affected less by the economic crisis and more by the Ukrainian problems. The Baltic States are afraid of a resurgent Russia. Yet Latvia has joined the Eurozone, and all three states (Latvia, Lithuania, and Estonia) have made significant economic progress as discussed in Chapter 20. Poland (Chapter 15), the Czech Republic (Chapter 17), and Slovakia (Chapter 18) are emerging from the fiscal slowdown in reasonable shape. Poland is doing exceptionally well and did not experience much of an economic crisis. These three states were, however, affected by decreases in demands from their major trading partner, Germany. With the exception of Poland, there seems to be a rise of Euro-skepticism in these states, and newer right-wing parties have developed, as seen in recent national and European elections. Slovenia and Slovakia are discussed in Chapter 18, and although Slovakia has made somewhat surprising development, Slovenia is doing less well than expected and has experienced more difficulties during the economic crises. All four states have been impacted by the Russian-Ukrainian crisis and fear a cutoff of their energy supplies. In contrast, Chapter 16 demonstrates that Hungary is pursuing a totally different path, one that deviates considerably from the rest of the EU. It is supporting Russia and sees it as an alternative model to the EU. Hungary did not experience the surge of economic well-being the other nations enjoyed in 2004 and is highly Euro-skeptic as a result. The UK (Chapter 7) and Denmark (Chapter 9) are the other more Euro-skeptic nations. Greece continues with its problems (Chapter 10), and the "no" vote in the July 5, 2015, referendum poses challenges to the existing structure of the EU and the credibility of the euro. Zahariadis suggests that the lack of leadership on both sides is exacerbating the confusion. There is some suggestion in Chapter 5 that Italy has lost its direction and is pursuing prestige power positions in the EU hierarchy over national economic interests. The Benelux countries (Belgium, the Netherlands, and Luxembourg; Chapter 6) remain resolutely pro-European although there has been a noticeable rise in right-wing parties, which support nationalist views and anti-immigration policies. The smaller states of the EU, Malta and Cyprus (Chapter 19), Slovenia, and Croatia (Chapter 22), are struggling with the economic slowdown and depend heavily on Germany. As Chapter 21 points out, Bulgaria and Romania continue as the most corrupt states in Europe and progress is slow, but trust in the EU institutions remains surprisingly high. Their greatest export is their young people, as is Croatia's, and they continue to emigrate westward in large numbers. Bulgaria in particular is dependent on Russian energy. Each chapter recounts different tales of European progress, and the concluding Chapter 23 recaps the relations between the EU and its member states and revisits the questions of Chapters 1 and 2 concerning which model the EU will follow in the future: federal, multilevel, or confederal. What is notable is that despite the crises, the normal, day-to-day activities of the EU continue, and the benefits of economic linkages are apparent in the greatly increased trade and growth of the EU average income. For many of the 28 member states, the EU remains the best option for future development, despite its problems and the constraints it places on them.

Conclusions: The Book's Perspective

The European Union is continuously evolving. So are the member states, and thus so are the relations between the EU and the member states and among the member states. Understanding these complex relationships is key to analyzing and explaining the EU's development. If we consider that confederation is a logical way to describe the state of the EU today, we can look at the nature of the relationship between the EU and its members in a new light, which allows for more explanations about the EU's development and direction. This volume explores the evolving relations among the 28 member states in the EU. We expect to gain more understanding about the Union as we look at how the states are reacting to the various crises that have recently occurred. A union that can stay together during the bad times and find creative solutions to its problems should become stronger, especially if states become used to working together and helping each other. Indications are that the EU will not disappear, but it could become less effective. Its policymaking ability could decrease. As the EU gets larger, will it federalize, confederalize, or dissolve? In addition to how the member states react to each other and to the EU, we also ask how each member state feels about its membership and its ideal union. Studying the member states individually and their relationships with the EU should help us better gauge the strength of the Union and its future direction and form.

Notes

1. Dinan (2006).
2. Churchill (1949), p. 197.
3. Monnet (1976).
4. The League of Nations had required unanimous voting for passing policy, and this requirement crippled the League by making it too hard to make decisions. See Ginsberg (2010)). Functional institutions associated with the UN included the International Monetary Fund (IMF) and the General Agreement on Tariffs and Trade (GATT).
5. Dinan (1999), pp. 10, 15, 19.
6. Since 2010, under David Cameron's Conservative and Liberal Democratic Coalition government, Great Britain has been trying to renegotiate its relationship with the EU.
7. Einhorn and Erfer (2006), p. 173.
8. Markou, Nakos, and Zahariadis (2006), p. 218.
9. Roy and Kanner, (2001).
10. See Lisbon Treaty at http://ec.europa.eu/archives/lisbon_treaty/index_en.htm (accessed March 11, 2014), for more information about this volatile period and the reforms the treaty introduced, such as a stronger European Parliament.
11. The euro is the single currency shared by (currently) eighteen of the EU member states, which together make up the euro area. The introduction of the euro in 1999 was a major step in European integration: more than 333 million EU citizens now use it as their currency.
12. European Union Labour Force Survey, Annual Results, issue number 14/20/2013, released July 2013 (accessed March 2014). This publication presents the main results of the EU Labour Force Survey for the EU-27 as a whole and for all member states for 2012.
13. Ibid.
14. Haas (1968).
15. Niemann and Schmitter (2004), pp. 46–47.
16. Moravcsik (1998).
17. Ibid.
18. Aspinwall and M. Schneider (2001).
19. Pollack (2003).
20. Hooghe and Marks (2001).
21. Ibid.
22. Risse (2001).
23. Schmidt (2006); Waever, (1998).
24. Ginsberg (2010), p. 65.
25. Ibid. For more discussion about federalism and the EU, see Fabbrini (2007), Goldstein (2001), and Buonanno and Nugent (2013). See also Majone (2006).
26. Hoskyns (2004), pp. 217–236.
27. For more information on all of these theoretical perspectives, the reader is encouraged to consult one of several excellent reviews of EU theory, such as Wiener and Dietz (2004) and Caporaso (1998).
28. McCormick (2011), p. 38.

29. Xiaokun Song, "Confederalism. A Review of Recent Literature," chapter 8, part 4: Federalism, Confederalism and Consociationalism. Available at http://poli.vub.ac.be /publi/orderbooks/federal/08song.pdf (accessed March 11, 2014).

30. Ibid.

31. Lister (1996).

32. McCormick (2011), p. 38.

33. Wallace (1982).

34. Hamilton and Madison, *The Federalist*.

35. Germany also had a confederation with a shared Federal Assembly and a common army, which lasted from 1815 to 1866.

36. Elazar (1998).

37. Forsyth (1981).

38. McCormick (2011), p. 36.

39. See McCormick (2013) and the Confederal vs. the Federal Model (Comparing federations and confederations) in Figure 1 p. 28, in *Why Europe Matters*, New York: NY: Palgrave MacMillan, 2013, p. 28.

2

What Is the European Union?

John McCormick

TO UNDERSTAND THE RELATIONSHIP BETWEEN THE EUROPEAN
Union (EU) and its member states, we ideally need a sound grasp of the
personalities of the partners involved. Unfortunately, pinning down and
agreeing on the meaning of the EU is a goal that has eluded scholars and
political leaders for decades. Not only has its character and reach changed
constantly over time, but numerous troubling questions face the EU as it
struggles to address the ongoing fallout from the crisis in the Eurozone, reflected in growing political and public doubts about the value and efficiency
of European integration.

Understanding the twenty-eight member states of the EU presents relatively few challenges. They contain all the conventional features of sovereign
states, including geographical territory, authority over that territory, political
independence, and legitimacy under international law. In terms of administration, most are unitary states with the bulk of power focused at the national
level, whereas some are federal states in which power is shared between national and local governments. But agreeing how best to understand the European Union is much less easy, if only because the conventional vocabulary of
political science, tied as it is to the state and interstate systems, seems unable
effectively to capture its personality.[1]

The precursor of today's EU was the European Economic Community
(EEC, 1958–1992), which was best understood as a free trade area with many
of the standard features of an international organization: voluntary cooperation, communal management, shared interests, and the use of institutions that
were designed to manage and coordinate policy while enjoying few if any independent powers.[2] The member states of the EEC were clearly free-standing
members of a club, were still politically and legally independent, were seen

by other states in individual rather than collective terms, and were free to leave the club if they wished.

The EU today is much more than a conventional international organization: it has greater reach and consequences, and it imposes deeper obligations on its member states. They still have their own national governments and make much national law and policy, but their freedom of action has been constrained by the demands of membership of the EU, and in some areas of policy, notably trade and competition, the EU is now better understood as a single unit. Just how far we can take that understanding, and how we should thus regard the EU, is debatable.

Much of the scholarly debate about the EU has come out of the field of international relations, which focuses on the ties among the member states and is interested in the extent to which the EU is still mainly intergovernmental or supranational. The former concept sees the EU as a meeting place in which representatives from the member states negotiate with each other in an attempt to achieve a consensus and pursue state interests while paying less attention to the broader interests of the community of states. The latter concept also sees the EU as the meeting place of the representatives of the member states but is based on the assumption that governments compromise state interests in the common good and transfer authority to institutions that work in the interests of the EU as a whole.

Since the 1990s, there has been more consideration, influenced by the thinking of scholars in the fields of comparative politics and public policy, of the EU as a political system in its own right.[3] But there are concerns about the absence of an unequivocal system of EU government and questions about the significance of this absence. While many Europeans have long hoped for the development of a federal United States of Europe, many others, in increasing numbers, oppose such a notion. Although there are federal qualities to the EU, it still falls short of the kind of federalism we see at work in the United States, Germany, Canada, or other federal systems.

Yet another option is to simply think of the EU as sui generis, or unique. In this spirit, Jacques Delors, the former president of the European Commission, is reputed once to have described the EU as an "unidentified political object." Although this would seem to create a new category into which to place the EU, it still begs the question of how and why it is unique. Having a category that contains just one example creates many analytical problems: to say simply that the EU is different without explaining the differences, for political scientists anyway, abrogates responsibility.

Sitting in the background of the debate about the EU is a fourth option that is routinely overlooked, yet which handily steers us away from the kind of federal Europe that so many oppose while offering an explanation that nicely summarizes most of the key features of the EU today. This is to think of the EU as a confederal system, or one in which member states come together to cooperate in areas of mutual convenience without creating a new level of government. Confederal institutions are relatively weak and the bulk of decisionmaking authority still rests with the member states. In these terms, the EU can best be seen as a union of states rather than a European superstate.

This chapter looks at the debate over how best to understand the EU, by first reviewing the debate over the personality of the EU, then looking at the balance of political responsibilities between the EU and the member states, then examining the features of the EU policymaking process, and finally discussing the qualities of the EU as a confederal union of states. Although it is true that the EU has never been formally declared to be a confederation, it has never been formally declared to be anything other than an effort to achieve "ever closer union" among its member states. The EU is both more than a conventional international organization and less than a federal United States of Europe. Just where this leaves it, and where it leaves the relationship between the EU and its member states, is a question that is yet to be settled.

Understanding the European Union

Pinning down the personality of the EU is not easy. There has never been anything like it before (none of the many other examples of regional integration around the world have involved the degree of cooperation found in the EU), and its character and structure have never been static. Its rules have constantly evolved, and its membership and the balance of power among EU institutions and member states has regularly changed, as have the functions, powers, rules, and goals of EU institutions and European integration more generally. J. P. Olsen noted the fluidity, ambiguity, and hybrid nature of the EU, arguing that it is always in the process of becoming something else and concluding that it may never actually reach a stable equilibrium.[4] John Peterson and colleagues argue that "about the only thing that can be safely predicted about [the EU's] future is that it is unlikely to remain static for long."[5] For their part, Brigid Laffan and Sonia Mazey write of "the stability of instability" in their study of the changing nature of integration.[6]

The challenge of understanding the EU is exemplified by the evolving personality of its institutions, which have either been assigned new powers by the treaties or have won new powers for themselves by the adept exploitation of legal and political opportunities. The balance of power between the Council of Ministers and the European Parliament has changed, for example, as the latter has exploited its moral advantages as the only EU institution directly responsible to the voters of the EU. The balance of institutional authority has changed with the relatively late creation (in 1974) of the European Council, the evolution since 1997 of the euro group of finance ministers charged with steering the euro, and the more recent creation in 1999 of a high representative for external relations and in 2009 (under the terms of the Treaty of Lisbon) of a president of the European Council.

The challenge of understanding the EU is further reflected in the difficulties of coming to grips with the manner in which policy is made at the EU level, studies of which are peppered with such adjectives as *arcane*, *complex*, *cumbersome*, *distinctive*, *dynamic*, *fragmented*, *inefficient*, *uneven*, *unique*, *unpredictable*, and *unstable*. Vincent Wright describes Brussels as a "decisional maze" and an "over-crowded policy arena."[7] Alexander Stubb, Helen Wallace, and John Peterson note the experimental nature of the EU policy system, which has meant that institutions and policymakers have operated in different ways from one policy to another and even from one issue to another, changing their approaches over time.[8] Jeremy Richardson concludes that the complexity of the EU policy process demands the use of multiple concepts from multiple models.[9]

Understanding the EU and its relationship with the member states might be easier if the EU had a formal constitution: a single, amendable, codified document that could function as a power map through the structure and responsibilities of the "government" of the EU. But with the death in 2005 of attempts to adopt a European constitution, the EU has had to continue to rely on a series of treaties, each one amending those that came before, and whose effects are constantly fine-tuned as a result of debates among the governments of the member states, struggles for influence among the major EU institutions, new laws adopted by the EU, decisions reached by the European Court of Justice, and the political and economic pressures of the international system. The treaties provide us with a series of policy principles and a list of the policy areas in which the EU is active, but they are not always exact on the balance of policy responsibilities between EU institutions and the member states (which varies from one policy area to another).

To further complicate matters, while policy studies at the national or subnational level have the advantage of being able to focus on the formal structures of government and the pressures to which those structures are subject, in the case of the EU there is no European government as such. Simon Hix and Bjørn Høyland argue that it is a political system but not a state because it does not have a monopoly on the legitimate use of coercion.[10] Seeking another channel of explanation, the term *governance* is often used in connection with the system of authority in the EU. This describes an arrangement in which laws and policies are made and implemented without the existence of a formally acknowledged set of governing institutions but as a result of interactions involving a complex variety of actors. The European institutions are not so much governing bodies as they are administrative bodies, and understanding them means trying to understand the interplay between the institutions themselves, the governments of the member states, interest groups, and many other sources of influence. Mark Pollack notes that the approaches of international relations and comparative politics have recently been joined by a third approach, which might be described as "governance without government," in which the EU is considered neither as a traditional international organization nor as a domestic political system, but as a combination of both.[11]

In its earliest years, the process of European integration was driven mainly by the member states. It was bottom-up in the sense that it was an accumulation of the decisions taken by the national governments of the member states: national interests were to the fore, decisionmaking was decentralized, member states were the source of most law and policy, and the European institutions had little independence. In short, integration was ultimately an intergovernmental endeavor.

As integration evolved, however, the balance changed: European interests became more important, decisionmaking became more communal, more laws and policies were developed by the EU institutions, member states became the target as well as the source of law and policy, and EU institutions developed greater independence. The European Union became increasingly institutionalized and formalized, and to understand the processes and pressures of public policy in Western Europe, it became increasingly important to study and appreciate policy at both the national and the EU level.

The difficulty of pinning down the political character of the EU is reflected in the manner in which competing models of the EU policy process have been proposed, but none have won broad support or agreement. The earliest, simplest, and purest of these models was the Community (it is accepted to refer to this a the "Community method" and so needs to be capitalized) method,[12] envisioned by Jean Monnet, one of the founders of European integration, who predicted that national policies would simply be replaced with European policies. But his thinking was based on the (flawed) assumption that there would be wholesale agreement on switching authority from the member states to the EU and a uniform transfer of authority across different policy fields.

In the mid-1990s, multilevel governance (MLG) began to emerge as a popular model for understanding the EU, describing a system in which power is distributed and shared horizontally and vertically among many different levels of government, from the supranational to the local, with considerable interaction among the parts.[13] Responsibility is shared at each stage of the decisionmaking process, with an emphasis on partnership and negotiation, rather than hierarchy.[14] It is actually not all that new as an idea, having already been hinted at by Donald Puchala when he argued that the European Community could be seen as "a multileveled system arranged in political layers from the local to the supranational," with complex organizational linkages binding center and peripheries, going upward and downward, and inward and outward.[15] Most problematically, however, MLG is not all that distinctive from federalism, if we define this as an administrative system in which authority is divided between two or more levels of government, each with independent powers and responsibilities. If there was one undisputed model of federalism, then the qualities of MLG might be clearer, but federalism comes in many different forms, and the concepts overlap in many areas.

More recently, attempts to understand the changing place of the member states have focused on the idea of Europeanization. Exploited far more often than it has been explained,[16] it can be defined as the process by which national policies and government structures have been changed and brought into alignment by European laws and policies, such that (as Robert Ladrech puts it[17]), the political and economic dynamics of the EU become part of the organizational logic of politics and policymaking at the national level. It is both vertical, in the sense that it affects the way policies are developed, and horizontal, in that it may have "a homogenizing impact" on institutions and practices across a wide range of state activities.[18] It may also have a harmonizing effect by bringing laws and practices into conjunction across different member states. Put another way, policy in the member states now develops in response to developments at the EU level as well as independent national decisions and judgments. The administrations of the member states have changed in response to the pressures of integration: by becoming responsible for implementing EU rules; by changing or abandoning existing policies, structures, and procedures; and by becoming involved in the work of EU institutions.[19]

Just how far the impact of Europeanization has been felt is difficult to measure; several studies have questioned the extent of the process,[20] whereas another study concludes that there has been neither wholesale convergence nor continuing divergence of national policy structures, but that there has been "domestic adaptation with national colors," in other words, a mixture of European and national pressures and features.[21] Although it is true that there is no longer a clear separation of the European and the national, neither are the two levels fully integrated, nor is there a clear differentiation of power and responsibility between the levels.

It has also been difficult to ascertain the extent to which the pressures that have led to changes at the national level have been uniquely or demonstrably "European." Clearly we can identify the effect of EU regulations that must be carried out on the ground in the member states or the effects of EU directives that must be translated into national laws, but there are many other pressures at work in Europe that lead to policy outcomes; these include globalization, the international trading regime, and the requirements of international law. Policymaking in the EU in recent years has been dominated by the need to respond to the fallout from the global financial crisis, which first broke in the United States in 2007, and from the crisis in the Eurozone, which broke in 2009, which, while more home-grown in nature, had many and complex roots. In short, isolating and distinguishing the effects of these pressures from the effects of Europeanization is no simple matter.

The Balance of Political Responsibilities

In unitary systems of government, such as those in Japan and most European states, the question of the balance of policy powers rarely arises; the national government dominates, and local governments tend to play a supporting role in such areas as education, health care, and public safety. In federal systems of government, however, such as the United States, Germany, Russia, and India, the picture becomes more complicated because powers and responsibilities are divided among national and local units of administration. In the United States, for example, the federal government has primary responsibility for defense and foreign policy, monetary policy, interstate commerce, international trade, and social security. State and local governments for their part have the majority of responsibility for education, policing, highways, and law enforcement, and the three levels of government share responsibility on issues such as welfare, health, and transportation. No level has exclusive powers in most areas; instead, there are overlapping circles of responsibility, with cooperation and vertical influence being greater in some areas than in others.

While the division of powers in the United States has reached a strong state of equilibrium, the division of powers in the EU changes constantly as the process of integration sees responsibilities shifting away from the member states and toward the EU institutions. The extent of the uncertainty is reflected in the different assumptions about how much law is now made at the EU as opposed to the national level. Critics of the EU have quoted numbers as high as 80 percent in their efforts to cast aspersions on the growing authority of the EU, and several scholars have adopted similar views. Giandomenico Majone, for example, has suggested that the EU sets more than 80 percent of the rules governing the production, distribution, and exchange of goods, services, and capital in the markets of the member states.[22]

However, a recent study by the library of the British House of Commons, which looked only at the British case, was able to conclude only that between 1997 and 2009, just under 7 percent of primary legislation in the UK and just over 14 percent of secondary legislation could be tied to the obligations of implementing EU rules. The report noted the unreliability of EU and national databases, the difficulty of differentiating the relative material impact of EU and national laws, and the different levels of impact that EU laws have from one member state to another. In summary, it determined that there was "no totally accurate, rational or useful way of calculating the percentage of national laws based on or influenced by the EU."[23] All that we really have is a series of clues regarding the relative political responsibilities of the EU and the member states, which can be found in three main places.

The first set of clues can be found in the treaties, revisions to which have given more clarity to the boundaries of the "competence" (responsibility) of the EU. But while Articles 3–6 of the Treaty on the Functioning of the EU provide what looks like a comprehensive listing of EU areas of competence (see Table 2.1 for a summary), the list is not always as clear or as complete as it might seem. Missing from that list, for example, are external relations and immigration, areas in which the EU is active. Environmental policy is listed in the treaty as a shared responsibility, but in practice it is now almost entirely made at the EU level, and it has had greater impact on those Eastern European countries that joined the EU with relatively little in the way of prior environmental law, and less impact on those Western European countries that have had the most influence on the development of EU law. While human health is listed in the treaty as a shared responsibility, health care is almost entirely a responsibility of the member states. Even in policy areas where competence is shared, it is not always clear how far it is shared; in some areas the EU has authority only to support or supplement the work of the member states.

The second set of clues can be found in the budget of the EU, although care must always be taken over how figures are interpreted, for two main reasons. First, the amount spent may be more a reflection of the outcome of political struggles than of real need. Thus the EEC long and infamously spent more on agricultural price supports than on any other area of activity, largely because France was able to win agreement on this at the time of the drafting of the Treaty of Rome and stubbornly refused to make significant concessions. Second, there is no direct link between spending and the amount of time and effort expended by government and policymakers. Immigration, for example, is a hot-button issue in the EU, but it does not demand spending significant funds, if only because dealing with immigration is a bureaucratic matter as much as anything.

Nonetheless, a review of the EU budget shows that agriculture has been a major priority of the process of integration, even if its share of spending has fallen (from 75 percent of the budget in the 1970s to 31 percent in 2015), while spending on cohesion policy (efforts to reduce economic disparities within the EU) has grown, accounting for nearly 35 percent of spending in 2015. The balance in 2015 went to rural development and the environment (11 percent), competitiveness (10.5 percent), and just under 6 percent on external policies. In short, when it comes to spending at least, the vast majority of the EU's attention appears to be focused on just two issues.

The third set of clues regarding the relative authority of the EU and the member states comes from a subject analysis of European law, which provides insight into policy areas where the EU is most active and where the member states, by implication, have most actively pooled authority. But care again has to be taken in assessing the numbers, because the reach and significance of individual laws varies: some cover a large area of ground and have major policy effects, whereas others are more focused in both policy and territorial terms. Some areas of policy also demand more technical and finely

Table 2.1 Balance of Policy Responsibilities in the EU and the Member States

Exclusive EU Competence[a]	Shared Competence	Responsibility of Member States
Competition	Agriculture	Broadcasting
Customs	Civil protection[b]	Citizenship
Fisheries conservation	Cohesion	Criminal justice
Monetary policy (Eurozone)	Consumer protection	Defense
Trade	Culture[b]	Education
	Development cooperation	Elections
	Economic policy[c]	Health care
	Educationb	Land use
	Employment policy[c]	Local transport
	Energy	Policing
	Environment	Postal services
	External relations	Tax policy
	Freedom, security, justice	
	Human health[b]	
	Humanitarian aid	
	Immigration	
	Industry[b]	
	Public health	
	Research and development	
	Single market	
	Social policy	
	Space policy	
	Tourism[b]	
	Trans-European networks	
	Transport	
	Vocational training[b]	

Sources: Extrapolated by the author from a listing in Articles 3 to 6 of the Treaty on the Functioning of the EU.

Notes: a. The EU also has exclusive competence to sign international agreements when provided for in EU law or when necessary to allow the EU to exercise its internal competence; b. The EU has powers to support, coordinate, or supplement actions of member states; c. The EU has some powers of coordination.

tuned pieces of law, hence the volume of laws adopted in a given area may be more an indication of the depth rather than the breadth of EU activity.

The data in Table 2.2 suggest that external relations is the dominant area of EU policy, but this is a policy area in which the member states still have substantial independence of action. The data also show a large number of active laws in the fields of agricultural, environmental, and competition policy, as well as the single (or internal) market, reflecting the priorities of EU interests. A more thorough study reveals that the EU has only been involved in specific elements of each of these policy areas, prompted as much as anything by the harmonization of member state laws and the need to remove the physical, fiscal, and technical barriers to free trade in support of the broad goals of integration.

The ongoing tensions between supranational and intergovernmental pressures have ensured that few policy areas have yet become the exclusive domain of the EU, and none of the areas of policy over which the member states still have most authority are entirely immune from the pressures and demands of integration. At the same time, the contradictory attitudes of member states to the process of integration have meant that different states have retained different levels of authority over different policy areas. Thus, all we can say with any certainty is that the process of integration has brought the EU to a point where responsibilities are shared, but the focus of

Table 2.2 EU Legislation in Force, by Subject

Subject	Number of Pieces of Legislation
External relations	3,936
Agriculture	3,324
Environment, consumers, and health	2,027
Competition	1,822
Industrial policy, internal market	1,696
Financial and institutional matters	1,382
Fisheries	1,277
Customs union, free movement of goods	1,019
Transport	787
Freedom, security, and justice	692
Free movement of workers, social policy	617
Common foreign and security policy	593
Economic and monetary policy	560
Science, information, education, culture	460
Energy	421
Regional policy	400
Right of establishment, provision of services	326
Taxation	192
Undertakings	125
People's Europe	25
TOTAL	21,681

Source: EUR-Lex website. http://eur-lex.europa.eu. (Accessed July 2014).

responsibility for some policy issues lies with the EU and the focus for others rests mainly with the member states to differing degrees.

Generally speaking, the focus of policy responsibility lies with the EU on economic issues, and it is now fair to say that economic policy in the EU is driven or influenced more by the work of the EU institutions than by the initiatives of the governments of the member states. "Economic policy" means more than the single market and consists of a variety of concerns that are central to the single market, related (1) to the need to ensure free trade among the member states, and (2) to the need for the member states to work in tandem in their dealings with external trading partners. The combination of the customs union and the single market has led to increased EU responsibility for issues such as environmental protection, consumer safety, the development of European transport and energy networks, labor issues, competition, financial services and banking, and telecommunications.

It is still too early to be sure of the long-term effects of the crisis in the Eurozone. The member states struggled to understand the precise causes of the crisis, which left them handicapped as they designed their policy response. There has clearly been a subsequent extension of the authority given to the European Central Bank to manage the euro, an extension of the mechanisms through which the EU institutions can work to ensure better management of national budgets, and a reduction in the abilities of states in the Eurozone to ignore the requirements of euro membership. Exactly what this means in terms of the relationship between the whole and the parts remains to be seen.

The Character of EU Policymaking

More clues regarding the political personality of the EU can be found in the character of its policymaking procedures. Public policy consists of the deliberate actions or inactions of government. When officials are elected or appointed into the bureaucracy, they (hopefully) have a sense of the problems faced by a society and of what they consider to be the most effective responses to those problems. The actions they pursue or choose to avoid constitute their policies, and when policies affect large and generalized segments of society, they become public. All policy systems have characteristics that are unique to their political, economic, and social circumstances, and the same is true of the EU, where any discussion about the nature of policymaking will typically include most or all of the following concepts.

Games and Competition

Politics everywhere is driven by struggles for power and influence, and such struggles are magnified in the EU by the extent to which member states and EU institutions compete. Guy Peters describes three sets of interconnected "games" being played out in the EU: a national game among member states, which are trying to extract as much as possible from the EU while giving up as little as possible; a game played out among EU institutions, which are trying to win more power relative to each other; and a bureaucratic game in which the directorates-general in the Commission are developing their own organizational cultures and competing for policy space.[24] The institutions and the member states have different definitions of the European interest, and they often sacrifice that interest on the altar of their own more narrow political and economic goals.

Spillover

Leon Lindberg described this as a process by which "a given action, related to a specific goal, creates a situation in which the original goal can be assured only by taking further actions, which in turn create a further condition and a need for more action."[25] In other words, as the European institutions have become active in one area of policy, so they have found that political, economic, and/or social forces have compelled them to become involved in additional areas of policy. This was particularly true of the single market program, where efforts to bring down barriers to trade found EU institutions making policy in areas that were not anticipated by the authors of the Treaty of Rome, such as consumer protection and the environment. Critics of the EU (like critics of the US federal government) charge that it has tried to become involved in too many policy areas; however, it has often had little choice; the creation of new programs has revealed or created new problems, which in turn have led to demands for supporting programs in related policy areas.

Institutional Fragmentation

Power in the United States is shared between multiple different institutions, but the links among them are firm and stable, and each represents a relatively clear constituency, whether it is local districts (the House of Representatives), the states (the Senate and state governments), or the federal government (the president). At the national level there is a relatively clear distinction between executive, legislative, and judicial responsibilities. In the EU case, by contrast, legislative power is shared between the Commission, the Council of Ministers, the European Parliament, and national legislatures. Executive power is shared between the Commission and the member states. Hussein Kassim argues that, "each institution is internally differentiated, and has its own methods, procedures, and culture, exercises varying degrees of power, and commands different resources."[26]

Subsidiarity

Although the concept of subsidiarity is at the core of the character of the EU, its precise meaning and implications are open to debate. An attempt at definition was made in the Treaty of Maastricht by insisting that the EU

should act only if "the objectives of the proposed action cannot be sufficiently achieved by the Member States and can therefore, by reason of the
scale or effects of proposed action, be better achieved by the Community"
(Article 5). In other words, let the EU do what it does best, and let the member states do what they do best. Though it is not always possible to agree on
what kinds of actions are more effectively or efficiently undertaken at one
level or another, negotiations and political pressures over the years have led
to an expansion of the body of policy areas that are considered part of the
"competence" (authority) of the EU. However, levels of authority vary from
one policy area to another and have typically changed over time, not always
as a result of deliberate policy decisions or changes to the treaties.

Informal Politics

Studies of politics and policy usually concentrate on the formal aspects of
administration, yet much of what is done by government falls into the sphere
of the informal, a sphere that Keith Middlemas argues is as critical to an understanding of how decisions are reached as the formal.[27] Just as an understanding of policymaking in the United States cannot be achieved without
looking at the role of legislative assistants, presidential advisers, interest
groups, and the media, so it is important to appreciate that in the EU case,
the Commission will often liaise with interest groups, experts, representatives of industry, and representatives of national government ministries and
local government. Each of the Commission directorates-general has become
used to working with external actors, people, and organizations that can provide it with the information most relevant to its work and that are most
likely to be involved in the implementation of EU law. There is nothing in
the treaties to say that the process should be so; these informal processes
have evolved out of need and circumstances.

Differentiated Integration

An ongoing feature of policymaking in the EU has been the extent to which
different member states have opted in or out of selected policy areas or have
moved at different speeds to achieve the goals of integration in a phenomenon known as differentiated integration. For example, not all EU member
states have adopted the euro, the UK and Ireland have not yet signed the
open borders Schengen Agreement, and several countries (notably Britain
and France) have moved ahead relatively vigorously on security issues while
others have been less enthusiastic, and several (including Austria, Finland,
and Ireland) have worked hard to maintain their neutrality. Alongside these
headline-making macrolevel examples of disagreement on policy, member
states are also moving at different speeds on the microlevel implementation
of European laws. Dirk Leuffen and colleagues argue that differentiated integration is likely to become a persistent feature of EU politics, such that to

fully understand the EU, we need to understand the level of policy centralization, the functional scope of integration, and its territorial reach.[28]

The Democratic Deficit

Most liberal democracies have high levels of public accountability, and
public opinion plays a vital role in policymaking; leaders will not always
proceed unless they can be sure that public opinion is on their side. The
same is not true of the EU, however, where secrecy surrounds much of the
work of the Commission and the Council of Ministers, where few policymakers are directly or even indirectly accountable to voters and where the
policy world is replete with examples of leaders proceeding even in the
face of hostile or indifferent public opinion. Examples include the adoption
of the euro in several countries where public opinion was opposed, and EU
leaders moving to ratify the draft EU constitution even when it was clear
that votes against it were inevitable. While public opinion has played an increasingly important role in EU policymaking with the growth of lobbying,
direct elections to Parliament, the creation of the European ombudsman,
and the Commission's efforts to promote transparency, the links between
policymakers and citizens are still poorly developed. The result is that policymaking in the EU remains largely an elitist, top-down phenomenon.

Incrementalism

Because of concerns over the loss of national sovereignty, the absence of a
consensus about the priorities of European integration, and the need for constant compromise, EU policymaking tends to be slow, cautious, and incremental. The process sometimes slows to the point where the critics of integration complain about Euro-sclerosis, but this is probably unfair. Although the
Community had many problems in the 1970s, and there have been many
teething troubles in the process of integration, breakthroughs have often been
made in that process, such as progress on the euro, convergence on foreign
policy, and agreement on the need for enlargement. All these initiatives
emerged incrementally from a combination of opportunity and need.

Some of these policymaking qualities are shared with conventional
states, but this particular combination of characteristics helps shed additional
light on the personality of the EU. With all this in mind, this chapter closes
with an analysis of the debate about the confederal qualities of the EU.

The EU as a Confederal Union of States

So far, then, we have reviewed the discussion over the personality of the
EU; reviewed the uncertainties over the division of political, legal, and policy responsibilities between the EU and its member states; and looked at
some of the features of policymaking in the EU. As noted earlier, the EU is

more than a conventional international organization, but it is also less than a federal United States of Europe. Exactly where it sits on the continuum between these two extremes has not yet been resolved to anyone's satisfaction, a problem that hinders attempts to understand the relationship between the EU and the member states.

In this final section, the argument is made that the EU is best understood as a confederation: an administrative system in which independent states come together for reasons of security, efficiency, or mutual convenience; retaining the powers they consider best reserved to themselves; and working together through joint institutions on matters such as foreign, trade, and security policy. Citizens are linked to these institutions indirectly through the governments of the states in which they live. Put another way, a confederation is a looser form of a federation, a union of states with more powers left in the hands of the constituent members. As Frederick Lister put it, if a federation is a union of peoples living within a single state, then a confederation is a union of states.[29]

To better understand confederalism, we need to briefly refer back to federalism. Although it has been very much a part of the political and theoretical debate about the EU, it has tended to crop up only in regard to either the end state championed by the more ardent Europeanists or the end state that critics of the EU most actively fear. Rather predictably, and in spite of decades of study, political scientists have failed to agree on exactly what a federation looks like, because although there are about two dozen in the world, they all apply federal ideas differently. Broadly speaking, a federation is a system of administration involving two or more levels of government with autonomous powers and responsibilities, in contrast to the unitary systems we find in states such as France and Sweden, where the balance and focus of power lies with the national government.

Anthony Birch long ago remarked that federalism was a concept with "no fixed meaning,"[30] and more recently Ronald Watts has warned that "there is no single pure model of federalism."[31] The waters of the debate about federalism have been further muddied by developments in several countries that have never formally declared themselves to be federations but where the transfer of powers to local units of government has resulted in a process of federalization; these include Argentina, South Africa, Spain, and the UK. As for claims of the federal qualities of the EU, opinion is divided. David McKay argues that the EU is "a species of federal state" with some clear federal qualities,[32] whereas Andrew Moravcsik has described it as "an exceptionally weak federation" because of its modest budget and bureaucracy, its lack of coercive force, and the constraints on its decisionmaking rules.[33] Michael Burgess argues that the EU might be described as "a classic example of federalism without federation" because it has been a repository of federal ideas and influences without becoming a formal federation.[34]

The idea that the EU might be a confederation has attracted much less attention, probably for several reasons. Any entity that looks like a confederation can simply be described as a weak form of federation; the confederal option pleases neither European federalists nor critics of European integration (who, respectively, want more or less integration); there is no standard, uniform, or simple model of confederalism to which we can refer for guidance; and history has shown that confederations typically evolve into federations or new states (and thus are widely seen only as temporary arrangements). Among the few examples of historical confederations, as mentioned in Chapter 1, are the United States from 1781 to 1789, Switzerland until 1789 and again from 1815 to 1848, and Germany from 1815 to 1866.

Not everyone rejects the idea that the EU might be considered a confederal system. Murray Forsyth argued in 1981 that the study of confederations in history revealed that the EEC was clearly an economic confederation in both content and form.[35] Lister later agreed, describing the EU as a "jumbo confederation" whose member states and governments continue to dominate the EU's institutions.[36] For Moravcsik (quoted already as describing the EU as "an exceptionally weak federation"), the EU is, "despite a few federal elements, essentially a confederation of member-states."[37] Majone agrees, arguing that the confederal model describes "precisely" the arrangement found in the EU and bemoaning the fact that confederalism has been "practically banned from the discourse about the future and finality of the Union."[38]

Other scholars take a middle path between federalism and confederalism. For example, Burgess suggests that the EU is not a federation in the conventional sense, but that it is "a political union with strong federal and confederal elements . . . [or] a new kind of federal-confederal union that we can classify as a 'new confederation' or a new federal model."[39] Charles Blankart argues that the EU is neither a confederation nor a federation, but is instead an "association of compound states," some policies being dealt with in a federal manner and others in a confederal manner.[40] Ronald Watts describes the EU as a "hybrid confederation-federation," noting its confederal roots in the powers of the Council of Ministers, its small budget, its legal basis in a series of treaties, and the policy powers kept by the member states. He sees its federal qualities in the work of the European Commission and the European Court of Justice.[41]

In terms of the more detailed qualities of the EU as a confederation, consider the following:

- There is no European constitution capable of being amended and developed by proposals from the EU institutions. The EU is instead based on treaties designed and developed by intergovernmental conferences. This takes it beyond the standard definition of an international organization, because it involves a higher level of commitment on the part of the member states but ensures that it stops short of a single European state.

- The EU has administrative institutions, but as noted earlier, they collectively amount to a system of governance rather than a system of government. The European Parliament is the exception to the rule, because it has a direct political relationship with the voters of the EU member states, but European Parliament elections are twenty-eight separate national elections contested by national political parties rather than EU elections contested by cross-national parties. For their parts, the European Council and the Council of Ministers are meeting places for representatives of the member states and can only do as much as those representatives will tolerate or as the treaties will allow, whereas the European Commission is a bureaucracy whose powers are defined by the treaties, and the job of the European Court of Justice is not to lead so much as to interpret the meaning of the treaties.
- The interests of the citizens of the EU member states are represented indirectly through their governments (with the exception of the elected European Parliament). The EU is often criticized for its lack of democracy, but to make its institutions truly democratic by allowing them to be directly elected would be to move the EU closer to the idea of a federal system. Voter interests are represented in the EU, but indirectly through the governments of the member states, a classic confederal idea.
- The member states of the EU are still distinct and independent political units under international law. They have their own national defense forces and national security policies, and they can still sign bilateral treaties with non-EU states. The relationship between the member states and the EU is quite different from the relationship between the federal government and the states in the United States; the president, Congress, and the Supreme Court collectively constitute a shared system of government, and there is relatively little that the states can do independently.
- Because there is no European state, citizens of the member states cannot legally become European citizens, still carry passports issued by the governments of their home states, and still have a higher sense of allegiance toward national flags, anthems, and other symbols. Any sense of European identity that they may have is compromised by the lack of agreement on exactly what it means to be European.
- Although an effort by a state within a federation to leave would be considered secession, and might result in conflict and even war, the EU is still very much a voluntary association, meaning that its members are free to leave if they wish. This is even confirmed in the treaties, even though nothing has been agreed on the details of how an exit would work or what the implications would be for the relationship between the "newly exited" state and its former EU partners.

When we ask "What is the EU?," it would be helpful to have a short and clear answer. It would certainly save us a great deal of often inconclusive discussion about what the EU means to its residents and those who relate to it from outside, and about how it relates to its member states. Unfortunately, in the absence of clear agreement on its personality and character, it is prone to being whatever we want it to be. Furthermore, it is prone to conflicting interpretations of its effects: for some it is a valuable exercise in cooperation that has helped sustain peace in Europe and opened up markets and opportunities, whereas for others, it has impinged dangerously on the sovereignty of its member states and the people who live in those states.

Conclusions

This chapter has been an attempt to pin down the nature of the political relationship between the EU institutions and the member states of the European Union. It has argued that the relative input of the two sides is complex, changeable, and often ambiguous and that the division of responsibilities between the EU and the member states remains unclear. While the balance of power lies with the EU in some policy areas and with the member states in others, there are significant differences in the balance of responsibilities on different issues within these areas.

It was argued more than twenty years ago that there were only three possible outcomes to the process of European integration:[42] a federal Europe, a Europe of states in which the member states played the main role, and a multispeed Europe in which levels of integration varied from one issue to another and from one member state to another. Not much has changed, because today there is little agreement to be found among politicians, the public, or scholars about which of these three, or any additional alternatives, applies to the EU. This chapter has suggested that the EU is best considered as a confederal system, but this is not a view that is widely held. The chapters that follow examine the relationship between the EU and each of the member states, casting more light on the nature of that relationship and on the balance of power between the two sides. They also discuss the personality of the European Union, asking if the EU and its member states might have more of a confederal personality or future than has been previously thought.

Notes

1. See discussion in Schmitter (1996).
2. Zweifel (2005).
3. Hix (1994).
4. Olsen (1997).
5. Peterson, Bomberg, and Corbett (2012), p. 225.
6. Laffan and Mazey (2006).

7. Wright (1996), pp. 151–152.

8. Stubb, Wallace, and Peterson (2003).

9. Richardson (2006), p. 23.

10. Hix and Høyland (2011), p. 12ff.

11. Pollack (2010), p. 35.

12. See Lindberg and Scheingold (1970).

13. See Hooghe and Marks (2001), and Peters and Jon Pierre (2004).

14. European Commission (1999), p. 143.

15. Puchala(1975).

16. K. H. Goetz has described the concept as "a cause in search of an effect"; See Goetz (2000).

17. Ladrech (1994).

18. Page (2003).

19. Kassim (2003).

20. For a brief review, see Page (2003). See also Graziano and Vink (2007).

21. Cowles, Caporaso, and Risse-Kappen (2001), p. 1.

22. Majone (1996).

23. Miller (2010).

24. Peters (1992), pp. 106–107.

25. Lindberg (1963), p. 10.

26. Kassim (2003).

27. Middlemas (1995). See also Andersen and Eliassen (2001a).

28. Leuffen, Rittberger, and Schimmelfennig (2012).

29. Lister (1996), p. 106.

30. Birch (1966), p. 15.

31. Watts, (2008), p. 1.

32. McKay (2001), pp. 8–10.

33. Moravcsik (2001), p. 186.

34. Burgess (2006), p. 226.

35. Forsyth (1981), p. 183.

36. Lister (1996), Chapter 2.

37. Moravcsik (2007).

38. Majone (2006), p. 136.

39. Burgess (2006), p. 239.

40. Blankart (2007).

41. Watts (2008), pp. 56–58.

42. Andersen and Eliassen (1993a), p. 7.

3

Germany: Architect of Europe

Carl Lankowski

GERMANY WAS THE MAIN TOPIC OF WORLD POLITICS FOR MUCH OF the twentieth century, and the European Union is properly interpreted as a response to Europe's "German problem." In contrast to the failure of the European union idea of the interwar period,[1] after the defeat of the Nazi regime, the US presence and a radically truncated Germany set the stage for a fundamental remodeling of the continent. Presented with the opportunity to reemerge economically and then politically in a system of pooled sovereignty, and from 1955 in alliance with its NATO partners, Germany and Europe prospered. The recovery program (the Marshall Plan) offered to Europe in 1947 was made contingent on German participation, and its overall aim was to reinstate Europe's ability to take charge of its own destiny.[2] The first phase of Europe's reemergence came in the 1970s and was capped by German leadership in two key areas. The common market launched by the Treaty of Rome required stabilization of exchange rates when the United States was no longer willing to defend the Bretton Woods fixed-rate exchange rate system it had created in the 1940s. Germany and France led the way to the European Monetary System (EMS) in 1979, a precursor of the Economic and Monetary Union (EMU) twenty years later.

Germany Interacts with the EU: How the EU Affects Germany and How Germany Influences the EU

The geostrategic impasse of the superpowers in the wake of the Cuban missile crisis was broken by the détente policy of a new West German government. This *Ostpolitik*, based on the notion of creating connections with Cold War adversary regimes in a series of small steps, captured the imagination of a new postwar generation of Germans and arguably led to the generalization of this policy in both blocs in the Conference on Security and Cooperation in Europe and the resulting Helsinki Accords of 1976, the functional equivalent of the European peace treaty that never was drawn up after World War II.

The signal moment in the West's grand strategy of containment, which rested on expectations of "a mellowing of Soviet power" after a competition between systems,[3] came with the implosion of the East German state in 1989–1990. The Soviet leadership accepted the primary goal of German statecraft since the 1950s because, in light of its Ostpolitik, in light of the attitudes of its new generation (featuring the pacifist Greens) and its integration into a European structure on the verge of pooling its currency, Germany no longer seemed threatening to it.

By the eve of the sovereign debt crisis that washed over the EU in 2010, Chancellor Angela Merkel had burnished Germany's Euro-friendly credentials, inter alia, by orchestrating the resurrection of the failed constitutional treaty in the form of the Treaty of Lisbon. It was a green Germany in a green EU that became greener still with the adoption of REACH, a comprehensive regulatory procedure and institutional infrastructure for chemicals, and the ambitious 20-20-20 program to address climate change by mandating EU-wide reductions in greenhouse gases, significant increases in the role of renewables in the energy mix, and efforts to raise energy efficiency in the EU. As part of its contribution, Germany launched its Energiewende (energy transition), which featured guaranteed access to the grid and a guaranteed price (feed-in tariff) to those willing to install solar panels or windmills. In the wake of a nuclear disaster in Japan, the German government mandated the decommissioning of all remaining nuclear power plants in Germany. When energy prices increased, so did the country's dependence on imported gas from Russia. But German policy vis-à-vis Russia embraced economic interdependence by design and was fully consistent with the spirit of Ostpolitik.

Drivers of German EU Policy

With this background in mind, let us turn to the critical drivers of Germany's relationship to the EU in the second decade of the twenty-first century.

The First Driver

Germany is the largest country in the size of its economy, export prowess, and population of the 28 EU member states. But Germany's population of about 81 million is only 16 percent of the EU's 506 million people and its GDP of €2.7 trillion in 2013 was only 20.6 percent of EU GDP (€13.1 trillion). The 18-member euro area had a population of 335 million in 2013, of which Germany accounted for just over 24 percent, whereas its GDP was about 29 percent of euro area GDP (€2.7/€12.9 trillion).[4] To the extent that

German elites desire to shape EU development, Germany's economic size, structure, and performance raise the issue of how to organize leverage, since outright dominance is clearly out of the question. The same is true for defending perceived economic interests in the EU context. Germany's leverage derives from its economic performance, manifested most obviously by its export prowess and associated current account surpluses that have exceeded 5 percent of GDP per year for the past decade, as well as its AAA sovereign bond rating and benchmark status for sovereign issue. Germany's economic interests in the EU are clear enough: much of its exports are bound for the EU. Given the magnitude of this export performance, it is also clear that German industry reaps enormous benefits from a lower exchange rate than would apply were Germany still to have the deutsche mark as its currency. Just like every other EU member state, German producers and consumers benefit from economies and politics of scale in the internal market. Under supranational authority, EU policy and law establishing a broadly common regulatory environment puts a specifically European stamp on commercial activity.

EU enlargement proved to be a major success in several respects for Germany. New members offered new markets, the largest and closest being Poland, whose early post–Cold War policy decisions transformed its economy, making it fit for German investment and export penetration. Germany became Russia's primary economic partner, but the German-Polish economic relationship is bigger still. Moreover, Poland's EU membership meant that the EU eastern external border was pushed away from Germany for the first time, reassigning external border sentinel duty from Germany to Poland. Poland's accession to NATO in 1999 had already relieved Germany's security situation.

The Second Driver

Like the rest of EU Europe, German society is being transformed by an aging population and a migration transition.[5] Milward, Romero, and Brennan argued persuasively that by the late 1950s, a central if somewhat understated aim of the European integration project was facilitating the defense and further development of the welfare state, by which they meant the large-scale entitlement programs that are mainly responsible for EU member states spending quotas of 45–55 percent of GDP.[6] Those programs have been built on the contributions and taxes of a large working population that continues to retire and begin drawing benefits by age sixty-six or younger, even as populations peak and begin to decline. Increasing fiscal stress is the result and is amplified by the recomposition of the workforce as well as regulatory preferences. Germany has not been spared these pressures, despite its current comparatively favorable unemployment figures. Total fertility in Germany has declined to around 1.4 live births per woman, below the point at which population is replaced. Most analysts expect a significant reduction of the German population to begin by 2030, along with an increasing proportion in retirees receiving state pensions. In justifying policy choices, Merkel frequently refers to the fact that the EU-28 account for 7 percent of the world's population, 25 percent of world output, and 50 percent of global welfare spending.

Immigration has blunted the incipient population decline, but problems of social integration have arisen and persist, creating political barriers to immigration with a significant EU dimension. Sources of the inflow have changed over the years. Article 48 of the Treaty of Rome (1957) authorized free movement of EC nationals in search of work and led to immigration from the first member states, especially Italians and Belgians. Later, Portuguese, Spaniards, and Greeks came. In anticipation of the "big bang" EU enlargement with ten new member states in 2004, Poles and other Central Europeans flocked to Germany. The same logic applied to Bulgaria and Romania after their accession in 2007. Germany also encouraged third-country nationals as *Gastarbeiter* (migrant workers) before 1973, recruiting mainly Turkish Turks and Kurdish Turks from the Anatolian interior. Workers were joined by their families even after 1973, and Germany now boasts a population of Turkish people of about 3 million, of which only a small fraction have attained citizenship. Added to these were waves of asylum seekers, many from the Balkans during the wars of the 1990s and later the greater Middle East and sub-Saharan Africa. German citizenship could be claimed by people with German ancestry living behind the Iron Curtain, and many *Übersiedler* (migrants) were welcomed to Germany before and after unification in 1990; previously, their linguistic and cultural connection to their new country had been tenuous at best. A large proportion of the immigration stream settled in Germany's cities, so although in 2013 the percentage of foreign-born in Germany was 8.8, it was much higher in urban areas.[7] Among the most prominent newcomers since 1991 have been Russians.

Though studies suggest there is no net fiscal effect of immigration, the presence of large numbers of non-native Germans has encouraged the perception that this population increases the fiscal imbalance. Foreigners are also blamed for high rates of unemployment in some sectors of the economy. Asylum seekers are not given work permits, so they are often targeted for abuse because they receive payments but do not contribute taxes. Again, like many Northern European countries, Germany went from a liberal asylum seeker intake regime to a very restrictive one in the 1990s. Discrimination aimed at *Ausländer* (foreigners), especially Turks, was pervasive, but in that decade, religious identities came to reinforce their perceived otherness, a trend that intensified after the terrorist attacks of September 11, 2011.[8] NIMBY (not in my back yard) protests against proposed mosque constructions have been common. When a Social Democratic–Green coalition government introduced a green card system for IT staff in short supply in Germany, the center-right Christian Democratic premier of Germany's largest state sloganized his opposition with the phrase "Kinder statt Inder" (Educate our youth instead of hiring Indians).

The Third Driver

The overall success of European integration is notable. It goes beyond issues involving social integration connected to immigration. Although those responsible for German statecraft are aware of and embrace European integration as the escape route from the awful past of economic depression, fascism, and war and as the path to security and prosperity now and for the foreseeable future, they also confront the daily reality of EU politics. The *acquis communautaire* has been developing, after all, for the better part of a century; there are approximately 120,000 pages of EU legal text and more than 1,700 directives in force. The European Court of Justice hears hundreds of cases each year and issues dozens of authoritative judgments. A sense of obligation and responsibility based on history plays out in institutions that have been developing since the 1950s and has transcended early idealism, although the relationship between pragmatic pursuit of national interests and idealism has never been mutually exclusive. Institutions and policymaking are intrusive across many policy fields and no longer novel. Regarding EU issues, in the 1998 Bundestag elections, Social Democratic chancellor candidate Gerhard Schröder campaigned on the slogan "im deutschen Interesse" (in Germany's interest). In the context of the costs of German unification borne mainly by West German taxpayers, Germany recoiled from its perceived role as *Zahlmeister Europas* (Europe's paymaster). Vis-à-vis the EU, Germany had become *stink normal*.

Active management is required to optimize benefits defined both in terms of politics—the representational, aggregative, and brokerage functions of politics in liberal democratic settings—and policy outcomes. More integration, in the sense of "Europeanization" of policy, frequently means more attention to the European dimension by national political leaders. This is not so much about a "choice for Europe" in any aspirational sense, as it is the answer given to the question: how do we deal best with this or that problem, given the options available to us at present. Therefore, the "choice for Europe" is not a matter of intentionality as much as it is a by-product of a setting which has become, over two or more generations, increasingly Euro-centric. At least at the policy level, an "ever closer union of European peoples" has become a statement of fact, whatever the manifestations of opinion polling. Indeed, the increasing relevance of EU Europe is averred by the very movements arrayed against it in the European Parliament elections of 2014, according to the polls.[9]

A Fourth Contemporary Driver

The gap between systemic requirements for smooth functioning and capacities and willingness to contribute in key areas, including incomplete EU structures, is another factor driving Germany's EU policy. Germany has had to adopt a much more pronounced leadership role in EU affairs. This has much to do with the perceived value of the EU by policy elites in Germany. It has also to do with serious challenges combined with relative resource abundance and Germany's "soft power." Expectations by relevant policy actors in EU institutions and member states—the demand side of leadership—makes up another dimension of more pronounced German leadership.

Financial Crisis: EMU Reconstituted

Crises have sometimes advanced European integration. Germany played a central role in managing the EU response to the worldwide financial and economic crisis dating from late 2008, but it also acted as architect-in-chief as the key issue was revealed to be less economic and financial capacity than structures of governance in the euro area. In that role, German decision-makers ensured continuity in the technical design of the evolving European edifice, at every stage mindful of the calculus of consent to German contributions within Germany, even though its positions evolved as its decision-makers encountered institutional and political constraints. More often than not, German preferences governed the EU's overall response. The country's influence was a steadying one.

In principle, the Economic and Monetary Union (EMU) has always been about coordination of fiscal policies. Whereas, the United States was able to climb out of the Great Recession on the basis of a relatively quick toxic asset cleanup (Troubled Asset Relief Program) and a reflationary stimulus of approximately $800 billion, the EU experienced great difficulty on both counts. The Maastricht Treaty on European Union centralized monetary policy for the euro area, but left both tax-and-spend policies and financial regulation in the hands of the member states. According to the treaty, member states were not to be bailed out of their debts by the EU. They were supposed to follow the Stability and Growth Pact, which specified deficit and sovereign debt limits that should have prevented the crisis. But once confronted with the sovereign debt crisis, it is telling that the aggregate sovereign debt to GDP ratio of the EU-27 (or euro area 17) has been lower than the US debt/GDP ratio. The euro area sovereign debt crisis, which subsided only after European Central Bank president Mario Draghi's intervention in the summer of 2012, manifested itself in the way it did because of the EU's deficient governance structure. The euro currency weakened only slightly against the US dollar between 2009 and 2012 and from the later date has been strengthening against the dollar, although it has declined substantially because of the European Central Bank (ECB) version of quantitative easing launched in January 2015. Europe's crisis came in large part from rules that assigned responsibility for debt to each issuing member state, a clear example of the disadvantage of confederal over federal solutions to macroeconomic shocks in a currency union. Unlike the United States, whose federal level also does not bail out its states, the EU lacks the automatic stabilizers of the US system, which compensate for economic shocks: flexible labor markets and significant geographic mobility, as well as countercyclical transfers from the large federal budget.

The EU response to crisis is a story of movement along a spectrum from confederal to the adoption of more federal solutions largely driven by the euro group. It features significant institutional change in the form of "banking union" elements, assertive ECB leadership as the EU lender of last resort, an enhanced fiscal rule book, and a reworking of the Stability and Growth Pact to strengthen both its preventive and corrective arms.

Tethered to its EU partners, Germany also experienced significant economic effects from the financial crisis. As GDP plunged by 4.7 percent from Q4/2008 to Q4/2009, mainly due to falling exports, the normal driver of growth in Germany, the government adopted two stimulus packages worth about 3.3 percent of GDP. That unemployment only increased by a fraction of the GDP decline was due to Germany's novel policy response of *Kurzarbeit*—short work—a scheme by which public authorities topped up half-wages paid in Germany's Mittelstand export sector.[10] Aside from the sharp export-related downturn in 2009, the main signs of economic crisis during the entire period under review consisted of media reports about what was happening elsewhere in the EU and a spike in immigration caused by the situation in other EU member states as well as external events, such as the Arab Spring.

The EU Sovereign Debt Crisis Starts in Late 2009 with Greece

Euro area member states worked together outside the treaty framework to stabilize individual member states that were caught up in the financial contagion following the initial rescue operation for Greece. The news of impending Greek insolvency from Socialist Greek Prime Minister Georgios Papandreou in early November 2009 was received as coalition negotiations were under way in Berlin following Germany's federal elections in September. Bond spreads between the German Bund and Greek sovereign debt rose precipitously on the news that Greek debt figures had been inaccurately reported and its current account deficit was running at an unsustainable level of nearly 13 percent of GDP. Papandreou turned to euro area partners for help, but the response requiring Germany's blessing took half a year to organize, raising the cost to participating countries. Agreeing to policy design and corresponding institutional innovation accounted for the slow response. On May 10, 2010, an EU rescue fund amounting to €750 billion was announced in an attempt to reassure investors that Greek debt remained viable and that EU member states would similarly support the bonds of other EU sovereigns. Triple-A rated euro group sovereigns raised the money outside the EU treaties in this special-purpose vehicle. The European Financial Stability Facility (EFSF) brought in €440 billion from the member states, each contributor responsible for an amount proportionate to the size of its economy. The German director-general for Economics and Finance in the Commission was entrusted with running it. Germany's EFSF share was 27 percent (€119.39 billion; France had the next largest share at 20 percent). In addition, the International Monetary Fund (IMF) was associated with a €250 billion stake, as well as €60 billion from the Commission. A program aiming to bring Greece onto a path of debt sustainability was offered a week earlier. Other programs followed for Ireland, Portugal, Spain, and Cyprus as bad debt of financial institutions in these countries was made good by the respective sovereigns, which were in turn encumbered, driving up the interest rates on their bonds and in extremis raising the specter of sovereign defaults.

A series of precedents had to be set to respond to the crisis, involving:

- Framing of the crisis—as a systemic event or discretely national
- Strategic direction—the balance between fiscal consolidation and growth
- Financial liability—who should pay for the adjustments
- Institutional development—what mechanisms should be put in place to lessen the risks of a similar crisis in the future

The policy dynamics are clearly spelled out in a remarkably prescient paper by Bergsten and Kirkegaard.

> Every policymaker in Europe knows that the collapse of the euro would be a political and economic disaster for all and thus totally unacceptable....Europe's key political actors in Berlin, Frankfurt, Paris, Rome, Athens, and elsewhere will thus quite rationally exhaust all alternative options in searching for the best possible deal before at the last minute coming to an agreement . . . the process relies on financial market volatility to incentivize solutions that will ultimately resolve the crisis. Europe's overriding political imperative to preserve the integration project will surely drive its leaders to ultimately secure the euro and restore the economic health of the continent.[11]

Germany Was from the Beginning a Willing Contributor to a European Solution

Germany's leadership sought to assign primary responsibility for dealing with the EU to individual member states. Germany wanted to preempt an alternative narrative that viewed the crisis as a systemic event requiring all parties to acknowledge their complicity in generating it. They wanted to participate in the adjustment process from a position of strength. Whatever the need for action, the national framing is also supported by governing treaty provisions, particularly the "No bail out" article (104b) of the Treaty on European Union specifically exonerating member states from sovereign debt incurred by their peers. Moreover, acknowledgment of the systemic character of the crisis could translate into joint responsibility for its resolution. In this, policy was consistent across all governments since the project of European integration was launched; Germany's position anchored the original limitation of grant-based social programs in the Treaty of Rome, alongside the establishment of the European Investment Bank, whose funds were to be repaid. In the same vein, responses to the Great Recession included proposals for stabilization of the euro area as a whole via joint (EU) issuance of bonds that could leverage the creditworthiness of AAA-rated countries like Germany and other Northern European euro area members. Germany rejected this approach on political as well as financial and technical grounds, though at least some portions of the Social Democratic and Greens opposition parties viewed the idea in a positive light.

German decisionmakers were clear about using rescue funds as leverage to advance cures for bad behavior in the euro area. Merkel's Free Democratic Party (FDP) coalition partner favored budget consolidation in the German domestic context, and the resulting €80 billion savings package and adoption of a constitutional provision designed to limit public debt were spun to project the moral force of example in demanding fiscal probity across the EU and eventuating of the Fiscal Pact signed by twenty-five member states in March 2012. The Germans understood the faulty logic of *Milchmädchenrechnung*— that what was true at the household level did not hold in the aggregate economy—but dismissed the relevance of this insight for political, economic, and Euro-strategic reasons. Politically, Merkel needed to accommodate the FDP. Economically, they could point to their own painful "internal devaluation" earlier in the decade and were able to turn the argument around by referencing the global reach of Germany's export performance. Euro-strategically, they wanted to use the crisis to advance reforms to improve the functioning of the euro area, closer to the ideal of an optimum currency area.

Defining membership of the euro area had been contentious in the 1990s. Finance Minister Wolfgang Schäuble advocated a core federated Europe concept consistent with a tighter, Northern European grouping. He returned to the idea in 2010 and was willing to cut Greece free.[12] Contingency plans were drawn up for "Grexit," an eventuality that turned on the outcome of an EU referendum-like Greek national election in May 2012. In the end, stringent conditions for assistance to Greece imposed by the Commission, the ECB, and the IMF (the troika)—reforms prioritizing fiscal consolidation—corresponded to the size of the effort, which was the largest sovereign bailout to date. German attitudes were more accommodating toward Portugal, Ireland, and

Spain. Germany mobilized a coalition of North European euro area states (mainly the Finns, Swedes, Danes, and Dutch) whose economic and financial policy preferences converged on several key positions.

Germany's strategy was demanding for relatively small countries/ economies like Greece, Portugal, Ireland, and Cyprus, but it was more difficult for larger ones like Spain. For a big country/economy like Italy, no politically feasible firewall could be mobilized. Italy's sovereign debt/GDP ratio was well over 100 percent already when it joined the euro area with the first group of members in 1999. When, during the 2010–2012 crisis, the Berlusconi government could not find the will to introduce reforms aimed at calming the markets and interest rates on its debt, and the EU could not credibly offer backing, the euro area faced an existential moment. Two responses ensued involving Italy's two "Super Marios." The first was to arrange a change in political leadership to mollify markets by policy reforms. Berlusconi was induced to step aside in favor of the former EU commissioner for competition policy, the Italian Mario Monti. This step was backed up by Mario Draghi's "whatever it takes" announcement, referring to ECB purchases of government bonds in the furtherance of its stability mandate. This act revealed divergent positions of the Bundesbank versus the German government, with the Bundesbank representative isolated in the ECB council with the view that the OMT (Outright Monetary Transactions) instrument to be deployed by the ECB was in fact fiscal support (prohibited by the treaty's no bailout clause) by another name. That divergence then emboldened German EMU skeptics to file another challenge in Germany's constitutional court. Germany's representative on the ECB council, Bundesbank chairman Jens Weidmann, resisted the policy, and German ECB executive board member Jürgen Stark resigned over it. The United States, sometimes with European connivance, also advanced the case for ECB action assiduously to Germany.[13]

According to German constitutional provision and several cases adjudicated before the Federal Constitutional Court, although Germany is constitutionally connected via Article 23 GG to the EU, the EU is understood as a *Staatenbund* (confederation), not a *Bundesstaat* (federation). The point is that pooling of sovereignty at EU level is permitted as long as the member states control the process. By this definition, the ECB has an ambiguous status, and there is some scope for differing interpretations of what is permissible between the ECB and German governmental authorities. The ECB is by design a federal institution, analogous to the US monetary system, with a central board and national (in the United States, regional) authorities. In the EU context, pooling sovereignty in monetary policy meant that Germany's partners would collectively control Germany's power to set policy. The price paid by the other EU member states for the euro was an ECB mandate based on the Bundesbank's monetary stability orientation (in contrast to the US Federal Reserve, which is also accountable for balancing monetary stability with low levels of unemployment). Subsequent to the launch of the new currency and the ECB, the Bundesbank carried on its institutional tradition as guarantor of this narrow mandate. An equally important element, also analogous to Germany's institutional landscape, consisted of the central bank's constitutional autonomy. Like the Bundesbank, the ECB was established beyond the reach of direct government influence. The corollary was that member states had to reorder central bank–government relations to conform to this model, in those cases in which governments possessed some directive authority over central banks—and this for the EU generally, not just euro area members. It was not coincidental that the ECB headquarters were set up next door to the Bundesbank's in Frankfurt. With this European watchdog role in mind, the Bundesbank continues to be a key institution for Germany's financial constitution.

Turning to the issue of institutional innovation and policy development to decrease the risks of Reinhart-Rogoff-type financial crises,[14] in the future, we start with the regulatory dimension to Germany's position. Offense was taken at careless practices of financial institutions in packaging securities and triggering the crisis, a reflex that has its source in the prudential culture of Germany's *Sozialmarktwirtschaft* (social market economy). It takes almost willful amnesia to forget the outrage resulting from hedge fund raids that left mass unemployment in their wake—part of what was derisively referred to as *amerikanische Verhältnisse* (the American way). Germany had no property bubble, but its banks were heavily invested in euro area sovereign debt in Greece and Iberia. Thus in the German context, it made sense to insist on private sector involvement—that is, investor losses, "haircuts"—in any bailout scenario to discourage the moral hazard of risky behavior. Of course, given the fragile state of the euro area, attempts to establish policy undertaken by Merkel and French president Nicolas Sarkozy at Deauville in October 2010 would make the crisis worse by spooking investors. The Deauville meeting stands out, nevertheless, as an example of Franco-German coordination in EU policy development, a central trope of European integration since the Schuman Declaration. In the case of the March 2013 bailout of Cyprus, Germany's underlying concern was use of the banking sector as a platform for Russian money laundering, that is, it was a regulatory more than an economic concern.

The same logic applied when the parties turned to updating the governance structure of the EMU. Attention to fiscal probity across the EU was the point of departure. Better monitoring and improved coordination with better preventive and corrective mechanisms figured centrally. The European Semester is complex,[15] but at core requires member states to submit government budgets to the EU for evaluation before introducing them to their own parliamentary authorities. Tightening of the Stability and Growth Pact was agreed on at the European Council on March 25, 2011, and ended up strengthening the role of the Commission through the reverse qualified majority voting rule. On the same day the Euro-plus Pact was announced, Berlin's initiative to tie access to the EFSF successor, the European Stability Mechanism (ESM), to structural reform programs among six euro area aspirants. Emphasis on aspirational fiscal consolidation continued with the Fiscal Compact of March 2012 (notably absent the UK, which held out to strike a better deal for the City of London's financial services sector).

Germany's position vis-à-vis the constellation of proposals, conventionally summarized under the heading of banking union, shows a similar pattern. Berlin went along with some EU federalization of bank supervision, but held out for a system that distinguishes between larger, systemically relevant and transnational entities versus the hundreds of smaller market participants, for which the reach of the new banking authority nested in the ECB will be indirect. Regarding resolution authority for failing banks, Berlin sought above all to avoid financial responsibility, and the result was a messy compromise both procedurally, involving a labyrinthine decision-making process, and in terms of the ramping-up period for accumulation of contributions from banks to fund the authority. In the end, Finance Minister Schäuble gave more ground to the European Parliament than he did to the other EU finance ministers. Finally, in light of the amelioration of the crisis from late 2012, the project of common deposit insurance has stalled, again, in Germany's case, because it wishes to avoid open-ended commitments.

Partisan Politics in Germany's Consensus-Oriented Polity Both Influenced and Was Influenced by the Euro Crisis

Alternating national governing coalitions, even with the same chancellor, produced different responses to challenges. At the start of the crisis, Germany was governed by a grand coalition of Christian Democrats (CDU-CSU) and Social Democrats (SPD) under CDU leader Angela Merkel's first chancellorship. Notwithstanding this policy success, Germany's political landscape changed in the September 2009 Bundestag election, which produced a demoralizing repudiation of the SPD, its lowest result in the era of the Federal Republic. In the new national government the SPD was replaced by the high-flying Free Democrats (FDP), a party of classical liberalism and industrial interests, ever a small party alongside the larger, more collectivist Christian and Social Democrats. Four years later, in September 2013, the FDP was cashiered in turn, and 2013 ended with the renewal of the grand coalition. Even as the financial crisis symptoms eased, the opponents drove Merkel's FDP coalition partner to ruin by upsetting its internal balance on EU policy, some of its members bolting from the party to form the Euro-skeptic Alternative für Deutschland (AfD) in the run-up to the 2013 Bundestag elections. An important factor in the rise of the AfD is the aforementioned framing of the discussion of the euro area crisis. Desperation in the euro area periphery, especially in the program countries—Greece, Portugal, Ireland, Spain—was interpreted moralistically as failures of those countries. Analysts and politicians suggesting that growth was as important a priority as fiscal consolidation found no hearing. Corollary criticism that persistently large German export surpluses implied a demand-suppressing and therefore growth-killing feature of its macroeconomic performance was similarly brushed aside.

Though Merkel's Christian Democrats also benefited from the FDP's problems, the FDP's disappearance from the Bundestag meant that Merkel needed a new coalition partner. Of the two available, the Greens or the SPD, it was the Social Democrats who made the cut. Though the AfD did not make it into the Bundestag—its 4.7 percent of the vote was just short of the 5 percent threshold for representation, it tapped and defined a current in the German electorate that virtually guaranteed its success in the May 2014 European Parliament elections. In this, the AfD did not even need the recent ruling of the German constitutional court abolishing the representational threshold for the EP election, as it achieved 7 percent. It managed this by mobilizing electoral support around figures with name recognition from industry and marrying its euro area populism (return to the deutsche mark), opposing any payout from German taxpayers to "undeserving" countries, to the primary concern of Europe's right-wing populists—unease about foreigners in their midst—without demanding the end of the EU. In the end, its appeal was a better defense of German interests in the EU than the government of the day. But the AfD could only ever be a protest party, since it is toxic to both the major parties in the German constellation. In the end, it succeeded as a spoiler, fatally undermining the liberal FDP in the national election of September 2013 as well as the 2014 European Parliament election. The FDP had functioned as the CDU coalition partner of choice since the 1960s. Its electoral demise in 2013, thanks also to a poor showing by the Greens, led to a return of the grand coalition with the SPD.

The EU policy implications of the grand coalition were politically integrative, interpreted as a signal of moderation. During the crisis, discussions within the SPD aired some support for euro bonds and growth stimulus, proposals consistent with an EU-systemic perspective. They were also consistent with transnational coalitions seeking to revise troika policy in the program countries and the preferences of governments in Germany's two biggest euro area partners, Italy and France. That these policies were mostly tactically deployed in the opposition is demonstrated in the coalition agreement with the CDU hammered out after the 2013 election and the continuation of Schäuble in the role of minister of finance.[16]

At Policy Level, German Preferences Meant the
ECB Assumed a Central Role in Crisis Resolution

Draghi's July 2012 "whatever it takes" statement was in essence an acknowledgment that given Germany's position, only the ECB was in a position to do something about the "doom loop" weighting down governments with outsized sovereign debt incurred by their own crisis response programs in response to the failure of national financial institutions. In the wake of the constitutional court's ruling on the OMT sovereign bond purchasing program, which deftly reassigned jurisdiction to the ECJ, even Bundesbank president Jens Weidmann signaled willingness to countenance a European version of quantitative easing, if circumstances demanded.

Indeed, by the end of 2014, the macroeconomic policy debate swirls around the specter of a Japan-like scenario of low growth linked to deficient demand and low lending levels. ECB policy aims at inflation of about 2 percent per year, but the actual figure hovers at about a third of that, making it all the harder for countries to service debt and emerge from programs. Italy and France have made common cause in trying to persuade the Germans to reflate and allow them to put off achieving their macro-targets agreed in council. But the euro area has been showing an export surplus, much of it accounted for by Germany. There is simply no appetite for change of monetary policy in the Bundesbank or the government in Berlin, even though export success is linked to upward pressure on the euro/US$ exchange rate (which depresses growth prospects further in most of the euro area).

Despite the array of federalizing measures generated by the euro crisis, they stopped well short of what was envisaged in the 1977 MacDougall Report. There were discussions about "fiscal union," but it was considered politically unachievable. Nevertheless, decisions in the euro area pointed in the direction of a transformed European architecture, not only in Germany's relentless pursuit of stronger EU fiscal governance cum implicit promises of assistance, which contributed to refashioning the matrix of norms to which member states are bound in new hybrid forms,[17] but also in sharpening the choices between more integration and less, reflecting the political pressure in the UK over Britain's future in the project and opening the prospect for a two-tier Europe—the more tightly integrated euro area and the rest, which might accommodate increasingly ambivalent aspirants like Turkey and someday Ukraine.

There is no question that Germany emerges from the Great Recession in a position of greater acknowledged power. In fact, German economic and financial power has been great since the 1970s at the latest. Although Germany has formulated a strategy for dealing with the financial and economic tsunami of 2009 and successfully used its leverage to implement it, it nevertheless did so in an environment defined by the existing matrix of European institutions—Council, Parliament, Commission, ECJ, and above all the

ECB—and used its leverage to define a new generation of EU financial regulatory agencies and fiscal surveillance mechanisms, not to mention the treaty-parallel crisis financial firewall, the ESM. This outcome reflects a willingness to marshal resources in a difficult political environment. That it also reflects German mainstream policy precepts and seeks to protect German interests should not be surprising. None of this makes Germany's contribution any the less "European." Systemic crisis revealed institutional design deficiencies that required remodeling. Enough of a European edifice already existed to channel responses into an architectural moment backed by resources of a well-endowed and successful actor, self-confident about its own design. The result is a regional version of the US role in fashioning an international economic and financial order out of the ruins of World War II.

Issues Remain

Hegemony requires buy-in by affected groups in a system like the EU whose structure and ethos (unity in diversity) encourages competing policy narratives and whose policy style awards inclusion. Crisis policy implementation produced countervailing movements, and not just in program countries. Far in advance of the 2014 European Parliament election, they articulated dissent and alternative policy ideas that did in fact find voice in EU policy forums. Indeed, attempts were made at the highest levels to persuade the German government to recalibrate priorities of fiscal consolidation versus growth at the Cannes G7 summit.[18] Yet German-inspired policy preferences were matched by significant EU institutional innovation, which again Europeanized decisionmaking.

Ukraine: Whither *Westbindung*?
Reemergence of Germany as *Zentralmacht*?

The integration project was created and has always functioned as a working peace system. The main narrative has been about taming German power.[19] Germany has clearly embraced an architectural leadership role in the Great Recession. But it has traditionally eschewed leadership in political-military affairs on the continent, let alone further afield. It has found comfort in designation as a civilian power and a trading nation. What happens when this civilian power architecture itself comes under threat? The crisis of Ukraine clearly raises this question.

At the February 2014 annual Munich Security Conference, German president Joachim Gauck delivered a speech acknowledging German responsibility for international peace and stability.[20] At that moment, hundreds of thousands of Ukrainian citizens on the Maidan in Kiev were expressing their preference for an EU association over one with Russia. In a few short weeks, Germany had to decide how to address Russian subversion of Ukraine—a naked invasion of Crimea, annexed to Russia within a week, and violence and intimidation in the remaining eastern and southern provinces of a country whose territorial integrity Russia guaranteed along with the UK and the United States in the 1994 agreement that removed nuclear weapons from the country. This was also a clear violation of the Helsinki Accords of 1976 and more broadly of basic international legal norms. Europe's postwar order—indeed, the whole meaning of European integration—was called into question.

Germany had begun to take responsibility for the security of Europe. In 1999, Germany's SPD-Greens government supported intervention (with NATO) in Kosovo. In 2001, Chancellor Schröder rallied his government behind the United States as it intervened in Afghanistan. But Schröder refused to follow the United States into Iraq in 2003 and abstained when the UN Security Council authorized intervention in Libya in 2011. Germany's position in the Libyan episode was described by FDP foreign minister Guido Westerwelle as an expression of Germany's culture of military restraint. It was a position that grated in Washington, Paris, and London, coming in the context of a major strategic challenge—and opportunity—in the so-called Arab Spring, and in light of Germany's dwindling military expenditures, NATO agreements on that score to the contrary notwithstanding. Against that background, Gauck's Munich speech attracted widespread attention. He acknowledged that Germany had sometimes sheltered behind other NATO partners in assuming responsibility for difficult problems and that the increasing complexity of challenges required a greater willingness to engage.

Germany's September 2013 election resulted in a return to the CDU-SPD grand coalition and a return to the foreign ministry of Frank Walter Steinmeier, architect of Germany's "modernization partnership" with Russia. The January 2014 Wehrkunde heralded the foreign policy debut of the new government, and German foreign policy was immediately tested with the crisis in Ukraine. For Germany, the issue was how to respond to a popular appeal backed by a significant part of the political class for Ukraine's westward orientation, taking the specific form of an association agreement with the EU in the context of the EU's European Neighborhood Policy (ENP). The Swedish and Polish governments had been advocating a policy of intensified engagement since the ENP was launched in the wake of Russia's invasion of Georgia in 2008. Russia president Vladimir Putin countered with an offer to Ukrainian president Viktor Yanukovych to join Russia's Eurasian Union project.

In November 2013, Yanukovych canceled Ukraine's expected signing with the EU and indicated he would take Ukraine into the Eurasian Union instead. This transformed the situation on the Maidan, which rapidly filled, with crowds sometimes approximating 1 million, demanding a Western-oriented Ukraine—one with better rule-of-law institutions, less corruption, and a better outlook for life chances. The blue and yellow of the Ukrainian flag flew alongside EU flags. Under intense pressure, Yanukovych agreed to meet protest leaders, and a Euro-Maidan agreement was signed and witnessed by German foreign minister Frank-Walter Steinmeier along with his French and Polish counterparts. It lasted scarcely twenty-four hours, undermined by Yanukovych's precipitate flight into Russian exile after a military action that killed nearly 100 on or near the Maidan. This left elected parliamentary leaders siding with the protestors in control, and they immediately appointed an interim president and prime minister with parliamentary backing and also set the date of May 25 for election of a new president, to be followed later by new parliamentary elections. With Russian connivance in the form of lightly disguised security forces on the ground, backed up by an estimated 40,000 combat troops massed on Ukraine's eastern border, separatists seized public buildings and in an atmosphere of coercion organized independence referendums, first in Crimea in March, which Russia formally annexed within a week, and then in Donetsk in May. NATO members reacted by threatening and then implementing a phased introduction of economic sanctions specifically targeting the Russian political leadership.

The crisis divided the German business leadership, political class, and commentariat. Germany's postunification relationship to Russia is heavily invested and complex. Germany is far and away Russia's biggest trade and investment partner, though Russia ranks eleventh, after Poland, as Germany's top trade partners. There are an estimated 6,500 German firms doing business in Russia. Then there is energy dependence, which at the time of this writing amounts to about 30 percent of gas consumption.

An agreement between Russia and the EU, the United States, and Ukraine was worked out on April 17 to disarm illegal groups, vacate occupied buildings, hold presidential elections as planned, and associate the Organization for Security and Co-operation in Europe (OSCE) with the process. Nevertheless, the situation on the ground continued to deteriorate. A small team of OSCE military observers, including four Germans, sent to eastern Ukraine on the request of the interim government was taken into custody by separatists. German senior diplomat Wolfgang Ischinger was brought out of retirement to lead another OSCE effort to deescalate, but Russia continued its relentless campaign to destabilize eastern Ukraine. In the weeks after Ukrainians went to the polls on May 25 in large numbers to elect "chocolate billionaire" Petro Poroshenko president, Russia introduced tanks, artillery, armored vehicles, and rocket launchers into Ukraine and on July 17, 2014, a Buk surface-to-air missile fired from that area brought down a commercial airliner, killing all 298 passengers and crew.

Successive rounds of sanctions against Russia were introduced in 2014, and on July 29, the EU announced a round of sectoral sanctions against key players in Russia's energy and arms economy and financial institutions, with Chancellor Merkel playing a central role. So far, she has succeeded in overcoming resistance in the SPD, the Foreign Office, and German industry, and on that basis prevailed among her peers in other EU member states.

Alternatives for Germany

The May 2014 European Parliament elections indicate that Euro-skepticism proved a bust in Germany. Even the AfD ended up supporting continued German membership, the overwhelming consensus position. And why not? Over the life of the seventh directly elected EP, Germany's position had established itself unequivocally as Europe's directive force in the crisis of the euro area. Under conditions of improving economic circumstances in Germany itself, neither AfD nor SPD were ever in a position to credibly argue that they would be better stewards of Germany's European policy. By mid-2014, AfD leader Bernd Lucke was successful in gaining membership for his group in the Tory-dominated European Conservatives and Reformists bloc in the European Parliament. Though unassailably logical with respect to alignment of their positions on European integration, the move put Chancellor Merkel and UK prime minister David Cameron at odds. Merkel then backed European People's Party European Parliament *Spitzenkandidat* Jean-Claude Juncker, a choice publicly repudiated by Cameron, as the next Commission president.

The euro area crisis will continue to challenge German leaders—the pain of adjustment in troika program countries continues to be a stern test of cohesion. Italian prime minister Matteo Renzi, alongside Merkel the biggest winner among centrist parties in the 2014 EP elections, did not waste much time in publicly petitioning for a change in euro area priorities from fiscal consolidation to growth. Still, if societal consensus in Germany on the EU makes up a European resource to be carefully husbanded, then it is hard to avoid the conclusion that Germany's government performed in an enlightened manner, according to need.

Over the same period, the EU in effect acted as a shelter for Germany in areas in which its government would rather not act—whether in Libya or Ukraine. In the past, German restraint has served Europe well. Gradual assumption of greater responsibility in response to proposals from its NATO and EU partners is the most reasonable course of action. Statements supporting that concept from Germany's political leaders in 2014, the early phase of the new national coalition government, can hardly be criticized.

But a debate is unavoidable in reassessing Germany's relations with Russia. For too long Germany's attitude toward Europe between itself and Russia has been hostage to its Russian policy, exhibited dramatically in the reaction of Russia to Ukraine's Euro-Maidan movement. Tensions between two fundamental principles of German policy—accommodation with Russia and a European order based on rule of law—have been brewing at least since the Orange Revolution. Now Germany must choose whether it can sacrifice the Euro-Maidan on the altar of its commitment to comity with Russia, when comity portends a sphere-of-interest politics that the whole concept of European integration was designed to transcend.

Some of its response will be articulated vis-à-vis renewed initiatives for EU energy policy. If it chooses to do so, Germany could advance its green agenda and at the same time promote solidarity with Poland and the rest of Eastern EU member states, deepen the EU internal market, and raise the profile of the EU as a global actor. What Germany can achieve and what Germany desires to achieve with respect to European integration are questions that may have significantly different answers. Former US ambassador to Germany John Kornblum is convinced that the outcomes we see are intentional, that "the solution to Germany's leadership dilemma is closer European cooperation" belongs to the several myths about German leadership.[21] It will be up to the Germans to prove him wrong.

Notes

1. Stevenson (2004), pp. 436–437 on Aristide Briand's plan in 1929 for a European Union.

2. Holborn (1951) and DePorte (1980).

3. Kennan (1947).

4. Figures in this paragraph are taken from Eurostat (2012) at http://epp.eurostat .ec.europa.eu/tgm/table.do?tab=table&init=1&language=en&pcode=tec00001& plugin=1 (accessed May 10, 2014).

5. See Castles and Miller (1993).

6. Milward, Romero, and Brennan (2000).

7. Eurostat (2012). Of the 8.8 percent, 3.5 percent came from other EU member states and 5.3 percent came from third countries. The overall percentage is not much different from that of the United States at the same date.

8. Members of an al-Qaeda cell operating out of Hamburg carried out the attacks on the World Trade Center and Pentagon.

9. The popularity of the EU waxes and wanes. In a poll released on May 12, 2014, less than two weeks before the European Parliament elections, the main takeaway point was "disillusion with the EU seems to be ending." See Stokes (2014).

10. Brenke et al. (2013).

11. Bergsten and Kirkegaard (2012).

12. Spiegel (2014).

13. Ibid.

14. Reinhart and Rogoff (2009), Preamble and Chapter 1, where the authors distinguish financial crises from other events.

15. Hallerberg (2011).

16. *Koalitionsvertrag zwischen CDU, CSU und SPD*, 18, Legislaturperiode (Stand 24.11.2013). European policy is listed as item six of eight, just before foreign and defense policy. The first three items are the economy, work, and public finance, respectively.

17. Armstrong (2013).

18. Spiegel (2014).

19. Katzenstein (1998).

20. Joachim Gauck, "Germany's Role in the World: Reflections on Responsibility, Norms and Alliances," speech at the opening of the Munich Security Conference (2014). Available at http://www.bundespraesident.de/SharedDocs/Downloads/DE /Reden/2014/01/140131-Muenchner-Sicherheitskonferenz-Englisch.pdf;jsessionid =20C8E1F055E3DC1DCCFE81D84804859D.2_cid379?__blob=publicationFile.

21. John Kornblum, "Five Myths about German Leadership," Carnegie Europe, May 27, 2014. Available at http://carnegieeurope.eu/strategiceurope/?fa=55699 (accessed May 27, 2014).

4

France:
Adjustment to the Euro System

Christian Deubner

THE MANNER IN WHICH THE FRENCH SEE AND INTERPRET EUROPE and European affairs in 2008 and after is strongly influenced by inherited paradigms dating from the European Union's formative period of the 1950s and 1960s. In consequence, even when looking at reactions to the crisis of the years 2008–2013, their political weight and connotations will only be understood when seen in their longer term political-institutional and economic context.

The Political and Institutional Heritage of French Integration in the EU

The specific advantages France drew from EU membership consisted in providing a firmly established regional cooperation and an institutional framework within which France could influence how it would take part in the liberalization of international economic exchanges. This framework was supposed to protect the French society and economy against excessive pressures resulting from this liberalization—in 2014 we would say "globalization"—and permit an adaptation adjusted to its own capacities. Nevertheless, membership in the EC/EU has never been a self-evident outcome of French politics. The idea of a French drawback from present levels of European integration continues to nourish the French euro-political debate, especially on the far left and the far right.

The ambivalence of French positions vis-à-vis EU integration finds part of its explanation in the six-decades-old contradictions between the policy objectives of its main political forces. On the one hand, there were the founding fathers, Robert Schuman, Jean Monnet, and the Catholic and centrist parties behind them who invented the first 1950 integration initiative and the community method with its supranational elements. These elements also mark the treaty for the European Economic Community (EEC of 1957), negotiated and signed by a socialist-dominated government. The founding fathers have their survivors in the main centrist party, Union pour la Démocratie Française (UDF) of today. But they remain a minority current of the political center-right, which is dominated by the neo-Gaullists. The French socialist fathers of the EEC survive in the Socialist Party in power in 2014.

Then came Charles de Gaulle, French president during the EEC's first formative decade of 1958 to 1969, opponent of the European Defence Community and the other European treaties, creator of the nationalist Rassemblement pour la France,[1] defender of a grand power role for France and enemy of supranationalism. The communists and other forces to the left of the socialists, together with the groups to the right of the Gaullists, were also opposed to European integration but were too small to gain direct influence on the construction of the EU. Once elected first president of the Fifth Republic in December 1958, de Gaulle stuck with the European integration treaties that he had earlier opposed, and he started to see France's interest in modernizing and liberalizing its economy within the EEC. He also succeeded early on in preventing more federalist orientations from being put into practice.[2]

The legacy of this period is contradictory, with France's biggest center-right party a staunch defender of European integration. Simultaneously, the idea of French uniqueness and grandeur, or at least of France's ability to go it alone, has remained to impede full acceptance of further progress of European integration.[3] In France there is almost no political force left in the whole spectrum that would accept federalism as a legitimate perspective of European integration. As for the Union altogether, Gaullism has bequeathed it, even before Margaret Thatcher, a strong element of intergovernmentalism.

Germany and French European Policy

The geopolitical reality of its neighborhood with Germany has been a (if not *the*) first-order determinant for France's choice of Europe. Every debate about France's economic and political weight and power in Europe takes Germany as its reference. Since the beginning of the Cold War in 1947, since the United States began to pressure for inclusion of West Germany into an anti-Soviet alliance in Europe, French postwar balance-of-power politics against a potentially stronger Germany became untenable. France's overwhelming impulse for security vis-à-vis its neighbor found expression in binding West Germany closely into the European integration project. This French reflex of reacting to increased German power with increased European integration willingness has remained active up to the present.[4]

De Gaulle initiated a special bilateral coalition of the two countries in 1962 to magnify their influence in Europe.[5] Because basic economic policy and institutional orientations of the two countries differ, EU policymaking has frequently become synonymous, for each government, with defining its respective attitude vis-à-vis the others' concepts and searching bilateral points of agreement to propose to the other member states. In the absence of agreement, the latters' support might also be sought—but with less chance of success—for a unilateral French or German proposal and against the other one.[6] The French financial crisis policies were strongly marked by this bilateralism.

The Instability of Popular Support for European Integration
The Failed Referendum of May 29, 2005

From the beginning the French have had a tumultuous relationship with European integration because the popular majority for more integration has always been rather slim, French politicians or electorates not hesitating to make dramatic decisions—or votes for that matter—against further progress in European integration. Nevertheless, most of the time France has been able to play a highly constructive and even crucially positive role for European integration.

This mixture of positions is present in French financial and euro crisis policy in 2008 and afterward. It has certainly contributed to the failure of the referendum of May 29, 2005, on the EU constitutional treaty of 2004, a referendum clearly lost because of strong reservations not against the EU as such but as it was perceived—and painted by the skeptics—to have become at that time. The promise of integration to France had been to soften globalization's negative effects for the French economy and render the process more controllable. But in the end, the decades since 1980 coincided with the inexorable increase of unemployment in France. The hope linked with European integration has often turned into outspoken fears that it might contribute to social degradation. These circumstances were clearly recognizable in the reasons given for the "no" vote in the 2005 referendum.[7] This EU was not found to deserve explicit solemn confirmation in a constitutional act.[8] One important heritage of that failure is the further strengthening of skepticism against European integration, with the Front National and the political left including parts of the governing Socialist Party as the two rallying points.

The financial and euro crisis came just a very few years after the failed referendum, and one may well ask whether it has confirmed French misgivings about deeper integration and whether the slim advance for the historic approval of integration in France may now be disappearing together with the political support for constructive or daring steps in further European integration. We will see whether France's reaction to the financial crisis of 2008 and after gives a clue to the outcome of this worrying uncertainty.

The Financial and Economic Upheavals of 2008 and After

Longer Term Elements, Europe, and the French Economy

As to the crisis of 2008 and after, the underlying economic and social issues also have a longer term history, which has to be taken into account, even in acknowledging important specific effects of the financial crisis of 2008. The newest pillar of the Union, namely, the common currency of the euro, has since its inauguration in 1999 become a crucially important element of the EU institutional frame in which French economic developments took place. It is not very difficult to assemble the basic elements underpinning the economic diagnosis because most experts across the board agree on them. Frequently they compare the French achievements and weaknesses with other large economies. Most of all, they refer to Germany. This analysis follows that example.

Status Quo Ante

The French economy has already seen its growth rate decrease over the past three decades, from 2.4 percent in the 1980s to 1.9 percent in the 1990s and 1.8 percent in the years between 2000 and 2007.[9]

French foreign trade deteriorated after an ascent in the 1990s: from balance in 2004 to a deficit of −2.2 percent in 2012. Over the same period, the share of French goods and services in international export markets has descended from 6 percent in 1994 to below 4 percent in 2012, whereas German exporters have preserved their share of 9–10 percent.[10] The receding growth rates and world market shares of France over the past decades were mainly a result of insufficient productivity progress from the high level reached in the 1990s and lagging innovation confronting high and further rising labor cost. Low and decreasing profitability of private companies, in particular in the manufacturing sector, was the result.

According to French economists, the insufficient profit margins in the French enterprise sector are what have prevented industrial firms from keeping up with their foreign competitors since the late 1980s, leading to deindustrialization and insufficient investment in technical progress. On the financial front, an important result is their higher indebtedness compared with their principal competitors in Germany.[11] Even so, until the end of the 1990s French international competitiveness—even if it decreased in terms of innovation and quality of French goods—could be upheld in terms of price, and consequently its balance of trade and of payments remained sustainable as well, even though with upward and downward fluctuations.

The explanation lay in France's freedom to manage its money's foreign exchange rate, with which the fallbacks in competitiveness could be compensated. Vis-à-vis the German mark, for instance, the French franc devalued by around 30 percent in every one of the four decades between 1949 and 1989.[12] After 1989 came the postreunification boom in Germany. For about a decade

French (and Italian) producers' exports grew quickly, even French firms' R&D improved, whereas German firms' competitiveness shrank due to high debt and excessive labor costs; France did very well without devaluation. But its firms did not use this window of opportunity for the necessary structural adaptations to the sharpened international competition.

This period ended at the turn of the century, with the start of the euro and a forceful corrective movement of cost control and debt reduction in German firms, supplemented by a political reform of the German labor market from 2003 onward. This resulted in a sustained catch-up movement, which erased the French advances of the 1990s. But at this moment, the advent of the euro (created on French initiative!) had deprived French economic policymakers of the instrument of devaluation. A sea change! That moment begins what Didier and Koléda call the "grande rupture" in economic competitiveness between French firms and their principal European competitors from Germany (and elsewhere).[13] Without the option of currency devaluation to support its exports, France resorted to more public spending and debt to compensate the resulting loss of demand.

The now more-than-a-decade-long loss of international market shares of French business, accompanied by increasing unemployment and indebtedness, is without precedent and concerns all industrial sectors. This alarming development already confronted the presidency of Jacques Chirac since 2002 and Nicolas Sarkozy since 2007; it persists under François Hollande since 2012. The onset of the crisis since 2008 added to but did not create these problems.

The Role of Politics in Economic and Social Affairs
Status Quo Ante
Domestic policy has played a big role in the creation of these economic dilemmas, first by closing its eyes to the new constraint created by monetary union, namely, to adapt in real terms so as to become and remain competitive vis-à-vis its partners in European and world markets. The reduction of profits has largely been caused by politics, principally linked to the big social policy innovation of this time: the reduction of the legal working time with constant remuneration, and also the excessive increase of more traditional legally fixed social cost components: the share of social security charges imposed on firms and the minimum wage, the SMIC. The SMIC is fixed by the government, which may but is not obligated to follow the proposal of an independent expert council. Accordingly political considerations play a role. Being higher in France, with €9.4 per hour, than in almost all other EU member states, the SMIC is frequently considered harmful for employment,[14] (Germany's new minimum wage is fixed at €8.5 for 2015). French industry together with commercial services have hourly labor costs (including employ-

ers' social charges) of €35.7, which lie clearly above those of their competitors among other large EU member states (Germany €32.9 in 2013–2014).[15] Only in the manufacturing industry does Germany retain a slight hourly labor cost advantage (€37.5) compared to France (€37.4).

In addition, the politicization of French trade unions and strike activity and the excessive proportion of public employment (see later discussion) certainly play important roles in restraining productivity progress. They are not dealt with in more detail here. The French employment rate before 2008 already hovered slightly below the average of the Eurozone countries. In comparison with the other large but more competitive economy of Germany, this had already been clearly too low, 64.8 percent versus 70.1 percent.[16] This made for a high unemployment rate of around 8–10 percent over the past twenty years, a rate that affects especially the young and the elder job seekers. On the eve of the crisis, Sarkozy started his presidency with about 8.5 percent unemployment in May 2007, with an improvement to 7.7 percent one year later.[17]

Crisis Effects

By August 2007, the first financial market turbulence had occurred in the United States. The effect of the US banks' subprime mortgage crisis in Europe was twofold: on the economic output and on the way it was interpreted. Particularly concerning the financial sector, the appreciation of risks deteriorated dramatically. Credit-financed economic activity, like investment, was hit, as well as the mortgage-fueled building booms of Ireland and Spain and the banks that had financed these activities. Highly indebted states saw their creditworthiness come under new scrutiny. For some of them, credit ratings worsened and the risk premium for their borrowing soared, like for Portugal and for overindebted Greece from the moment of the first explicit avowal in autumn 2009. The same fate overtook Spain and Ireland after they shouldered the costly bailouts of their banks.

Everywhere in Europe asset values, investment, and demand tumbled and recession set in. Figure 4.1 shows this clearly in the gray columns (Italy is missing, but it moved in the same direction). Interestingly, France was less affected at the beginning than were many other European countries. After still growing by 2.3 percent in 2007 followed a dip of 0.1 percent in 2008 and 3.1 percent in 2009. Probably this comparatively low ratio was due to its growth depending more on domestic consumption and less on exports (27 percent of GDP), compared with Germany (48 percent), Ireland (83 percent), and the Netherlands (76 percent),[18] and to the lesser exposure of its banks to subprime assets, compared with the UK and Germany, among others.[19] Renewed growth of 1.7 percent and 2.0 percent in 2010–2011 followed, but a new descent to around zero in 2012 dashed the hopes for an end of the crisis.[20] Nevertheless, over the crisis years, the cu-

Figure 4.1 Differences in the Success of First-Year Crisis Management, 2008–2009 (second quarter)

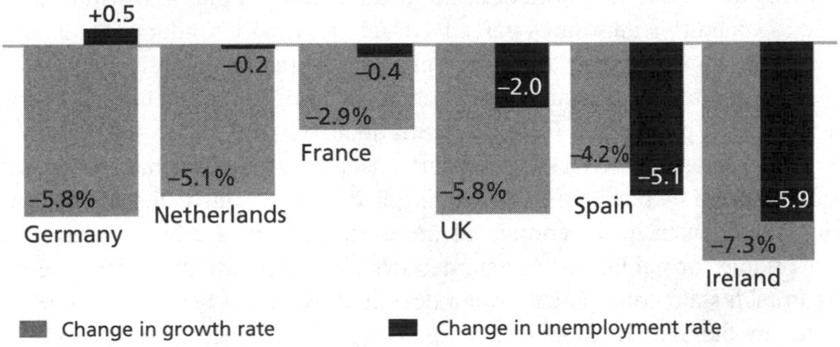

+0.5

−0.2   −0.4
−2.9%
        −2.0
France
              −4.2%
−5.1%   −5.1
−5.8%   −5.8%   Spain   −5.9
Germany   Netherlands   UK
                                        −7.3%
                                        Ireland

■ Change in growth rate   ■ Change in unemployment rate

Source: Böckler Impuls, No. 14/2010; data from European Trade Union Institute (2010).

mulative loss of national economic output was below the Eurozone average. Further down we will see that there was a price to pay for this relative advantage, in terms of higher public debt.

As with the economy in general, deterioration of employment was at first not very marked because of the quick activation of a state-subsidized stabilizing mechanism, the partial unemployment regime. In other EU member states like the Netherlands, Germany, or Italy, analogous systems existed and held the employment effects under control. But also these regimes are costly and help push indebted governments like the French one closer to the limits set by the EMU's Stability and Growth Pact (SGP) and by the financial markets.

In any case, by year's end 2009, this regime lost its effectiveness in France: unemployment had climbed from the 7.7 percent the year before to 10 percent. After dropping by about 0.5 percent in 2010–2011, it climbed again in 2012. President Hollande took office with about 9.7 percent unemployment in May and finished the year with 10.3 percent, and the rate stayed at about that level until spring 2014. This was about twice the rate in Germany at that time.[21]

Public Finances
Status Quo Ante
Public spending in France represented around 55 percent of GDP before the crisis, the second highest ratio among Organisation for Economic Cooperation and Development (OECD) countries after Denmark. The country stands at the third place in the EU for its tax and contribution ratio, with al-

most 45 percent of GDP. The OECD, the EU Commission, and many leading independent experts consider these levels excessive and harmful for growth and job creation and doubt that the country's public institutions are able to spend this enormous part of GDP in a growth-conducive manner.[22]

Public employment, an important cause of public spending, represents 21.9 percent of the national workforce and is way above the OECD average of around 16 percent (or Germany with about 11 percent).[23]

In addition to its excessive proportions, public spending has increasingly been financed by borrowing. Borrowing had become much cheaper for countries like France, in the context of the euro, making it more attractive and supportable for public and private debtors alike. Already during this decade, the French state continuously ran a deficit above the 3 percent of GDP permitted by the SGP, to support lagging growth and finance its far-flung public services. The public debt climbed from around 55 percent in 2000 to 70 percent in 2008. At the onset of the crisis, then, French public finances were already on a negative path, which put their sustainability in question.

Crisis Induced

After lying above the 3 percent limit already up to and in 2008, France's deficit climbed to 5.4 percent in 2009 (according to Commission forecast in January 2009). For new sovereign debt, it already paid a small risk premium of 0.5 percentage points above Germany in the same year. By 2012 its deficit had sunk to 4.9 percent and by 2013 to 4.3 percent, still far above the Eurozone's obligatory 3 percent. In 2011 three years of crisis policy necessitated public outlays for (among other tasks) bank rescue, economic stimuli, increased unemployment aid, and the subsidization of short work schemes, adding 15 percentage points to the public debt level, which reached 85 percent. In spring 2014 it stood at 93.6 percent,[24] the seventh worst place in the Eurozone, and continued to increase.

For public finances, which even before 2008 were insufficient to fund government expenses year after year without recourse to deficit spending in excess of SGP limits, these tendencies must be seen as very alarming, especially when the debt level and service requirements had climbed constantly since the 1980s. The minimum foreseeable consequence was that France lost its triple-A rating, a risk French central bankers and finance ministry officials had fretted about since 2010. Standard & Poor's did indeed downgrade France one notch in January 2012, and in November, half a year after the election of Hollande as president, Moody's followed suit.[25] Nevertheless, government bond yields have remained exceptionally low in comparison with the Eurozone. One hypothesis of this chapter is that the financial market actors see France as so closely allied with Germany inside the Eurozone that Germany would never let it become insolvent.

The French and the Challenges of EU Membership
The Public Debate About the Crisis
and the Key Role of the Euro System

The challenges resulting from the crisis concerned the national French policies in the financial, economic, and social arena. Making the proper choices between protecting or rescuing the banks and stimulating consumption and employment, demanding sacrifices from some and helping others, was and is bound to create intense political debate and conflict at the domestic level. The presidential election campaign of 2011–2012 and its result bore rich testimony to this.

Given the membership of France in the EU and the extraordinary dimensions and scope of the required policy measures, the government had also to pay special attention to the EU rules, especially concerning the Internal Market and the euro system. In fact, the relationship of France to the euro system quickly developed into a key determinant of domestic crisis policy, which influenced all debates, and also became the principal issue of French European policy. Public opinion concerning the proper crisis policy could therefore also be understood as public opinion vis-à-vis the euro and French European policy and vice versa. The basic tenets of public opinion vis-à-vis European integration and its further deepening had already fully developed in the years preceding the 2005 referendum and were reflected in its results.

Crisis Induced

In 2013, new French polls on Europe continue to reflect these tenets, which have become even more pronounced and prevalent.[26] The results are clear enough: by autumn 2013, a majority of the French did not want to strengthen the EU's competences any further. Almost a fourth of them wanted to end the European integration adventure. Asked to whom they wanted to entrust the competence for dealing with the financial and economic crisis, namely by means of social security and of economic and employment policy, the French clearly favor their national government, for which these topics should be top priority. The EU received its strongest support for taking care of relatively less immediate concerns like the environment or research and innovation.

The Political Parties

How are these positions distributed among the French party spectrum? As became noticeable on the occasion of the referendum campaign, they were marked by the growing cleavage between the defenders and the increasingly numerous opponents of a further deepening or even preservation of EU integration. On the right, this cleavage separates the anti-European and ever more powerful Front National from the Union pour un Mouvement

Populaire (UMP) plus center parties. But certain smaller and Euro-skeptic parties had been part of Sarkozy's presidential alliance and could well be needed for a future rightist candidate again.

On the left, the referendum confirmed that this divide passed through the middle of the governing Socialist Party, of which the clearly larger part supported the Constitutional Treaty, but which a sizable second part opposed, together with other parties of the left united in the Front de Gauche. Seven years after the referendum, in the 2012 presidential campaign, the positions toward European integration have grown even more negative. The socialist president was elected with the help of the political left, which in 2005 had opposed the Constitutional Treaty, together with a part of his own governing Socialist Party.

Consequently, Hollande has seen himself even more hindered than was Sarkozy, from any simple compliance with existing EU rules and acceptance of their economic policy logic. In fact, he felt constrained to take an explicitly different approach to the European issue. In the composition of his first government of May 15, 2012, these constraints became visible in that it still fielded four ministers who had belonged to the anti–EU constitution group in 2005 (Foreign Minister Laurent Fabius, Industry Minister Arnaud Montebourg, European Affairs Minister Bernard Cazeneuve, and Minister for the Social Economy Benoît Hamon). In another visible sign, this time for the government's swing away from the left under Prime Minister Manuel Valls since April 2, 2014, Montebourg and Hamon have resigned.

The Compliers

The center-right parties and a sizable portion of the experts in the public debate defend policies that try to render domestic anticrisis strategies compatible with respect to the reformed euro system rules and procedures, which we also call the "European semester" now and then. As to general economic policy, this includes a social market economy approach with a good dose of competition—largely compatible with Internal Market rules—and the submission of all government intervention (even in crisis time) to these rules and to the oversight of the European Commission. Even if none of these political forces except perhaps the small liberal center (MODEM, for example) support this approach at 100 percent, the UMP appears the most closely aligned with these principles, more than either the political far right or the left.

This part of the political spectrum is also relatively more prone to support compliance with the European semester, especially with respect to the deficit limit. After all, the reform of this system was carried out in very close cooperation of the Sarkozy administration with the other member states of the Eurozone. French participation in the euro is considered a central achievement of French European policy; no member state must be permitted to leave.[27]

The Compliers Plus "Solidarity"

The socialist majority party (PS) and a clearly larger portion of the country's experts in the public debate defend a similar social market economy approach for France, but with substantially more state-directed and interventionist tendencies. In addition, the PS's left-wing spokespersons, like the ex-Minister of Industry and Economy Arnaud Montebourg, demonstrated a much more explicit skepticism vis-à-vis the principle of competition constitutive for the EU's Internal Market approach. They tried to impose a more voluntary industrial policy of the government, even against the EU Commission.

The rules governing the euro system enjoy the declared respect of the socialists. Again this respect is much more explicitly mitigated than on the political center right. First concerning the fiscal pact signed by president-elect Hollande's predecessor. Hollande opposed this pact. Even though he was not able to impose its renegotiation vis-à-vis the co-signatories and it was ratified by his majority, his disagreement with this central piece of euro group coordination came explicitly on record. Second, concerning the Commission's new competence—written into the European semester with French assent—of giving member states in excessive deficit explicit policy guidance how, and how quickly, to repair their public finances. The French government opposed the application of this new Commission competence to its own fiscal and economic policy. It wants to retain more autonomy in economic policy decisionmaking for itself than the European semester conceded.

In a large section of the party, these reserves are complemented by a principled skepticism concerning the corrective action demanded by these rules in case of excessive deficits or debts, especially if it occurs in an economic downturn. In this opinion, national responsibility must be complemented with a stronger element of collective EU responsibility: for instance by funding national sovereign debt via Eurobonds guaranteed by all euro member states collectively, according to need and not to the 3 percent deficit criterion. Further, an EU-funded growth package should be added, together with a stability mechanism (also EU-funded), to bail out not only overindebted euro member states but also private banks in need of help.

Two "Fronts" of Refusal, on the Right and on the Left

For the more than 20 percent of the electorate that vote for the far right or far left, the exit from the euro or even from the EU has been the declared option for many years, a position that was reinforced by the crisis and the reactions of the French government. For the far right Front National, the exit from the euro is the basic orientation, together with national tariffs for imported goods. Exit from the EU itself is stipulated if these measures cannot be imposed (election program Marine Le Pen).[28] Its economic policy line thus reflects a more general leftist policy turn, mixing national redistributive policies with tax cuts at the local level.[29]

For the far left of the Front de Gauche (which included the Communist Party), the program of its presidential candidate in 2012 insisted that the euro must become a currency that can be created by the European Central Bank in the volumes needed by the euro states, to stimulate their growth. Capital controls must be instituted at the EU's borders. Social welfare must be protected against any cuts and even increased; demand must be stimulated to aid future growth again. The Lisbon Treaty and the Fiscal Pact have to be revoked.

Parties and Elections

For more than twenty years, election results have shown that the Euroskepticism of the far right has been more attractive for the French electorate than that of the far left, most recently in the elections for municipal counselors in March 2014, when the governing Socialists suffered a humiliating defeat at the hands of the center right parties, and the Front National with 7 percent of the countrywide vote advanced far beyond the result of the far left.[30] Even worse for France's pro-European politicians were the European elections of May 25, 2014. Whereas the Front National achieved its best electoral performance ever (25 percent), the two major mainstream parties, the Socialist Party (PS) with 14 percent and the center right UMP with 20 percent, found themselves simultaneously weakened and destabilized. The situation is most serious for the PS.[31]

France's Future Relationship to Europe: Biting the Bullet on Monetary Union
A Shared Heritage Between Left and Right

The Monetary Union project was initiated and advocated by French Socialist president François Mitterrand since the middle of the 1980s, to regain French influence on a European monetary system de facto dominated by the Bundesbank. After 1990 this also became one more case of strengthened—reunified—Germany being bound even closer into European bonds by France.[32] The Treaty of Maastricht of 1992, which introduced it, was already bitterly contested by the left wing of Mitterrand's own party, and the referendum ratifying it was won by the smallest of margins.[33]

We said earlier that France's attitude to the euro system had become the touchstone of French European policy. After the loss of customs and quotas, currency sovereignty had been at the heart of preserving French competitiveness within the EU. Oversized public finances and unbridled public borrowing were allowed to finance a strong French state and the French social model. In euro-land, the loss of exchange rate adjustment and the limitation of public borrowing since 1999 exposed the weaknesses on both fronts. The financial crisis of 2008–2009 increased the visibility of this situation even more and brutally increased the urgency for French politics to carry out real adjustment to the realities of the Eurozone. The French state, the French way in finance, economy, and social affairs—all of them central elements of French identity—could not remain unchanged in the process.

During the euro's first twelve years, it had fallen to Mitterrand's successors from the political center-right, Chirac and Sarkozy, to start adjustment. They attempted a measure of real domestic economic and social policy change to adapt France to the new conditions. Given that the necessary adaptations must cut deeply into the vested rights in social and economic policy, and given the prevalent refusal of deeper economic integration, these attempts had very limited success.

Chirac's reform attempts addressed retirement and labor market policies, and both failed in the face of huge popular protests and opposition from the political left. Sarkozy did not want to risk the same kind of confrontation. He succeeded with initiating a number of more modest reforms, which aided compliance with the euro system, that is, to raise the pension age, reduce the bloated bureaucracy, increase the effective working time, and reduce public expenses. And Sarkozy played a substantial role in the euro system reforms.

The Center Left Facing the Task

Since 2012 it is up to Mitterrand's party, the center left, to bite the bullet of adjusting France to the monetary and economic realities of 2014. It could feel motivated by the experience of Social Democrat Gerhard Schröder's 2003 turnaround to market-oriented labor politics in Germany. This experience is a powerful reminder that leftist leaders can make leftist electorates swallow reform pills that they refuse to take from the right, even if they lose office afterward, as happened to Schröder. Hollande can either try to refuse compliance with the euro system created since 2010 and demand further reform, or comply with and adapt to it, in reverting from the PS's former ideological refusal and beginning structural reforms to improve the real competitiveness of the French economy. Many of the socioeconomic weaknesses highlighted further up would need to be addressed by such a strategy. He can also try a combination of the two.

Choosing the second option means going against the majority of the French electorate and a large number of the PS's own politicians. Sympathizers and ideology push in the other direction, together with far left and far right, toward the first solution. Accordingly, in his campaign and in the domestic politics of his first year (2012), Hollande encouraged expectations that he might choose the option of noncompliance and new demands. He began with pushing through a string of leftist measures he had promised during the election campaign, including a 75 percent top income tax rate; increased taxes on companies, wealth, capital gains, and dividends; a higher minimum wage; a partial rollback of a previously accepted rise in the pension age; and an increase of public employment. All this would please the most leftist part of his electorate. But very soon his popularity with larger parts of the electorate was harmed by the inexorable progression of unemployment in spite of his promises to the contrary, the introduction of new taxes for broad segments of the population to finance the election promises, and the hesitating implementation of the tax on very high incomes. Other election promises remained unfulfilled.[34]

On the other hand, the new president had also seen—but unlike the incumbent Sarkozy avoided to mention in his campaign—the economic wall against which France was slowly driving, consisting of high and ever-mounting public debt, a worsening loss of international competitiveness, and rising trade deficits, and of France's cost problem and the lurking risks for the French banks in Southern Europe. Even though he had kept silent about the painful efforts necessary to meet these challenges, efforts that would also bring France more into line with the constraints of the euro system, he knew about them and already had the government order an authoritative report on French competitiveness in early summer 2012.

Only in autumn did Hollande start to speak in public about the gravity of France's lack of competitiveness. The report was submitted to his prime minister in November.[35] Certain benefits it promised for business—the reduction of social policy contributions, partial tax exemption for employing minimum salary recipients, and an increase of VAT—could not fail to raise virulent opposition among Hollande's adherents. These proposals further increased his unpopularity.

Viewed from the EU vantage point, the crucial importance of the French case for the future of the euro system appears evident. Before entering directly into this issue, other challenges that confronted the member states including France in autumn 2008 must at least be mentioned. First, other EU member states were hit as badly as France (or even worse) in their economic and social development by the crisis of 2008 and after. This provoked a series of uncoordinated and urgent countermeasures in national financial and economic policies, which more or less directly threatened the preservation of the single market and the euro system, what is often called the *acquis*.

Second, the necessity to react to the crisis by European policy also created incentives for governments to recast EMU structures according to their preferences and advance in the "Europeanization" of additional parts of their financial-economic policies remaining under full national competence. France was no exception and successfully defended its interests. Of the many problems resulting for French policy out of these challenges, three are briefly mentioned:

1. Preservation of the single market; bank restructuring demanded special attention by the European Commission Directorate General for competition. Here, France joined with other member state governments to control the European Commission's action.

2. Recasting the EMU structures; the establishment of a "Euro-Summit" can be considered a special French achievement.

3. Europeanization of as yet national competences; the first EU coordination of fiscal stimuli organized under the French presidency was an important step forward. It also helped in holding France's stimulus obligations down in 2008–2009.

Recasting the Euro System

However, as shown, recasting the euro system has proven to be the most important and far-reaching of the new challenges, where the principal issues of French economic and financial policy merge with the future perspectives of this system itself. Given that the French policy choices vis-à-vis the euro system were principally made in a number of hard-fought compromises with Germany, this bilateral relationship is also closely involved with recasting the euro system.

There are several different French contributions to this new euro system. The largest and most sustained of them came from 2008 to 2012 during Sarkozy's presidency. His cooperation with the other EU member states in countless crisis sessions, punctuated by bilateral meetings with Angela Merkel of Germany (which led to the nickname "Merkozy" for the EU's crisis leadership duo) led to the construction of a new euro system. It consists of rule-bound budgetary and fiscal policy coordination with a strong monitory and correctional role for the Commission, designed to be highly constraining and prevent future debt crises within the Eurozone (principally the Six-Pack and Two-Pack, plus the Fiscal Pact). While this was favored by Germany, the other elements of the system were favored by France, namely a German renunciation to the no-bailout principle plus a new important element of euro group solidarity, that is, a bailout system and emergency fund (ESM) for preventing euro monetary system insolvencies, and a strong role of the Eurozone summits in crisis management.[36]

The preceding paragraphs about the three basic options open to Hollande and about the "compliers-plus-solidarity" orientation taken by his governing majority up to spring 2014, show that this presidency's official Eurozone policy in fact conforms to the third option to reconcile both approaches: Comply credibly enough to keep France in the system, increase France's margins by simultaneously pushing back against the rigor of EU rules, and constrain and re-create more room for negotiation in the euro system's coordination on the one hand, and on the other, add more elements of collective euro group solidarity: Eurobonds and a more substantial growth fund.

Two citations illustrate this two-pronged approach. The Commission on May 29, 2013, opted to concede a second extension (to 2015) of France's delay for meeting its budget deficit target, but demanded more adaptation efforts. "France should make its pension system sustainable and improve its business environment." Yet in France the Commission's advice struck a nerve. Hollande observed tartly that the Commission

> "cannot dictate to us what we have to do. . . . On structural reforms, especially pension reform, it's for us and only us to say what is the right way to attain the objective." Mr. Hollande's response seemed a touch ungrateful, given that the Commission had sweetened its proposed medicine by giving France two more years. . . . But it illustrated how some politicians find it hard to adjust to the new schema for fiscal discipline and economic governance that has evolved in the euro-zone during almost five years of unrelenting crisis.[37]

Shortly before having to ask the Commission for a third extension of this adaptation delay, in May 2014, Hollande's new prime minister Manuel Valls declared on April 8, 2014, in his first government policy statement in the Assemblée, that he "did not want to ruin growth, otherwise neither our deficits would diminish nor would unemployment be reduced. Evidently our public accounts must be set right, but without breaking our social model or our public services. Otherwise the French people would not accept it."[38] After the European elections in May 2014, the strengthened position of socialist Italian prime minister Matteo Renzi—himself a staunch defender of this compliers-plus-solidarity orientation, which he has strongly defended in EU councils[39]—has revived French hopes for realizing this two-pronged strategy after all.

This is a risky path. The new euro system of coordination, painfully constructed over the years 2010 to 2012 against much opposition and in a difficult compromise between Paris and Berlin, has the explicit objective to do away with member states' former options to negotiate and avoid full compliance. This was the price to pay for getting important new solidarity elements in the EMU. For conceding additional steps in the same direction, the architects of this system wanted first to be convinced of France's and other member states' willingness and ability to comply fully with this system.

Conclusions

In April 2015, as this text is finalized for printing, it has become evident that France's halting economic growth will not permit reduction of its deficit to the promised 3 percent in 2015, not in 2016, and probably not even in 2017. France is already in the process of asking for a fourth extension of the EU's deadline for returning to the 3 percent deficit limit. The acceleration in April 2014, of the more competitiveness-minded and industry-friendly growth policy begun in autumn 2013 by Hollande, upheld even after the dramatically lost municipal and EU elections and against the open rebellion of numerous Socialist MPs against the new government's 2015 budget and against its first economic reform law, the "loi Macron," does not yet go fast and far enough.[40] (Emmanuel Macron is the successor of former economy minister Arnaud Montebourg.)

But seeing France explicitly take its own time by evading full compliance with the calendar demanded by the Commission will seriously damage the credibility of its willingness to play by the rules. As France is among the EMU's most important players and architects, this will damage the new system's credibility.

France would also incur a domestic price for such a "success," the most evident one being the further extended periods of servicing and repaying its increasing debt, eventually at higher costs in the future if Germany were seen to distance itself from French policy. The less evident but more important price would be domestic, by reducing pressure on all political, social, and economic defenders of the status quo. Rendering France more adapted to the global competition must leave some groups less well off in the short run. To accept this and impose change requires pressure and necessity from outside. Otherwise, France may have to wait for its next socialist president before it can try again, that is, if the euro system of 2015 survives until then.

The third key element of France's European crisis policy, after its domestic socioeconomic policies and its role in the euro system, has always been its relationship with Germany. Germany accepts rule-bound controllable solidarity obligations in the Eurozone in exchange for "hard" fiscal policy coordination. Would and could its elites go along to break this link and accept the open-ended negotiated transfers and debt guarantees that France demands? Will it even continue to support the status quo solidarity pillars installed before 2014 if France does not comply? These questions remain unanswered.

Notes

1. The Rassemblement pour la France has today become the Union pour un Mouvement Populaire (UMP), which unites the traditional Gaullists with other sympathizing rightist parties. In Spring 2015, the Gaullist Party changed their name to Les Républicains.

2. The crisis of the empty chair, July 1965–January 1966, was when France imposed the Luxembourg Compromise on its partners, conceding a veto to every member state that saw "important interests" endangered (Müller-Brandeck-Bocquet [2004], p. 26). A good short account of the two contradictory approaches of France to European integration can be found in Chagnollaud and Quermonne (1996), p. 705ff.; the currency reform of 1958 (Plan Pinay-Rueff) confirmed de Gaulle's willingness to adapt France to the challenge of intra-European liberalization, see Chelini (2001).

3. Chagnollaud and Quermonne speak of the Fifth Republic "oscillating" between the two strategies of integration and of cooperation (1996, p. 705). They follow up with a short account of each of these strategies (p. 706ff).

4. The Germany issue is best dealt with in Müller-Brandeck-Bocquet (2004), pp. 14, 28, 283.

5. Krotz and Schild (2013), p. 115.

6. Ibid., for instance p. 20ff.

7. Useful information about the electorate's opinions in the public opinion poll by TNS-Sofres and Unilog for *Le Monde*, RTL, and TF1, carried out by phone with a representative sample of the population, was published in *Le Monde*, no. 18770 (May 31, 2005).

8. Deubner (2005).

9. *France Stratégie* (2014), p. 2. One of the best critical overviews on the discussion in this section is found in OECD (2013).

10. *France Stratégie* (2014), p. 4.

11. Didier and Koléda (2011), p. 74–75.

12. Ibid., p. 23.

13. Ibid., p. 18, 103.

14. For the minimum wage, see Le Monde, "Augmenter le smic détruit des emplois," interview with Paul Champsaur, Le Monde.fr, June 22, 2012; data from de.statista.com for 2013.

15. According to Eurostat, March 19, 2014.

16. See http://epp.eurostat.ec.europa.eu/statistics_explained/images/d/db/Employment_rate%2, (accessed June 2014).

17. See http://epp.eurostat.ec.europa.eu/tgm/table.do?tab=table&init=1&language =de&pcode=tsdec450&plugin=1 (accessed June 2014).

18. Data from the World Bank.

19. The biggest early losses from these subprime assets hit Swiss, UK, and German banks, in that order, from February 2007 to May 2008, see http://news.bbc.co.uk /2/hi/business/7096845.stm (accessed April 14, 2014).

20. *France Stratégie* (2014); also see http://data.worldbank.org/indicator/NY.GDP .MKTP.KD.ZG.

21. See http://epp.eurostat.ec.europa.eu/tgm/table.do?tab=table&init=1&language =de&pcode=tsdec450&plugin=1.

22. Very explicitly in this sense: OECD (2013), p. 33ff.

23. Ibid., p. 31.

24. INSEE, general government debt according to Maastricht criteria; see http://www.insee.fr/en/themes/info-rapide.asp?id=40.

25. *Financial Times* reporting, on January 13, and November 19, 2012.

26. *France Stratégie* (2014), p. 27.

27. "UMP Election Program Nicolas Sarkozy. Lettre de Nicolas Sarkozy Aux Français" (2012), http://ump-34.org/uploads/media/lettre-aux-francais-2012.pdf (accessed April 14, 2014).

28. Election program of Marine le Pen, Europe (2012). Front National, http://www.frontnational.com/le-projet-de-marine-le-pen/politique-etrangere /europe/Election prog (last accessed April 15 2014)

29. Evans and Ivaldi (2014).

30. Ibid.

31. Grunberg (2014).

32. Müller-Brandeck-Bocquet (2004), pp. 84ff. and 106.

33. Ibid., pp. 118ff.

34. See http://www.luipresident.fr/engagement/relancer-lunion-politique-europeenne -avec-angela-merkel-11384; or "Les 60 promesses de Hollande, un an après," *Le Nouvel Observateur*, May 6, 2013, available at http://tempsreel.nouvelobs.com/politique/hollande -un-an-a-l-elysee/20130430.OBS7741/les-60-promesses-de-hollande-un-an -apres.html.

35. See http://fichier.europe1.fr/infos/rapport_de_louis_gallois_sur_la_competitivite.pdf.

36. Deubner (2011).

37. "Europe Will Struggle to Swallow Economic Medicine," *Financial Times*, May 30, 2013.

38. "L'ambitieuse feuille de route de Manuel Valls," *Le Monde*, April 8, 2014 (translated by C. Deubner).

39. See "Renzi Hits Back at Bundesbank Chief," *Financial Times*, July 4, 2014, as one of numerous articles.

40. For a good overview, summing up these various recent developments, see *Financial Times*, "Emmanuel Macron vows to push through French economy reforms," February 26, 2015.

5

Italy:
The Maze of Domestic Concerns

Federiga Bindi

ITALY IS TRADITIONALLY KNOWN AS BEING A "PRO-EUROPEAN country." In this chapter we explore what this really means and whether it translates to effective influence in EU decisionmaking. In doing so, we first briefly look at how the relations between Italy and the EEC/EU have evolved over time; second, we discuss how domestic institutions have adapted to deal with EU policymaking; third, we analyze the Italian presence and negotiating strategies in the EU institutions. In each part, concrete case studies are presented.

Italy and the European Communities
in Historical Perspective
Italy ended World War II as a loser, leading to regime change and the new Republican Constitution (January 1, 1948). Prime Minister Alcide De Gasperi and Foreign Minister Carlo Sforza saw in Robert Schuman's 1950 proposal an important political and economic opportunity for Italy: they were convinced that to balance domestic instability, a strong counterweight of international dimensions was needed. Yet most of the country did not favor this option. Only the trade unions looked upon the European Communities with some interest. De Gasperi and Sforza decided to take the risk and make Italy a European Coal and Steel Community (ECSC) founding member.

In Messina in June 1955, the six ECSC foreign ministers called for further integration, and France's prime minister Pierre Mendès-France, fearing that the Italy would "export" its unemployment, tried to prevent Rome from joining. Dramatic international events then provided the necessary impetus for sealing the negotiations: the invasion of Hungary (November 4, 1956) and the nationalization of the Suez Canal (July 20, 1956). Thus, in March

1957, the treaties creating the European Economic Community (EEC) and Euratom were signed in Rome. In Italy, the invasion of Hungary had a lasting effect on domestic politics as the Socialist Party (PSI) sharply criticized the Soviet Union's intervention and broke its alliance with the communists, thus becoming pro-European. The Communist Party joined in supporting European integration by the end of the 1970s.

In July 1970, the Italian Franco Maria Malfatti was named EEC Commission president; he resigned less than two years later to stand for political elections in Italy. Despite the fact that other commissioners have also resigned early, Malfatti's departure is held up as an example of the Italians' lack of trustworthiness, undermining the role of future Italian commissioners. France eventually used this argument to strip Italy of the agriculture portfolio, the main one at the time.

In October 1973, the third Arab-Israeli conflict erupted. One repercussion in Europe was an increase in oil prices, and Italy was hard hit. For the first time, Italian politicians blamed the European Community for its economic difficulties, which also conveniently offered a sort of justification for the country's lack of respect for EEC deadlines and obligations. The end of the dollar's convertibility into gold also hit Italy, weakening the national currency, the lira. The EEC member states tried to protect themselves through the "European Monetary Snake," created March 7, 1972, but it was not enough for Italy. Once the European Monetary System (EMS, 1978) came into force, Italy was forced to ask for partial opt-outs. Italy's European counterparts, especially Germany, stigmatized these systemic weaknesses and called Italy the European Cinderella (or the "sick one"). Similarly, within the Common Agricultural Policy debates, Italy was disadvantaged by its lack of a global agriculture strategy and its patchwork domestic agriculture organization. Italy counted just one triumph in this period: it succeeded in establishing the European Regional Fund in 1973, thanks to British support and despite the German refusal to fund it until Rome proved capable of using the financing in an efficient way.

The long "Euro-sclerotic" period finally ended in the mid-1980s. Meanwhile, European political geography had changed with the elections of François Mitterrand in France (1981) and Helmut Kohl in Germany (1982). Despite personal and political differences, they became the heart of Europe, and only the skillfulness of Italian leaders like Giulio Andreotti avoided Italian sidelining. In the first semester of 1985, Italy held the EEC presidency. Foreign Minister Andreotti unlocked the stalemate on fisheries and fishing quotas that were blocking Spain and Portugal from signing the accession treaties and, on the wake of Altiero Spinelli's 1984 Draft Treaty, made convening an Intergovernmental Conference (IGC) to reform the EEC treaty the presidency's priority. However, at the European Council in Milan (June 28–29, 1985), the UK and Greece opposed the idea. After a tense debate, the Italian presidency took the unprecedented move to ask for a vote, in which Greece, Denmark, and the UK were defeated and the IGC was summoned. Despite the difficulties, the Single European Act was agreed on in December 1985.

That same year, Italy gained an important victory over the so-called Delors package. The package introduced the idea of a fourth source of income for the EEC budget, calculated in terms of gross national product (GNP), which Italy strongly opposed, as it was bound to be penalized. Despite yet another change of government, Italy managed to hold firm on this issue and finally, thanks to Kohl, a compromise was reached: Italy's proposal to calculate the fourth resource on the difference between the GNP and value added tax (VAT) revenues was accepted.[1] On the other hand, Italy's poor implementation record for the directives needed to complete the single market caused difficulties. In Italy, some blamed the problem on the EEC for failing to match Italian interests, while asking and succeeding in obtaining a two-year delay in the liberalization of capital movements.[2]

A year of great change in Eastern Europe was 1989. The transformations had lasting consequences on Italian domestic politics, too. On July 1, 1990, the day that marked the beginning of the monetary union between the two German republics, Italy again held the EEC presidency. The Italian presidency gave top priority to the preparation of the IGC for the European Monetary Union (EMU). To that end, Prime Minister Andreotti proposed holding an informal European Council meeting in Rome (October 27–28, 1990) where, notwithstanding UK opposition, the Carli Report on the EMU was approved. This eventually led to Margaret Thatcher's defeat and resignation at home (November 28, 1990). John Major replaced her, and Andreotti and his foreign minister, the socialist Gianni De Michelis, used their personal and political networks to secure a successful formal meeting of the European Council in Rome (December 14–15, 1990), thus managing to successfully convene two IGCs to reform the treaties.

Later, speculators attacked the Italian lira and the British pound sterling. On September 4, 1992, Italy was forced to raise its interest rates and had to devalue by 7 percent. Then, on September 17, both the Italian lira and the British pound sterling had to leave the EMS. As Italy progressively drifted from the EU following two subsequent sets of enlargements, to the north in 1995 and to the east in 2004, its old ruling parties were wiped away by history. The end of communism had in fact made the old Italian parties redundant and led to the rise of new political actors such as Forza Italia, the Northern League, as well as postcommunist and post–Christian Democrat parties. In March 1994, a right-wing coalition led by Silvio Berlusconi won the elections, and this Italian government expressed rather anti-European sentiments. In his first speech to Parliament, Berlusconi aggressively declared that Italy was to play "a leading role in the framework of the European Union."[3] Under pressure from the postfascists in the coalition, his government even tried to oppose Slovenia's EU membership.[4] For the first time, an Italian government was isolated in Europe; none of the coalition parties belonged to major European political families, and a number of European counterparts objected to the presence of Alleanza Nazionale (the postfascists) in the government. Berlusconi learned his lesson and devoted much of his party's energy in the following years to becoming a member of the European People Party.

The Italian EU presidency of 2003 started with a major incident. On July 2, Berlusconi was attending the plenary of the European Parliament to present the presidency's priorities. During the discussion, the German Member of European Parliament (MEP), Martin Schulz, aggressively attacked Italy for its immigration policies and for Berlusconi's conflicts of interest between his own business and political activities. Berlusconi, in turn, overreacted, essentially accusing Schulz of being "like a Nazi," creating a serious diplomatic row with Germany and gravely endangering the beginning of the Italian presidency.[5] Soon afterward, the president of the European Convention, Giscard d'Estaing, presented the "Draft Treaty establishing a Constitution for Europe" to the Italian presidency. To complete the EU reform process, it was now necessary to convene another IGC. Opinion diverged about how to proceed, and negotiations were not easy. Italy recognized that the primary obstacle to an agreement was the question of qualified majority voting, due in particular to the opposition of Spain and Poland (though Poland was not yet an EU member state). Italy's strategy, therefore, was to reach a compromise on this point above all, hoping that the resolution of all other outstanding problems would follow smoothly. Unfortunately, these efforts were useless. Without French or German support, Italy faced deadlock. Unable to make a proposal that would be acceptable to everyone, it issued a statement declaring that negotiations had failed and asking the Irish presidency to continue consultations.

After five years in power, Berlusconi was narrowly defeated in the legislative elections. Back in power, Romano Prodi sought to relocate European integration at the center of Italian foreign policy. In so doing, he followed the tradition and the strategic approach of the Christian Democrat governments of the past: that is, equating the European interest with the national one, thereby somehow taking a step backward.[6] The discussion on the national interests had meanwhile progressed, especially while Massimo D'Alema was prime minister (1998–2000), leading to a shared consensus on the idea that national interests must be defended in Brussels.

The case of the redistribution of seats in the post-2009 European Parliament, however, shows a gap between words and reality. Under the new Lisbon Treaty (2009), the number of Italian MEPs was to be cut on the principle that the number of MEPs should be calculated on the basis of the number of residents in a given country, rather than on the number of voters.

According to this system, Italy would have six fewer MEPs than with the previous system and, most important, fewer MEPs than France. The European Council meeting in Brussels on June 21–23, 2007, approved the Lamassoure Report, but when word reached the Italian press, people protested vehemently. Calls were made for Italy to use its veto. There was general outrage again when the European Parliament approved new provisions in the Lamassoure Report on October 11, 2007. Yet according to a witness at the meeting, the two Italian representatives in the European Council, Prodi and his foreign minister, D'Alema, were not even present. Apparently, while the new numbering was being approved, they were outside the meeting room, trying to resolve a domestic political problem. Eventually, a diplomatic solution was found. One more MEP was added to the final number, the formula being "750 plus the president," and that extra MEP was promised to Italy.

Handling the Economic Crisis of 2008 and After in the Italian Way

Prodi's tiny majority in Parliament did not create the foundation for a long reign; the Prodi II government fell after less than two years. In May 2008, Berlusconi was back in power, essentially concentrating on domestic politics and leaving European policy and most foreign policy to Foreign Minister Franco Frattini. By that time, European policy again was a consensual policy, as a unanimous vote in the Italian Parliament to ratify the Treaty of Lisbon showed on August 31, 2008. When the economic crises started to hit Europe, Berlusconi initially denied it was affecting Italy, too.[7] Ironically, however, the rising spread of the Italian economic crisis (and sexual scandals) forced him to resign in November 2011.

The two subsequent prime ministers, Mario Monti (2011–2013) and Enrico Letta (2013–2014), both gave the EU high importance. Italian president Giorgio Napolitano chose both for their supposed "international credibility,"[8] which should have helped them address the economic crises. Monti's government was particularly focused on it, yet his approach of mainly horizontal cuts and an increase in taxes may have cut the public debt but did not help overcome the economic crises, with Italy progressively sinking deeper into it.[9] In EU policymaking, given Monti's distrust of his foreign minister, Giulio Terzi, the minister for EU affairs, Enzo Moavero, a former advocate general at the EU Court of Justice (ECJ), got free rein to move the core of EU policies to the presidency of the Council. He subsequently focused on reducing the Italian gap in EU legislation enactment and litigation cases with the EU Commission. Moavero worked well in coordinating with Italians (MEPs, permanent representatives, etc.) in Brussels; however, interministerial coordination in Rome lingered, and the inability of the two governments to control Parliament led to an impasse.

Then Matteo Renzi, the youngest ever prime minister of Italy, took office in February 2014. Contrary to Monti and Letta, Renzi did not have previous experience in foreign and European policies and tended to consider them dependent variables of domestic politics, with special attention to relevant photo ops. In a way, his approach to European politics recalled the 1994 Berlusconi for his confrontational approach to Europe. Renzi particularly emphasized a supposed Italian "leading role in Europe" and his other mantra— "Europe cannot dictate to Italy what to do." He skillfully mixed highly rhetorical references to Europe, seen as the natural venue for his own generation, with virulent attacks on dull-witted "European bureaucrats." In July 2014, he did not hesitate to cause a diplomatic row when his counterparts failed to support his foreign minister, Federica Mogherini, as European Union High Representative (EUHR). Despite advice to change candidates or change portfolios, Renzi did not give up until he got what he wanted. He presented the appointment as the ultimate Italian victory. Whether it was in the best Italian interest to have the foreign policy portfolio rather than an economic one, few in his entourage questioned. One immediate price that Italy had to pay were sanctions on Russia, which are a heavy burden for Italian business.[10] Having Mogherini named to the EUHR post meant taking a tougher stance on Russia following the Ukraine crises. Mogherini was in fact initially opposed by many EU member states for her pro-Russia attitude.[11] Renzi adopted a similar attack strategy for the European economic crises:[12] Domestically, he used an odd rhetorical mix of pro- and anti-Europeanism— "European bureaucrats cannot tell Italy what to do"[13]—while asking for growth policies in the European Council.[14] As a result, in November 2014, the EU Commission decided to postpone its judgment on Italy's, France's, and Belgium's budgets until early March 2015.[15]

Italy's Domestic Institutions and EU Decisionmaking
The Italian Constitution and EU Law

The Italian constitution does not deal with the EU in an organic way. The legal basis for the delegation of powers to the EU is Article 11 of the constitution, which was designed in anticipation of UN membership. The 2001 constitutional reform then "constitutionalized" the relationship between the regions and the EU, yet without rethinking the whole EU–Italy relation in an overall, coherent framework. The relation between EEC law and national law has also been rocky: for a long time both legal doctrine and the Italian Constitutional Court's rulings did not recognize the principle of supremacy of EEC law over national law and supported the principle of the separation between the two juridical systems. Only in 1984 did the conflict between the Italian Constitutional Court and the ECJ finally came to an end, with the *Granital c. Ministero delle Finanze* ruling.[16] This setting, coupled with the inefficiencies of the Italian bureaucracy and the parochial attitude of most Italian politicians, concurred in making Italy a passive actor in EU policymaking.

The Italian Parliament and EU Affairs

The Italian Parliament was also slow to realize the importance of actively dealing with EU policymaking. From the early Community years until the Single European Act, the Italian Parliament maintained a low level of Europeanization with weak structural adaptation and minimal time and energy devoted to the scrutiny of EC law. The EEC was seen as a part of foreign policy and therefore considered primarily a matter for the government and namely for the Foreign Ministry. For a long time, the two branches of the Parliament, the Chamber of Deputies and the Senate, did not even establish standing committees for European affairs or set up specific scrutiny procedures. In both houses, EC legislation and policies were reviewed, sporadically, by the committees for foreign affairs through the normal parliamentary procedures, leading to significant backlogs in the implementation of EC directives and to the European Court of Justice repeatedly condemning Italy for its failure to implement EC law correctly or in a timely fashion. The Single European Act and the expected wave of directives for the completion of the Internal Market finally provided the catalyst for a radical reorganization of internal decisionmaking on EU matters.

Between 1987 and 1989, the Italian Parliament adopted two laws, providing a framework for domestic decisionmaking on EEC affairs: the so-called Fabbri Law[17] and the La Pergola Law.[18] Together, the two laws introduced a number of innovations: they redefined the government's structures for coordinating the national position on EU policies, they made it the government's duty to transmit EC draft legislation to Parliament, and they formalized the Parliament's right to adopt resolutions on EU matters. The La Pergola Law also set up the "Annual Community Law," a mechanism for the systematic and timely implementation of EU legislation. As a result, both the Senate (in 1988) and the Chamber of Deputies (in 1990) adapted their internal rules of procedure to take advantage of the opportunities offered by the new legal framework: special procedures were established to deal with EC policies and standing committees were empowered to express their position on EC proposals. In practice, however, the reforms had a limited impact and Parliament's influence on EU affairs remained marginal.

The Treaty of Amsterdam and subsequently the Constitutional Treaty thus triggered a new wave of reforms. The reforms, embodied in the national legislation ratifying the Treaty of Amsterdam[19] and in the changes introduced by the "Community Laws"[20] for 1995–1997, expanded the scope of parliamentary scrutiny, obliging the government to forward all draft EU legislation, including (then) second- and third-pillar acts. They also simplified and rationalized government reports on EU affairs[21] and introduced a "soft version" of "parliamentary scrutiny reserve."[22] The Chamber of Deputies significantly revised its internal rules of procedure in 1997 and in 1999; the Senate did so in February 2000 and 2003. These changes addressed a number of issues left unresolved by the post–Single European Act reforms as well as some newly emerging issues, signaling a qualitative change in the Italian Parliament's approach to EU matters.

The accumulation of amendments to the Fabbri and La Pergola Laws had, however, fragmented the legal framework into a plurality of sources, raising some issues of clarity and consistency. In response to these factors, the parliament adopted the so-called Stucchi-Buttiglione Law,[23] which consolidated and clarified the legal framework for Italian participation in EU decisionmaking, replacing the Fabbri and La Pergola Laws and their subsequent amendments. The Stucchi-Buttiglione Law provided for a comprehensive definition of the domestic decisionmaking processes as related to EU affairs.

In a short span of time, the Italian Parliament has thus successfully addressed many issues that had remained unresolved for years, gradually putting in place a well-developed scrutiny system in which the standing committees specializing in EU affairs play the leading role. It has expanded the scope of its scrutiny of EU policies, is kept regularly informed of developments in EU affairs, and has developed specific procedures for scrutiny and fact-finding; it has even protected its prerogatives by introducing a scrutiny reserve system. Thus, the Italian Parliament's role in EU affairs moved away from primarily implementing EU directives toward a more positive and proactive role in shaping the national position on draft EU legislation. Yet although the Parliament now has a new system of scrutiny reserve, it is used infrequently. This is what Law 234 (2012),[24] which took over three years to negotiate (2009–2012), intended to accomplish. Law 234 is a comprehensive normative law regulating the ensemble of the relations between the EU and Italy at all levels (national, regional, local). On paper, it establishes the ultimate framework, the highest level of institutional maturing and Europeanization that Italy has ever reached.

There are now two different kinds of legal provisions: the so-called European Delegation Law and European Law. The European Delegation Law shall only be used to enact EU directives and decisions into domestic law: by February 28, the government shall send the bill to the Parliament; in case of need, it can introduce a second one July 31. European Law, on the contrary, has no set deadlines and shall be used whenever needed to adapt (or repeal) national law that contrasts with EU law. If needed, the government can also introduce "urgent bills" to deal with other aspects of EU law as they emerge, such as to implement ECJ rulings, remedy cases of infringement of EU laws brought about by the European Commission,[25] or deal with EU norms of particular political, social, or economic relevance.

The 2013 European Delegation Law and 2013 European Law were approved in July 2013, making up for part of the delays accumulated in the previous years. Yet by March 2014, Italy had again piled up as many as 120 infraction procedures.[26] The Italian Parliament adopted the European Delegation Law 2013 and a European Law 2013 in September 2014. The 2014 European Delegation Law was enacted in October 2014.[27] Also in 2014, Italy's deficit in directives' implementations amounted to 0.7 percent, finally equaling the EU average.[28] Complying with the Treaty of Lisbon, Law 234 also further increased the potential influence of the Italian Parliament in EU policymaking law. The government now has to inform the Parliament about its positions and take into account eventual recommendations by the Parliament. Whether this will actually happen is too early to tell. It does not look good, though, considering that the ECJ has just condemned Italy to pay €40 million for failing to tackle the dumping of illegal waste.[29] In a clear lack of understanding of EU procedures and rules, the minister for environment responded that Italy was not going to pay a cent.[30]

The Executive and EU Affairs

In Italy, the Ministry of Foreign Affairs (MAE or Farnesina, for the building that houses it) has traditionally played the main role in EU affairs. There are a number of explanations: the initial idea that the European Communities were a classic international organization, the supremacy of the Council in EU decisionmaking, the uncertain distribution of tasks among ministries until the reforms of the 1980s and 1990s, and the Farnesina's technical superiority in linguistic and negotiating skills. The centrality of the MAE was also consistent with the coordination tasks given by the founding fathers to the General Affairs Council (GAC), for a long time formed by the foreign ministers, before giving way to the EU ministers. (Coincidentally, Italy was the last country to adapt: only in late 2011, and then EU Minister Moavero rightfully became the Italian representative in the GAC.)

Gradually, the MAE's supremacy in European affairs eroded, to the advantage of the presidency of the Council. Three subsequent laws[31] increased the Italian prime minister's responsibilities for Italy's participation in the EU, in line with the increasing role of the European Council at the EU level. In 1999, the prime minister was entrusted with the coordination of the Italian Council of Ministers, relations with other institutions (such as the Parliament), and relations with EU institutions. Many of the day-to-day duties in EU affairs, starting with the enactment of EU law into national law, are, however, delegated to the minister for EU policies.

The minister for the coordination of EC policies, as he was initially called, is a minister "without portfolio" and thus is attached to the presidency of the Council. The position was created in 1980, then suppressed in 1995 by Prime Minister Lamberto Dini, who assigned its tasks to the undersecretary of state for economics, and reintroduced in 1998, when Prime Minister D'Alema entrusted the new Ministry for EU policies to Enrico Letta who, despite his young age, used his knowledge of EU affairs to elevate the role of the ministry. Since then and until Renzi's government (2014), all governments have included a Ministry for EU Policies. Yet only a few had Letta's technical competence and passion for the issue: Ugo La Malfa (2005–2006), Emma Bonino (2006–2008), Enzo Moavero (2011–2014), and Sandro Gozi (from 2014), are among the few.

Formally, the ministers for EU policies' tasks have not changed significantly over the years; the main focus is the incorporation of EU law into national law. The ministry also deals with ECJ cases; promotes the professional training of public officials in EU affairs; disseminates information about the EU; (in theory) promotes the careers of Italian citizens in the EU institutions; represents Italy in the Council for the Internal Market; and coordinates the involvement of the other branches of the Italian public administration and of the social parties in EU policymaking. Until November 2011, however, the minister for EU policies was included in the delegations attending the GAC or the European Council, a fact that has at times undermined its role both domestically and at the European level, due to opposition from the MAE.

The minister for EU policies has the logistical support of the Department for EU Policies. Located at the presidency of the Council, this department was introduced in 1987 by the Fabbri Law. Its fortunes have varied over the years, though it has generally always suffered from understaffing. Although initially only the foreign affairs ministers were to be involved in European affairs, today virtually no national ministry can avoid dealing with the EU. Yet unlike in other EU countries, most Italian ministries still lack "European offices" or units charged with negotiating and implementing EU law. In general, while EU enactment is mostly coordinated by the various legislative offices, the negotiating phase, if it is dealt with at all, is coordinated in any number of ways, and often ends up in the hands of the diplomatic advisers. This has partially changed with the application of Law 234 (2012), as shown shortly.

For years, the lack of intraministerial coordination together with the typical Italian interministerial rivalry have prevented any real chance of creating an efficient system of interministerial coordination on EU affairs. In 2005, one of the important changes brought by the Stucchi-Buttiglione Law was the creation of an Interdepartmental Committee for Community and European Affairs (CIACE). The idea was to create a sort of cabinet for EU affairs at the presidency of the Council, as other countries had done. Staffed by some twenty people, individually chosen for their commitment and expertise and drawn partially from the Department for EU Affairs, the CIACE was given the task of finally enabling the government to coordinate and deepen its actions on issues of relevance to Italy. Regions and local communities were also invited to participate. The CIACE functioned at two levels: the political level and the technical level. However, the political level slowly moved from the ministers themselves to their aides.

The CIACE did a good job coordinating the Italian position on a number of relevant cases. A case in point is the 20-20-20 Climate-Energy Package, where the CIACE managed to conciliate rather opposite views of the different ministerial departments across two opposite governments.[32] However, it had a number of weaknesses. First and foremost, the establishment of an interdepartmental coordination body did not coincide with the introduction of corresponding facilities in each ministry. The coordination work performed by the CIACE was not adequately supported by all the units it intended to coordinate. Second, the CIACE was understaffed and could only manage to coordinate the ascending phase of community law in a limited number of cases, leaving many negotiating areas completely uncovered. Third, the involvement of the regional governments in the coordination effort was fraught with difficulties, despite the progressive increase of the regions' powers and prerogatives in matters of EU and foreign affairs. Last, the CIACE did not always succeed in framing its positions quickly enough to keep pace with the European decisionmaking process. The CIACE worked well as long as its founder, Massimo Gaiani, who also served as diplomatic adviser to the minister of EU affairs, led it (2006–2011). After his departure, however, the CIACE stopped working, following a common pattern in the Italian public administration: the incapacity of real institution building. Consequently, Law 24 (2012) introduced another interministerial coordination body: the CIAE (Inter-ministerial Committee for European Affairs). However, as long as Moavero stayed as minister for EU affairs (February 2012), he did not bother to convene it, claiming that he could more efficiently bring EU issues directly to the Council of Ministers.

As mentioned, for the first time since 1998, Renzi marked a discontinuity by not naming a minister for EU affairs, instead having Gozi serve as undersecretary at the presidency of the Council. Gozi, a former EU official turned politician, resumed the CIAE both at the technical and political levels and tried to ensure that each ministry finally created its own intraministerial coordination bodies[33] as mandated by Law 234. Yet the EU Department, with its staff of seventy-five, still suffers from understaffing. Gozi also partially followed on the path inaugurated by Moavero by attending most General Affairs Councils, a long-due measure that for too long had being prevented by the opposition of the Foreign Ministry, fearing a reduction of its influence in EU affairs, but which is key for an efficient coordination of EU affairs domestically. Following tradition, he also represents Italy in the Single Market Council. A member of Parliament, and one of the Law 234 proponents, he also enjoys good relation with its EU Committee.

The Italian Regions and EU Affairs

One of the CIACE's weaknesses was the absence of some of the Italian regional governments, which are still lagging behind in EU affairs. Suffice it to say that since 2002, the Italian regions have not succeeded in spending all of the structural funds allocated to them. Despite a massive (and costly) presence in Brussels, only few regions have the necessary political weight and economic might to have any direct impact on EU policies at the EU level. These include Lombardy and the regions of central Italy led by Tuscany, Emilia-Romagna, and to a lesser degree, Veneto, Piedmont, Liguria, and Puglia.

Law 234 (2012) was aimed at upgrading the regions' participation in EU decisionmaking and EU law implementation. The government must take the State-Regions' Conference's advice in formulating its position (it can, however, proceed if the conference does not gives its opinion within thirty days), and the conference now has the possibility to ask for a scrutiny reserve, just like the Parliament (a thirty-day time limit applies here, too). Regions also acquired the right/duty to directly implement EU directives. However, should they fail to act past the deadline, the state can step in. This still seems to be needed as about a third of the EU law infractions are caused by problems in the regions.[34]

Negotiating Strategies and Alliances

How Italy Attempts to Maximize Its Voice in EU Policymaking

According to Andrew Moravcsik, European high politics are determined by the convergence of domestic policy preferences in the largest member states: the UK, Germany, and France.[35] Italy is therefore excluded from the group of the leading countries that count. Nevertheless, there have been important cases of high politics in which Italy has played a crucial part. Two good examples are the Single European Act (1985) and the Treaty of Maastricht (1991–1992). But the case of the 2003 IGC shows that although the Italian presidency had technically prepared the IGC very thoroughly, the lack of German and French support eventually caused the negotiations to fail.[36]

In theory Italy is on the same footing as the UK, France, and Germany with regard to voting in the Council, inasmuch as they are all "big" countries, but the reality is different. A country's ability to pool its votes with those of other countries obviously enhances its ability to enforce its positions; in a multilateral environment, it is important to act in conjunction with others and work within a framework of alliances. Ultimately, a country's ability to move on the complex multilateral chessboard depends on the professional skills of the players. Negotiating methods used in the Council are akin to those of traditional multilateral diplomacy, despite the innovative nature of the EU initiative. A multilayered and lengthy process makes decisions difficult to reach and often requires procedural ploys such as "very selected meetings," "confessionals," and "package deals." It has also become customary to debate the most controversial issues on the agenda at lunchtime, possibly in the presence solely of the ministers, when the more controversial issues can be turned from technical to political, and giving an expert chair the chance to win larger support than in an open debate. However, when ministers are nonspecialists or do not speak English well, the risk is, as has often been the case with the Italians, that they may find themselves endorsing decisions they cannot subsequently deliver.[37]

A member state is successful in European negotiations if it has properly defined goals and credible players and if it uses them to formulate and pursue consistent strategies. Properly defining one's goals demands efficient underlying coordination. For many years until the CIACE was established, Italy's weakness was a lack of interdepartmental coordination. In its absence, Italy's negotiating positions were often defined by its permanent representatives on the eve of the Council meetings. Italian diplomats have experienced this situation as both a source of frustration and as an opportunity. While the absence of properly defined national positions enabled Italy's representatives to enjoy a broader negotiating spectrum, in the long run this situation has undermined the nation's credibility in the EU arena. A credible player is one who, regardless of rank, role, or position, is well known around the negotiating table for his or her authoritative standing at home or in the institution he or she represents at the community level. In some cases these individuals manage to stave off difficulties thanks to their personal credibility. In other cases, the lack of continuity in the representatives sent to Brussels by different departments can cause serious damage. This situation has frustrated Italian diplomats, an elite corps within the Italian civil service, but it has also provided an opportunity for them to play a greater role in EU negotiations than their European colleagues do.

Unfortunately this parochial standpoint typifies the Italian political classes at all levels and allows them to avoid addressing European issues. By *parochialism*, I mean Italian politicians' tendency to give priority to local over national issues and, even more detrimentally, over European and international issues. Italy's ministers and undersecretaries tend to delegate their attendance at Council meetings to their underlings to a far greater extent than do their European counterparts. The result of this practice is that the person attending ministerial-level meetings is often the permanent representative, which means that Italy has a far weaker negotiating capacity, as mentioned in the case of the reduction of Italian MEPs.

Two additional factors need to be considered: the degree of flexibility in negotiations and a country's propensity to use its veto power. While the Council has hitherto worked behind closed doors, and individual member states' positions are never (officially) disclosed, it is also the case that the member states' flexibility in negotiations varies. Italy's representatives, for example, usually enjoy a higher degree of flexibility than do Danish and Swedish representatives, who often have no option but to go along with the positions approved by their parliaments.[38] Italy's representatives on the Council now have the theoretical option of resorting to the parliamentary scrutiny tactic. Nevertheless, parliamentary scrutiny is not something the Italian Parliament fully appreciates; as far as I know, it has only been used once.

The other factor is a country's use of its veto power. While qualified majority voting is the official method of reaching decisions in the Council, in practice there is still a desire to reach a consensus whenever possible. Formal votes are mostly taken only when a member state or a minority group of states, not enough to constitute a minority bloc, insists on vetoing a proposal. The member states that tend to use their veto power include the UK, the Scandinavian countries, Germany, France, and, since the recent enlargement, Poland. Italy, on the other hand, tends not to. Even when some parties were calling for it during the Treaty of Lisbon negotiations, Italy did not use its veto. Breaking with tradition, Renzi de facto used his veto power with regard to the Commission's nominations in July 2014. He finally obtained Mogherini's nomination as EUHR but in exchange gained a bully reputation that is likely to hurt him in future negotiations.

Finally, there is the "cross-table bargaining" technique, which requires member states to be in control of the situation at every negotiating table (in other words, they need a strong degree of domestic coordination) and invest heavily in bilateral diplomatic relations. Former prime and foreign minister Andreotti, for instance, was well known for forging ties with the "small" and "medium-sized" countries, so that by the time the Council meeting was held, he could rely on those countries to vote with Italy. Yet the lack of coordination at the national level has made it difficult to employ cross-table bargaining strategies. There is also an ethical aspect that needs to be highlighted, which has carried some weight in the past. This is Italy's desire to emphasize the difference between the EU and other international organizations, such as the United Nations. In these other forums, which are solely in the Foreign Ministry's hands, Italy often succeeds with cross-table bargaining.

Italy does not appear to be part of any stable alliance. Although the six larger member states (the UK, Germany, France, Italy, Poland, and Spain) have regular consultations, they cannot be considered to have a stable alliance. Jan Beyers and Guido Dierick studied the negotiating patterns of a representative sample of working groups within the Council, showing the importance of two particular variables in the choice of allies by the member states' representatives.[39] The first variable is a player's credibility: the round of informal negotiations varies according to the players' nationality and the perception of their credibility. Southern countries, with the partial exception of Spain, are defined as "peripheral" and are less sought after as allies. Countries deemed to be the most desirable as allies are the ones holding the rotating presidency and the "major" countries, except Italy. If a country is seeking allies in Southern Europe, it will most likely prefer Spain's representatives over Italy's. The authors argue that the reason for this lies in the "lack of consistency" in Italian policymaking: Italy's representatives are not perceived as reliable, and neither are they considered to be strategic allies. It also appears that sociogeographic homogeneity is more highly valued by the Northern European member states than by the southern states. According to the authors, the representatives of the northern countries (Germany, Denmark, Benelux, the UK, and Ireland) tend to communicate mainly among themselves rather than with representatives of the southern countries. The southern countries' representatives also interact mainly with each other, but their interaction (unlike that of the Scandinavian countries) tends not to constitute a full-fledged network. There is no stable cooperation among the countries of Southern Europe, despite the fact of the closeness of their interests and their substantial convergence on several issues.

During the "First Republic," Italy was part of a stable framework of alliances under Christian Democratic (DC) leadership, comprising the Benelux countries and Germany. Yet Italy has slowly lost its allies beginning in the mid-1990s. The disappearance of the old political parties revolutionized that framework, leaving Italy frequently excluded from the core group of countries that carry weight and exert influence; a lack of stable alliances has proven to be extremely costly. The first Berlusconi government (1994–1995) was a spectacular example of the consequences of losing allies. That government, which comprised not only Berlusconi's party, Forza Italia, but also the Northern League and the postfascist National Alliance, found itself up against a wall of obstructionist resistance from its European partners. When his European counterparts met their respective European political families before the European Council (and on other occasions), Berlusconi was totally isolated. It is no coincidence that Berlusconi's first priority, once out of government (1996–2001), was to get Forza Italia into the European People's Party (EPP), thus pegging his party to a framework of stable European alliances.

Italy and Foreign Policy: The EU High Commissioner Position Versus National Interests and Russian Sanctions

The first thing that Renzi did was firmly anchor his Democratic Party into the European Socialist Party (PES) in February 2014, of which he became the major stakeholder after gaining 41 percent of the votes in the European Parliament elections in May 2014. He then decided to almost immediately cash in his credit by forcing his PES colleagues to support Mogherini's candidacy as EUHR. Incidentally, Mogherini was the person who closed the deal between the PES and the Italian Democratic Party.

Last but not least, while other countries put the promotion of their national interests before political loyalties, in Italy the reverse is often the case. Domestic divisions make it more difficult to appoint Italians to strategic posts. In addition, traditionally Italians tend to prefer "status" posts over "authoritative" positions: "armchair politics" has been one of the axioms of the Italian diplomatic tradition and political culture. When the opportunity arises to appoint Italians to fill international posts of responsibility, Italy's governments often choose undistinguished candidates from their own parties over qualified, rather than possibly winning, candidates from the other side of the political divide. Or they put up a fight at the domestic level. A case in point is related to the position of the EUHR, seemingly an Italian obsession. Former prime minister D'Alema twice tried to self-candidate, in 2009 and 2014. In 2009, despite being supported by the Berlusconi government for the sake of pure domestic politics, he met the opposition of the Eastern European countries because of his past as a Communist Party leader (supposedly he speaks better Russian than English), as well as US (and Israeli) reservations about his views on the Middle East and Russia. His very own European political family, the socialists, finally turned him down. In 2014 again D'Alema tried to float his name, notwithstanding that Italy had already named Mogherini as a candidate to the post. As mentioned, despite that opposition to Mogherini's candidacy by a number of European partners,[40] the candidacy was finally imposed by Italy, not without taking prisoners. In particular, in having Mogherini appointed to the post, Renzi discarded the possibility of having Letta named at the rather more influential post of EU president. Fearing a potential threat to his political leadership in Italy, Renzi abruptly ousted Letta from the government in February 2014. Relations between the two remain rocky.[41]

In other European countries we see the opposite approach: when it comes to international appointments, governments search for their best national candidate, regardless of political affiliation. Two examples of this have been the appointments of Javier Solana (a socialist) to the post of "Mr. CFSP" (Common Foreign and Security Policy) by a government headed at the time by José Maria Aznar (a member of the People's Party) and the appointment of Pascal Lamy (a socialist) by the French president Jacques Chirac (a conservative), as director general of the World Trade Organization. This practice of Italian politicians—namely, their failure to consider the national interest and promote that interest at the European level—is part of an approach to politics that hampers Italy's participation in the EU decisionmaking process.

Conclusions

Without doubt, since the early 2000s a process of Europeanization has been characterizing the main Italian institutions: Parliament, government, and the regions. Yet this was not enough to change the mind-set of Italian policymakers. Italy's image as an unreliable country is proving hard to bury. There are both historical and more recent grounds for this. On a continent where history weighs heavily, Italy is still the country that changed sides in both world wars. This historical perception is further strengthened in the suspicious eyes of European partners when they see Italy's wavering positions, for example, in the matter of alliances. Many other Europeans have networks of alliances that remain stable over time, with homogeneous geographic and socioeconomic interests. But for twenty years Italy has played the game of shifting alliances. Furthermore, Italy seems to be wavering today between its past as an honest European broker and giving way to temptations of power, with the result that its conduct is increasingly perceived as unpredictable.

Our last task is therefore to try to understand why the changes have been incomplete and what prospects lie ahead. Until the mid-1990s, Italy's difficulties were largely attributable to its unstable governments, lack of government cohesion, inability to implement a learning process, and political culture.[42] Italy's greater political stability between 1996 and 2011 has made it possible for the country to embark on a series of reforms encompassing the executive and the legislature, as well as the regional governments, and these changes have enabled the country to make major strides forward. There remained, however, a lack of government cohesion and a problematic political culture. Taken together, they prevented Italy from achieving the prominent position that it might otherwise occupy in European relations.

Since 2011, Italy has returned to political instability, with three different nonelected governments seizing power in a row, with a high level of infighting among the different government coalitions' parties. Without a widespread external perception of stability, there cannot be any beneficial fallout from the political and administrative system, particularly with regard to the complex management of European affairs. In a climate of political instability, in fact, bureaucracy becomes the most important variable. In Italy, civil servants do not fail to remind us that politicians come and go, while they stay. This enhances resistance to change, explaining for example why the creation of the CIACE did not trigger a series of reforms within the various ministries and why, once CIACE's founding director left, it ceased to function.

One of Renzi's main goals is a comprehensive reform of public administration.[43] Others before him had tried and failed. As Gozi bluntly told the Parliament,[44] there still is an urgent need to change the administrative culture in Italy. If this change does not happen, change and positive action will continue to be limited to the will and leadership capacity of single actors. This way Italy will never be a relevant actor at the EU level and will continue implementing what others decide in Brussels.

Notes

1. Ferraris (1996), pp. 341–342.
2. Ferraris (1996), pp. 243–245.
3. *Il Sole 24 Ore*, May 17, 1994.
4. *Il Sole 24 Ore*, July 17, 1994 and July 31, 1994.

5. *European Voice*, July 3, 2003.

6. In an early speech in front of the Italian Parliament (May 18, 2006), Prodi affirmed: "We are convinced that the Italian national interest and the European interest are one and the same. We are convinced that Italy will count—even in relations with its greatest ally—only if it counts in Europe. We will work to put Italy back among the leaders of a new Europe" (see http://www.camera.it).

7. See http://www.6aprile.it/featured/2011/11/04/berlusconi-in-italia-non-ce-la -crisi-i-ristornati-sono-pieni-video.html.

8. See http://temi.repubblica.it/limes/con-monti-litalia-riconquista-la-credibilita -internazionale/32317.

9. See http://scenarieconomici.it/il-bilancio-del-governo-monti-valutazione-finale -il-peggior-governo-della-2-repubblica-valutazione-analitica-delle-performance-dellitalia -rispetto-alla-ue-di-tutti-i-governi-2/.

10. See http://www.affarinternazionali.it/articolo.asp?ID=2844.

11. See http://www.europeanvoice.com/article/federica-mogherini-italys-scape-goat/.

12. See http://www.matteorenzi.it/idee/.

13. See http://www.lastampa.it/2014/08/10/italia/politica/renzi-non-prendo-ordini -dalleuropa-xXMsNyAHuHmkurn45MfDXJ/pagina.html.

14. See http://www.europaquotidiano.it/2014/10/22/renzi-4/.

15. See http://www.reuters.com/article/2014/11/27/us-eu-budgets-exclusive-id USKCN0JB11520141127.

16. Ruling 170 of June 8, 1984, where the Constitutional Court finally declared that national judges have to apply EC norms whenever they conflict with national legislation.

17. Law 183 (1987).

18. Law 86 (1989).

19. Law 209 (1998).

20. Community Laws are omnibus laws that shall be passed annually to implement EU directives.

21. Law 25 (1999).

22. Law 422 (2000).

23. Law 11 (2005).

24. "Norme generali sulla partecipazione dell'Italia alla formazione europea e all'attuazione della nermativa e delle politiche dell'Unione europea," L. 234/2012, in G.U. no. 3, 4 (January 2013).

25. Article 37, Law 234 (2012).

26. In a hearing of the Undersecretary of State for European Affair Sandro Gozi in front of Italian Parliament, April 29, 2014.

27. Law 154 (2014) in GUCE (*Official Journal of the European Union*, Italian) no. 251, October 28, 2014.

28. The Single Market Scoreboard: Italy 2013–2014. Available at http://ec.europa .eu/single-market-scoreboard.

29. See http://www.theguardian.com/world/2014/dec/02/eu-court-fines-italy-illegal -waste.

30. See http://www.repubblica.it/ambiente/2014/12/02/news/rifiuti_corte_di_giustizia _ue_condanna_italia_sanzione_di_40_milioni-101920712/.

31. Laws 400 (1988), 300 (1999), 59 (1997).

32. Bindi (2011), pp. 182–190.

33. "Nuclei di valutazione."

34. Hearing at the EU Affairs Committee in the Italian Parliament, October 1, 2014.

35. Moravcsik (1991), pp. 41–84.

36. The EU governments began an IGC on October 4, 2003, to revise the draft constitutional treaty that had been adopted by the European Convention on July 10. During the IGC session of December 12–13, 2003, however, the EU heads of state and government failed to agree on the Council voting system. On June 17–18, 2004, the European Council finally brought the IGC to a conclusion.

37. Blondel and Thiebault(1991).

38. Spence, David: Negotiations, coalitions and the resolution of interstate conflict pp. 256-267 in Westlake & Galloway, D., ed., 2004 (338=9. edition)

39. Beyers and Dierick(1998).

40. See http://www.dw.de/eu-summit-fails-to-reach-agreement-on-top-jobs/a -17791114.

41. See http://www.huffingtonpost.com/federiga-bindi/knock-on-wood-matteo-renzi _b_4783224.html.

42. Bindi and Cisci, (2005).

43. See http://www.washingtonpost.com/opinions/is-italy-finally-ready-for-radical -reform/2014/02/17/807842fc-95ac-11e3-afce-3e7c922ef31e_story.html.

44. Hearing the EU Committee of the Italian Parliament, October 1, 2014.

6

Belgium, the Netherlands, and Luxembourg: Challenging European Integration

Karen M. Anderson

BELGIUM, THE NETHERLANDS, AND LUXEMBOURG ARE FOUNDING European Union members, and EU membership continues to be a cornerstone of domestic and foreign policy. All three countries enthusiastically supported the introduction of the euro and have been among the most pro-integrationist EU members. Support for EU membership and further integration is high among political elites and the public in Belgium and Luxembourg, whereas important groups in the Netherlands have begun to question core aspects of European integration.

Belgium continues to be one of the most pro-integration member states, and the location of the central EU institutions in Brussels brings significant economic benefits to Belgium. Belgian EU membership must also be viewed in the context of the country's slow transformation from a unitary into a federal state. Belgium's 10 million inhabitants include three ethnic groups: French-speaking Walloons, Dutch-speaking Flemish, and a small German-speaking minority. The three regions (Flanders, Wallonia, and Brussels) each have their own government and legislature, and govern policy areas such as housing, employment, energy, infrastructure, environment, spatial planning, and transport. Federalism complicates Belgium's relationship with the EU level because the regions participate in many aspects of EU policymaking and implementation. At the same time, Belgium's multilingual federalism is often viewed as a model for what a (con)federal Europe might look like.

In the Netherlands, EU membership remains an article of faith, but public skepticism for further integration has increased significantly. The Dutch rejection of the Constitutional Treaty in 2005 was a foreboding of more spectacular manifestations of Dutch ambivalence concerning EU membership. The rise of the anti-EU, right-wing populist Freedom Party (PVV) and widespread dissatisfaction with the EU's bailouts of Greece,

Portugal, and Ireland in 2010 and 2011 are the latest signs of this trend. However, it would be a mistake to conclude that the Dutch no longer support EU membership. Indeed, public support for Dutch EU membership remains high, but EU membership has become much more politicized in the past decade, and Dutch voters increasingly view the workings of EU institutions with suspicion.

Luxembourg is one of the two smallest member states, with 470,000 inhabitants.[1] Like Belgium, Luxembourg benefits from the location of important administrative functions in the country: the European Court of Justice (ECJ). As an extremely small state, Luxembourg has historically sought means of cooperating with neighboring states for economic purposes, most notably in its currency and customs union with Belgium in 1922 and its membership in the Benelux Customs Union established in 1948. EU membership and Luxembourg's pro-integration stance are logical extensions of this long-standing orientation.

How and in What Areas Does the EU/EC Affect the Benelux Countries?

From the outset, the Benelux countries' participation in the European integration process has been shaped by their status as small, open economies located between two much more powerful states, Germany and France. The importance of market access for the Benelux countries can hardly be exaggerated: according to World Trade Organization statistics, the Netherlands was the fifth largest merchandise exporter in the world in 2013 and seventh in services. The Netherlands is also the second largest exporter of agricultural products in the world. Belgium is ranked twelfth in merchandise and fifteenth in services exports. The internal market is also hugely important for all three economies—the 72.8 percent of Dutch exports went to other EU countries in 2013, 70.1 percent of Belgian, and 80.7 percent of Luxembourgian. By contrast, 55.7 percent of Germany merchandise exports were destined for the EU market.[2] In short, the three Benelux countries have vigorously supported European integration as a means of guaranteeing access to European markets and of constraining the dominance of more powerful states.

A closer look at the budgetary implications of EU membership is one way of approaching the issue of how the EU influences each country. All three countries are net contributors to the EU, with Belgium and Luxembourg benefiting disproportionately from the location of core EU institutions in Brussels (European Commission, European Council, Economic and Social Committee, and Committee of the Regions) and Luxembourg (ECJ, General Court, Court of Auditors, and European Investment Bank).

Until 1990, the Netherlands was a net beneficiary of EU funding, and the country's status as one of the EU's largest net contributors has had a significant impact on Dutch voters' more skeptical attitude toward EU policies and the functioning of EU institutions (see later discussion). In December 2005, the European Council decided to reduce the contributions of the Netherlands, Germany, Austria, and Sweden. The decision means a €1 billion reduction in the Dutch net annual contribution. The member states had to ratify the decision, which took until 2009. The rebate was then applied retroactively, resulting in the large decrease in 2009. Even with this rebate, the Netherlands is still a net contributor. In 2009, the Netherlands' net contribution was €900 million (€3.2 billion contribution minus about €2.3 billion in receipts). Forty percent of payments received by the Netherlands were related to the common agricultural policy, whereas about one third came from Structural Funding.[3] In 2013, the Netherlands' net contribution had risen to €2,675.1 million (0.45 percent of gross national income, GNI), Belgium paid €1,541.1 million (0.20 percent of GNI), and Luxembourg paid €69.4 million (0.22 percent of GNI).[4]

Dutch income from the EU budget is forecast to decline in the 2014–2020 Financing Framework, largely because of of reductions in EU spending on the Common Agricultural Policy (CAP) and Cohesion Policy. Dutch agricultural payments are forecast to decrease by about 7 percent for the period 2014–2020 compared to 2007–2013. Dutch payments from the Structural Funds will decrease by about 25 percent for the same period.[5] Belgian and Luxembourgian shares of cohesion spending and agricultural policy are likely to show similar declines.

The Benelux countries are net contributors to the EU budget largely because they receive little funding from the two largest EU budget items: the Common Agriculture Policy, which is now classified under the Natural Resources (along with fisheries and rural development) category in the budget, and Cohesion Policy. In 2013, Belgium received 4.2 percent of Cohesion funding, the Netherlands 3.5 percent, and Luxembourg less than 1 percent. Agricultural support played a larger role until the 1980s, but today the Benelux countries are among the EU members that receive the smallest amount of CAP funding.[6] In 2013, Belgium received 1.2 percent of the Natural Resources budget, the Netherlands 1.7 percent, and Luxembourg less than 0.1 percent.[7]

As noted, the workings of the EU budget have taken on great political significance in the Netherlands, but not in Belgium and Luxembourg. Citizen and elite displeasure with the growing size of the Netherlands' net contribution to the EU has spilled over into both supranational and national politics. In 2005, the Netherlands joined forces with two other net contributors, Austria and Sweden, demanding a rebate modeled on the British one. The Council responded in 2005 with a decision granting all three countries reduced annual contributions for the 2007–2013 financial planning period.[8] Keeping the rebate beyond 2007–2013 has been a major issue in Dutch politics. The 2010 coalition agreement between the Liberal Party (VVD) and the Christian Democrats (CDA) expressed the intention to not only make the rebate permanent but also increase it.[9] The Dutch rebate has become an article of faith for all of the mainstream political parties.

The effects of financial crisis on the Dutch economy caused the downfall of the Liberal–Christian Democratic minority government in April 2012. The government depended on the support of the right-wing populist, anti-EU Freedom Party (PVV). The PVV opposed some of the tough austerity measures the government proposed to keep the government deficit in line with the Stability and Growth Pact and withdrew its support. The move was not entirely unexpected given the PVV's obstructionist, Euro-skeptical stance and its success in pulling the government toward a less positive orientation concerning EU membership.

Dutch EU membership was a major issue—for the first time ever—in the 2012 election campaign. The PVV played an important role in this; party leader Geert Wilders asserted that the elderly (because of cuts in pensions) should not have to bear the financial burden of dictates from unelected bureaucrats in Brussels. Wilders portrayed austerity policies as something dictated by Brussels that would redistribute from deserving groups in the Netherlands (the sick, pensioners, etc.) to undeserving groups in profligate EU member states (Greece and other Mediterranean countries). The PVV campaigned on a manifesto titled "Their Brussels, Our Netherlands," and even advocated Dutch exit from the Eurozone and the EU. The established parties did not follow Wilders's anti-EU line, but they were more critical of the EU than in the past. In particular, the mainstream parties (Liberals, Labour, Christian Democracy) advocated reining in some of the EU's powers and improving the efficiency and legitimacy of EU institutions.[10] On the left, the Socialist Party also campaigned on an anti-EU message, increasing pressure on the centrist parties concerning the impact of the EU on the Dutch political economy.

Political parties' declining enthusiasm or outright hostility (in the case of the PVV and Socialist Party) resonated with voters. Opinion polls in 2012 showed high levels of support for EU membership, but growing dissatisfaction with the effect of EU membership on the Netherlands. The share of Dutch respondents who view EU membership positively dropped from 47 percent in 2008–2009 to 40 percent in the third quarter of 2013; the share who think it is a good thing that the Netherlands has the euro during the current economic crisis dropped from 45 percent to 29 percent in the same period; and the share who think the Netherlands has relinquished too much power to the EU increased from 47 percent to 59 percent between the end of 2012 and the third quarter of 2013.[11]

The 2014 elections to the European Parliament threatened to become another victory in the PVV's attempts to complicate the Netherlands' relationship with the EU. During the campaign, Wilders announced his intention to attack the EU from within by forming an anti-EU bloc within the Parliament in alliance with the French National Front and the Italian Lega Nord. In addition, he began to openly call for a Dutch exit from the EU—"Nexit." A British consultancy was hired to estimate the benefits of leaving the EU and reintroducing the guilder, though few experts and national politicians took the results of the study seriously. Wilders even staged a publicity stunt in Brussels right before the election in which he cut out a star (to represent the Netherlands) from the EU flag. The PVV did not perform as well in the election as forecast, so his plans did not come to much. However, mainstream political parties cannot afford to ignore the PVV's anti-EU message. In June 2013, Prime Minister Mark Rutte issued a memorandum setting out a list of fifty-four competencies that the EU should leave to the member states.

One of the most important ways that EU membership shapes the political economies of the Benelux countries is via the Stability and Growth Pact. In the wake of the sovereign debt crisis, the member states have strengthened budget surveillance procedures. The European Semester was adopted by the Council in 2010 to streamline and improve the coordination of fiscal and employment policy as part of the governance architecture of Europe 2020. Early 2011 saw the kick-off the new European Semester that gives the Union stronger oversight concerning national budgets and national reform programs. The semester process aims to strengthen fiscal policy coordination by empowering the Commission to evaluate fiscal policy and reform agendas before national budget cycles begin.

This unprecedented fiscal supervision of national budgets has been particularly important in Belgium and the Netherlands, but for different reasons. The Netherlands has historically been a strong proponent of fiscal discipline, and it usually backs the strict "ordo-liberal" approach advanced by Germany. The Dutch approach to sound finance means that there is political consensus around the goal of budget discipline and reduced public debt. In contrast, Belgium has struggled for several decades to achieve budget discipline and manageable debt levels. Indeed, qualifying for European Monetary Union (EMU) was defined as a national project requiring extraordinary policymaking, and it dominated Belgian politics in the mid-1990s.[12] This was no easy task given that in 1993, the budget deficit hovered around 7 percent, while the debt ratio reached its highest level ever, at 137.9 percent of GDP. The run-up to the EMU in the late 1990s provided the government with the political capital necessary to secure approval for major reforms of the welfare state designed to reduce public expenditure.

The constraints of EMU have had a profound impact on Belgian fiscal policy. Until the late 1990s, Belgium was a case of increasing deficits and public debt. Indeed, federalism and the challenges associated with governance in a multiethnic polity created incentives for politicians to prioritize public sector expansion over fiscal discipline. For Belgium, qualifying for EMU was a high-stakes political project. On the other hand, qualifying for EMU was a national priority of such importance that failure was impossible for political elites to contemplate. The overriding importance of participating in such a significant European project enabled political actors who under other circumstances might have opposed budget consolidation measures to agree to painful cuts.

The impact of the EMU budget constraint on Belgian public finances has been substantial. Between 1995 and 1998, Belgium reduced its budget deficit from 3.9 percent to 1.6 percent of GDP. In the same period, the public debt to GDP ratio fell from 131 percent of GDP to 117 percent of GDP, a reduction of 16 percent.[13] By the end of 2004, the public debt to GDP ratio had decreased by 40 percent, and in 2003 gross debt fell below 100 percent of GDP (down from 137 percent of GDP in 1993).[14] In 2004 and 2005, the government budget was roughly in balance, in sharp contrast to the early 1990s when deficits of 7 percent were not uncommon.

The 2008 financial crisis threatened to reverse Belgium's progress concerning budget discipline and reducing public debt. By 2009, the deficit reached 5.6 percent of GDP, activating the EU's Excessive Deficit Procedure. The Council gave Belgium until 2012 to rein in the deficit, and the introduction of the European Semester's surveillance tools increased the pressure to cut the deficit. Belgium's Stability Programme aims to achieve budget balance by 2012 and keep the debt to GDP ratio below 100 percent. As recently as 2007, the debt to GDP ratio was 84 percent, and it had climbed to 99.6 percent in 2012.[15] The Belgian fiscal consolidation program includes painful cuts to social programs like pensions and unemployment benefits and has not been popular with voters. Indeed, Belgians staged a general strike in December 2014 that shut down key sectors of the economy, most notably transportation.

The financial crisis also caused a sharp deterioration of public finances in the Netherlands. The deficit reached 5.1 percent of GDP in 2010, and public debt rose to 63.4 percent of GDP.[16] As already noted, the government's fiscal consolidation program failed to secure support in Parliament in 2012, largely because the PVV portrayed cuts to Dutch social benefits as unfair given the Netherlands' contribution to the bailout of Greece. The September 2012 election brought a Liberal-Labour majority coalition to power, which is firmly committed to budget consolidation. Budget consolidation packages adopted since 2012 have brought significant cuts on social spending and moderate tax increases.

To summarize, the Benelux countries are among the most affluent and trade-dependent EU members, so the impact of European integration is seen most clearly in access to the internal market and participation in the Eurozone. All three are founding member states, and clear majorities support EU membership. However, the Netherlands has embarked on a much more Euro-skeptical path than Belgium and Luxembourg. EU membership is now a highly politicized issue in Dutch national politics, whereas Belgian and Luxembourgian voters view EU membership as a beneficial, more or less uncontested element of the political and economic environment.

How Do the Benelux Countries Influence EU Policies?

Belgium, the Netherlands, and Luxembourg are small countries, so they cannot hope to shape the EU agenda like the larger countries do. However, EU decisionmaking institutions amplify the influence of small member states, and the Benelux countries have used this to their advantage. First, political elites from the Benelux countries have long occupied prominent positions in European institutions. Paul Henri Spaak, a former Belgian prime minister, was one of the architects of European integration in the 1950s and 1960s; the former Dutch finance minister Wim Duisenburg was the first president of the European Central Bank; Luxembourg's Jacques Santer was president of the Commission from 1995 to 1999; Belgium's Herman van Rompuy served as the first president of the European Council; and Luxembourg's prime minister Jean-Claude Juncker is the president of the current European Commission.

Aside from this more individualized path of influence, there are two central avenues for EU members to try to influence EU policymaking: agenda-setting during the rotating presidencies and voting and coalition building in the European Council and Council of Ministers. The rotating presidency is especially important for small states like the Benelux countries, and they have exploited this to push their own policy agenda at the EU level. Indeed, two notably pro-integration treaties were signed during Dutch presidencies: the Treaty of Maastricht (1992) and the Treaty of Amsterdam (1997). In December 2001, Belgium occupied the presidency when the Laeken Declaration convened the European Convention on the draft Constitutional Treaty.

The Benelux countries have historically used the presidency to advance their pro-integrationist agenda. This is still largely true of Belgium and Luxembourg, but the Netherlands pursued a decidedly less integrationist program when it held the presidency for the last time, in 2004. Although the main priorities of the Dutch presidency were enlargement, economic growth, increased security, budget reform, and a more effective role for the EU in the world, Hans Labohm argues that the Dutch presidency was rather uneventful: "It laboured under an interruption of continuity caused by the start-up of a new European Parliament, the accession of new members, which still have to settle down, the resignation of the old Commission and the delays in connection with the acceptance by Parliament of new commissioners."[17] Nevertheless, the Dutch presidency completed accession negoti-ations with Romania and Bulgaria; the heads of government reached agree-ment to start accession negotiations with Turkey on October 3, 2005; and the European Council adopted an action plan to improve measures to com-bat terrorism. Member states also decided to strengthen the EU's military and civilian capabilities so that it can engage in crisis management outside its borders in accordance with its security strategy.

Luxembourg took over the presidency in the first half of 2005. The presidency started optimistically but ended in crisis. The French and Dutch rejections of the Constitutional Treaty, as well as the failed attempt to reach a compromise on the EU budget, overshadowed the other modest accom-plishments. During the presidency, the EU reformed the Stability and Growth Pact and set new objectives in terms of public development aid at the EU level. On the international agenda, the Luxembourg presidency im-proved EU transatlantic relations culminating in the meeting of February 22, 2005, in Brussels with President George W. Bush and a follow-up EU–United States summit thereafter.

It is instructive to compare the budget deal brokered under the British presidency with the proposal made by Luxembourg during its presidency. Prime Minister Juncker advocated a larger budget than Tony Blair proposed during the British presidency in December 2005, clearly reflecting Luxem-bourg's pro-integrationist agenda. Juncker's proposal was €871 billion for the 2007–2013 budget period, whereas Blair's initial proposal was €850 billion.[18] Luxembourg's budget proposal not only included more money, it would also have frozen and eventually phased out the British rebate. More-over, the Luxembourg proposal left the CAP more or less intact.

The Belgian position was very close to Luxembourg's, and the Nether-lands joined the British in pushing for a smaller EU budget and fundamental CAP reform.

The Dutch in particular have adopted a hard-line position on EU budget issues, particularly their own budget contribution and the implementation of the Growth and Stability Pact (GSP). With the United Kingdom, Austria, and Sweden, the Netherlands was part of the "Gang of Four" pushing for budget-ary reform in the first half of the 2000s. Since the adoption of the GSP, Dutch finance ministers have promoted effective implementation of the GSP and voted for tighter implementation in the Council of Ministers. Belgium and Luxembourg have not pursued a similar policy stance; both countries prefer to increase the EU's financial resources. For example, Belgium explicitly supports increasing EU financial resources by increasing the EU's "own re-sources," currently set at a maximum of 1.24 percent of the EU's GNI.[19]

Eastern enlargement has decreased the number of opportunities for the Benelux countries to use the rotating presidencies to promote their interests. Not only does each country have to wait longer for its turn at the presidency, but starting in 2010 each must coordinate its presidency with two other member state presidencies. Luxembourg is scheduled to hold the presidency in the second half of 2015, and is part of the presidency trio for 2014–2015 that includes Italy and Latvia. The Netherlands has not held the presidency since 2004, and will form a trio in 2016 with Slovakia and Malta. Before Eastern enlargement, member states had to wait about seven years for their turn at the presidency. The postenlargement cycle is twelve years.

Belgium was the last Benelux country to occupy the presidency, in 2010, as part of a trio with Hungary and Spain. The financial crisis dominated the presidency, so Belgium played an important role in brokering the introduction of stronger economic governance tools and more effective coordination of economic policy. The Belgian presidency also emphasized implementation of the Lisbon Treaty (in force since December 2009). Two important parts of this effort were the application of new budget procedures for the 2011 budget and the introduction of the European Citizen's Initiative. The latter was introduced by the Lisbon Treaty and allows citizens who collect a specific number of signatures supporting their efforts to petition the Commission to consider legislation on a particular topic.[20]

National Positions in the Council of Ministers

The Benelux countries are pro-integration,[21] but each tends to prioritize a different set of issues in intergovernmental bargaining, and each country relies on a different set of procedures in formulating its bargaining stances. Erik Jones argues that the consensual nature of domestic policymaking in the Benelux countries produces a complicated relationship between national and EU-level politics.[22] In all three countries, political institutions are designed to facilitate consensual decisionmaking, and this means that multiple actors are incorporated into the decisionmaking process via bipartite or tripartite organizations like the Social Economic Council in the Netherlands. Belgium is an extreme case in this respect because federalism complicates the formulation of a coherent Belgian position in the Council of Ministers. The constitutional reform of 1970 introduced the first elements of a federal structure, and this process was completed in 1993.[23] Two additional major reforms (in 2001 and 2011) devolve important tasks from the federal to the regional and community level, including important social welfare functions.

At the administrative level, the Benelux countries differ in the ways they coordinate EU policymaking. Whereas the responsibility for preparing, deciding, and implementing EU dossiers in Luxembourg rests with only a few people, the Netherlands and especially Belgium are characterized by a complex system of coordination. In Luxembourg, coordination is officially the responsibility of the Ministry of Foreign Affairs. However, as Danielle Bossaert notes, "Usually, the officials who are in the charge of a certain EU dossier have a large degree of independence in their field and, when working within their ministry, they will generally co-operate with their minister, with whom they have direct contact in person or by telephone."[24] Because the country is so small, civil servants in the Luxembourg administration dealing with EU policy often know each other personally, and this means that the Ministry of Foreign Affairs organizes only a few regular coordination meetings.

In the Netherlands, the requirements of coalition government prevent the formulation of a strong central political direction. Instead, ministers normally have a large degree of autonomy. A characteristic of the decision-making in Dutch Cabinets is that all members are collectively bound by the final outcome. When negotiations are conducted within the Council of Ministers, the Dutch position must be formulated by the Dutch Cabinet. The formulation of this view, to be discussed in meetings of the Cabinet, is prepared by interdepartmental coordination committees, the so-called departmental proches. The most important departmental committee with a formal status with regard to European affairs is the Coordination Committee for EU and Association Problems (CoCo). The chair of the committee is the minister for foreign affairs; the vice chair is the minister for economic affairs. The other members of CoCo are high-ranking departmental officials. However, subcouncils of the Cabinet deal with important problems with the preparation and implementation of Community policies that are part of the overall policy of the government. An important subcouncil in this respect is the Council for European Affairs, presided over by the prime minister. The other members include ministers, state secretaries, and the permanent representative in Brussels. Conclusions of the CoCo, as well as those of the Council for European Affairs, are discussed in meetings of the cabinet.[25]

Due to its federal and constitutional entities, Belgian ministerial departments at the federal level have their own European coordination structures. In addition, there are several interdepartmental coordination bodies. At the political level, the Minister for Foreign Affairs is responsible for Belgium's EU policy. At the administrative level, the Ministry of Foreign Affairs and Ministry of Economic Affairs are the coordinating ministries. The Economic Affairs Ministry takes place in an interdepartmental committee known as the Inter-Ministerial Economic Committee (IEC). Next to representatives from several ministries there are representatives of both the communities and the regions. Whereas the IEC deals with technical issues, the European coordination meetings in the Ministry of Foreign Affairs deal with the political dimensions of issues.[26]

Trend and Prospects

Ratification of the Constitutional Treaty is a good example of how the Benelux countries' approaches to European integration have diverged in the past decade. The ratification process in Belgium and Luxembourg was relatively trouble-free,[27] with comfortable majorities in both countries voting "yes" either in Parliament or in a national referendum. These outcomes reflect both countries' continued support for deepening European integration. In contrast, Dutch voters' resounding "no" to the constitution on June 1, 2005, demonstrates the Netherlands' deep ambivalence about the future direction of European integration.

The structure of Belgian federalism means that seven legislative assemblies had to ratify the constitution. Both houses of the Belgian Parliament ratified it in April 2005 by wide majorities, and four of the five regional assemblies have also approved the constitution.[28] Belgians have historically had very positive attitudes toward European integration, and support for the constitution was high. In January 2005, 70 percent of Belgians said they favored the constitution, and even after the French and Dutch "no" votes, support climbed to 77 percent in autumn 2005, the highest in the EU.[29]

Citizens in the Benelux countries continue to view EU membership favorably, even if they diverge concerning the effectiveness of European institutions and the desirability of further integration. In Autumn 2013, 81 percent of Luxembourgians thought that their country was better off in the EU than outside. Seventy-seven percent of Dutch and 71 percent of Belgian respondents also viewed membership favorably. Support for the euro is similarly high: 79 percent of Luxembourgians (the highest level in the EU), 74 percent of Belgians, and 71 percent of the Dutch support the euro. Trust in the EU as a whole is much lower. Fifty-six percent of Belgians, 42 percent of Luxembourgians, and 38 percent of Dutch respondents expressed trust in the EU. The three countries diverge concerning their view of how well democracy works in the EU, however. Forty-three percent of Dutch respondents think democracy works well in the EU, whereas 64 percent of Luxembourgians and 61 percent of Belgians think so.[30]

As discussed, the period since 2000 in the Netherlands has been marked by an ambivalent attitude among elites and the public toward the EU. The EU and Dutch membership became politicized, and parts of the political establishment began to criticize the direction of European integration and the Netherlands' pro-integration stance. The rise of the populist politicians Pim Fortuyn in 1992 and Gert Wilders in the 2000s accelerated this trend. Fortuyn and Wilders capitalized on voter disenchantment by questioning some of the unwritten rules of Dutch politics, including multiculturalism, consensus politics, and European integration. Voters and politicians are now much more likely to voice their skepticism about issues like immigration and institutions like the EU.

Dutch voters' rejection of the Constitutional Treaty must be viewed against the background of the Fortuyn and Wilders revolution and the Netherlands' evolution from net beneficiary of EU funding to the largest per capita contributor in 2003. Nevertheless, the Dutch result was devastating: 61.5 percent of the electorate voted "no." The Dutch "no" was different from the French "no," however. Whereas the French electorate voted against the modernization of the Common Agricultural Policy and the subsidies for French farmers, Dutch voters felt insecure. French voters expressed their reluctance toward the discipline of the free market, against the services directive, whereas Dutch citizens voted against the way Europe works and how Europe is administered.

A central irony of the referendum is that a large number of voters (49 percent) favored a European constitution, but many still voted against it.[31] According to the most recent polls, the most important reason for voting "no" was lack of information. Thirty-two percent of respondents said they did not have enough information to vote "yes." Lack of information also kept many citizens from voting.[32] According to the same Eurobarometer poll, the second most important reason for voting "no" was potential loss of national sovereignty. Voters' view of the European Union also heavily influenced the vote. Regardless of how someone voted, his or her view of the EU was the most important factor affecting his or her vote: 31 percent said that this was the key element influencing their vote.[33] Indeed, the referendum result closely resembles Dutch attitudes toward the EU.

EU membership remains an article of faith in the Netherlands, Belgium, and Luxembourg. However, the Netherlands' increasing skepticism about the functioning of European institutions, especially the Stability and Growth Pact and the budget, means that the Benelux countries are no longer as close to each other on European issues as they once were. Belgium and Luxembourg remain staunchly pro-integration, but the recent Dutch ambivalence means that it now resembles the strong Euro-skeptics Sweden, Austria, and the United Kingdom.

Notes

1. The smallest member state is now Malta, with 400,000 inhabitants.
2. See http://stat.wto.org/CountryProfile/WSDBCountryPFReporter.aspx ?Language=E (accessed January 9, 2015).
3. Arkestijn (2010).
4. See http://ec.europa.eu/budget/financialreport/2013/foreword/index_en.html.
5. Tweede Kamer der Staten-Generaal (2013–2014), p. 218.
6. Ibid. Dutch farmers benefited from the CAP in the first three decades after the EC was established. Even though the Dutch agricultural sector remains substantial, Dutch farmers receive comparatively little CAP aid.
7. European Commission (2014a), p. 123.
8. The Netherlands and Sweden receive lump sum payments resulting from reductions in their yearly GNI contribution, and Austria, Germany, the Netherlands and Sweden receive reduced VAT call rates. See Council Decision of 7 June 2007 on the system of the European Communities' own resources (2007/436/EC, Euratom).

9. The Liberal–Christian Democratic government governed until 2012 as a minority coalition with the support of the anti-EU, anti-immigrant populist party PVV.

10. Van Kessel and Hollander (2012).

11. Dekker and den Ridder (2013), p. 19.

12. This section draws on Anderson et al.(2007).

13. Belgian Minister of Finance, "The Stability Programme of Belgium 1999–2002. Available at http://www.eu.int/comm/economy_finance/about/activities/sgp/country /countryfiles/be/be19981999_en.pdf.

14. Belgian Ministry of Finance, "The Belgian Stability Programme 2005–2008. Update." Available at http://www.eu.int/comm/economy_finance/about/activities/sgp /country/countryfiles/be/be20042005_en.pdf.

15. Kingdom of Belgium, "Belgium's Stability Programme (2013–2016)".

16. Kingdom of the Netherlands, Stability Programme of the Netherlands, April 2014.

17. Labohm (2004), p. 1.

18. The final compromise agreed in December 2005 was €862 billion.

19. See Kingdom of Belgium, Federal Public Service, Foreign Affairs, Foreign Trade and Development Cooperation, *Activity Report 2012*, p. 38.

20. See the information on the presidency website, http://www.eutrio.be.

21. As noted, the Netherlands has recently backed away from this stance.

22. Jones (2005).

23. In contrast to many other federal states, Belgium became a federal state because of centrifugal tendencies: a unitary state separated into parts rather than the more common pattern of autonomous regions uniting into a federation. See, for example, Hooghe (2004).

24. Bossaert (2003), p. 303.

25. Pappas (1995).

26. Franck, Leclercq, and Vandevievere (2003).

27. The Belgian ratification process is not yet complete. The Flemish regional parliament still has to vote. The largest party in parliament, the right-wing nationalist Flemish Interest, opposes the constitution, but this is not likely to prevent ratification.

28. The Brussels regional parliament voted "yes" on June 17, 2005; the German Community Parliament voted "yes" on June 20, 2005; the Walloon regional Parliament voted "yes" on June 29, 2005; and the French Community Parliament voted "yes" on July 19, 2005.

29. Eurobarometer 64 (2005).

30. European Commission, Standard Eurobarometer 82, Public Opinion in the European Union.

31. All opinion data are from Eurobarometer 63.4, Spring 2005, Netherlands.

32. Flash Eurobarometer, "The European Constitution: Post-Referendum Survey in The Netherlands." http://ec.europa.eu/public_opinion/flash/fl172_en.pdf.

33. Ibid.

7

The United Kingdom:
Reacting to Crises

Janet Mather

THE EUROPEAN UNION'S "AWKWARD PARTNER" HAS BECOME
rather more awkward following the economic crisis of 2007 for two primary reasons. First, in 2010, a coalition government (composed of both
Conservatives and Liberal Democrats) was established, albeit dominated by
a Euro-skeptic Conservative Party and under the leadership of a Conservative prime minister. Second, it was possible to interpret the economic crisis
as emanating from the European Union, thereby giving additional strength
of purpose to the Euro-skeptic or, more accurately "Euro-phobic," members
of the Conservative Party and their supporters. At the same time and for the
same reason, the anti-EU party, the UK Independence Party (UKIP) gained
legitimacy for its primary political agenda, leading to yet more pressure on
the mainstream Conservative leadership. The result of these events has
been a reopening of the entire question of the UK's membership in the EU,
the outcome of which is still uncertain.

This chapter discusses the crisis in terms of its political effect on the
UK and, more specifically, the relationship between itself and the EU. Second, the chapter looks at the issues that have made EU membership problematic in mainstream politics for the first time since 1974. Third, it explains how the partial misnomer "the Euro crisis" was dealt with in the UK,
and fourth, it discusses the 2014 European election results. It concludes by
discussing the future of the UK in the European Union.

The Economic Crisis, the UK, and the EU

The economic crisis hit both Europe and North America, but it had a UK
dimension in the costs to the state resulting from the behavior of individual
banks and their executives, including such individuals as Fred Goodwin

("Fred the Shred") of the Royal Bank of Scotland and Matt Ridley of Northern Rock. Their irresponsible approach to investment added weight to the financial crisis in the UK and resulted in bank nationalizations (Northern Rock; Bradford and Bingley) and recapitalizations (partial nationalization) of both Royal Bank of Scotland and Lloyds Banking Group.[1] A recession was formally declared in January 2009.

The economic crisis as a whole had a number of consequences for UK governance. It enabled discourse on the economic system, it raised the question of deficit, and it affected the approach taken by both the media and the government toward the EU. These issues themselves had at least two outcomes that were indirect as well as direct. First, to some extent the crisis made a division between the UK and other "austerity economics" member states and those that, like France, took a less definitive position on the economic cure for an economic malady. For example, the coalition's "Programme for Government" laid out unmistakably where the emphasis on restoring the UK's finances would lie: "We will significantly accelerate the reduction of the structural deficit over the course of a Parliament, with the main burden of deficit reduction borne by reduced spending rather than increased taxes."[2]

By contrast, François Hollande, on gaining the French presidency in 2012, stressed his belief in debt reduction tempered by development: "To overcome the crisis that is hitting it, Europe needs projects. It needs solidarity. It needs growth. I shall propose to our partners a new pact combining the necessary reduction in public debt with the essential stimulation of the economy."[3] The "Programme for Government" did not raise the question of who was responsible for the economic crisis but did state firmly that closer integration with the EU's economic and monetary policy was not an option: "We will ensure that Britain does not join or prepare to join the Euro in this Parliament."

In addition, it was made clear that the UK government would not accept any transfer of "sovereignty" (undefined), and that no suggestions about further transference of powers to the EU would be accepted without a referendum. To that effect, the "Programme" proposed amending the 1972 Communities Act and the European Union Act requiring such referenda, as well as an act of Parliament needed to provide the amendment. The amending act received the Royal Assent on July 19, 2011. Interestingly, in view of later events, the "Programme" was also unequivocal that the coalition support further enlargement of the EU, an issue that had long been part of Conservative Party policy.

Second, although the euro's problems had a relatively limited effect on the UK, since it is not a member of the Eurozone, it did enable a comparison to be made between the EU's economic policies and those of the UK. It was implied that the EU's policies were significant in causing the crisis, rather than emphasizing that despite using a different currency, the UK recovery was to some extent dependent on the Eurozone's. In turn, emphasis on the supposed link led to a less positive approach by the media and by the coalition government from 2010 onward toward the EU. In much of the reporting, little was made of the fact that the problem was caused by incautious behavior on the part of the banks, nor of the possibility that it was light regulation of the banks that enabled the incautious behavior in the first place. Instead, emphasis was laid on the EU's methods of coping with the crisis, while criticizing the former Labour government's profligacy as a cause of the situation.[4] This criticism was presented despite the agreement among most analysts that the behavior of US and UK banks and their lending of substantial but unsustainable loans had been the primary initial cause, while liberalization of financial markets, supported by the Conservatives, had enabled banks to use deposit accounts to sustain their investments.[5]

Criticism of the EU's policies focused on the bailouts. Oddly, no comments were made about the decision, political rather than economic, that had been made to enable some of the EU states to accede to economic and monetary union despite the fact that they did not meet the Maastricht criteria. Instead, more simplistically, the question of "why should the UK help bail out countries that are social democratic high spenders and are the Eurozone's responsibility anyway?" was implied. This was despite the fact that the UK was not required to contribute directly. As the *Daily Mail*, a right-wing tabloid newspaper, suggested when the question of a bailout for Greece was first discussed in 2010 (before the UK general election): "Officials in Brussels claimed British taxpayers would not have to contribute to the rescue deal but critics said it was obvious such a large bailout would have impact around the European Union bloc—including the UK."[6] The UKIP Member of European Parliament and leader, Nigel Farage, was "certain that Britain will bear the brunt" of the bailout.[7] In the end, however, the UK was not involved directly, and the Eurozone financed the deal.

When it came to the second Greek bailout in 2011, David Cameron, by then the UK prime minister, won a "victory" over Germany in Brussels by arguing successfully that it should be financed from the Eurozone, not from the EU budget to which the UK contributes 12 percent. There does not appear to have been much difficulty here, since Angela Merkel, the German chancellor, had already agreed that the Eurozone would meet the cost.[8]

However, 2011 continued to be a difficult year for the coalition's European policy. In December, as Andrew Gamble notes, Cameron fought doggedly for specific guarantees for the City of London before he would contemplate the idea of a fiscal compact to save the euro becoming a formal part of a new European treaty. No agreement was reached, and Cameron did not win favor from his fellow European leaders, but he did succeed in appeasing his backbenchers and the Euro-skeptic tabloid press.[9] In the meantime, the twenty-six (then) other EU leaders decided to draw up an "accord" without the UK.

Despite his approach, it became clear that Cameron was not prepared to risk the failure of the Eurozone. Both he and George Osborne, the UK chancellor, have encouraged fiscal union. Gamble comments:

> They have taken this position not because they wish Britain to be part of the eurozone, but because they fear that if the Eurozone disintegrates there will be catastrophic consequences for British banks and the British economy. In the worst-case scenario, the world could be tipped into a full-blown depression. In these circumstances it has apparently suddenly become a vital British interest for the eurozone to survive, and to do so by embracing fiscal union.[10]

However, their stance did not please Cameron's Euro-skeptic members and supporters, while equivocating on the contents of a potential new treaty similarly displeased his fellow European leaders.

Coping with the Crisis

The issue of EU membership can serve as a distraction from the problems the crisis has caused for the UK. It may also serve as a distraction from the relative failure of the coalition government to deal with the crisis, which was alarmingly evident in the form of both media headlines and governmental action.

As noted, nationalization and partial nationalization of the banks was needed, but it was insufficient, and the government's aid to the financial sector resulted in a total of £1,162 billion of government money provided to the banks at its peak. The total scale of the bailout was estimated by the governor of the Bank of England to be almost £1 trillion.[11] The National Audit Office comments that "if the support measures had not been put in place, the scale of the economic and social costs if one or more major UK banks had collapsed is difficult to envision."[12] The overall cost to the taxpayer has not been fully calculated so far, but the total was £20 billion by April 2013.[13]

Initially, it appeared that Cameron's government would present a less harsh version of liberal Conservatism than had Margaret Thatcher's. Cameron had agreed, as party leader before the election, that the public sector should share increased income with the private sector.[14] For Thatcher, on the other hand, public expenditure was a problem that needed resolving. It prevented private enterprise from flourishing; it encouraged individuals to rely on the state rather than on their own resources. Her answer (in part) was to cut back. In contrast, the Labour governments from 1997 to 2010, while embracing the rhetoric of the limited state, had actually increased public spending substantially, particularly in the areas of health and education, although they had also embraced the notion of encouraging competition from the private sector within all public spending areas. In doing so, however, most of the welfare state's primary spending sectors had become reasonably cushioned. The effect was to make the welfare state a target for a government that wanted to make savings.

Hence, after the collapse of UK banks after 2007 and further financial crises, Cameron and Osborne, his chancellor-to-be, became more critical of Labour's approach. Shortly after its election, in October 2010, the coalition's Spending Review referred to its predecessors' "unsustainable public spending" that had "unbalanced" the UK economy.[15] Austerity was to be the answer, not just to the problem of the "unbalanced" economy but also to the problems of the UK deficit and, in turn, the economic crisis.

Overspending, then, rather than undertaxation, was the coalition's target. Osborne planned to reduce borrowing and achieve almost three quarters of the required savings from reductions in the public sector with the remainder by means of tax increases, although initially the National Health Service was to be excluded from the cuts.[16] Jobs would be lost, he conceded, but that, as Norman Lamont had said in the early Thatcher years, would be "a price worth paying" and only a temporary issue anyway, because the private sector would create sufficient jobs to replace those lost in the public sector.

A second prong of financial policy (although introduced by the previous Labour government and determined by the independent Bank of England's Monetary Policy Committee [MPC], involved purchasing assets (also known as "quantitative easing" [QE] or "injecting money into the economy").[17] QE is regarded as an "unconventional method" of bank activity[18] and is used only when interest rates are already low. While the Bank of England calculated that the first round of quantitative easing increased UK gross domestic product by 1.5 percent,[19] the main criticism has been that the policy added up to giving banks a lot of extra money, which they used in doubtful speculation, and thereby increased inflation.[20] The hope was that the banks would use the additional money flow to support small and medium-sized enterprises and thereby increase employment, but this did not happen, and the government instead introduced "credit easing," guaranteeing cheaper borrowing by the banks, funded by taxpayers.[21] However, the MPC complained in April 2014 that bank lending to business was still weak.[22]

Third, as noted, the government focused on low interest rates, making the assumption that this would encourage people, as well as financial institutions, to borrow—particularly in terms of mortgages. This policy, however, has not been entirely successful, given that house prices have risen considerably, so that people are unable to afford mortgages even at low interest rates. In addition, low interest rates discourage saving and can lead to individuals either spending instead (with a consequent effect on demand-led inflation) or investing in riskier projects to obtain a better return on their money. In particular, low interest rates have a negative impact on people with fixed incomes, especially pensioners.

On the whole, the response of the coalition to the economic crisis has not been impressive. Nevertheless, there are currently signs of recovery. The Confederation of British Industry (CBI) reported that a survey of 405 manufacturers showed that there had been high growth in orders in the first three months to April 2014, the fastest since 1995, and that the numbers employed had risen at the strongest rate since October 2011.[23] However, the signs may be misleading. The MPC noted that while unemployment had fallen (although it was still over 7 percent), about half of the reduction was due to the increase in self-employment and that credit conditions for small businesses were still stringent. It also noted that although sales overall had increased, this did not apply to housing, where loans had fallen by 10 percent.[24]

The Coalition and the UK in the EU
The "Europe" Issue

As Down and Wilson note, it is common within the EU for parties to downplay the "Europe" issue, although this was not the case between 1997 and 2001, because the Conservatives thought that they reflected the public's views on the EU more accurately than their opponents did.[25] From 2005 onward, however, it appeared that the Conservative Party had recognized that although the public might be Euro-skeptic on the whole, "Europe" was not their priority. It was not a priority in the 2010 election campaign, and, with the Conservatives' subsequent alliance with the Liberal Democrats, the most pro-European of the other main parties, to form the coalition, it might have been thought that the government would continue to moderate its views on the EU.

However, it has not, for at least three reasons. As implied already, it is possible that Conservative strategists thought that the financial crisis was of sufficient concern to the public to warrant more attention on the EU (despite the tenuous connection it had with the crisis) to the extent of publically disagreeing with its coalition partners. There is also a possibility that the government was becoming concerned about the attractiveness of the anti-EU UKIP. Or it is possible that the Conservative leadership had little choice, given the increasing demands of some of its backbenchers and supporters, already in danger of alienation because of the failure of the Conservative Party, after thirteen years out of office, to form an overall majority government.[26]

The EU and Immigration

Evidence for the second notion may be found in the coalition government's approach to immigration. Hoops et al. point out that immigration is a divisive issue between the EU and its member states, since it contrasts the EU's vision of pluralism and unification with its states' instinctive preservation of national unity.[27] The issues of both asylum and immigration are generally regarded as needing to be dealt with sensitively in the UK, however—not least because there is a substantial difference between the electorate's perception of the scale and the reality. An Ipsos-Mori opinion poll found that public concern about immigration in the UK is significantly higher than in other EU member states.[28] UK respondents (almost two-thirds of them in 2011) fear overcrowding, particularly from "foreign-born" people, far more than do the residents of equally populous states such as France and Germany.[29] Curiously, there is preliminary evidence to suggest that popular attitudes toward immigration trump even concern over the economy. Recent findings from the British Social Attitudes survey show that 77 percent of the public wants less immigration; even though less than half of them (47 percent) think that it is bad for the economy.[30] It appears that UK citizens' objections to immigration are deep rooted rather than rational. It should also be noted that neither the surveys nor popular attitudes distinguish between immigrants from outside the EU and people from within the EU who may be staying only temporarily to live and work in the UK in accordance with one of the fundamental freedoms established in the treaty.

On average, according to Ipsos-Mori polls, people think that over 30 percent of people living in the UK are immigrants. The actual figure is 13 percent.[31] Ipsos-Mori note that the UK respondents "overestimate more wildly than most" of their fellow Europeans in the countries studied. Immigration is also more likely to be looked on negatively in the UK than in other European states.[32]

Although it is difficult to decide why any UK government chooses to give prominence to particular issues, no government for the past thirty years has managed a term without at least one major piece of immigration/asylum legislation.[33] Either the problem is greater than it appears or governments are in fact practicing populism, to distinguish themselves from their main opponents in the Conservative case,[34] and to try to neutralize the potential threat of far right parties, currently UKIP. In the run-up to the European elections, UKIP leader Nigel Farage (who has been an MEP since 1999) was particularly keen to play on popular sentiment on any issues that had an EU or international aspect.

There are more people coming into the UK than are leaving it. The majority of immigrants are from India, but the second largest number is from Poland.[35] In fact, the "Polish plumber" became shorthand for fears expressed by both the media and some members of the public that "British" jobs were being lost as a result of EU-related immigration.[36] The reason there were a relatively large number was because most of the other EU member states at the time of Poland's entry into the EU (and that of nine other Central and Eastern Europe and Mediterranean states) decided to put an embargo on the freedom of movement of persons (as enshrined in the treaty) for the first seven years after membership.[37] In 2004, under Blair's last Labour government, the decision was made not to ban citizens from the new member states. The result, not unexpectedly (except, it appears, on the part of the government) was that those Central and Eastern Europeans gravitated to the UK, having little choice as to other Western EU destinations. It enabled writers for the more right-wing tabloids to claim that the government had lost control—not just of immigration per se but of immigration from the new EU member states. Hoops and his coauthors calculated that there were ninety-eight feature articles in the *Daily Mail/Mail on Sunday* opposing the government's stance on immigration from Central and Eastern European countries between April 2006 and March 2007.[38] For example, Melanie Phillips in the *Daily Mail* used the opportunity to disparage the Labour government:

> Many of the immigrants in contention are white people from eastern Europe. The argument is not about the desirability or otherwise of immigrants but the numbers who are coming in. . . . Mr. Blair thought that on immigration, as on so many other issues, he could pull the wool over people's eyes. He has made a major error.[39]

At any rate, the government was not prepared to welcome the Bulgarian and Romanian entrants in 2007 on the same terms as the earlier ones, and the issue died down for a time. It was resurrected between 2013 and 2014, but the issue was not so much the numbers but the treatment of workers from the EU.

In 2014, restrictions on the number of Romanians and Bulgarians acceding to the "freedom of movement" within the EU were lifted. There was a media panic, presumably at the thought of an influx of Romanian/Bulgarian tradesmen and their dependents, ignoring the fact that Romania's (at around 21.5 million) and Bulgaria's (about 7.5 million) population added together was considerably less than Poland's (about 38.2 million).[40] The *Daily Mail*, citing a University of Reading "secret" report, predicted that "Britons could find their jobs are squeezed in some areas, while community tensions could rise as the new wave of migrants fight for work with other Eastern Europeans who have been settled in Britain for a decade."[41]

In fact, the report (which was not secret, according to one of its authors, Christian Nygaard[42]), commissioned by the South East Strategic Partnership for Migration, showed only that the southeast of England was likely to be a favored destination for (any) East European immigrants because of the job opportunities for skilled workers, of which Bulgaria had a relatively high proportion. Nevertheless, the report estimated that Bulgarian and Romanian immigration would have little negative effect on UK unemployment rates. It noted previous research had demonstrated that new arrivals were more likely to replace earlier migrants; that immigrants tended not to claim state benefits (particularly Bulgarians and Romanians, in fact); that there was a tendency for them to take up "hard-to-fill" job vacancies; and that many immigrants were in the country temporarily.[43]

Whatever the reality, the coalition issued a series of announcements to reassure voters that the welcome received by new EU immigrants would be cool. As Cameron commented, in a press conference during the European Council meeting in December 2013, he supported enlargement and believed it to be one of the EU's greatest strengths, but he continued: "We must return it to what the EU first envisaged; the free movement of workers ready to work hard and get on in life, not the free movement of those after the best benefit deal."[44]

Demonstrating what Cameron meant by that, in late 2013, the government announced that new immigrants would not be able to claim housing benefits or out-of-work benefits unless they had previously worked for three months, while job seeker's allowance would only be payable for a maximum of six months and a minimum earnings level would be introduced before income support would be available.[45] Cameron said: "Accelerating the start of these new restrictions will make the UK a less attractive place for EU migrants who want to come here and try to live off the state."[46] In addition, the government intends to bring in new charges for some National Health Services.[47] EU law, however, expressed in a 2009 Guidance from the Commission, already allows inter-EU immigrants to access host country's benefits only after working for three months, stating that they must not become a burden on their host country's social assistance system and they must have comprehensive sickness insurance coverage. The Guidance also permits member states to determine their provision of benefits in relation to the applicant's personal circumstances, which include duration of residence and habitual reliance on or, conversely, financial contributions toward the host state's social assistance.[48]

Perhaps more should be understood by Cameron's choice of words than by governmental actions. If it intended to encourage anti-immigrant voters to vote for Conservative candidates rather than UKIP in the European elections, it probably needed to do more. Shortly after the coalition announcement, Farage told the *Daily Express*, another right-wing tabloid, that "in terms of [EU] immigration, . . . I would suggest that for up to a five year period we don't have people coming to settle until we sort out the mess [*sic*]."[49] Nevertheless, an IPSOS Mori poll carried out for British Future in February 2014 showed that 68 percent of correspondents thought that Bulgarian and Romanian immigrants should be welcomed as long as they "learn the language, work hard and pay taxes, fit in and be part of the community."[50] The inference that might be drawn from this news is that the immigrants might be welcome as long as they cannot be distinguished from citizens of longer duration in the UK!

Euro-Skepticism and Referenda
Evidence for the third possibility, the increasing demands from Conservative Euro-skeptics, may be found in parliamentary activities from the election in

2010 until April 2014. Since the coalition came into government, over twenty private members' bills have been put forward that could be described as "anti-EU," from requesting an audit on the EU's costs and benefits[51] to bills asking for withdrawal,[52] involving seven different members of the House of Commons and three members of the House of Lords. None of the bills stand any chance of becoming laws under UK parliamentary procedures, but they do indicate the attitude of the current Conservative Party in Parliament. They have also given backbenchers an opportunity to demonstrate their views. For example, as Philip Cowley and Mark Stuart note, the government had no difficulty in defeating one bill for an immediate referendum on EU membership in October 2011, but it defeated it with the highest number of rebels to that date (eighty-one, with up to nineteen abstentions) including two parliamentary private secretaries, despite a three-line whip on the issue.[53] It was the largest rebellion ever on "Europe."[54] As Cowley and Stuart also point out, it was one of twenty-two EU rebellions up to that date, involving a total of sixty-three Conservative MPs.[55]

As John Fitzgibbon notes, it is not just the Conservative backbenchers and members that apply pressure to the government. He has researched the activities of a number of "hard" Euro-skeptic civil society organizations in the UK from the early 2000s onward. These organizations, while apparently campaigning now for a referendum on EU membership, are in Fitzgibbon's view aiming for UK withdrawal from the EU.[56] He emphasizes, though, that the groups, most of them opposing the exercise of a particular EU polity competence, are essentially civil, that is, non–party-affiliated, organizations,[57] although he also notes that they are supported by a national tabloid and Conservative backing newspaper, the *Daily Express*.[58]

The pressure, then, on the Conservative part of the coalition has been substantial, and it appears that the prime minister, who has expressed moderate views on EU membership, has either chosen to or has had to harden his stance after the European Parliament (EP) elections.

The European Parliament Elections

The EP elections, often considered to be "second-order" elections, enabling voters to express their opinion about their government, rather than about their MEPs, were held in May 2014 in all EU states.

The UK Public

The eightieth edition of *Eurobarometer*, published before the European elections, showed that only the people of Cyprus of the EU-28 were more inclined than the British to think that their state would be better off out of the EU, with 56 percent of Cypriots and 50 percent of the British agreeing with the statement.[59] The average among the EU-28 was 38 percent. The survey also showed that UK citizens had a lower number (37 percent) who disagreed compared with Cyprus's citizens (40 percent).

How the UK public would vote in those circumstances has been drawn to the attention of academic commentators, as well as politicians and journalists. According to Down and Wilson's analysis, the EU public in general has become more politicized and more divided about the EU over the past twenty years. They commented that this was because issues relating to economic integration (market liberalization) and cultural integration (immigration, multiculturalism) divide supporters of the national community and proponents of integration. The problem, they thought, was that the public has a very limited understanding of the EU and could easily be made afraid of the implications of membership, so that once divisions in public opinion had been established, it might be difficult to remove them.[60] With that in mind, it may be noted that *Eurobarometer* 80 indicated that 13 percent of UK citizens (compared with 4 percent of Cypriots) registered a "don't know" on whether they think that the UK would be better off outside the EU. If Down and Wilson are correct, the issues of the economic crisis (market liberalization) and of EU immigration (cultural integration) could both be assumed to be significant in setting anti-EU views and increasing them.

However, there are other factors to be taken into consideration. First there is the rise of new and more extremist parties. Armen Hakhveridan and his colleagues agree that lower-educated people in particular tend to be more skeptical than the better educated, partly because of the idea that EU integration threatens national identity and cultural integrity.[61] They note that extremist parties, particularly since the greater speed of integration since the Treaty of Maastricht, exploit those fears because they are likely to be Euro-skeptic.[62] From this, it may be suggested that some parties (UKIP would be an example in the UK case) draw their lifeblood from Euro-skepticism and exist primarily to exploit and benefit from it. If "lower-educated" people (and higher-educated ones too, for that matter) have nebulous fears validated by a national political party, the two may become symbiotic, voters feeding from the party and feeding the party in exchange.

As will be shown, the outcome of the UK elections to the EP, taken with the discussion on immigration, help substantiate the arguments of Down and Wilson and Hakhveridan et al. Second, the impact of the mass media should be considered. Katjana Gatterman, looking at reporting on the EP, shows that there is comparatively low media coverage by the UK, although articles tend to be longer than those in other states' media. However, she finds insufficient evidence to conclude that the relative coverage is low because of low public support.[63] Nevertheless, Hakhveridan et al. consider that the framing of EU news coverage is significant, given that when it is negative, support in general drops among those most susceptible, that is, those who are less politically sophisticated.[64] Pippa Norris, according to Hakhveridan et al., finds that the mass media are consistently negative about the EU, whereas Catherine De Vries, also cited by Hakhveridan et al., comments that EU actors are evaluated negatively, although she thinks that coverage is neutral.[65]

This commentary is helpful, but it does not (nor does it intend to) give much indication as to the extent that the UK public is influenced by the mass media. There is an extensive debate on this subject, including whether the media leads or follows public opinion. For the purposes of this chapter, however, it may be noted UK citizens tend to be negative about the EU, and that they also tend to read mass circulation tabloid newspapers, most of which are Euro-skeptic. It could also be conceded that politicians on the whole tend to be concerned about what is published and who reads it. In any event, it appears either that the tabloids were influential or that they were good forecasters.

Third, it was shown already that there is a strong civil society movement against the EU, here fueled not so much by crises as by fears of the EU's exploitation of its competences. In an era of declining deference toward political parties (particularly governing political parties), nongovernmental organizations may contribute toward legitimizing public opinion as well as, and sometimes better than, political parties.

The EP Election Results

The EP election results were not very surprising. UKIP won the highest number of seats, followed by Labour, then the Conservatives. The Liberal Democratic Party, the "junior partner" in the coalition, lost all but one of its former eleven seats, while the Green Party (which holds one seat in the UK Parliament) won three seats in total, an increase of one. Figure 7.1 shows the distribution of seats across the UK.

Figure 7.1 Distribution of Seats, EP Elections, 2009 and 2014

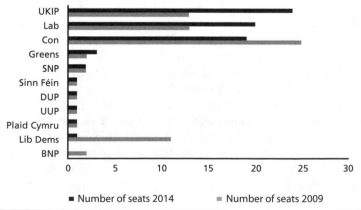

Source: http://www.results-elections2014.eu/en/election-results-2014.html.

The average turnout was, not unexpectedly, low at 34.19 percent. Conservative support fell from 27.9 percent in 2009 to 23.05 percent in 2014, while Labour support rose from 15.8 percent in 2009 to 24.43 percent in 2014. The electorate collectively combined punishment of the governing parties (particularly the Liberal Democrats, who had lost their traditional support because of their supporting role to the Conservative majority in the coalition) with the media-predicted upsurge in support for UKIP whose share of the vote rose from 15.8 percent in 2009 to 26.6 percent in 2014. Figure 7.2 shows how support was distributed among the parties in 2009 and in 2014.

All in all, the results of the election demonstrate a decline in support for the ruling governmental parties and a reduction in the support for the EU. In 2014, in England, Scotland, and Wales, twenty-seven seats, as opposed to twenty-nine in 2009, are held by parties that could be described as pro-EU (with reservations in some cases), including Labour, with forty-three seats held by parties that are on the whole anti-EU to some extent, as opposed to forty in 2009, including the Conservative Party.

Impact of the EP Elections
Although the difference between the numbers of seats is not great, there are three matters of concern for the future of the UK in the EU. First, the highest level of anti-EU support has coalesced around one party, UKIP (note that the British National Party lost support and won no seats in 2014). Inasmuch as UKIP continues as a united party, there is a potential for an anti-EU stance to solidify among the public as well.

Second, the Conservative position on the EU has hardened since 2009. The text of the Conservative manifesto for the EP elections in 2009 was not

Figure 7.2 Distribution of Party Support, EP Elections in England, Scotland, and Wales, 2009 and 2014

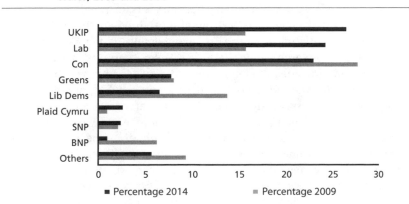

Source: http://www.results-elections2014.eu/en/election-results-2014.html

very positive, underscoring the need for reform, but it did stress the Conservative commitment to the Single Market, devoting a whole chapter to it and emphasizing the four freedoms as "crucial to our economic success,"[66] while praising past and future EU enlargement as "highly successful."[67] By contrast, the 2014 manifesto asserted its "victories" against the EU.[68] Enlargement was supported but only with the proviso "with new mechanisms in place to prevent vast migrations across the continent."[69] The Single Market was relegated to page 15, and later in the manifesto, it was claimed that its integrity could only be protected "by insisting on protections for those countries that have kept their own currencies."[70] Surprisingly, the manifesto even included a reference to the unwanted interference of such European institutions as the (non-EU) European Court of Human Rights!

Third, it may be concluded that the UK's anti-EU representatives in the EP have increased not only in number but also in intensity, while the fact that the numbers have grown demonstrates a rising Euro-skepticism among the UK public. More problematically, there is evidence from recent polling that voters have conflated their concerns about their future in post-crisis Britain with fears concerning the EU. In a *Guardian*/ICM poll, published in June 2014, 46 percent of respondents, the highest proportion, cited immigration "undercutting British workers" at the root of their fears.[71] In answer to a separate question about which action a UK government could take to "bolster faith in politics," 26 percent, again the highest proportion, selected "curbing immigration." The poll did not differentiate between EU and non-EU immigration, but EU immigration has been at the forefront of recent government policies and pronouncements.

The Future of the UK in the EU
Referendum?

In a speech made at the Bloomberg headquarters in London in January 2013, Cameron first announced his intention to hold an "in-out" referendum, after renegotiating the terms of membership, if the Conservatives were elected to government in 2015. While he expressed his desire for "flexibility" in terms of EU integration and distanced himself from "ever closer union," he was otherwise positive about the EU, stating that he wanted the EU to be successful, with the UK as part of it. Cameron pledged that "when the referendum comes let me say now that if we can negotiate such an arrangement, I will campaign for it with all my heart and soul."[72] Interestingly, that promise has been removed from the government's official website,[73] and since then the tone has become increasingly Euro-skeptic.

At first sight, renegotiation appears to need treaty change, and it is hard to imagine the UK's success, given that an EU à la carte has been ruled out since the Treaty of Rome. But this is to ignore the "real world" of politics, in which national leaders tend to water down their demands on an international community to avoid potentially difficult or embarrassing situations. In March 2014, the Conservative Party EP election manifesto set out seven points that would need "renegotiation" (p. 13):

- Powers flowing away from Brussels, not always to it
- National parliaments able to work together to block unwanted European legislation
- Businesses liberated from red tape and benefiting from the strength of the EU's own market, the biggest and wealthiest on the planet, to open up greater free trade with North America and Asia
- Our police forces and justice systems able to protect British citizens, unencumbered by unnecessary interference from the European institutions, including the European Court of Human Rights
- Free movement to take up work, not free benefits
- Support for the continued enlargement of the EU to new members but with new mechanisms in place to prevent vast migrations across the Continent
- Dealing properly with the concept of ever closer union

The issue of powers flowing away from Brussels would be a matter for treaty agreement, but the UK does not need to renegotiate this, since all states would be involved in any proposals of increasing EU powers and unanimity would be required. As noted, the European Court of Human Rights is not an EU institution, which makes its appearance (the only European institution named) in the list curious. Free movement to take up work is already subject to constraints regarding benefits. Enlargement is unlikely to be a matter for consideration in the near future. What is also striking about the list is the number of qualifying words: *greater* free trade (presumably a reference to the US–EU Transatlantic Trade and Investment Partnership already being negotiated), but the EU is already committed to greater free trade. *Unnecessary* interference—does that mean that the UK would consider some interference necessary? Finally, the adverb *properly*: does this mean more or less close union?

It is perhaps unfair to analyze or read too much into the wording of an election manifesto, but if this is the list on which the Conservative Party wants to base its renegotiation of the UK's terms of membership, it would not prove to be too difficult to fulfill. The government could then claim successful renegotiation, but in reality the electorate would be voting on more or less current terms of membership, as they were in 1974.

However, in October 2014, Cameron was said to have raised the stakes by reversing his support for the "four freedoms," apparently no longer essential for economic success, suggesting that a cap on migration from the EU would be required.[74] Both the outgoing and the incoming EU Commission presidents pointed out that it was unrealistic to expect a renegotiation of the fundamental basis of the treaty. José Manuel Barroso responded that "Any kind of arbitrary cap [on migration] seems to me to be not in conformity with European laws."[75] Speaking at a press conference after the EP had appointed his Commission team, Jean-Claude Juncker commented that: "As far as the freedom of movement is concerned . . . I do think this is a basic principle of the EU since the very beginning and I am not prepared to change this because if we are destroying the freedom of movement, other freedoms will fall in a later cause. So I am not ready to compromise in an irresponsible way."[76] Since Cameron must understand the nature of the treaty, if he does support making a cap on EU immigration part of the renegotiation, either he is prepared to allow the UK's exit, since it is unlikely that the other member states would agree to remove one of its fundamental principles, or he is obliged to sound as if he would to appease anti-EU MPs in his party, two of whom have already defected to the UKIP. Either way, the UK's relationship with the EU may depend on the outcome of the 2015 general election.

The government moved from defeating a private members' bill for an in-out EU referendum to requesting one. In 2014, Cameron asked Conservative backbenchers to consider reintroducing a private members' referendum bill, with a date for the event, if they won the top four places in the members' ballot in summer. Robert Neill obliged, and a bill progressed to a second reading although it was unable to go any further since no money resolution was passed, and parliament has now been prorogued. Nevertheless, the government was prepared to invoke the Parliament Act (which prevents a veto from the House of Lords in certain circumstances) if necessary to force through the legislation, since it wanted the referendum date to be in law before the Conservatives fought the next general election.

Referenda are not constitutionally binding in the UK, although this has not mattered so far, since no referendum has yet delivered the "wrong" result.[77] Nevertheless, a referendum in which the public delivered the outcome that the government did not support might well still be politically (if not constitutionally) binding. May 2015 elections resulted in the Conservative Party winning an overall majority of twelve seats, and it immediately announced its intention to hold a referedum on EU membership before 2017, after renegotiation of terms.

Currently, the results of such a referendum are unpredictable, but it appears from the evidence that any government that wants the UK to remain in the EU has a lot of work to gain the public's trust in the EU as an institution. It will not be assisted by an increasingly popular UK "out" party,[78] or by the majority of the UK mass media, nor by an increasing number of civil society organizations that are campaigning against individual EU competences.

How Fares the "Awkward Partner"?

Currently in the UK, any love of the EU is one that dare not speak its name. Conservative MPs' hatred of the EU may be freely expressed, but it can never measure up to the vitriol of the unambiguously anti-EU UKIP. Nevertheless, there are some avenues that are open to a government that are not available to a party without representation in Parliament. One of those options is playing the awkward partner, as Stephen George once called the UK in the EU.[79] Current commentary from Conservative MPs and ministers on the EU have stretched this definition somewhat. For example, there is the question of the European Arrest Warrant. The government decided to opt out of over 130 EU criminal justice measures (a decision opposed by the House of Lords),[80] then immediately opt back into thirty-five of them. There was, however, considerable pressure from the backbenches not to include the European Arrest Warrant among those to be reinstated,[81] although the grounds for opposition are not clear.

Another example was the current prime minister's refusal to endorse Juncker as the next president of the European Commission, allegedly threatening at a European Council meeting that the UK could withdraw from the EU if he were appointed.[82] The grounds were that Juncker was an old-style EU federalist, but it may be that Cameron objected not so much to Juncker, but to the fact that he was the EP's candidate. The Council's acceptance of the nominee may be construed as evidence of the growing strength of the EP and therefore of an increasingly "federalized" EU.

There is a tradition for UK prime ministers to veto a favored nominee for the presidency of the Commission on the grounds that they were too federalist. John Major refused to back Jean-Luc Dehaene in 1990, and the ineffectual Jacques Santer was appointed instead. Guy Verhofstadt was blocked by Tony Blair in 2004, and José Manuel Barroso was chosen in his place. However, this time is different because Cameron's position received little backing from the other EU states, including Germany. The outcome of Cameron's attempted veto may be problematic if the other EU states decide that Cameron's tactics are too heavy-handed and un-European.

Such negotiations or games are frequently played at the EU level as anywhere else, with an individual's political capital providing the stakes. However, the trick is to win, and the UK formerly had a good track record of winning. Political capital can thus be retained, although there is still likely to be a price to be paid. How much of a price is debatable. Daniel Naurin and Rutger Lindahl argue that there is little evidence that a state that opts out of EU competences is less successful in negotiations within the Council of Ministers, given that there is no great sense of Europeanization therein.[83] In this case, however, Cameron lost, and it is not so much the Council of Ministers that is likely to react negatively to UK awkwardness but the Commission (headed by Juncker despite Cameron's opposition), the

EP, and perhaps most significant, the majority of the European Council's members. No doubt, if the UK stays within the EU, life will go on more or less as usual, in time at least. But if the UK does decide to leave, it is hard to see from where the goodwill that will be necessary for the nation to retain the benefits of the single market will come.

Conclusion

This chapter considered the issues that have affected the UK within the EU at a particularly difficult and challenging time. It has shown that the UK government has shown a tendency to blame the EU for its economic difficulties on occasion, in relation to both bailouts and EU-generated migration. The chapter also showed that the political climate—from government, politicians, the media, civil society, and the public—has chilled since the last EP elections and that the outcome of the 2014 elections demonstrated the cooling. The chapter finally discussed the outlook for the UK within the EU, expressing concern about the future, particularly if the UK population decides in a referendum that they wish to leave it—should that choice be put to them.

Notes

1. National Audit Office, "The Treasury's Support to the Banks," 2014. Available at http://www.nao.org.uk/highlights/taxpayer-support-for-uk-banks-faqs/ (accessed April 10, 2014).

2. Her Majesty's Government, "The Coalition: Our Programme for Government (HM Government)," 2010. Available at https://www.gov.uk/government/uploads/system/uploads/attachment_data/file/78977/coalition_programme_for_government.pdf (accessed March 3, 2014).

3. François Hollande, "Inaugural Speech," May 15, 2012, p. 19. Available at http://ambafrance-us.org/spip.php?article3469 (accessed March 3, 2014).

4. This approach could have been intended to lay the foundation for austerity policies in terms of the coalition government's public spending, or it could have been a continuation of a UK government's general attitude toward its predecessors of an opposing party.

5. Kingdom (2014).

6. K. West, "Greece Gets £22bn Bailout to Help Stabilise Vulnerable Euro," *Daily Mail*, March 12, 2010.

7. N. Farage, "UK Taxpayers Will Pay 'Tens of Billions' of Euros for Greek Rescue," 2010. Available at http://www.ukipmeps.org/blog_view_60_%95-UK-taxpayer-will-pay-tens-of-billions-of-euros-for-Greek-rescue.html (accessed March 3, 2014).

8. A. Grice, "David Cameron Wins 'No Greek Bailout' Battle," *Independent*, June 24, 2011.

9. Gamble (2012).

10. Ibid., p. 469.

11. Kingdom (2014), p. 570.

12. National Audit Office (2014).

13. Ibid.

14. Lee (2011), p. 61.

15. HM Treasury(2010), p. 6.

16. Lee (2011), p. 63.

17. QE is a means of injecting money into the economy whereby the Bank of England creates new money electronically and uses it to buy government bonds from private investors, for example, banks, pension funds, and insurance companies, with the assumption that the sellers will use the money received to buy other assets, for example, corporate bonds and shares, that would have a higher yield. In the long run, this is expected to reduce borrowing costs, thus creating demand, as well as encouraging the issue of new equities, and so on. These activities should stimulate spending while keeping inflation at the government's target of 2 percent and increasing confidence. In particular, it is expected to reduce mortgage rates, which are set with reference to the yields from government bonds.

18. Joyce, Tong, and Woods (2011).

19. Ibid.

20. H. Stewart, "Quantitive Easing—The Key Questions," *Guardian*, October 6, 2011.

21. Ibid.

22. Bank of England, Monetary Policy Committee, "Minutes of the Monetary Policy Committee Meeting 09 April 2014," 2014. Available at http://www.bankofengland.co.uk/publications/minutes/Documents/mpc/pdf/2014/mpc1404.pdf (accessed April 10, 2014).

23. Confederation of British Industry, "Optimism Among Manufacturers Sees Fastest Rise Since the Early 70s—CBI Survey: Strong Growth Reported in Orders and Jobs," 2014. Available at http://www.cbi.org.uk/media-centre/press-releases/2014/04/optimism-among-manufacturers-sees-fastest-rise-since-the-early-70s-cbi-survey/ (accessed April 15, 2014).

24. Bank of England Monetary Policy Committee (2014).

25. Down and Wilson (2010), p. 468.

26. Evans (2012), p. 479.

27. Hoops et al. (2010), p. 9.

28. Duffy and Frere-Smith (2014), p. 10.

29. Ibid., p. 13.

30. L. Marshall, N. Joyner, and J. Barclay, "More Than 3 in 4 Want Reduction in Immigration: But Fewer Now Believe Immigration Is Bad for the Uk Economy," 2014. Available at http://www.natcen.ac.uk/news-media/press- British Social Attitudes releases /2014/january/more-than-3-in-4-want-reduction-in-immigration/ (accessed April 22, 2014).

31. Duffy and Frere-Smith (2014), p. 22.

32. Ibid.

33. The 2014 Immigration Act intends to limit immigrants access to services, facilities, and employment and makes it easier to deport all immigrants. It was recently passed through Parliament.

34. Hoops et al. (2010), p. 12.

35. Duffy and Frere-Smith, (2014), p. 7.

36. Hoops et al. (2010).

37. The only states that did not were the UK, Sweden, and Ireland.

38. Hoops et al. (2010), p. 13.

39. Melanie Phillips, "Immigration and the Demonising of Decency," *Daily Mail*, April 11, 2005.

40. All population numbers are from the World Population Review. Available at http://worldpopulationreview.com (accessed April 21, 2014).

41. J. Petre and S. Walters, "Exposed: What They Didn't Tell You About New Wave of Migrants Heading for Booming Britain," *Daily Mail*, December 28, 2013.

42. Nygaard quoted in "Expert Comment: How Will Lifting European Union Border Controls Impact Bulgarian and Romanian Workers?," University of Reading, January 3, 2014. Available at https://www.reading.ac.uk/news-and-events/releases/PR557255.aspx.

43. Nygaard, Pasierbek, and Francis-Brophy (2013), pp. 3–6 *passim*.

44. David Cameron, "Press Conference at the European Council 12.20.2013," 2013. Available at https://www.gov.uk/government/speeches/european-council-december-2013-david-camerons-press-conference (accessed April 21, 2014).

45. David Cameron, "Accelerating Action to Stop Rogue EU Benefit Claim," press release, 2013. Available at https://www.gov.uk/government/news/accelerating-action-to-stop-rogue-eu-benefit-claims (accessed April 22, 2014).

46. Ibid.

47. BBC News, "Bulgarian and Romanian Immigration—What Are the Figures?," May 14, 2014. Available at http://www.bbc.co.uk/news/uk-politics-21523319 (accessed April 21, 2014).

48. European Commission, "Communication from the Commission to the European Parliament and the Council on Guidance for Better Transposition and Application of Directive 2004/38/EC on the Right of Citizens of the Union and Their Family Members to Move and Reside Freely Within the Territory of the Member States," 2009.

49. Nigel Farage, "Farage Calls for Five-Year Immigration Ban," *Daily Express*, January 7, 2014.

50. Ipsos Mori for British Future, "The State of the Nation 2014," 2014, p. 18. Available at http://www.britishfuture.org/wp-content/uploads/2014/01/State-of-the-Nation-2014.Final_.2.pdf (accessed April 7, 2014).

51. "European Union, Audit of Benefits and Costs of UK Membership) Bill."

52. "United Kingdom, Withdrawal from the European Union Bill".

53. Cowley and Stuart, (2012), p. 402.

54. Ibid., p. 403.

55. Ibid., p. 404.

56. Fitzgibbon (2013), p. 115.

57. Ibid., p. 105.

58. Ibid., p. 114.

59. Commission of the European Communities (2013), p. 68.

60. Down and Wilson, (2010), p. 83.

61. Hakhverdian et al. (2013), p. 2.

62. Ibid., p. 4.

63. Gattermann (2013), p. 11.

64. Hakhverdian (2013), p. 13.

65. Ibid., p. 7.

66. The Conservative Party, "Vote for Change: The Conservative Manifesto," 2009, p. 11. Available at http://www.conservatives.com/~/media/Files/Downloadable%20Files/Euro%20Election%202009/euro-manifesto.ashx.

67. Ibid., p. 23.

68. The Conservative Party, "Conservative Party European Election Manifesto 2014," 2014. Available at http://www.conservatives.com/~/media/Files/Downloadable%20Files/MANIFESTO%202014/Large%20Print%20Euro%20Manifesto_English.ashx (accessed June 2014), p. 2.

69. Ibid., p. 14.

70. Ibid., p. 24.

71. C. Clark and M. Taylor, "Insecure Britain: Poll Shines Light on Nation's Economic Anxiety," *Guardian*, June 17, 2014.

72. *New Statesman*, "David Cameron's Speech on the EU: Full Text," January 23, 2013. Available at http://www.newstatesman.com/politics/2013/01/david-camerons-speech-eu-full-text (accessed October 26, 2014).

73. D. Cameron, "EU Speech at Bloomberg," 2013. Available at https://www.gov.uk/government/speeches/eu-speech-at-bloomberg (accessed October 26, 2014).

74. G. Parker and A. Barker, "David Cameron Floats 'Emergancy Brake' on EU Immigration," *Financial Times*, October 16, 2014. The article reports that the prime minister's office dismissed the suggestion as speculation, but that the idea had been discussed by senior Conservatives for some time.

75. J. Picard, "Barroso Says Immigration Cap Would Be Against EU Law," *Financial Times*, October 19, 2014.

76. N. Watt, "Juncker Tells Cameron: You Can't Destroy EU Migration Rules," *Guardian*, October 23, 2014.

77. The referendum on Scottish independence, which itself would have raised interesting questions about EU membership, had the "yes" vote won, was defeated by 50 percent to 45 percent.

78. UKIP won its first parliamentary seat in a by-election in October 2014, although the candidate was a Conservative who resigned his seat after defection to UKIP. In addition, the result in another by-election indicated a slide toward UKIP, although it was held by Labour.

79. George (1990).

80. Under Protocol 36 to the EU Treaty, the member states have to decide whether to opt in from the measures before December 1, 2014, when they become subject to the European Court of Justice and the Commission's enforcement powers. The UK government decided to opt out of all, but opt in to those that it favored.

81. A. Grice and N. Morris, "Conservative Whips Warn of Backbench Revolt on European Arrest Warrent," *Independent*, October 23, 2014.

82. N. Watt, "Merkel Vents Anger at Cameron's Withdrawal Threats over Juncker," *Guardian*, June 10, 2014.

83. Naurin and Rutger (2010).

8

Ireland:
Cranky Rebel or Good Soldier?

Richard B. Finnegan

TO STATE THAT THE PLACE OF IRELAND IN WORLD POLITICS IS modest is not to engage in irresponsible hyperbole. Nor is Ireland's place in the European Union (EU) one that should be exaggerated. The Republic of Ireland's 4.6 million people are on an island the size of Maine, set apart geographically from the center of Europe. We should begin with the recognition that the importance of the European Union to Ireland is considerably greater than the importance of Ireland to the EU. A senior member state of the EU since 1973, Ireland has been pro-Europe until recently and has benefited as much or more than any member state. Yet Ireland's posture has been altered recently by two negative votes on EU treaties, the economic collapse of the banks and subsequent bailout by the EU and the International Monetary Fund (IMF), tax and compliance issues, and a diminished voting presence.

For Ireland the primary impact of the EU has been in the economic realm, first by fostering growth especially through the Single Market, the Common Agricultural Policy (CAP) and the Structural Funds, tax policy, and then, most recently, the provision of funds to prevent Ireland from defaulting on its sovereign debt. Ireland's entry into the EU played an important part in its relationship to Great Britain and developments in Northern Ireland.[1] Abortion, women's rights in the area of social policy, and Irish neutrality in the security domain have been distinctive policy issues for Ireland.

Economic Impact

On January 1, 1973, Ireland's entry into the EU not only connected the Irish economy to those of the states of the EU but also forged a relationship that symbolically diminished the primacy of the Irish link to Britain. That psychological break should not be underestimated given the long and antagonistic colonial relationship between the two countries, especially given the tensions in the north of Ireland at that time. Ireland becoming among the most "European" of the member states is not unrelated to departing the British orbit. EU entry shifted Ireland's balance of trade from the almost exclusive focus on the UK to a more balanced distribution of exports and imports to and from the EU states.

In 1979 Ireland opted to join the European Monetary System (EMS). Britain chose not to enter. After 1992 Ireland then opted to join the Eurozone, and the euro currency introduced in 2002 in another of a series of important policy choices that moved Ireland closer to Europe. The surge of growth in the Irish economy was in part a function of Ireland's membership in the EU. The Irish rate of growth from 1987 to 2000 was 140 percent, whereas the United States in this period grew 40 percent and the EU zone 35 percent. Ireland's growth earned the country the sobriquet the "Celtic Tiger." In thirty years Ireland transitioned from a relatively closed and backward agricultural economy to an open globalized economy.[2] Rejecting protectionism and adopting incentive planning after 1959, Ireland began shifting the basis of the economy to industry and service and shifted industrial development from reliance on a paucity of domestic capital to attracting foreign direct investment.[3] A surge of agricultural economic growth after entry into the EU also came from the benefits of the Common Agricultural Policy to the farmers of Ireland and their access to new markets.[4]

The grants from the Structural and Regional Funds, designed to bring the poorer regions of the EU up to the standards of the more well-off sections, assisted the development of the west of Ireland and the infrastructure within the country. From its entry in 1973, Ireland has received more of the EU Structural Funds per capita than any other state.[5] The funds have been important for Ireland's medium-term financial planning and have been considered successful in public infrastructure development, such as improving freight handling at Dublin Airport, building roads, dredging Waterford Port, the treatment of wastewater, and coastal protection schemes. In fact, the border and western region counties of Ireland still qualified for some European Regional Development Fund regional cohesion funds up to 2004 because that area earned only 72 percent of the EU average gross national product (GNP). Capturing these EU funds looked a bit contrived, however, as the government divided Ireland into two regions, cleaving the poorer border, midland, and western (with the notably upscale acronym BMW) regions from the more prosperous east. It appeared to some EU members that Ireland was "subsidy shopping" by economically gerrymandering the country.

By 2000, some EU members, notably Germany, France, and the Netherlands, viewed Ireland's economic growth as "caused" by EU subsidies and felt it was no longer reasonable for Ireland to be receiving them. The Germans were reluctant to pour more money into the Structural Funds for the more well-off areas, and suggested criteria such as participation in the euro or high annual rates of growth as disqualifications for getting funds. Bolstering this argument was the fact that the Civil Society Funds provided by the EU to Ireland from 1989 to 2000 did amount to about 2.6 percent of GNP.

Irish economists, however, argue that Structural Funds have actually accounted for about 2 percent of the Irish GNP growth while the remaining 6 percent to 8 percent or more during the "Tiger" years had been spurred by foreign and domestic investment in computers, software, and pharmaceuticals. Moreover, GNP overstates Irish growth as it counts earnings from foreign firms that are repatriated.[6] Ireland also still has a very high poverty rate among industrialized nations. Despite Ireland's stellar economic growth over the years from 1995 to 2008 almost a quarter of the country's population still face potential poverty. Social Welfare Minister Seamus Brennan said the report showed how many people still "struggle on the margins of society."[7]

Ireland's then low rate of corporate taxation, 10 percent, also became a point of contention with France and Germany in the late 1990s and remains so. The number of new industries locating in Ireland was clearly disproportionate to its small size compared with the size of the industrial economies of France and Germany. This disparity led to a call for a harmonization of corporate tax policy in the EU as a whole. The Irish government, not surprisingly, resisted this pressure and still does.

The fairly quick transition to an EU Single Market converged with a critical take-off point in the Irish economy. The possibility of entering the Single Market encouraged investment by Japanese and US firms in Ireland providing an increased source of foreign direct investment. The growth of indigenous industry in Ireland had been spurred by a change in Irish investment policy after 1984. Innovation practices had put the Irish economy in a particularly advantageous position.

Irish companies were not prepared for foreign competition at the time of entry into the EU, but they were better prepared in the late 1980s to take advantage of the EU market, evaluating their strengths and weaknesses and their potential expansion into sectors previously closed to them.[8] Greater entrepreneurial scope, especially in services such as banking (ultimately to the detriment of the government of Ireland) and aviation, ensured that the Irish economy was poised to exploit the Single Market as well or better than most.

The adoption of a series of national plans that set targets in the realm of taxation, inflation, interest rates, and employment became the hallmark of the government's management of the economy from the mid-1980s until 2008. Political scientist Brigid Laffan called this development "a process of learning how to manage internationalization and the emergence of international governance" through the use of the social partnership.[9] The Irish national planning documents had the major sectors agreeing to constraints on wage increases, tax policy, and social services. All sectors recognized that a small economy must maximize domestic policy consensus to be internationally competitive.[10] The evidence is clear that membership in the EU has benefited Ireland's economy in numerous tangible and intangible ways, facilitating the double-digit economic growth rate from 1995 to 2002.

The Role of Women

As a traditional society, women in Ireland had been excluded from the corridors of power and the halls of commerce, yet at the same time they held an especially venerated place in the society as the center of the family and as the conservators of religious and social values. An emerging woman's movement in Ireland and the EU directives in the 1970s on equality of pay, equality of opportunity, social benefits, employment, and retirement benefits had the effect of changing the rights of women. These directives led to substantial changes in legislation in the 1970s that guaranteed the equal treatment of women in the workplace and prompted the creation of the Employment Equality Agency to monitor and foster equality of opportunity for women. Ultimately, a 1998 Equality Act that eliminated all forms of discrimination in Ireland superseded the equality legislation of the 1970s.

The issue of abortion was particularly difficult for Ireland and came to involve the EU Court of Justice (ECJ) in determining Irish law. Though abortion was illegal in Ireland since 1861, pro-life groups feared that there would be a judicial decision or legislation in Ireland that would allow abortion. The Eighth Amendment, Article 40.3.3, forbidding abortion, was passed in a referendum in 1983, after a rather bitter campaign. Abortion counseling clinics providing nondirective information were then challenged by the Society for the Protection of the Unborn Child in 1988 as being in violation of the Eighth Amendment. The Irish courts took the position that the amendment, as it forbade abortion, also forbade providing information about abortion. The Irish Supreme Court also found that providing information about travel for an abortion was illegal. The case was appealed to the ECJ, which decided in 1991 that information about abortion services available in one community member could be available to citizens of another member state, and European Court of Human Rights decided that people in EU countries were free to travel to another member country, whatever the purpose of their visit, under Article 10 of the European Convention on Human Rights. The cases in Ireland were *Attorney General v. Open Door Counseling* in 1988 and the *SPUC v. Grogan and Others* in 1989. The European case was *Open Door Counseling, Well Women's Centre and Others v. Ireland* in 1992.

In the 1992 "X Case," Irish courts differed on the meaning of the wording of the amendment, and ultimately the Irish Supreme Court determined that the young woman, a minor, could have an abortion as her threat of suicide put her life in danger. The issue became moot when the young woman miscarried. The European Court decisions and the X Case led to referenda being held on three additional amendments to the Irish constitution in 1992. The two that passed were those that had been generated by the EU court decisions as the Ninth Amendment guaranteeing travel throughout the EU and the Tenth Amendment recognizing the right to the dissemination of information on abortion. Thus, the constitution of Ireland was amended in accord with the decisions of the EU courts. The European court also requested that Ireland produce some sort of regulation or legislation that clarified what constitutes meeting the test of allowing an abortion under the X Case ruling and such very restrictive legislation was finally passed in 2013.

Neutrality and Ireland

The 1996 white paper on Irish foreign policy *Challenges and Opportunities Abroad* notes: "The extent to which Ireland . . . has come to express its foreign policy through the medium of the European Union." Membership in the EU has definitely enhanced the diplomatic status of Ireland. A small state on the perimeter of Europe, Ireland has direct and regular access to the policy elites of all the major countries of the continent. The rotating presidency of the EU Council of Ministers gave Ireland high-profile visibility as Dublin focused on the issues it chose to emphasize during its term in 2012. Participation in the EU brings Ireland into development and trade policy issues in the global arena that would be beyond the country's scope as an individual state.[11] Reflecting this importance, the permanent delegation to the EU in Brussels is the largest of all Irish diplomatic missions, especially in light of the fact that Ireland is generally under-represented abroad. The smaller states of Europe maintain about twice the number of overseas missions and twice the number of diplomats.[12]

Irish neutrality had emerged as a pragmatic response to political conditions in the 1930s, as Ireland could not and would not ally with Germany before and during World War II and would not ally with Britain either as long as the island was partitioned. Joining the EU raised the question of neutrality as Article 224 of the Treaty of Rome specifies that the European Community could take common action during war, which would clearly imply actions that could ultimately be inconsistent with Irish neutrality. When entry was put before the Irish people in a referendum, the economic pragmatists, such as Prime Minister Sean Lemass, argued that there was no threat to Irish neutrality in joining the Community. The Irish public, to the degree that neutrality entered their consideration at all, overwhelmingly opted for economic pragmatism and voted for entry into the Community in 1973.

In practice since 1970, European Political Cooperation (EPC), the 1986 Single European Act (SEA), and the Maastricht Treaty of 1992 established the Common Foreign and Security Policy formally as part of the new EU structure. In 1982, the European Community imposed economic sanctions on Argentina in support of Great Britain after Argentina invaded the Falkland Islands. The Irish went along with the sanctions until the British were prepared to invade the island. The government of Prime Minister Charles Haughey opted out at that point, saying that continuation of Irish sanctions was inconsistent with their policy of neutrality in the context of armed conflict. Though doing so created friction with London, other European Community members did not challenge the Irish action.

In 1986, the Irish government adopted the Single European Act through legislative approval rather than using a national referendum as required for an amendment to the constitution. The Irish Supreme Court decided in the 1987 case *Crotty v. A Taoiseach* that the SEA codifying European political cooperation did require an amendment to the constitution for ratification. When Ireland approved the SEA through a constitutional amendment in 1987, it lodged a statement with the EU on neutrality, declaring that the act: "does not affect Ireland's right to act or refrain from acting in a way which might affect Ireland's international status of military neutrality."[13] Ireland, for example, failed to join NATO's Partnership for Peace in 1994 as an assertion of "neutrality" though Austria, Finland, and Sweden, other European and EU neutral states, did join. The perception of the general public is that neutrality was seen as something threatened by the EU. Such views helped contribute to the rejection of the Treaty of Nice in 2001, discussed shortly.[14]

The foreign policy white paper *Challenges and Opportunities Abroad* was clear enough, stating that since 1973 "successive governments have indicated that they would be prepared to enter into discussion with other member states on the development of common arrangements in relation to security and defense matters." Finally, the white paper indicates that the ratification of the Maastricht Treaty bound Ireland to a "Common Foreign and Security Policy."[15]

The government made clear in a position on the Treaty of Amsterdam in 1998 that it was willing to participate in an EU "common defense policy." In 1999, at the Helsinki Summit, the EU members agreed to the creation of a rapid reaction force (ERRF) of 60,000 troops, and the Irish government pledged up to 850 troops and 80 police to the ERRF. Moreover, the mission of the ERRF was defined by the 1992 Petersberg Tasks, which allow only humanitarian and peacekeeping responsibilities. The European diplomatic corps was created to provide Europe with a single foreign policy voice and structure. Though no threat to Irish neutrality, it does signal a greater shift to diplomatic unity, however fragile, in the EU and away from the members' unilateralism.

Though fully supporting the EU sanctions on Russia, Ireland found the situation in the Ukraine close to the situation in Northern Ireland—similarities that were raised by commentators. It was not completely parallel (few cases are), but close enough to see that that the ethnic Russians in east Ukraine and their affinity to Russia were not unlike the unionists of Northern Ireland and their affinity to Britain, and the position of Kiev, calling for an end to resistance, was not unlike that of traditional Irish Republicanism calling for a united Ireland. Vladimir Putin was doing no more than what the British had done for years in support of the unionists. Does Northern Ireland offer any lessons? The resolution may involve some level of devolution and perhaps joint citizenship, rather than complete secession or complete control by Kiev. As it turned out, Northern Ireland was not, as Margaret Thatcher once proclaimed, "as British as Finchley," and eastern Ukraine may not be as Ukrainian as Kiev.

Ireland's Policy Process and the EU

The Irish political style in the EU is reactive and focused, centralized, and neocorporatist. The Irish bureaucrats are very comfortable with the EU style of policymaking as it replicates the policymaking style in Ireland: a relatively small elite from the government and peak organizations discuss and negotiate policy issues as those issues wind their way through the EU bureaucratic process. Irish bureaucrats are not, however, movers of policy proposals and tend to work at shaping the proposals of others. They tend to focus their resources on a few critical areas of policy that are highly important to Ireland, such as agriculture, food, or, until recently, financial services. Some interest groups, such as large farmers and industrial organizations, have also thrived in the Brussels environment. As Laffan states, "Groups in Ireland can play nested games at the national level and connected games in the Brussels arena."

The Irish policymaking process was relatively unprepared for entry into Europe and led to deficiencies in the Irish–EU interface. Since 1987, Ireland has fallen behind most member states in rate of timely implementation of the laws and regulations establishing the single European market. The sheer weight of the EU legislation and the absence of legal specialists and bureaucratic support have prompted the Commission to institute proceedings against Ireland on implementation of EU directives at a rate disproportionate to its size and population.[16]

Until 2002, the Irish parties and Parliament have had relatively little influence on Ireland–EU matters. Laffan notes of the Parliament: "The committees are dependent on the Department of Foreign Affairs for information and positions," which is, of course, the point.[17] Neill Nugent stated: "The fact is that in Ireland EU policy tends to be in the hands of a small, government dominated, network of politicians and officials who listen to Parliament only as they see fit."[18]

The defeat of the Nice referendum in 2001, discussed shortly, triggered a significant change in the policy process. A new position of minister of state for European affairs was created. Since July 2002, that minister chairs an Interdepartmental Co-coordinating Committee on European Affairs that is host to senior civil servants. This committee serves as a distant early warning system for problematic issues that could arise from EU matters and meets with a cabinet subcommittee on European Affairs every two weeks to discuss EU policy. Within the Dáil, a new Select Committee on European Affairs was set up and has the task of sifting through the EU policy documents. The new structures and process bring EU policies under much greater scrutiny, communication, and cooperation among legislators, cabinet officials, and bureaucrats than heretofore had occurred. The creation of the National Forum on Europe in 2002 not only educated the public but also educated the representatives from the political parties. The participation of legislators in the forum brought the level of sophistication of Dáil members to a higher degree than had been done by the earlier committees.

The line between domestic law and European law in Ireland and all the members is increasingly blurred, and in Ireland, EU court decisions have affected such issues as gay rights, women's rights to equal pay, equal opportunity, pensions, and access to services in another member state. A British judge has said that it is "like an incoming tide. It flows into the estuaries and rivers. It cannot be held back."[19]

One case can illuminate the expansion of EU regulation, the resistance of the Irish government and the Irish courts to EU policy, and finally the need to adapt Irish law to EU regulation. The issue concerned the claim of an individual to the application of European human rights standards in the elimination of discrimination against homosexuals in Irish law.

A high-profile member of the Irish Senate, David Norris, brought a case to the Irish court in 1977 challenging sections of the 1861 Offences Against the Person Act, which outlawed buggery, and an 1885 act that criminalized "gross indecency" between men. Norris argued that the provisions of these acts were in violation of Article 40 of the Irish constitution that guaranteed the rights of the individual. Norris was represented, as it happens, by Mary Robinson, who was later to be elected president of Ireland in 1990. The High Court rejected Norris's claim in 1980, arguing that sex should be confined to lawful marriage and sex outside of marriage, and, of course, sex between people of the same gender, is wrong and not in accord with the "Christian and democratic nature of the state." An appeal to the Irish Supreme Court brought the same decision. The Supreme Court also suggested that homosexual behavior was a threat to marriage and the Court had a responsibility to "guard with care the institution of marriage."

A gay man from Northern Ireland, Jeffrey Dudgeon, said his rights under the European convention were violated by police harassment. The European Court of Human Rights had ruled in Dudgeon's favor in 1981. The Dudgeon case provided grounds for Norris to appeal his case to the European Court of Human Rights, which narrowly found in his favor in 1988 on the grounds of a violation of his right to personal privacy. The Irish government in 1993 introduced the Criminal Law (Sexual Offences) Act, which repealed the relevant portions of the 1861 and 1885 acts and reserved criminal penalties for offenses against males or females less than seventeen years of age.

As the first two decisions of the Irish courts revealed, given the religious and cultural attitudes in Ireland in 1977, there was little likelihood that the legislation on homosexuality was going to be changed. The presence of the European Convention on Human Rights and the capacity of a citizen to appeal to the European Court of Human Rights brought EU pressure to bear on the Irish government and the Irish courts to bring about a reformulation of individual rights in Irish law.

The Rejections of EU Treaties

Certainly the first dramatic impact of Ireland on the chain of developments in the EU was the Irish rejection of the Treaty of Nice in 2001 and the even more dramatic Irish rejection of the Treaty of Lisbon in 2008. The Irish had been seen as firmly committed to Europe from the time of entry up to the adoption of the euro. More than 60 percent of Irish voters had approved the referenda on various EU treaties from 1972 to 1998. Public opinion polls and the Eurobarometer polls regularly indicated that the Irish people believed EU membership was a good thing for Ireland and that the country had benefited from the EU.[20] Thus, the result of the referendum in June 2001 in which the Treaty of Nice was defeated by 53 percent to 46 percent, with a very low voter turnout of 35 percent, came as a shock to both the Irish government and the other EU members. The shock was amplified by the fact that the government, the major parties, business associations, labor, farm organizations, and media all favored the treaty and did not foresee the outcome at all. The opponents were mobilized by a variety of issues. Some were specifically Irish, for example, an EU threat to Irish family values through the potential availability of abortion.

The inclusion of the Charter of Fundamental Rights with the Treaty of Nice referendum did not add to the clarity of the debate. The issue of abortion also lurked behind the opposition to the charter, as did same-sex marriage. So few voters had voted "yes," and so many had stayed home, that it meant a very large number of Irish people were unwilling to unhesitatingly vote for another EU treaty. On closer analysis it turned out that the reason most voters either did not vote or voted "no" was that they had a lack of understanding and a lack of information about the treaty.[21]

The Ahern government was stung by the vote in June 2001 and, after being reelected in May 2002, responded quickly. At the Seville Summit Ireland secured the agreement of EU members to declarations that sought to make clear the Irish position on neutrality. The government created the National Forum on Europe, a body composed of representatives of the different groups and parties in Ireland with the express purpose of informing the media, politicians, and the public about the EU. The government then put the Treaty of Nice to the public again in October 2002. With 49.5 percent of the voters turning out, 63 percent approved and 37 percent voted "no." Polls in Ireland showed that the voter's grasp of the issues in the treaty went from 37 percent before June 2001 to 64 percent in October 2002.

The debate did not end there, however, as the proposed new constitution for the EU in 2005 triggered renewed opposition in Ireland. The opposition held the view that the new EU constitution would expand the fundamentally humanitarian Petersberg Tasks to combating terrorism and would include mutual defense clauses that would commit the member states to military security actions. These developments reflected the different view of international and European security since 9/11 and the Iraq War and found expression in Javier Solana's *A Secure Europe for a Better World.*[22]

The Treaty of Lisbon was the next test. Unlike earlier referenda, there was a vigorous, well-organized, and well-financed campaign against the treaty orchestrated by the organization Libertas under the leadership of Declan Ganley. The guesstimates of Libertas spending on the campaign range from €1.3 to €1.8 million.[23]

Due to the Crotty decision, Ireland was the only country to submit the treaty to a referendum, as all the other members sought approval through their national parliaments. In Ireland, the issues in the debate leading up to the vote in June 2008 again included the purported threat to neutrality. The European Charter of Fundamental Rights attached to the treaty again was seen by conservative Catholic groups as potentially opening the door to forcing Ireland to "legalize abortion, gay marriage, prostitution and euthanasia. All of these claims were factually erroneous."[24] The "No Campaign" also focused on the democratic deficit in the EU policy process and the threat of an even greater erosion of Irish sovereignty. The persistent criticism of the Irish corporate tax rate of 12.5 percent also rankled the Irish

At the time the vote was approaching, Prime Minister Bertie Ahern was facing tribunals that were revealing his corrupt financial dealing. He did not put his full attention and weight behind the "yes" campaign. As a result of the tribunal's findings he resigned in 2008. The new prime minister, Brian Cowen, had only one month before the vote on the treaty. In June 2008, 53 percent of the public went to the polls and rejected the treaty by 53.4 percent to 46.6 percent and sent a shock around the capitals of Europe. The most cited reason given by the public after the vote was lack of information (22 percent), about double the next reason, to protect Irish identity (12 percent), and cited about four times as often as any of the other twelve reasons.

The reaction to the Irish referendum vote was mixed. Some argued that the Irish vote should be respected, and the treaty shelved, in the same manner as the Dutch and French referenda did to the new EU constitution in 2005. Others worried that the Irish vote would derail the whole process of reforming the EU treaties and both President Nicolas Sarkozy of France and Chancellor Angela Merkel of Germany flew to Ireland after the vote to express their dismay and see what could be done to remedy the situation. The Irish government was embarrassed.

The vote was also a problem for Europe because the member states faced the mirror image of Ireland's problem: what were they to do with a state that rejected the institution's structure? Politically more volatile was the idea fostered by the Irish vote that if referenda were held in other states, the public would also reject the Treaty of Lisbon, most notably the Euroskeptic countries of Hungary and the UK. The Irish vote in turn raised the argument that the political elites and the Brussels bureaucrats were insensitive to public will, and the persistent perception of a EU democratic deficit was highlighted. The other European states made it clear that the treaty was not subject to renegotiation or adding special provisions for Ireland. The Irish government developed a campaign to inform the public and mustered a significant effort to clarify the misrepresentations.

In October 2009, another referendum was held, and the swing from negative to positive was 20 percent. The turnout was 59 percent and the "yes" vote was 67.1 percent and the "no" vote 32.8 percent, and the treaty was submitted to the Dáil for approval. The fallout from the two votes, however, made many Irish uneasy in that the clear will of the public in 2008 was deemed to be unacceptable and the government had to go back to the public again. What if the public had rejected the treaty one more time? Were they going to keep holding referenda until they got the results they wanted?

The Nice and Lisbon episodes were symptomatic of changing attitudes on the part of the Irish public toward the EU. From the first referendum in 1972 the positive vote on EU treaties has diminished:

	Yes (%)	No (%)
1972 Accession	83	17
1987 SEA	70	30
1992 Maastricht	69	31
1998 Amsterdam	62	38
2001 Nice I	46	54
2002 Nice II	63	37
2008 Lisbon I	47	53
2009 Lisbon II	67	33

Eurobarometer polls and public opinion polls in Ireland up until 2010 were consistently positive on the EU, with the Irish ranking second to the

Netherlands in 2007 in viewing membership in the EU as a good thing and ranking first among the member states in feeling that Ireland has benefited from EU membership. The Irish, however, along with the Spanish, British, and Portuguese, were among the most poorly informed about the EU.[25] The sharpest turn in Irish attitudes came after the EU/IMF bailout in 2010.

The Collapse of the Celtic Tiger

Rather than one Celtic Tiger, there were really three. The first was a product of policies adopted after 1960 and had a growth spurt during 1960 to the 1970s. The cumulative impact of these developments led to the second Celtic Tiger, a high-productivity, high-export economy that hit its peak between 1995 and 2001. The third Celtic Tiger ran from about 2001 to 2008 and was based on domestic demand, a construction boom in property based on low interest rates, extensive consumer debt, bank corruption and debt, and government debt. The second and third Celtic Tiger periods merged in the minds of external observers of Ireland, the Irish people, and, most dangerously, the delusionary Fianna Fáil Irish government of 1997 to 2011. Why this huge boom in construction? There are several answers, and among the most important was the fact the major developers and the leaders of the Fianna Fáil party were very close. Developers were showered with incentives. "There were incentives for the developers of hotels and holiday camps, of private hospitals and nursing homes, of holiday cottage schemes, of third level educational buildings and student accommodation blocks, child care and park and ride facilities, of multi-story car parks and refurbished flats."[26] As journalist David Lynch commented, "Only sand castles seemed to have been overlooked by Fianna Fail."[27] Then again, the whole boom after 2001 was a sand castle. An example was the tax incentive to build hotels that produced an increase in hotel rooms in the third Celtic Tiger years of 150 percent while tourism increased by 70 percent. The €330 million of government spending on hotel construction produced so many hotels that they could not fill them with guests and, as Fintan O'Toole points out, by 2009 the occupancy rate was 53 percent. The hotels were half-empty, and the hotel building industry had been a bonanza to the construction developers but not the hotel business.[28]

The tax largesse was not confined to Irish developers. In 1987, Prime Minister Haughey decided to set up a new International Financial Service Center in Dublin that would attract companies with a very low tax rate of 10 percent that was upped to 12.5 percent in 2005, still about two-thirds lower than that of the United States or the countries of the European Union. The limited regulation and oversight was an additional bonus for the more than 1,200 banks, brokers, and insurance companies that set up offices in the International Financial Service Center. By the early 2000s, the amount of money parked in Dublin was enormous, and the tax revenue to the government produced €1.2 billion. "By 2003 Ireland was the main global location for money market mutual funds, a total of $125 billion in these funds were domiciled in Dublin, overtaking the former homeland of the Cayman Islands. In the same year Dublin's investment funds industry, valued at $480 billion, surpassed London's. Hedge fund managers certainly liked the place: by 2004, over $200 billion in hedge fund assets were being serviced in Dublin."[29] Many of these companies were merely offices that were located at the International Financial Service Center for channeling corporate profits through Ireland at the low tax rate, while the actual management of the companies was located elsewhere. Ireland's reputation suffered as the international financial community began to see the absence of regulation as an invitation to fraud. The Irish government chose to look the other way and in fact increased the tax incentives for firms to locate at the International Financial Service Center with the more generous 2004 Finance Act.

Major Irish banks, operating in a relatively unregulated environment, began to lend increasingly large sums to developers and homeowners to the point that was well beyond their reserve capacity to cover should the loans go bad. The developers and bankers kept designing increasingly expensive schemes and making millions in the process without any sense that this form of growth might have limits.

The property bubble was unique in comparison with other property bubbles. Housing in Europe boomed during the 1990s and 2000s with prices in Italy rising 50 percent from 1985 to 2006, France by 75 percent, and the UK by 140 percent, but in Ireland the increase was 250 percent. In the United States, house values went up 50 percent in the ten years from 1996 to 2006, whereas in Ireland the increase was 172 percent. It was a true bubble in that the increase in prices bore no relationship to increases in the consumer price index as new house costs increased seven times faster than inflation, four times the increase in the cost of building materials, and five times the rise in average industrial earnings.[30] Consumer debt rose from about 40 percent of gross domestic product (GDP) in 1994 to 110 percent of GNP in 1999, to 145 percent in 2004, and finally, by 2008, to a figure of over €400 billion, 250 percent of GNP. Two-thirds of this debt was connected to property. The escalation of personal debt and mortgage-related debt both doubled in the five years from 2004 to 2008.[31]

Brian Cowen, the finance minister, became prime minister in 2008 as the property bubble burst and the economy unraveled. He was among the Panglossians who kept asserting that economic conditions in Ireland were fine up through 2008, until it became clear how big the financial disaster was. Without knowing the size of the bank debt, he then decided the government should take on the debt of the banks to maintain financial credibility, and the bank debt became sovereign debt. The government spent months denying that Ireland needed to be bailed out by the EU. But the yield on the Irish ten-year bond climbed to 9.26 percent in November 2010, hitting an all-time high since the launch of the euro in 1999.

The three-year €85 billion rescue plan with the IMF, European Central Bank, and EU was agreed on in November 2010 with strict conditions attached. The plan required a €15 billion austerity program from the government as well as €5 billion out of its own cash resources and €12.5 billion out of the National Pensions Reserve Fund. Of the overall amount, €17.5 billion was to save the banks, although observers correctly noted the ultimate cost of the bank bailout would be closer to €50 billion. Fifty billion euros was for the government's finances, which were bleeding red. For the money to be released, Dublin had to undergo quarterly reviews, performed by a team of inspectors from the European Commission, the European Central Bank, and the IMF. The average interest rate of the loans was 5.8 percent and, though better than the bond rate, resulted in one-fifth of the government's revenues going to interest payments.

The Irish public did not perceive the loans as necessary but as money that was forced on them at a high interest rate to protect the euro and the debts of German banks that had lent the Irish banks a lot of money. The burden was apparent to the Irish people, who held demonstrations in Dublin in November 2010, decrying the harsh costs imposed on workers and taxpayers. Organized by the Irish Congress of Trade Unions, it was the first major public signal of disapproval by the Irish people. The general mood was dark as the Irish public realized the extent of the recession as jobs were lost and the economy declined. Trust in government was at a low point: in little more than a year, from 2009 to 2010, public trust more than halved from 20 percent to a figure of 8 percent and, more than that, it was also the lowest level of any European state.[32] Politicians, especially Gerry Adams of Sinn Féin, saw the bailout as a flawed plan forced on them and the public and that Ireland was being victimized to save the euro.

The 2011 election brought a new government in Dublin as the Fianna Fáil party, which had presided over the crisis, was decimated and a coalition government of Fine Gael and Labour took over. However, the large EU powers viewed Ireland's management of its economy as barely more competent than Greece and were taken aback by the apparently bottomless levels of bank and government debt. In 2011, Dublin was denied the base point reduction that was granted to Portugal and Greece. France and other EU states still object to the 12.5 percent corporate tax rate and would not grant relief on the loans until Ireland raised the tax rate. Ireland chose to swallow hard and work its way out of the debt.

Crucial decisions that would normally ensue after such an electoral change in Ireland in 2011 were constrained by the power of the external agencies that controlled the bailout funds, the euro interest rate, and the re-funding of capital-poor banks.[33] Ireland had little more recourse than to petition for the better terms, which were finally granted in 2012 after Greece's, Spain's, and Portugal's debts proved to be more troublesome than those of Ireland.

Prime Minister Enda Kenny tried to secure some debt relief and still protect Ireland's 12.5 percent corporate tax rate. This process triggered several rebuffs from the EU finance ministers. Attention then shifted to the creation of a new financial authority by the EU to deal with the crisis. Fear of another rejection arose when the Irish voters had to approve an EU Fiscal Compact in 2012 that was designed to constrain government spending among the member states. This compact emerged from the stability and growth agreements of 1997, which required EU governments to have a budget deficit of no more than 3 percent of GDP and government debt of no more than 60 percent of GDP. These benchmarks were not met by most members even before the economic crisis of 2008. The EU Fiscal Compact was signed in 2011, ratified in 2012 by member states, and went into effect in 2013. The policies in the pact represented the German position that governments with so much deficit spending required austerity to foster confidence in their management of sovereign debt. This position, held by Angela Merkel, was inflexible and has had the effect of very sharp cuts in Irish government salaries, employment, services, and welfare.

In a tough battle for public approval, the government argued that the long-term interest of Ireland was in the Eurozone and should not be a party to the failure of the euro and risk the loss of future funding from the EU. Those who opposed signing believed that the Eurozone was going to collapse at some point in the future, and the Irish people should not suffer any more by following the policies of the German Central Bank. The Irish voters did not reject the Fiscal Compact in June 2012 despite the hardships they had been suffering and despite the fact that the compact only promised more austerity. The vote was 60.29 percent for, 39.71 percent against and allows Ireland to access the European Stability Mechanism, the Eurozone's permanent $618 billion bailout fund. Only countries that ratify the fiscal treaty can access those funds.

The Irish policy of being a good soldier finally paid off in July 2012, when a summit of Eurozone leaders in Brussels pledged to examine the situation of the Irish financial sector. Kenny hailed the deal as a major victory for the taxpayers of Ireland. The deal was also a major victory for Kenny, who had campaigned on the need to restructure Irish debt but had been rebuffed repeatedly by the EU finance ministers. In 2013 Ireland cut loose from the EU loans and offered Irish bonds to the financial markets; these drew a low interest rate, indicating that they were perceived as considerably less risky than in 2008.

The year 2013 also marked the year that Ireland was president of the Council of the European Union. While for Ireland the financial pressure was foremost, the Irish presidency did have a significant agenda for job creation in the unemployment-racked EU states, negotiations on a United States–EU free trade agreement that the Kenny said would shape global trade for the next fifty years. The assessments of the Irish presidency were favorable as the Irish bureaucrats were skilled at this work because Ireland had held the presidency a number of times before.

May 2014 brought the European parliamentary elections. The Irish vote was of course a chance to reward or punish the performance of the parties on the domestic front. The government was a coalition of the Labour Party and Fine Gael, and the candidates of both parties lost support through the peculiarities of redistricting Ireland from twelve seats to eleven, and the transferable vote led to Fine Gael gaining four of the eleven seats despite a drop from the last EU election of 6.8 percent in their vote, down to 22.2 percent. The Labour Party went from 13.9 percent to 5.3 percent and gained no seats. Fianna Fáil, despite having the same percentage of votes as Fine Gael, 22.2 percent, garnered only one seat. The big winner as a party was Sinn Féin, which went from 11.2 percent of the vote to 19.5 percent and went from no seats to three. The most surprising outcome was the collective vote for independent candidates that jumped from 17.3 percent to 25.6 percent and earned three seats. The Irish voters had punished the coalition government due to harsh economic conditions, but that punishment really fell on the Labour Party. The voters rewarded Sinn Féin, a party that had been a strident critic of the EU bailout and the harsh conditions that accompanied those euros. Perhaps most surprising was the fact that the largest percentage of the vote went to independents, also critics of the bailout, and could be read as a disappointment with all the established parties. The Irish version of Euroskepticism took the form of anger at the politicians and bankers who put Ireland in the crisis and the pain the Irish taxpayers had to bear to get them out of it, while few went to jail and many ordinary people lost their jobs and their homes. The EU bailout brought no relief to ordinary people but in fact brought cuts in pay and in services.

The voice and representation of Ireland in the EU as a whole will be diluted by the expansion of the EU and the changes wrought by the Treaty of Lisbon. Some fear that the secular values of other European states potentially might be imposed on Ireland through the instrument of the EU. The EU democratic deficit creates a sense of marginalization in the ordinary citizen. Ultimately, the Irish public may be participating in both a form of Euro-fatigue as well as a form of Euro-anger over the terms of the debt bailout. The persistent and often acrimonious exchanges over the interest rate on Irish debt and grumbling over EU oversight of Irish economic policy are seen as an abdication of economic sovereignty to EU overseers. These issues have dominated Irish relations with the EU since the 2010 bailout. Finally, only in 2014 did the Irish economy begin to recover with a growth rate of 3.4 percent and a projected growth rate for 2015 of over 4 percent.

Conclusion

The broader issues that Ireland will face in the future retain some that have been central to Irish concerns, such as the CAP, and others that will be a function of the development of the EU vertically and horizontally. Increasing pressure to adjust and renationalize the CAP payments will be a major agenda item for Ireland, which will resist changes in the CAP. The same is true for the equalization of corporate taxes across all the member states, for it will directly undermine one of the engines of Ireland's growth—low corporate taxes.

Despite protocols in the EU treaties designed to preserve Irish religious and moral values, some will always fear that a secularized EU will seek to change Ireland's laws through the adoption of the Charter of Fundamental Rights or through interpretation of EU rights or directives sometime in the future. Though the Seville Declarations would seem to settle the status of Ireland on neutrality and European security and defense, there are those who see that posture as potentially problematic in a changing global system.

Finally, the expansion of the EU has shifted Ireland's small representation, 13 seats in a 626-member European Parliament, to even the even smaller representation of 11 seats of 732. The expansion of the EU will mean an inevitable shift in the duration and sequence of the presidency of the European Council and the opportunity for Ireland to hold such a leading role in Europe, and for that matter the world, for six months within each six years, will diminish. The adoption of qualified majority voting in the EU Commission on certain issues will inevitably expand and make Ireland's 7 votes out of 345 relatively inconsequential. Despite the defeat of the constitution in France and the Netherlands in 2005, the issues of the balance of power between the EU and the member states, the Charter of Fundamental Rights, the consolidation of the treaties into a constitution, and the role of the national parliaments versus the EU will remain on the agenda of the member states and will force Ireland to recalculate where it fits in the EU of the twenty-first century. The Irish may move to a more Euro-skeptic posture and be more sensitive to the idea of restructuring the EU in a more decentralized direction. Nevertheless, Irish attitudes have changed, and the effects will be far-reaching as the generations removed from World War II and experiencing the rebirth of nationalism undermine the supranationalism of the EU.

Notes

1. On Northern Ireland, in the early 1970s, the Republic of Ireland brought a case against Great Britain over the treatment of prisoners in Ulster. In 1978, the European Court of Human Rights ruled against the UK. The judgment of the court was that the UK authorities in Ulster had not engaged in torture but had engaged in "inhumane and degrading treatment" of Irish Republican Army (IRA) detainees. The result was embarrassing to the British, who had argued that what was done to the prisoners was not torture but interrogation necessary for national security. After the hunger strikes of 1981, the European Parliament initiated hearings and reports on Northern Ireland.

2. Reid (2004), p. 248, citing the globalization index of the journal *Foreign Policy*, noted that Ireland ranked number one in globalization in the early 2000s.

3. See Wiles and Finnegan (1993) and Finnegan and Wiles (1995), pp. 50–55.

4. O'Donnell (2002), p. 5.

5. FitzGerald (2003), p. 158.

6. O'Donnell (2002), p. 16.

7. Quoted in EU Business, "Almost a Quarter of Irish Face Risk of Poverty: EU Survey."

8. Wiles and Finnegan (1993), pp. 127–208.

9. B. Laffan and R. O'Donnell (1998), pp. 157–158.

10. Ibid., p. 165.

11. Irish Department of Foreign Affairs (1996).

12. Laffan and O'Donnell (1998), p. 157–158.

13. Keatinge (1991), pp. 151–157.

14. Keatinge and B. Laffan(1999), pp. 283–310.

15. IGC 96 Task Force, European Commission (1996), pp. 51–52.

16. Laffan.

17. Laffan and O'Donnell (1998), p. 169.

18. Nugent (1994), p. 418.

19. Lord Justice Denning, quoted in Chubb (1992), p. 51.

20. Coakley, (2005).

21. O'Mahoney (2004), p. 27.

22. Solana (2003).

23. Laffan and O'Mahoney (2008), p. 117.

24. Ibid., p. 117.

25. Ibid., p. 129

26. O'Toole (2010), p. 118.

27. Lynch, (2010), p. 157.

28. O'Toole (2010), p. 118.

29. Ibid., p. 129.

30. Ibid., p. 104.

31. Ibid., p. 116.

32. Hardiman (2012), p. 224.

33. Mair (2011), p. 296.

9

Denmark:
Its European Dilemma

Marlene Wind

EUROPE IS AT A CROSSROADS. SEVERAL MEMBER STATES AND IN particular the Eurozone countries seek closer integration after the financial crisis. Where will that leave Denmark and other smaller economies outside the euro area? These and many other questions are addressed in this chapter.

Denmark applied for membership to the European Community (EC, after 1992 the EU) for the first time in 1961 together with the UK, and Denmark's accession to the EC was closely linked to that of Britain. The UK was Denmark's largest market, and Denmark simply could not afford to remain outside of the community if the UK decided to join. The close relations with Britain meant that when France blocked British membership in 1961, and again in 1967, Denmark withdrew its application as well. However, in 1971, when the Charles de Gaulle era ended and the French position toward British membership changed, the Community accepted Denmark's application for membership, along with those of the UK and Ireland. After a national referendum on membership, Denmark joined the EC on January 1, 1973.

As a small, independent democratic state with an open economy dependent on trade with its neighboring countries[1] and with a large agricultural sector, Denmark had already, in the aftermath of World War II, demonstrated its commitment to international cooperation in areas such as trade, defense, and security. It was a strong supporter of the creation of the United Nations in 1945 and became a member of NATO in 1949. Denmark was moreover one of the founding members of the General Agreement on Tariffs and Trade (GATT) and since 1960 a member of the British-sponsored European Free Trade Area (EFTA), which was (and still is) a less committed type of cooperation compared to the EC. Adding the EC to the list of memberships of international organizations would, it was believed, bring major economic benefits and market access, including membership to the customs union. Also participation in the Common Agriculture Policy was considered beneficial for Denmark.

Even though the economic advantages of EC membership were apparent, and the politicians who were pro–EC membership had a strong case, joining the EC was a controversial issue in Denmark. The left-wing parties and a large portion of the Danish public were either opposed or very skeptical about membership. In the run-up to the referendum in 1972 a heated debate went on with the "yes" campaign putting forward the economic arguments while the "no" campaigners focused on the risk to national sovereignty and a potential weakening of the Danish welfare state.[2] The importance given by the Danes to the question of membership was evident from the exceptional high turnout in the referendum where 90.1 percent went to the polls. With 63.3 percent voting in favor and 36.7 percent against, the results of the referendum demonstrated that a strong skepticism toward the European integration project had taken root in Denmark. This Euro-skepticism has accompanied Danish EC/EU membership ever since.

Referenda and Opting Out

According to the 1953 Danish Constitution, sovereignty may be ceded to international organizations either by an overwhelming majority in Parliament (five-sixths majority) or by a parliamentary majority backed by a national referendum. Denmark has held referenda on EU issues seven times. The most recent referendum was on the EU's Unified Patent Court, for which the Danes voted in favor on May 25, 2014. The referendum was called because Parliament could not reach the necessary five-sixths majority to join the Court. Even though few citizens really understood the Patent Court, neither the right-wing Euro-skeptic party the Danish People's Party nor the left-wing Euro-skeptic party the Unity List would support Danish membership in the EU's Unified Patent Court. Table 9.1 shows a list of the referenda held in Denmark since 1972 on EU issues.

A key event in Denmark's relations with the EU was the referendum in 1992 on the Treaty of Maastricht establishing the European Union. While the Danes had voted "yes" to the Single Market Act in 1986, a majority vetoed the Treaty of Maastricht, sending shockwaves throughout Europe and the Danish political establishment.[3] The Edinburgh Agreement was the solution to bring the Danes on board so they would vote in favor of the Treaty of Maastricht in May 1993. The agreement contained four Danish opt-outs from the Treaty of the European Union (TEU or the Treaty of Maastricht) in the following areas: the single currency, a common defense policy, supranational cooperation in justice and home affairs, and Union citizenship. The latter lost its relevance with the Treaty of Amsterdam,[4] but the other three are still effective more than twenty years after they were established.[5] The

Table 9.1 Danish Referenda on EC and EU Issues

Date	Issue	Turnout (%)	Yes (%)	No (%)
October 2, 1972	Danish membership in the EC	90.1	63.3	36.7
February 27, 1986	Single European Act (indicative)	75.4	56.2	43.8
June 2, 1992	Treaty of Maastricht	83.1	49.3	50.7
May 18, 1993	Treaty of Maastricht and Edinburgh Agreement	86.5	56.7	43.3
May 28, 1998	Treaty of Amsterdam	76.2	55.1	44.9
September 28, 2000	Danish accession to the third stage of the EMU (Eurozone membership)	87.6	46.8	53.2
May 25, 2014	Unified Patent Court	55.9	62.5	37.5

Source: http://www.eu-oplysningen.dk/dkeu/dk/afstemninger/afstemning/.

negotiations with the other member states for the Edinburgh Agreement and the subsequent "yes" vote in 1993 had been made possible by the so-called national compromise between all the major political parties in Denmark at the time, including the Socialist People's Party, which had advocated a "no" to the Treaty of Maastricht in the 1992 referendum. This broad consensus in Parliament on Denmark's EU policy provided stable ground for Denmark in the following years to pursue a pragmatic and dualistic EU policy. It made it possible for the country to preserve its autonomy in selected areas while at the same time attempting to maximize its influence in the EU.[6]

With the national compromise in place, Denmark entered into the Schengen Agreement in 1996, and after the Danish government had actively participated in the negotiations of the Treaty of Amsterdam, the Danes voted "yes" to this treaty in 1998.[7] Then in 2000, after the positive result of the referendum on the Treaty of Amsterdam, the Social Democratic government, led by Prime Minister Poul Nyrup Rasmussen, attempted to remove the opt-out from the common currency to pave the way for Danish membership in the Eurozone. However, as in the case of the Maastricht referendum, the pro-EU parties' campaign was not in line with the majority of the public and 53.2 percent voted "no" to Danish membership in the Monetary Union. Since then, neither the conservative-liberal governments in office from 2001 to 2011 nor the succeeding social democratic–social liberal government has dared bring the opt-outs to a referendum, even though it has been a declared priority in all government programs to remove them.

With the euro crisis amending the single currency, this opt-out has been put on hold. However, the situation is different when it comes to the justice and home affairs opt-out, which includes police cooperation, policies on immigration and asylum, and related issues. The entering into force of the Treaty of Lisbon in 2009 put pressure on the justice and home affairs opt-

Table 9.2 The Danish Opt-Outs

The Edinburgh Agreement of December 12, 1992, signifies the other member states' acceptance of Denmark's nonparticipation in specially defined areas:

Common Defense	Denmark does not participate in the elaboration and implementation of decisions and actions that have implication within the areas of defense.
Economic and Monetary Union	Denmark will not participate in the third phase of the Economic and Monetary Union. Therefore Denmark will not be a member of the Eurozone.
Citizenship	Union citizenship cannot replace national citizenship.
Freedom, Security, and Justice	Denmark only participates in EU judicial cooperation at the intergovernmental level.

Source: Kelstrup, Martinsen, and Wind (2012), Box 13.1, p. 423.

out because it was decided to move this policy area from intergovernmental decisionmaking to supranational. So far Denmark has been able to participate in police cooperation (Europol) because it was kept at an intergovernmental level, but with the elevation of cross-border police cooperation to the supranational level, the justice and home affairs opt-out forces Denmark to step out of Europol. The pro-EU parties in Denmark see this as an unfortunate situation, and it has led to a political agreement between the major pro-EU parties stating that regardless which of the leading parties wins the national elections in 2015, there shall be a referendum on amending the justice and home affairs opt-out within the first quarter of 2016.[8] Table 9.2 provides an overview of the opt-outs.

How and in What Ways Does the EU Influence Denmark?
EU and Domestic Politics
An important aspect of member states' relations with the EU is the place of EU issues in the domestic political sphere. The national compromise between the pro-EU parties on the goals and terms of Danish membership has made it possible to keep questions relating to the EC/EU separate from ordinary domestic politics. EU policy issues have rarely decided national elections, and at the same time, national politics have played a minor role in EU elections.[9] Moreover, one could say it has provided the shifting Danish (often minority) governments with a stable base for conducting a coherent EU policy and thereby strengthened the governments' positions in EU negotiations. In the coming years, things may be changing in this respect, however, as EU policies impose more and more on national policy areas. Some examples include social issues, where foreign workers claim social benefits when working in Denmark; nondiscrimination issues and issues re-

lating to social dumping and the minimum wage; and all policy areas that touch on the so-called Nordic welfare model.

Another aspect of the dissociation of EU issues from domestic politics has to do with the political movements against or skeptical of EC/EU membership, which were created alongside the traditional political system and have not been represented in the Danish Parliament but have gained seats in the European Parliament. The Popular Movement against the EU (Folkebevægelsen mod EU), created at the time of the first referendum on EC membership in 1972, and the June Movement (Junibevægelsen), created in the heydays of Euro-skepticism in 1992, are examples. The People's Movement against EC/EU won four seats in the European Parliament in the first popular elections in 1979 and up until the mid-1990s accounted for the largest number of Danish members of the European Parliament (MEPs). Since 2004, the electoral support for the two movements has diminished, and in 2009, the June Movement dissolved itself after not winning any seats in the 2009 EP elections, while the Popular Movement against the EU only won one seat in the 2009 and 2014 elections. What made the popular movements stand out was exactly that they did not seek representation in the national parliament. One might say they functioned as a "bypass" directing EU skepticism away from the national parliament and directly into the European Parliament.

The dissociation of EU politics from domestic politics has not meant that EU issues are not debated in Denmark, but that they have mainly been confined to the frequent EU referenda and the elections for the European Parliament. This situation has, however, changed over the past years. As mentioned briefly, developments, primarily at the EU level, have led to EU politics being increasingly entangled with the national political sphere. Some scholars argue that EU politics has actually been "normalized."[10]

The elections in 2001 brought an end to nine years of Social Democratic government. The entry into office of a Liberal Conservative minority government, with Anders Fogh Rasmussen as prime minister, marked a change, not least because the new government's powers rested on parliamentary support from the right-wing EU-skeptic Danish People's Party. The Liberal Conservative government could, however, still rest its EU policy on the established pro-EU consensus with the opposition parties. Nevertheless, the strong position of the Danish People's Party, which became even stronger in the 2005 national elections, meant that the government had to strike a careful balance between continued influence in and adherence to what was decided in Brussels while not provoking the party whose mandates it relied on for staying in power. As we shall see, this balancing act became very hard in regard to the (restrictive) Danish immigration policy introduced during the Liberal Conservative government's time in office from 2001 to 2011 and with respect to meeting Denmark's commitments as a member of the Schengen Agreement.

Even though Denmark is often seen as a "reluctant European,"[11] at the same time it has been "the good pupil" in the European class and is known as an obedient complier with EU rules and directives.[12] Denmark's transposition deficit is among the lowest in the EU, with only 0.2 percent of all directives relating to the Single Market overdue in 2014. Thus, when it comes to timely transposition, Denmark clearly meets the deficit target of 1 percent set by the member states.[13] Furthermore, the number of infringement cases relating to Single Market legislation pending against Denmark is almost half (seventeen in 2014) of the EU average (thirty in 2014).[14] Denmark's high level of compliance and excellent transposition record can be explained by the political capacity of the centralized Danish public administration to coordinate and smoothly transpose EU law into the national legal order.[15]

There exist, however, exceptions to the rule of Denmark being the obedient complier, but these have more to do with a misfit between EU law or principles and the values dominating the domestic political sphere than the capacity of the public administration.[16] One example of this was the misfit between the EU citizenship directive, adopted by the Council and the European Parliament in 2004, and the strict immigration laws, especially those concerning requirements for family reunification, which the Liberal Conservative government introduced after it came into power in 2001. The implementation of the directive would undermine the restrictive Danish rules for family reunification, adopted by a majority in Parliament, which were the most important issues for the right-wing Danish People's Party supporting the government. The problem was that the government had voted "yes" and supported the directive when it was adopted at the EU level, perhaps not really understanding the implications for its own immigration law. However, when it was realized that there was a clash, the directive was not implemented into Danish law for years.[17] Not until a court case on the directive originating in Ireland, did Denmark finally, and very reluctantly, comply with the citizenship directive.

Another example of how EU politics and domestic politics clashed during the time of the Liberal Conservative government, and where the government found it difficult to strike the balance between adherence to EU policies and ability to satisfy its parliamentary base, concerned an agreement made on the reintroduction of border control in Denmark. In 2011, the Danish People's Party launched a demand to reintroduce border control and managed to negotiate an agreement with the Conservative Liberal government about introducing "permanent customs control in Denmark," as it was phrased. The agreement was not only a breach of Denmark's commitments as a member of the Schengen area, it also breached the EU principle of free movement. Evidently it caused outrage in the other EU member states, not least in Germany, Denmark's neighbor to the south, and the European Commission threatened to raise a case against Denmark at the European Court of

Justice for breaching EU law.[18] The solution to the controversial agreement, which caused a dispute with the European Commission lasting several months, came when a center-left government was voted into office at the general elections in autumn 2011. The first thing the new Social Democratic–led government did was roll back the decision to reintroduce border control in Denmark.[19] The agreement of reintroducing border control was a blot on the picture of Denmark as the obedient complier to EU law. It also demonstrated a shift in the way Danish EU policy is dealt with domestically and how the parliamentary success of the Danish People's Party has indicated that EU politics can no longer be kept apart from national politics, but has found its way into the core of the domestic political sphere.

The EU and the Danish Judiciary

Denmark's membership of the EU entails an acceptance of a EU supreme court, the European Court of Justice (ECJ) in Luxembourg, which has the final word when a conflict arises between, for instance, a member state and the Commission on the proper implementation and administration of EU law. The ECJ (and the Commission) can also hand out significant fines if EU law is not upheld.[20]

This judicial system is important because it actually makes the EU effective and EU law binding, predictable, and real to citizens and businesses. The judicial set-up, however, is something of a challenge for a country like Denmark, which has no tradition of judicial review of national legislation at the national level.[21] The Danish national courts normally never disregard what a majority in the Danish Parliament decides (it has only happened once in 165 years when the highest court set aside a statute that was in conflict with the Danish constitution). Denmark, as well as the rest of the Nordic countries and to some extent the UK, subscribe in practice to a so-called majoritarian democracy, as opposed to constitutional democracy, where judicial review by courts is considered essential.[22] This means that the ECJ is often regarded as a rather problematic institution and is often criticized by the Danish public and parliamentarians who generally hold the view that only elected bodies, like parliaments, can have true democratic legitimacy.

In the past few years, increasing numbers of rulings by the ECJ have been the subject of intense debate in Denmark and have, in many ways, made its workings more visible to the Danes. The court rulings on issues such as the right of EU citizens and their spouses to residence in any EU member state despite the member states own immigration laws (the Metock case of 2008), the right for EU citizens employed in Denmark to receive educational grants from the Danish state when studying in Denmark, and the eligibility of EU citizens living in Denmark to receive family allowances such as child benefits from the Danish state, are controversial to many Danes because they touch on some of the core components of the highly tax-based Danish welfare state.[23] All these cases have brought attention to the fact that judgments by the ECJ may have direct impact on Danish policies and even set aside what a majority in Parliament has already decided.

The EU and the Danish Economy

When Denmark entered the EC in 1973, it meant vast economic benefits for the Danish agricultural sector. From the early 1980s until the enlargement in 2004, Danish agriculture received large subsidies from the EU's Common Agricultural Policy (CAP).[24] This also meant that for many years Denmark received more money from the EU budget than it contributed. Reforms of the CAP and the model for calculating the member states' contributions to the EU budget have changed the equation, and Denmark has recently been a net contributor.[25]

Judging the influence of the EU on the Danish economy solely on the basis of whether Denmark is a gross or net contributor would be to simplify matters however. More important than the amount of money flowing between the EU and Denmark are the effects of the Internal Market on the Danish economy. Bringing down trade barriers, establishing common effective laws and regulations and thereby increasing competition within Europe have had an enormous impact on a small open economy like that of Denmark. Added to these benefits comes the EU's ability to negotiate collectively for trade agreements with third parties, such as the current trade talks between the EU and the United States. According to a recent German study measuring the effects of twenty years of the Internal Market on the member states, Denmark is the country whose economy has gained the most. Calculations show that the annual gain in real gross domestic product (GDP) per capita in Denmark has been €500 in the period from 1992 to 2012.[26]

Another aspect to consider when looking at the EU's influence on the Danish economy is that Denmark is not a member of the Eurozone. However, the Danish currency is fixed to the euro via the Exchange Rate Mechanism II.[27] The mechanism was made to ensure that exchange rate fluctuations between the euro and the currencies of the non-Eurozone members did not disrupt economic stability within the Single Market. The advantage for Denmark of entering into this agreement is the stability and predictability of the Danish currency (the krone) and the opportunity to easily join the euro should the Danish opt-out from the single currency be removed. This arrangement also means, however, that the European Central Bank has indirect influence on the exchange rate of the Danish currency.

Denmark was not totally clear of the financial crisis that hit in 2008, but the economy was not as badly affected as other EU member states. Tables 9.3, 9.4, and 9.5 show that compared to the Eurozone, Denmark is doing relatively well on the OECD's fiscal indicators such as growth in GDP, fiscal balance,

Table 9.3 GDP Growth, percentage

	2008	2009	2010	2011	2012	2013	2014	2015[a]
Denmark	–0.8	–5.7	1.4	1.1	–0.4	0.4	1.4	1.8
Euro area	0.2	–4.4	1.9	1.6	–0.6	–0.4	1.2	1.7
OECD	0.2	–3.5	3.0	2.0	1.5	1.3	2.2	2.8

Source: OECD, "Denmark—Economic Forecast Summary," May 2014. Available at http://www.oecd.org/eco/outlook/denmarkeconomicforecastsummary.htm. (Accessed August 7, 2014).
Note: a. 2015 figures are forecasts made by the OECD.

Table 9.4 Fiscal Balance, percentage

	2008	2009	2010	2011	2012	2013	2014	2015[a]
Denmark	3.3	–2.8	–2.7	–2.0	–3.9	–0.9	–1.5	–3.0
Euro area	–2.1	–6.3	–6.2	–4.1	–3.7	–3.0	–2.5	–1.8
OECD	–3.5	–8.4	–8.0	–6.5	–5.9	–4.6	–3.9	–3.2

Source: OECD, "Denmark–Economic Forecast Summary," May 2014. Available at http://www.oecd.org/eco/outlook/denmarkeconomicforecastsummary.htm. (Accessed August 7, 2014).

Table 9.5 Unemployment Rate, percentage

	2008	2009	2010	2011	2012	2013	2014	2015[a]
Denmark	3.5	6.0	7.5	7.6	7.5	7.0	6.8	6.7
Euro area	7.5	9.4	10.0	10.0	11.2	11.9	11.7	11.4
OECD	6.0	8.1	8.3	8.3	7.9	7.9	7.5	7.2

Source: OECD, "Denmark–Economic Forecast Summary," May 2014. Available at http://www.oecd.org/eco/outlook/denmarkeconomicforecastsummary.htm. (Accessed August 7, 2014).
Note: a. 2015 figures are forecasts made by the OECD.

and the unemployment rate from the year 2008 and onward. Denmark has coped with the financial crisis rather well and is now turning its economy around despite the krone being closely pegged to the euro.

How and in What Ways Does Denmark Influence the EU?

The influence of a state is a strange issue to discuss because it can be measured in many ways. Often Denmark has been presented as a role model, that is, when the discussion falls on the advantages of the welfare state and a flexible labor market (here the issue of "flexicuraty" is often mentioned). Other times the efficiency and competence of Danish civil servants is held up as giving Denmark a comparative advantage compared to its relatively small size. Below I focus on some of the more conventional ways of looking at influence in the EU by highlighting the institutional dimensions.

Influence via the Council

With a population of 5.5 million, making up 1.1 percent of the total EU population, Denmark is a smaller member state and has traditionally focused on making use of the relatively privileged powers enjoyed by small states in the Council. Accordingly, Denmark has taken an intergovernmental approach advocating unanimity and has been hesitant about institutional reforms that would alter the balance between the large and small member states in the Council or provide the European Parliament (EP) with more powers at the expense of the Council.

Despite its reputation as a "reluctant European," Denmark has sought, formally and informally, to be actively involved in the everyday negotiation processes in the Council of Ministers.[28] Moreover, research on the impact of the Danish opt-outs on the work of the Danish officials in Brussels and the Danish negotiation strategy has shown that Danish civil servants have tried hard to compensate for the opt-outs with efficiency, credibility, and constructive cooperation to avoid any negative effects on Denmark's relations with Europe.[29] Danish officials have thus worked with everything available to avoid Denmark's marginalization.

The Danish government and civil servants are, however, not entirely free to negotiate on Denmark's behalf in the Council. Thus, before the Danish ministers depart for Brussels to negotiate in the European Council or the Council of Ministers, they must present the items on the Council agenda to the Danish Parliament's European Affairs Committee and collect a mandate for the government's negotiation position. The Danish EU decisionmaking process has built into it a comprehensive scrutinizing system where the Danish Parliament keeps a tight rein on the government's EU policy. The parliamentary scrutiny ensures, in particular, that there is no majority in the Danish Parliament against the government's EU policy, which is important in Denmark because of the long-standing tradition of minority governments.[30]

When the Parliament's European Affairs Committee was created at the time Denmark joined the EC, it was the first of its kind. The committee has proven effective as a democratic body keeping oversight of Denmark's EU policies and has inspired other EU member states to create similar committees. There exists, however, some concern that EU legislation today covers so many areas that having just one parliamentary committee dealing with EU issues is far too little. Hence, it has been argued that all parliamentary committees ought to deal with and integrate EU policy areas into their day-to-day work, and what is really needed is sufficient institutional support to make them capable of handling it.[31] While being a way of securing representation of the (majority) of the Danish voters' interests in the EU, the comprehensive scrutiny by the Danish Parliament can at times also limit the Danish government's flexibility in EU negotiations and occasionally make negotiations cumbersome.

The Rotating Presidency

The rotating presidency of the Council is an arrangement that provides small member states like Denmark with the opportunity to be in charge of the EU's decisionmaking process for six months. Although it is administratively a tough job for many of the smaller states, Denmark has managed to gain respect from the other states for its efficient running of presidencies. This was especially the case when during its presidency in 2002, Denmark successfully concluded the accession negotiations with candidate countries of Central and Eastern Europe, leading to the enlargement with ten new member states in 2004.

When Denmark held the presidency again in the first half of 2012, the financial crisis dominated the EU's political agenda, and it was difficult to make room for traditional Danish favorite issues (e.g., the environment) in the program. Instead, the Danish presidency was occupied with producing results that would help Europe tackle the financial crisis and secure the euro that Denmark is herself not a part of. The Danish presidency managed to finalize the negotiations on the "two-pack," which included regulations aimed at monitoring potential economic problems in the Eurozone countries[32] and acted as a mediator in the negotiations of the Fiscal Compact between the Eurozone countries and those outside the Eurozone.[33] What is worth noting about the results is that Denmark was able to orchestrate these important negotiations on fiscal issues in spite of its opt-out from the single currency. Most of these issues were closely tied with Internal Market regulation, however, where Denmark is a full-fledged member state.

The Influence of the Danish Public
via the European Parliament

The Treaty of Lisbon extended the powers of the European Parliament vis-à-vis the Council. Hence, the importance of the direct European elections as a mechanism for ordinary European citizens to influence the EU, or at least as a way to express their views, increased when the Treaty of Lisbon entered into force in 2009. Even though the turnout for the European Parliament elections in Denmark is not as high as for the referenda on EU issues or the national elections, a rather large share of the electorate make use of their right to vote for an MEP to represent them.

The Euro-skeptics have, as mentioned earlier, always done well in the European elections in Denmark. The public support for the popular movements against or skeptical of EC/EU membership may have withered in recent years, but as Table 9.6 shows, this development does not mean that Euro-skepticism has declined. On the contrary, in the European elections in May 2014, the right-wing Danish People's Party, known for its harsh Euro-skeptic policy, increased its share of the votes with 11.3 percentage points, thereby doubling the party's number of seats in the European Parliament. Table 9.6 shows the results of the European elections in Denmark since 1979.

Table 9.6 Results of European Parliament Elections in Denmark, 1979–2014

Party	1979	1984	1989	1994	1999	2004	2009	2014
Social Democrats	21.9 (3)	19.5 (3)	23.3 (4)	15.8 (3)	16.5 (3)	32.6 (5)	21.5 (4)	19.1 (3)
Social Liberal Party	3.3 (0)	3.1 (0)	2.8 (0)	8.5 (1)	9.1 (1)	6.4 (1)	4.3 (0)	6.5 (1)
Conservative People's Party	14.1 (2)	20.8 (4)	13.3 (2)	17.7 (3)	8.5 (1)	11.3 (1)	12.7 (1)	9.1 (1)
Centre Democrats	6.2 (1)	6.6 (1)	8.0 (2)	0.9 (0)	3.5 (0)	—	—	—
Justice Party of Denmark	3.4 (0)	—	—	—	—	—	—	—
Socialist People's Party	4.7 (1)	9.2 (2)	9.1 (2)	8.6 (1)	7.1 (1)	7.9 (1)	15.9 (2)	11.0 (1)
Liberal Alliance	—	—	—	—	—	—	0.6 (0)	2.9 (0)
June Movement	—	—	—	15.2 (2)	16.1 (3)	9.1 (1)	2.4 (0)	—
People's Movement against the EC/EU	21.0 (4)	20.8 (4)	18.9 (4)	10.3 (2)	7.3 (1)	5.2 (1)	7.2 (1)	8.1 (1)
Danish People's Party	—	—	—	—	5.8 (1)	6.8 (1)	15.3 (2)	26.6 (4)
Christian Democrats	1.8 (0)	2.7 (0)	1.1 (0)	2.0 (0)	1.3 (0)	—	—	—
Denmark's Liberal Party	14.5 (3)	12.5 (2)	16.6 (3)	19.0 (4)	23.4 (5)	19.4 (3)	20.2 (3)	16.7 (2)
Left Socialists	3.5 (0)	1.3 (0)	—	—	—	—	—	—
Progress Party	5.8 (1)	3.5 (0)	5.3 (0)	2.9 (0)	0.7 (0)	—	—	—
Turnout	47.8%	52.4%	46.2%	52.9%	50.5%	47.9%	59.5%	56.3%
EU Average	63.0%	61.0%	58.5%	56.8%	49.6%	45.7%	43.2%	42.5%

Source: Folketingets EU-Oplysning and Danmarks Statistik. See also Kelstrup, Martinsen, and Wind 2012; and Bischoff and Wind 2015.

Note: The numbers in parentheses indicate the number of seats obtained.

The success of the Danish People's Party should be seen in the context of the intense debate about free movement of workers and welfare tourism in the EU that has taken place during the past couple of years in Denmark (and in other EU countries). The party has also been able to present itself as the defender of the Danish people's (national) interests in the EU while portraying the pro-EU parties and the business establishment as elites living in a remote world with no understanding of ordinary people's worries. The effectiveness of the Danish People's Party's tactic became apparent when traditional pro-EU parties in the 2014 European election campaign were suddenly spending a lot of energy on anti-EU issues and started using slogans such as "We take care of Denmark in the EU."[34] With regard to the question of welfare tourism, the EU's principle of free movement of workers within the Union and its potential impact on the generous Danish welfare state have increasingly become hot topics in domestic politics and have received much attention in the media. Since the enlargement with the Central and Eastern European countries in 2004 (an enlargement that Denmark supported wholeheartedly) concerns have been raised about social dumping and uneven competition. Workers from the much poorer member states have entered the Danish labor market quite massively in recent years, mainly because their skills are highly praised by Danish employers. But stories have also surfaced about poor Eastern European workers traveling to the west mainly to gain the benefits of these countries' high wages and safety nets, including significant social benefits in the case of unemployment. The much-debated rulings by the ECJ, mentioned earlier, have fanned the fires for such concerns and given fuel to the EU skeptics' arguments about the EU as a threat to the tax-financed Danish welfare state.

The Danish Euro-skepticism is not as straightforward as the results of the EP elections and the content of the public debate make it seem. Certain ambivalences among the Danes toward the EU can easily be traced. Thus, at the same time the Danes are voting for EU-skeptic politicians to represent them in the European Parliament, they are among the most vigorous supporters of membership in the EU. They are also among those who have the most trust in the European institutions, and 74 percent say that the EU helps tackle global threats and challenges.[35] What seems to be of concern to the Danes is the deepening of the political integration with more decisions taken at the EU level, the possibility of any more ceding of sovereignty to supranational structures or institutions, and Danish membership of the European Monetary Union.

Future Trends and Prospects

The EU is very different today compared to when Denmark entered the EC in 1973. Not only has it enlarged and now includes twenty-eight member states, it is also a very different and more dispersed Union than what was originally foreseen. Not all countries can participate in all areas of cooperation, such as the common currency, and not all countries are willing to do so even though they are eligible. Denmark has significantly contributed to shaping a European Union of different speeds and areas of cooperation by voting "no" to the Treaty of Maastricht in 1992.[36]

Up until the financial crisis however, the EU was largely still characterized by some kind of companionship. In principle, one waited for the slowest ship in the convoy[37] before new integrationist steps were taken, and the slower ships were in most cases the UK, Denmark, or Sweden. As many analysts see it, however, this way of moving forward is no longer possible. The crisis has made most member states, in particular those belonging to the Eurozone, aware of the need for a much more integrated EU.

The fact that the EU stands at a crossroads at the moment also means that Denmark and other noneuro countries soon will be asked to openly announce where they see themselves in relation to the EU ten years from now. This announcement will be crucial for the influence Denmark will have on the future architecture of the EU. Does it see itself as a part of the core of the EU where the Eurozone countries and the other "pre-in" countries are placed (or strive to be); or is it on its way out altogether, perhaps accompanying the UK? A third option could be to place itself in one of the outer circles of European cooperation. However, such a "wait-and-see" position signals hesitation and doubt of what the country wants from its membership altogether. As has been suggested, this strategy served Denmark well earlier, but since the Eurozone countries are now convinced that the only way to consolidate the common currency is through more integration, a continued hesitant strategy could prove fatal. As described by the former highest legal adviser to the European Council Jean Clause Piris in his book, *The Future of Europe: Towards a Two-Speed EU* (2012), steps toward more union in the Eurozone will have implications for cooperation between not only the so-called in-countries but also for the rest of the EU. The problem is that the old European house will gradually transform. The integration of the Eurozone could, in other words, change the entire European edifice, which is why it is so important for Denmark and other non-Eurozone countries to place themselves wisely in the new European architecture in the coming years. It is obvious that the EU today is far from just being for collaboration on economic matters, and the latest developments with the Banking Union and the strengthening of the common currency club illustrate where things may be moving.

Conclusion

With the plans for a Banking Union and further integration of the Eurozone, there are clear signs that European integration is moving toward a more flexible and multidimensional Europe—in other words, an EU consisting of multiple rooms and multiple speeds. The countries outside the Eurozone, including Denmark, by all accounts will not be able to follow such radical, federal integration steps. If a core of countries moves toward more Europe and closer economic cooperation, the countries not currently in favor of more integration will be in danger of becoming even more marginalized than they are today. So far Denmark has sent mixed signals to the rest of the EU on this issue. On the one hand, it states that it wants to join the core at some point, but its opt-outs say otherwise. Furthermore, the skepticism toward the EU among the Danish citizenry is still a major factor, which makes it difficult for an otherwise EU-positive government. Without the willingness of the public, it is unlikely that the politicians will dare to try— again—to dissolve the Danish opt-outs and commit Denmark entirely to the European project. Four Danish members of the European Parliament put it very clearly: "The stage is set for the creation of a core-EU and a periphery-EU. Each country must, of course, decide for itself which part of the EU it wants to be a part of. But it has to be discussed and decided, also in Denmark."[38] The EU is currently in the process of separating the willing from those not willing to integrate further. If Denmark is not careful and aware of its signals, it may end up—in the eyes of others—hemmed in with the British and their exit strategy. The former Danish minister of foreign affairs, Uffe Elleman-Jensen, strongly warned against sending the wrong signals. As he put it at a conference in Copenhagen in 2012: "We would like to say to the British: We followed you into the EC, but we have no plans whatsoever to follow you out."[39]

Notes

I would like to thank my research coordinator, Majka Holm, for help with fact-checking this chapter. I would also like to recognize the help of two student assistants, Line Bachmann and Jens Bang Larsen.

1. About two-thirds of the Danish products are exported to EU member states.

2. Kelstrup (2014).

3. Besides the major political parties, many interest organizations, such as the Confederation of Danish Industries, and Danish agriculture had vividly advocated a "yes." See, for instance, Kelstrup (2014).

4. Denmark's opt-out on Union citizenship stipulated that Union citizenship could not replace national citizenship. This supremacy of national citizenship over Union citizenship was written into the Treaty of Amsterdam in 1998 and hence the Danish opt-out no longer relevant.

5. They can only be changed by referendum.

6. Kelstrup (2014).

7. Ibid.

8. Statsministeriet, Aftale om Danmark i Europol (Agreement on Denmark in Europol). Agreement made between the government (the Social Democrats and the Social Liberals) and the Liberal Party, the Conservative People's Party, and the Socialist People's

Party, December 10, 2014. Available (in Danish) at http://www.stm.dk/_p_14101.html (accessed December 17, 2014).

9. Svensson (2002), pp. 733–750. It has been suggested that the outcome of the referendum on membership of the Eurozone in 2000 had a bearing on the defeat of the Social Democratic government in the national elections in 2001.

10. Anders Wivel, "While the UK Considers a 'Brexit', Danish Eurosceptics Continue to Be Reluctantly Pragmatic over EU Membership," LSE EUROPP blog, December 3, 2014. Available at http://blogs.lse.ac.uk/europpblog/2014/12/03/while-the-uk-considers-a-brexit-danish-eurosceptics-continue-to-be-reluctantly-pragmatic-over-eu-membership/ (accessed December 8, 2014).

11. Wind (2010).

12. Falkner et al. (2005).

13. It is the ministries themselves who report to the European Commission when a directive has been implemented, and this is often only a reporting of whether an executive order has been written and signed in time. Hence, knowledge of the actual implementation of EU law—that is, how and when EU law is "felt" on the ground in the sense of actually being practiced in the field with concrete effects for citizens, companies, municipalities, is still limited and a research field under development.

14. European Commission, "Single Market Scorecard Reporting per Member State, Denmark, Reporting Period 2013–2014," 2014. Available at http://ec.europa.eu/single-market-scoreboard (accessed December 6, 2014).

15. Wind (2014).

16. Ibid.

17. Ibid.

18. For a thorough analysis of the agreement on reintroducing border control see Wind (2012).

19. Wind (2012).

20. Microsoft received a fine of €561 million. See European Commission, press release, "Antitrust: Commission Fines Microsoft for Non-compliance with Browser Choice Commitments," March 6, 2013. Available at http:// http://europa.eu/rapid/press-release_IP-13-196_en.htm.

21. Wind (2009).

22. The distinction between the two types of democracy draws on the distinction made by Dworkin (1996).

23. Information about the concrete cases can be found at Folketingets EU-oplysning. Information about eligibility to family allowances: http://www.ft.dk/samling/20131/almdel/sau/spm/25/svar/1088111/1325364.pdf. Information about the European Court of Justice ruling about eligibility to receive educational grant from the Danish State, "SU-Case"/C-46/12 LN: http://www.eu-oplysningen.dk/upload/application/pdf/c366de7d/12E43.pdf. Information about the Metock Case, C-127/08: http://www.eu-oplysningen.dk/dokumenter/efdomstolen/domme/anlaeggelse/2008/C127_08/.

24. Nedergaard (2014).

25. An overview of the member states' contributions to the EU budget in the period 2000–2013 is available at http://www.eu-oplysningen.dk/fakta/tal/nettosaldo/. An interactive map illustrating the contributions by each member state since 2000 can be found at http://folketinget.vertic.com/eudata/nettobidrag (accessed December 17, 2014).

26. Petersen and Böhmer (2014).

27. Denmark joined the Exchange Rate Mechanism II along with the other non-Eurozone members in 1999 when the Eurozone countries entered the third phase of the EMU.

28. Pedersen (2014).

29. Adler-Nissen (2014).

30. Leaflet about the European Affairs Committee of the Danish Parliament published by Folketingets EU-oplysning. Available at http://www.euoplysningen.dk/upload /application/pdf/77305369/euo_europaudvalg_jan2012_uk_web.pdf%3Fdownload%3D1 (accessed December 2014).

31. Kasper Kaasgaard, "Tænketank: Europaudvalgets mandat er et gummistempel" (Think Tank: The European Affairs Committees Mandate Is a Rubber Stamp), Altinget, November 11, 2014. Available at http://www.altinget.dk/eu/artikel/taenketank -europaudvalgets-mandat-er-et-gummistempel (accessed December 2014).

32. Udenrigsministeriet, "Europa I Arbejde: Resultaterne Af Det Danske Formandskab for Rådet I Det Første Halvår af 2012" (Europe at Work: Results of the Danish Presidency of the Council in the First Half of 2012). Available at http://eu2012.dk /da/NewsList/Juni/Uge-26/~/media/5E9581B7697745B6A035975ADCB616AF.pdf (accessed December 2014).

33. All members of the Eurozone and all the non-Eurozone members except for the Czech Republic and the UK signed the Fiscal Compact.

34. This was the slogan in the 2014 electoral campaign of the candidates from the Conservative Party, which traditionally has been among the pro-EU parties.

35. Standard Eurobarometer 81, Public Opinion in the EU, Spring 2014. Available at http://ec.europa.eu/public_opinion/archives/eb/eb81/eb81_publ_en.pdf (accessed December 15, 2014).

36. For this argument see the study by K. Lamers and W. Schaüble as mentioned in Wind (2003).

37. This phrase was first used by the former British Premier John Major in a speech in Leiden in 1994.

38. *Berlingske Tidende*, October 23, 2012.

39. Conference on the twentieth anniversary of the adoption of the Danish opt-in, Copenhagen University, organized by the Centre for European Policy (CEP), University of Surrey, and the Danish newspaper *Politiken*.

10

Greece:
Austerity and EU Influence

Nikolaos Zahariadis

SOON AFTER THE SACKING OF TROY, ODYSSEUS, THE HERO OF Homer's *Odyssey*, reaches the island where Calypso lived. Having lost his ship and crew, exhausted and distraught, Odysseus refuses her hospitality but eventually relents and lives with her for seven years. However, he always longs for his home in Ithaca. Calypso refuses to let him go. The issue is resolved when Athena intervenes and asks Zeus to order his release. What would have happened if Athena had not intervened? What if Odysseus accepted Calypso's generosity and stayed, partly content with his fortune but always secretly scheming to return home? What if Calypso's love ran its course and she realized Odysseus was not the man she thought he was? This chapter considers the possibility of this alternative ending to the story. For their own reasons, Calypso (the European Union) and Odysseus (Greece) have decided to unite their fortunes. But at some point Calypso finds out Odysseus lied to her. This is the moment of truth and Calypso's subsequent wrath.

In October 2009, George Papandreou, the newly elected Greek Socialist prime minister, announced to stunned voters that he had made a mistake. Having to go back partially on his campaign promise that "money is available," he instructed the finance minister, George Papakonstantinou, to identify the budget shortfall and come up with recommendations about how to address it. In the same breath, Papandreou promised extra subsidies for low-income families and retirees, no rise in the prices charged by public utilities, increases above the rate of inflation in wages, and extra funding for public investment to rise to 5 percent of gross domestic product (GDP). What he did not say was how all this would be accomplished.[1] In the meantime, "if a crisis emerges in one country, there is a solution. . . . Don't fear for this moment, we are equipped politically, intellectually and economically to face this crisis scenario," declared Commissioner Joaquín Almunia in March 2009, responding to talk of an impending crisis in the Eurozone.[2] Both policymakers were obviously wrong. Why did it happen, and how has Greece been affected by the EU's response?

This chapter traces the evolution of the Greek sovereign debt crisis. Placing the issue within the framework of common pool resources (CPRs), it examines how and why it began and charts the consequences since the first and second Greek bailout packages were signed.[3] I make three arguments: The medicine may be more toxic than the illness; problems related to the lack of administrative capacity and widespread corruption may demonstrate that Greece has been asked to do too much, too soon; the crisis is unlikely to be resolved within the current timeframe (Bailout I was supposed to end in 2013; Bailout II is expected to end in 2015).

Problems Involve an Interaction of National and Supranational Failure

The issue is very important. Because the EU monetary system (Eurozone) is tightly coupled, there is a high risk of contagion and cascading damage in an environment of global crisis and toxic assets. The solvency risk maintained by a very small part of the whole Eurozone economy (Greece accounts for only 2 percent of the total EU output) can potentially spread to the rest quickly. When one country's rating is downgraded, it has a significant negative effect on the sovereign bond spreads of other countries with relatively weak fundamentals. Evidence of strong spillover effects runs asymmetrically both ways: a Greek downgrade affected Ireland, Portugal, Italy, and others, much more than their downgrade affected Greece.[4] For this reason, response must be timely. Problems cannot be isolated and corrected. The EU at large must deal them with systemically; the Greek problem is a European problem.

First is a brief overview of how widespread corruption and internal politics added to institutional and leadership flaws at the EU level leading to the crisis. The implementation of the first and second bailout packages is then briefly sketched to isolate impediments and obstacles. Analysis of the consequences of austerity follows to give a better sense of political dynamics and social effects. Finally, the chapter offers concluding thoughts on Greek lessons for the future prospects of European integration.

The Impending Crisis

Although international institutions viewed with alarm Greece's deteriorating public finances, they did little in public to highlight the severity of, let alone prevent, the coming storm. The rationale was not to instill panic and precipitate the very crisis they were warning about. The moral hazard was obvious.

Coming down hard on the country would bring about the very crisis that is being avoided. Not saying anything would be encouraging the same profligate behavior. But in the end, both the European Commission and the International Monetary Fund (IMF) spoke out. There was a very real concern that damage caused in Greece might cascade to other Eurozone members. In March 2009, the European Commission censured Greece for excessive deficit in 2007, but it still spoke in glowing terms about the high levels of past economic growth. Later that year, the IMF issued a warning in its 2009 country report and the early warning exercise, but its recommendations were ignored. The country was heading toward national elections in a few months. The next government would settle the issue. Then conservative prime minister Kostas Karamanlis spoke about the need for reforms, but he did not make a strong case for it during the campaign, as if he feared the consequences. A confident Papandreou dismissed talk of an impending economic crunch and proceeded to promise populist raises in wages and retirement benefits.

To understand the dynamics of the financial crisis, developments are framed within problems arising from collective action and CPRs.[5] CPRs are natural or manmade resources sharing two attributes: the difficulty of excluding individuals from benefiting from these resources and rivalry, which means that benefits consumed by one individual are subtracted from those available to others. Public works, such as transport or environmental projects, and public services, such as health, education, and pensions, raise collective action problems that are present in CPR environments. In addition, risk sharing within the Economic and Monetary Union (EMU) system gives rise to similar issues. The EMU institutionalizes collective responsibility and provides incentives that decrease the likelihood of national fiscal accountability precisely because risk is spread over several countries. Institutional efforts to recalibrate the balance, risk undermining collective solidarity. The framework is, therefore, useful in identifying institutional shortcomings that have led to the sovereign debt crisis.[6]

CPRs raise uncomfortable dilemmas for consumers and providers: free riding, which leads to problems of underinvestment and overconsumption, and rent seeking, which leads to lack of transparency and corruption. Because it is difficult or costly to exclude users, consumers of CPRs tend to overconsume. Health facilities, for example, may be inundated with patients seeking affordable care. The EMU followed similar logic. Countries with relatively weaker finances suddenly saw their creditworthiness go up when they entered the EMU because risk was now shared with other countries with stronger finances. That led to a spending spree. Both consumers and providers of CPRs have incentives to abuse the public purse and promote lack of transparency to hide the true cost of transactions.

To overcome the problems of mismanagement, corruption, and overconsumption, Ostrom argues there must be, among other things, transparent monitoring, consistent enforcement of graduated sanctions, and effective leadership in managing the system.[7] Greece and the EU failed in all three areas. Mismanagement and corruption appeared endemic to the Greek system. In a recent report, the European Commission cites a Eurobarometer survey on perceptions of corruption that places Greece at the very top among member states on degree of corruption (99 percent as opposed to an EU average of 76 percent).[8] Sixty-three percent of those surveyed believe it affects their daily lives (as opposed to an EU average of 26 percent). The same report cites another conclusion reached by the Council of Europe in 2010, which finds significant legal, judicial, and institutional impediments in fighting Greek corruption effectively. Three years (August 2013) after those recommendations were published, only one of them was implemented satisfactorily.

Papandreou admitted, "We developed a lot of corruption at the highest levels and we did not take the structural measures to change our economy, to move our economy, to make it more competitive."[9] Much like Mikhail Gorbachev, the last Soviet leader, he tried to steer anger at the previous government so his reforms would gather momentum. Like Gorbachev, he overestimated his skills and underestimated the magnitude of the task. He haplessly tried to reassure investors by announcing a string of austerity measures lowering wages and reducing benefits. But the numbers told a different story: he had lost control of the economy.

The two main Stability and Growth Pact (SGP) indicators, budget deficit and public debt, skyrocketed. First, deficit data needed to be revised by the government's own admission of flawed reporting (see Figure 10.1). Although it was a time-honored Greek tactic to blame the previous government so as to "buy" voter goodwill for impending austerity, voter discontent and allied disaffection were sharp and unrelenting. The Greek Finance Ministry initially revised the 2009 figures from 6 percent (already in breach of SGP rules to a staggering 12.5 percent, later revised to a final 15.6 percent) of GDP. Moreover, on sectoral and individual firm levels, things looked really bad. In the case of Hellenic Railways, where there is talk of a future sale, losses outpaced revenues by eight to one in 2009. The company had a debt of €10 billion backed by taxpayers, requiring annual interest payments of €500 million.[10] Together with public hospitals, the fifty-two state-run companies (DEKO) lost €18.3 billion in 2009 (a figure not included in official deficit data), an increase of 72.6 percent from 2008.[11] Interestingly, in September 2011, members of Elstat, the general accounting office, accused its director and government officials of artificially inflating the budget deficit in 2009 (which Eurostat approved) to make it look bigger than it otherwise would have been for political gain![12]

After staying at just over 100 percent of GDP throughout the early 2000s, public debt began to rise in 2006. It accelerated by over 6 percent in

Figure 10.1 Government Budget Deficit in Selected Eurozone Countries, 2001–2013

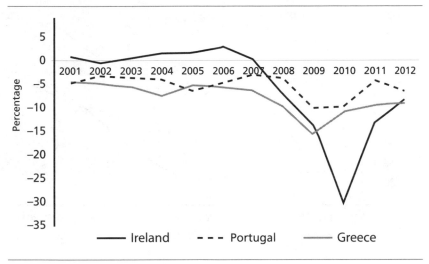

Source: Eurostat

2006 to reach an estimated level of 157 percent in 2012. Part of the reason for the acceleration since 2009 is the gargantuan amount borrowed as a result of the bailout packages. The same is true for other bailed out countries (see Figure 10.2). The problem with Greece was not that it was the worst in all indicators; the Irish debt, for example, has accelerated fourfold since 2001 while the Greek debt went up by only 50 percent! The problem was that it had both a high deficit and a high public debt.

But there was more. Excessive borrowing in the 2000s took the pernicious form of external borrowing by the mostly (to that point) low-indebted private sector. According to data from the Bank of International Settlements, consolidated foreign claims of banks on Greek debt reached $161 billion by December 2010.[13] About half of it was owed to banks in France and Germany, although much of the amount owed to the French was in the form of assets (Greek banks were bought and since sold) while amounts owed to German banks consisted largely of securities.[14] International debt securities nearly doubled from $192.8 billion in December 2008 to $358.9 billion in March 2011.[15] The reason was simple. The Greek government needed to raise about €55 billion in 2010 to refinance existing debt and keep paying salaries and pensions; most of this amount was front-loaded into the first six months. Furthermore, household indebtedness increased sevenfold from roughly 10 percent of GDP in 1995 to almost 70 percent in 2010.[16] Simply put, Greeks borrowed heavily, mainly from foreign sources, to finance largely private consumption.

Figure 10.2 Public Debt in Selected Eurozone Countries, 2001–2012

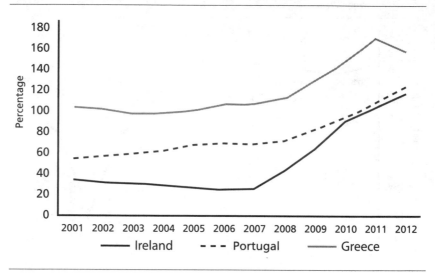

Source: Eurostat

There was one more element. The global economic crisis that had befallen the United States spread like wildfire to the rest of the developed world. It acted as a policy window, creating the requisite environment within which the Greek crisis would unfold.[17] First, because of the US meltdown, investors put their money in safer investments, mostly in Europe. As a result, the value of the euro rose relative to the US dollar, causing some to speculate the time had come for it to eclipse the dollar as the world's premier reserve currency. In such an environment, it was natural for currency speculators to wonder whether that was really the case. Second, Dubai World, the conglomerate owned by the government of the Gulf emirate, asked creditors in November 2009 for a six-month debt moratorium, rattling financial markets and leading to sharp increases in risk aversion.[18] The fact that the Greek fundamentals took a turn for the worse jolted the system, but it would likely have not been the fatal blow it turned out to be in the absence of the broader global economic crisis. Investors doubted Greece's ability to manage its own economic affairs and demanded a higher rate of return. Greece could not afford to refinance its debt obligations with sharply increasing interest yields (in April 2010, rates on ten-year Greek bonds shot up to over 1,000 basis points above the German benchmark; Figure 10.3) and following successive credit downgrades by rating agencies to essentially junk status, the country had to activate the bailout package it had since negotiated with its creditors and the IMF.

Figure 10.3 Greek Government 10-Year Bond Yields, 2009–2013

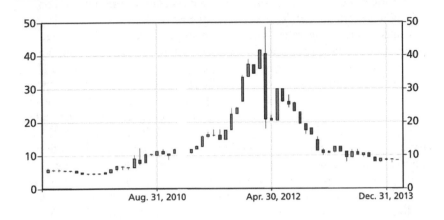

Source: Tradingeconomics.com

Implementing the Two Bailout Packages

In May 2010, the Greek government activated a rescue package, amounting to €80 billion from bilateral EU sources and €30 billion from the IMF, monitored and disbursed quarterly on the basis of progress on indicators assessed by the IMF, the European Central Bank (ECB), and the European Commission (the so-called troika). The point was to temporarily help Greece generate primary surplus to meet obligations to external creditors at a reasonable interest rate. In return, Greece agreed to a series of painful measures designed to reduce the public sector, cut salaries and pensions, raise the retirement age, open "closed" professions (such as lawyers, engineers, pharmacists, and others), and increase revenues through value-added tax (VAT) (up to 24 percent) hikes on all goods and services and with better collection processes. Overall, the measures amounted to 14 percent of GDP over three years.[19]

Despite some initial success, the economy began to sputter by February 2011. Two reasons mainly contributed to this result. First, the economic downturn turned out to be far steeper than anticipated.[20] Part of the reason had to do with the global economic environment and more significantly Greece's main trading partners. One of the main aims of the bailout package was to make Greek products more competitive. As the IMF's lesson-drawing exercise revealed, "Greece was to stay in the euro area and an estimated 20–30% competitiveness gap would be addressed through wage adjustment and productivity gains."[21] This is why wage cuts were implemented. In the absence of national currency devaluation, countries in the EMU have labor costs as the only lever to recalibrate their competitiveness.[22]

There are two problems with this rationale. First, labor costs are linked to exchange rates, which may not be in equilibrium at the time of conversion. When Portugal and Greece entered the EMU, they adopted widely undervalued conversion rates while Germany accepted an overvalued exchange rate.[23] The expectation, therefore, would be that once the euro is introduced among them, costs would appreciate in the former two and depreciate in the latter, which is what data show. Second, there was the assumption that Greece would export and partners would buy. But if partners are themselves in a recession or are unwilling to boost domestic demand (as some policymakers throughout Europe, the United States, and the IMF have advised), even if Greece could produce more efficiently, it could not have generated income because few were willing (or able) to purchase Greek products. Moreover, wage cuts stifled domestic demand without any clear plan on how to make the economy grow. In the case of bailout packages, the logic of austerity assumes there is inefficient allocation of resources. But if resources are cut when both the public and the private sectors are heavily indebted, there is no domestic actor left to "carry the torch."

Second, Greek leaders failed to take ownership of the political program despite rhetoric to the contrary. Reforms stalled because of strong political opposition from affected groups and the governing socialists. For example, having assessed Greek progress, troika representatives noted significant delays, unwillingness, and indifference on the part of ministers to implement measures. Although they noted complications from the steep recession, they insisted that it was a matter of coordination and political will. In one case, they encountered a minister who, responding to their complaints about delays, retorted: "The Memorandum is only indicative."[24] In another instance, a prominent member of the cabinet admitted he had not read the bailout package because it was rushed (Parliament was given only three days to debate and pass it) and he had no time to do it.[25] Although there was a kernel of truth in the bailout being rushed, the excuse appeared to fuel suspicion that the political elite were unwilling to do the necessary. Evangelos Venizelos, then finance minister and now socialist leader, admitted that the problems of Greece were not just economic, they were mainly political.

The ability to buffer Greece and prevent cascading damage from reaching other member states seemed to complicate Greece's rescue effort. The more the country borrowed, the less it was able to accomplish.[26] Despite a new bailout package with some debt relief in July 2011 (20 percent of privately held debt would be written off) and more strings attached, Greeks seemed unable to meet their targets.

Creditors were divided. Germany and Holland pressed for more losses to be imposed on private debtholders while France and the ECB feared that would spark renewed sales of shares in banks holding (not just Greek) bonds of peripheral countries.[27] Germany's Free Democrats, the government's junior partners, publicly speculated that Greece should be expelled from the Eurozone. Charles Dallara, head of the Institute of International Finance, a global consortium of banks and investment houses, openly worried about the lack of EU leadership: the euro's successes "are being masked and undermined by parochialism and nationalism."[28] President José Manuel Barroso called for a new Eurobond, an option strongly opposed by Germany. The cacophony and hesitation among Europe's political leaders made matters worse.

The main reason for this division was national leadership and EU institutional failure. Creditor decisions were driven largely by national electoral calendars and voter discontent, especially in Germany, where Chancellor Angela Merkel faced tough state elections, in every one of which her party experienced losses, and a skeptical public wondering why it should pay for Greek profligacy. She invoked Article 125, which states that there is no obligation to bail out EU member states. However, she failed to adequately take into account that if the eventual aim was to save Greece (and it turns out that it was), uncertainty caused by indifference or political delay would undermine confidence in the euro and increase the final bailout amount.[29] Moreover, she did not explain that the rescue package also conveniently saved German, French, and other creditors who stood to lose billions from Greek insolvency. In fact, bailout disbursements go into a fund not managed by the Greek government, which ensures obligations to external creditors are met first before any money is left over for the country. In an honest but muted effort, Peter Böfinger, an economic adviser to the German government, has admitted that billions in Eurozone bailouts are going primarily to German banks: "It is not primarily about the problem countries, but our own banks, which are heavily involved with loans there."[30]

To be fair, creditors had good reason to worry. On the one hand, SGP rules were reformed in 2005 to accommodate national political circumstances and needs.[31] Leaders had good reason to fear them, for they proved to be terribly inconsistent in applying sanctions! They were quick to sanction (but not fine) Portugal in 2002, but not France or Germany in 2003. The lack of consistently applied sanctions and subsequent reinterpretation of the rules led to acrimony and confusion. Even European Commission president Romano Prodi called them "stupid" in 2002, while Pascal Lamy, then trade commissioner, viewed them as "crude and medieval."[32] On the other hand, Greeks also gave them fodder. Greece made a mockery of transparency by reporting false data. Moreover, Greek leaders worked with a dysfunctional and complex budget system. Kevin Featherstone reports that in 2009 "the government budget was based on some 14,000 separate 'budget lines' where each 'line' represents grouped items of expenditure within part of the public administration."[33] Policymakers simply had no idea where the money went. They didn't even know how many people were employed in the public sector. That is why a special census was set up in July 2010. According to the latest data, the number of regular full-time employees in November 2013 stood at 603,319, down from 667,374 in December 2010.[34]

The tax code has traditionally contained ambiguous language and numerous exemptions and deductions, narrowing the tax base, increasing the likelihood of political favoritism, and giving rise to corruption and discontent. Without appropriate reforms, higher taxation increases tax evasion because of disproportionate effects on different population groups. For example, broadening VAT revenues under certain conditions would fall disproportionately on the poor because they pay more for food or fuel than do rich households. Unless they are compensated in some way through exemptions and thresholds, there will be serious equity problems. Using the UK example, John Hills notes: "But in the context of fiscal consolidation, the aim is revenue-raising, so by definition what would be available for compensation would be much more limited, leaving a larger proportion of low-income households exposed to losses."[35] Despite repeated claims to sensitivity to vulnerable groups, this is indeed what many in Greece claim has happened.

Tax evasion during periods of fiscal consolidation may go up for two reasons.[36] First, producers evade taxes to continue financing their operations. Second, consumers simply seek to maintain the same lifestyle in light of nominally lower disposable income. Both may estimate that the drawback of penalties does not outweigh the benefit of avoiding bankruptcy, especially when administrative capacity is lacking. The vicious circle of lower revenues leading to less economic activity and more austerity has not gone unnoticed. But the obligation to meet short-term targets has increased tax evasion, fueling public discontent and increasing the political cost of reform.

As a result, a second bailout package was (re)negotiated in October 2011. Papandreou realized he would have to take additional and even harsher austerity measures to satisfy creditors. So he proposed a referendum to seek a fresh mandate and legitimize the results. However, the French president and German chancellor humiliated the Greek prime minister, summoning him to the G-20 meeting in Cannes and publicly castigating him about not being previously consulted. They also told him when to hold the referendum, if he insisted, and what it should state. Although this was done in the name of solidarity, it is hard to imagine why there is surprise in not taking political ownership of the program. Commissioner Olli Rehn perceptively admits, "We need leadership. . . . [But] without democratic legitimacy, all the best intentions are doomed to fail."[37] But legitimacy stems from voter involvement, which appears in the Greek (and other bailout cases) not to have been sought.

In the meantime, labor discontent led to the resignation of Papandreou and the formation of a transitional government led by a technocrat, Lucas Papademos, whose job was to negotiate the second bailout package. It was agreed in February and ratified in March 2012. It envisioned broadly similar measures as the first package with modified targets, different assumptions (for example, a deeper recession), and a backload of fiscal measures to tackle the deflationary impact of 2012. The aim was still "to strengthen the core social safety net to protect the most vulnerable" amid cuts in social transfers and to restore financial stability through the capitalization of banks and a restructuring of government debt.[38] The gargantuan amount of €130 billion would again be provided on exceptional basis outside the European Stability Mechanism, setting aside €30 billion just to restore banks to financial health.

It is interesting to elaborate on the 53.5 percent "haircut" on privately held debt for two reasons. First, it was the largest in world history. Second, it differentiated between senior and junior holders, with juniors being private owners of Greece's government debt and seniors being sovereign owners. Essentially, it imposed losses on banks and other owners without many of them being represented at the table. Negotiations were conducted with a group of large commercial banks. The haircut had significant repercussions. On the one hand, it satisfied (not only) German demands that the private sector share the cost of the bailout. On the other hand, because small individual investors had no say, the haircut had two devastating consequences. It evaporated the savings of private and non–central government agencies in Greece, such as municipal governments and universities, who by law were required to invest in sovereign bonds. They had to take a haircut but were not included in the recapitalization package. In addition, Cypriot banks took a hit, having invested heavily in Greek government bonds. That led to the subsequent demise of Cypriot banks and the EU rescue in March 2013.[39]

The second package has been more successfully implemented, partly because it drew on the experience of the first and partly because the Commission set up the Special Task Force for Greece.[40] It is a group that includes sixty individuals from different EU countries and the Commission and provides technical advice to the Greek government and assists in coordinating the implementation of specific reforms. Assistance is grouped in twelve policy domains, ranging from tax collection and migration to transport and employment schemes. Different countries and institutions provide advice on different reforms, such as tax collection and public health advice by German authorities, administrative reform by French agencies, tax audits of large taxpayers by Spanish experts, health advice by the World Health Organization, and employment service schemes by experts from Britain and Sweden. In total, 431 missions have been supported from September 2011 to May 2014, involving projects totaling 2,392 expert days.

The CPR logic predicts negative consequences for managing common pool resources in the absence of transparent monitoring of consumption, lack of enforced sanctions, and leadership failure. The Greek case makes clear all three factors contributed and exacerbated the sovereign debt crisis.

Social and Political Consequences

The results of five years since the onset of the sovereign debt crisis are not encouraging despite some progress. Greece was able to show a primary budget surplus in 2013 of €1 billion (in line with targets but above the expected amount).[41] Much-needed reforms are taking (or have taken) place in administration, energy, and closed professions, such as trucking, pharmacists, and taxis. After many years of false starts, the sale of assets in ports and portions of public utilities are mostly on track. The public sector's wage bill is shrinking as employees have taken pay cuts to the tune of at least 25 percent, retired, or been laid off. But two areas still need serious attention.

First, the social cost to Greece has been enormous. The most important and immediate problem is not the budget deficit but unemployment. Figure 10.4 tracks unemployment in Greece and Germany (as a benchmark) since 2004. What is interesting is that up to 2008, Greece had similar and at times lower unemployment. Since the crisis began, German unemployment has shrunk to the second lowest in the EU, while Greek unemployment has skyrocketed to the highest. Although Greek jobs have not migrated to Germany, it is difficult for Greek voters not to perceive the results in a quasi-zero-sum manner: the crisis has produced clear winners and losers. The distance in job prospects between northern and southern Europe has widened significantly.

Figure 10.4 Unemployment in Greece and Germany, 2004–2013

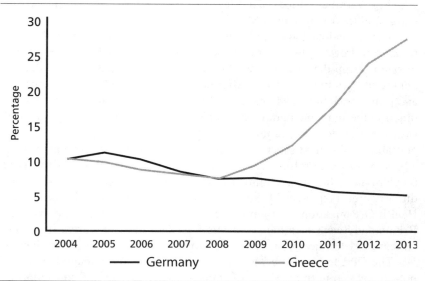

Source: Eurostat

Note: 2013 figures for Greece refer to December 2013

Moreover, for all the talk of protecting the most vulnerable, it is difficult to imagine how that can be accomplished. Rates of unemployed youth (defined as less than twenty-five years old) have increased dramatically in Greece from 33 percent in 2010 to 52.3 percent in 2014.[42]

Unemployment also has a strong link to suicide and mental illness (depression). Using official Elstat figures, the Greek nongovernmental organization dealing with suicides, Klimaka, reports an increase in Greek suicides from 328 in 2007 to 477 in 2011. It is an increase of 43 percent, turning Greece into a world champion in suicide rate growth![43] Other studies report a strong correlation between economic hardship and spikes in clinical depression and mental disorders in the country.[44] According to one study by the Institute for Mental Health Research at the University of Athens, the number of Greeks suffering from clinical depression was over 12 percent in 2013, a rise of almost 400 percent from 3.3 percent in 2008.[45] The authors point to the need for urgent thoughtful and targeted employment measures to partially reverse this trend.

Second, Greek economic recession is approaching Depression-era levels. Figure 10.5 shows the rate of constant economic growth. Despite gargantuan bailout money and significantly higher rates of indebtedness (see Figure 10.2) Greece has entered its sixth year of recession, having lost almost 26 percent in real economic output since the recession began in 2008! By comparison and according to Bureau of Economic Analysis data, the US economy

Figure 10.5 Real Economic Growth in Greece and Germany, 2004–2014

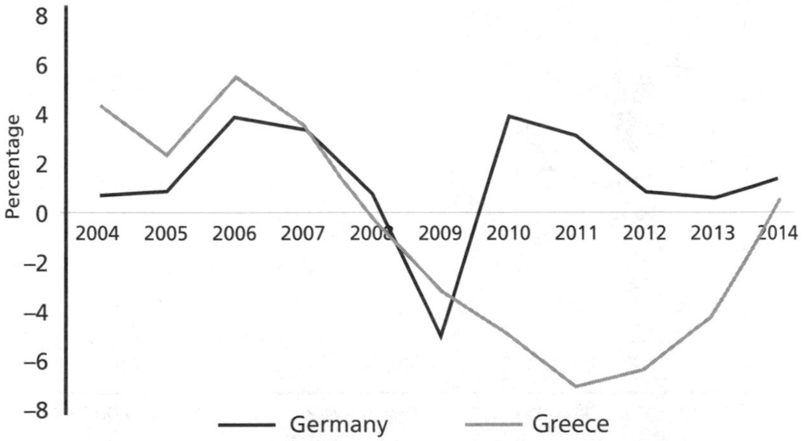

Source: IMF, World Economic Outlook (April 2013)

Note: Figures for 2013 and 2014 are estimates

lost 27.9 percent real GDP from 1929 to 1932.[46] The first year of Greek growth is projected to be 2015 with an anemic 0.6 percent if all assumptions hold. Banks have stopped making new loans, despite recapitalization, because nearly 30 percent of their loans are at or near default.[47] Using Germany as a benchmark, Greece was doing slightly better until both countries dipped into a recession in 2008. However, since the crisis hit they have followed opposite trajectories. Still, the country is left with no credible economic growth plan other than what is included in the second bailout package, which refers mostly to gains from liberalization measures.

Equally interesting are the political consequences. Figure 10.6 tracks estimates of electoral influence (defined as likelihood to vote for a political party) of four major parties. The trajectories of the parties are fascinating. The governing socialist electoral appeal began to decline after the government signed the first bailout package in 2010. What is interesting is that other parties did not necessarily pick up voter discontent. Voters simply punished the government for austerity measures. The real changes came between April 2011 (when Greece began to negotiate revised targets and a new bailout package) and January 2012 (right before the new bailout package was signed). The socialist PASOK (Panhellenic Socialist Movement) "bled" votes as citizens realized more and harsher measures were in the works. Many of those voters went to the Radical Left (Syriza), which promised to reverse the measures (most notably layoffs in the public sector) and renegotiate a "fairer"

Figure 10.6 Estimate of Electoral Strength of Four Major Greek parties, 2010–2014

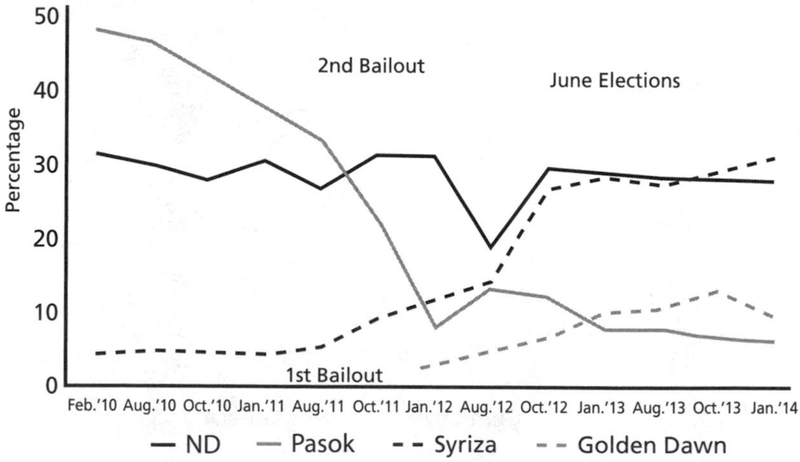

Source: Publicissue.gr

package with creditors. Votes also leaked from the center-right New Democracy (ND) to Golden Dawn, an extreme right party whose nationalist and xenophobic platform appealed to an increasing group of scared voters.

National elections in May and June 2012 fed speculation of the so-called grexit (the prospect of Greek exit from the Eurozone). The coalition government between ND, the Democratic Left (which later withdrew), and PASOK put an end to such speculation. However, national elections raised two very important points. First, they elevated the Radical Left from obscurity to the position of main opposition party. Streams of disaffected PASOK voters flocked to Syriza, whose platform is reminiscent of the early populist days of Andreas Papandreou. The trend accelerated in the 2014 elections to the European Parliament, when Syriza finished first with 26.5 percent of the national vote and five more seats relative to ND's 22.7 percent and three fewer seats.

The crisis reform dilemma is obvious.[48] When national leaders face a public catastrophe, they are pushed and pulled in two opposite directions. They are asked to respond to the crisis, which essentially calls for returning to the familiar old days and to reform the country not to make the same mistakes that precipitated the crisis in the first place. Evidence from Greece shows that leaders will choose the path of least resistance to placate voters and mostly undermine the structural reforms they are "asked" to implement.

Second, the appearance and strong polling of the extreme right is a troubling sign. Its steadily rising electoral appeal in hard times is quite logical. With jobs disappearing and grim economic prospects for recovery, voter wrath turns on those with no voice, mostly illegal migrants and the troika, who have "imposed" this fate on people. What is interesting is not that ND has lost appeal due to expected consequences from governance decisions (their appeal, Figure 10.6 shows, has remained surprisingly flat), it is the beginning of political polarization of society. Support for the main center-left party has collapsed. PASOK lost 20.6 percent and six seats since the last European elections in 2009. The Radical Left has a platform of nebulous social justice, economic growth, and jobs for all that has begun to resonate more strongly among disillusioned voters. More ominously, the extreme right continues to appeal to increasing numbers of disaffected voters. In 2014, it gained three seats and 9 percent of the vote (in the 2009 European election it got 0.5 percent) despite charges of criminal activity (extortion, blackmail, and murder) and a leadership crackdown since September 2013.[49]

New Developments in Relations Between Greece and the EU

By late spring 2014, the governing (New Democracy–PASOK) coalition teetered on the brink of collapse. Despite registering a primary budget surplus (a necessary bailout target), unemployment remained stubbornly high at 26 percent while the economy was still in recession. In this context, two elections took place in May 2014. In local elections, the governing parties performed reasonably well, keeping many mayoral positions but losing the important governorship of the Attica region to the Radical Left. While local issues featured prominently in local elections, elections to the European Parliament were fought along national lines, more specifically perceived on the government- (and EU-) imposed austerity and heavy taxation. Normally, the EP elections are considered a bellweather of support for national government policies, but they were strongly contested this time and won by the Radical Left, which increased its share of the vote by 21.9 percent since 2009, and finished first with 26.6 percent, gaining five more seats (six seats in total). Alexis Tsipras, Syriza's leader, declared victory, proclaiming the outcome robbed the government of "political and moral legitimacy" if it continued with austerity policies.[50] In response, the conservative prime minister, Antonis Samaras, reshuffled the cabinet in a vain attempt to inject new dynamism and, more important, bring economic results. Following an unsuccessful attempt to borrow from international investors, the country's politicians were unable to elect someone to the post of president of the Hellenic Republic, leading to the dissolution of Parliament (as prescribed by the constitution) and national elections in January 2015. The elections brought a new left-right coalition government composed of Syriza and the right-wing party of Independent Greeks.

Today, the country finds itself in political chaos. Society is heavily polarized between those demanding an end to austerity now and those who view painful reforms as the necessary precondition for ending austerity. Unable to reform and bereft of realistic plans to end the crisis, politicians are caught in a vicious circle of despair: austerity generates opposition, which slows down reform, the lack of which leads to suboptimal outcomes and more austerity. The resulting uncertainty has dampened voter expectations, destroyed the social fabric by undermining trust in political institutions, increased indebtedness (despite €240 billion in bailout aid and some debt forgiveness, Greece's debt hovered at 175 percent of GDP in 2014, some 62 percent higher than in 2009), and given rise to populists promising an exit from the Eurozone (and possibly the EU) as panacea.

Moreover, negotiations with creditors have reached a bitter stalemate. Greeks complain of unreasonable demands, while some analysts believe creditors no longer "trust the Greeks to keep their word, nor the European Commission to hold them to it."[51] In the meantime, an email from the Bank of Greece estimates, among others, that during the first 100 days of the new leftist government €30–35 billion has been taken out of banks, €3 billion in structural funds has been frozen due to the public sector's inability to co-finance projects, and another €3 billion in payments to the private sector has been delayed by the government. These losses must be added to the lack of economic activity because of uncertainty over negotiations with creditors, leading to an explosive mix of social and economic calamity. In addition, the impending agreement is likely to include significant new taxes and fees to shore up public revenues as the government seeks to balance them against losses from declining economic activity and voter demands for more public sector jobs and benefits. To make matters worse, the government led by Syriza appears eager to reach an agreement but faces an open revolt by some extremist party members, increasing political uncertainty and suspicion of lackluster implementation no matter what the new agreement may include. No one in Greece seems to know how to overcome this political morass or to get the economy back on its feet.The depth of the crisis, and more important, its duration, unfortunately demonstrate the dubious quality of Greek political leadership and the paucity of Greek and EU ideas about how to end it.

Greece in the Age of Austerity

This chapter analyzed the Greek sovereign debt crisis and the implementation of the subsequent bailout packages. It was shown the crisis was a combination of Greek and EU leadership and institutional failures. The findings have implications for policy theory and the future of European integration.

Five years after the first bailout package, results are not encouraging. True, some progress has been made in terms of fiscal consolidation and administrative reforms. However, job prospects remain bleak while the capacity to raise needed additional revenues is nonexistent. According to Parliament's Budget Office, the current model of tax collection cannot be maintained due to social exhaustion, putting in doubt the sustainability of generating budget surpluses in the coming years.[52] An even more troubling prospect is the exodus of many well-educated and skilled Greeks in search of job prospects elsewhere, mostly in northern European countries and Australia. The flight of young scientists may undermine efforts to restructure the economy. Data show that 90 percent of new Greek companies created in 2012 were in low value-added sectors, such as restaurants, bars, and clothing retail stores.[53] At the same time, many of the scientists may not return once Greek economic conditions improve, weakening the prospects of sustainable long-term prosperity.

Moreover, responding to flaws exposed by the sovereign debt crisis, there has been greater centralization of rules (including stronger and deeper imposition of bailout conditions over time) accomplished by mostly intergovernmental processes. The bailouts were driven by and implemented according to national political concerns. Not only have the different timescapes exposed fundamental political and economic problems,[54] they have led to a different integration method, what Uwe Puetter has called "deliberative intergovernmentalism."[55] It refers to the process of making decisions at the EU level in a slower but more deliberative fashion. The Greek case shows that to be only partly accurate. True, intergovernmentalism appears to be on the rise in the sense that national rather than supranational actors seem to be in control of the process, but it is not deliberative. Rather, the new process is power-political in the sense that decision outcomes reflect mostly preferences of creditors, not debtors. In the absence of robust and widely accepted EU leadership,[56] such changes will surely test confidence in European institutions and the likely individual or national benefits from loyalty to this type of European architecture.

The bailout packages and their Greek implementation raise an impossible paradox. On the one hand, it is argued that political ownership of reforms and democratic legitimacy are a necessary prerequisite for measures to take effect. On the other hand, stringent conditionality rules imposed by creditors undermine voter efficacy. Greece is no longer a sovereign country in the traditional sense because laws and policies are dictated by rescue packages and not by voter preferences. Moreover, measures designed to address systemic flaws, such as the Fiscal Compact, which entered into force in 2013, complicate this notion of quasi sovereignty. They tighten fiscal rules and create surveillance and correction mechanisms to prevent future crises while retaining a noncredible no-obligation-for-bailout clause.[57] In the EMU that is logical and desirable, but in practice it implies countries will still not be bailed out (highly unlikely) while national budgets are now subject to external influences in non–voter-accountable ways. In other words, as Fritz Scharpf perceptively observes, "EMU member states cannot expect any help from the European level in managing macroeconomic imbalances that are induced by European monetary impulses that fail to fit the specific conditions of the national economy."[58]

The problem will no longer be Greece, whose voters have had to accept the effects of policies without much hint of debate or consultation. The problem will be larger countries such as France or Germany. Because the new rules link the fate of different countries even tighter, increasing the chance of cascading damage next time, will their voters accept external interference? Research has so far shown that in countries with widespread corruption, trust in European institutions tends to be higher as compensation for internal deficiencies even if these institutions are not directly accountable to voters.[59] In countries of low perceptions of corruption, with a system of low voter efficacy, and in times of crisis, will voters place similar trust in the effectiveness of European institutions? To return to Calypso, the relationship between Calypso (EU) and Odysseus (Greece) has changed but not necessarily for the better. Her wrath, however justified, has pernicious side effects. In her quest to bring the two sides closer together, she may have set in motion the process that drives them apart.

Notes

1. *To Vima*, "The Immediate Economic Aims" (in Greek), October 12, 2009. Available at http://www.tovima.gr/politics/article/?aid=294516&wordsinarticle=%

CF%80%CE%B1%CF%80%CE%B1%CE%BD%CE%B4%CF%81%CE%B5%CE%
BF%CF%85%3b2009 (accessed February 2, 2014).

2. Quoted in Manolopoulos (2011), p. 220.

3. Ostrom (1990).

4. De Santis (2012).

5. Manolopoulos (2011).

6. Zahariadis (2013a).

7. Ostrom (1990).

8. European Commission, "Greece: Annex 8 to EU Anti-Corruption Report," February 3, 2014. Available at http://ec.europa.eu/dgs/home-affairs/what-we-do/policies/organized-crime-and-human-trafficking/corruption/anti-corruption-report/docs/2014_acr_greece_en.pdf (accessed April 7, 2014).

9. Quoted in Larry Elliott, "No EU Bailout for Greece as PM Promises to 'Put Our House in Order,'" *Guardian*, January 28, 2010. Available at http:// www.guardian.co.uk/business/2010/jan/28/greece-papandreou-eurozone.

10. Alexandra Kassimi, "Indebted Transport Derailed," *Kathimerini*, April 7, 2010.

11. Kathimerini, "Instructions of Austerity to DEKO by the Ministry of Finance" (in Greek), September 11, 2010. Available at http://news.kathimerini.gr/4dcgi/_w_articles_politics_100005_11/09/2010_414660 (accessed April 7, 2013).

12. Evangelos Lazaridis, "Conflict in the Independent Statistical Authority," *To Vima* (in Greek), 2011. Available at http://www.tovima.gr/opinions/article/?aid=423380&wordsinarticle=Cexqcams (accessed April 7, 2014).

13. Ibid.

14. Ibid., Table 9C.

15. Ibid., Table 11.

16. Zahariadis (2013a), p. 278. De Grauwe makes a similar argument, noting "the fundamental cause of the sovereign debt crisis" was unsustainable private debt "with the possible exception of Greece." See De Grauwe, (2013), p. 5. I argue the interaction of both did Greece in.

17. Kingdon (1995).

18. Gibson, Hall, and Tavlas (2011).

19. International Monetary Fund (2010).

20. International Monetary Fund (2013a).

21. Ibid., p. 1.

22. For example, see Dohse, Krieger-Boden, and Soltwedel (1999).

23. Wyplosz (2013), p. 7.

24. Dimitra Kroustalli, "Greece Reaches Its Limit," *To Vima* (in Greek), April 9, 2011. Available at http://www.tovima.gr/politics/ article/?aid5417697 (accessed February 8, 2014).

25. Ibid.

26. Zahariadis (2012).

27. Peter Spiegel and Quentin Peel, "Split Opens over Greek Bail-Out Terms," *Financial Times*, September 28, 2011. Available at http://www.ft.com/intl/cms/s/0/69902e72-e926-11e0-af7b-00144feab49a.html?ftcamp5rss&ftcamp5crm/email/2011928/nbe/WorldNews/produc t#axzz1dhjJyctT (accessed April 8, 2012).

28. Quoted in A. Beattie, "Europe's Successes Underminded by 'Parochialism,'" *Financial Times*, September 14, 2014. Available at http://www.ft.com/intl/cms/s/0/393be280-dedf-11e0-9130-00144feabdc0.html?ftcamp5rss&ftcamp5crm/email/2011915/nbe/BrusselsBrief/product#axzz1dhjJyctT (accessed February 8, 2014).

29. For example, see Featherstone (2011) and Jones (2010).

30. Quoted in Stephan Schultz and Philipp Wittrock, "Parade of Ego-Europeans," *Spiegel Online*, May 12, 2011. Available at http://www.spiegel.de/wirtschaft/soziales/0,1518,762097,00.html (accessed June 15, 2012).

31. Heipertz and Verdun (2010).

32. Quoted in Andrew Osborn, "Prodi Disowns 'Stupid' Stability Pact," *Guardian*, October 18, 2002. Available at http://www.theguardian.com/business/2002/oct/18/theeuro .europeanunion (accessed February 8, 2014).

33. Featherstone (2011), p. 196.

34. Ministry of Administrative Reform and E-Government, 2014. Census of Public Sector Payroll. Available at http://apografi.yap.gov.gr/apografi/Flows_2013.htm.

35. Hills (2013), p. 86.

36. De Santis (2012).

37. Quoted in Peter Spiegel, "Brussels' New-Found Aggression Raises Hackles," *Financial Times*, November 7, 2011. Available at http://www.ft.com/intl/cms/s/0/a3cc10fc -0964-11e1-a2bb-00144feabdc0.html#axzz1daViK5yq (accessed December 20, 2011).

38. International Monetary Fund (2012), p. 1.

39. Interview with Cypriot academic on January 16, 2014.

40. Special Task Force for Greece, *Seventh Activity Report*, July 2014, p. 22. http://ec.europa/eu/archives/commission_2010-2014/president/pdf/qr7_en.pdf.

41. Liz Alderman, "Greece Has a Budget Surplus, a Respite That Could Be Short-Lived," *New York Times*, February 4, 2014. Available at http://www.nytimes.com /2014/02/05/business/international/greece-has-a-budget-surplus-a-respite-that-could -be-short-lived.html?_r=0.

42. Eurostat, "Unemployment Rate by Sex and Age Groups." http://appsso.eurostat .ec.europa.eu/nui/show.do?dataset=une_rt_a&lang=en. Accessed on April 13, 2015.

43. Klimaka, "10 September: World Day for Suicide Prevention" (in Greek), September 10, 2013. Available at http://www.klimaka.org.gr/newsite/ (accessed February 7, 2014).

44. For example, see Christodoulou and Christodoulou (2013) and Economou et al. (2013).

45. Institute for Mental Health Research, "Stigma: The Biggest Obstacle to Preventing Suicide" (in Greek), 2013. Available at http://www.epipsi.gr/pdf/Suicide%2010-09 -2013%20-%201.pdf (accessed February 8, 2014).

46. Bureau of Economic Analysis, http://www.bea.gov/national/index.htm.

47. Alderman (2014).

48. Join and Hart (2003).

49. Helena Smith, "Greek Golden Dawn Member Arrested over Murder of Leftwing Hip-Hop Artist," *Guardian*, September 18, 2013. Available at http://www.theguardian .com/world/2013/sep/18/greece-murder-golden-dawn (accessed February 8, 2014).

50. Helena Smith, "Leftwing Syriza Party Triumphs in European Elections in Greece," *Guardian*, May 25, 2014. Available at http://www.theguardian.com/politics /2014/may/26/syriza-european-elections-greece.

51. Paul Taylor, "Greece may have Blown Best Hope for Debt Deal," Reuters, April 12, 2015. http://www.reuters.com/article/2015/04/12/us-eurozone-greece-deal-analysis -idUSKBN0N306W20150412. Accessed on April 13, 2015.

52. Alderman (2014).

53. Kimitris Katsikas, "Brain Drain: A New Challenge for the Eurozone," *Euractiv.com*, November 26, 2013 (accessed November 26, 2014).

54. Dyson (2009).

55. Puetter (2012).

56. Posner and Blöndal (2012).

57. Wyplosz (2013), pp. 34–37.

58. Scharpf (2011), p. 33.

59. Muñoz, Torcal, and Bonet (2011).

11

Portugal and Spain: The Limits of Convergence

Sebastián Royo

PORTUGAL AND SPAIN JOINED THE EUROPEAN UNION (EU) AT THE same time in 1986. This momentous event had profound implications for both countries and contributed to the transformation of their political, social, and economic institutions. The first two and half decades of membership were generally extraordinarily positive for them. The 2007 crisis, however, has been devastating for the Iberian economies.

This chapter explores the impact of EU membership for Portugal and Spain, with particular focus on the recent Eurozone financial and economic crisis. It analyzes the effect of European integration on both countries' economies and explains differences in economic performance in the years prior to the crisis, emphasizing the limits of convergence. Furthermore, it examines the crisis and the role of the EU and the importance of the domestic actors in the process. Indeed, although the dominant view in Europe has been that the crisis in Portugal and Spain reflects fiscal indiscipline, the reality has been far more nuanced. In the years prior to the crisis, both countries suffered divergent competitiveness and record external imbalances. Yet for Spain an additional core problem was excessive lending, which led to a European bailout for the country's banking system in 2012, whereas for Portugal fiscal indiscipline was a major contributing factor that led to a full-fledged EU–International Monetary Fund (IMF) bailout package in 2011.

Prior to the crisis, the economic modernization of Iberia was simply remarkable. However, as I examine here, since the beginning of the new century their economic performance diverged. This divergence is particularly striking because the performance of both economies was quite similar in the first thirteen years following their accession to the EU. This chapter argues that one of the fundamental reasons for the poor performance of the Portuguese economy between 1999 and 2006 was the lack of fiscal discipline and the failure in the adoption of ad hoc measures to try to control the deficit.

Indeed, the Portuguese and Spanish economies experienced a boom in the second half of the 1990s, when nominal short-term interest rates converged to those set by the European Central Bank (ECB). In both countries, the rates fell more rapidly than inflation, which contributed to increased domestic demand (and in the case of Spain to a real estate bubble). This growth, however, would have required a concomitant prudent fiscal policy, which, in the case of Portugal, did not take place.

Furthermore, one of the most generalized misinterpretations regarding the current crisis in Southern Europe is attributing it to wildly mismanaged finances. Many policymakers across Europe still insist that irresponsible public borrowing caused the crisis, and this in turn has led to misguided solutions. In fact, that interpretation is incorrect. In Spain, the current crisis did not originate with wildly mismanaged finances. On the contrary, as late as 2011, Spain's debt ratio was still well below the European Monetary Union (EMU) average: whereas Spain stood at less than 60 percent of gross domestic product (GDP), Greece stood at 160.8 percent, Italy at 120 percent, Portugal at 106.8 percent, Ireland at 105 percent, Belgium at 98.5 percent, and France at 86 percent.

Indeed, the fiscal position of Spain prior to the crisis was reasonably robust, as it ran a budget surplus in 2005, 2006, and 2007. It was only when the crisis hit and the real estate market collapsed that the fiscal position deteriorated markedly and the country experienced huge deficits. Prior to 2007, Spain seemed to be in an enviable fiscal position, even compared with Germany.[1] In the end, however, the country could not escape the dramatic consequences of the crisis, and fiscal conditions deteriorated markedly after 2007.

Despite the fundamental institutional design problems of the EMU— which did not include a fiscal union, a European joint bank regulator, or a system to deal with financial institutions in stress—this chapter shows that the crisis had profound domestic roots in both Iberian countries. It seeks to account for the fiscal divergence between Portugal and Spain in the years prior to the crisis as a way to illustrate the limits of external pressure and the ability of the *acquis communautaire* to force change. As we will see, EU membership has had enormous impact on both countries. Yet governments still had leeway to implement their own policies (and even avoid European ones). These decisions have affected their economic performance and in the case of Portugal and Spain paved the ground for the devastating crisis that both countries have experienced since 2007.

The chapter proceeds as follows. The first section examines the impact of EU integration in both countries. The next section examines the economic divergence between Portugal and Spain during the 2000–2007 period. The third section examines the reasons for the performance differences between the two countries, focusing in particular on their fiscal policies. The following section analyzes the domestic factors that led to the 2007 crisis. The chapter closes with some lessons from the Iberian experiences.

Background: How Has the EC/EU Affected Portugal and Spain

January 1, 2014, marked the twenty-eighth anniversary of Portugal and Spain's accession to the European Community (EC). European integration followed the establishment of democracy in Portugal and Spain in the 1970s, a precondition for EC membership. By the 1970s, their relative isolation from Europe had spearheaded their desire to become part of the EC, and most Portuguese and Spaniards supported the integration process. Indeed, in the second half of the past century, the EC epitomized in the eyes of Iberian citizens the values of liberty, democracy, and progress absent in their country. In addition, although some economists expressed reservations about the impact of EC membership, most Iberian entrepreneurs knew that their future lay in Europe and the modernization of their countries was contingent on European integration. Hence, belonging to the European club was a mission to be pursued.[2]

Surprisingly, however, membership negotiations lasted seven years. The negotiation process was hindered by political instability in both countries, and for Portugal, it was also marred by some of the decisions (including the nationalization of important sectors of the economy) that were made during the revolutionary period that followed the 1974 coup. Slow progress in the talks was also attributed to contentious bargaining over sensitive issues, such as migrant workers, agriculture, fisheries, and particularly textiles.[3] French opposition to enlargement (based particularly on concerns over the impact of Spanish agriculture) further delayed the final agreement. The final obstacles to accession were removed in subsequent negotiations throughout 1984–1985. The treaties of accession were signed in 1985, and Portugal and Spain joined the EC on January 1, 1986. This long-awaited development had profound consequences for the EC and for both countries.[4]

Since their accession, Portugal and Spain have played an important role in the process of European integration and have become, again, important actors in the European arena. They have contributed decisively to the development of an institutional design of the European Union that has been largely beneficial to their interests and have participated successfully in the creation and implementation of the Single Market and the EMU. Indeed, membership to the EC has brought many benefits to both countries.[5]

From a political standpoint, Portugal and Spain have undergone profound transformations. Accession was viewed as a mean to consolidate political and economic reforms, and as a push for modernization. In both countries integration was viewed by the political and economic elites as the best way to consolidate the fragile structures of Iberian democracies, and therefore Europeanization and democratization were considered complementary processes. Indeed, the EC played a significant role in the success of the democratization process. First, the EC had a demonstrative and symbolic influence because Iberian citizens associated the EC and its member countries with the values of democracy and freedom. In addition, the EC had important indirect levers, such as the democratic precondition for EC entry. Finally, the repetitive refusals to consider the Iberian applications for membership during the Franco-Salazar/Caetano years strengthened the positions of opposition groups and economic actors supporting democracy, and European governments exerted considerable bilateral pressures to follow through with the democratization process.[6]

Consequently, the democratic regimes installed in the 1970s have lasted far longer and attained a greater degree of stability than earlier democratic episodes, and EC membership finally ended the relative political isolation of both countries. Indeed, membership paved the way for the complete incorporation of Portugal and Spain into the major international structures of Europe and the West, as well as the normalization of these countries' relations with their European partners. Hence, from a political standpoint, EU integration has been an unmitigated success, as both countries have consolidated their democratic regime and institutions.

The process of European integration has also influenced sociological and cultural developments. Both countries attempted to come to terms with their own identities, while addressing issues such as culture, nationality, citizenship, ethnicity, and politics. At the dawn of the new millennium, it would not be an exaggeration to say that the Spaniards and the Portuguese have become "mainstream Europeans." EU integration, however, has also brought significant costs in terms of economic adjustment, loss of sovereignty, cultural homogenization, and fears, which have been exacerbated by issues such as size, culture, and nationalism.

From an economic standpoint, entry into Europe has contributed to the modernization of the Iberian economies. Although EC/EU membership has not been the only reason for this development (in both countries the economic liberalization and modernization processes started in the 1950s and 1960s), European integration has played a critical role. Indeed, the perspective of EC integration gave a final push to the modernization and liberalization of the Iberian economies. The perspective of EU membership acted as an essential motivational factor that influenced the actions of policymakers and economic actors, thus acting as a catalyst for change, as Portugal and Spain took unilateral measures in preparation for EC accession, including increasing economic flexibility, industrial restructuring, the adoption of the value-added tax, and trade liberalization.

At the same time, the fact that most citizens supported integration facilitated the implementation of (in many cases quite painful) micro- and macroeconomic reforms, which allowed the political and economic actors to adopt economic policies and business strategies consistent with membership and the *acquis communautaire* (which at the time of accession included the custom union, the VAT, the Common Agriculture and Fisheries Policies, and the external trade agreements, and later the Single Market, the European Exchange Mechanism [ERM], and the EMU).

Overall, EC/EU membership has had a very significant effect on economic policies. In this area, it has constrained significantly the economic strategies of the Portuguese and Spanish governments. In both countries, with a strong history of state intervention in the economy, the Single Market, the EMU, and the EU competition policies have diminished the state role in the economy and constrained policy options. They have forced these governments to deregulate their economies, privatize public companies, and eliminate subsidies that had been used to sustain noncompetitive industries.

As a result of EU accession, trade barriers to the EU have been eliminated; markets and prices have been deregulated and liberalized; the labor market has been the subject of limited deregulatory reforms; a privatization program was started in the early 1980s to roll back the presence of the government in the economy and increase the overall efficiency of the system; and competition policy was adapted to EU regulations.[7] In the 1990s, the desire of both countries to participate in the EMU led to the implementation of policies that resulted in fiscal consolidation and the independence of their central banks.

In terms of static effects, EU membership offered opportunities for both trade creation and trade diversion. Portugal's and Spain's trade with the community has expanded dramatically over the past two decades. In addition, the process of market liberalization that followed the implementation of the Single European Act (SEA) contributed significantly to the increasing internationalization and openness of the Portuguese and Spanish economies, which increased from less than 40 percent in Spain and 25 percent in Portugal in 1986 to 65 percent and 35 percent, respectively, in 2003.[8]

Moreover, membership has also brought about important dynamic effects. Portugal and Spain with relatively good infrastructure, an educated and cheap labor force, and a market of millions of potential consumers offer an attractive production base.[9] As expected, one of the key outcomes of integration has been a dramatic increase in foreign direct investment in both countries, from less than 2 percent to more than 6 percent of GDP in the decade following their accession.

One of the main consequences of these developments has been a reduction in the economic differences that separate each country from the European average. Table 11.1 shows the evolution of the economic convergence.

An additional outcome of EU membership has been to give Portugal and Spain additional macroeconomic credibility. When both countries joined

Table 11.1 Economic Convergence

Economic Convergence	Portugal	Spain
Year of Joining the EU	1986	1986
Transfer of Cohesion Funds as Percentage of GDP (at 2004 prices)	2.20	1.30
GDP per Capita PPP at the Year of Joining as Percentage of EU-15 Average	54	71.90
GDP per Capita PPP in 2013 as Percentage of EU-15 Average	67.90	86.10
Number of Years to Reach the EU-15 Average at Present Trend (2013+)	43	22

Source: Ameco database, December 2013, European Commission.

the ERM (in 1992 for Portugal and 1989 for Spain), the escudo and the peseta became more respectable because they became effectively pegged to the deutsche mark. Following the crises of the ERM and the devaluations of 1992 and 1993, credibility was reestablished when it became clear that both countries would qualify to join the EMU at the outset. The EMU effects were very important: both countries had to maintain their exchange rate peg within the ERM, keep inflation low, reduce their budget deficits to less than 3 percent of GDP, and try to cut the public sector debt to below 60 percent of GDP. The Iberian governments were forced to tighten fiscal policy, use privatization revenues to pay down debt, and liberalize their economies further. The culmination of this process was the largely unexpected participation of both countries in the EMU. Indeed, Portugal and Spain fulfilled the conditions established by the Treaty of Maastricht, and on January 1, 1999, both became founding members of the EMU. This development confirmed the nominal convergence of both countries with the rest of the EU.

The first few years of EMU membership were very successful for both countries, particularly Spain (see Table 11.2 for economic performance). However, data from Tables 11.1 and 11.2 show that nominal convergence advanced more quickly than real convergence. Indeed, Portugal and Spain's European integration revealed both convergence and divergence, nominal and real. Since 1997, inflation in Spain has exceeded the EU average every year. In Portugal, real convergence slowed down each year since 1998, turning negative in 2000, with both real and nominal divergence decreasing until 2006.

Explaining the Economic Divergence

Portugal's divergence is particularly striking because the performance of both economies was quite similar during the first thirteen years following their accession to the EU. Indeed, between 1994 and 2000, the growth in

Table 11.2 Economic Summary, Portugal and Spain, 2006–2015

Indicator	2006	2007	2008	2009	2010	2011	2012	2013	2014*	2015*
Portugal										
GDP (% change)	1.448	2.365	-0.009	-2.908	1.936	-1.25	-3.225	-1.351	1.166	1.4512
Inflation (% change)	3.043	2.423	2.651	-0.903	1.389	3.557	2.777	0.44	0.668	1.19
Unemployment (%)	7.657	7.985	7.592	9.469	10.797	12.739	15.653	16.252	15.65	15.05
Structural Balance (% potential GDP)	-3.796	-4.172	-5.371	-9.181	-9.035	-6.634	-4.098	-3.107	-2.66	-1.708
Net Debt (% GDP)	58.558	63.658	67.49	79.672	89.569	97.769	114.022	118.397	119.915	119.224
Current Account Balance (% GDP)	-10.685	-10.102	-12.638	-10.919	-10.582	-7.016	-2.018	0.532	0.83	1.174
Spain										
GDP (% change)	4.075	3.479	0.893	-3.832	-0.203	0.052	-1.643	-1.22	0.868	0.962
Inflation (% change)	3.563	2.844	4.13	-0.238	2.043	3.052	2.436	1.526	0.271	0.838
Unemployment	8.525	8.275	11.3	18	20.075	21.65	25	26.375	25.54	24.9
Structural Balance (% potential GDP)	1.314	0.559	-5.629	-9.964	-8.416	-8.011	-5.723	-4.902	-4.374	-3.672
Net Debt (% GDP)	30.654	26.7	30.801	24.749	33.177	39.717	52.692	60.444	65.697	69.427
Current Account Balance (% GDP)	-8.961	-9.995	-9.623	-4.828	-4.491	-3.803	-1.12	0.702	0.755	1.374

Source: International Monetary Fund, World Economic Outlook Database, April 2014.
Notes: * Estimate.

income per capita was 3.1 percent in Spain and 3.1 percent in Portugal. Yet since then, instead of catching up, Portugal fell behind, with GDP per capita decreasing from 80 percent of the EU-25 average (without Bulgaria and Romania) in 1999 to just over 70 percent in 2006; labor productivity, still at 40 percent of the EU average, has shown no growth since 2000. Portugal's per capita GDP fell far behind Spain, and since 2000, the Czech Republic, Greece, Malta, and Slovenia surpassed Portugal. Moreover, Portugal was the first member of the EMU to be threatened with sanctions by the EC under the Growth and Stability Agreement (GSA) for violating the excessive deficit provisions. The country became, in the words of *The Economist*, "the new sick man of Europe."[10]

Although there are other factors that help explain economic divergence between both countries,[11] there is growing consensus that different fiscal policies, within the constraints imposed by the Growth and Stability Pact, played a central role. Since Spain and Portugal became founding members of the EMU, monetary policies were no longer in the hands of their national governments and therefore could help account for differences in performance between both countries. It is now widely accepted that increases in government consumption adversely affect long-term growth, and also that while fiscal consolidation may have short-term costs in terms of activity, they can be minimized if consolidation is credible by implementing consistent decisions that deliver solid results.

Both the Portuguese and Spanish economies experienced a boom in the second half of the 1990s, boosted by the considerable fall in interest rates, when nominal short-term interest rates converged to those set by the ECB. This growth, however, would have required a concomitant prudent fiscal policy, which, in the case of Portugal, did not take place. On the contrary, the cyclically adjusted primary balance fell from 1.2 percent of GDP in 1994–1996 to –0.6 percent in 1999–2001. At the same time, the combination of expansionary fiscal policies and insufficient structural reforms did not prepare the country for the economic downturn.

Indeed, one of the fundamental reasons for the poor performance of the Portuguese economy between 1999 and 2006 was the lack of fiscal discipline and the failure in the adoption of ad hoc measures to control the deficit. On the other hand, Spain was one of the most disciplined countries in Europe and was able to maintain a margin of maneuver that allowed fiscal policy to be used in a countercyclical way (see Table 11.3).

There is widespread consensus that Portugal's biggest mistake was its "chronic fiscal misbehavior."[12] Vítor Constancio, governor of the Bank of Portugal, acknowledged that "when in 2001 we had these big shocks to growth, tax revenues dropped and suddenly we were in a situation of an excessive deficit. . . . The sudden emergence of budget problems led to a big revision of expectations about the future."[13] As seen, largely as a result of

Table 11.3 Fiscal Position of Portugal and Spain Before the Crisis, 2000–2008

% of GDP	2000	2001	2002	2003	2004	2005	2006	2007	2008
Portugal									
Structural Balance	−4.047	−4.864	−4.468	−4.744	−5.178	−5.616	−3.894	−3.26	−3.805
Net Debt	41.974	46.386	48.118	51.218	53.282	57.954	58.771	63.658	67.361
Spain									
Structural Balance	−1.121	−1.752	−1.118	−0.975	−0.97	−1.599	−1.275	−1.133	−5.034
Net Debt	50.265	47.541	44.007	41.319	38.583	34.705	30.53	26.52	30.484

Source: International Monetary Fund, World Economic Outlook Database, October 2009.

this revision of expectations, the Portuguese economy contracted by 0.8 percent in 2003. The deficit reduction, on the contrary, is credited by Fernando Teixeira dos Santos, finance minister, with restoring "Portugal's credibility in international markets and strengthen[ing] confidence in the economy."[14] The improvement in the financial position of the budget allowed the government to cut the VAT from 21 percent to 20 percent in July 2008 to stimulate the economy. Hence the Portuguese experience shows that countries that want to join the Eurozone need to have a "comfortable budget position because that will give [room] for maneuver once inside."[15] Not surprisingly, of the cohesion countries, the ones that have done better in the decade and a half prior to the 2007 crisis were those who maintained fiscal discipline: Ireland and Spain, which either maintained a budget surplus or reduced their budget deficits to comply with the SGP, while reducing their total expenditures vis-à-vis GDP. Portugal, as noted, was the exception.

Tracing the Role of Institutions, Ideas, and Interests
The experience of Portugal and Spain in the EU demonstrates the limits of external pressure and the ability of the *acquis communautaire* to force change. As we have seen, after almost two decades of economic growth following their EU accession in 1986, Portugal experienced poor economic performance since the beginning of the twenty-first century, struggled with the Stability and Growth Pact, and violated its fiscal deficit rules. Institutions, ideas, and interests are crucial in understanding these outcomes.[16]

Institutions. Defined as the set of rules, formal and informal, that actors generally follow, institutions are crucial to the understanding of the behavior of economic actors and policy outcomes. From an institutionalist standpoint, there were a number of factors that helped account for the limits of convergence.

First, there was a problem of temporal inconsistency, which was a key factor to account for the fiscal problems examined in the previous section. Indeed, in Portugal prior to 2005, political instability has been the pattern; there were four prime ministers between 1995 and 2005 and the previous three prime ministers resigned before their terms were over for various reasons. One of the key differences between the countries was that in Spain there was remarkable economic policy stability after the crisis of 1992–1993. There were few economic policy shifts throughout the 1990s and first half of the 2000s, despite changes in government. Between 1993 and 2007, there were only two ministers of finance, Pedro Solbes (from 1993–1996 and 2004–2008) and Rodrigo Rato (from 1996–2004);[17] the country only had two prime ministers (José María Aznar and José Luís Rodríguez Zapatero).[18] More important, each of the last three governments completed its mandate, and there were no early elections.

In Portugal, António Guterres was prime minister between October 28, 1995, and April 6, 2002, and the previous three prime ministers resigned before their terms were over for different reasons. Furthermore, the Ministry of Finance position was a revolving door, bringing instability to the economic policy portfolio, with ministers often resigning in protest for their inability to reign over their colleagues or control fiscal policies and expenditures. Between 1990 and 2005, there were ten ministers of finance and on average they served less than two years in the position. In the end, the credibility of economic policies (and fiscal policies in particular) was undermined by the relative political instability that prevailed in Portugal during the first half of the decade.

Ideas. Defined as "causal beliefs," ideas have not been able to counter Portugal's history of fiscal misbehavior. Ideas define goals and strategies and shape the understanding of political problems. Indeed, the national discourses that generate and legitimize change in policies remain distinct in Portugal and they still matter as primary sources of political behavior. Differences in national discourses extended to the EMU project itself. Part of the business community led by the Confederação da Indústria Portuguesa and the Associação Portuguesa de Bancos as well as the Communist Party and its closer union, the Confederação Geral dos Trabalhadores Portugués; even the president's economic counsel and many independents closer to the Socialist Party and members of its Euro-skeptic wing publicly criticized the convergence criteria in the early 1990s because they considered them as hurtful for the real convergence process. In the absence of strong consensus on EU and EMU membership, it is not surprising that there was even less consensus on the implementation of the necessary policies to succeed in Europe. Therefore, in this context the sound public policy paradigm was never dominant in Portugal, and no major group or political party strongly supported it.

In Spain there has been a much stronger consensus about economic policymaking, and the central bank has been able to play a central role influencing policy. Since the transition to democracy, domestic elites seized on liberal economic arguments to promote an agenda of institutional reform, largely influenced by domestic politics and interests. Economic reforms served the specific objectives of a small group of reformers within the central bank, with long ascendance in Spanish policymaking circles since the last years of the Franco regime. The result was the perpetuation of a pattern of accommodation between state elites and private bankers that had characterized Spanish financial regulation and economic policymaking since the transition to democracy.[19]

In addition, in Spain, the policy stability described before was reinforced by the shared (and rare) agreement among the Conservative and Socialist leaders regarding fiscal consolidation (the balance budget objective was established by law by the Popular Party), as well as the need to hold firm in the application of conservative fiscal policies and the achievement of budgetary fiscal surpluses. Indeed, fiscal consolidation happened to a degree in which Spain became the paradigmatic model of a country applying the budget surplus policy mantra.

Interests. Finally, the role of interests is also essential to understand the fiscal outcomes described in the previous section. Interest groups attempt to influence policy. Until the global crisis hit Portugal in 2008 and the country faced the risk of default, there was limited change in domestic incentives or external pressures, and the supporters of sound fiscal policies, like the Bank of Portugal or the Ministry of Finance, have not been sufficiently empowered. On the contrary, entrenched interest groups, like the civil servants, and the labor unions, were able to exercise effective veto power over any attempt to impose fiscal discipline. Workers' rights are enshrined in the constitution, one of the legacies of the transition to democracy.

In sum, institutions, ideas, and interests help explain why the opportunity for sustained structural reform and improvement in fiscal discipline afforded by the euro was largely lost, which made Portugal a victim of the "euro holdup." Table 11.4 summarizes these findings.

The Crisis and the Limits of Convergence

Though Spain entered the crisis in a relatively robust fiscal position, in the end, fiscal prudence was not enough. When the impact of the crisis intensified in 2008, Spain seemed to be in an excellent fiscal position, yet the country's structural or cyclically adjusted deficit turned out to be much

Table 11.4 Summary of the Main Findings

Policy Domain	Independent Variable: EU	Intervening Variable 1: Institutions	Intervening Variable 2: Interests	Intervening Variable 3: Ideas	Dependent Variable: Domestic outcome
Fiscal Policy	Prior to 1999: TEU, fiscal convergence criteria After 1999: Stability and Growth Pact	Domestic institutional change (1990s onward) (P, S) Limit: institutionalization of "chronic fiscal misbehavior" (P) Ministry of Finance weak and with revolving door (P) Fiscal constitution unchanged (P) Temporary inconsistency and instability (P) Failure of semi-rigid institutional mechanisms (P, S) Stengthening of Central Bank and Ministry of Finance (S) New fiscal constitution (S) Decentralization (S) Stability and policy continuity (S)	Limited change in domestic political incentives or external pressure (1990s onward) (P) Veto power for some groups (P) Insufficient empowerment of sound fiscal policy supporters (i.e., Bank of Portugal and Ministry of Finance) (P) No effective veto power (S)	Limited change of fiscal policy paradigm domestically (1990s onward) (P) Spread of the sound public finance paradigm, but fiscal and political elites lacked incentives or external pressures to enforce it (P) Central Bank and Ministry of Finance strong influence in sound public policy paradigm (S) Paradigm internalized by political elites (S) Consensus among leading parties (S)	Accommodation Fiscal adjustment in the run-up to EMU (1999); looser policy afterward to 2005; severe fiscal adjustment after 2008 (P) Opening of protocal for violation of SGP (P) Fiscal consolidation and new fiscal contitution (S) Budget surplus and record low debt (S)

Notes: P = Portugal; S = Spain

higher than its actual deficit (see Table 11.2). Spain was one of the European countries that had experienced a huge increase in property prices (the UK and Ireland are other notable ones) and a boom in property development. That created a big bubble and a very large crash. The property boom was associated with financial excesses, which were fostered by an illusion of prosperity that proved unfounded and unsustainable.[20]

The problem in Portugal and Spain was the giant inflow of capital from the rest of Europe, and the consequence was rapid growth and significant inflation. In fact, the fiscal deficit was a result, not a cause, of Spain's problems. When the global financial crisis hit the country and the real estate bubble burst, unemployment soared and the budget went into deep deficit, caused partly by depressed revenues and partly by emergency spending to limit human costs.

The conditions for the crisis in Spain were created by excessive lending and borrowing by the private sector. The problem was not public debt, but private. Indeed, Spain experienced a problem of ever-growing private sector debt, which was compounded by the reckless investments and loans of banks (including the overleveraged ones) and aggravated by competitiveness and current account imbalances. In Spain, the debt of private sector (households and nonfinancial corporations) was 227.3 percent of GDP at the end of 2010; total debt increased from 337 percent of GDP in 2008 to 363 percent in mid-2011.

A Sharp Decrease of Competitiveness

While the focus during the current euro crisis has largely centered on the fiscal challenges, it is essential to note that there was a serious problem with competitiveness in these two countries prior to the crisis. EMU membership meant, in fact, that the economies of member states should converge in productivity (e.g., that the Portuguese and Spaniards would in effect become more like the Germans). However, the gap between German and Portuguese and Spanish productivity increased, rather than decreased, over the past decade; as a result, Germany developed a large surplus on its current account; Portugal and Spain (and the other periphery countries) had large current account deficits that were financed by capital inflows (see Table 11.5).[21]

As noted before, EMU membership fostered a false sense of security among private investors. In this regard, during the years of euphoria following EMU membership, prior to the financial crisis, private capital flowed freely into Portugal and Spain and, as a result, the countries ran current account deficits around 10 percent of GDP. In the case of Spain, these deficits helped finance large excesses of spending over income in the private sector (and notably, not so much in the public sector). These capital inflows could have helped Portugal and Spain invest, become more productive, and "catch up" with Germany. Unfortunately, in the case of Spain, they largely led to a massive bubble in the property market, consumption, and unsustainable levels of

Table 11.5 Trade Balance of Portugal and Spain Before the Crisis, 2000–2008

Current Account	2000	2001	2002	2003	2004	2005	2006	2007	2008
Portugal	-10.3	-10.3	-8.2	-6.4	-8.3	-10.3	-10.7	-10.1	-12.6
Spain	-3.9	-3.9	-3.2	-3.5	-5.2	-7.3	-8.9	-9.9	-9.6

Source: International Monetary Fund, World Economic Outlook Database, September 2011.

borrowing. The bursting of that bubble contracted the country's real economy, and it brought down the banks that gambled on loans to real estate developers and construction companies. Again, the problem for Spain (and Ireland) was not caused by irresponsible fiscal policy, but instead by irresponsible banking practices leading to the accumulation of unsustainable liabilities.

At the same time, the economic boom also generated large losses in external competitiveness, and Portugal and Spain failed to address well-rooted structural problems and the challenge of competitiveness. As a result, costs and prices increased, which in turn led to a loss of competitiveness and large trade deficits. This unsustainable situation came to the fore when the financial shocks that followed the collapse of Lehman Brothers in the fall of 2007 brought "sudden stops" in lending across the world, leading to a collapse in private borrowing and spending, and a wave of fiscal crises.[22]

The Financial Crises in Spain

Between 2008 and 2010, the Spanish financial system, despite all its problems, was still one of the least affected by the crisis in Europe. During that period, of the forty financial institutions that received direct assistance from Brussels, none were from Spain. In December 2010, Moody's ranked the Spanish banking system as the third strongest of the Eurozone, behind only Finland and France, above the Netherlands and Germany, and well ahead of Portugal, Ireland, and Greece. Spanish regulators had put in place regulatory and supervisory frameworks that required higher provisioning, which provided cushions to Spanish banks to initially absorb the losses caused by the onset of the global financial crisis.

Nevertheless, this success proved short-lived. In the summer of 2012, Spanish financial institutions seemed to be on the brink of collapse and the crisis of the sector forced the EU in June 2012 to devise an emergency €100 billion rescue plan for the sector. Indeed, the collapse of the real estate market eventually led to a traditional banking crisis, and by September 2012, the problem with toxic real estate assets had resulted in the intervention and nationalization of eight financial institutions. Altogether, by 2012, the reorganization of the sector had involved €115 billion from the Spanish government.

There are a number of factors that help account for the deteriorating performance of the Spanish banks after 2009.[23] The first one was the effect of the devastating economic crisis on Spanish banks. As we have seen, since 2008 the country has suffered one of the worst recessions in history: in 2010, Spain's GDP fell by 3.6 percent, the worst performance since data have been compiled; the public deficit reached over 11 percent; public debt increased from 36 percent to 50 percent; and housing construction fell by 20 percent. In 2014, unemployment stood at over 26 percent, and the debt is expected to reach 100 percent of GDP. These deteriorating economic conditions have had a severe impact on the banks' balance sheets.

Second, banks were also being affected by concerns over the country's sovereign debt. Spain seems to have fallen into the "doom loop" that afflicted Greece and Portugal and led to their bailout. The sustainability of the Spanish government debt affected Spanish banks (including BBVA and Santander) because they have been some of the biggest buyers of government debt in the wake of the ECB long-term refinancing operation liquidity infusions (the percentage of government bonds owned by domestic banks reached 30 percent in mid-2012).

An additional crucial factor that helps explain the financial crisis in Spain was the collapse of the real estate sector. As we have seen, Spain had a huge property bust. This led to a very traditional banking crisis largely driven by bad property lending (in some cases caused by political cronyism). Land prices increased 500 percent in Spain between 1997 and 2007, the largest increase among the OECD countries. The result of the collapse of the real estate sector had a profound effect in banks: five years after the crisis started, the quality of Spanish banks' assets continues to plummet. The Bank of Spain classified €180 billion as troubled assets at the end of 2011; banks are sitting on €656 billion of mortgages of which 2.8 percent are classified as nonperforming. Overall nonperforming loans represented 13.4 percent of all loans in May 2014 (or €193 billion euros).

Spanish banks were also suffering the consequences of their dependence on wholesale funding for liquidity since the crisis started, and in particular their dependence on international wholesale financing, as 40 percent of their balance depends on funding from international markets, particularly the ECB. Moreover, the crisis has also exposed weaknesses in the policy and regulatory framework. The most evident signs of failure was the fact that the country adopted five financial reforms in three years and it implemented three rounds of bank mergers. The results of these reforms have been questionable at best. Finally, the current financial crisis can also be blamed on the actions (and inactions) of the Bank of Spain. At the beginning of the crisis, the Bank of Spain's policies were all praised and taken as model by other countries. Time, however, has tempered that praise and the Bank of Spain is now criticized for its actions and decisions (or lack thereof) during the crisis. The bank chose the path of least resistance: alerting about the risks but failing to act decisively.

Conclusions

Much of the focus during the Eurozone crisis has been on the fundamental institutional design problems of the EMU, which did not include a fiscal union, a European joint bank regulator, or a system to deal with financial institutions in stress. These deficiencies go a long way toward explaining the crisis of the Eurozone. However, this chapter shows that the crisis had profound domestic roots in both Iberian countries. They squandered the privileges of EMU membership, and this created resentment from their European neighbors.

This chapter has attempted to illustrate the limits of external pressure and the ability of the *acquis communautaire* to force change. It has shed light on the divergent economic performance of the Portuguese and Spanish economies between 2000 and 2008. During those years, Spain's per capita income reached the EU average, but Portugal's remained stagnant. As we have seen, one of the key differences to account for this development was their fiscal policy. The chapter has argued that institutions, ideas, and interests help account for differences in fiscal policies.

However, the current crisis exposed the weaknesses of both countries' economies and economic models (see Table 11.4). Despite the significant progress and achievements in the two decades of EU membership prior to the 2008 crisis, the Portuguese and Spanish economies still faced serious competitive and fiscal challenges. Unfortunately, the economic success of both countries fostered a sense of complacency, which allowed for a delay in the adoption of the necessary structural reforms that would have been required to succeed in the Single Market and the monetary union. Both Portugal and Spain still have considerable ground to cover to catch up with the richer EU countries and improve the competitiveness of their economies.

In the end—and this is the paradox—fiscal prudence in Spain was not enough either, because it failed to address well-rooted structural problems and the challenge of competitiveness.[24] As we have seen, while the Spanish economy performed significantly better than the Portuguese one between 2000 and 2008, this success was a mirage. The collapse of the construction sector that followed the global financial crisis of 2008 had dire consequences because the country had already suffered a sizable loss of competitiveness. Moreover, the technological capacity of Spain's tradable good industries was weak, and much of the country's investment efforts went into the production of nontradables, particularly buildings. In both countries, industries were relatively vulnerable to competition from cheaper wage producers in Central and Eastern Europe and Asia, and productivity growth has been low, which will make it harder to restore competitiveness. Finally, (unlike Portugal) wage bargaining was quite rigid in Spain and, above all, unresponsive to conditions in the Eurozone. While unitary labor costs remained fairly stable in Portugal, they increased significantly in Spain, further eroding its competitiveness.

Despite the ongoing fixation on fiscal discipline and austerity to address the crisis, this chapter shows that in Spain the debt crisis did not originate with wildly mismanaged finances. Indeed, the escalating deficit since 2008 was a result, not a cause, of Spain's current problems. Moreover, both countries faced serious competitiveness problems prior to the crisis. In this regard, piling austerity measures on top of one another, as they have been doing in both countries, will not be enough. The Iberian economies are shrinking at a faster rate than forecasted for reasons outside the countries' control. The ratio of Portugal's debt to its economy was 107 percent when it received the bailout and it is expected to reach 118 percent by 2014. In Spain it was 36 percent before the crisis and is expected to reach 100 percent in 2011. In this context, further adjustment of the deficit is undesirable and will exacerbate market tensions. These countries need automatic stabilizers to work.

The political costs of austerity have manifested throughout the crisis (the ruling parties at the outset of the crisis, the Spanish PSOE and the Portuguese PS, lost power) and in the May 2014 elections to the European Parliament (see Table 11.6). The result was particularly striking in Spain, where the two leading parties suffered staggering losses (for the first time since the establishment of democracy thirty-five years ago they failed to win a majority of votes), and Podemos, a new political party that did not exist three months before the election, emerged as the fourth most voted party, thus shaking the foundations of Spanish politics. The impact of this election on European politics and the process of European integration remain to be seen, but they show that European leaders can ignore their voters only at their own peril.

The experience of these countries before the crisis shows that EU and EMU membership have not led to the implementation of the structural reforms necessary to address these challenges. On the contrary, particularly in Spain, EMU membership contributed to the economic boom and a real estate bubble (estimated at 30 percent) fueled by record low interest rates, thus facilitating the postponement of necessary economic reforms. This challenge, however, is not a problem of European institutions but of national policies. The Stability and Growth Pact was unable to address Portugal's fiscal challenges and fiscal prudence, and in Spain did not lead to the reforms that should have addressed the country's competitiveness problems (nor did Portugal's chronic fiscal misbehavior). Indeed, the process of economic reforms must be a domestic process led by domestic actors willing to carry them out.

The Iberian experience illustrates that EU/EMU membership brings challenges and opportunities. Membership by itself did not lead to the implementation of the structural reforms necessary to address fiscal and com-

Table 11.6   Elections to European Parliament, 2009 and 2014

Party	2014 Vote %	2014 No. of Seats	2009 Vote %	2009 No. of Seats
Portugal				
PS	31.4	8	26.5	7
PSD/CDS-PP	27.7	7	31.7	8
CDU (PCP-PEV)	12.6	3	10.6	2
MPT	7.1	2		
B.E.	4.56	1	10.7	3
CDS-PP			8.3	2
Spain				
PP	26.0	16	42.2	23
PSOE/PSC	23.0	14	38.5	21
IU-ICV-EUIS-BA	9.9	6	3.7	2
UPyD	6.5	4	2.8	1
Podemos	7.9	5		
CEU	5.4	3		
EPDD	4.0	2		
C'S	3.1	2		
LDP	2.0	1		
Primavera Europa	1.9	1		
CpE			5.1	2
EdP-V			2.5	1

Source: European Parliament, http://www.results-elections2014.eu

petitiveness challenges. Success is not automatic, and there are no guarantees. Indeed, membership helps those prepared to exploit its benefits. There has to be strong coherence between EU/EMU institutions and domestic policies, and hence governments need to balance prudent policymaking, control labor costs, and make structural reforms.

The crisis has had an earth-shattering effect in both countries at all levels: economic, political, institutional, and social. One of the main casualties has been to their political institutions that have been battered badly. But the process of institutional degeneration preceded the crisis, and it was one important element that led to the crisis.[25] Both countries will also have to undertake a profound upgrade of their institutional framework to address the political and economic reforms they need.

In Spain the institutional crisis even affected the monarchy. Members of the royal family were heavily criticized over questionable decisions, and a daughter of King Juan Carlos and her husband were embroiled in a corruption scandal involving influence peddling, leading in part to the abdication of the king in favor of his son, Felipe. With growing discontent and opposition to the monarchy, this unexpected decision sought to stop the hemorrhage and attempted to rebuild public support for the institution. Subsequent polls from the Center of Sociological Research seemed to confirm Spanish citizens' support for the new king.

One important challenge for both countries will be the decision over the degree of decentralization. In Spain the quasi-federal system established by the 1978 Constitution is being questioned, and demands for independence have been growing in Catalonia (which has already called for a referendum in November 2014) and the Basque Country. In Portugal, a much more centralized country, demands for decentralization have been growing as well. Finding the right balance in ways they take advantage of the diversity of their countries, while maximizing the benefits of decentralization and minimizing its costs, will be crucial for both countries.

In the summer of 2014, growing domestic as well as geopolitical tensions cast further clouds over the economic recovery of both countries. In Portugal, the collapse of the country's main bank, Banco Espirito Santo, caused by $5.36 billion in nonperforming loans that the bank made to its struggling group companies, caught the country by surprise and raised fundamental questions about the supervision and oversight of financial institutions. The bank was in effect nationalized, but investors' confidence was shattered. The crisis in Ukraine, over which Spain had played a dovish role throughout, led to the imposition of sanctions. Russia's decision to ban agricultural products from the EU was bound to severely affect Spain: agricultural exports from Spain to Russia represented €440 million in 2013 (the fifth largest in the EU). The Spanish government was working with Brussels to identify ways to limit the damage to agricultural producers.

Still, there are important reasons for optimism. Despite the challenging international economic environment, Iberian companies have been quite successful at diversifying their export markets and investments, increasing the technology content of their exports, and adding value to their products. To consolidate a new growth pattern based on value added and productivity, both countries will have to achieve a massive upgrade of their productive base that will allow them to move up in the value chain. To do this, they need to improve productivity, develop a more flexible economy with a better-educated labor force, achieve higher savings and investment, and develop a more efficient public sector.

Notes

1. See Royo (2013a).
2. Sebastian Royo (ed.), *Do Isolamento a Integação*. Lisbon: Instituto de Ciencias Sociais da Universidade de Lisboa, 2004, pp. 95–96.

3. Dinan (2010), pp. 104–109.

4. Royo and Manuel (2003), Royo (2003).

5. Earlier versions of parts of this section have been published in Royo (2004) and Royo (2003).

6. Geoffrey Pridham, "European Integration and Democratic Consolidation in Southern Europe," in António Costa Pinto and Nuno Severiano Teixeira, eds., *Southern Europe and the Making of the European Union* (New York: Columbia University Press, 2002), pp. 185–186.

7. Royo (2003), pp. 291–292.

8. Data from the European Commission.

9. Royo (2003), p. 292.

10. "A New Sick Man of Europe: Portugal Comes in at Bottom of the European Economic Growth League," *The Economist*, Apr 12, 2007.

11. Royo (2010), pp. 209–254.

12. Martin Wolf, "Struggling to Tackle Bad Fiscal Behaviour," *Financial Times*, April 8, 2008, pp. 1–2 (special section on Investing in Portugal).

13. "Concerns about Divergence 'Overlook Ability to Change,'" interview with Vítor Constancio, governor of the Bank of Portugal, *Financial Times*, May 16, 2008, p. 2.

14. Interview in *Financial Times*, see "Tough Cuts to Strengthen Confidence," in *Financial Times*, April 8, 2008, p. 2 (special section on Investing in Portugal).

15. Interview with Constancio (2008), p. 2.

16. This section borrows from Royo (2013a, 2013b).

17. Prior to them, Carlos Solchaga had been in the position between 1995 and 2003.

18. Prior to them, Felipe González was prime minister for almost fourteen years, between 1982 and 1996.

19. Sofia A. Pérez, *Banking on Privilege*. Ithaca, NY: Cornell University Press, 1997.

20. This sections borrows from Royo (2013a).

21. Simon Johnson, "The End of the Euro: What's Austerity Got to Do with It?," *Baseline Scenario*, June 21, 2012. Available at http://baselinescenario.com/2012/06/21/the-end-of-the-euro-whats-austerity-got-to-do-with-it.

22. Wolf (2008), pp. 1–2 (special section on Investing in Portugal).

23. See Royo (2013a).

24. For a detailed analysis of the reasons, impact, and lessons from the crisis, see Royo (2013a, 2014).

25. Royo (2013a)

12

Austria: Broadly Pro-European

Zdenek Kudrna

THE IMPACT OF RECENT CRISES ON THE POLITICAL DISCOURSE, AS well as economic indicators, is clearly discernible in Austria, although it is one of the least affected countries within the European Union (EU). The country recently returned to the top of the list of wealthiest European nations, with high living standards and low unemployment rates.[1] As in numerous past crises, its unique system of social partnership served it well. At the same time, there are signs of growing strains that put pressure on the long-established patterns of cooperation. During the past two decades of its EU membership, Austria became ever more closely integrated with neighboring countries and the global economy. It is one of the largest beneficiaries of the Single Market, which allowed its firms to expand and succeed, especially in the postcommunist member states that joined the EU after 2004.[2] However, the integration also created the potential for cross-border contagion as shocks from other economies and financial sectors propagated toward Austria. Similarly, although the free movement of workers has benefited the Austrian society and economy, it also created tensions that manifest themselves in support for anti-immigration policies.[3]

Austrian authorities managed the recent crises rather well, proving their reputation for pragmatism and cooperation. The unique system of social partnership that manages internal conflicts, coordinates social and economic policies, and maintains the external competitiveness of Austria proved to be well adapted to the euro area circumstances. It allowed the country to reap the benefits of the single currency while avoiding the risks that plagued many of the southern members. At the same time, the euro crisis and migration pressures undermined public support for traditional political parties that form one of the key pillars of the social partnership system. The 2013 elections might be the last instance where the traditional parties of the "grand coalition" achieve a majority. This trend was also borne out by the 2014 European elections that confirmed support for smaller parties, including the populist right.

In 2015, Austria celebrates twenty years in the EU, where it quickly attained a place among the core countries. Its political stability, robust economic performance, as well as policymaking capacity enabled it to shed its newcomer status, despite occasional setbacks, such as the informal sanctions imposed by other EU members in 2000 after the right-wing populist party entered the government.[4] In the EU, Austria is particularly active in environmental policy, financial crisis management, and matters related to enlargement and neighborhood policies.

The EU Influence on Austria

Austria has developed a unique system of governance that relies on a strong public sector, extensive social partnership, and consensual policymaking.[5] This system was at the core of Austria's transformation from a poor country during the interwar period to one of the richest European countries today.[6] It facilitated the country's adaptation to the EU and euro area membership and enabled it to take advantage of EU membership opportunities while also managing related risks. At the same time, globalization and Europeanization and change in Austrian politics has put the system under increasing pressure.

The social partnership is the core institution of "democratic corporatism,"[7] which provides formal institutional representation for workers, employers, farmers, and other unions through chambers with compulsory membership. All positions in each chamber are filled through democratic elections.[8] Their primary task is wage bargaining, but negotiations cover issues of cooperation on technical innovations, education and vocational training,[9] as well as management of public services, and administration of the social security system, pensions, and family policies. The law then requires the government to consult with social partners on all economic and financial issues before it presents any legislative proposals.[10] Consultations are highly regularized; hence, actors can rely on informality and confidentiality, which increases the chances of arriving at a consensual solution likely to be accepted by respective social partners and in the Parliament.[11]

The social partnership is also instrumental for the management of the public sector that is one of the largest in the EU: 47 percent of annual gross domestic product (GDP).[12] It offers comparatively generous social transfers, a complex network of public services, and a comprehensive regulatory framework covering many aspects of life. A dense, multilevel system of federally, *Länder* (state), and locally funded organizations dominate all segments of public services from education, health care, and kindergartens to collective housing, public transportation, and environmental protection. The public sector is a key contributor to the high standards of living.[13] Despite growing concerns about its inefficiencies[14] and related corruption scandals,[15] the arrangement continues to be endorsed by society.[16]

Wage bargaining is at the heart of the social partnership. It guarantees modest minimum standards and provides considerable upward flexibility, which is reflected by large wage differences between sectors, enterprises, and job types.[17] It traditionally follows the lead of the metalworking industry, which sets a benchmark for other sectors, regions, and enterprises. Since this sector is exposed to German and global competition, it keeps the benchmark wages aligned with productivity and prevents unit labor costs from deteriorating to uncompetitive levels.[18] The close integration with German and other EU economies and participation in the European Economic Area that transferred most of the EU's economic *acquis* prior to 1995 membership explain the ease of economic adaptation to the Single Market. The necessary reforms focused on modernization of the public administration and upgrading personnel skills necessary for functioning within the EU's multilevel governance.[19]

Austrian EU membership coincided with the onset of the eastern enlargement process that brought eleven postcommunist countries, many of them immediate neighbors of Austria, into the EU. This presented Austrian firms with new competition, but also enormous opportunities. They became one of the most active participants in the privatization and restructuring process in the postcommunist countries. Many medium-sized firms became regional multinationals when they took control of major firms in manufacturing, retail distribution, telecommunications, utilities, and banks across Central and Eastern Europe (CEE). This expansion also prevented foreign takeover of Austrian firms, which tend to be small by global standards, by larger multinationals. More important, it allowed them to extend production and supply chains to countries with substantively lower labor costs, which was instrumental for their sustained global competitiveness.

The entry of low-wage and low-tax CEE economies into the EU induced some internal reforms as well. Social partners agreed to reduce corporate taxation and the overall tax burden,[20] while ensuring that the combination of competitive advantages, such as political stability, efficient administration, and the good quality of education and vocational training, motivated domestic firms to keep the high value-added operations in Austria and limit outsourcing to the labor-intensive, lower-value-added parts of the production process. Maintaining these advantages remains high on the agenda, as illustrated by the increase in research and development funding at the onset of the financial crisis.[21]

At the same time, evolving EU rules continue to erode some traditional competitive advantages. In 2014, after sustained pressure from Germany and other EU countries, Austria and Luxembourg finally agreed to stop vetoing the EU tax transparency scheme. This will undermine the bank secrecy rules that allowed foreign bank customers to keep untaxed funds in

Austrian bank accounts. Similarly, many utility industries that were sheltered from competition before Austria's EU membership are increasingly
liberalized and exposed to competition within the EU and globally.

The single currency is the third most important source of EU influence on
Austria after the *acquis communautaire* and enlargement. The country was
well prepared due to historical links with Germany, with which it formed a de
facto monetary union because the Austrian schilling had been pegged to the
deutsche mark since the 1980s.[22] Austria complied with the Maastricht criteria
and joined the single currency in the first wave. The central bankers, managers, entrepreneurs, and trade union leaders were all used to operating within
the confines of hard currency policy and low inflation. The social partnership
system is traditionally benchmarked to German policies, which keeps the
wage raises broadly in line with productivity increases. Hence, it prevented
any build-up of macroeconomic imbalances and competitive disadvantages
that recently undermined the southern euro area economies.

Overall, the economy was well positioned to deal with the challenges
of EU membership, eastern enlargement, and the euro. Austria entered the
EU as the country with the highest standards of living and was outper-
formed by Ireland, Denmark, and the Netherlands during the precrisis
decade.[23] However, since all other EU economies suffered more during recent crises, Austria returned to the top in 2012.[24] Similarly, throughout its
EU membership, Austria was always among the five EU countries with the
lowest unemployment rates. Since 2010, it has the lowest unemployment
rate in the EU and, along with Germany, the lowest youth unemployment.
At the same time, even the lowest figures in the EU represent the highest
rate of unemployment that Austria experienced since 1960s.[25]

However, maintaining the high living standards and low unemployment
coincided with persistent public finance deficits and growing indebtedness.
Ever since Austria entered the EU, its government finances were always in
deficit and in five separate years exceeded the 3 percent Maastricht limit.
The public debt grew from around 68–75 percent of GDP, although just before the crisis it almost reached the 60 percent Maastricht limit, 60.2 percent of GDP in 2007.[26] The public finance data indicate a need for fiscal
consolidation, which will present a renewed challenge for the social partnership. This will come on top of the increasing strain within the society,
which has already been manifested in recent election results.

The unique system of social partnership was traditionally supported by
a stable party system, dominated by the center-left Social Democrats (SPÖ)
and the center-right People's Party (ÖVP). During the post–World War II
decades, these two parties typically governed together in a "grand coalition" with a large majority.[27] However, in the 1999 parliamentary elections,
the SPÖ suffered a heavy defeat, to which the ÖVP responded by forming a
coalition government with the populist right-wing Freedom Party (FPÖ).

This led not only to the imposition of informal sanctions on the Austrian government by the remaining EU members but also to the undermined effectiveness of the traditional social partnership.[28] The sanctions faded quickly, although the uneasy coalition lingered for nearly seven years.[29] The restoration of the grand coalition after 2006 elections stabilized the traditional arrangement again.

However, long-term challenges to the social partnership persist. As the shift of competences from the national level to the EU level intensifies in response to the euro crisis and other developments, it leaves the social partners in Vienna with a decreasing number of policy options.[30] Moreover, the increasing diversity of the Austrian economy and society makes it more difficult to capture and reflect interests of important social groups within the traditional institutions of the social partnership. An increasing proportion of voters, including those with a migration background, feel underrepresented and excluded from the system, which often motivates their voting against established parties. Moreover, there is a growing concern about corruption among political elites.[31]

In the past, groups such as the liberal professions, civil servants, or bankers were able to free ride on the moderation policies of social partnership.[32] They could increase their nominal income above average while profiting from the low inflation secured by the system as long as they remained small enough. Disproportional wage increases of some groups undermine the solidarity among the traditional social partners, which is necessary for wage moderation and sustained competitiveness. Moreover, free-riding groups in important sectors, such as banking, may impose additional costs on firms in important export sectors, thus harming their productivity and competitiveness as well as eroding the purchasing power of households.[33] Hence, it is crucial to maintain and extend the inclusiveness of the chambers and parties to prevent accumulation of benefits to politicians and privileged groups. The most recent elections suggest that nearly half of the electorate seems to think that the established elites are failing at this task.

The 2013 parliamentary elections resulted in an all-time low vote for the parties of the grand coalition, the SPÖ and ÖVP. They defended their combined majority by a margin of 0.8 percent, while a quarter of the vote went to the populist antiestablishment parties, with an anti-immigration and anti-EU agenda. The election campaign was dominated by the issues of economy, welfare, and corruption.[34] The SPÖ and ÖVP focused on above average economic performance during the crisis, while the opposition parties emphasized primarily the corruption combined with an environmental agenda (Greens) or welfare issues that implicitly referred to an anti-immigration agenda (FPÖ). The new parties added a liberalization agenda (NEOS) and Euro-skepticism (Team Stronach).[35] In the end, neither corruption nor Euro-skepticism became the most prominent issues as voters stuck to the traditional party competence ascriptions.[36] However, the lowest ever turnout (74.9 percent), the smallest ever vote, especially among the younger generations of voters, for the two dominant parties and two new parties in the Parliament suggest that the next elections may reshape the traditional party politics that underpins the social partnership.

Overall, the EU influence on Austria over the past two decades was channeled by successive adaptations to the EU membership, enlargement, the euro, and recent crises. The central political and economic institutions were well equipped to steer these adaptations in such a way that enabled Austria to become one of the largest beneficiaries of the Single Market and single currency, while successfully containing many related problems.[37] At the same time, changes in the external environment related to globalization and the EU, as well as internal factors stemming from increasing diversity, undermine the social, political, and economic basis of the social partnership system. The perceived gaps in its legitimacy and effectiveness combined with future fiscal challenges may force dramatic changes as early as in the next parliamentary elections.

Austrian Influence on EU

Almost entire generations of voters, politicians, and decisionmakers have been directly participating in the day-to-day operations of the EU since 1995. As a result, Austria advanced from newcomer status and achieved a standing comparable to some of the smaller founding members, despite occasional setbacks such as the 2000 informal sanctions. The country has successfully chaired two EU presidencies, in 1998 and 2006, and its representatives are fully integrated within the EU and euro area decisionmaking structures. Although there were only nineteen Austrian members of European Parliament (MEPs), Othmar Karas was elected a vice president of the European Parliament and Hannes Swoboda became the president of the important Socialists and Democrats Group in 2012.

Unlike most EU countries, Austria is not a member of NATO but remains committed to the neutrality principle, which, despite its roots in Cold War agreements, became part of the national identity. It allows Austria to position itself as a neutral player and offer a convenient location for mediation in international conflicts, which is often an active contribution to a broader EU foreign policy. Recent examples include mediation events regarding Russia and Ukraine (2014), the Iranian nuclear program (2014), and the United States–Russia spy exchange (2010). At the same time, Austrian foreign policy, especially during the 1980s Bruno Kreisky era, used to be even more pronounced than today, when it is closely aligned with the EU.

The Austrian concept of neutrality does not prevent participation of its armed forces in the peacekeeping missions sanctioned by the UN Security

Council. Hence, Austria keeps participating in international initiatives such as with NATO-led forces in Afghanistan and UN peacekeeping operations. It also participates in the EU security missions, such as policing in Kosovo.

Austria became a core participant in the environmental coalition of EU member states. It consistently supports initiatives to increase environmental standards and leverages its leadership in renewable energy generation within the EU. At the same time, it strongly opposes nuclear energy, banned by law in Austria, as well as any fracking initiatives. This creates tensions with some of the neighboring new member states, such as the Czech Republic, Slovakia, or Poland, that are generally more supportive of both fracking and nuclear energy. Austria is also a staunch opponent of genetically modified foodstuffs and the EU leader in organic farming.

Austrian authorities supported the EU enlargement policy, although the consequent issue of increased migration remains politically sensitive. Austria supported the 2004, 2007, and 2014 eastern enlargements that created extensive economic opportunities and stabilized neighbor countries. It continues to support EU enlargement in the western Balkans and neighborhood policy in Eastern Europe, although it remains firmly opposed to EU membership for Turkey.

At the same time, Austria utilized the temporary measures protecting its labor market from the influx of workers from the postcommunist EU member states to the maximum.[38] Free movement of workers remains an important political issue due to concerns about possible exploitation of the social welfare system, competition in the labor market, and integration of migrant populations. The high levels of support for the anti-immigration rhetoric of the FPÖ induces the government to align closer with EU countries such as the UK and France that occasionally question existing EU rules on freedom of movement. However, Austria's social system is better protected against so-called benefit tourism, because it is based primarily not on residency but contributions, and, unlike other countries such as Germany, migrants in practice receive less social benefits than do native recipients.[39] Similarly, labor migrants concentrate in sectors such as elder care, construction, tourism, and agriculture that could hardly operate without them, which limits their effect on labor market competition and employment. Nonetheless, like many other EU countries Austria struggles to integrate its especially non-EU migrant populations into its education system and labor market, which keeps the issue on the policy agenda.[40]

The political divisiveness of the migration issues is also clearly observable in the results of the 2014 elections to the European Parliament. The FPÖ anti-migration and anti-euro ticket gained a fifth of the total vote and four MEP seats out of eighteen.[41] That is two more than in 2009, but at the same time, much less than some earlier polls had predicted.[42] The ÖVP and SPÖ coalition managed to achieve a 51.1 percent majority, while the Greens got three MEPs and the new liberal party NEOS one. Overall, the Austrian contribution to the far-right rise in the EP remained sizable but contained.[43]

In summary, after two decades in the EU, Austria is fully integrated within the EU governance structures and makes strong contributions especially in foreign, environmental, and enlargement policies. It benefits from the economic side of European integration, but struggles with integration of migrants, which fuels the Euro-skeptic vote in national and European elections. The recent crises also aggravated this skepticism toward European integration.

Austria in the Midst of Recent Crises

The impact of the global financial crisis on Austria was relatively modest in comparison with other EU countries, but it was by no means negligible. The economy avoided excessive macroeconomic imbalances that deepened the crisis on the EU's southern and eastern periphery. However, it was highly exposed to financial contagion through its banking sector, which was the main source of troubles during the financial and euro crises and which may be exacerbated further by the Ukrainian crisis and sanctions imposed by the EU on Russia.

In 2009, Austrian authorities responded to the financial crisis by stimulating the economy through increased spending. The government introduced a series of social measures, including abolishing university student fees, introducing a thirteenth month of family allowances, increasing social care subsidies, providing payment for some nursery school fees, and halting or postponing several price increases. It also stimulated demand in labor-intensive industries, such as construction, by accelerated investment into infrastructure and offering subsidies for renovation and thermal insulation of buildings. In line with the focus on competitiveness, the government also sustained funding for universities and increased the budget for the promotion of research and development.[44]

The labor market measures included a *kurzarbeit* (short time) scheme providing subsidies for up to two years encouraging firms to employ people for shorter working hours rather than dismiss them during the downturn.[45] The opportunities for job training for the unemployed were also increased. Furthermore, the government provided special loan guarantees of up to €300 million to facilitate lending to companies that form the core of the Austrian economy and are collectively the largest employers. The stimuli helped the economy rebound from the recession-level 3.9 percent decrease in GDP in 2009 to surprisingly strong growth of 2 percent in 2010.[46] The quick return of growth reduced the social benefit outlays and boosted tax revenue, which helped contain the government deficit and debt. Austria also remained in the small group of stable euro area countries that retained high credit ratings and could provide credible guarantees for stabilization schemes, such as the European Financial Stability Facility and later the European Stability Mechanism. However, the return of recession after 2011 pushed Austria toward fiscal consolidation.

The government passed a consolidation package in 2012 to meet the commitments under the Stability Program submitted to the European Commission. The aim was to balance the budget by 2016 with a combination of tax increases and budget cuts. The package introduced a tax on the sale of property, a "solidarity surcharge" on high earners, and the closure of several tax loopholes. However, most of the savings were to come from austerity measures, such as pay and hiring freezes in the public sector, cuts to pension increases, and reduced eligibility for early or disability retirements.[47] At the same time, the government remained committed to the support for research and development, thermal insulation subsidies, and large infrastructure investments, particularly railways. The new government that came to power in 2013 is likely to introduce further austerity measures due to the escalating costs of banking failures and increasing public indebtness.

Maintaining the financial stability of banks throughout recent crises proved to be the most serious challenge for Austrian authorities. Internal stagnation and external expansion left the banking sector dangerously exposed to shocks, just before it suffered from the global financial crisis, euro crisis, and the Ukrainian–Russian turmoil. So far, the Austrian banks and authorities have managed these crises well, while also making a distinctive contribution to the stabilization within the EU and in its southeastern neighborhood.

Austria was "overbanked" by the time of its EU entry in 1995. There were too many small banks, ill-prepared to take advantage of the Single Market and technological innovations.[48] They would be likely targets for acquisitions by larger European financial groups. However, banks responded to the new circumstances with domestic consolidation and expansion to the postcommunist countries.[49] They developed a unique business model of the second-home market by forming a closely linked network of locally incorporated banks, rather than relying on cross-border services or a mere branch network.[50] This novel business model was a crucial for understanding the Austrian response to the financial and economic crisis on the eastern periphery of the EU.

The eastern expansion was very successful and profitable before the crisis, but left Austria exposed to the economies of Hungary, Romania, Serbia, and Ukraine that fell into deep recession in 2009. Over €200 billion, equivalent to about 70 percent of GDP, was at risk in these countries, which came on top of the risk exposure to the domestic economy that shrank by 6 percent in 2009. The Austrian authorities responded quickly by providing potential funding of up to €100 billion in October 2008 for capital and funding guarantees to the banking sector. The guarantee calmed market fears, the large banks sustained access to borrowing from international investors, and after a brief spike the interest rates normalized. In the end, only 2.4 percent of the money allocated for bank support was used.[51]

However, the potential for disaster was much greater, both for Austria and the CEE countries. International markets nearly panicked on October 2008, after economist and *New York Times* columnist Paul Krugman published a blog headlined "Eastern Europe 2008 = Southeast Asia 1997," drawing attention to eastern Europe's foreign currency loan exposure that could turn to crushing losses for Austrian banks. These fears were exaggerated because global financiers lacked understanding of both Austrian banks and CEE countries, some of which, such as Poland, the Czech Republic, or Slovakia, remained stable and their banks profitable throughout the crisis. Nonetheless, there was the potential for extremely damaging panic, which authorities had to address.

In February 2009, Austria's minister of finance proposed an EU-level rescue fund of €150 billion, and Hungary's prime minister lobbied for an even larger package of €240 billion at the subsequent extraordinary summit of EU leaders.[52] These efforts were rejected by the large EU countries, which saw it as a specific problem of a few member states that did not require an EU-level response. However, Austrian and other Western banks with a strong presence in CEE countries faced sustained pressure as nervous international investors were reluctant to do business with them. Moreover, as some of the EU member states' governments bailed out their banks, they initially included provisions that limited financing of their subsidiaries in other EU and CEE countries.[53] There was a risk that some of these banks would "cut and run" from their foreign markets, which would hurt not only these host economies but also other transnational banks present in CEE markets, including those from Austria.[54] Austrian banks and authorities responded to this threat with a successful private-public initiative that partially substituted for the yet-to-emerge banking union.

The scheme, formally titled the European Bank Coordination Initiative, is better known as the Vienna Initiative and bears an imprint of Austrian capacity for cooperation and mediation of competing interests. In November 2008, the three largest banks, which were also most exposed to CEE, got together and wrote a letter to the European Commission asking for assistance in preventing the spread of banking nationalism that could induce the bank withdrawals from other EU countries.[55] The letter, supported by the Austrian Central Bank and supervisory authorities, was also sent to international organizations active in CEE countries.[56] These joined together and helped develop a series of agreements for Latvia, Hungary, Romania, Serbia, and Bosnia-Herzegovina. Transnational banks agreed to continue financing their CEE subsidiaries, while the CEE governments reiterated their compliance with reform requirements imposed by the International Monetary Fund (IMF). In addition, the Commission clarified that bailout clauses that restrict financing of bank subsidiaries and branches in other EU countries are illegal under Single Market law.[57] The IMF, European Bank for Reconstruction and Development, and European Investment Bank contributed a €33 billion loan package to support foreign bank lending in CEE countries.[58]

The Vienna Initiative tamed the panic in financial markets in the CEE region and averted further escalation of instability. In the end, only two minor banks withdrew completely from the CEE countries, while all large banks from Austria, France, Germany, the Netherlands, Belgium, and even crisis-stricken Greece stood behind their subsidiaries.[59] However, it did not change the underlying problem of large exposure to potential bank instability between home countries of transnational banks such as Austria and the host countries in CEE, whose banks remained dependent on capital from their foreign parent bank. Authorities in Vienna tried to limit this exposure with several new rules, including limits on new lending to foreign subsidiaries set only to 110 percent of its local deposits.[60] This new rule was not compatible with the aim of the Vienna Initiative, and it triggered the protests of host countries, eventually inducing the Commission ruling that such measures were incompatible with the Single Market, and Austrian authorities demoted its status to mere recommendation. Nonetheless, the episode illustrated the contradictory motivations of member states' authorities that on one hand try to find a cooperative response to the crisis but on the other hand need to protect their national interests.[61]

Government guarantees and the Vienna Initiative successfully stabilized the banking sector as a whole. Yet three smaller banks became insolvent and had to be nationalized during 2009. The most serious case was the Hypo Alpe Adria, the sixth largest bank that expanded aggressively into Balkan countries and employed questionable business practices that included involvement in several corruption scandals in Croatia. Its expansion was supported by a state guarantee provided by the government of the Austrian province of Carinthia, which was at the time dominated by populist FPÖ politicians. However, the province was never in a position to pay billions of euros if the guarantee was called upon. Hence, when the bank failed, Austrian federal authorities had to step in and take over losses, created by irresponsible decisions of the provincial government. This doubled the public deficit from 1.5 to 3 percent in 2014 alone and pushed the state debt of Austria toward 80 percent of GDP.

The government imposed the "solidarity tax" on bank balance sheets and imposed other fees on the financial sector in an effort to recoup some of the costs of bank restructuring.[62] It also supports the initiative of eleven EU countries that consider implementation of the financial transaction tax, which is a controversial initiative with uncertain prospects of being adopted.[63] However, these initiatives increased the tax burden on banks beyond the levels of Germany and other neighboring countries, which may undermine Vienna's status as the regional financial center. The Hypo Alpe Adria scandal and high taxes are illustrative of the increasingly ambivalent relationship to banking, which was a boon during the precrisis decade but became a major burden after the crisis erupted. Moreover, there are further losses to come if the Ukrainian crisis and EU-Russian conflict escalates.

Ukraine was a source of losses ever since the onset of the financial crisis, but Russia accounted for nearly a half of the net profit of Austrian banks in 2013. Austria also remains more exposed to Ukraine and Russia than any other banking sector in the EU.[64] A protracted conflict in the Ukraine will deepen losses, but escalating EU sanctions on Russia are a real threat, especially if they result in some forced exit or even some form of expropriation. Moreover, all other CEE economies are likely to suffer from the loss of Russian and Ukrainian export markets, therefore export-oriented firms might not be able to repay loans to local subsidiaries of Austrian banks. In short, after six years of fending off one threat after another, there is no sign of relief for Austrian banks and financial authorities.

Austrian Support for Federalizing Reforms

While the series of recent crises had a relatively modest effect on social and macroeconomic stability in Austria, the banking sector was persistently a source of major concerns and losses. At the same time, Austria has benefited enormously from the expansion of its firms and banks throughout the enlarged EU and beyond. This makes the country a firm supporter of EU and euro area reforms, such as the banking union, which preserves the economic benefits of international cooperation while containing its potential risks and costs.[65] However, these reforms tend to centralize macroeconomic and financial policies on the EU level, thus pushing the EU past the confederal model as outline in Chapter 1.

The EU model that emerges from the postcrises reforms is better characterized as contingent federalism or federalism by exception.[66] The so-called six- and two-pack reforms[67] of macroeconomic oversight as well as the banking union[68] have centralized oversight and decisionmaking on economic affairs, which brought the EU closer to federal-like arrangements. However, no reforms so far have introduced any automatic stabilizing mechanism, such as common unemployment insurance or some kind of cyclical adjustment mechanism, which are a hallmark of fiscal federalism. The European Stability Mechanism or the Single Resolution Fund can provide temporary fiscal support to participating EU countries stricken by financial or economic crisis. However, any such support is always contingent on identification of the source of the problem and commitment to reforms that would prevent its reoccurrence. Hence, all the new federal-like aspects of the reformed EU governance framework can only be used in exceptional circumstances and include no automatic fiscal transfers.

Austria, like all other EU member states, is likely to support further centralization in those areas where it seems in its national interests. At the same time, it will argue for more flexibility, a more confederal approach, in all those areas where it prefers to protect national specifics. The outcome in each policy domain depends on complex bargains within the EU decision-making system. Nonetheless, it is fair to conclude that in response to recent crises, Austria supported federalizing reforms that moved the EU, and in particular the euro area, further from any confederal model of governance.

Conclusion

Throughout the recent crises, Austria remained exceptionally stable. As in the past, its unique institutional framework of social partnership served it well. Before the crisis, it helped prevent a build-up of any macroeconomic imbalances that could undermine Austrian competitiveness and make the economy excessively vulnerable to external shocks. During the crisis, the social partnership underpinned the economic stimulus in 2009, followed by very gradual fiscal consolidation during the subsequent years. As a result, Austria was able to preserve its high living standards and low unemployment.

The banking sector proved to be the single most important threat to economic stability. Austrian banks expanded to other EU and non-EU countries in CEE very successfully and profitably during the decade before the crisis. However, this exposure was a source of major uncertainty among international creditors, who initially failed to differentiate among the stable and ailing CEE countries and failed to understand Austrian banks' long-term commitment to these economies. The risk of panic was contained by the Vienna Initiative, masterminded by Austrian actors and supported by the Commission and international financial organizations. The initiative proved to be a useful contribution to the stabilization of the eastern periphery and the neighborhood of the EU. At the same time, the domestic bank–supporting measures could not prevent a failure of three smaller banks, of which the case of Hypo Alpe Adria generated lasting economic and political consequences.

Nonetheless, Austria required no external support as did a number of EU countries on the southern and eastern periphery. To the contrary, its fiscal strength enabled it to make a contribution to the credibility of the European Stabilization Mechanism and other management measures that the EU created to assist stabilization of crisis-stricken banks and countries. At the same time, Austria is also set to benefit from recent EU reforms. The banking union, and especially the emerging single resolution mechanism, provides an additional layer of potential support for its large international banking sector. Hence, the financial panic regarding Austrian exposure to other economies is less likely to repeat itself, even if the Ukrainian and Russian crises continue to escalate.

Recent crises have dented the trust and support of the EU and the euro within the electorate.[69] The traditional parties of the grand coalition narrowly defended an overall majority in the 2013 elections, and a fifth of the votes in the 2014 European elections went to Euro-skeptic parties. Over time, these trends may challenge the traditional social partnership arrangements as well as Austrian cooperation on the EU level. However, there is currently no serious discussion of a major change of policy toward European integration, and Austria remains committed to the euro and the EU.

Notes

I thank Patrick Müller, Gerda Falkner, and Anna Durnová for helpful comments on earlier draft of this chapter and Veronika Pollak for comments and useful sources. All remaining mistakes are mine.

1. Eurostat, "Statistics Database," 2014. Available at epp.eurostat.ec.europa.eu /portal/page/portal/statistics/search_database. See also note 24.
2. See Breuss (2013) and Petersen, Bohmer, and Weisser (2014).
3. Dolezal and Zeglovits (2014), Aichholzer et al. (2014).
4. Falkner (2001).
5. Traxler (1998).
6. Nowotny (1993).
7. Katzenstein (1985).
8. OECD (2013), p. 94.
9. See Crouch and Traxler (1995). The multilevel social partnership is complemented by compulsory participation of trade unions in supervisory boards of larger enterprises.
10. OECD (2013), p. 94.
11. The Council for Economic and Social Questions, which consist of chambers' representatives and independent experts, establishes common evidence and analysis on economic and social questions. It operates on a consensual basis without voting, and its joint reports on economic and policy issues often serve as blueprints for government legislation.
12. OECD (2013), p. 91.
13. Ibid., p. 94.
14. Fischer, Gönenç, and Price (2011).
15. Dolezal and Zeglovits (2014).
16. OECD (2013), p. 95.
17. Ibid., p. 94.
18. Scharpf (1987).
19. Falkner and Hunt, (2006).
20. Austria is one of the few high-tax OECD countries that reduced the share of taxes in GDP after 2000. See OECD (2013), p. 96.
21. EIU (2013).
22. Traxler (1998), p. 258.
23. Eurostat (2014). Ranking of living standards refers to the GDP per capita figures expressed in purchasing power standard that enables cross-country comparison. Luxembourg tops these rankings, but since its economy depends largely on nonresidents, it is omitted from the comparison.
24. Eurostat (2014).
25. Ibid.

26. Ibid.

27. Rose (2000).

28. OECD (2013), p. 96.

29. Falkner (2001).

30. Scharpf (2010), Fernandes and Maslauskaite (2013).

31. Dolezal and Zeglovits (2014), pp. 4–5.

32. Nowotny (1993), p. 14. Mayer, Andersen, and Muller (2001).

33. OECD (2013), p. 96.

34. Dolezal and Zeglovits (2014).

35. Kritzinger (2014).

36. Dolezal and Zeglovits (2014), Aichholzer et al. (2014).

37. See Breuss (2013), Petersen, Bohmer, and Weisser (2014), and Mattern et al. (2012).

38. Germany and Austria requested a gradual phase-in of the free movement of workers from new member states. See Bohle and Husz (2005), p. 90.

39. Huber and Oberdabernig (2014).

40. European Commission, "Recommendation on Austria's 2014 National Reform Programme," 2014, p. 7. Available at http://ec.europa.eu/europe2020/pdf/csr2014/csr2014 _austria_en.pdf (accessed August 15, 2014). Eurostat, "Unemployment Rate for Non-EU Citizens Notably Higher Than for Nationals in the EU28," news release (2014), p. 2.

41. As part of the EP reform following the recent EU enlargements, the Austrian contingent was reduced from nineteen to eighteen parliamentarians.

42. Kritzinger (2014).

43. Treib (2014).

44. EIU (2011), p. 11.

45. Bock-Schappelwein, Mahringer, and Ruckert (2014).

46. Eurostat (2014).

47. EIU (2011), pp. 1–24.

48. Mayer, Andersen, and Muller (2001).

49. Oesterreichische Nationalbank (2004), p. 23.

50. Epstein (2014).

51. EIU (2011).

52. Epstein (2014).

53. Ibid., p. 853.

54. Kudrna and Gabor (2013), p. 553.

55. Epstein (2014).

56. These organizations included the European Bank for Reconstruction and Development, the International Monetary Fund, the International Finance Corporation, the World Bank, and the European Investment Bank, which eventually were all involved in the Vienna Initiative.

57. European Commission (2008a).

58. EBRD, EIB, and World Bank Group (2011).

59. Ibid.

60. EBRD (2013), p. 54.

61. Kudrna (2012), p. 289.

62. KPMG, "Bank Levies: Comparison of Certain Jurisdictions," 2012. Available at www.kpmg.com/Global/en/IssuesAndInsights/ArticlesPublications/Documents/bank -levy-9v2.pdf (accessed July 24, 2013).

63. Schneider (2014), pp. 1–3.

64. J. Ficenec, "Banks Most Exposed to Russia Sanctions," *Telegraph*, August 6, 2014, p. 1.

65. Kudrna (2014), pp. 14–18.

66. Enderlein et al. (2012).

67. The six-pack introduced or amended the following tools of macroeconomic coordination: European Semester, Medium-Term Budgetary Objectives, Commission run warning system, Excessive Deficit Procedure also covering debt, Excessive Imbalance Procedure, and Alert Mechanism Report for macroeconomic surveillance. The two-pack enhanced some of these further by implementing a Fiscal Compact (a.k.a. Treaty on Stability, Coordination and Governance) in euro area countries.

68. The banking union consists of the three pillars: the Single Rulebook, Single Supervisory Mechanism, and Single Resolution Mechanism. Complementary financial reforms consist of the European System of Financial Supervision, which introduced European Supervisory Authorities and European Systemic Risk Board as well as thirty legislative packages reforming various aspects of financial market regulation. See European Commission (2014b).

69. Eurobarometer (2013), p. 2, indicates that the positive view of the EU fell from 34 percent of Austrian respondents to 25 percent between late 2007 and late 2013, while the negative view increased from 30 percent to 34 percent. The positive view remains below and the negative above the respective EU averages.

13

Sweden:
A Non-Euro Member
Losing Influence

Leif Johan Eliasson

SWEDEN'S SECOND DECADE AS AN EU MEMBER DIFFERED FROM ITS
first. A significant part of the first ten years were spent adapting—specifically,
moving from being a small country with a large state mentality and perceived
moral superiority to a normal state among others, as well as modifying and
updating its security and defense policies as part of the European Union's
Common Security and Defense Policy (and to be compatible with NATO
standards).[1] Sweden has settled in as a constructive albeit Euro-skeptic, reform-
minded member state with strong public finances. Its experiences during the
global fiscal crisis, Eurozone turmoil, and Europe's banking and sovereign debt
crises were also different from most other states.[2] Sweden suffered a deep but
brief downturn in 2008–2009, followed by two years of growth rates equaling
many emerging markets. Swedish private sector companies flourished, while
the state continued its privatization of publicly owned assets. Several previously adopted structural changes buttressed public finances and helped consumer purchasing power during the recession. In the early 1990s Sweden introduced a dual income tax, combining a flat tax on capital with a progressive
income tax. Nationwide school vouchers preceded privatization of the post office, railroads, armaments industry, and motor vehicle inspections. The public
pension system was overhauled in 1998, replacing a defined benefit with a defined contribution system while making automatic adjustments for longer life
expectancy. This left Sweden as one of the few states not pressured to reduce
payments or reform the pension system during the crisis. Sweden was also one
of only four states not exceeding the EU's debt limit of 60 percent of gross domestic product (GDP) in 2012 and 2013, thus avoiding a Commission monitored excessive debt program.[3] Thanks to balanced budgets, solid finances, and
some additional reforms during the crisis (discussed later), national debt and
unemployment are projected to be lower by 2017 than they were in 2009.

One would expect this mid-sized country with the EU's seventh largest economy to exert influence in the EU. Sweden has long been considered an active and highly respected EU member, a perpetual advocate of efficient EU governance, improved environmental policies, and expanded free trade agreements. Being an EU member in good standing traditionally helps command respect among fellow members;[4] Sweden is continuously among the best in implementing EU directives and following EU regulations.[5] Yet the country's influence on EU economic and fiscal issues has declined dramatically, and other members of the Council of Ministers (hereinafter Council) and their representatives are increasingly skeptical of Sweden's positions and proposals on fiscal policies and related reforms because of its refusal to commit to further fiscal, monetary, and banking integration. Sweden is also frequently lumped with Britain as a permanent outsider on many other issues.

This chapter first places Sweden's approach to and relationship with the EU in its domestic context. Thereafter, the focus turns to the economy, banking, employment, and social policies, and how they have been affected by EU membership and the financial crisis. The final part looks at how remaining outside the euro, with no intentions of joining, has reduced Sweden's influence in the EU, leaving it with an uncertain future.

Background

Swedes have long cherished their distinctive ideals of low socioeconomic inequality, pragmatism over ideology, publicly funded investments, and social pacts, where the state, trade unions, and employers cooperate. *Folkhemmet* (people's home) is a well-established domestic metaphor for "the Swedish model" dating back to welfare expansion and industrial investments in wake of the 1930s Great Depression, and refers to comfort, familiarity, security, and high-quality public services. Sweden's success, with expansive growth, high living standards, low crime, no military conflicts, and internationally recognized quality manufacturing and diplomatic prowess, led Swedes to adopt a perceived social superiority, a sense of "exceptionalism."[6] As a consequence, Swedes cherished neutrality and remained skeptical of Europe's three C's (Catholicism, conservatism, capitalism).

The neutrality argument waned after the Berlin Wall fell and the EU's Treaty of Maastricht lacked a common defense clause. Yet the decisive factor for EU membership was a severe recession that started in 1991. With a banking crisis, skyrocketing unemployment, and accompanying budget deficits, all intensified by the tumultuous turns in Europe and export declines following the fall of communism, the major parties decided the benefits of membership outweighed the financial contributory obligations of a rich member country. EU membership negotiations required far-reaching market reforms in previously protected sectors, as well as new fiscal and monetary policies.

Finance, justice, commerce, agricultural, and social policy laws and regulations have been the areas most affected by EU membership.[7] Domestically institutionalized expectations of consensus-based policymaking (long overriding the legally stipulated simple majority needed for foreign policy decisions), which carry high opportunity costs for dissension, were manifest in new legislative committees. Swedish parliamentarians now monitor how ministers carry out their duties in the Council through an all-party parliamentary body: the EU Advisory Committee (EUAC). Though not concerned with legislative bills, it may call public hearings on any topic decided in the EU. The EUAC's weekly meeting, where the committee adopts recommendations (read: instructions) on policy issues, is attended by the cabinet minister(s) due to participate in the following week's specific Council session(s). If the government strays from EUAC's position (which has occasionally occurred since 2000) it must provide Parliament with a written explanation of its reasoning. Moreover, the government is required to continuously keep Parliament informed of the work in the EU. This is done through annual written reports and the biannual parliamentary EU debates.

Sweden joined the Union on practical grounds, as a necessary means to improve its global reach and enable a small country to gain economically and politically through the strength of a large union. The results have not been disappointing. Macroeconomic indicators are stellar, capital income has soared, and Swedes enjoy among the highest national median income in the world. The country has run annual surpluses most years since 2002, lowering the debt from 70 percent to a mere 39 percent of gross domestic product (GDP) by 2012; government spending as a share of GDP was reduced 23 percent. In many areas Sweden is now among the most market-oriented of all European states.

The reasons for Sweden's strong economic performance go much deeper than expanded markets through EU membership; they include well-functioning capitalist institutions (including property rights), deep trust in public institutions, regulatory and judicial transparency, meritocracy, solid public finances, and strong banks generating confidence to spend and invest.[8] Swedes trust their public institutions and politicians: the national tax authority and police both enjoy high approval ratings, and the national enforcement and collection agency is disliked by only 8 percent of the population. Swedes' trust in government is not that of a fool's ignorance but stems from a sustained culture of transparency, openness, and abiding by laws, reinforced by a fiercely independent investigatory press that continuously scrutinizes public affairs. Public right-to-know laws are among the most extensive in the world.[9] Add in unabated gender equality, semi-autonomous public agencies that implement most public sector policies, and very few politically appointees, and you have an efficient public sector that can rapidly and effectively implement reforms.[10] Swedish public administration departments and agencies have always operated largely independently of the national government. This autonomy enables flexibility, quick responses, and an adaptive approach to a changing regional and international environment, exemplified by volatile financial, economic, and labor markets, as well as new EU treaties. These positive traits are recognized internationally, as Swedish public servants, widely perceived as honest and skilled, also permeate international organizations and agencies. In addition to institutions, Swedes' curiosity, honesty, and flexibility are critical to explaining the ease and determination with which they carry out reforms, including large structural reforms. Companies, citizens, and policymakers consistently welcome new ideas, enthusiastically experimenting in areas deemed less than optimally efficient. International consumer brands have also recognized this, frequently using Sweden to test consumer responses to new products. In short, institutions matter; institutionalized trust is crucial. In southern Europe more people trust the EU more than they do their own government; in the north it's the opposite. The farther north in Europe one goes, the less corruption and more effective public services one finds.

There is deep-seated support for European integration, if not the euro, in Swedish society, but Swedes have a complex, even ambivalent relationship with the EU.[11] The country's economic success has gradually removed any lingering social and cultural hesitancy toward the three C's, and Swedes' liberal attitude on social issues and personal behavior (reproductive rights, marriage) turned out not to be threatened by EU membership, especially as many Catholic-dominated Southern and Eastern European countries have liberalized substantially. Domestic opinion of the EU tends to fluctuate with the state of the economy, and most Swedes recognize the EU's importance for Swedish exports, and its role in enhancing Sweden's international influence. European federalism remains dreaded in Sweden, and, reflective of the successes of its domestic reforms, most Swedes take a skeptical view to the EU's perceived bloated bureaucracy and perceived wasteful spending on agriculture and profligate Southern European states. General support for membership reached above 50 percent in annual surveys only once between 1996 and 2012, despite support among the highly educated, the politically interested, and those on the ideological center right; however, the country has not raised the prospect of leaving the EU, nor is there much domestic support for such a move.[12] When directly asked whether to leave (rather than whether EU membership is good for the country), a majority of Swedes consistently wish to remain in the EU, a trend unchanged during the financial and sovereign debt crisis.[13] Swedes' general support for the EU actually declined less than in Eurozone countries, again implying that support for the EU and developments in the Union appear highly correlated with domestic economic developments, which in turn work well because of efficient Swedish institutions.

How EU membership has impacted Sweden: The Economy

Access to the internal market and EU's free trade agreements with other states have greatly benefited Swedish companies by boosting sales, spurring employment, and aiding growth. The value of Swedish exports equal 48 percent of GDP, with 70 percent of exports going to Europe (2013), even though this ratio is slowly declining as North America and Asia assume a larger share. The 2008–2009 recession exposed the export economy's vulnerability to slowdowns in foreign markets with GDP declining 4 percent in 2009. Yet exports to North America and Asia, as well as Germany, soon rebounded. One reason is that many Swedish export products tend to have few substitutes. Sweden is a high-tech, high value-added, export dependent nation where the engineering industry accounts for half of all industrial output and exports.[14] Information technology, health, and life sciences are also big sectors, and most Swedish products benefit from reputational advantages: the country and its products are highly regarded around the world.[15]

Many of the structural reforms required of other states during and after the crisis had been implemented in Sweden prior to 2008, including banking and pension reforms. Swedish banks are also highly regarded. They are deemed safe, with triple-A ratings and significant profits. After the 1991–1993 banking crisis, including a state bailout and the creation of a bad bank to handle underperforming assets, the sector was completely overhauled. Capital requirements were raised, retail rather than investment banking became the focal point for the largest banks, and cost efficiencies were adopted (most Swedes now do mobile and online banking). Capital balance sheets grew strong, and bank profits have risen every year since 2010. By 2013, the combined assets of the four largest Swedish banks were four times the country's GDP, while their share prices were up almost 30 percent, and all were triple-A rated; none had problems raising capital, and all increased dividends.[16] Several leading banks (SEB, Nordea, Swedbanken) invested heavily in the Baltic, so when Lithuania, Estonia, and especially Latvia suffered severe recessions in 2008–2010, losses ensued. Yet Swedish banks coped well because of the Swedish requirements of tier 1 capital ratios higher than the prevailing Basel II requirements.[17] The housing market in Sweden suffered few direct repercussions from the mortgage problems in the United States or peripheral European markets, but strong domestic performance and low interest rates spurred home purchases, and Swedish households saw their property prices soar about 25 percent between 2006 and 2012. All major banks capped lending at 85 percent of property values, with further limits proposed by the government in 2014 to prevent a potential property bubble. The government has continuously sought to ensure that taxpayers would not be left with a hefty bill should a large bank run into other trouble. As the EU adopted higher tier 1 requirements than agreed by the Basel III Committee, Sweden joined the UK in successfully ensuring that states were allowed to set even higher requirements; Swedish banks are required to have a 12 percent leverage ratio of tier 1 capital from 2015, almost twice the Basel Committee requirements for 2019.[18]

Since 2001, the Swedish Central Bank has maintained a neutral position on the exchange rate of the krona, refusing to intervene directly in currency markets to stabilize or weaken the krona; a position that has won it praise internationally. Between 2007 and 2009, the central bank cut its benchmark interest rate more than the European Central Bank or the US Federal Reserve (in real terms), and as the Swedish economy rebounded in 2010, it raised interest rates to contain inflation.[19] The Swedish Central Bank also established new credit lines for banks and financial institutions, twelve-month low-interest loans with an expanded list of assets acceptable as security, and new swap lines with other central banks; it injected a total equivalent to 9 percent of GDP into the economy.[20] These extensive and decisive actions lowered rates and received positive market reactions.

Previously enacted public sector reforms generated strong public finances, thus removing any threat of austerity-based cuts to public services such as pension, unemployment insurance, education, research, or even foreign aid, while allowing greater support for innovation and creating an attractive environment for foreign investments. To both help domestic export companies and attract new investments, the corporate profit tax (already lower than in many other EU states) was cut to 22 percent in 2013, resulting in a cumulative lowering of the rate by one-third over sixteen years. Foreign investments grew 12 percent at the height of the euro crisis (2010) when the rate stood at 26 percent, with half of investments coming from outside Europe; a lower rate will likely attract even more investments.[21] Innovative start-ups generating new technology products in health, medicine, information and communications technology, and life sciences have led Sweden to consistently rank as one of the most competitive countries, with Stockholm ranked as one of the world's top ten most competitive cities, a position it is projected to retain until at least 2025.[22] *Fortune* magazine wrote, "The Swedish capital is especially good for software, research and development and its business-friendly policies."[23] Other reforms helped domestic growth. Wealth and inheritance taxes were abolished in 2006 and 2007, and the residential property tax a year later; along with high levels of personal savings, these fiscal policy reforms spurred consumer spending and domestic investments. Sweden also spends more than most on research and development, which has helped generate new products, services, and successful companies. Finance Minister Anders Borg explained,

> If you have a high wealth tax and an inheritance tax, people emigrate because it becomes too costly to own a company. Ownership is a production factor. Entrepreneurs are a production factor. Yes, these people are rich and you can

obviously argue that we want to encourage social cohesion. But it is also problematic if you drive out entrepreneurs from your country, because they are the source of job creation.[24]

Dozens of major international companies opened shops or expanded their presences in Sweden in 2012–2013.[25] Domestic creativity and entrepreneurship grew alongside foreign investments during the crisis. For example, technology and innovation combined to generate new desired products based on Swedish culture and history, including smartphone apps and games (Swedes make more per person than any other country).

From 2006 to 2013, Sweden implemented numerous tax cuts for individuals and corporations; adopted national job training programs; simplified, decentralized, and cut welfare payments; and incentivized health services. The results in health care included dramatic cuts in waiting time and improved outcomes. The debt shrank from 45 percent of GDP in 2007 to 38 percent in 2012, while the median national income rose nearly 5 percent.[26] The economy grew 6 percent in 2010, 4 percent in 2011, and 2 percent the following year; the current account surplus averaged 6 percent in 2010–2012.[27] Inflation peaked at 3.1 percent in 2010, before falling and remaining below 2 percent; Sweden's economy (inflation adjusted) was 8.5 percent larger in the fourth quarter of 2013 compared with the same quarter in 2008. The result of stellar growth, low inflation, and reformed taxes was a real net income growth averaging 1.5 percent annually in 2007–2012.[28]

In sum, Sweden's floating currency and skillful monetary policies helped with a steady rebalancing of trade and economic growth, but so has well-functioning markets, reformed public services and entitlements, widespread trust in public institutions, and regulatory and judicial transparency.[29]

Unemployment

The Eurozone crisis affected Swedish employment as export markets were in recession. With stable fiscal policies but stubbornly high unemployment (compared with precrisis levels), growing skills shortages, and uncertainty about the external environment, especially in Europe, the government acted on social benefits reforms, tax cuts, and job training programs.[30]

Over two-thirds of Swedish workers belonged to a union in 2011 (unchanged since 1970 and one of the highest levels in the Organisation for Economic Co-operation and Development). Membership has distinct and recognized advantages as unions negotiate wages through collective bargaining agreements (there is no national minimum wage, and the state stays clear of wage disputes) and also administer most unemployment insurance (contingent on the recipient actively seeking work). Roughly 30 percent of Swedes do not qualify for contributory-based unemployment insurance (administered by unions) and have to rely on state-based assistance programs.

Willingness to work has always been an eligibility requirement for state unemployment insurance, housing assistance, heating assistance, and other welfare provisions, and assistance is provided through transfers, services, in-kind services, and cash (for food and clothes) equivalent to nearly 60 percent of net national median income. The pressure on these programs increased during the recession (demand rose 13 percent in 2009) as unemployment worsened. The percentage of the labor force on disability insurance also rose sharply, straining social expenditures.

During the brief recession, trade unionists worked actively with employers to find ways to save jobs while remaining competitive. Swedish trade unions value free trade and globalization, recognize the necessity of a company remaining competitive, and work with the employers and employer unions to improve competitiveness.[31] Cooperative efforts notwithstanding, and despite having the highest employment levels in the EU, unemployment rose to 9 percent in 2010 before gradually declining to 8 percent by mid-2014. Even so, there was still slack in the economy. While the economy was growing at 3 percent, skills shortages held back even higher growth; many sectors had significant problems finding employees. Sweden's continued growth will depend on its ability to address skills shortages and associated wage pressures; some companies in the engineering and medical sectors offer unprecedented signing bonuses. Restrictions on foreign skilled labor have been lifted; attaining a work permit is relatively easy for engineers, computer scientists, medical personnel, and other skilled labor.[32]

The wage system in Sweden is completely left to labor market participants, with employer-employee unions agreeing to sector specific wages and benefits (the latter within the realm of national legislative and EU minimum levels). In 2011, the government brought together all social partners to discuss how to make the labor market even more flexible, yet inclusive, bringing marginalized recent immigrants and/or low-skilled citizens back into the workforce. A structural budget surplus allowed for labor market initiatives as well as tax cuts, a rare combination on a continent dominated by austerity, tax hikes, and cuts to public spending. There were also other reforms to spur the economy. Tax credits for the poorest, equaling up to a month's extra earnings, were approved in 2012, followed a year later by the fifth increase in income tax credits in seven years. The threshold for paying taxes was raised, and pensioners' tax obligations were lowered. Sweden's prime minister commented that "Sweden is in a position of strength that allows fiscal policy to support measures for growth and jobs . . . the tax credit alone is expected to create 13,000 new jobs . . . wage earners are going to have more money in their pockets."[33] In 2013, the conservative-led coalition government agreed to create 14,000 new adult vocational training slots by the end of 2014, along with 8,000 practical work experience and labor market training places (where government pays most of the expenses for companies training workers) and 2,800 new seats in engineering and nursing degree programs.[34]

One of Sweden's core problems is a high rate of sick leave, which feeds into permanent disability claims.[35] Short-term sick leave is low, but 50 percent of those on sick leave remain absent for more than six months, with many eventually moved over to disability insurance.[36] In 2004, this applied to 14 percent of the working-age population.[37] By late 2006, the government decided to reform eligibility for sick leave and oversight of claims, while simultaneously adopting long-term changes in education by promoting diverse skills and job mobility in early ages to allow people with certain disabilities to move into other suitable jobs. By the time the crisis hit in 2008, the rate of disability claims had fallen, but as unemployment increased, the total percentage of the workforce receiving some social insurance stood at over 20 percent. Sick leave benefits were then again changed in 2010, from an unlimited duration to a maximum of 550 days, with intermittent assessments of an individual's work capacity. Those on disability are now allowed to earn substantial income while initially keeping their benefits; employers may apply for substantial subsidies (equal to twice the employer's expenses) when hiring long-term unemployed or individuals on sickness, rehabilitation, or disability benefits.[38]

How EU Membership Has Affected Sweden: The Political Arena

The Rise of the Extremists

The absences of a unified EU immigration policy and the lack of burden sharing for asylum seekers has contributed to major political developments in Sweden. Like many other EU states, Sweden has experienced the rise of a populist far-right party. The Swedish Democrats (SD), a nationalist, anti-immigrant, anti-EU party with roots in neo-Nazism, emerged from the fringes, ascending on waves of discontent with rising unemployment to secure over 10 percent in the May 2014 European Parliamentary elections (matching the results of the only Swedish party advocating European federalism, the liberal People's Party) and over 12 percent in the fall 2014 national elections. The party initially seized on a widely publicized case decided a few years prior to the 2010 elections as indicative of EU policies overriding sovereignty, forcing a race to the bottom and displacing Swedish workers, especially as European financial markets were tumbling and Swedish export orders began to decline. The case included a Latvian construction company that won a contract to renovate a Swedish school but brought in Latvian workers at Latvian wages (40 percent lower than Sweden's collectively bargained wages), and where the European Court of Justice ruled that EU law on free movement of workers supersedes the right to collective action (taken by Swedish unions).[39] In the 2010 national elections, the SD received 5.7 percent of the votes, capturing 20 out of 349 seats in Parliament, thus depriving the ruling conservative-led coalition of its own majority.[40] The government, with support of the opposition SD, allowed in hundreds of thousands of refugees in the years leading up to the 2014 election (more per capita than any other EU member), and tensions over generous immigration policies and poor assimilation (especially for North African and Middle Eastern asylum seekers) mounted. Some analysts have pointed to a fraying social model, where the combination of having the most generous pace of immigration in the developed world (over 17 percent of the population is now foreignborn; most are non-European), stubbornly high unemployment (8 percent in 2014; 16 percent in immigrant-born communities), and generous social benefits, is straining resources and increasing social friction. Race-based attacks have risen, and in 2013, street violence erupted in suburbs of Stockholm, with gangs (mostly unemployed youths) burning cars and throwing rocks at police. The public has frequently blamed the EU for Sweden's social problems and the high level of EU asylum seekers ending up in the country.[41] Partly in response to lackluster EU action, Prime Minister Fredrik Reinfeldt declared that any Syrian refugees making their way to Sweden would be granted asylum, while asking Swedes to "open their hearts" to immigrants.[42] This, along with the financial crisis, rising Swedish unemployment, and generous EU bailouts fueled discontent and fueled support for the SD. The 2014 fall general elections were further evidence of immigration skepticism. While 48 percent of Swede's expressed satisfaction with the center-right coalition just before the election, and 45 percent said a new government would not do better, the SD gained a king-maker role in Parliament after these elections.[43] Both the coalition government and the opposition parties have refused to formally work with the SD, thus limiting their influence on policy. However, the rise of the SD shook Swedish politics unlike anything since World War II. Parliament has allocated additional funds to integration projects while calling for better enforcement of EU solidarity rules on asylum, including burden sharing.[44]

How Sweden Influences the EU:
The Euro and EU Integration

Swedes rank their country's ability to influence events in Europe as a vital reason for membership.[45] The crisis amplified this perspective: Swedes perceive themselves as a responsible country with sound finances and proper policies which others should follow, and domestic perceptions of Swedish influence is vital for the government's ability to pursue certain policies.[46] The successful resolution of its 1991–1993 banking crisis served as a model for Ireland's and Spain's attempts at resolving their own banking crises. Relations with the UK, Finland, the Baltic states, and increasingly Poland also appeared strengthened in the debate over austerity versus stimulus. The fact that many structurally distinct but in practice overlapping bodies (e.g., the European Council, EcoFin, the Commission, central banks, various committees) were involved in addressing the initial steps of the fiscal-turned-sovereign-debt crisis and banking union provided many opportunities for Swedish representatives to influence decisions on, for example, bailouts and the EU budget (discussed later). Sweden supported the bailouts of Southern European states and signed the EU's Fiscal Compact, while advocating fiscal responsibility for euro and noneuro states alike, and stressing the urgency of structural reforms in distressed countries.

Sweden has long been perceived as pragmatic, effective, and reliable, devoid of the ideological underpinnings prevalent in France or Germany—in other words, a country with whom others have liked to cooperate.[47] With strong public finances, solid banks, and extensive domestic structural reforms, Swedish leaders were not shy with their ideas, championing supply-side economics while declaring "Europe's problems are fundamentally long-term and structural, with faltering competitiveness, over-regulated service sectors, labor markets with little flexibility, and low potential growth. Temporary stimuli do not solve these structural problems."[48] Sweden joined other Northern European states in advocating austerity measures and structural reforms in peripheral and/or high-deficit states, while voting for the IMF and EU loan programs. Borg urged the Southern European states to enact far-reaching structural reforms to calm markets and raise competitiveness, even publicly criticizing Greece's timid steps, vacillation, and lack of public sector reform.[49] It is a bluntness that won both praise and criticism, but some diplomats argue that Borg's comments conveyed the frustrations of many others, including German Minister Wolfgang Schäuble, who were unable to express their feelings publicly.[50] Why? Having a well-run, noneuro country with a history of Greek immigration bring attention to Greece's performance shifts the focus away from the main paymaster, Germany (as well as others, such as the Netherlands and Finland). For Sweden it builds up political capital with those states that ask Sweden to speak tough. Sweden also needs countries such as Greece and Italy to succeed as Europe continues to be Sweden's largest export market.

This was evident when Sweden agreed to let the Treaty on the Stability, Coordination and Governance in the Economic and Monetary Union (Fiscal Compact) be part of the EU as long as noneuro members had some ability to veto plans affecting them. Sweden joined others (Britain, Poland) in insisting that noneuro states be given access to Eurozone meetings when discussions pertain to European competitiveness, the architecture of the euro, and other related issues in the treaty.[51] After Britain's veto, the Fiscal Compact became an intergovernmental treaty. Sweden signed and ratified the agreement while reserving the right to apply articles only of its choosing. The reasons for signing an agreement lacking any compulsory action was that Sweden desires deeper relations with other EU states and wants to be perceived as a constructive member, even if the population (currently) rejects euro membership.[52]

In the year-long wrangling over the 2014–2020 EU budget, Sweden assumed a tough stand, scolding the initial proposal by the Commission and countering with calls for a 15 percent cut over seven years.[53] Sweden sided with Britain in pushing for the reallocation of available funds, opposing new transfers of power to the Commission (except when enhancing the service sector of the internal markets), and the financial transaction tax, while supporting comprehensive trade and investment agreements without exempted sectors.[54] Sweden argued for cuts partly because it opposed expanding the budget when cuts were demanded of many member states, but also because it was deemed an opportune time to cut wasteful agricultural subsidies while increasing allocation to productive areas such as research and development, foreign affairs, and justice and home affairs. Sweden was very pleased with reallocations that occurred and the slight reduction in the size of the budget.

Small achievements aside, remaining outside the euro is gradually diminishing Sweden's standing in the EU. While leading Swedish companies as well as centrist and right-leaning parties support adopting the euro, the public does not. Membership was rejected in a 2003 referendum, and opposition to joining the euro hit an all-time high in December 2012, with only 9 percent desiring the euro.[55] The krona is not in ERM2 (the required pre-euro stage), in contrast to, for example, Denmark, which tied its currency to the euro shortly after its launch. Sweden has met all economic and inflation criteria and lacks the legal opt-out awarded Denmark and Britain, but it has some incompatibilities in the legal basis of the Swedish Central Bank with the Treaty on the Functioning of the European Union Articles 123 and 130, particularly its lack of clear independent powers of appointment, reporting, profit allocation, and monetary financing (credit and guarantees).[56] The required changes for EU treaty compatibility are easy to implement, but retaining existing provisions provides the Swedish government a legal cover. The Commission has been increasingly flexible interpretation of euro membership, realizing that politically, at least during the crisis, that it was better left to the countries themselves to decide when they are ready to apply; Sweden's refusal to change its laws is causing consternation in the EU, evident in the Commission's annual euro convergence reports and in discussions with officials.[57] One official in the Council referred to Sweden as an "irritant." "In the grand scheme of things, it is not feasible to stay with one foot in and one foot out," "It does not mean that they have to adopt the euro immediately, but on the Swedish side they need to show a more constructive role."[58] With the rank-and-file of the main opposition party, the SD, remaining firmly opposed to the currency, the Conservative-led coalition government joined the opposition in declaring the issue off the agenda for the next Parliament, ending in 2018.

This stance has unequivocally weakened Sweden's position vis-à-vis other members on issues, which will shape the future integration process, such as banking union and fiscal integration in the Eurozone.[59] For example, Sweden has continuously pushed for a clear separation, a firewall, between monetary policy and banks, and was disappointed when the December 2013 European Council agreement on banking union failed to achieve this. The agreement also fell short of an efficient and credible backstop; Sweden argued the agreed structure would be too slow, too cumbersome, and fail to sever the vicious ties between sovereigns and banks.[60] A spat between the Swedish and Dutch finance ministers erupted, where they disagreed on whether the Council decision on the banking union was sufficient to resolve failing banks, resulting in a rare public display of real underlying tensions.[61] Traditional Northern European allies are increasingly exasperated with the Swedes, telling them to take a stance and stick to it: "Join the euro if you want a say." French representatives think Sweden has become ultraliberal, way too Anglo-Saxon for France or anything they perceive as acceptable for Europe.[62] According to one senior diplomat "Germany's confidence has risen dramatically since the start of the crisis, reflected in an unprecedented brashness on policy positions. If you are not willing to integrate further, to join the euro, the Germans are increasingly less interested in your position. As spillover will naturally occur into other policy areas among the core euro-group, this German strength will be clear." Even Denmark enjoys more receptiveness; it is a well-known secret that the Danes are considering abandoning most of their opt-outs (justice and home affairs, defense, and the euro). The Danish government has also publicly acknowledged that a de facto two-speed EU is emerging as the Eurozone countries integrate and speed ahead, leaving other members with less influence on the direction of the EU.[63]

Conclusion

Sweden straddles the divide in the EU. It supported the Commission's six-pack in 2010 because it addressed state finances, aiming to rectify budget deficits through joint oversight and recommendations. During its second decade in the Union, Sweden has worked for deeper economic integration, free trade, and a stronger internal market; it punched above its weight in foreign affairs and supported closer foreign policy and defense cooperation. Yet Euro-skepticism has grown, and with a populace increasingly skeptical of integration in areas other than the common market, Sweden's position is one of growing isolation. Among the main parties only the Left and the SD are calling for Sweden to leave the EU, but their presence has stifled any discussion of Swedish support for further EU political or monetary integration until after the next general election in 2018. This will make influencing the future direction of the EU increasingly tough. Noneuro members may have to choose whether to join the core by adopting the euro or be relegated to the periphery. However, opposition runs so deep in all but certain elite groups that Sweden's economy would likely have to be near its 1991 state for the country to reconsider the common currency; under such circumstances it is highly unlikely that Sweden could meet the fiscal and macroeconomic membership criteria for the common currency.

Notes

The author thanks Nemanja Nikolic for assistance with this chapter.

1. Eliasson (2006).

2. This chapter draws on seven personal discussions on background with officials from the three countries' Permanent Representations to the EU.

3. European Union Council, "Regulation Amending Regulation (EC) No. 1467/97 on Speeding Up and Clarifying the Implementation of the Excessive Deficit Procedure," EU Commission No. 1177, 2011. Available at http://ec.europa.eu/economy_finance /economic_governance/ (accessed November 8, 2011)..

4. Alistair Scrutton, "One Foot In, One Foot Out—Sweden's EU Role Under Scrutiny," Reuters, 2012. Available at http://www.reuters.com/article/2012/12/19/sweden -eu-idUSL4N09R3Q620121219 (accessed December 19, 2012).

5. European Commission, "National Implementation Measures Notified to the Commission," continuous. Available at http://ec.europa.eu/eu_law/directives/directives _communication_en.htm.

6. See, for example Dörfer (1992), p. 605; Ingebritsen (1997), p. 246; Anderson (1996); Cramér (1998).

7. Halje (2012). She estimates that 30 percent of laws and regulation are the result of or tied to EU directives.

8. Swedish exports declined slightly as imports rose from key markets in Europe and North America as the krona strengthened 22 percent vis-à-vis the dollar and euro 2009–2013 (source: http://scb.se).

9. One rather amusing example was conveyed to me by a representative of one of the largest lobbying firms in Brussels. On behalf of a client, the firm had been trying to get hold of a proposal circulated in the Council and headed for the Parliament, and all the normal avenues led to nothing. The Swedish office assistant was then asked to call up her national representative at the Council and ask, as a Swedish citizen, for the document. Thirty minutes later, it was delivered to her inbox.

10. Holmberg and Sommerstein (2013), Holmberg, Weibull, and Oscarsson (2010).

11. Holmberg (2013).

12. The highest educated citizens remain consistently supportive of EU membership. Holmberg and Vernersdotter (2013), see also pp. 10–13; Tallberg (2013).

13. Holmberg (2012), European Commission, "Standard Eurobarometer 70, spring 2013, p. 70. Available at http://ec.europa.eu/public_opinion/archives/eb_arch_en.htm.

14. CIA, "World Fact Book," 2013. Available at https://www.cia.gov/library /publications/the-world-factbook.

15. Corporate Excellence—Centre for Reputation Leadership (2012), Reputation Institute, "Canada Has the Best Reputation in the World According to Reputation Institute's 2013 Couuntry Reptrak Study," press release, 2013. Available at http://www.reputationinstitute.com/frames/events/2013_Country_RepTrak_Press _Release_Final.pdf (accessed September 6, 2012).

16. Richard Milne, "Swedbank Finds 'Utility Banking' Pays Dividends," *Financial Times*, June 11, 2013. Available at http://www.ft.com/intl/cms/s/0/320d29aa-d07e -11e2-a050-00144feab7de.html#axzz2nxVpSbbj.

17. Swedish banks focused on safe retail banking, eschewing credit growth and risky investments, leaving them with ratios of 12–17 percent by 2012, much higher than other European banks.

18. In 2013 the government was discussing ratios of 15 or 20 percent by 2020. Johan Carlström and Niklas Magnusson, "Borg Tells Swedish Banks to Gird for Buffer Rule Topping 12%," *Bloomberg News Online*, May 21, 2013. Available at http://www.bloomberg.com/news/2013-05-21/borg-tells-swedish-banks-12-capital -requirement-may-be-raised.html (accessed May 23, 2013).

19. The central bank rate went from 4.75 percent in 2008 to 0.25 percent in mid-2009, before rising to 2 percent in 2011.

20 Elmér et al. (2012).

21"Stockholm's Top 5 Foreign Investments Trends," *Swedish Wire*, March 28, 2011. Available at http://www.swedishwire.com/business/9121-stockholms-top-5 -foreign-investments-sectors.

22 Economist Intelligence Unit in Johan Nylander, "Retail Brands Flood into Stockholm—Apple, Prada, Zara Home, Habitat, Michael Kors, Sephora, Stella Mccart-ney, Picard, River Island," *Swedish Wire*, December 10, 2013. Available at http://www.swedishwire.com/business/19058-retail-brands-flood-into-stockholm -apple-prada-zara-home-habitat-michael-kors-sephora-stella-mccartney-picard-river -island-starbucks. In the same article, Professor Stephane Garelli, director of the IMD World Competitiveness Center that ranked Sweden the most competitive country in Europe said, "Europe's competitiveness is declining, but Switzerland, Sweden, Germany and Norway are shining successes." A respected independent judiciary, strong constitutional guarantees of property rights and freedom of speech, a well-educated workforce, low capital gains and corporate tax rates, and an open trade-based economy are key factors in making it one of the world's most competitive states. See World Economic Forum rankings at http://www.weforum.org/issues/global-competitiveness.

23. Omar Akhtar, "Seven Best New Global Cities for Startups," *CNN Money Fortune*, September 19, 2012. Available at http://money.cnn.com/gallery/technology /2012/09/19/startups-global-cities.fortune/3.html (accessed September 19, 2014).

24. Quoted in Fraser Nelson, "Sweden's Secret Recipe Advice from a Successful— and Tax Cutting—Finance Minister," *Spectator*, April 14, 2012. Available at http://www.spectator.co.uk/features/7779228/swedens-secret-recipe/?fwcc =1&fwcl=1&fwl.

25. "GfK Study Shows Uneven Distribution of Purchasing Power Across Europe," GfK press release, November 4, 2013. Available at http://www.gfk.com/news-and-events/press-room/press-releases/Pages/purchasing-power-europe-2013-14.aspx.

26. The cost of financing its national debt dropped 80 percent from 1998 to 2013.

27. World Bank data at http://data.worldbank.org/indicator/BN.CAB.XOKA.CD /countries.

28. OECD data at http://www.oecdbetterlifeindex.org/countries/sweden/; Nylander (2013).

29. Swedish exports declined slightly as imports rose from key markets in Europe and North America as the krona strengthened 22 percent vis-à-vis the dollar and euro 2009–2013 (source: http://scb.se).

30. Sweden was the first country to introduce universal school vouchers in 1993, but as PISA results showed declining results in 2009, new reforms were introduced in 2011 for compulsory school, upper secondary school, and higher education.

31. "Unions, Inc.: Unions Are in Trouble. But Some Are Learning New Tricks— from the Bosses," *The Economist*, April 6, 2013. Available at http://www .economist.com/news/international/21575752-unions-are-trouble-some-are-learning -new-tricksfrom-bosses-unions-inc.

32. "Why Coming to Work in Sweden Has Never Been Easier," *The Local*, July 13, 2011. Available at http://www.thelocal.se/20110713/34918.

33. Finance Minister Borg and Prime Minster Reinfeldt quoted in Richard Milne, "Sweden Unveils Further Stimulus Package as Election Looms," *Financial Times*, September 18, 2013. Available at http://www.ft.com/intl/cms/s/0/e407e96a-2038-11e3-9a9a-00144feab7de.html#axzz2t8a6J5qh.

34. European Commission, "Sweden's National Reform Programme 2013 Europe 2020—The EU's Strategy for Smart, Sustainable and Inclusive Growth," 2013, p. 4. Available at http://ec.europa.eu/europe2020/pdf/nd/nrp2013_sweden_en.pdf.

35. Thulesius and Grahn (2007).

36. OECD (2009), p. 16; 9 percent were on disability insurance in 2012, and by 2013 20 percent of the working age population received some social assistance.

37. OECD (2009), pp. 8–9.

38. Ibid., p. 24.

39. Court of Justice of the European Union (2007), case Case C-341/05, Laval Un Partneri Ltd V Svenska Byggnadsarbetareförbundet, Svenska Byggnadsarbetareförbundets Avd. 1, Byggettan, Svenska Elektrikerförbundet." Available at http://curia.europa.eu/juris/document/document.jsf?text=&docid=71925&pageIndex=0&doclang=EN&mode=lst&dir=&occ=first&part=1&cid=735937 (accessed December 18, 2007).

40. Another neo-Nazi party gained 2.8 percent of the vote in a regional election in 2010, thereby becoming the first national-socialist party to gain elected seats since World War II. While racist groups declined from 2008 to 2012, neo-Nazi and nationalist parties nonetheless gained traction. "Nazi Activity Increases in Sweden: Report," *The Local*, December 18, 2013. Available at http://www.thelocal.se/20131218/nazi-activity-increases-in-sweden-report.

41. For example, Holmberg (2012).

42. Summer speech, August 15, 2014. Available at at http://www.tv4play.se/program/nyheterna?video_id=2918957.

43. Swedish Radio poll, August 25, 2014. Available at http://sverigesradio.se/sida/gruppsida.aspx? programid=83&grupp=12794.

44. "EU Countries Must Share Responsibility for Refugees, Sweden Insists," *EurActive*, March 10, 2014. Available at http://www.euractiv.com/justice/sweden-eu-countries-share-respon-news-533998..

45. Holmberg (2012).

46. Interview with government adviser, Stockholm, 2012; see Jerneck (2013), esp. p. 3.

47. Naurin and Lindahl (2010).

48. Finance Minister Borg, *Dagens Nyheter*, May 29, 2013.

49. Finance Minister Borg at the German Marshall Fund, February 13, 2012. Available at http://www.youtube.com/watch?v=dwC3z3qTx9Q.

50. Sweden supported Germany's proposed contracts between states and the Commission, where loans would only be provided in exchange for structural reforms.

51. Treaty on the Stability, Coordination and Governance in the Economic and Monetary Union, available at http://european-council.europa.eu/media/639235/st00tscg26_en12.pdf.

52. Alistair (2012); confirmed in personal communication in Brussels.

53. EU Affairs Minister Ohlsson, Foreign Minister Bildt, and Prime Minister Reinfeldt publicly stated that "cuts should be three or four times as much," "no deal will be possible on the basis," "It was a distinctly backward-looking EU budget proposal. . . . Are they aware of a changing world out there?" "Unrealistic. They have to be lowered,"

in Andrew Rettman, "Sweden Emerges as Top EU Budget Hawk," *EUObserver*, October 31, 2012. Available at http://euobserver.com/economic/118046.

54. Ibid.

55. Holmberg and Vernersdotter (2013).

56. European Commission, "Convergence Report," 2012, pp. 145–146. Available at http://ec.europa.eu/economy_finance/publications/european_economy/2012/pdf/ee-2012-3_en.pdf..

57. The Commission is more careful after being burned by Greece's dubious accounting when it was allowed to join in 2001, which came back to hurt the Greeks and the Eurozone in 2010 when Greece needed the first of two bailouts.

58. Senior official quoted in Scrutton (2012). This was confirmed by several EU diplomats in personal conversations.

59. "Its political commitment to the EU is being tested," "Sweden needs to rethink its relations with the EU, otherwise it risks being more side lined." Diplomats quoted in Scrutton (2012).

60. "Though it is a long-term process of building a solid structure, this solution we worry is very complex and fails to provide a confidence boost to the European economy." Finance Minister Borg, December 18, 2013, Brussels. Available at http://www.youtube.com/watch?v=-SH3ezxdwl4.

61. Borg and Dijsselbloem interviews on December 19, 2013, see, for example, http://www.youtube.com/watch?v=-SH3ezxdwl4 and http://www.youtube.com/watch?v=BhkDixv-iTw (accessed January 4, 2014).

62. An extreme example of rejecting noneuro states includes a failed attempt by the French and Swedish finance ministers to coauthor an opinion piece on structural reforms. The French ministry found the first Swedish draft so Anglo-Saxon, borderline libertarian, that it found no reason to even reply. Personal communication, 2013.

63. Helle Thorning-Schmidt, speech at the College of Europe, 2012, and "Interview in Altinget.dk," 2014. Available at http://www.altinget.dk/artikel/132265-thorning-fordel-hvis-danmark-kommer-med-i-euroen.

14

Finland:
An End to Domestic Consensus?
Tapio Raunio

FINLAND'S INTEGRATION POLICY CAN BE CHARACTERIZED AS FLEXI-
ble and constructive. Successive governments have constantly underscored
the importance of being involved in the process when decisions that con-'
cern Finland are taken. According to the political elite, national interests
can be best pursued through active and constructive participation in European Union (EU) decisionmaking. Underlying this stance is a conviction
that strong and efficient European institutions and common rules can best
protect the rights and interests of smaller member states, as intergovernmental processes tend to favor the larger member states.

Pragmatism and adaptability are the leading qualities of Finland's EU
policy, behavioral traits obviously influenced by Cold War experiences.
Finnish integration policy thus stands in striking contrast to the policies of
Denmark and Sweden (and, of course, Norway and Iceland), both of which
have been far less supportive of further integration. Finland is the only
Nordic country that belongs to the Eurozone, with the single currency
adopted without much political contestation. The earlier policy of neutrality
or military nonalignment has been compromised or abandoned altogether as
Finland has played an active part in the further development of the EU's
Common Foreign and Security Policy (CFSP).[1]

However, the recent euro crisis has certainly shaken the foundations of
this pro-integrationist approach, bringing to the surface the internal divisions that exist among political parties and the public over Europe. In particular, the crisis ushered in an era of unprecedented domestic politicization
of Europe, with this contestation over Eurozone bailout measures and the
further development of integration affecting the work of Parliament, government, and even Cabinet formation. Moreover, the current war in Ukraine
has led to questions about Finland's foreign policy, especially in relation to

243

Russia, and to what extent Finnish external relations are tied to European-level decisions. The domestic debates have clearly revealed the tensions between those favoring a more supranational EU and those more in line with a confederal vision of Europe.

Joining the "West" for Economic and Security Reasons

When the Cold War ended and the Soviet Union collapsed, Finland wasted no time seizing the opportunity to become fully engaged in European integration. While joining the European Community (EC) was not on the political agenda during the Cold War, Finnish industry, especially the influential wood-processing sector, had expressed its preferences by investing heavily in Western Europe.[2] Finland applied for membership in the European Economic Area in 1990 and joined it in 1994. Application for EC membership followed suit in March 1992. Finland joined the EU at the beginning of 1995, following a membership referendum held in October 1994 in which 57 percent voted in favor of entering the Union.[3] While the pro-EU camp argued that by joining the Union, Finland would merely be maintaining or consolidating its place among West European countries, there is little doubt that especially among foreign observers the "Western" identity of Finland had been far less clear. Indeed, the significance of EU membership for Finland should not be underestimated, for it clearly constituted a key element in the "process of wholesale re-identification on the international stage."[4]

Economic factors were strongly emphasized in the membership debates. Finland is heavily dependent on trade, and the demise of the communist bloc increased trade dependence on the EU countries. Apart from trade concerns, the heavy recession of the early 1990s, including the instability in monetary policy and the devaluation of the markka, further convinced the industry and the trade unions of the importance of joining the EU. The rather uncertain political situation in Russia brought security concerns to the fore. Although security policy considerations were often downplayed during the referendum campaign, there is no doubt that the security dimension was a key factor behind the decision of both the elite and the voters to support EU membership.

From the start of EU membership in 1995 until the outbreak of the euro crisis, Finland had a relatively broad consensus about Europe among its political parties. The divisive nature of the EU membership referendum held in 1994, however, indicated that the commitment to integration that prevailed among the political parties was not shared to the same extent by the electorate. There was a notable lack of congruence between the citizens and the political parties, with most parties considerably more supportive of the EU than their supporters were.[5] Hence it is not surprising that overall the Finnish parties kept a fairly low profile in integration matters, with the rules of the national EU coordination system—based on building broad domestic elite consensus, including often between the government and opposition parties—contributing to the depoliticization of European issues.[6]

The Euro Crisis: Politicization of EU Affairs

Economic factors played a key role in the decision to join the EU, and, if anything, the euro crisis has further convinced at least the political and economic elites of the value of the Internal Market and monetary stability. As one of the Eurozone countries with a triple-A rating, Finland has supported tight budgetary discipline, emphasizing that the success of the single currency and European economy depends on the performance of national economies. But while Finnish governments have consistently supported various euro area rescue and coordination measures from bailout payments to the Fiscal Compact and the banking union, they have certainly needed to pay closer attention to the mood at home.

In the run-up to the 2011 elections to the Eduskunta (the unicameral national parliament), the problems affecting the Eurozone triggered heated debates, and the EU—or more precisely the role of Finland in the bailout measures—became the main topic of the campaign. The decision to rescue Greece from its near bankruptcy and the related euro stabilization measures resulted in unexpectedly heated debates in the Eduskunta, and just before the 2011 elections, when first Ireland and then Portugal followed the path of Greece and required bailout measures, the debate intensified. It is fair to say that no other EU matter has produced similar tensions in Finland since joining the Union. While the opposition parties as well as a notable share of backbenchers from the governing parties were clearly angered by the EU's response to the crisis, the debates were also strongly influenced by the upcoming elections. The more Euro-skeptic parties (the Finns Party, the Christian Democrats, and the Left Alliance) and the main opposition party, the Social Democrats, led the attack on the government. The Social Democrats adopted a high-profile position against lending money to Greece, demanding that the banks and investors get involved in resolving the crisis, and the opposition parties in general voted against the aid measures.

Particularly the Finns Party had an electoral incentive to capitalize on the crisis. It is the only party represented in the Eduskunta that has consistently been opposed to European integration, and also the only party that has systematically used the EU as a central part of its campaigns and political discourse. The Finns Party has forcefully attacked the consensual modes of decisionmaking and demanded public debates about Europe, calling for an end to "one truth" politics. Indeed, it was the "outsider" position that enabled the Finns Party to benefit from these developments. Because the party was not part of the consensual arrangements, it could attack the existing status quo and the bailout measures with more legitimacy and credibility than could its competitors.

The election result was nothing short of extraordinary, producing major changes in the national party system and attracting considerable international media attention. The Euro-skeptic and populist Finns Party[7] won 19.1 percent of the votes, a staggering increase of 15 percent over the 2007 elections and the largest ever increase in support won by a single party in Eduskunta elections. All the other parties represented in the Eduskunta lost votes. In light of the debates and campaigning during the 2011 elections, the "six-pack" National Coalition–led government came under serious political pressure to defend national interests in Brussels. Finland has demanded bilateral guarantees on its bailout payments; attempted, on its own, to reject the 85 percent majority decisionmaking in the European Stability Mechanism, demanding unanimity instead; and together with the Netherlands blocked the entry of Bulgaria and Romania into the Schengen Area. This represented at least a temporary change to the bargaining strategy of Finland in the EU, which has mainly been characterized by pragmatism and the desire to build compromises. Overall, it appears that the emphasis on national interests and the role of smaller member states has become more pronounced in Finland in recent years, and the success of the Finns Party has clearly pushed the other parties in the direction of more cautious EU discourse.[8]

Governmental EU Coordination: Increasing Focus on the European Council and the Eurozone

The politicization of Europe also applies to the Finnish government and the Eduskunta. Turning first to the government, the domestic EU coordination system has remained basically unchanged since Finland joined the EU. It was strongly influenced by the Danish model, which appealed particularly because of its emphasis on broad societal consensus and parliamentary scrutiny. Indeed, the publicly stated priority of the Finnish EU coordination system is to manufacture national unanimity or at least broad elite consensus, which can arguably be translated into additional influence in EU-level bargaining.

Overall, Finland's EU coordination system is formalized. Individual officials work according to established vertical and horizontal forms of interaction within a clearly defined administrative structure.[9] The ministerial EU Committee in Finland, officially titled the Cabinet Committee on European Union Affairs, defines the national position in politically, financially, or legally significant EU matters. The Finnish Cabinet EU Committee is chaired by the prime minister (PM) and is open to all ministers, which makes it well suited for building compromises between governing parties. Despite being formally only a preparatory body, the ministerial EU Committee in practice approves Finnish positions ahead of Council and European Council meetings. The EU Secretariat,[10] originally located in the Foreign Ministry, was transferred to the PM's office in 2000, reflecting the fact that the government and the PM lead EU policy. The principal duties of the EU Secretariat include ensuring the smooth functioning of the national coordination system, supplying timely instructions to the Finnish Permanent Representation together with competent ministries, and acting as a secretariat to the Cabinet EU Committee and the Committee for EU Affairs in Finland.

How has the euro crisis affected intra-Cabinet EU coordination in Finland?[11] The analysis is based on all protocols (agendas) of Cabinet EU Committee meetings from 1995 to 2012 ($N = 696$) and on interviews, carried out in April–May 2013, with key civil servants who either currently work or have worked in the EU Secretariat. The number of meetings, on average thirty-nine meetings per year, has not varied significantly, notwithstanding a moderate increase since the beginning of the euro crisis (forty-three to forty-five meetings a year in 2009–2012). The average number of ministers present is ten, with little yearly variation except for 2011, the high point of the euro crisis, when thirteen ministers on average were present.

Regarding the distribution of issues in the Cabinet EU Committee, the agendas are divided into three categories of matters: (a) individual EU matters and European Council meetings, (b) Council meetings and informal ministerial meetings, and (c) cases pending before the European Court of Justice. Group a consists largely of so-called general affairs, including negotiations on EU enlargement, preparation of the multiannual budgetary frameworks, and institutional issues such as treaty reforms (36.5 percent of issues for group a). EU external affairs are also commonly debated by ministers (12.4 percent), as are economic and financial issues, especially in recent years (14.2 percent). Other EU policy sectors are discussed, clearly less often, as individual agenda points. European Council meetings figure prominently in Cabinet EU Committee protocols (8.3 percent of issues in group a), especially since 2009, reflecting the increased frequency of European Council meetings. Overall, the European Council agenda significantly influences the agenda of the national ministerial EU Committee. This empowers the PM, charged with presenting the European Council agenda and the tentative national positions to fellow ministers, and the EU Secretariat, whose task it is to prepare the background document. Another important group of issues coordinated by ministers are Council meetings and informal ministerial meetings at the EU level. It is established practice that every Council meeting is coordinated in the Cabinet EU Committee. General affairs and foreign affairs are once again dominant, accounting for 29.1 percent of issues discussed in group b. Ecofin Council/Eurogroup and the Agriculture and Fisheries Council also form an important part of all Council meetings coordinated in the ministerial EU Committee (12.8 percent for both).

EU membership has substantially increased the workload of the Finnish cabinet, and this has reinforced the delegation of issues to civil servants and the need for the Cabinet to be more selective when planning its agenda. Governmental EU coordination mainly revolves around important and horizontal EU matters such as treaty reforms or European Council meetings or topical highly salient issues like the euro crisis. Individual laws or legislative packages are discussed by ministers only when they have far-reaching political or financial consequences, like the EU climate and energy package approved in 2008. Reflecting changes in EU governance, the focus has shifted increasingly to European Council and Eurozone summits. The increasing significance of the European Council and of the euro crisis in shaping the agenda of the ministerial EU Committee also implies that individual ministers have more freedom to maneuver in their own jurisdictions.

The findings offer strong support for the thesis about the empowerment of PMs, with the stronger role of the European Council particularly reinforcing the domestic leadership of the PM.[12] European integration and euro area decisionmaking in particular have also clearly strengthened the position of finance ministers, a cross-national development already under way even without any direct effects of EU governance. On a more positive note, the euro crisis has clearly politicized and enlivened debates in the ministerial EU Committee. Overall, it appears that the agendas of EU institutions, more precisely those of the Council and the European Council, largely shape the ministerial EU Committee agenda, with basically all issues routinely "'downloaded" from the European level.

Contestation in the Parliament

The parliamentary EU scrutiny model has remained essentially unchanged since Finland joined the EU. This applies to both the procedures guiding scrutiny and the actual level of scrutiny.[13] When scholars have ranked the effectiveness of the various parliamentary EU scrutiny mechanisms, without exception the Eduskunta has been categorized as one of the strongest parliaments.[14] The Finnish scrutiny model has also been exported abroad. The parliaments of at least the Baltic countries, Hungary, and Slovenia examined it closely when preparing for EU membership, adopting several features of the Finnish mechanism in their own scrutiny models.

Two interconnected features of parliamentary EU scrutiny stand out as particularly relevant: government scrutiny and parliamentary unity. These features need to be understood in the context of the major constitutional reform that has radically transformed Finnish politics. The new constitution, which entered into force in 2000,[15] completed a period of far-reaching constitutional change that curtailed presidential powers and brought the Finnish political system closer to a pure parliamentary regime.[16] Hence EU membership presented a challenge for the Eduskunta, concerned about seeing its newly won powers weakened as a result of the political dynamics of regional integration. The goal was to guarantee the Eduskunta as powerful a position in EU decisionmaking as possible for any national legislature, with the parliament closely studying the work of the existing scrutiny systems in national legislatures, particularly that of the Danish Folketinget.[17] In fact, the role of national parliaments has been an important theme in Finnish EU discourse. Finnish governments and members of parliament have repeatedly argued that national parliaments are the primary channel for providing democratic legitimacy to EU decisionmaking, with the European Parliament complementing the role of domestic legislatures.

The scrutiny model is primarily designed for controlling the government in EU affairs, with emphasis on mandating the Brussels-bound ministers in the Grand Committee, the European Affairs Committee (EAC) of the parliament. The main procedural rules, relatively proactive engagement, delegation of scrutiny to specialized committees, strong information rights, and confidential ministerial hearings in the EAC aim at facilitating government accountability. The Grand Committee coordinates parliamentary work on EU issues and speaks on behalf of the Eduskunta in such matters (with the exception of those questions that specifically require plenary approval). This emphasis on government scrutiny in the EAC has clearly affected plenary involvement in EU affairs, which, at least until the euro-crisis, was very limited.

The Grand Committee aims at unanimity. This consensus-seeking approach applies to the conduct of committee meetings and to EAC decisionmaking. Overall, the processing of EU matters in the Eduskunta can be characterized as pragmatic, with little if any public conflict between or within the political parties. In addition to the consensus-building logic of the domestic EU coordination system, the fragmented party system, with no party winning more than 25 percent of the votes in elections as a rule, also facilitates ideological convergence between political parties. But perhaps most important, the government-opposition dimension has not been anywhere near as significant in EU affairs as it is in domestic issues. The objective is to produce unanimous committee opinions instead of decisions that pit the governing parties against the opposition. It is expected that MPs do not force votes to be held and do not add dissenting opinions to the committee minutes or statements.

The outbreak of the euro crisis and the 2011 elections certainly triggered a considerable politicization of European integration in the Eduskunta, thus challenging the institutional norms of parliamentary engagement in EU affairs. In contrast to previous lack of European debates, between 2010 and 2012, on average eighteen EU debates took place per year, with 63 percent of them focusing on the euro area.[18] More interesting are interpellations that have become the standard form of confidence vote. Between 1995 and 2014, a total of seventy-two interpellations were tabled. Before 2010, only two were EU-related, with both of them dealing with the Common Agricultural Policy and its effect on Finland. However, since the outbreak of the euro crisis the opposition has tabled five crisis-related interpellations. The first of these was signed by the Left Alliance, and the other four were put forward by the Finns Party. Although problematic for the government (and by extension for EU decisionmaking), these developments are good news in terms of democracy and the level of public debate. The parliamentary debates about the Eurozone are arguably the first time that the government has been forced to justify and defend its EU policies in public and when the opposition has attacked the government publicly over its handling of EU matters.

Examining Grand Committee decisionmaking and outputs, we can see a clear change from 2010–2011 onward. Between 1995 and 2013, the EAC issued eighty-two reports, twenty-five of which included a dissenting view (a total of forty-three dissenting opinions, as many reports had more than one dissenting view). Eighteen dissenting opinions were issued up to 2009, and twenty-five during 2010–2013. Particularly since the 2011 elections, the dissenting views have been put forward by the two opposition parties, the Finns Party and the Centre. The clear majority of the post-2010 dissenting opinions have been added to statements on economic and financial affairs. Individual MPs or discontented minorities can also add their dissenting views to committee minutes. Between 2002 and 2013, the EAC held 722 meetings, with the minutes of only 30 containing such dissenting views. However, until 2009, just four meetings had a dissenting view, with the remaining twenty-six from the 2010–2013 euro crisis period (many of the meetings' minutes indicated more than one dissenting opinion), and most of them are signed by the Finns Party. With the dissenting opinions added to EAC statements, the overwhelming majority of the post-2010 dissenting opinions, disclosed in committee minutes, dealt with economic and financial affairs. The third numerical indicator is EAC voting, and data for 2007–2013 show that in both 2007 and 2008 there were five votes, in 2009 eleven, in 2010 seventeen, in 2011 thirty-two, and in both 2012 and 2013 thirty-five. After the 2011 elections, the two opposition parties demanded voting, and the overwhelming majority of votes have been on euro crisis–related issues. Hence the euro crisis ushered in a new era of more contested EAC and parliamentary decisionmaking in EU affairs.

Ukrainian War and the "Special Relationship" with Russia

For centuries, Finland has been a borderland in between East and West, as a part of Sweden, as part of Russia, and then from 1917 on as an independent state trying to find its position.[19] During the Cold War, Finland had close economic and political ties with the Soviet Union, consolidated in the Treaty of Friendship, Cooperation and Mutual Assistance signed in 1948. The treaty placed limitations on Finnish armed forces, and prohibited military cooperation with any country hostile to the Soviet Union. The Cold War entailed a delicate balancing act, with priority to good relations with the Soviet Union reconciled with democratic political institutions at home and integration into markets in the West. While the direct interference of the Soviet leadership in Finnish politics has often been exaggerated, the Finnish political elite nevertheless were always forced to anticipate reactions from Moscow, which set firm limits on Finland's cooperation with Western European and Nordic countries.

Another tenet that grew out of Finnish history was that of a small state, and by the early 1990s, the Finns had become used to living in a world where state sovereignty and national security formed the uncontested starting points for political life. Finnish foreign policy was very much driven by the policy of neutrality, and this culminated in 1975 when Finland hosted the Conference on Security and Cooperation in Europe. From the mid-1960s at least until the mid-1980s, this foreign policy line enjoyed virtually unanimous political and public approval. During the long reign of President Urho Kekkonen (1956–1981), foreign policy was personally identified with the president, who was more or less visibly supported by political elites within the Soviet Union. Political debate and contestation on foreign policy were rare during this era of compulsory consensus that placed a premium on maintaining amicable relations with the Soviet Union.[20]

Concerns about national security certainly influenced voting behavior in the 1994 membership referendum, but at the same time it was understandable that many commentators in Finland and abroad questioned whether the "special relationship" with Russia, which in economic terms had been very important for Finland, would hinder Finland's participation in the CFSP. Others in turn argued that even when operating in the EU context, Finland should strive to maintain strong bilateral relations with Moscow. Since joining the EU, Finland has actively supported the development of the CFSP, particularly regarding crisis management, and the policy of neutrality or military nonalignment has been compromised or even abandoned altogether in the face of European-level security cooperation and commitments.[21]

However, the current war in Ukraine has certainly brought to the fore the special relationship with Russia, including whether Finland can or should have bilateral ties with Moscow. Economically, Russia is a hugely important trading partner for Finland, and hence the sanctions imposed by the EU are hitting Finland particularly hard. Nonetheless, Finland has supported the EU's line, with the government and President Sauli Niinistö underscoring that there is no other option. Niinistö's active role during the crisis is also interesting because of the dual leadership system, with Finland's foreign policy co-led by the president and the government.

Moving Away from Semi-Presidentialism

European integration has acted as a catalyst for constitutional change, providing a major exogenous factor for reducing the powers of the president and strengthening parliamentary democracy. Since relations with the Soviet

Union were at the top level primarily based on negotiations between the Finnish president and the leaders in the Kremlin, the dissolution of the Soviet empire reduced the importance of such personalized foreign policy leadership. It was perceived that there was a poor fit between a president-led system and the demands of EU membership, with the PM and the government better positioned to coordinate national EU policy and represent Finland in Brussels. This question was very important in terms of parliamentary accountability, as the president has no obligation to inform the Eduskunta.

Without constitutional change, the president would have led national integration policy and would have been Finland's main representative at the European level. Therefore, the constitution was amended before EU membership. According to Section 93 of the new constitution, the government is responsible for EU policy, with foreign policy leadership shared between the president and the government:

> The foreign policy of Finland is directed by the President of the Republic in co-operation with the Government. However, the Parliament accepts Finland's international obligations and their denouncement and decides on the bringing into force of Finland's international obligations in so far as provided in this Constitution. The President decides on matters of war and peace, with the consent of the Parliament.
>
> The Government is responsible for the national preparation of the decisions to be made in the European Union, and decides on the concomitant Finnish measures, unless the decision requires the approval of the Parliament. The Parliament participates in the national preparation of decisions to be made in the European Union, as provided in this Constitution.
>
> The communication of important foreign policy positions to foreign States and international organizations is the responsibility of the Minister with competence in foreign affairs.

European policy thus belongs almost exclusively to the jurisdiction of the government. The competence of the government covers all EU matters, but in the CFSP the government must act in "close cooperation" with the president. Co-leadership in foreign policy is in turn executed through the Cabinet Committee on Foreign and Security Policy and the essentially weekly dialogue between the president and the PM and/or the foreign minister.[22]

National or European Foreign Policy?
Without any doubt the biggest challenge has been drawing a clear line between EU policy and foreign policy matters. The strong links between EU policy and foreign affairs make such categorizations inherently difficult, as national foreign and security policies are increasingly influenced by European-level coordination processes and policy choices. While the effectiveness of CFSP can be questioned, it is plausible to argue that the linkage between the two

levels—national foreign policies and EU's external relations—will become stronger in the future.[23] Hence it is completely logical that the president has tried to legitimize his or her role in EU affairs and particularly CFSP matters through the strong linkage between European and foreign policies. For the president to genuinely lead foreign policy, he or she must also be actively involved in EU policy. To quote President Tarja Halonen (the president from 2000 to 2012): "It is not possible to discuss foreign and security policy without considering the influence of the Union. EU penetrates everything."[24] This in turn produces tensions and conflicts between the president and the government. The president has attempted to influence national integration policies, particularly in CFSP matters, while the government defends its turf and has adopted organizational and procedural practices that explicitly marginalize the president, especially during the preparatory stage of the policy process.

Perhaps the best example is after autumn 2005, when the government introduced the Act on Military Crisis Management and certain associated acts (HE 110/2005). According to the proposed law, the president, as the commander-in-chief of the defense forces, would have decided on Finland's participation in EU-led crisis management operations. However, the Constitutional Law Committee disagreed, stating that the government should take the decision regarding both participation and deployment of national units for the operations. The committee emphasized the strong interdependence between the preparatory work carried out in the EU institutions and the national decision on participation. It would be illogical if the government was responsible for the earlier stages of the policy process and the president for the decision on whether to participate, as the latter is obviously influenced by the former. But the committee was not unanimous, and importantly, the majority of the experts heard by the committee, mainly professors of law with long-standing expertise on constitutional questions, felt that the president should decide on Finland's participation.[25]

Relations with Russia provide another good example. Constitutionally bilateral relations with foreign states fall under the co-leadership of Section 93, but Finnish-Russian relations are increasingly influenced by the EU, not least because trade policy is in the competence of the Union. As a result, presidential activism toward Russia has not always been welcomed by the government. The president and the PM have had several behind-the-scenes disputes about who is the leading actor toward Russia. During the Ukrainian war, the division of labor appears to have functioned smoothly, with the PM representing Finland in the EU and the president engaging in bilateral talks with his Russian counterpart.

But the problem that really symbolized these jurisdictional conflicts was the policy of two plates: dual representation in the European Council. The Constitutional Law Committee decided, prior to EU membership, that the

PM should represent Finland in the European Council. However, according to President Martti Ahtisaari (1994–2000), the president should have the right to decide on his participation in the European Council. In May 1995, PM Paavo Lipponen announced a statement, formulated jointly with the president's office, according to which the PM will always attend the European Council meetings along with the president as he or she chooses. Until the Lisbon Treaty entered into force, Halonen participated in the majority of European Council meetings.[26] When the president attended the European Council, the foreign minister had to leave the meeting room, despite the fact that agenda items had been prepared by the PM's office (perhaps together with the Foreign Ministry) and was within the competence (jurisdiction) of the government. Moreover, dual representation arguably made it more difficult for foreign observers to understand who leads Finnish EU policy. It is probable that not all of the politicians in the European Council, or the media covering the meetings, knew the wording of the Finnish constitution.

The Lisbon Treaty formalized the position of the European Council as one of the EU institutions, and this provided an "external" solution to the policy of two plates. After the Lisbon Treaty entered into force, each country was to be represented in the European Council by either the PM (head of government) or the head of state. The government and the Eduskunta agreed that the PM would represent Finland. According to the government's new bill for amending the constitution (HE 60/2010), the PM would represent Finland in the European Council and in other EU meetings where the political leaders of the member states are represented (such as informal meetings between the leaders of member states and summits between the EU and third countries). However, to the extent that this is possible within the EU framework, the government could in exceptional circumstances decide that the president would also represent Finland in EU meetings. The presence of both the PM and the president would, the argument goes, indicate that the issue is of particular salience to Finland and would also strengthen the country's bargaining position. Hence, according to a constitutional amendment (Section 66) from 2012, "The Prime Minister represents Finland on the European Council. Unless the Government exceptionally decides otherwise, the Prime Minister also represents Finland in other activities of the European Union requiring the participation of the highest level of State."

Concluding Discussion:
Federalist Actions, Confederal Discourse?

Considering the relatively narrow majority in favor of joining the EU in the referendum held in 1994, the traditionally state-centric political culture, and low public support for the EU, Finland would seem to have all the key preconditions for adopting a more intergovernmental approach to European integration. Yet the situation is very much the opposite, with successive Finnish governments consistently in favor of deeper policy integration and increasing the powers of supranational institutions. Finland can therefore with good reason be categorized as an integrationist member state.

This chapter showed how the euro crisis destabilized Finnish integration policy. The outbreak of the euro crisis coincided with the campaign for the 2011 Eduskunta elections and revealed the fragile basis of the domestic (elite) consensus over Europe. That consensus was fragile because public opinion has consistently been more critical of integration than political parties. Moreover, most parties are internally divided over the EU, and hence there was always the potential for mobilization and a clear demand for a party with a more critical view of European integration. The euro crisis and the success of the Finns Party have influenced domestic EU discourse, which is certainly more cautious, downplays any moves toward further centralization, and emphasizes the role of national interests. Yet at the same time the Finnish government, with some reservations, has supported various euro area coordination instruments and bailout packages. The policy choices are thus federalist, but domestic discourse is confederal.

The euro crisis did bring, at least temporarily, an end to the domestic depoliticization of Europe. There is now more contestation over integration, and importantly much of this party-political conflict takes place in public in the plenary debates in the Eduskunta and in printed and electronic media. This is certainly a highly positive development when considering that Europe as an issue had remained depoliticized in Finland for such a long time. The euro crisis has also at least partially changed how EU affairs are handled in Helsinki. Voting has become more common in the EAC of the Eduskunta, with the votes reproducing the government-opposition cleavage characterizing plenary decisionmaking and with the losing opposition minority adding its dissenting opinions to the reports and minutes of the committee. Inside the Cabinet, the crisis has produced livelier EU debates, but at the same time, the government has needed to prioritize, with intra-Cabinet EU coordination focusing very much on the European Council and euro area coordination instruments at the expense of other EU questions. This empowers the PM, whose domestic leadership has also been bolstered by constitutional changes that have further marginalized the president.

The Finnish experience indicates that there can be a rather poor fit between semi-presidentialism and EU governance. In several semi-presidential countries both the government and the president are involved in national foreign and/or European policy, particularly in Finland, France, Lithuania, Poland, and Romania.[27] In these countries the standard constitutional solution is that of government presiding over EU affairs, with the president either alone or together with the government directing foreign policy. National foreign policies are increasingly influenced by and linked to the EU, and hence the foreign policy powers of the presidents are circumscribed by the ongoing development of the CFSP. It therefore appears that in semi-presidential systems domestic strains will be the more or less inevitable outcome when the formal rules vest the direction of foreign and/or EU policy conjointly in the president and the government. At the same it must be emphasized that despite tensions and occasional public conflicts, foreign policy co-leadership has functioned rather smoothly in Finland. It is also probable that the constitutional amendments from 2012, particularly the fact that the PM alone represents Finland in the European Council, have clarified the rules of dual leadership.

Despite the increased domestic contestation that has also affected national EU policy, it is unlikely that the euro crisis will result in more long-term changes to Finland's role in the Union. The basic equation remains the same: Finland joined the EU for economic and security reasons, and if anything the euro crisis and the Ukrainian war have underscored the importance of the European framework for advancing national interests. In terms of the future of Finnish EU policy, the main question concerns the Finns Party, particularly if they enter the government. Although the current debate is characterized by concerns about securing national influence, the debate is about how to achieve that inside the EU, not about whether life would be better inside or outside the Union. Policy questions that featured in the membership debates and influenced voting behavior in the membership referendum, such as agriculture, foreign and security policy, and economic policy, are nowadays very much approached through the EU context, with debates focusing to a large extent on the compatibility of domestic and EU policies and on the policies to be adopted at the European level.

Notes

1. Raunio and Tiilikainen (2003), Tiilikainen (2006).
2. Väyrynen (1993).
3. Pesonen (1994); Arter (1995); Jenssen, Pesonen, and Gilljam (1998).
4. Arter (2000).
5. Mattila and Raunio (2005, 2012).
6. Raunio (2005), Johansson and Raunio (2010).
7. The party adopted its current English name in August 2011. Until then it had been known as the True Finns. According to the party leader, Timo Soini, the simpler name is intended to emphasize the fact that the party represents ordinary citizens. Soini also felt that the old name had an extreme right or nationalistic slant to it. The exact translation of the Finnish name of the party, Perussuomalaiset, would be "common Finns" or "ordinary Finns."
8. Raunio (2012b).
9. Lampinen, Rehn, and Uusikylä (1998), Kinnunen (2003), Laffan, (2006), Hyvärinen (2009), Johansson and Raunio (2010), Hämynen (2011), Hyvärinen and Raunio (2014).
10. The official name since 2013 is the Government EU Affairs Department.

11. Hyvärinen and Raunio (2014).

12. Johansson and Tallberg (2010).

13. Raunio (2015).

14. Karlas (2012, Winzen (2013), Auel, Rozenberg, and Tacea (2015).

15. The Constitution of Finland, June 11, 1999 (731/1999). https://www.finlex.fi/fi/laki/kaannokset/1999/en19990731.pdf

16. Nousiainen (2001), Paloheimo (2003), Raunio (2011).

17. Jääskinen (2000).

18. Auel and Raunio (2014).

19. Tiilikainen (1998), Alapuro, (2004).

20. Arter (1987).

21. Raunio and Tiilikainen (2003), Jokela (2011), Palosaari (2011).

22. Tiilikainen (2003), Raunio (2008).

23. According to the Venice Commission, this was foreseen by the drafters of constitution: "In defining the area of governmental primacy by reference to an entity, the EU, whose competence is continually shifting/expanding, the framers of the Finnish Constitution have deliberately provided for a growing area of primary governmental competence in foreign policy. The growth of common positions and strategies in the EU common foreign and security policy (CFSP), e.g. as regards what has traditionally been a crucially important part of Finnish foreign policy, its relationship with Russia, means that issues previously regarded as purely bilateral will now be regarded, depending on the circumstances, as partially, largely, or wholly, within the Government's primacy." Venice Commission, "Opinion on the Constitution of Finland," Opinion No. 420/2007, Strasbourg, April 7, 2008, p. 14.

24. Arto Astikainen, "Presidentti ei voi olla reservissä," *Helsingin Sanomat*, December 24, 2003.

25. Niskanen (2006, Niskanen (2009), pp. 141–45.

26. Niskanen (2009), pp. 175–86.

27. Raunio (2012a). Currently twelve out of the twenty-eight EU member states are semi-presidential. These countries can be divided to two categories: those where the president has genuine powers in foreign and/or EU policy (Finland, France, Lithuania, Poland, Romania, perhaps Croatia) and those where the government essentially decides such matters alone (Austria, Bulgaria, Ireland, Portugal, Slovakia, Slovenia).

15

Poland: A Skillful Player

Artur Gruszczak

TEN YEARS OF POLAND'S MEMBERSHIP IN THE EUROPEAN UNION (EU) have brought positive effects. Poland has strengthened its position in the Union thanks to the pro-European policy of the ruling Civic Platform Party, relative resilience to the economic crisis, and support for a general reform of the European integration process. It would be an exaggeration to call Poland a "Euro-enthusiastic" country. Rather, it is fair to depict Poland's role in the EU as a smart player advocating for more effective reforms of the Union and seeking, at the same time, to safeguard its national interests without running the risk of being marginalized on the main stage of the political competition between EU member states.

Poland aimed to take advantage of her surprisingly good economic performance throughout the EU's period of instability to have a say on the overall state of the Union, including the developments in the Eurozone, to which Poland did not belong. It promoted closer cooperation with countries of Eastern Europe, particularly Ukraine, seeking to pull post-Soviet states into the Union and offering them a permanent program of cooperation and assistance called the Eastern Partnership.

Poland has also experienced the positive consequences of EU membership. As a major beneficiary of the EU's Common Agricultural Policy (CAP) and the cohesion policy, it made tremendous progress in such areas as economic modernization, communication and transportation, local development, and agriculture. Polish society was among the most enthusiastic about the EU and European integration. Support for Polish membership in the EU remained at the 80 percent level, which was particularly telling when compared with the rising nationalist and anti-European movements and parties in other member states trying to discredit the achievements of the European integration and highlighting negative outcomes of the Eastern enlargement.

Poland's Relations with the EU
Stability Under Liberal Rule

When Poland joined the EU, the ruling leftist coalition assumed a cautiously reformist attitude about the future of the Union. However, in the final stage of the negotiations, Polish authorities did not mask their disappointment at being pressed hard by Brussels to accept poor conditions of membership. The parliamentary and presidential elections of September–October 2005 strengthened these sentiments. Two center-right parties won the parliamentary elections: the Civic Platform (PO) and the Law and Justice Party (PiS). Contrary to a general expectation of a "great coalition" built by the two winners, the PiS decided to form an alliance with two small Euro-skeptic parties. The presidential race ended in a rather unexpected victory for Lech Kaczynski supported by the PiS (headed by his twin brother, Jaroslaw). The new executive, as well as the majority in the parliament, consisted of politicians who criticized certain provisions of the Constitutional Treaty, preferred NATO over the European Security and Defence Policy, and denounced EU restrictions against new member states in such areas as free movement of persons and services, CAP, and tax policy. Likewise, Kaczynski declared that his presidency should contribute to an active policy regarding European integration, but he meant in loose intergovernmental projects, seeking to protect Warsaw's interests.

The new Polish executive and legislature clearly preferred an intergovernmental and not a supranational Union. In effect, it clashed with big EU powers seeking the reinforcement of EU institutions and law, most of all Germany and more gently with France. Polish-German relations rapidly deteriorated over numerous bilateral and European issues such as federalization of the EU, legal reform of the Union, energy issues, cooperation with Russia, and historical disputes. The resistance to the Constitutional Treaty provoked growing criticism from the majority of the member states. Following the French and Dutch "no's" to the treaty, the Kaczynski government attempted to direct the debate on a reform treaty on the intergovernmental track. As a result, Poland was marginalized in the EU, along with the Czech Republic, as an anti-European country. The Polish government finally approved the reform treaty negotiated in June 2007 but left open the question of its ratification.

The Polish prime minister, Donald Tusk, signed the reform treaty in Lisbon. He represented the new ruling coalition formed after early parliamentary elections were held in October 2007 and following an acute crisis in the PiS-led political formation. Tusk led the victorious PO, supported by the Polish Peasant Party (PSL), with a strong dedication to alter patterns of governance established by the PiS and reorient Euro-skeptic policy to pro-European active engagement in the current and future developments in the EU. His government lowered the earlier profile presented in Brussels, especially in its relations with the Commission, which were often strained on such issues as environment, public support of state-owned industrial companies, climate change, fundamental rights, and sexual minorities.

A "cohabitation difficile" between Tusk and Kaczynski provoked numerous disputes about internal political, social, and economic issues as well as foreign policy. President Kaczynski opposed the ratification of the Lisbon Treaty. Only when Poland along with the Czech Republic remained alone in opposition to the treaty did he decide to sign the ratification law. Poland was optimistic about its future; the signs of economic crisis diagnosed in 2007–2008 were obscured by ambitious plans of liberal reforms fueled by EU funds and foreign direct investments. Poland prepared an impressive show as a dynamic, modern, European country, during its Council presidency in the EU in 2011 (second half) and for the European Football Championship in June 2012 (co-organized with Ukraine). Officials from city councilpersons to the president of the republic were eager to use the soccer tournament as a national showcase, adding government spending to EU funds. The crisis that hit the EU in 2009 was not very acute and painful in Poland. The economic dynamics generated by large-scale public and private investment, high demand on the internal market, low labor costs, and floating national currency immunized the national economy from the contagion coming from the south of Europe. Poland regained its importance in the EU thanks to patient and consistent activities undertaken by Tusk and Foreign Minister Radoslaw Sikorski. They normalized the relationship with Germany, improved that with France, and strengthened ties with the UK. Likewise, Poland improved relations with the Russian Federation and took contentious issues to its EU policy agenda. This proved especially effective when Poland, jointly with Sweden, put forward a plan for the Eastern Partnership dedicated to six post-Soviet republics, which the European Council adopted during the Prague summit in May 2009.

Such a pro-EU foreign orientation did not negatively affect the traditional Polish-US alliance. Poland kept considering the United States as its strongest ally and guarantor of its national security. Despite embarrassing decisions taken by the new Barack Obama administration (resignation from the missile shield in Europe, reset in US-Russia relations despite the Georgian war in 2008, reduction of US troops in Europe), Poland consistently supported US global strategy. Polish diplomats were helpful in the Middle East and North Africa, and Polish soldiers fought in Afghanistan with their US brothers in arms.

Thge stability of liberal rule was shaken by the tragic events of April 2010, when a Polish airplane crash killed ninety-six people near Smolensk, Russia. This catastrophe was more than a human tragedy, it was a political earthquake because the passengers belonged to the top political and military establishment, and included President Kaczynski, the chief of the army general staff, and other senior military officers, the president of the National Bank of Poland, government officials, and eighteen members of the Polish parliament.

Despite accusations by the Law and Justice opposition party, of the Tusk government's neglect and lack of proper security during the flight, the PO candidate Bronislaw Komorowski won the presidential contest in July 2010. "Benign cohabitation" between the president and the prime minister facilitated carrying out the political and economic plans of the ruling party. Economic recuperation in 2010 and 2011 strengthened the PO at home and abroad. The Polish presidency in the Council was well prepared and had administrative and organizational success. The general elections in October 2011 demonstrated the strong position of the ruling coalition. The PO won 39 percent of the ballots and the main opposition party, PiS headed by Jaroslaw Kaczynski and cultivating the memory of his deceased brother, obtained 30 percent of the vote. The PO's partner, the PSL, came fourth, with the support of 8.5 percent of the voters, sufficient to sustain the ruling coalition.[1]

Despite electoral victory, the PO was far from complacent. It did not improve its position in the parliament and still had to gain support from its minor partner, the agrarian PSL, which was reluctant about many reform proposals the PO put forward. The economic crisis reached Poland, and even if it did not bring about painful consequences, it destroyed the conviction of the country passing unscathed through the muddy waters of economic recession around Europe. Alarming forecasts and growing social costs for the neglected reforms induced the government to engage in unpopular undertakings. First, the government embarked on pension reforms. In May 2012, the Polish parliament adopted a new pension law to reduce the share of contributions transferred to private pension funds and raise the retirement age to sixty-seven for both men and women (instead of the current sixty-five for men and sixty for women). The reform did not affect the farmers' social security scheme, hugely subsidized by the state. In a dramatic move to reduce public debt, the parliament passed in December 2013 a bill to reform the private pension fund sector. As a result, the government seized privately run pension funds in February 2014 and transferred them to state control. This decision was strongly criticized by numerous social groups, institutions, and experts. Estimates indicated that the real pension value after the reform will be significantly lower than before, and the decrease could reach 30 percent.

The row over pension reforms reflected a more serious problem in Polish politics and society. Much of the population had not seen the fruits of the transformation and resented the beneficiaries, identifying them with the political class, economic oligarchs, and "cheaters" or "dodgers" abusing state resources. An echo of protests in many cities in the West could also be heard in Warsaw and other major cities. In September 2013, thousands of protesters, organized by the Solidarnosc trade union, marched through Warsaw, demanding more jobs, higher pay, and no increase in the retirement age. Polish "time for outrage" was, however, politicized and linked to the PiS. Nevertheless, it was a resounding outcry against the incapacity of the government and the ruling coalition to effectively tackle rising joblessness, an inflexible labor market, poor employment conditions, and difficult career opportunities, especially for young persons. It was also the voice of protest against the "arrogance of the ruling elite," its moral and human decadence, selfishness, and lack of responsibility for the state. A wiretapping scandal erupted in June 2014 and confirmed the general mood in society. Private conversations among top politicians, recorded in secret by undisclosed persons and leaked and published by one of the most popular weeklies, plunged Poland into one of the worst crises since the PO came to power.

Public opinion was shocked by the dirty language of the conversations, the instrumental approach to national interests, and the covering of costs of meals for private meetings in restaurants with public money. Tusk was embarrassed by disparaging remarks about Poland's allies, especially the United States. The Tusk government narrowly won a confidence vote in the parliament in late June 2014, yet the prospects for the PO to regain its dominant political position were grim.

The "Green Island on a Red Sea": Poland's Economy During the EU's Economic Crisis

The recession that hit the EU at the end of the first decade of the 2000s did not substantially affect the Polish economic system. This somewhat puzzling phenomenon was subject to numerous analyses that did not result in a convincing explanation. This confusion was due to the fact that Poland's post-2004 development has been following a largely autonomous path determined to a considerable degree by incentives coming from EU membership as well as internal dynamics of political, social, and economic processes. Poland joined the EU at the start of its second wave of economic acceleration in the post-1989 period. A decline in Poland's growth rate at the beginning of the first decade of the twenty-first century stimulated both important corrections of government economic policies and structural changes in enterprises. The reform of public finance, institutional progress triggered by the upcoming EU membership, and strengthening of domestic financial markets established a solid basis for modernization and growth. This was crucial for the improvement of the quality of the business environment and innovation capabilities as well as for the reinforcement of export-oriented sectors and their ability to compete in the demanding EU common market.

Structural adjustments, introduced in the years preceding Poland's accession to the EU, brought positive effects in the early years of membership. The Polish economy successfully merged into EU structures and made a smooth transition into the Internal Market, despite external economic factors that were unfavorable, the constant rise in oil and raw energy prices, jumps in production costs and prices, as well as the decline in EU economic development. Thanks to financial inflows from the EC budget, dynamic growth in Polish exports, and a "preaccession consumption boom," the national economy experienced a boost contributing to a 5.9 percent gross domestic product (GDP) growth rate in 2004, 6.2 percent in 2006, 6.8 percent in 2007, and a still impressive 5.1 percent in 2008.

Contrary to the fears of a strong inflationary leap due to significant price differences between Poland and other EU countries, the rate of inflation started to decline slowly by the end of 2004, reaching 1.5 percent in July 2005.[2] The index of consumer prices oscillated between 1.3 percent in 2006 and 4.2 percent in 2008. The rapid drop in the unemployment rate was probably the most meaningful indicator of the upheaval on the labor market caused by membership in the EU. Economic development driven by the common market, EU funds, and demand in the Internal Market generated new jobs in industry and services. In parallel, the opening of labor markets in several of the member states caused a huge new wave of emigration. As a result, unemployment fell from 19.1 percent in 2004 to 13.9 percent in 2006 and to a record low 7.1 percent in 2008.[3]

Positive indicators of economic revitalization could not, however, conceal the evident structural deficiencies of the Polish economic system[4] revealed by declining labor productivity (from 4.2 percent in 2004 to 3.0 percent in 2006 and 1.3 percent in 2006)[5] and an exceptionally low rate of labor participation and a dramatically low percentage of high-technology exports in total manufactured exports (3.3 percent in 2004, 3.7 percent in 2006, when the world average indicator was 20.9 percent and 20.8 percent, respectively, and in the EU it was 17.7 percent and 18.4 percent, respectively).[6]

Regardless of the structural impediments, the pre-2009 high economic dynamics were due to the following factors: positive midterm effects of preaccession adjustment and transformation processes; noticeable improvement of the quality of microeconomic management; flexibility and adaptability of small and medium enterprises to the new business environment; greater input of local governments in regional development; and institutional, financial, and investment benefits resulting from EU membership.

The global financial meltdown, which hit the EU between 2009 and 2010, did not provoke major shocks in Poland. Its economy looked healthy, and EU funds reinforced positive trends in local, regional, and national economic development. Foreign trade flourished and the financial balance did not engender alarming reactions. Certainly, the Polish economy, as part of the EU common market and thereby an element of the global economic system, felt the negative consequences of the recession, yet it was far from the dramatic scenarios unfolding in Southern Europe. Macroeconomic indicators worsened, GDP growth rate dropped to 1.6 percent in 2009, the inflation rate reached 4 percent, the deficit of the current account was slightly reduced to 3.9 percent, but the general government deficit rose sharply from 1.9 percent of GDP in 2007 to the alarming 7.5 percent in 2009. The public debt ratio also worsened, despite significant efforts to reduce the debt undertaken since joining the EU. The foreign direct investment inflow decreased significantly, from €17.2 billion in 2007 to €9.3 billion in 2009.

Nonetheless, Poland stood out on the economic map of the EU, especially when compared with countries such as Greece, Portugal, and Spain, which were experiencing sovereign debt crisis, bank default, ballooning budget deficit, and severe recession. Poland was largely untouched by the crisis, mainly because it relied far less on easy credit from Western European banks to support domestic spending and because it took steps to rein in government deficits.[7] Hence, Poland seemed immune to the contagion effects, no bailout was needed, no harsh austerity measures were under consideration, and the economy kept growing. This induced Tusk to announce gloatingly at a press conference in May 2009 that while other EU nations were in recession, Poland was the only state enjoying "positive growth." Poland was the green island on a red map![8]

Economic Challenges

The following years were a mixed picture for the Polish economy's performance during the Eurozone crisis and the EU common market's hard times. Despite Poland's relative resilience since the beginning of the economic crisis, its economy weakened significantly between 2012 and 2013. Initially, growth recuperated and reached 3.9 percent in 2010 and 4.3 percent in 2011. However, the economy slowed down in the following years: to 2 percent in 2012 and 1.6 percent in 2013, evidently experiencing the results of the recession in the EU and the weakened demand from its major trading partners, namely, Germany, France, and the UK. Private consumption weakened and investment decreased as a result of fiscal consolidation and lower EU cofunding, growing unemployment, and subdued wage growth.

The Tusk government, and especially Finance Minister Jacek Rostowski, made efforts to sustain economic growth by increased public spending, mostly in investments, while reducing the budget deficit and maintaining public debt below the threshold established in the constitution of Poland at 60 percent of GDP.[9] The Plan for Development and Consolidation of Public Finance for 2010-11, released in January 2010, was intended to apply existing prudential and remedial procedures if the debt ratio to GDP was between 50 percent and 55 percent. In fact, pressure to increase public spending continued, resulting in EU-funded investments and nationwide programs of infrastructure development in the areas of communication and transportation (motorways, railroads, airports, and railway stations), as well as construction and modernization of sports facilities in preparation for the European Football championship in 2012. Public debt grew rapidly after

2008, reaching 50.9 percent of GDP in 2010 and an all-time high of 56.2 percent in 2012.[10] This alarming situation prompted the government to set forth plans for macroeconomic structural adjustment and reform, which also included an agenda for pension reform, privatization, and broadening tax bases.

The first signs of recovery were seen in late 2013. Real GDP growth was higher than projected and forecasts for the upcoming years were even more optimistic (3 percent in 2014 and 3.4 percent in 2015). Industrial production growth recovered from −2.8 percent in the last quarter of 2012 to 4 percent in the second quarter of 2013, 5.9 percent in the last quarter of 2013, and 5.2 percent in the first quarter of 2014.[11] The budget deficit fell from a record high 7.8 percent in 2010 to 5.1 percent in 2011 and 3.9 percent in 2012, to slightly increase to 4.3 percent in 2013.[12] The Polish government continued its policies of cutting the budget deficit and sticking to the target of 3 percent of GDP for 2015.[13] The unemployment rate started to steadily decrease from 10.5 percent in May 2013 to 9.6 percent in May 2014, and fell below the EU average.

Despite economic success during the EU's difficult period of stagnation and financial imbalance, Poland faces numerous challenges and demanding tasks in the near future. They stem mostly from the rising social and political costs of the negligence of structural reforms in industry, agriculture, the social welfare system, the labor market, and the R&D sector. The government needs to address short- and midterm sustainable economic development as well as overall patterns of modernization and growth. Labor productivity is still low, whereas average incomes have grown steadily. Exports, regardless of the impressive increase in volume, are still low as measured per capita. Poor spending on science and research and development (in 2012 expenditure on R&D reached a mere 0.9 percent of GDP whereas the EU average was 2.1 percent) and lagging investment in the IT sector contribute to the low percentage of high-technology exports and limited competitiveness of Polish products on world markets. In 2014, the Innovation Union Scoreboard placed Poland twenty-fifth out of the EU's twenty-eight countries, beating only Latvia, Romania, and Bulgaria. According to the European Commission, Poland's relative strengths are in human resources, whereas relative weaknesses are in linkages, entrepreneurship, and innovators.[14] Investment and saving rates are definitely below EU levels. Between 2004 and 2011, the average saving rate was only 17 percent of GDP and the average investment rate was 21 percent. High outflow of manpower is partly a reaction to labor market segmentation, which is exceedingly high, largely because of differences in the tax treatment of contracts under the civil code versus those signed under the labor code. Companies hesitate to offer employment contracts to evade high social insurance contributions, which create a tax wedge between labor cost to the employer and worker pay. The economy is still overregulated, and the market is subject to administrative decisions and bureaucratic restraints. Poland ranks only forty-first and forty-fifth, respectively, on Transparency International's Corruption Perception Index and the World Bank's Ease of Doing Business Index.

Poland missed the spillover effects of the 2008 global economic crisis and functioned quite smoothly through the EU's period of recession, but not because of the strong stimulus for comprehensive structural reforms. Rather, Poland has preserved certain systemic impediments, which probably will have a significant impact on the chances of modernization and sustained growth in the years to come.

"It Pays to Be in the EU"

Poland joined the EU with a reputation as a tough player acquired during the negotiations period. Such areas as agriculture, regional policy and structural funds, budget, and finance were treated by Polish officials as if they were battlefields where Poland had to struggle with EU representatives in defense of national interests. The label as a pro-US, Euro-skeptic, agricultural country initially restrained Polish activities in the EU institutions and auxiliary bodies.

The fact that Poland joined the EU as a relatively poor and underdeveloped country, though with solid grounds for sustained development and modernization, predetermined its principal goals and strategic blueprints in the first years of membership. Polish authorities in 2004–2006 concentrated on the best use of transitional resources from the preaccession and facility funding (like ISPA, SAPARD, PHARE, Cash Flow facility, Schengen facility) and a smooth absorption of major funds, namely, Cohesion Funds, CAP direct payments, and Rural Development Program funds. The EU funding in that period totaled €9.4 billion while Poland's contribution to the EU budget amounted to €4.9 billion. The next financial perspective in 2007–2013 made Poland one of the biggest beneficiaries of the EU's budget. Net transfers in that period accounted for €68.7 billion (total allocation was €101.5 billion, and Poland's contribution to EU budget was €32.8 billion).

The inflow of EU funds to Poland will slightly increase in 2014–2020, as the EU budget for that period, approved by the European Parliament in November 2013, set the allocation for Poland at €105.8 billion, including €72.9 billion in the cohesion policy framework and €28.5 billion as CAP subsidies. Therefore, Poland is going to be the biggest beneficiary of EU financial assistance of all the member states, not just the biggest recipient of the cohesion funds, as was the case in 2007–2013. This entails rosy prospects for modernization and closure of gaps between less developed areas and the leading regions within Poland, as well as reducing distance to EU average levels of development, welfare, education, and infrastructure. Poland's capacity to absorb EU funds is fairly good. As of the end of

2013, Poland managed to draw 67.9 percent of its allocated EU funds for the period 2007–2013 (only Estonia and Lithuania did better in the group of Central and Eastern European member states).[15] The overall number of projects carried out within the framework of the cohesion policy since Poland joined the EU has amounted to 185.000, and the total sum of EU funding was around €65.3 billion. These projects were mainly for transportation (38.2 percent), research and development (15.8 percent), human capital (14.4 percent), and environmental protection (11.9 percent). The total number of applications for EU funds, under cohesion policy and structural funds and registered by the national implementing authority came to 298,000 by July 20, 2014. Their overall value was estimated at around €135 billion, which illustrates the scope of activities across various sectors of the economy and society, as well as the engagement of the state at local, regional, and central levels in the stimulation, financing, and management of EU-funded projects. It is worth underscoring that the EU contributed 70 percent to the completed projects, meaning the state's financial contribution to those projects was €30 billion.[16]

EU funds boosted economic growth and contributed greatly to Poland's overall development. Macroeconomic indicators demonstrate the progress that has been made since Poland obtained its EU membership. Certainly, the dynamics of growth, development, and modernization were generated before 2004 due to tremendous efforts made in the tortuous but transformative decade of the 1990s. Poland's cumulative GDP growth in the period 2004–2013 was 48.7 percent (EU: 11 percent) and in the "crisis years" 2008–2013, GDP increased over 20 percent.[17] GDP per capita, measured in Purchasing Power Standard, rose from 48.8 percent of the EU-27 average in 2003 to 66.9 in 2012. The value of Polish exports to the EU grew threefold, from €38.4 billion in 2003 to €114 billion in 2013. The trade with the EU made up three-fourths of the total value of the foreign commercial exchange. Poland reduced its negative balance of trade with the EU, amounting to €3.3 billion in 2003 and built up a healthy surplus of €24 billion in 2013. The share of the Polish exports to the EU in the country's GDP was 35.6 percent in 2013 (a growth of 8.7 percent compared with 2003).[18]

The structure of Polish exports to the EU reflects Poland's position in the EU, its global division of labor, and its involvement in international supply chains. In 2012, mechanical engineering products accounted for 39.1 percent of the total value of Polish exports, chemical products 14 percent, agricultural and food products 12.3 percent, and metallurgical products 11.7 percent. The agricultural sector deserves attention. The heavy inflow of EU CAP subsidies not only resulted in a significant improvement of the standard of living of farmers but also contributed to a growing effectiveness of agricultural production and an impressive dynamics of exports. Since Poland entered the EU, Polish food and agricultural exports increased fourfold (from €4.1 billion in 2003 to €17.5 billion in 2012), with the trade turnover with EU countries rising from €0.4 billion in 2003 to €4.2 billion in 2012. Poland became another breadbasket in the EU, delivering numerous products to regional and local markets, such as grain, meat, dairy products, fresh fruits, and frozen food.

Direct and indirect effects of funding and assistance to Poland had a positive feedback. Much of the money allocated from EU resources went back to the major contributors to the common budget. According to the Polish Ministry for Regional Development, every euro granted to the Visegrad Group countries (V4: Poland, the Czech Republic, Slovakia, and Hungary) in cohesion funds resulted in €0.61 return in the form of additional exports from EU-15 ("old member countries"). Direct benefits for the period 2004–2015 were estimated at €8.64 billion and referred to construction services and mid- and high-tech exports. Indirect profits were estimated at €66 billion. Interestingly, Ireland got the biggest compensation (299 percent) in relation to its contribution to cohesion funds for V4 countries. Luxembourg got 136 percent and Germany 125 percent.[19] Poland's foreign minister Sikorski often outlined the positive effects of the eastern enlargement on the European Union and its major countries. In his speech at the German Council on Foreign Relations in Berlin in November 2011, he pointed out that the volume of trade between the "old" EU-15 and "new" EU-10 grew significantly and that exports from Germany to EU-10 skyrocketed from €15 billion in 1993 to €95 billion in 2010.[20]

EU funds contributed to a significant improvement, thanks to heavy investment of public and EU financial resources in communication technologies and infrastructure, transportation, local development, and research and development. *The Economist* diagnosed the sources of Polish achievements in the following words:

> The biggest single contribution to Poland's success, however, was its effective use of EU membership. The Poles were quick to see the opportunities in the EU's structural and cohesion funds as well as the benefits of improving their own governance and transparency. Poland fought harder than Romania, Bulgaria and its Visegrad peers against corruption, especially in public procurement, and has a decent record of using structural funds as a result.[21]

This description discusses benefits drawn from membership in the EU. There were, however, examples of problematic outcomes of EU membership, which had both positive and negative consequences for Poland.

The migration issue provides an interesting case of relative cost-and-benefit assessment of the effects of the enlargement. In a historical perspective, Poland was the country of origin of millions of migrants who dispersed around the world. Numerous push and pull factors stimulated emigration from Poland throughout the twentieth century. Migration became a synonym of wealth, well-being, and prestige. Remittances flowing from emigrants to their families in Poland became important sources of additional incomes. With the beginning of capitalist transformation, migration flows weakened, but after the mid-1990s, the tendency of increased emigration reappeared, due to the hardships of economic reform, new opportunities in foreign labor markets, and legalization of seasonal employment in some EU member states. In 2003, approximately 400,000–450,000 Polish employees worked legally in EU member states and an additional 100,000–120,000 stayed illegally. Most of the latter worked as seasonal workers in construction, farming, and housekeeping.

Before the eastern enlargement, in the "old" member states, the principle of free movement of persons was abused by the citizens of new member states and caused negative financial, organizational, and political repercussions. All of them, except for the UK, Ireland, and Sweden, applied for transition periods in opening their labor markets, anticipating an invasion of cheap Polish manpower.

According to experts in migration policy, "Interestingly, whereas after 1989 the volume of potential East to West migration was first overestimated, this new labour migration was initially underestimated, particularly migration to certain countries."[22] In 2005, the total number of Polish economic migrants rose to 670,000, and in 2008 it exceeded 1 million. Experts from the Polish Academy of Sciences estimated the number of emigrants in the period 2004–2013 at 1.05 to 1.1 million. There were also another half a million seasonal migrants. The Polish Central Statistical Office estimated the total number of Polish migrants in the EU at 1.72 million in 2012.[23] Poles took a special liking to the British islands. *The Economist* reported, "The 2011 [UK] census counted 579,000 [Poles], a tenfold increase from a decade earlier. Many more have come and gone: since 2002 almost 1.2m Poles have been issued with National Insurance numbers. But that still leaves a lot of settlers."[24]

Outflow of Poles after enlargement augmented demographic problems experienced since the beginning of the transformation. Poland's population, according to official census and data provided by the Central Statistical Office, had remained stagnant since 1990. The number of inhabitants remained constant, ranging from 38.2 million in 1990 to 38.6 in 2000 and 38.5 million in 2013.[25] This stagnation stemmed from divergent "natural" factors: a low fertility rate (one of the lowest in the EU), a low natural increase rate, and a shift of the female fertility peak to an older age group. Social and economic determinants were equally important: relatively low living standards, especially of young people and families, poor child care services, limited child support incentives, and an inflexible labor market triggered by a high unemployment rate among young people.

The human capital loss was partially compensated by remittances transmitted to Poland. It is estimated that the total value of the remittances in the years 2004–2013 amounted to €36 billion, which equaled 60 percent of net transfers from the EU budget to Poland.[26] The remittances accounted for about 2.5 percent of Polish GDP in 2007, although the value of transfers decreased after 2008, and their contribution to the GDP fell to 1.6 percent in 2013.

Social attitudes toward the EU, European integration, and Poland's membership in the Union have been positive, with a clear tendency of growing support for the EU in such areas as economy, security, and infrastructure. The general support for Poland's membership has remained high since 2006, above 80 percent, noting a slight decrease in 2013, to 72 percent in May, but reaching a record 89 percent in March 2014. The percentage of opposition has never exceeded 21 percent and has generally maintained the average level of 10 percent. Concurrently, individual perception of benefits and costs of Polish membership has shown a solid positive assessment.

Europe Must Be Defended

When Poland entered the EU, it had the reputation of being a "difficult" or "obstinate" member. Doubts about Poland's role in the Union concerned economic structures, its social system, and political configurations as well as its geopolitical position and historically based aspirations. Initially treated as an awkward partner,[27] after the 2005 elections and the government change, it earned the popular label of Euro-skeptic, pretentious, and even quarrelsome newcomer. Indeed, the priorities of the Kaczynski government were underpinned by national interests and hesitance toward supranational developments of European integration. Poland was interested in the maximization of financial advantages and defended the traditional composition of the EU budget while appealing for its expansion.

The Kaczynski brothers applied the policy of "selective integrationism."[28] They were supporting loose intergovernmental projects on security issues (like the return to the idea of European forces closely linked with NATO), free movement of persons (eastern enlargement of the Schengen Area), or energy issues (the proposal of an EU energy policy "musketeers pact"). Likewise, they opposed a European constitution, struggled for a "defederalized" reform treaty, and were hesitant about the prospects for reinforcement of community institutions. They also felt threatened by Russia's hardened position (embargo on Polish food imports and gas pressure on the neighboring Ukraine, also affecting supplies to Poland) and were disappointed by the tolerant and open-hearted attitude to Russia among the majority of EU members, with Germany and France at the forefront. For Polish executives, the Russian-German project of the Baltic Sea pipeline (Nord Stream) was particularly dangerous to Polish sovereignty and energy security, whereas Western member states saw it as an opportunity to widen the gas supply system in the EU.

Following early elections in October 2007, the new government broke with its predecessor's foreign policy and declared a firm pro-European stance. Prime Minister Tusk in his inaugural address to the Sejm (the lower house of parliament) defined the bases of his government's EU policy in the following statement:

> We want to pursue Polish interests inside the European Union but we also want . . . to present the Polish vision of further growth of the whole European Union. We believe . . . that deeper cooperation within the European Union and its expansion are a burning interest of the entire community, including Poland. The European Union . . . should be a superpower, it should be an organization— with our country as its important member—which is respected all over the world and should be the main, central actor in global events.[29]

Foreign Minister Sikorski in his speech at the German Council on Foreign Relations in Berlin said that the member states "have to decide whether we want to become a proper federation, or not."[30]

The strategic goals of Tusk government's new European policy included:

1. The strengthening of Poland's role in political decisionmaking in the EU through active participation in the major reform projects
2. The promotion of the solidarity principle as a "Polish brand" in the EU and, at the same time, the means to better defend Poland's national interests
3. The reinforcement of the EU neighborhood policy, especially in its eastern dimension, to mitigate negative consequences of Russia's policy in Central and Eastern Europe

The first objective was highly demanding, given the marginalization of Poland in the years 2005–2007. Tusk started from rapprochement with Germany, pledged his support to Germany's ideas about reforming the EU, and sought to revive the Weimar triangle (Polish-German-French cooperation in political and security matters). He strongly supported the Lisbon Treaty and did his best to break Kaczynski's resistance to the ratification of the treaty in Poland. He presented himself as a strong advocate for further reform to the European integration process, believing that the Lisbon Treaty would make the EU more effective. Although the Lisbon Treaty made the rotating Council presidency politically irrelevant, the Polish government assumed that the presidency would be a good opportunity to voice concerns about the "state of the Union."

Piotr Maciej Kaczynski evaluated Poland's position holding the presidency in the Council: "Their leverage over the European Council was similar to every other country's leverage over the European Council. Their leverage over the Euro group was non-existent and an initiative to participate in the Euro group meeting was denied. The Poles were soldiers in the war on the crisis in the Eurozone, . . . but they were not among the generals who met on 21 July 2011 as a summit of the heads of state or government of the Euro area member states."[31]

Regardless of its relative weakness, the Tusk government was deeply engaged in the general debate on rescuing Europe from acute financial crisis and economic recession, salvaging the single currency, and strengthening fiscal discipline across the EU. Poland gave considerable support to the idea of a fiscal pact, agreed formally at the EU summit ending the Polish presidency period. It promoted the so-called six-pack as a flagship project to improve economic governance and reform the Stability and Growth Pact. It signed on to the European Fiscal Compact and seemed to be interested in the reinforcement of institutional and financial tools like the envisaged establishment of a European Systemic Risk Board and a European System of Financial Supervision.

The second goal of Poland's EU strategy was to promote solidarity as the overriding principle of cooperation and integration within the Union. Solidarity was often identified with the Polish tradition of resistance against communist dictatorship as well as a potent social movement, which liberated Polish society and contributed to the demise of the Soviet bloc. This is why Tusk and representatives of his government presented solidarity as a Polish brand, an example of the power of trustful, loyal cooperation among equal partners. Hence, solidarity as a principle of European integration embedded in EU law[32] was conceived as a protective measure against self-interest and free riding of individual member states. Solidarity was also a means to defend Poland against the major powers in the EU. Despite alliance with Germany and good relations with the UK, French plans for loose political cooperation in the EU toward a two-speed integration with the Eurozone at the core made Poland afraid of being marginalized in the EU.

Poland was a party to the Treaty on Stability, Coordination and Governance, signed on March 2, 2012, by the leaders of all Eurozone members and eight other EU member states, mostly because the provisions of this document highlighted the devotion to the common principles regarding the sharing and bearing of costs of economic recovery. Moreover, during the negotiations of the fiscal pact, Tusk insisted that noneuro countries attend the European Monetary Union summits. He succeeded in pushing through, with German support, a so-called Polish amendment to be guaranteed in the pact.[33] At the same time this was an opportunity for Poland to gain influence in the decisionmaking processes within the Eurozone and the EU as well as to refute an allegation of giving up the adoption of the euro as a long-term strategic goal. Nevertheless, Poland's prospects for joining the Eurozone remained distant. Experts emphasized that global and European economic turbulence added to the Maastricht convergence criteria additional criterion for euro adoption, namely, the stabilization of the euro area.[34] Moreover, the crisis led to a slump in public support for adoption of the single currency. According to a poll published in November 2014, 68 percent of Poles believed that switching to the euro would be bad for the Polish economy.[35]

The third strategic objective is focused on regional and neighborhood issues. Poland jointly with Sweden presented in May 2008 the Eastern Partnership (EaP) scheme as a long-term project to bring six post-Soviet republics from the east of Europe closer to the EU and assist them in structural reforms. Some member states were not enthusiastic about the proposal. For some, like France, it was a competing project with the French-proposed Union of the Mediterranean. For others, like Italy and Greece, it could endanger EU cooperation with Russia.[36] Poland's engagement in the EaP project could also be explained by strong support for Ukraine's pro-European orientation, especially following the NATO refusal to open its door to this country and the Russia-Georgia war in August 2008, which was perceived in Poland as dangerous evidence of Russia's neoimperialist tendencies.

Konstanty Gebert from the European Council on Foreign Relations observed in February 2012 that "Poland was able to convert its own concerns over the situation east of its borders into a legitimate EU concern, by co-sponsoring, with Sweden, the Eastern Partnership policy (EaP). Even if it has recently registered several failures, with Belarus becoming more repressive, Ukraine following suit, and the Arab Spring replacing the East with the South on Europe's radar screen, concern with the Eastern neighborhood remains an area of Polish expertise."[37]

Long-term efforts to associate Ukraine and other EaP countries with the EU culminated in the summit of the EaP in Vilnius in November 2013. Ukraine's president Viktor Yanukovych declined to sign an association and free trade agreement. An editor of *The Economist* claimed at that time that the success of the EaP depends on Ukraine.[38] This is only partially true. Other participants in the EaP, especially Georgia and Moldova, have an impressive record in their reforms. This enabled them to sign association agreements in June 2014. Moldova, a veritable leader of the EaP group, has made tremendous progress in social, economic, and political spheres. Ukraine, regardless of the complex internal situation and the armed conflict in the eastern part of the country, also managed to conclude association agreements. It was Poland who pledged consistently strong support for these successful EaP members and contributed to their impressive achievements.

The first decade of Polish membership in the EU has witnessed significant evolution of the government position on the EU and the attitudes toward the dynamics of European reform. The feeling of being a second-category member state, distrust for EU institutions, and fear of domination of the big EU powers gave way to the conviction of positive effects of the membership in multiple areas as well as the assumption of making the EU an arena of strengthening Poland's European and international position.

Consolidating Poland's Role in the EU

Poland has built a relatively strong position in the EU. A total financial and economic meltdown was averted. Poland has become "Europe's biggest construction site."[39] The Polish economy has largely Europeanized. About three-fourths of the country's goods and services are exported to and consumed in Europe. More than 90 percent of the stock of inward foreign direct investment originates from Europe.

However, Poland had been critical about the performance of the member states in the realm of economic and fiscal discipline and their poor compliance with the principles set in the pact. Sikorski emphatically claimed that the pact "has been broken 60 times!"[40] As a result, Poland engaged in difficult negotiations on the reform of the Stability and Growth Pact. As a non-Eurozone country, Poland had to broker demanding and often rigid positions taken by the leading member states and watch over her own interests and avoid marginalization. From the Polish point of view, the EU must improve economic policy coordination to avoid huge internal imbalances.

A paradox of Polish membership in the EU is the fact that the old economic model inherited from the communists was preserved and only partially modified in the first stages of the 1990s transformation. It was based on a relatively low value-added energy- and labor-consuming industry, keeping Poland low on the value-added ladder. Even before entering the EU, Poland was incorporated into the German supply chain, and now it plays a key role, due to geographical proximity, improved transportation infrastructure, and low labor costs. According to experts of the International Monetary Fund, this has significant positive macroeconomic effects for Poland yet has also considerably increased its exposure to the German business cycle and global shocks.[41]

Conclusion

Geopolitically, Poland's traditional position between Germany and Russia escalates dilemmas of cooperation and conflict. Germany has turned into Poland's biggest and most important economic and political partner, whereas Russia, after the annexation of Crimea and open interference in Ukraine, is considered to be the biggest threat to stability in Europe. Meanwhile, both Germany and Russia cooperate in economic, financial, military, and diplomatic arenas and are hesitant about Polish efforts to strengthen the Ukrainian authorities and exert pressure on Russia, including diplomatic, economic, and financial sanctions. Without substantial support from the EU, Poland puts at risk economic and energy security. Significant energy imports from and agricultural exports to Russia make Poland vulnerable to geopolitical tensions surrounding Russia and Ukraine. In the years to come, Poland should consolidate its position as an important and reliable player in the EU, while defending the Eastern Partnership and intensifying cooperation with its neighbors.

Notes

1. Deloy (2011)
2. Eurostat, "Euro-Indicators Tables," various releases. Available at http://ec.europa.eu/eurostat/web/euro-indicators/consumer-prices/euro-indicators-tables.
3. Eurostat, "Unemployment Rate by Sex and Age Groups—Annual Average." Available at http://appsso.eurostat.ec.europa.eu/nui/show.do?dataset=une_rt_a&lang=en.
4. See Orlowski (2004), pp. 34–35.
5. Eurostat, "Labour Productivity—Annual Data." Available at http://appsso.eurostat.ec.europa.eu/nui/show.do?dataset=nama_aux_lp&lang=en.
6. World Bank, "High-Technology Exports (% of Manufactured Exports)." Available at http://data.worldbank.org/indicator/TX.VAL.TECH.MF.ZS/countries/1W-PL?display=graph.
7. See Bakker and Klingen (2012), p. 44.
8. Piotr Maciej Kaczynski, "Poland in the EU: The Green Island," Ministry of Foreign Affairs of the Republic of Poland, 2012. Available at http://www.msz.gov.pl/en/foreign_policy/europe/european_union/poland_ineu/poland_in_eu/poland_in_eu.
9. The Constitution of the Republic of Poland of 1997 provides in Article 216.5 that: "It shall be neither permissible to contract loans nor provide guarantees and financial sureties which would engender a national public debt exceeding three-fifths of the value of the annual gross domestic product." Under the Public Finance Act of 1998, three additional safety thresholds and adjustment requirements were defined. If public debt is higher than 50 percent of GDP but below 55 percent, the budget for the following year must not propose a higher deficit-to-revenue ratio than in the current year. If the debt is between 55 percent and 60 percent, the budget must not increase the ratio of central government debt to GDP in the subsequent year. If the debt exceeds 60 percent, any government borrowing is forbidden in the following year. See Rutkowski (2007), pp. 2–3.
10. Trading Economics, "Poland Government Debt to GDP." Available at http://www.tradingeconomics.com/poland/government-debt-to-gdp.
11. OECD, "Key Short-Term Economic Indicators," OECD.StatExtracts. Available at http://stats.oecd.org/index.aspx?queryid=21762.
12. Eurostat, "General Government Deficit (-) and Surplus (+)." Available at http://ec.europa.eu/eurostat/tgm/table.do?tab=table&plugin=1&language=en&pcode=teina200.
13. Christian Lowe, "Poland Needs More Belt-Tightening to Hit Deficit Target: OECD," Reuters, March 10, 2014. Available at:= http://www.reuters.com/article/2014/03/10/oecd-poland-idUSW8N0LT01820140310.
14. Hollanders and Es-Sadki (2014).
15. Jedlicka and Rzentarzewska (2014), p. 7.
16. Ministry for Infrastructure and Development of the Republic of Poland (2014), p. 35.

17. Ministry of Foreign Affairs of the Republic of Poland, "Poland's 10 Years in the European Union," based on Eurostat data, 2014. Available at: http://www.msz.gov.pl /resource/ef26c779-74e4-4a0c-aa73-0a9d3c8b695c:JCR.

18. Ministry of Foreign Affairs of the Republic of Poland, "Social and Economic Impact of Poland's Membership of the European Union (1 May 2004–1 May 2013)," 2013. Available at https://www.msz.gov.pl/resource/1f6677e7-cc34-45ab-9587-446ca 4f33428:JCR.

19. Ministry for Regional Development of the Republic of Poland, "Jak kraje UE-15 korzystaja polityki spojnosci realizowanej w krajach Grupy Wyszehradzkiej?," Warsaw, April 26, 2012. Available at https://www.mir.gov.pl/aktualnosci/ministerstwo /Documents/Paryz_inf_prasowa.pdf.

20. Radek Sikorski, "Poland and the future of the European Union," Ministry of Foreign Affairs of the Republic of Poland, presented in Berlin, November 28, 2011. Available at http://www.mfa.gov.pl/resource/33ce6061-ec12-4da1-a145-01e2995 c6302:JCR.

21. "Poland's Second Golden Age: Europe's Unlikely Star," *The Economist*, June 28, 2014, p. 13. Available at http://www.economist.com/news/leaders/21605910-poland -just-had-best-25-years-half-millennium-its-transformation-remains.

22. Engbersen et al. (2010), p. 10.

23. Slany and Solga (2014). In a report on the balance of ten years of Polish membership in the EU, the overall number of emigrants is considerably higher, amounting to 2.4 million (including circular and seasonal migration). See Polskie 10 lat w Unii. Raport , p. 203.

24. "The Polish Paradox," *The Economist*, December 14, 2013, p. 64. Available at http://www.economist.com/news/britain/21591588-britons-loathe-immigration-principle -quite-immigrants-practice-bulgarians.

25. This tendency is particularly striking if we compare Poland with Spain—a country with a similar population in 1990 (38.8 million people). The number of inhabitants (in millions): in 1995: Poland, 38.6, Spain, 39.4; in 2000: Poland, 38.6, Spain, 40.2; in 2005: Poland, 38.2, Spain, 43; in 2010: Poland, 38.5, Spain, 46; in 2013: Poland, 38.5, Spain, 47.3.

26. Polskie 10 lat w Unii. Raport, p. 17.

27. Szczerbiak (2012).

28. Antoni Podolski, "Between Samara and Brussels: Poland's European and Eastern Policy in the First Half of 2007," Monitoring of Polish Foreign Policy Report. Available at http://csm.org.pl/pl/publikacje1/category/46-2007?download=395:poland -s-european-and-eastern-policy-in-the-first-half-of-2007.

29. Donald Tusk, "President of the Council of Ministers,"rspeech presented to the Council of Ministers (Poland), Office of the Prime Minister, November 2007. Available at https://www.premier.gov.pl/en/news/news/president-of-the-council-of-ministers.html.

30. Sikorski (2011).

31. Kaczynski (2011), p. 9.

32. The relevant provisions are contained in Article 4 (3) of the Treaty on the European Union, although solidarity, identified with loyalty, is present in other provisions of the treaties. See Klamert (2004), pp. 12–19.

33. Adelina Marini and Ralitsa Kovacheva, "The Polish Amendment in the New Fiscal Treaty," *Euinside*, February 1, 2012. Available at http://www.euinside.eu/en /news/the-polish-amendment-in-the-new-fiscal-treaty.

34. Kawecka-Wyrzykowska (2013), pp. 59–60.p

35. CBOS Public Opinion Research Center, Concerns related to the introduction of the euro. Available at http://www.cbos.pl/EN/publications/reports/2014/151_14.pdf.

36. Adamczyk (2010), pp. 201–202.

37. Gebert (2012).

38. "Charlemagne: Playing East Against West," *The Economist*, November 23, 2013, p. 33. Available at http://www.economist.com/news/europe/21590585-success-eastern-partnership-depends-ukraine-playing-east-against-west.

39. Orenstein (2014).

40. Sikorski (2011).

41. International Monetary Fund (2013b), p. 5.

16

Hungary:
Embracing Euro-Skepticism

Tamas Novak

CENTRAL AND EASTERN EUROPE (CEE) HAS BEEN EXPERIENCING A deep economic and political transformation since the beginning of the 1990s. The new economic and political pattern that started to develop within the region was based on the liberal market economy model and aimed to open up markets and integrate the region into the world economy and the North Atlantic security structure. In the pre-accession years, the European Union (EU) served as an external anchor that helped the economic and political transformation of the CEE countries. Each country aimed to enter the EU as soon as possible. The coercive pressure to comply with EU rules and regulations was an important factor in the fast and successful adjustment to the new conditions of democratization and marketization of the economy.

The first years of EU membership saw diverging economic performances unfolding in the countries that joined the Union in 2004. Convergence prospects became very different. Hungary is a country where the clearest contrast can be observed in recent years in comparison with the previous decade in terms of economic policy, international economic and political relations, and managing EU affairs. There is a sharp dividing line between the policies pursued before and after entering the EU in 2004 and before and after 2010.

Concerning the 2004 dividing line, its most important feature is the diminishing political stability between 2004 and 2010. Six months after accession, the prime minister was displaced because of increasing dissatisfaction from within his own party.[1] Every effort was made to prevent the return of FIDESZ-KDNP (FIDESZ, the Hungarian Civic Alliance, and its coalition partner, the Christian Democratic People's Party)[2] to office and this goal led to budgetary overspending and spiraling public debt. After winning the elections again, MSZP (the Hungarian Socialist Party) and its coalition partner SZDSZ (Alliance of Free Democrats) were suddenly faced with double pressure. The leaked speech of the prime minister in September 2006 admitting budgetary tricks and lying to the voters had severely damaged the government's image, destroyed the prime minister's credibility, and ignited mass protests across Hungary and rioting in Budapest.[3] This political crisis was concurrent with the macroeconomic stabilization attempts soon after the elections, which were triggered by fiscal and monetary imbalances. This economic and political pressure had greatly restricted the government's room for maneuvering. In 2008, prior to the crisis, the coalition government had broken up due to the success of a referendum initiated and promoted by the opposition,[4] but the smaller coalition partner (SZDSZ) continued to support the government. In March 2009 when the severe effects of the economic crisis became noticeable and Hungary seemed to be isolated after requesting an IMF-EU loan, the prime minister stepped down as he felt he would not be able to achieve much success in the elections in 2010. It was clear to everybody that an early election would lead to a catastrophic defeat for the governing parties, and this concern made it possible for the minority government, led by Gordon Bajnai, to survive for a year.

The other sharp dividing line is associated with the parliamentary elections in 2010. As a result of the turbulent political and economic period that had developed since 2004, the popularity of the governing parties plummeted. The opposition parties won the elections with a super-majority (two-thirds of the seats). The strong support behind and the overwhelming parliamentary majority of FIDESZ-KDNP coupled with marginalized opposition forces made it possible to put into place a completely new program relative to previous years. It has to be noted that this landslide victory was not only due to the economic crisis and crisis management but also to the domestic political problems, the lack of credibility, and the unclear strategy of the earlier governments between 2006 and 2009.

The Impacts of the 2008 Economic Crisis on Hungary

In Hungary, economic difficulties had emerged much earlier than the 2008 crisis. Large overspending since 2001 led to very high public debt levels in comparison to other Central European states. Because of the high budget deficit, the country was put under the Excessive Deficit Procedure immediately after joining the EU. By 2006 and after the parliamentary elections, it had become evident that the economic trends were unsustainable, and this realization triggered macroeconomic stabilization to improve the balance sheet of the country. The several waves of budget consolidation since 2006 had significantly weakened GDP growth even prior to the crisis. Although Slovakia, the Czech Republic, and Poland delivered above 5 percent GDP growth for years after EU accession, Hungary was not able to achieve any

sizable GDP growth in 2007 and 2008 (see Table 16.1). Falling incomes
and expensive financial resources (because of the high interest rates caused
by the large external financial exposure of the country) led to near economic stagnation despite the relatively favorable global economic trends
prior to 2008. As a result, convergence prospects for Hungary worsened in
regional comparison. These already weakened economic foundations were
then hit hard by the crisis of 2008.

In addition to the unfavorable growth prospects, the increasing role of
foreign currency–denominated household and corporate loans had presented great risks to the economy, which later became hardly manageable in
comparison with any of the other Visegrad (V4) countries. The exchange
rate risk that materialized due to the devaluation of the domestic currency
has been one of the most negative implications of the economic crisis and
the chosen economic policy of the 2010 government, which prolonged the
effects of the crisis.

Another specific feature that also differed from the prospects of the
other V4 countries related to the room available to the fiscal policy for maneuvering. The international financial position of Hungary was shattered
when Lehman Brothers went bankrupt and the international confidence and
liquidity crisis developed. International financial liquidity was of utmost
importance for the country because a large share of the public and private
debt was denominated in foreign currency and domestic savings were low.
Because of these pressures, the government asked for the support of international organizations. After very rapid negotiations, Hungary received a
US$25.1 billion IMF-EU-World Bank loan to secure the stable financing of
the external debt even if the financial markets were disrupted.[5]

This loan created a financial protective net for Hungary and started to
restore confidence subject to economic stabilization measures. The loan required disciplined economic policy and improving or not significantly increasing budget deficit from 2009—a year when the crisis-driven decline of
GDP was the steepest. Due to this need for stabilization measures, the room
of the fiscal policy for budgetary spending was much narrower than in

**Table 16.1 GDP Growth Rates in the Visegrad 4 Countries Prior to
the Economic Crisis (% change over previous year)**

	2004	2005	2006	2007	2008
Czech Republic	4.9	6.4	6.9	5.5	2.7
Hungary	4.8	4.3	4.0	0.5	0.9
Poland	5.1	3.5	6.2	7.2	3.9
Slovakia	5.2	6.5	8.3	10.7	5.1

Source: Eurostat.

other countries in the region. Public debt levels in the whole CEE EU region—except for Hungary—were low, and this allowed for a significant deficit rise to apply countercyclical instruments without jeopardizing state finances. In 2009–2010 at the deepest point of the crisis—in line with the Keynesian solutions to pursue active state spending—fiscal spending skyrocketed in Slovakia and Poland while the Czech Republic followed somewhat less ambitious fiscal policies, which was reflected in less favorable GDP data, too.

Formed in spring 2009, the new Hungarian government introduced several significant austerity measures immediately to restore confidence. These were particularly difficult and cost a lot in terms of GDP growth (see Table 16.2) and household income.

The government introduced stabilization measures in the form of spending cuts and tax increases when the GDP shrank significantly. The double pressure of stabilization and the large GDP drop made short-term growth prospects even worse but started to create a more competitive environment for the long term at the expense of a significant income squeeze. After a series of tough adjustment measures, a healthier economic base and macroeconomic balances were accomplished, although poverty had started to spread over large segments of the population by this time due to falling incomes and increasing unemployment rates. The crises, the already weak growth potential, and the falling external demand led to a large GDP drop of close to 7 percent in 2009 (see Table 16.3). Because of the lack of budgetary stimuli, the rebound, which generally follows such a big GDP decline, was much more prolonged than in most of the countries in the region.

Beside the government's difficult political situation and the deep impact of the economic crisis, another important political trend had started to emerge with the 2009 EU parliamentary (EP) election that was indicative of a transformation of the party structure and had several important implications later on. The result of the EP elections confirmed that the governing

Table 16.2 General Government Deficit (% of GDP)

	2008	2009	2010	2011	2012	2013
Czech Republic	−2.1	−5.5	−4.4	−2.9	−4.0	−1.3
Hungary	−3.7	−4.6	−4.5	4.3[a]	−2.3	−2.4
Poland	−3.7	−7.3	−7.6	−4.9	−3.7	−4.0
Slovakia	−2.4	−7.9	−7.5	−4.1	−4.2	−2.6

Source: Eurostat.

Note: a. The 2011 budget surplus in Hungary was the result of the redirection of private pension fund resources into the government budget. This later led to the elimination of the obligatory private pension pillar, which was established in 1997 with the aim of long term restructuring of the pension system.

Table 16.3 GDP Growth in the Visegrad 4 Countries from 2009
(% change over previous year)

	2009	2010	2011	2012	2013	2014
Czech Republic	−4.8	2.3	2.0	−0.8	−0.7	2.0
Hungary	−6.6	0.8	1.8	−1.5	1.5	3.6
Poland	2.6	3.7	4.8	1.8	1.7	3.3
Slovakia	−5.3	4.8	2.7	1.6	1.4	2.4

Source: Eurostat.

parties were weakened tremendously, the strength of the largest opposition party (FIDESZ-KDNP) was enormous, and the far-right party (Jobbik) began to gain strong ground particularly in specific regions in the country. The 2010 parliamentary elections only reinforced the political changes that were becoming apparent in the 2009 EP elections (see Table 16.4).

Changing Government Policies After 2010 and Relations with the EU

The new government that came to power in 2010 (FIDESZ-KDNP) won more than two-thirds of the parliamentary seats, which had two fundamental consequences. First, it empowered the government to execute its economic, social, and foreign policy without any significant control from the parliament. Second, from a legislative point of view, it meant that the government had the power to change any laws or the constitution without consultation or negotiation with the opposition parties[6] and sometimes almost on a daily basis according to its political interests.[7]

Table 16.4 Party List Votes in 2009 EP Elections and
2010 Parliamentary Elections

EP Elections, 2009		Parliamentary Elections, 2010	
Party	Votes (%)	Party	Votes (%)
FIDESZ-KDNP	56.36	FIDESZ-KDNP	52.73
MSZP	17.37	MSZP	19.30
Jobbik	14.77	Jobbik	16.67
MDF	5.32	LMP	7.48

Source: http://www.valasztas.hu.
Notes: MDF, Magyar Demokrata Fórum (Hungarian Democratic Forum; LMP, Lehet Más a Politika (Politics Can Be Different) green, liberal party.

A Completely New Government Strategy and Approach

Along the road to membership, Hungary—like other Central European countries—was aiming to comply with the *acquis* as soon as possible. After the early years of the 1990s, the driving force behind democratization and economic transformation was associated with the continuous integration of the region into the Euro-Atlantic structures, including both NATO and the European Union. During this period, the transformation seemed unstoppable, and the only question was when the process of catching up would result in a substantial rise of household incomes. In the preaccession years, the most important drive behind economic and political transformation and foreign policy orientation was the EU. The accession objective was achieved in 2004, and the previously unanimously supportive environment for the EU changed, the motivating and disciplinary force of the membership perspective vanished. This change was coupled with three unfavorable trends.

First, Hungarian domestic politics became very complicated; objectives became obscure and difficult to follow. A second problem was apparently related to the lack of strategic vision on how EU membership could be part of a long-term development strategy for the country. Short-term objectives—mostly in the form of rapid infrastructure development financed from EU transfers—and lack of consent among political parties on long-term development goals made the elaboration of a viable strategy impossible. The third challenge was related to developments in the EU, namely, the strategic problems regarding its future. At the turn of the millennium ambitious plans and strategies were formulated including enlargement or the Lisbon strategy, not to mention the introduction of the euro, but by 2004–2005 no further plans were on the table.

When the dynamic phase of eastern enlargement ended, there were clear signs of destabilization in parts of the CEE as a result of unfulfilled expectations mostly concerning living standards.[8] Voices questioning the success and rationale of more than twenty years of transformation and EU accession started to become stronger and questioned the competence and efficiency of the EU. Hungarian convergence was either slow compared to Poland and Slovakia or the absolute level of development lagged substantially in comparison to the Czech Republic (see Table 16.5).

As a result, skepticism developed regarding the success of economic transformation; negative perceptions of the EU's role in convergence strengthened, which made the emergence of very divergent strategies regarding relations with the EU possible. Parallel to the "not so promising" economic developments in the EU, the (temporary) crisis resistance observed in some emerging countries was now being seen as a more successful model. In Hungary, government politicians started voicing opinions about the need to develop economic and political relations independent

Table 16.5 Per Capita GDP at Purchasing Power Standard (EU-28 = 100)

	2004	2005	2006	2007	2008	2009	2010	2011	2012	2013
Czech Republic	79	80	81	84	82	83	81	83	82	82
Hungary	62	62	62	61	63	64	65	65	65	66
Poland	49	50	50	53	55	59	62	64	66	67
Slovakia	57	60	63	67	71	71	73	73	74	75

Source: Eurostat.

from the influence of the "declining" West (EU) and to make new and stronger ties with fast-growing emerging regions.[9]

Given this framework, a new narrative emerged in Hungary. Its most important elements were the following. The whole transformation project was based on Western ideologies and principles that did not seem to be in the interest of the Central European countries (e.g., the basic principles of the Washington Consensus, supported by renowned Western, mostly US advisers): international corporations investing in Hungary only extract their "extra" profits and disregard the true interests of the country. The EU uses double standards when applying economic and political rules and regulations requiring "new" and weak members to exhibit better performance than older and large members.

The new Hungarian government was able to redefine its policies against everything that had been pursued previously. It is not an overstatement to call the system of priorities a turning point in the Hungarian post-transformation phase from almost all aspects of policy, including but not limited to the government's EU strategy. The following basic strategic principles can be identified.

The first feature of the new government's strategy. It attempts to disregard the consequences of globalization. To serve this objective, it applies open or indirect protectionist measures, which follow the reasoning of economic theories that address the risks and problems through the negative effects of liberalized international economic environment and include preference given to domestic companies over stronger foreign competitors, the need for the capacity to define domestic development policy directions, and protection against foreign monopoly or oligopoly situations. At the same time, this principle acknowledges the importance of foreign-owned manufacturing firms by concluding so-called strategic agreements to guarantee their continued operation in Hungary and prevent their relocation to other business locations.

The next important characteristic is the "big country approach." Small countries with relatively unfavorable endowments of production factors generally cannot successfully repeat the economic policy and international strategies of large economies. The primary objective of this approach in Hungary is to become independent from international organizations and, in a broader perspective, get rid of any international and domestic critics, including the EU institutions. In extreme cases it may include control of the media and nongovernmental organizations.[10] As a result, conflicts with the EU also increased over very diverse issues ranging from sectoral taxes to media regulation. These conflicting fields are best reflected by the infringement proceedings, which included some very sensitive political issues.[11] The history of Central Europe proves that smaller, semi-peripheral countries with only a limited domestic market can very easily be marginalized in the international system due to their own faults or unfavorable internal and external conditions.

The third basic principle. This is the objective of establishing a state-dominated economy by strengthening new domestic monopolies. Besides full direct control of economic developments, strong authority over other social processes (culture, education) is also an important objective. The role of the Hungarian state grew after the crisis. There are, however, two different strategies for a stronger state: the first strategy aims at enhanced and more efficient regulation while ensuring neutral regulation and improving the business environment and competition (for example, in the case of the Baltic states). The other strategy basically aims at direct state involvement in the economy to change market positions. This involvement had precedents in several countries during the crisis with a view to handling very difficult crisis-related situations.[12]

It is also important to see the government's long-term growth and competitiveness goals, as these greatly influence the specific instruments and measures introduced by the government, not least as a response to the economic crisis. One objective is to gain cost advantage in production by ensuring a cheap labor force. This objective is served by the measures introduced in education, such as shortening the compulsory period of schooling. Then, employees become much more dependent and less mobile, while their chances of employment in higher value-added activities like services and modern industrial production decrease. As a result, they can only be employed in low value-added jobs, that is, by the assembly lines of manufacturing firms. If this labor is cheap enough in comparison with other European states, some firms might consider locating their production in Hungary instead of moving elsewhere. In addition, it is thought that cheap production may improve Hungary's position in Central European competition for foreign direct investment.

Thus, building up a system of clientelism[13] and making the increasing share of households and domestic enterprises dependent on government policy are important objectives. Widespread clientelism is not at all a novelty in Eastern and Southeastern Europe; its presence in Hungary is increasingly evident due to the centralization efforts of the state. This perspective has important implications for the mentality of citizens and business owners regardless of the size of their businesses. It can reinforce the belief that the success of doing business or getting additional benefits is dependent on total loyalty. To make matters worse, it can easily mislead large circles of the population to believe that the way to success is not by innovation, creativity, and competition but by involvement in the new monopoly and oligopoly positions and the redistribution of existing wealth and power within society. The process accelerated after the 2014 parliamentary elections, which strengthened the positions of the government and weakened he possible alternatives.

An additional important principle. This principle relates to the budget position and revenues. The primary objective is to make necessary revenue available by resorting to instruments that might only affect small groups and do not increase direct taxation on the population. This option offers quite a different approach to other mainstream crisis management instruments used in many countries, for example, Spain, Portugal, the Baltic states, and Greece. It is aimed at internal devaluation by decreasing wages and social transfers. The idea is to unlink the government from possible increases of household burdens by heavy taxation of the corporate sector (mostly foreign-owned firms that operate in services sector) or by the application of indirect instruments (value-added tax, bank transaction taxes, etc.). To reach this goal, one of the instruments applied was the flat tax, which primarily affected the poorest, who had previously not paid taxes. Ultimately and collectively household income was on the rise. The other important instrument is the forced public utility price cut, which was more than often coupled with the "nationalization" of the service providers.[14] The government refers to this policy as something that hurts large European businesses (several utility firms were fully or partly in foreign hands), which seek protection from the European Commission.[15] According to government rhetoric, the Commission primarily serves business interests, and, therefore initiates infringement proceedings against Hungary for breaching EU law.[16]

Relations Between the EU and Hungary

EU-Hungarian relations became tense immediately after the new government came into power in 2010. When it took office, the government thought it could manage the relatively high budget deficit and continues to pursue a policy that did not entail further austerity measures on households. However, as the country had been under the Excessive Deficit Procedure for several years, loosening the fiscal policy was not allowed by the European Union. From this point on, the government started to apply instruments that were called "unorthodox." It introduced significant sectoral taxes, eradicated the private pension funds, and accumulated assets were redirected into the budget or used to reduce government debt. An additional set of unorthodox measures related to the increasing state involvement in the economy, which was coupled with overtaking private firms and an increased role in price controls. At the same time, the super majority in the parliament allowed for substantial modifications of existing legislation including the enactment of a new Fundamental Law that replaced the previous Constitution.

According to the EU's evaluations, since 2010, democratic institutions and democracy have been under attack by the government's legislative steps, which violated the Copenhagen criteria.[17] The Copenhagen criteria, however, were never as effective as Brussels claimed they were. They were too general and were applied too inconsistently. EU elites presumed that if new members were capable of adhering to the rules governing the EU's common market, they could be certified as full-fledged liberal democracies.

The European Commission formulated objections against some of the Hungarian moves that were thought to violate European values, but in fact the possibility for intervention was extremely unlikely given the lack of legal and political instruments. Only violating the rules of the common market could be punished, after a very long procedure, and the excessive deficit procedure gives some possibility for leverage over certain countries and issues. At best, Brussels was able to address political problems only indirectly.[18] It must be noted that in theory it is possible to curtail membership rights if a country violates fundamental rights and/or European values, but it is very difficult to imagine this taking place. The final decision has to be taken by the EU member state governments, which may consider such steps to be precedents that can later be turned against other states. Other instruments, such as pressure by heavyweight EU politicians, did not work either. Open criticism was quickly turned around by the government, which accused the EU of applying double standards and only increased anti-EU sentiments.[19]

The toughest criticism came in mid-2013 in the Venice Commission of the Council of Europe's report on the problems of the amendment of the Hungarian Fundamental Law.[20] According to its conclusion, "Taken together, these measures amount to a threat for constitutional justice and for the supremacy of the basic principles contained in the Fundamental Law of Hungary. The limitation of the role of the Constitutional Court leads to a risk that it may negatively affect all three pillars of the Council of Europe: the separation of powers as an essential tenet of democracy, the protection of human rights and the rule of law."[21] A few weeks later, on July 3, 2013, after one and a half years of investigation, the European Parliament accepted the so-called Tavares Report.[22] This report listed all the steps considered undemocratic since Hungary's change of government in 2010.[23]

The Tavares Report

This report was the strongest official criticism of Hungary's undemocratic changes, and it put a new system of monitoring and assessment in place. The most important four elements are those that set up the monitoring system and can provide the basis for procedures in other countries.[24]

Article 2, Alarm Agenda, requires the European Commission in all of its dealings with Hungary to raise only Article 2 issues until such time as Hungary comes into compliance with the report. This Alarm Agenda effectively blocks all other dealings between the Commission and Hungary until Hungary addresses the issues raised in the report.

"The Commission, the European Council and the European Parliament will each delegate members to a new committee that will engage in a close review of all activities of the Hungarian government relevant to the Tavares report."[25] The new system creates monitoring that is deeper and more comprehensive than the Excessive Deficit Procedure, which simply checks whether the budget deficit numbers are acceptable, without looking into qualitative issues.

The establishment of the Copenhagen Commission, consisting of several independent experts, was entrusted with the task of reviewing compliance with the Copenhagen criteria against which the "new" member states were assessed prior to accession.[26]

The Tavares Report holds out the possibility of invoking Article 7 if the Hungarian government does not comply with the monitoring program and reform its ways.[27]

The Reaction of the Hungarian Government

The Hungarian government did not accept[28] the Tavares Report and quickly enacted its very offensive "Resolution on the Right of Hungary to Equal Treatment."[29] As a follow-up, the Tavares Report contributed to the EU's implementation of procedures against countries that are thought to be violating fundamental rights and obligations. In March 2014, "a new EU Framework to safeguard the rule of law in the European Union" was initiated.[30] It is aimed at safeguarding the rule of law when other solutions are not working. According to this,

> The new EU Framework will address situations in which a systemic threat to the rule of law emerges in a Member State. If this threat cannot be effectively addressed by the safeguards and mechanisms which exist at the national level, there is a reason for the EU to step in. In such situations, the Commission will use the Framework if the existing instruments at EU level, in particular infringement proceedings and the mechanisms of Article 7 of the Treaty on European Union cannot be applied.

In summary, Hungarian policies and recent developments in EU-Hungary relations triggered the creation of a new instrument and procedure, which later may strengthen the possibility of the EU's ability to enforce member states to comply with the Copenhagen criteria. It is a clear improvement of EU law in safeguarding fundamental values and principles.

Hungary's Changing Relations with the EU

The popularity of the government has not been damaged by the conflicts with the EU. Quite the contrary: owing to the government's interpretation of the EU criticism and the weakness of opposition parties, the government has been able to increase its popularity in the electorate. It also embarked on a strategic move to strengthen economic ties with the "Eastern countries" when it concluded a €10 billion state loan agreement in early 2014 with Russia to build two more nuclear power generators. The aim of this and many other attempts to improve economic relations with so-called emerging countries of the East was to gain additional growth impetus and use both the resources of the EU and the capital investments and loan facilities of Eastern countries. Hungary as a small peripheral country does not have many advantages in global competition and therefore is influenced by dominant international economic and political powers. This situation can be best utilized only if these international powers follow similar economic and political principles and values. Currently this is not the case. The government has been very fortunate that Hungary, as a member of the EU, is entitled to public EU transfers regardless of the values or policies it pursues, as long as certain minimum indicators are met. Hungary must meet the 3 percent GDP deficit rule at all costs, as compliance is very important to secure the continuous inflow of EU development funds. EU transfers currently (in 2013–2014) finance around 90 percent of public investments. In this specific case, it is possible to take advantage of financing from two divergent powers at the same time (the EU and Russia-China) in the short to medium term. On the other hand, and in the long run, it may have serious implications structurally and in terms of technology and innovation.

Using its strategic orientation, rhetoric, and the changes in the electoral system,[31] in April 2014, the government again won an overwhelming (two-thirds) majority of the parliamentary seats in the general elections. It seemed that the master plan of Prime Minister Viktor Orbán was finally achieved. He had positioned his party in the middle of the political arena and himself as the defender of democracy against the far-right party Jobbik. At the same time, the totally fragmented "left," which has been unable to formulate coherent economic and political messages, is not able to pose a serious threat to the government. This narrative is so strong that in the EP elections the governing parties were able to reinforce this pattern as they had won more than 50 percent of the votes (see Table 16.6).

Table 16.6 Results of Votes for Party List in April 2014 Parliamentary Elections and June 2014 EP Elections

Parliamentary Elections, April 2014		EP Elections, June 2014	
Party	Votes (%)	Party	Votes (%)
FIDESZ-KDNP	44.87	FIDESZ-KDNP	51.48
MSZP-EGYÜTT-		Jobbik	14.67
DK-PM-MLP	25.57	MSZP	10.90
Jobbik	20.22	DK	9.75
LMP	5.34	EGYÜTT-PM	7.25
		LMP	5.04

Source: http://www.valasztas.hu.
Notes: MSZP-EGYÜTT-DK-PM-MLP (left parties)

After winning the parliamentary elections, it was anticipated that the government would not be facing any major challenges in the coming years. However unexpected it was though, a sense of dissatisfaction with the government had soon started to grow. This change in attitude was fundamentally caused by three events: political mistakes committed by the ruling parties on the domestic scene; increasing international pressure on the government prompted by its authoritarian politics; and the emergence of sharp dividing lines within the governing elite.

One of the political miscalculations made involved a range of attacks—including exercising political pressure and the planned discriminative taxation—against selected media outlets. But contrary to government expectations, some of the concerned parties started to defend themselves with unexpected success. This had led to increasing criticism of the government on some influential television outlets, and later in newspapers. Without overestimating the impact of this phenomenon, it can safely be concluded that the critical voices that focused on alleged corruption cases and the inexplicable affluence of several key government figures had started to erode the popularity of the government. The second mistake concerns measures that triggered mass protests against the government. The most controversial such plan was the introduction of the so-called Internet tax, which was considered unacceptable by a large number of people—independent of political orientation. In addition to this broad popular dissatisfaction, the planned Internet tax was seen by many as evidence of the government's nondemocratic approach to the freedom of information. In both cases the government had to revoke its proposals or modify them significantly, but the losses of political goodwill require more long-term remedies.

At the same time, international criticism started to intensify, first because of the infamous speech of the prime minister praising the notion of

the "illiberal state,"[32] which resonated somewhat oddly in a new EU country. The vision of the illiberal state prompted external criticism at a very
high level, including a statement by former US president Bill Clinton.[33] The
other internationally criticized issue was the Hungarian government's policy toward Russia. The prime minister stated that the Russian relationship
was simply a business matter. This declaration coincided with the escalation of conflict in Ukraine with alleged active Russian involvement. The
third sensitive issue concerned the government attitude toward NGOs,
which began to change in the summer of 2014. This policy once again had
led to serious warnings for Hungary including statements by US president
Barack Obama.[34] These tensions led to the cooling of US-Hungarian relations and resulted in travel bans on several Hungarian public officers.[35]

Still, probably the most surprising turn of events was the development of
the increasingly evident lines of division within the governing elite. The most
important cracks seemed to have affected the relationship between the prime
minister and his former business ally, who had played a decisive role in the
financial survival of FIDESZ in the 1990s and who had then greatly benefited
between 2010 and 2014 from publicly financed projects. The tensions led to
an open "war" between different groups within the governing elite, which
caused increasing uncertainties among government supporters.[36]

All these developments eroded the popularity of the governing parties.
The growing dissatisfaction has led to strengthening support for the far-right
party, Jobbik. The traditional left parties remained weak but, given the falling
support for the government, their relative position has also improved. Given
these significant and unexpected changes since the 2014 elections, the political context for the next few years has become much more obscure than anyone
could have anticipated. The political fight between FIDESZ-KDNP (governing parties), Jobbik (the far-right), and the Left (traditional and "new" left)
will be extremely fierce over the next two or three years, which without a
doubt will severely disturb relations between Hungary and the EU.

The Citizens and the EU

The Euro-skepticism of Hungarians has been different in many respects
from their Western counterparts. While in the "old" member states skepticism is mostly based on what is seen as a democratic deficit in the EU, in
Hungary the problems were articulated, for several years, more in terms of
the quality of domestic democracy. Prior to the EU accession, Hungarians
were barely satisfied with their domestic institutions' democratic properties
and performance compared to EU institutions. It had very much to do with
the belief that after the accession, Hungary would soon become similar to
the more developed member states, especially in terms of living standards.
The EU was attractive for citizens from a number of perspectives. The sit-

uation changed rapidly after EU accession when it became clear that the path to convergence would be difficult and much longer than anticipated.

During this period Euro-skeptic sentiments grew, and a new pattern emerged: the political elite continued to support integration and the EU itself, while the citizens became disillusioned and less supportive. The fundamental reason behind these different attitudes was that on the macro-level benefits were tangible (e.g., in terms of infrastructure development or other EU-financed projects), but on the micro-level, in the everyday life of the people, these benefits remained unseen. Continuous economic stabilization efforts led to stagnation of wages, and the crisis hit the population significantly in terms of unemployment and real wages. This disillusionment contributed to the increasing popularity for the far-right Jobbik party, which gained momentum in the 2010 and 2014 elections.

The new government changed its approach to economic policy, which in 2011 had contributed to the second wave of the economic recession. In addition to the unfavorable economic developments, which were mostly based on measures that seriously damaged the country's growth potential, especially through falling investments, political conflicts (already analyzed) also emerged between the government and the European Union. These conflicts were used by the government to blame the EU for economic problems. According to the official interpretation, bad Hungarian economic performance was the consequence of the Eurozone crisis (which was not true given that the overwhelming majority of CEE member states were not in recession and performed much better than the Eurozone). In the government communication, the EU became an enemy, and an increasing share of the population started to share this view. At demonstrations that were organized by the supporters of the government, huge masses would gather under their most important slogan of "Hungary will not be a colony of the EU." The opposition parties generally condemned this approach, and at their rallies, attended by fewer supporters than the progovernment rallies, the EU was verbally supported, and EU flags were waved. In Hungary, there are no EU flags used at official government events, and during the 2014 election campaign, the far-right Jobbik party burned EU flags.

Owing not least to the government's communication on the EU and also to the relatively strong position of the far right, opinion polls in autumn 2013 indicated that only 32 percent of the population considered EU membership good, 22 percent of respondents said it was an absolute disaster, and 39 percent remained neutral or skeptical.[37] Data show that a large share of the population is either neutral or opposes EU membership, but this view is not very different from the EU average. However, the results show significant differences when comparing Hungary's Euro-skepticism with that of other CEE member countries. According to such a comparison, Hungary has been the second most Euro-skeptic country in the region after the Czech Republic.

Euro-skepticism in Hungary has one distinctive ideological feature: it is fundamentally different from the type held by the so-called free market or liberal Euro-skeptics. Euro-skeptics in Hungary may agree with other free market or liberal Euro-skeptics. The difference, however, is that the Hungarian Euro-skeptics attach something more to the argument: not only is Brussels nontransparent, overly complicated, overburdened by rules, and overregulated, it is also waging a war against Hungary. There has been growth in Hungary of "populist" or "nationalist" Euro-skepticism despite the fact that Hungary was the third largest beneficiary of the EU's 2007–2013 budget regarding per capita transfers.[38]

Conclusions

Hungarian perspectives about the EU have changed considerably over the previous decades. For several years it was thought that EU membership would guarantee the unstoppable development of democracy and a liberal economic system. Later this view was increasingly coupled with the belief of rapid economic development as a result of becoming part of a large Single Market, which delivers higher growth rates through improved market access, cheaper financing, and increasing competitiveness. Although these beliefs were strong, the need to adjust to the EU was an important driving force behind domestic political and economic development. When the domestic political situation became less stable around the time of accession and particularly when the economic crisis hit the country, this view of the EU changed. The primary objective was now to maximize the positive implications of the financial transfers that could be drawn while guaranteeing the freedom and flexibility for domestic political maneuvers. From this goal, it also follows that the current government's political strategy is to increase the independence of member states in making their policies and strengthen the intergovernmental nature of the EU.

The 2014 Hungarian government considers present EU integration to be "too deep." It believes that the original objectives of economic and political transformation of the new members and the convergence of living standards among the EU member states have not been achieved. It perceives that the EU was not able to manage the impact of the crisis in quite the same way that some large and not so democratic emerging countries were able to achieve. These perceptions weaken Hungary's commitments and obligations to the EU. Moreover, most of the more developed countries were unable to meet the Maastricht criteria immediately after the crisis broke out, and rules seemed to be meaningless when large countries faced hardships.

Hungary is clearly among the countries that want unlimited freedom in its policy instruments. The policy changes of recent years, without exception, and the processes after EU accession indicate that strategic questions relating to the future of Hungary in the EU remain unanswered. There is only one definite objective in mind: the transfers coming from the EU budget have to be spent in full. The strategy since 2004 has been limited to preserving a positive transfer balance as much as possible, coupled with increasing conflicts with the EU over substantive issues. This approach explains why Hungary has not dealt much with the prospective future of the EU and did not participate in any initiatives to deepen integration, including the adoption of the euro.

Notes

1. The governing coalition performed poorly in the 2004 European Parliamentary elections: Opposition leader FIDESZ got 47.3 percent and the leading government party (MSZP, Hungarian Socialist Party) collected 34.3 percent of the votes. Coalition party leaders thought there was no other solution to invigorate the government than to replace Prime Minister Péter Medgyessy with Ferenc Gyurcsány.

2. They ruled as a coalition government between 1998 and 2002 and since 2010.

3. Hungarian Prime Minister Ferenc Gyurcsány delivered a speech in Balatonőszöd in May 2006 to MSZP members of the National Assembly of Hungary. This meeting was supposed to be confidential, but it was taped and was later leaked. According to his words: "There is not much choice. There is not, because we have fucked it up. Not a little but a lot. No European country has done anything as boneheaded as we have. It can be explained. We have obviously lied throughout the past one and half, two years. It was perfectly clear that what we were saying was not true. . . . And in the meantime, by the way, we did not do anything for four years. Nothing. You cannot mention any significant government measure that we can be proud of, apart from the fact that in the end we managed to get governance out of the shit." BBC World Service, http://news.bbc.co.uk/2/hi/europe/5359546.stm, May 26, 2006. Accessed: April 20, 2015.

4. The referendum in early March 2008 was held on revoking medical and tuition fees. The proposals would cancel government reforms that introduced doctor fees payable per visit and medical fees payable on the number of days spent in hospital (co-payment) as well as tuition fees in higher education. All three were supported by the majority of voters.

5. For the details and objectives of the loan see https://www.imf.org/external/pubs/ft/survey/so/2008/car102808b.htm.

6. In Hungary, for the modification of the most important laws including the constitution, a two thirds majority is required. This solution was the result of negotiations between key parties in 1990 to guarantee the stability of the basic legal instruments and to protect them from frequent changes by a simple parliamentary majority.

7. The prime minister called the Fundamental Law, which entered into force at the beginning of 2012, strong as granite. It was then modified quite substantially five times in the next two years.

8. Hamilton (2013), p. 310.

9. Kałan, (2013), p. 2. "The Orban government has made enhanced Asian ties a cornerstone of its foreign policy and its diplomatic efforts have concentrated increasingly on reinforcing the country's contacts with a large part of the continent, from Northeast Asia through Central Asia and Transcaucasia, to the Persian Gulf."

10. One of the allegations against Hungary in terms of the rule of law by the EU was related to media supervision. Regarding the nonprofit sector, the government expressed its will to control any foreign support to civil organizations, for example, the Norway Grant (http://www.norvegalap.hu/en/cimoldal) — the attack of which war-

ranted the hearing by the Norwegian Ministry of Foreign Affairs of the Hungarian Ambassador in Oslo in June 2014.

11. Cases C-286/12 and C-288/12 of the European courts were particularly sensitive politically. The first was on the national scheme requiring compulsory retirement of judges, prosecutors, and notaries on reaching the age of sixty-two and the second on prematurely ending the term served by the supervisory authority for the protection of personal data. In both cases the Curia found that Hungary had failed to fulfill its obligations.

12. To name just a few examples: the solution offered by Iceland to the banking crisis; partial or full nationalization of private pension funds in several countries; different forms of quantitative easing, such as in the United States; Europe also starting to change its monetary instruments; massive bailouts in different sectors, most importantly in the banking industry, or sectoral taxes introduced by many countries (although at very different rates); and very expensive bailouts in the Eurozone to save countries from sovereign default. These interventions are creating precedents to which any country can refer later as instruments to be used in exceptional circumstances.

13. The trend of increasing clientelism was mentioned as a potentially positive development in Hungary by the president/CEO of the Hungarian Initiative Foundation in the United States, Tamás Fellegi (he was formerly the National Development minister between 2010 and 2012) as long as it supports the increasing wealth of several rich Hungarians. According to him, the longer term positive implications may overcome the negative side effects if clientelism does not spread beyond normal levels (Márton Galambos,, "Interview with Tamas Fellegi," *Forbes*, Hungarian edition, June 2014. http://forbes.hu/).

14. Intense debates can be pursued on the effectiveness and implications of different ownership forms. However, one thing stands out clearly: according to international experiences, forced ownership transformation definitely carries substantial risks. The dilemma is as old as the history of economic thinking: what is more beneficial, direct state involvement in the economy or the strong but normative regulation of markets?

15. According to the government spokesmen: "Multinational corporations and Hungary's left-wing opposition parties attack the *rezsicsökkentes* (public utility bills cut) and direct certain entities in Brussels to convince the European Commission to deliberately attack Hungary." See more (in Hungarian) at http://www.fidesz.hu/hirek/2013-06-29 /hoppal-a-fidesz-kitart-a-rezsicsokkentes-mellett/.

16. By cutting utility prices the government pushes these firms in the red. After a while they are expected to give up their business and sell it to the government. This process has recently been accelerated.

17. The Copenhagen criteria provide the rules that define whether a country is eligible to join the European Union. The criteria require a state to have the institutions to preserve democratic governance and human rights, have a functioning market economy, and accept the obligations and intent of the EU. Summaries of EU legislation: Glossary: http://europa.eu/legislation_summaries/glossary/accession_criteria_copenhague _en.htm. (Accessed: 20 April, 2015).

18. See more on this and similar considerations in Müller (2014).

19. The EU was compared to a colonial power in 2012. A "war of independence" was declared against Brussels. See, for example, "Hungary: Orbán Wasteland," editorial, *Guardian*, July 14, 2013. Available at http://www.theguardian.com/commentisfree/2013 /jul/14/hungary-viktor-orban-wasteland-leader.

20. Venice Commission, "Opinion on the Fourth Amendment to the Fundamental Law of Hungary Adopted by the Venice Commission at Its 95th Plenary Session, Venice, 14–15 June," CDL-AD(2013)012-e, 2013. Available at http://www.venice.coe .int/webforms/documents/?pdf=CDL-AD(2013)012-e.

21. Ibid., p. 32, para. 145.

22. The Tavares Report is by far the strongest and most consequential official condemnation of the FIDESZ consolidation of power after 2010. The report was accepted by 370 EP members against 248 and 82 abstained. The government alleged that the report was a result of conspiracy between socialist and liberal parties against a center-right party. In fact, the number of votes against the report was much less than the number of center-right MPs, but as the voting was not open, it is unclear who voted for and against it.

23. European Parliament resolution of July 3, 2013, on the situation of fundamental rights: standards and practices in Hungary (pursuant to the European Parliament resolution of February 16, 2012) (2012/2130(INI)). The key points receiving criticism were the Fundamental Law and its transitional provisions, extensive use of cardinal laws, accelerated legislative procedures, practice of individual members' bills, parliamentary debate, weakening of checks and balances, Constitutional Court, parliament, Data Protection Authority, independence of the judiciary, the electoral reform, media legislation, respect of the rights of persons belonging to minorities, freedom of religion or belief, and recognition of churches.

24. The Tavares Report has been thoroughly analyzed by Kim Lane Scheppele in several papers, see, for example, "In Praise of the Tavares Report," *Hungarian Spectrum*, July 3, 2013. Available at http://hungarianspectrum.wordpress.com/2013/07/03/kim-lane-scheppele-in-praise-of-the-tavares-report/.

25. See para. 85 of the Tavares Report, available at http://www.europarl.europa.eu/sides/getDoc.do?pubRef=-//EP//TEXT+REPORT+A7-2013-0229+0+DOC+XML+V0//EN.

26. The Hungarian government continuously claimed that the European institutions (and the international organizations in general) used double standards against Hungary. The Copenhagen Commission was modeled on the Council of Europe's Commission for Democracy through Law (the Venice Commission). Its neutral approach would be guaranteed by the composition of the Commission.

27. Article 7 describes a procedure through which an EU member state can be deprived of its vote in the European Council. It was considered to be useless because it was extreme and too dangerous, as it would have set a precedent.

28. See more on that in "Remarks of the Government of Hungary on the Report of the European Parliament on the Situation of Fundamental Rights in Hungary," available at http://www.kormany.hu.

29. The resolution states the European Parliament contravenes European values and led the bloc on a dangerous path by approving a report on the state of fundamental rights in Hungary. The resolution added that the Tavares Report "arbitrarily defines requirements, arbitrarily introduces new procedures and creates new institutions which stand in violation of Hungary's sovereignty guaranteed in the EU Treaty." The document is available in English at http://www.kormany.hu.

30. It is also important to mention that the problems of the quality of democracy or the business environment have been confirmed by other international indicators. To mention a few: the Democracy Index 2011 by the Economic Intelligence Unit has described the situation as follows: "Some negative trends have recently got worse. Hungary perhaps the prime example among the EU's new member states in the region." (EIU 2012, p. 21). According to the data, the democracy index for Hungary has shrunk further in 2012. It is interesting to note that between 2010 and 2012 in the V4 countries, only Hungary lowered its score and occupied the worst position among these countries with lowest index value, whereas in 2008 Hungary preceded Slovakia and Poland (EIU 2013, p. 11).

31. European Commission, "European Commission Presents a Framework to Safeguard the Rule of Law in the European Union, March 11," press release, IP/14/237.

32. For more details on the changes see "Legal But Not Fair (Hungary)," *New York Times*, April 13, 2014. Available at http://krugman.blogs.nytimes.com/2014/04/13/legal-but-not-fair-hungary.

33. Orban wants to build 'illiberal state,' BRUSSELS, 28 July 2014, https://euobserver.com/political/125128.

34. "The Hungarian Prime Minister—they owe a lot to America—he just said he likes authoritarian capitalism but he's just saying 'I don't want to ever leave power.' Usually those guys just want to stay forever and make money." (Former US president Bill Clinton; The Daily Show with Jon Stewart; 18 September 2014)

35. "From Hungary to Egypt, endless regulations and overt intimidation increasingly target civil society." (Remarks by President Barack Obama at the Clinton Global Initiative. http://www.whitehouse.gov/the-press-office/2014/09/23/remarks-president-clinton-global-initiative).

36. "The United States said yesterday (20 October) six Hungarians had been banned from entering the US, as a warning to Budapest to reverse policies that threatened to undermine democratic values."

(Washington introduces Russia-style sanctions against Hungarian officials. 21 October, 2014. http://www.euractiv.com/sections/global-europe/washington-introduces-russia-type-sanctions-against-hungarian-officials).

37. "I grew up at the time when the Soviet Union was still here and I don't have pleasant memories of the activities of the Russians in Hungary. I can't really see any difference between the behavior of the former Soviets and the political behavior of today's Russians. . . . I did not join Orbán to build another dictatorship to replace the old one. I'm no partner in such an enterprise." Lajos Simicska, former ally and favorite oligarch of Viktor Orbán, February 6, 2015, various media outlets, for example: http://hungarianspectrum.org/2015/02/06/a-different-kind-of-media-war-lajos-simicska-versus-viktor-orban/).

38. According to the data collected by TARKI Social Research Institute, Hungary.

39. At the same time, it is important to note that being able to call down the maximum amount of monetary transfers does not say much about the impact the money may make as it very much depends on the efficiency and the objectives of use.

17

The Czech Republic: Finding Its Way

Eleanor E. Zeff, Ellen B. Pirro, and Kieran Williams

WHEN THE CZECH REPUBLIC JOINED THE EUROPEAN UNION (EU) ON May 1, 2004, it did so with as much official fanfare as the other acceding states despite its reputation as a Euro-skeptic country. In the referendum on EU membership in June 2003, 77 percent of voters were in favor of joining. Public figures of great authority, such as former president Václav Havel, had long argued the benefits of accession, not least as a symbolic return to the Western fold, although the more persuasive arguments seem to have been economic (that membership would attract investment and create jobs).[1] Once inside the Union, however, the Czech Republic's ambivalence, latent in the low turnout (55 percent) of the 2003 referendum, asserted itself to the point of obstructionism, with the fate of the Treaty of Lisbon hanging on the will of Havel's Europhobic successor, President Václav Klaus, and a decision of the Czech Constitutional Court. The country's economic performance lurched from boom to bust, and scandal-fueled volatility in the party system led to a series of shaky coalitions, one of which fell while chairing the EU Council in 2009. The first ten years of Czech Republic membership in the EU is thus a mixed picture, and the country is still trying to work out its vision of the Union and its place in it.

Relations Between the Czech Republic and the European Union
Political Background of Czech–EU Relations
Two problems plagued Czech politics in the decade after accession. The first, as in the interwar republic, was the inability of governments to make it through an electoral cycle. From 2004 to 2014, there were nine governments under eight prime ministers. A second problem was episodic conflict between prime

minister and president, owing to the uncertain boundaries of the latter's power and propensity to intervene in policies or appointments of special interest.

The party problem. With at least four parties always able to qualify for seats in the more important lower house of the legislature, and none able to govern alone, each election raised new concerns about political stability and efficacy (see Table 17.1). Although this situation was hardly unique to the Czech Republic, government formation was complicated in two ways. The first was the enduring presence of the Communist Party of Bohemia and Moravia (KSČM), a relatively unreformed (and EU-ambivalent) successor to the party that ruled Czechoslovakia from 1948 until 1989. It was able to attract from 10 to 18 percent of the vote and occupy 22–41 of the 200 seats in the lower house.[2] Regarding the KSČM as "un-coalitionable," the other parties had to find a path to a working majority among the remaining seats, which could be arithmetically very challenging. After the June 2006 election resulted in an evenly divided parliament, a fragile coalition could not be cobbled together until the following January. Over the next two years it survived four votes of no confidence, but was felled by a fifth in March 2009 and replaced with a one-year caretaker Cabinet under the director of the state statistical office.[3] The 2010 elections produced a reconfigured center-right coalition that collapsed after revelation of massive corruption in the prime minister's office, and early elections were held for the second time since 1989.

The second complicating factor has been the irruption of anticorruption protest parties since the 2010 election, splitting or displacing the centrist minor parties that had previously helped the two pillars of the postcommunist system, the leftist Social Democrats (ČSSD) and liberal-conservative Civic Democrats (ODS), get to a majority.[4] ODS, badly damaged by scandal, by the 2013 elections was relegated to fifth place in a seven-party parliament. Surging to second place on 18.6 percent was ANO (Yes), led by Andrej Babiš, a billionaire agroindustrialist, while the populist movement Dawn of Direct Democracy, founded by another entrepreneur, Tomio Okamura, broke through with almost 7 percent. That the performance of these new entities did not map easily onto the left–right economic axis that had underpinned Czech party competition in the past was taken as a reaction "to the crisis of established parties and a general dissatisfaction of the voters with the performance of the incumbent political elite."[5]

The fall of the corrupt ODS-led government in 2013 was further confirmation of the "privatization of the Czech party system with the brokerage of state–corporate interests dominating all the main political parties,"[6] while the short duration of Cabinets impeded a sustained policymaking cycle. One saving grace is that because the upper chamber, the Senate, follows the US practice of staggered elections for six-year terms, it is never dissolved like the lower chamber and has been able to develop a better

Table 17.1 Prime Ministers, Governments, and Coalition Parties in the Czech Republic, 2002–2014

Prime Minister	Parties Involved	Dates
Vladimir Špidla	Czech Social Democratic Party (ČSSD), Christian Democrats (KDU-ČSL), and Freedom Union–Democratic Union (US-DEU)	July 2002–Aug. 2004
Stanislav Gross	SSD, KDU-ČSL, and US-DEU	Aug. 2004–April 2005
Jiří Paroubek	SSD, KDU-ČSL, and US-DEU	April 2005–Sept. 2006
Mirek Topolánek	Civic Democratic Party (ODS)	Sept. 2006–Jan. 2007
Mirek Topolánek	ODS, KDU-ČSL, and Green Party (SZ)	Jan. 2007–May 2009
Jan Fischer	Nonpartisan caretaker Cabinet supported by ODS, ČSSD, and SZ	May 2009–July 2010
Petr Nečas	ODS, Tradition-Responsibility-Prosperity (TOP 09), and Public Affairs (VV) (VV later split and a faction, LIDEM, stayed in the coalition)	July 2010–July 2013
Jiří Rusnok	Caretaker Cabinet supported by ČSSD and KDU-ČSL	July 2013–Jan. 2014
Bohuslav Sobotka	ČSSD, ANO (Yes), and KDU-ČSL	Jan. 2014

rhythm of work; as a result, its committees for EU affairs were judged to be the only ones of any in the new Central European member states able "to achieve some degree of importance in the process of formulating national positions on European legislative proposals."[7]

Rogue bulls. From the first provisional Czechoslovak constitution in 1918, the delineation of presidential power has been contested and unsettled. The first two men to hold the office in the interwar republic, Tomáš G. Masaryk and Edvard Beneš, tried to combine personal authority, patronage, and interpretation of the constitutional text to maximize their power.[8] The postwar decades, during which real power was vested in the first secretary of the Communist Party, resulted in a reduction of the presidency to little more than a ceremonial figurehead. The current office, as established in the 1993 constitution, reflects the wishes of its first postcommunist occupant, Havel: it ensures the president a potentially meaningful role in government formation and in the appointments of other significant actors such as members of the central bank's governing board and—subject to Senate consent—justices of the constitutional court. His signature is also needed for the ratification of treaties, and he can send legislation back to the parliament or refer it to the constitutional court.[9]

One informal limitation on the president's authority was his election not by the people directly but by an electoral college of the two legislative chambers. Havel's successor, Klaus, struggled to win the necessary majorities when he stood for election in 2003 and 2008, and in 2013 the Czech Republic, like Slovakia, shifted to popular election. Opinion polls found that the public welcomed the constitutional change and wanted to see it also result in an overall shift from parliamentary to semi-presidential political system.[10] The direct mandate and sense of public expectation emboldened the winner, Miloš Zeman, to try a more assertive approach in constitutional areas that had always been gray, such as whether he had to automatically appoint someone nominated to a ministerial post by the governing parties or could refuse in the same way he could return a bill to the legislature.[11]

More destabilizing than any hair-splitting over constitutional details, however, was the way Klaus and Zeman reconceived the presidency as a bully pulpit. Havel had modeled it on the (West) German presidency as exemplified in the early 1990s by Richard von Weizsäcker, as a place from which to exhort the nation to searing self-examination, unflinching confrontation with history, and moral/spiritual renewal. Klaus and Zeman turned Havel's bold candor into a relentless drive to shock, insult, and offend. Klaus took on the guise of the nasty professor, especially to crusade against the worldwide scientific consensus that climate change is man-made, and he frequently clashed with premiers and ministers of left and right over the EU, Russia, and greenhouse emissions.[12] Zeman's manner was of a tipsy uncle who could suddenly slip into profanity during a weekly radio address.[13] Whereas Havel saw it as his duty to invite the Dalai Lama for a state visit regardless of diplomatic fallout, Zeman hoped to roll out the red carpet for Uzbek dictator Islam Karimov and Russian president Vladimir Putin in 2015. Even before Zeman visited China in October 2014 and disavowed Tibetan and Taiwanese independence while refusing to lecture his hosts on human rights, one commentator was lamenting the loss of the "Havel brand."[14]

Economic Background of Czech–EU Relations

Historically one of the most advanced industrialized economies of Central Europe, the Czech Republic is highly exposed and dependent on trade. If we measure the ratio of trade to gross domestic product (GDP), the Czech Republic had one of the highest in the first years after accession, surpassed only by other small- and medium-sized member states such as Ireland, Belgium, Estonia, and Slovakia. Slovakia was also the only country more dependent than the Czech Republic on other EU member states to buy its exports, with only 20 percent going to countries beyond the Union.[15] Germany is the Czech Republic's major partner and accounts for about one-third of all Czech exports.[16]

A very large share of exports came from the machinery and automotive industry, thanks to the presence of three major carmakers: Škoda Auto Mladá Boleslav, part of the Volkswagen Group, which in 2007 accounted for 7.5 percent of all Czech exports;[17] TPCA Kolín, a joint venture of Toyota and Peugeot Citroën; and Hyundai Nošovice. Škoda Plzeň remains a globally competitive producer of trams and trains; in 2014, for example, it won the contract to modernize the trolleybus fleet of the US city of Boston. The energy giants (ČEZ, Unipetrol, and RWE) and petrochemical industries were major contributors to GDP but raised environmental concerns, given that the Czech economy had the fourth greatest "energy intensity" (the amount of energy needed to produce one unit of GDP) in the EU.[18]

All of these strengths were long standing and traditional, and the EU counseled the Czechs not to rest on their laurels. The Union as a general policy urges its members to foster domestic innovation drivers, primarily through robust research and development networks, and in this regard the Czech Republic was graded as performing below its potential. The lion's share of research and development funding came from foreign-owned companies or the EU itself via the Czech government's Technology Agency.[19]

Of possible economic consequence is the fact that the Czech Republic was not a member of the Eurozone to which so many of its exports went. This was not inevitable; at the time of accession, the official Czech position was that it would aim to meet the Maastricht convergence criteria by 2010, and polling from the early 2000s found that Czechs favoring the euro were in a majority somewhat smaller than in Slovenia and Slovakia but greater than in Latvia and Estonia, all countries that eventually gave up their national currencies.[20] In contrast to support for EU membership, however, attitudes to the euro turned out to be soft, easily moved by events and sustained elite hostility, especially as articulated by Klaus.[21] Support plunged from around 70 percent in 2002 to 20 percent a decade later.[22] With the return of the Civic Democrats to power in 2006, the Czech government abandoned its timetable of joining the Exchange Rate Mechanism the following year, setting no new date to aim for. President Klaus steadily used his power of appointment to pack the central bank's governing body with economists from his think tank, who could be trusted not to rush the country out of the koruna.[23]

Although keeping the koruna raised transaction costs for the republic's major exporters, it had the benefit of reducing demand for cross-border loans, which in other new member states contributed to the devastating credit crisis after 2008.[24] Nevertheless, new accession states enjoy no opt-out from the obligation to prepare for adoption of the euro, so the Social Democrat–led government in 2014 announced 2020 as the new target date. As part of the preparations, it would seek parliamentary approval to accede to the Treaty on Stability, Coordination and Governance in the Economic and Monetary Union (the "Fiscal Compact" or the "Fiscal Treaty" owing to its strong emphasis on balanced budgets) developed in 2012 for Eurozone countries, from which the Czech Republic, Croatia, and UK had abstained. At the time of this writing, the Czech Senate had approved the treaty but the lower house had not, and the government would need at least nine votes from opposition parties to reach the mandatory three-fifths majority.

How and in What Ways Has
the Czech Republic Influenced the EU?
The EU Presidency

The Czech Republic assumed the EU's rotating presidency in January 2009. Enormous resources—time, personnel, and half a billion Czech korunas—were invested in showing that a second postcommunist country (after Slovenia) had the administrative capacity to convene 200 gatherings, including seven summits; manage sessions of the Council of Ministers in all permutations (and in emergencies, such as to address the flu pandemic); and represent the Union internationally.[25] The presidency was also an opportunity for the Czech Republic to push a policy agenda: further liberalization of movement of services and deregulation of business, elimination of remaining restrictions on movement of workers from new member states, energy security, the European Neighborhood Policy toward former Soviet countries, and EU-US relations.[26] These middle- to long-term policy goals, however, quickly had to yield to the pressing events of the day: the global financial crisis, disruption of Russian natural gas supplies to fifteen member states owing to a payment dispute with Ukraine, and fighting between Israel and Hamas in Gaza in the first half of January.

Some of the original agenda could be salvaged—the gas crisis, for example, had been months in the making and could be enlisted to underscore the need for the EU to commit to lessening its dependence on Russia and launching an Eastern Partnership (officially, at a Prague summit on May 7). On the economic regulatory side, the Czech presidency crafted a compromise between Germany and France to reduce value-added tax rates in labor-intensive service sectors (such as restaurants) and persuaded Belgium and Denmark to lift their restrictions on workers from new accession countries. But they failed to convince the more important Germany and Austria to open their labor markets before 2011 and were unable to broker a deal between the Council and Parliament on the working time directive's maximum weekly hours (forty-eight versus sixty to sixty-five).[27] In keeping with their center-right government's ideology, the Czechs discouraged state bailouts, quashing Hungary's suggestion of a €300 billion fund to prop up banks in new member states.[28] While the Czechs led the March 2009 Council to reject new forms of national protectionism and the June Council to beef up the European Central Bank's oversight powers, it was not able to win changes in the deep structure of financial regulation.[29]

The Gaza conflict consumed the Czech diplomatic service's energy, diverting it from its intended transatlantic focus (an "informal" summit was held with US president Barack Obama on April 5 and an EU-Canada summit a month later). The Middle East involvement bore no commensurate results; as one appraisal put it, the Czech presidency "acted as an agenda manager (promoting a closer EU-Israeli relationship) when there actually was a demand for an intra-EU mediator (forging a common position on who will speak for the EU and what message to convey and in what tone) and a collective representative acting as an impartial mediator in the Gaza conflict."[30] Simultaneously, the Czech deputy prime minister responsible for the presidency was having to spend an inordinate amount of time defending a painfully unfunny art installation in the EU's Justus Lipsius building, sponsored by his government, which depicted the member states in unflattering stereotypes.[31] Particular offense was taken by Bulgaria, which was depicted as a Balkan squat toilet; Czech President Klaus personally wrote to his Bulgarian counterpart to apologize.

A far more serious setback came on March 24, when the ODS-led government lost a vote of no confidence. Although it would have been customary for a truce to be called in domestic politics when a country held the EU presidency (as in Slovenia in 2008), the opposition Social Democrats persisted in peeling away defectors from the governing parties. Taken aback by the criticism that followed, the Social Democrats signaled a willingness to allow Prime Minister Mirek Topolánek to finish out the EU presidency, an idea vetoed by Klaus. (Klaus had cofounded Topolánek's ODS in 1991 but on moving to the presidency had distanced himself from it, publicly criticizing Topolánek as insufficiently neoliberal and Euro-skeptic.[32]) When no alternative majority could be assembled in the deadlocked legislature, the major parties and the Greens agreed on a caretaker Cabinet of experts on May 8. Responsibility for the EU presidency was assumed by a new deputy prime minister, Štefan Füle, a former ambassador to NATO (and a future EU commissioner), whereas the new foreign minister, Jan Kohout, had been a Czech ambassador to the EU.[33] This solution minimized disruption. On handing the presidency over to the Swedes on July 1, the Czechs felt that even with mixed results on the policy side, they had acquitted themselves well, especially given the preceding "hyperactive" French presidency and Nicolas Sarkozy's reluctance to relinquish control of EU business.[34]

The Lisbon Treaty

In the background of the Czech EU presidency was the fate of the Lisbon Treaty, which had been called into question by Ireland's "no" vote in 2008. The French presidency had already negotiated arrangements to placate Irish concerns, so the Czechs were spared the burden of implementing the treaty and rescuing it. The Czech legislature was only just getting to its own vote on the treaty, with the lower house approving it on February 18, 2009, and the Senate doing so on May 6. At that point it went up the hill to Prague Castle for signing by President Klaus, who refused to act until the constitutional court, like its counterpart in several other member states, had decided that the treaty did not conflict with national legal norms.[35] Klaus, in keeping with his long-established persona as a neoliberal Thatcherite, had never openly opposed membership of the EU but preferred a bygone pre-Maastricht community of strict intergovernmentalism and national vetoes.[36] When he was still prime minister in 1996, his government had been the second to last of the associate states to submit a formal application for membership; in 2003, newly installed as president, he was the only head of an applicant state not to campaign actively for a "yes" vote in the referendum on membership.[37] Although he avoided any reckless behavior during the Czech EU presidency, he coldly downplayed its significance and in February 2009 told the European Parliament that the EU's deeper integration would be an irrational "revolutionary experiment" that would impose central direction at the expense of market forces and endanger the positive achievements of postwar European reconstruction. It was just the latest iteration of Klaus's hallmark insinuation that EU *dirigisme* was akin to the failed Soviet command economy,[38] but members of the European Parliament, unaccustomed to hearing such talk in their chamber, replied with booing or walking out.[39]

Keen to delay signing the treaty as long as possible in the hope that an election might be called in the UK that would lead to a negative British referendum, Klaus encouraged senators to petition the constitutional court on September 29, 2009. A challenge had already been filed in 2008 regarding specific elements in the treaty, which the court had unanimously found to be compatible with the country's constitution.[40] The new challenge was to the treaty in its entirety, asking in particular that the court strike down any transfer of competences infringing the "untouchable" essence of sovereignty, such as "decision-making on the income and expenditure of the Czech budget, . . . the definition of criminal offences, sanctions and the conditions of the criminal responsibility, guaranteeing the public order in the Czech Republic and decision-making with exceptional/extraordinary impact on the cultural and social life of the Czech Republic."[41] The justices were no more willing than before to pin down the elusive "substantive core" of the constitution and declined to determine which competences the republic could not surrender or share with an international organization.[42]

By this point, Polish president Lech Kaczyński (himself a critic of Europeanization) and Ireland had dropped their resistance; with no UK referendum imminent, Klaus finally signed the treaty on November 3, 2009. To save face, he had insisted that the European Council meeting at the end of October acknowledge that nothing in the EU Charter of Fundamental Rights (which the treaty would make solemnly binding) could be cited against the decrees issued at the end of World War II to expel Czechoslovakia's Sudeten Germans, lest their descendants try to reclaim confiscated property.[43]

Euro-Skepticism in the Czech Republic

As a prominent figure in Czech politics from 1990 to 2013, Klaus had a tremendous impact on the formation of public opinion and tapped into a strand of that opinion that was anxious about the loss of sovereignty and national identity so soon after the end of Soviet hegemony. He did not single-handedly inject Euro-skepticism into the discourse,[44] even if he was one of its most forceful and articulate proponents, especially after his party fell from power in 1997 and used a long spell in opposition to sharpen its image as defender of the national interest.[45] But only a small segment of the elite and the wider population could be described as Euro-skeptic to the point of Europhobic; in the six years before accession, polls consistently found between 70 and 80 percent reporting that they would vote in favor of joining the EU.[46] Later, even as Klaus himself drifted to advocating withdrawal from the EU and shifted his allegiance from ODS to the anti-EU party Heads Up!,[47] few followed him, as indicated by the abject failure in national and European Parliament elections of parties like Heads Up! It is telling that when ODS left the main conservative bloc in the European Parliament in 2009 it joined the British Conservatives in the new European Conservatives and Reformists faction, not the more radically antifederalist Europe of Freedom and Democracy group.[48]

In the Council of Ministers, the Czech Republic was not a disruptive presence; early statistical analysis turned up very few instances of "no" votes by Czech ministers—only four from 2004 to 2006, well below the average for all member states (9.8), pre-2004 member states (11.2) and new member states (7.7).[49] Roll-call analysis of Council voting also placed the Czechs in the middle of a distribution of countries, grouped neither with Sweden, Denmark, the Netherlands, and Finland at one end nor Portugal, Poland, Spain, Italy, and France at the other.[50] When the relaxation of unanimity voting was being debated, the Czechs were more (not less) willing than older member states such as France to extend qualified majority voting to sensitive areas.[51]

The more popular self-description among Czechs would be "Euro-realist," and it would not be confined to the right side of the spectrum—many on the left would be just as wary of too great a loss of national control.[52] Even when Social Democrats replaced Civic Democrats in power, there was relatively little change in priorities with regard to the EU agenda other than "perhaps a slight rebalancing towards a vaguely defined social dimension."[53] Czechs were not exceptionally harsher in their opinion of the EU's workings than were the inhabitants of other member states. A 2009 survey found that more Czechs were satisfied with "the way democracy work[ed]" in the EU (57 percent) than it did at the national level (48 percent); when compared with satisfaction levels across the member states (then only twenty-seven), the Czechs were close to the average with regard to democracy in the EU (56 percent satisfied) and more critical of their domestic politics (on average 53 percent satisfied).[54] Even as a 2014 Eurobarometer found 61 percent of Czechs tending "not to trust" the EU, and only 12 percent believing that the EU would be able to take effective action to solve economic problems, it also found 82 percent agreeing that the EU member states should work together more to tackle the economic and financial crisis.[55] In any event, many studies found that EU issues received very little space in party electoral manifestos or press coverage of campaigns and were rarely in the forefront of voters' minds as they cast their ballots.[56]

How and in What Ways Does the EU Affect and Interact with the Czech Republic?

Compliance with the EU *acquis* is not merely a matter of transposing it into domestic law in a timely fashion; it is also about meaningful implementation, enforcement by dedicated agencies, and provision of trustworthy venues for citizen complaint, such as courts and tribunals. Four broad cultures of compliance have been identified, with the best cases in the "World of Law Observance" family (Denmark, Finland, and Sweden). Next comes the "World of Domestic Politics" countries in which implementation and enforcement are on par with the World of Law Observance, but there is more controversy about which parts of the *acquis* to transpose, depending on "the fit with the political preferences of governing parties and other powerful players"; this cluster contains Austria, Belgium, Germany, the Netherlands, Spain, and the UK.[57] Several of the oldest member states (France, Luxembourg, Greece, Portugal) fall into a dismal "World of Transposition Neglect," in which the political process and sluggish bureaucracies fail to keep pace with the *acquis* even while paying lip service to it. Then there is the "World of Dead Letters," covering the Czech Republic and other new member states but also Ireland and Italy: formal transposition might take place promptly, but then the implementation and enforcement suffer from insufficient institutionalization, such as labor inspectorates and equal treatment authorities, or from a lack of public confidence in the judicial system (especially in the Czech Republic).[58]

The mixed record emerges from the EU's surveillance mechanisms, which have become ever more elaborate since the onset of the financial crisis in 2008. Within the general recommendations made to the entire Union, Commission staff tailors subsets of advice to individual states, primarily in areas relating to budgeting, growth, competitiveness, and the quality of public administration. In the case of the Czech Republic, many of the shortcomings are perennial ones already being flagged in preaccession progress reports, and not products of the more recent crisis. For example, while the central government has moved to a multiannual budgeting process, it has not always respected spending ceilings, nor has it integrated the budgeting of regional and local governments or developed "strict rules" regarding their debt.[59] As of 2014, reform of the pension and health systems and higher education still lagged, and an act on the civil service was woefully overdue. The EU's recommended shifts in tax burden (away from labor and onto housing and "green" taxes) had not been acted on, as the forging of a coalition in 2013 between the Social Democrats and ANO required both sides to set aside their very different preferences for tax policy. While the general rate of unemployment remained low, it was high for certain groups, especially mothers of young children, owing to the lack of affordable pre-school facilities. The EU average percentage of children under the age of three in formal day care was 30 percent, in the Czech Republic it was only 5 percent. This contributed to the Czech Republic having the fourth largest gender gap in employment and pay.[60]

A related perennial concern was the Roma minority. Of the 300,000 Roma believed to live in the Czech Republic, the Commission estimated that 80,000–100,000 were socially excluded.[61] Czech authorities had always been willing to draw up national integration plans that looked admirable on paper, and the Czech EU presidency was the first to organize a discussion of the Roma in the Employment, Social Policy, Health and Consumer Affairs Council; the EU Platform for Roma Inclusion was launched in April 2009 by a former Czech prime minister, Vladimír Špidla, in his capacity as Commissioner for Employment, Social Affairs and Equal Opportunities.[62] The will to put the fine talk into practice, however, was less robust, even after the European Court of Human Rights issued its landmark 2007 judgment condemning segregated schooling.[63]

However, compliance should not be viewed only through the Commission's critical report cards; the Czech government's ambitious National Reform Program and its 2014–2020 Strategy on Social Inclusion, both adopted in January 2014, will go a long way to addressing these shortcomings if—and it is a big if—they are implemented. Also, case studies of specific policy areas can provide a rounded perspective of everyday practice in all its subtlety. An important example is environmental policy. Given the Czech Republic's inheritance of a horrifically polluted landscape from the socialist period, environmental recovery was a self-evident but low priority in the 1990s, when the emphasis fell on the transition to market forces. Preaccession transposition of the environment *acquis* in 1999–2002 forced the Czechs toward more stringent and potentially costly rules. The enormity and speed of those legal changes, combined with uncertainty about the capacity of the state to enforce them, would be grounds to fear that they would become yet another batch of dead letters. That they did not is clear from case studies of the impact of three EU directives (the Environmental Impact Assessment Directive and the Directives on the Conservation of Wild Birds and the Conservation of Natural Habitats, Wild Fauna and Flora). That they had real teeth was thanks largely to vigilant Czech nongovernmental organizations, which alerted the Commission to infringements or lack of timely implementation; most Commission warnings to the Czech authorities were then settled without having to be referred to the European Court of Justice.[64]

How Has the Czech Republic Weathered the 2008 Economic Crisis and Interacted with the EU Institutions?

Like most of the states that joined in 2004, the Czech Republic experienced a postaccession economic surge thanks to full access to the Single Market, the basket of liberalizing reforms required for EU membership, and capital inflows,[65] making the country overall a sizable net recipient from the EU budget. Even the small Czech agricultural sector (about 3 percent of GDP) experienced an overnight boost courtesy of the Common Agricultural Policy, making a chronically loss-making sector profitable, apart from the restrictive impact of the EU sugar quota on Czech sugar beets.[66] The impact of accession would have been even greater had the Czech state had the programs and capacity to request and absorb more funds from Brussels.[67]

The global crisis in 2008 put an end to the already decelerating growth of the Czech economy, which contracted by 4 percent in 2009. As in much of the EU, recovery was slow and sluggish, with another dip into recession in 2012–2013; overall, in the twenty-three quarters from the third of 2008 to the first of 2014, Czech average GDP growth was negative (–0.1 percent), whereas neighbors stayed in positive figures (Germany 0.7 percent, Slovakia 1.3 percent, Poland 2.9 percent).[68] The outlook from 2014 was for annual growth to return to the 2.5 percent range for coming years.[69] As rebounds in Central Europe go, this is one of the least impressive: as of summer 2014, Czech GDP had yet to reattain its 2008 level, whereas neighbors had surpassed theirs, in the case of Poland by more than 15 percent. Only Hungary had fared worse.[70]

On the brighter side, Czech unemployment remained at rates lower than the average for the EU and was projected to fall to 6.1 percent by 2015.[71] Czech society continued to have one of the lowest levels of income inequality in the Union, and the percentage of the population in or near the poverty line (understood as below 60 percent of the median wage) rose only slightly, from a pre-crisis 5.6 percent to 7 percent in 2011.[72] Per capita GDP (PPS) for the Czech Republic stayed above 80 percent of the EU average throughout the lean years, second only to Slovenia among postcommunist countries. Private debt as a percentage of GDP (around 80 percent) was lower in the Czech Republic than almost any other Central European member state.[73] Having already been through a banking crisis in the mid-1990s, Czech financial institutions were in good order and adequately capitalized when the 2008 crisis hit (although the EU criticized the lack of access to equity financing for small- and medium-sized enterprises). These trends helped the country get through the recessions without major unrest, terrorism, or a rise in support for extremist parties.

In its response to the crisis, the Czech government, like all member states, had to move in concert with the EU's Europe 2020 strategy (launched in 2010 to spur growth and job creation) while coming under an Excessive

Table 17.2 Czech Economic Indicators, Various years

	2004	2009	2012	2013
GDP growth (%)	4.4	−4.1	−1.3	−0.9
Exports (million of euros)	1,722.7	2,138.6	3,128.2	3,188.3
Unemployment rate (%)	10.2	9.24	9.36	8.17
Inflation rate (%)	2.8	1.0	3.3	1.4

Source: Czech Statistical Office.

Deficit Procedure in 2009 when the shortfall in government revenue approached 6.6 percent of GDP. Since the center-right parties that took power in 2010 were fiscally hawkish, EU expectations tallied with domestic elite intentions and the deficit was reduced to 1.5 percent of GDP by 2013. Satisfied that the gap would remain below the 3 percent threshold in the near future, the EU took the Czech Republic, along with Slovakia, off its watch list.[74]

The Czech Republic, Russia, and Ukraine

Owing to its history of invasion and occupation by great powers, including the Soviet Union in 1968, the Czech Republic is commonly expected to be uniformly critical of any threat to smaller nations' sovereignty and integrity and wary of Russia generally. Foreigners tend to be surprised if a Czech official voices a more forgiving line on the Kremlin, and in the Czech Republic itself, speculation can arise that such a person might be a paid agent or spending too much time at the Russian embassy. Such was the response in some corners to President Klaus's remarks on the 2008 Russo-Georgian conflict that seemed to put the blame largely on Georgia, and his tolerance of Putin's authoritarianism. Klaus was nothing if not consistent in his post-presidential reaction to developments in Ukraine in 2014, being careful to place the blame not on Ukraine or on Russia but on the West for allegedly forcing Ukraine into choosing between Brussels and Moscow and thus needlessly provoking a confrontation.[75]

Klaus's stance can be explained easily as another of the many ways in which he was distinguishing his presidency from that of his predecessor, Havel, whose advocacy of human rights Klaus derided as naive, counterproductive "do-goodery." Like US social conservatives, Klaus embraced Putin as "one of us" in the culture wars. Also against Havel, Klaus defined himself as a defender of the right of nation-states to resist the pressure of international organizations and their norms, especially to resist a vague humanitarian justification for warfare without express UN authorization. While speaker of the lower house in 1999, Klaus (like many Czech officials) had refused to support NATO's operation against Serbia in Kosovo, and (like officials in several EU countries) he had not welcomed Kosovo's declaration of independence in 2008. To him, Russia's actions in Georgia and Crimea were the West's comeuppance for trashing the traditional comity of nations.[76]

Klaus was not alone. Many Czech officials, on the left and right, have expressed a pragmatic approach to Russia, for the simple reason that before summer 2014 it received 3–4 percent of the Czech Republic's exports (making it the seventh largest buyer of Czech goods and the largest outside the EU). In turn, Russia was the sole supplier of natural gas, and in 2013, the 760,000 Russian visitors to the Czech Republic represented 10 percent of tourist traffic, second only to Germans.[77] Trips by Czech presidents to Russia (and Central Asia) were largely commercial in intention, and Klaus was on close terms with entrepreneur Petr Kellner, whose investments in Russian precious metals, insurance, and banking helped make him the richest man in the Czech Republic. When the EU was formulating its sanctions on Russia in summer 2014 in response to the fighting in eastern Ukraine, the Czech government lobbied successfully for exemption of trade in strictly civilian goods, in the hope of minimizing blowback into the machinery, motors, and electronics sectors that dominated Czech exports. It was inevitable, however, that sales of Czech cars would be hurt by the sharp devaluation of the ruble that accompanied the conflict.[78]

Although differences could be teased out in the opinions of President Zeman, Prime Minister Bohuslav Sobotka, and Foreign Minister Lubomír Zaorálek regarding the proper response to events in Ukraine, they moved within fairly narrow parameters. The Czech Republic, after all, had business interests in Ukraine also, which would only grow if Ukraine were put on the path to EU membership. The Czech Republic was already the fifth largest EU exporter to Ukraine in 2013, and in relative terms its €1 billion in exports compared favorably with Germany's €5 billion. Whereas it ran trade deficits with Russia, with Ukraine it was surpluses, and the elimination of import tariffs through an EU association agreement signed in June 2014 would save Czech firms an estimated €20 million.[79] The lure of greater opportunity, combined with outrage at the downing of a Malaysian airliner over separatist-held eastern Ukraine in July 2014, was enough to keep Czech policy in step with that of the EU.

A Belated National Conversation

The Czech "choice for Europe" has been said to be driven not so much by ideology, public opinion, or domestic interest groups as by a broadly held feeling of vulnerability rooted in a sometimes traumatic history and exposure to globalization.[80] Even Klaus while in public office never advocated any alternative to EU membership, the rank-and-file and regional barons of his ODS were less Euro-skeptic than its leaders, and the relatively brief experience of holding the EU presidency in 2009 had profound Europeanizing effects on the Czech civil service.[81]

Even if the Czech Republic is more wedded to the EU than it might like to admit, it has yet to figure out what it wants the EU to become and what the Czech place in it will be. In recognition of this, in 2014, the government set up a national convention to coordinate input from state agencies, think tanks, trade associations, unions, and parliamentary committees to arrive at a Czech vision of its place in the EU. Even if it achieves no consensus on major paradigmatic questions—the EU as federation or confederation or still looser free-trade area—it should serve at least as a belated opportunity for systematic consideration of the options and their ramifications.

Notes

1. Hanley (2004), Lyons (2007).
2. Lach et al. (2010).
3. Haughton, Novotná, and Deegan-Krause (2011), p. 395. On nonpartisan Cabinets, see Hloušek and Kopeček (2014).
4. Hanley (2011).
5. Hloušek and Kaniok (2014), p. 12.
6. Innes (2014), p. 100.
7. Knutelská (2011), p. 336.
8. Orzoff (2009).
9. On Havel's use of that power, see Havlík, Hrubeš, and Pecina (2014).
10. Kudrna, "Jen krok od poloprezidentského systému," *Hospodářské Noviny*, September 24, 2013. Available at http://jankudrna.blog.ihned.cz/c1-60861980-jen-krok-od-poloprezidentskeho-systemu.
11. "Pawel Uhl: Musí nebo nemusí?," *Jiné Právo*, December 14, 2013. Available at http://jinepravo.blogspot.com/2013/12/pawel-uhl-musi-nebo-nemusi.html.
12. Jiří Pehe, "Existuje česká zahraniční politika?," September 30, 2014. Available at http://www.aktualne.cz.
13. Jan Wirnitzer, "Zeman v centru pozornosti. Přehled výroků, jimiž rozbouřil společnost," *Mladá fronta Dnes*, November 23, 2014.
14. Martin Fendrych, "Značka Havel končí. Zahraniční politika se zemanizuje," *aktuálně.cz*, May 14, 2014. Available at http://nazory.aktualne.cz/komentare/znacka-havel-konci-zahranicni-politika-se-zemanizuje/r~fd7e2a8ada8211e38cb6002590604f2e/.
15. Haughton (2009), pp. 1380–1381.
16. Czech Republic, Ministry of Business (2014).
17. Haughton (2009), p. 1378.
18. European Commission (2014d), p. 26.
19. Ibid., pp. 23–24.
20. Allam and Goerres (2011), p. 1413.
21. Kaniok and Hlousek (2014). See also Pechova (2012).
22. Roberts (2014), p. 933.
23. Kopeček (2012), p. 244; Šlosarčík (2011), p. 26.
24. Jacoby (2014), pp. 58–59.

25. Matějková (2012), p. 216.
26. Šlosarčík (2009a), p. 8.
27. Beneš and Karlas (2010), pp. 72–73.
28. Copeland (2014), p. 481.
29. Beneš and Karlas (2010), pp. 74–75.
30. Ibid., p. 78.
31. Matějková (2012), pp. 219–221.
32. Kopeček (2012), pp. 224–227.
33. Šlosarčík (2009a), p. 7.
34. Matějková (2012), p. 218.
35. On the many cases spawned by the treaty, see Wendel (2011).
36. Kopeček (2012), p. 228.
37. Hanley (2008b), p. 193, 202–203.
38. Ibid., pp. 191–193.
39. Kopeček (2012), p. 230.
40. Bříza (2009).
41. Šlosarčík (2009b), p. 3.
42. Komárek (2009).
43. Kopeček (2012), p. 237, Puchalska (2014).
44. Rakušanová (2007).
45. Hanley (2008b), pp. 195–196.
46. Roberts (2014), p. 932.
47. Jiří Kubík and Robert Čásenský, "Za vším špatným u nás je Unie, vystupme z ní, vyzývá Klaus," *Mladá fronta Dnes*, October 3, 2013.
48. Bale, Hanley, and Szczerbiak (2010).
49. Hosli, Mattila, and Uriot (2011), p. 1256.
50. Mattila (2009), pp. 849–850.
51. Kratochvíl (2004).
52. Hanley (2008a).
53. Haughton (2009), p. 1385.
54. Hobolt (2012), p. 92.
55. European Commission, "Standard Eurobarometer 81: Public Opinion in the EU," spring 2014.
56. Haughton (2014). On the narrowly economic focus of press coverage, see Urbániková and Volek (2014).
57. Falkner (2010), p. 114.
58. Ibid., pp. 103–104, 107–108, 113.
59. European Commission (2014d), p. 11.
60. Ibid., pp. 17–18.
61. Ibid., p. 21.
62. Ram (2012), pp. 1196, 1198.
63. D.H. and Others v. The Czech Republic (Grand Chamber), Application no. 57325/00. The failure to follow up was detailed in Amnesty International (2010).
64. Baun and Marek (2013).
65. Jacoby (2014), pp. 56–60.
66. Tomšík (2010), p. 115.
67. Šlosarčík (2011), pp. 27–28.
68. Martin Slaný, "Česko zaostává za sousedy," *Newsletter Institutu Václava Klause*, July–August 2014, p. 1.
69. "Zpráva o realizaci Národního programu reforem České republiky 2014 a doporučení Rady pro rok," *Vláda*, November 24, 2014, p. 4.

70. Slaný (2014), p. 1.
71. "Zpráva o realizaci" (2014), p. 5.
72. Antošová, Skálová, and Birčiaková (2013).
73. Jacoby (2014), p. 61.
74. Council of the European Union, "Council Closes Excessive Deficit Procedures for Belgium, Czech Republic, Denmark, Netherlands, Austria and Slovakia," press release 11089/14 (June 20, 2014).
75. Václav Klaus, "Ukrajina byla zneužita ke konfrontaci," *Newsletter Institutu Václava Klause*, July–August 2014, p. 3. Klaus suggested that Ukraine had left itself open to misuse owing to its failure to undertake economic and political reform after 1991, and Klaus's adviser Jiří Weigl similarly saw Ukraine as a cautionary example of corrupt, oligarchic rule in a country artificially assembled by the Soviets ("Ukraina mezi Evropou a Ruskem," *Newsletter Institutu Václava Klause*, July–August 2014, p. 4).
76. Kopeček (2012), pp. 118–120, 246–251.
77. Kratochvíl et al. (2014), p. 23.
78. Ibid., p. 17.
79. Sekce pro evropské záležitosti Úřadu vlády České republiky (2014), pp. 1, 5.
80. Haughton (2009), p. 1388.
81. Šlosarčík (2009a), p. 10.

18

Slovenia and Slovakia: A Tale of Two States

Peter Loedel

It was the best of times, it was the worst of times, it was the age of wisdom, it was the age of foolishness, it was the epoch of belief, it was the epoch of incredulity.

—Charles Dickens, *A Tale of Two Cities*

SLOVENIA AND SLOVAKIA SHARE SOME COMMONALITIES THAT make them useful to compare within one chapter. Both transitioned into the European Union (EU) in the large 2004 enlargement that included many post-Soviet Eastern and Central European member states, and both joined the Eurozone relatively soon thereafter (Slovenia in January 2007 and Slovakia in January 2009). Leading up to enlargement, both countries experienced the multiple conditions imposed on them by the accession process. Both had no option but to transpose EU directives into domestic legislation, setting the path for Europeanization.[1] One can also note the strong differences between the countries and the unique and rich histories of each as they have experienced very different paths to economic and political development. Even with Europeanization, and with both countries dutifully transposing EU directives and laws, there has been wide variation of implementation based on respective national approaches and traditions.[2]

Interestingly, Slovakia's membership in the EU appeared initially in doubt, whereas Slovenia had made steady progress all along. Today, through the ongoing adjustment and crisis brought on by the Great Recession and the Eurozone sovereign debt crisis, Slovakia appears to be the stronger member of the EU, relatively stable politically and aligned on economic and monetary matters with Germany. In a surprise role reversal, Slovenia seems to be the more troubled EU member, perhaps another domino to fall off the debt cliff in the ongoing Eurozone crisis. Slovenia's political climate is also quite unstable, now with the fourth government in the past six years and governed by yet another new political party reacting to ongoing corruption and economic problems of the small state. Indeed, it is a tale of two states, good times and bad times, a belief in the euro's power and the incredulity of the Eurozone. What will be the outcome of this particular tale? Will it be further confederation or possible disintegration?

With ten years of membership in the EU complete, both countries are heavily Europeanized—economically, politically, and in terms of identity. On a wide range of fronts, both find their governments, policy structures, and bureaucratic structure show the Europeanization effect to be more pronounced than might be expected.[3] Ministries responsible for transposing many EU directives tended to institutionalize centralized oversight in legislative planning and review. In a large public opinion survey of the member states conducted by the European Commission in November 2013,[4] Slovenia and Slovakia typically fit on the moderately Euro-enthusiastic or supportive end of the spectrum. When asked whether they felt like citizens of the EU, 70 percent of Slovakians and 61 percent of Slovenians answered in the affirmative. Even with the ongoing strains of the Eurozone crisis, over 50 percent of respondents in both countries signaled that they were still optimistic about the future of the EU. There really is no option other than "Europe" for both countries. Slow and steady deepening, with a possible leap toward further confederation, could indeed be a likely outcome.

Despite these optimistic trends in public opinion, 88 percent of Slovakians and 96 percent of Slovenian citizens state that their economic situation is bad, with unemployment, the general economic situation, and rising prices identified as the most important issues facing their countries. Both countries face serious issues, although Slovenia's situation appears more problematic. Over the past ten years, the citizens of each country have seen both the gains brought about by EU membership and pains of integration and loss of significant policy autonomy. Although it is difficult to envision disintegration, it is not too difficult to see further paralysis within the EU and the Eurozone. This paralysis will affect these two countries in ways likely to deepen the bouts of mistrust and pessimism about Europe's future.

What about the euro and membership in the Eurozone specifically? Despite the effects of the Eurozone-induced economic problems, Slovenians and Slovakians do not tend to blame the euro for the ill effects. When asked the question, "Having the euro is a good or bad thing for your country?," 56 percent of Slovakians and 55 percent of Slovenians indicated "a good thing."[5] Roughly a third of the population still thinks it is a bad thing, but the results indicate that the euro itself is not identified as the central problem for the citizens of these countries. Additionally, 69 percent of Slovakians and 67 percent of Slovenians indicate that the euro is a "good thing" for the EU. Whether thinking about the impact of the euro on their own country or on the EU, strong majorities of each country's citizens still view the euro positively.

Furthermore, citizens of each country are supportive and interested in developing greater and wider macroeconomic coordination. Overall, 72 percent of respondents across the Eurozone indicated they would support a higher degree of economic and budget policy coordination. A strong 72 percent of Slovenians and 59 percent of Slovakians indicated support for further Eurozone coordination. Correspondingly, across the Eurozone area, 79 percent of respondents indicated a need for significant reform to improve economic performance, and nearly three-quarters of respondents indicated that economic reforms would be more effective if they were carried out in a coordinated way at the EU level. Sixty-eight percent of Slovenians and 62 percent of Slovakians shared similar views on greater coordination. Reforms required because of Eurozone macroeconomic adjustment were also strongly supported by Slovakians (80 percent indicated "agree" to the question about the need for significant reforms to improve the performance of the economy) and by Slovenians (85 percent). Notably, Slovakians were the most inclined, across all Eurozone member states, to indicate support for specific sector reform (labor, market, education, etc.) that had been demanded as part of the macroeconomic adjustment brought on by the Eurozone crisis.

What does all this suggest? Citizens of both countries recognize the importance and need to continue along the pathway of economic reforms as members of the Eurozone and see the need to develop greater Eurozone macroeconomic coordination at the EU level. Notably, the European Parliament election outcomes in May 2014 in both countries indicated stability and consistency in support for pro-European centrist Christian Democratic and Social Democratic parties. There were no sharp left or right swings in the electorate in May 2014. Despite the hit of the Great Recession and the possible default of Slovenia, there does not seem to be an alternative pathway for either country. Further integration and Europeanization are the only real paths forward.

How each country would respond to the quest for further integration, perhaps to a more confederal model, still remains to be seen. As this chapter develops, both countries have seen the rise of populist and nationalist parties opposed to deeper European integration. But the reality of membership in the EU and the Eurozone suggest a very narrow policy framework within which both countries operate. Politicians frequently announce that they will follow policies focused on the nation's interest, but soon subscribe to Commission or Eurozone mandates to resolve some serious macroeconomic imbalances. This chapter evaluates the progress in two critical policy arenas for clues to the pathway ahead. I first explore the economic and monetary policy effects of the Eurozone crisis as it overshadowed most other policy issues for each crisis. After evaluating the policy responses, I provide a summary account of each country's response to the Eurozone crisis, the EU's effect on each, and the respective paths that each might pursue into the future.

Slovakia and Slovenia: An Economic Snapshot of the Eurozone Crisis

In terms of the economic imperative of joining the EU and signaling their intent to join the Eurozone countries within a reasonable time frame, Slovenia and Slovakia appeared headed in two distinct directions. In 2006, Slovenia appeared to have its fiscal house in order and emerged set to join the Eurozone sooner than Slovakia would. Moreover, Slovenia's growth rates remained solid and steady, and it appeared ready to develop as one of the stronger economies among the 2004 enlargement group. Slovakia, on the other hand, appeared stable but was still beset by larger political instability and economic constraints, including a heavily industrialized and state-subsidized economy that would weigh heavily on any easy inclusion into the Eurozone and stable finances. Yet there was still optimism that the countries would enter the Eurozone, predicting accurately that Slovenia would join in 2007 and Slovakia, speeding "toward the European Monetary Union (EMU)," just two years later.

However, an overview of some of the key larger macroeconomic data illustrate just how the tables have turned on each country. Slovakia, and not Slovenia, appears the model child of adjustment and management, given the Great Recession and the painful shocks to the European economy. Slovenia appears incapable of addressing an ongoing banking crisis and unable to truly restore balance to its accounts. Slovenia would undoubtedly favor a more confederal EU if it meant ongoing access to financial support. Moreover, Slovakia has become a vocal (albeit limited in power) voice for adjustment to be imposed on weaker member states. Although it is difficult to ascertain the exact projection of such reservations on its view of a federal or confederal Europe, Slovakia's sharp "no" vote in March 2011 to the bailout fund program indicated that it did not appear to be favorably inclined to support a larger and more powerful federal union if that meant Greece and others would have access to the European (and Slovakian) purse strings.

Figures 18.1 and 18.2 (Slovenian and Slovakian government deficit as a percentage of gross domestic product [GDP]) and Figures 18.3 and 18.4 (Slovenian and Slovakian debt/GDP ratio) illustrate vividly the hollowing out effect of the Great Recession on each country's finances.

Budget deficits tend to provide a rather stark annual visual of the effect of the Great Recession. In the case of Slovenia, with its nearly perfect budget balance at the onset of the Eurozone crisis in 2008, the effect has been steady and sharp. Slovenia immediately fell onto the watch list (as did most Eurozone members) as budget deficits quickly exceeded the 3 percent

Figure 18.1 Slovenia Government Budget, as percentage of GDP

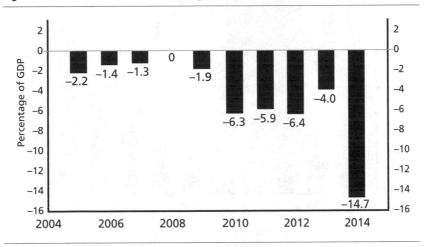

Source: Tradingeconomics.com/eurostat

Figure 18.2 Slovakia Government Budget, as percentage of GDP

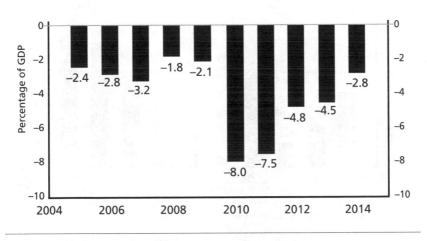

Source: Tradingeconomics.com/eurostat

cutoff. As will be discussed later, Slovenia has been halting in its approach to reform internally, hamstrung by the nature of its surprisingly large state-owned sector (relative to the size of its economy) and the political infighting and corruption scandals over the past six years. As a result, the shock-

Figure 18.3 Slovenia Government Debt to GDP, as percentage of GDP

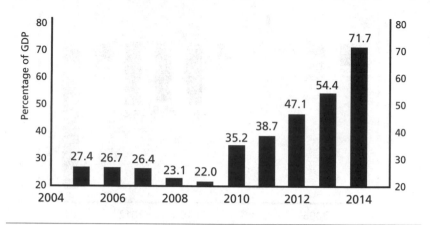

Source: Tradingeconomics.com/eurostat

Figure 18.4 Slovakia Government Debt to GDP, as percentage of GDP

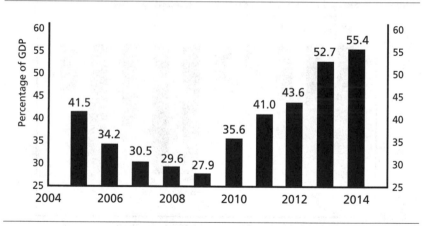

Source: Tradingeconomics.com/eurostat

ing 2014 budget deficit of 14.7 percent of GDP indicates an economy tee-tering on bankruptcy. Slovakia was not without its own problems, but was able to steadily maintain some momentum of economic reform and adjust-ments to tamp down on its deficits. With a forecasted 2.8 percent budget deficit/GDP in 2014, Slovakia finds itself liberated from the Commission's list of economically problematic members.

The figures for debt to GDP ratio show some similar stories but again highlight the longer-term struggles for Slovenia. Slovenia's debt to GDP ratio has now exceeded the 60 percent cutoff and shows no signs of slowing. In fact, the debt balance has doubled in the last year, quite a remarkable (albeit negative) feat for such small economy. Again, political paralysis and large financial and bank debt overhang make the road forward especially difficult. Slovakia is not without its own concerns, although the country remains under the 60 percent cutoff. Debt levels shot up noticeably with the onset of the Eurozone crisis, but have leveled off somewhat in the past two years. A fall back into Eurozone recession could exacerbate lingering areas of concern with its finances. But Slovakia remains a surprisingly stable and core member of the Eurozone member states.

The following section briefly updates the impact of the Eurozone crisis and Great Recession on each country in the period 2008 to 2014 and how each responded differently, in part reflecting how they politically preferred to handle their respective economic problems. I also examine the nature of the EU's effect on each country and further highlight the narrow policy parameters imposed on them. Whether one agrees or disagrees with these policy prescriptions—and we know the critics of austerity are vocal and strong—the outcomes are clear. Slovakia has emerged relatively stable and safely under the Eurozone-mandated debt and deficit criteria, part of the "hard" Eurozone countries, closely aligned with Germany. The situation in Slovenia is more complicated and potentially explosive. Slovenia's inability to fundamentally address its finances for the long haul have set it up for a potentially very hard landing, especially if the Eurozone heads back into recession.

Slovenia: Accession and the Great Recession

After gaining recognition by the EU as an independent republic of Slovenia on January 15, 1992, the path toward Europe was clear. Owing to its long-standing cultural and commercial ties to Western Europe, Slovenia's inclination to join the EU was virtually assured. By the time the EU promulgated the Copenhagen criteria in 1993, Slovenia was already a strong candidate for membership. The resolution of a dispute with Italy over the right of foreigners to buy property in the country allowed Slovenia to sign a Europe Agreement with the EU in 1996. At the December 1997 Luxembourg European Council, Slovenia was invited to be among the first six applicant states to initiate formal accession talks.

Negotiations on the various chapters of Slovenia's Accession Treaty began in February 1998 and proceeded relatively smoothly and quickly compared with the talks involving other applicants. For example, Slovenia was the first state to close talks on the environment and was among the three leading countries regarding the number of accession chapters it had successfully negotiated by autumn 2001. As with the other applicant states, talks on accession chapters with financial implications were the most problematic for Slovenia. However, with only 4 percent of its workforce employed in the agricultural sector, matters related to the Common Agricultural Policy (CAP) were resolved without much trouble. Slovenia's most fundamental concern in the accession talks was that it might end up as a net contributor into the EU budget after accession. Owing to its relative economic prosperity, Slovenia was already receiving the lowest amount of preaccession financial assistance from the EU per capita compared with other recipients. Slovenia's status as a net receiver from the community budget was guaranteed at least until the end of 2006 through the negotiation of support from the CAP, Structural and Cohesion Funds, as well as annual lump-sum payments. In the end, both the turnout (60.2 percent) and "yes" vote (89.61 percent) were relatively high for Slovenia's referendum on joining the EU.

Slovenia's political debates have largely shifted back and forth between the center-left Liberal Democrats (LDS) and the center-right Slovenian Democratic Party (SDS). The LDS held power through the first years of the emerging and stable multiparty parliamentary democracy. The LDS delivered on NATO and EU membership and looked set to win elections again in 2004. Surprisingly, the SDS won a plurality of seats and formed a coalition government with three smaller parties (conservatives, Christian Democrats, and pensioners). The LDS shifted into opposition for the first time. Despite the shock of an SDS upset, the desire of the electorate for change signaled a healthy competition within the mostly centrist-minded electorate.

As the economic turbulence unleashed itself across the EU, it had strong destabilizing effects on Slovenian politics. From 2008, when the center left took over, through the most recent election of July 2014, Slovenia experienced its fourth government, shifting between successive right and left governments seeking solutions to the crisis. The culmination of inherently unstable multiparty governments headed up by the center-left LZJ-PS (Positive Slovenia Party) as well as internal party conflicts between the popular Ljubljana mayor Zoran Janković, corruption-riddled Janez Janša, and the brutalizing effects on the Slovenian economy over the same period led to the shocking election outcomes of July 2014. Political newcomer and law professor Miro Cerar's anticorruption, slightly anti-EU Populist Party garnered the highest number of votes. Regardless of the outcome, the ability of Cerar's new party to govern within the divided multiparty system remains to be seen.

Matej Klarič and Miroslav Stanjojevič argue that significant changes occurred in the social dialogue and collective bargaining with the onset of the economic crisis.[6] The once highly coordinated Slovenian political and social system has begun to unravel. A more unilateral political response by opposing political parties on the left and right have essentially remained unsuccessful in resolving the economic and social crisis. The authors argue that these unilateral efforts have only further enhanced political instability and led to serious political crisis. With the election surprise of July 2014, the political crisis will likely continue. Parliaments have been transformed from primarily a legislative body to a mediating and supervisory body. Though overall the parliament has become stable in its structure and formal rules as well as its professionalism, at the end of the second decade the stability has been undermined and weakened.[7]

What is clear is that the EU's pressure on respective Slovenian governments to further reduce spending, privatize, and reform the banking system remained sharp and focused. There does not appear to be too much room to govern outside of the parameters foisted on successive Slovenian governments. We now turn to that story.

Slovenia's Economic Response and EU Pressure

During the period leading up to accession and the onset of the Eurozone crisis in 2007–2008, Slovenia pursued a macroeconomic policy intent on financial and monetary stability. By all measures related to Eurozone stability, by 2008 Slovenia maintained an envious budget balance as well as a mere 22.5 percent of debt to GDP ratio, gold standards by all Eurozone members. By 2014, the numbers had shifted sharply in the other direction: 14.7 percent of budget deficit to GDP and 71.1 percent debt to GDP. What happened?

Much like other countries hit hard by the global recession, Slovenia's economy remained dependent on exports. With the sharp and sudden drop in export revenues, Slovenia's still heavily state-controlled and -subsidized economy was exposed. Moreover, the banking system, centralized and linked into the same highly integrated Eurozone real estate market, was hit hard. Successive Slovenian governments sought to hold, protect, and subsidize the banks to keep them afloat. Although this strategy provided some short-term protection, by 2012–2013, the banks were in a near free fall. Slovenia was one of the last EU member states to force banks to clean up and clear out their bad debt. As a result, 2013 saw the swift and sudden collapse of the Slovenian banking system, leading the government to narrowly avoid an IMF bailout.

The underlying factors explaining the particular problem of the Slovenian banking system (and entire economic structure) lie in the unwillingness to reform prior to 2008. Zuokui Liu notes the following key factors as critical to understanding the Slovenian predicament:[8] banks that were extremely nationalized, extensively regulated, and riddled with poor corporate and political governance; the real estate crisis that eroded the assets of the banks; and the government's slow response to developing a comprehensive bailout strategy.

By 2012–2013, 18.2 percent of all loans were deemed nonperforming, and the international rating agency downgraded Slovenian debt from A2 to Baa2, just two notches away from a junk rating. The banking system is essentially majority-owned by the government through three of the biggest banks: NLB (New Ljubljana Bank), NKBM, and Akanda. NLB holds the dominant position in the banking system with thirteen regional banks attached to the NLB, controlling nearly 90 percent of the banking system in Slovenia. While the government has sought to reduce its control, this has been a very slow process. The banks are tied heavily to the construction industry, which suffered greatly from the overall economic downturn. Similar to many European economies, once the trickle became a flood of bad loans, infusions of more capital from the government, and more economic instability and crises, the debt accumulated to a point that today appears unsustainable. The debt-fueled growth of the 2004–2008 period, the "golden years" of Slovenia's EU membership and Eurozone accession set them up for collapse.[9]

The Slovenian economy quickly fell into recession. By 2009, the GDP decreased by 8 percent on an annual basis. The lack of political consensus, which ultimately is needed to develop a comprehensive strategy and framework for restructuring the Slovenian economy, failed to materialize. At first, the center-left government undertook austerity measures that attempted to set the country on proper footing. Some efforts by the Slovenian central bank to increase capital requirements, a move demanded by the EU, led to a further credit crunch. These programs were heavily criticized by Positive Slovenia to the point where the country was politically paralyzed in 2011. Various referendums signaling strong opposition to the reforms further prevented the government from acting. Elections in 2011 did bring the center-right into power, but it did not provide enough of a consensus overall to fundamentally reform the banking system. The political back-and-forth in 2012 over whether to create one state-owned "bad bank" company to take over the nonperforming assets of a large chunk of bad debt led to further delays in arriving at a solution. The political approach to the crisis prevented the government from implanting any systematic reforms. In addition, a deal struck with labor unions, after heavy protests, further postponed the possible additional referendum on reforms that would likely have thrown Slovenia into further crisis. But it only delayed harsher measures to come.

Ironically, Slovenia's membership in the EU, and then the Eurozone by 2007, led to a massive inflow of credit. The process of monetary accession especially contributed to the convergence of interest rates toward the level prevailing across the Eurozone. Slovenian debt was equal in the minds of investors to that of any other Eurozone member state. This enabled the Slovenian banks to get access to cheap credit from abroad and ultimately depend on foreign capital. Linking their monetary policy within the Eurozone thus made the economy even more dependent on the vagaries of international financial markets, which of course turned on Slovenia shortly. A classic case of a sovereign debt crisis was born. While many analysts in 2013 did not predict an imminent collapse, the "domino" of Slovenia was clearly wobbling.[10]

Adding pressure, of course, to the dire developing situation in Slovenia was the EU, particularly the Eurozone's monetary watchdogs. In April 2013, the euro-group finance ministers called on Slovenia to cut more from the budget and stated that deficit reduction was to date "inadequate." The Commission also demanded that new borrowing be less than 3 percent of GDP by 2015. Olli Rehn, EU monetary affairs commissioner, called the situation serious but manageable, but that the clock was ticking. Cuts were called for to public sector wages, pension and social security systems, education, and health care, along with privatization of state-owned industry and increased taxes. The government managed to push through some reforms, including an increase of 1 percent in the value-added tax and further privatizing state-owned industry, including fifteen larger companies. Such measures were noted by the EU as moving in the right direction. But up for sharp debate in 2014 was the decision to privatize the giant Telekom and the Mercator supermarket chain, owned in part by the government. No resolution was achieved on these two larger state-owned companies. As a result, the so-called bad bank program remains in limbo as the European Commission assesses the stress tests for these banks, which have not yet been completed.

Squeezing the parameters of policymaking were the Commission's "two-pack" regulations, which entered into force on May 30, 2013. These regulations included specific provisions on closer monitoring of euro area member states in the Excessive Deficit Procedure (EDP). These provisions aim to ensure that member states take corrective action in a timely and durable manner by increasing the scope and frequency of information to be submitted to the Commission and the Council for their review. Specifically, the legislation establishes a system of graduated monitoring, which includes regular reporting by the concerned member state every three or six months, according to the stage of the procedure. This regular reporting will allow the early detection of a member state at risk for not correcting its excessive deficit by the deadline set by the Council. If such a risk exists, the Commission may issue a recommendation to the member state to take further or different action. The two-pack also requires euro area member states entering the EDP to draft economic partnership programs, which provide a roadmap for structural reforms considered instrumental to an effective and lasting correction of the excessive deficit.

The latest European Commission review of the Slovenian economy states up front and clearly that the country "continues to experience *excessive macroeconomic imbalances which require specific monitoring and continuing strong policy action*."[11] As a result, the Commission maintains rigid monitoring of the policies of the Slovenian government. A continued reading of the most recent highly detailed monitoring report is littered with EU oversight concepts: Alert Mechanism Report, In-Depth Review (IDR), and surveillance under the Macroeconomic Imbalance Procedure. The Alert Mechanism Report in particular signals the initial screening device helping identify Slovenia's macroeconomic imbalances and provides the IDR the status of policy measures taken to address those imbalances. The primary takeaway from the most recent IDR is that Slovenia cannot escape the pressures and policy prescriptions of the EU.

While Slovenia so far has been just able to escape tapping into the EU's financial rescue facilities, it cannot escape the prying eyes of the Commission's oversight. Policy prescriptions are specific, unrelenting in focus, and difficult to avoid. Challenges include a durable and sustained repair of the banking sector, addressing the level of state ownership, bringing public finances onto a sustainable path, improving export performance and competitiveness, and enhancing corporate profitability and viability. The prescription for addressing the challenges are straight from the austerity playbook: further privatization, cuts in fiscal spending, pension reform, containing labor costs, deregulation of certain industries and sectors, and addressing the ongoing corruption crises. As we have seen, the demands of being placed in the EDP have been met in part with compliance and in part with a modest bit of resistance by the public and politicians. Slovenia is balancing on a high-wire act for the foreseeable future, with the weight of EU compliance, oversight, and austerity on the one hand and the demand for a slower pace of reform coming from the public and politicians on the other.

The austerity measures have had a decidedly sharp effect on the average Slovenian citizen. Unemployment rose quickly to more than 10 percent in 2013, and the average Slovenian family spent 25 percent of their income on food alone. The economy shrank by a projected 4.9 percent in 2014, with unemployment rising to 14 percent and exports dropping by 2.5 percent for the year. The depreciation of the euro and the ongoing recovery in the Eurozone should support the country's external sector and generate some economic growth. With some growth, the new government has pledged to meet the targets, but that approach would likely slow down some of the previous government's debt reduction programs and further stifle consumer demand. Despite the protestations of Cerar's new government to adjust the programs imposed by the EU, it is highly unlikely they will be able to carve out a new path that is decidedly far from the existing path. In July 2014, the government agreed to privatization procedures to support the partnership agreement between the government and the European Commission, which will enable Slovenia to draw on EU Cohesion funds within the 2014–2020 framework. The partnership agreement complements the Commission's Alert Mechanism Report and IDR by requiring compliance with the policy prescriptions developed within.

Slovakia: Accession and the Great Recession

Following its peaceful separation from the Czechoslovakian federation on January 1, 1993, the Slovak Republic experienced a rocky road to EU membership under the semi-authoritarian government of populist and nationalist Vladimír Mečiar and his Movement for a Democratic Slovakia Party. Slovakia's Europe agreement with the EU was signed in October 1993 but did not enter into force until February 1995. Its formal application for EU membership came in June 1996 but was not well received in light of the corruption in Slovakia's privatization process and virtual censorship of its media, as well as Mečiar's pro-Russian orientation and skepticism of both NATO and the EU. Mečiar's hold on power started to unravel after he assumed presidential powers amid a constitutional crisis created when Michal Kováč resigned from that office without a designated successor. This power play prompted protests at home and abroad, including criticism from the EU. Amid this political climate, the elections of September 1998 swung against Mečiar, allowing a broad coalition to form under the leadership of Mikuláš Dzurinda and his center-right Slovak Democratic and Christian Union, backed by a diverse mix of smaller parties.

The European Commission seized on the turning point on Slovakia's political landscape and, seeking to support Dzurinda, provided an optimistic report on the country's membership aspirations. The government worked quickly to implement the reform agenda and the country was included among the six states endorsed by the December 1999 Helsinki European Council to start formal accession negotiations. The talks began in 2000, and the government accelerated economic reforms and closed various chapters of accession. By October 2001, negotiations on twenty chapters had been completed, signaling that Slovakia had caught up with the so-called first-wave countries. Difficulties remained in some sectors—energy, competition policy, and taxation—and corruption and handling of EU financial assistance clouded some of the progress. However, by the end of 2002, at the Copenhagen European Council, Slovakia was primed for accession. Dzurinda was returned to power in parliamentary elections in fall 2002. In May 2003, 92.46 percent voted "yes" to joining the EU, with turnout a low 52.15 percent. In 2004, Slovakia joined in the largest enlargement in the EU's history.

Despite the success of steering Slovakia toward EU membership, Dzurinda's government suffered some instability as a result of the government's candidate for the presidential election failing to win. The government relied on a shaky coalition of smaller and some Euro-skeptic parties, including the left-leaning and populist Direction Party led by Robert Fico. Unemployment was stubbornly high throughout the adjustment period leading to EU membership and after. Many Slovakians began to question some of the government's initiatives and how they negatively impacted average citizens.

Entry in 2009 into the Eurozone brought about some notable changes in the macroeconomic structure of the Slovakian economy. In addition, Slovakia came to understand Eurozone membership as an important tool in reversing the feelings of isolationism experienced during the Mečiar period.[12] Exchange rate risks and instability lessened, borrowing costs fell (like in all Eurozone countries), and the outlook for growth was good. Annual real GDP growth in 2007 stood at a remarkable 10.5 percent. Even into 2008, when the first inclinations of a major crisis were brewing, Slovakia's GDP stood at 5.8 percent for the year. Slovakia was not immune to the predictable shocks brought about by the crisis: weakened access to foreign direct investment and international finance, weakened export markets, shrunken domestic credit markets, and plummeting consumer confidence. Unemployment rose notably, from 10 percent in 2008 to 15 percent in 2011, especially in regions (rural and in the east) where gains had always been slower.

Yet Slovakia was able to recover more quickly than other countries, most notably Slovenia. Slovakia's fiscal policies were headed in the direction favoring macroeconomic stability and modest fiscal imbalances. A much more cautious lending policy of banks prevented the large-scale boom and bust of the real estate market as occurred in Ireland and Spain. Some regained stability within the Eurozone, in particular Germany, where Slovakia's economy is strongly connected via foreign direct investment, and export markets helped create some modest growth. Labor productivity but a jobless recovery helped push Slovakia forward. Low inflation, low public debt, and output growth provided enough cover for rating agencies, which downgraded Slovakian debt from A+ to A. But compared to Slovenia, Slovakia remained a center of stability in a larger sea of Eurozone crisis. Not surprisingly, Slovakia's relative "strength" and stability manifested itself into some intense political debates.

The Eurozone sovereign debt crisis and the subsequent intense debates surrounding the Greek bailout and the creation of a European Financial Stability Facility (EFSF) were no different in Slovakia. However, Slovakia was in a much different financial and macroeconomic position. Unlike Slovenia, Slovakia maintained a steady course of macroeconomic policy focused on stability as well as steady reforms aimed at boosting export growth and competitiveness. While real GDP growth fell sharply in 2009 (−4.9 percent on an annual basis), growth jumped back in 2010 and 2011 to 4.2 percent and 3.3 percent, respectively. From this perspective, of growth and lower debt and deficit levels than many states within the Eurozone, Slovakia's debate on bailout turned on internal politics and elections. From the beginning of 2010 until the end of 2012, when the parliament approved the final EU Fiscal Compact with near unanimity, there was a tug-of-war debate about the wisdom of the bailout and financing schemes.

In May 2010, the Social Democratic Party (SMER) led by its chairman and Prime Minister Fico, approved a loan to Greece as part of the larger bailout package. The Slovakian minister of finance announced that the decision to support the contract was based on the desire to ensure "Eurozone stability."[13] The voting was delayed, however, because of the desire to see the upcoming parliamentary elections conducted, which would essentially provide a mandate one way or another. Unfortunately for the SMER, and despite winning the most seats, a conservative and right-wing coalition of four parties had a majority and agreed to form a coalition. In August 2010, three of the four parties in the coalition voted against the package while SMER pulled their votes of support. As a result, Slovakia became the only Eurozone country that refused to support the first bailout of Greece. The new prime minister, Iveta Radičová, argued that the more responsible and relatively poorer countries like Slovakia should not be asked to contribute to bail out the less responsible and richer countries of the Eurozone, aiming at the "moral hazard" of bailing out irresponsible partners. That said, a second vote to support the larger EFSF indicated that Slovakia's concerns about the Eurozone and debtor countries were focused more on individual states (like Greece) and not with the larger Eurozone project. All parties voted in support of the proposals.

More instability emerged as a second vote in October 2011 to approve the expansion of the EFSF to €780 billion was delayed and ultimately failed in the parliament. For a second time, Slovakia was the only Eurozone country that refused to support the expansion. Radičová used the vote as a vote of no confidence in her government, hoping that the threat of a collapsed government would secure enough votes. One of the small coalition parties, the liberal Freedom and Solidarity Party headed by Richard Sulík declined to support the vote. With SMER sitting patiently on the sidelines, and again withholding votes of possible support, the measure failed. Two days later, with guarantees that the new elections would take place, SMER provided enough votes to finally approve the Slovakian portion of the EFSF increase. In March 2012, new parliamentary elections were held and SMER again gained a majority and formed a single-party government. SMER was then able to deliver two key votes of support in June 2012 for the new European Stability Mechanism that replaced the EFSF. The government was also able to approve the last critical piece of the tumultuous Eurozone institutional changes in December 2012, the EU Fiscal Compact that would hopefully provide the architecture to prevent the next crisis.

What is the main lesson to be learned from the two-year period of dramatic and surprising votes and government changes? First and foremost, while some more conservative and right-wing parties, tapping into populist and nationalist sentiment, maintained a sharper line in terms of the divide over whether to help countries in crisis, Slovakia expressed a moderate streak of support for the various Eurozone programs and institutions to address the sovereign debt crisis. The only notable exception was the first Greek bailout vote. The center-left SMER party benefited politically from the instability over the two-year period. While Fico is often regarded as a populist, he has steadfastly voted and supported pro-European policies and expressed an interest in deeper integration within the EU, even at the potential cost of a further loss of national sovereignty. That said, he does not fully support austerity as the solution to the financial and economic crisis. Instead, a balanced package of economic growth spurred by more intense public investment and conditional support based on some measured structural reforms over longer periods of time would provide the right pathway to future economic growth. That more balanced approach is one that has resonated with other Eurozone member states still caught in the trap of EDP.

Moving Forward: Ukraine and the Larger Question of "Europe"

The 2014 summer and fall crisis over the EU's response to the events in Ukraine revealed some interesting dynamics that have developed. Empowered by its relative economic success and more closely aligned with Germany and the other stable Eurozone states, Slovakia now has greater policy choices to influence the direction of Europe's response. Moreover, Slovakia also now retains relatively more autonomy over those policy choices. Slovenia, largely without much policy leeway, remained mostly quiet and without any real significant input into the EU's response. With its economy in distress, Slovenia advocated options that generated minimal impacts to its system.

Slovakia, which is almost entirely dependent on Russian oil and gas, was among the nations hit hardest by Russia's 2009 cutoff of gas traveling through Ukraine to Europe. Now, given some of its economic prowess, it can secure supplies from the West if needed. In addition, with lower overall global oil prices, Slovakia can tap into the global market in ways it could not before. Moreover, Slovakia signed a memorandum with Ukraine, the so-called reverse flow agreement that sends gas back to Ukraine. Prime Minister Fico said his country is ready to meet its commitments. The maximum volume of such reverse deliveries is estimated at 10 billion cubic meters of gas a year. The Voyany-Uzhgorod pipeline, which became operational on September 2, 2014, will allow gas transportation from Slovakia to western Ukraine. The very real and symbolic effort of Slovakia to build an EU gas bridge to Ukraine should not be underestimated in Slovakia's increasing influence in the region.

That is not to say that it can disregard the effects of any Russian cutoff. The Ukrainian crisis has created more risk for investors in Slovakia, and projections for future economic growth have been cut. But the ability to play a leading role in negotiations with the Russians over the flow of gas to the EU has also demonstrated Slovakia's key role as an intermediary. "Why should we jeopardize the EU economy that begins to grow?" Fico asked at a news conference. "If there is a crisis situation, it should be solved by other means than meaningless sanctions."[14] Fico's position with Russia has always been pragmatic and, some have argued, too soft. But given its border with Ukraine and the potential for real negative spillover effects on Slovakia, Fico will likely stick to walking a fine geopolitical tightrope between harder EU positions toward Russia and those advocating a more cautious approach. Such a position is reflected in the EU failure to impose additional tougher sanctions on Russia in late 2014. Moreover, a gas exemption to earlier EU–US sanctions signified the need to target sanctions carefully. One can ascertain from these developments that the Slovakian position has influenced EU policy toward the Ukrainian crisis, perhaps a sign of the relative importance of Slovakia within the region.

For Slovenia, the crisis in the Ukraine could not have come at a worse time. Teetering in financial crisis, the effects of the limited EU–US sanctions have hurt Slovenian tourism, exports, and the agricultural industry. Similar concerns regarding the flow of gas and oil to Slovenia, most notably the development of the South Stream pipeline to the west, also frame the perspective of officials. In 2013, Slovenia maintained a trade surplus with Ukraine and Russia. As 2014 ended, Slovenian exports to Ukraine and Russia were projected to fall by €200 million because of the Ukrainian crisis, and that figure may grow if the conflict escalates. Slovenian exports to Ukraine already dropped by 13 percent in the first five months of 2014, compared with the corresponding period in 2013. Exports to Russia fell by 20 percent.[15] As a result, Slovenia has also pursued a more cautious and pragmatic approach to resolving the Ukrainian crisis.

The approach taken by Slovakia and Slovenia toward the Ukrainian crisis, along with the countries' divergent paths following the economic recession of 2008 and lingering Eurozone crisis, indicate the inherent problems facing any effort to further strengthen EU confederation. While the influence of these two countries on the direction of EU policies may be low, the policy approaches of each indicate the larger divisions with the EU and the difficulty in forging a stronger EU institutional shift that would signal movement toward confederation. Slovakia has emerged as a pragmatic balancer in terms of some deeper economic integration to deal with the Eurozone crisis while hesitating on a stronger EU approach toward Russia and the Ukrainian crisis. Slovakia's role as a geopolitical bridge between the core of Europe and the outlying Central and Eastern European countries struggling with economic and political instability will likely continue to increase. Slovenia's approach, more limited and dependent on others, will likely follow the Slovakian approach. While the tale of two countries remains accurate as developed in this chapter, the ties that bind these two together remain: progress and regress, advancement and retreat, and stability and instability. Within that push and pull dynamic, it is difficult to envision a smooth path forward for either country, to say nothing of more strongly committing to the larger EU project.

Notes

1. Gorton, Lowe, and Zellei (2005).
2. See, for example, Falkner (2010).
3. Zubek and Staronovo (2012).
4. European Commission (2013b).
5. European Commission, "The Euro Area, Flash Eurobarometer 386," November 2013. Available at http://ec.europa.eu/public_opinion/flash/fl_386_en.pdf.
6. Klarič and Stanjojevič (2013).
7. Mansfeldová (2011).
8. Liu (2013).
9. "The Slovenian Banking and Debt Crisis," *Troika Watch*, April 8, 2014. Available at http://www.troikawatch.net/the-slovenian-banking-and-debt-crisis/.
10. Cyrus Sanati, "Forget Latvia. Slovenia Is the Next Euro Domino," *Fortune*, June 7, 2013.
11. European Commission, "Macroeconomic Imbalances: Slovenia 2014," Occasional Papers on the European Economy no. 187, March 2014, p. 3. Emphasis in original.
12. Pechova (2012).
13. Golias and Jurzya (2013).
14. "Slovakia Grumbles as EU Begins Crisis Russia Food Ban Talks," *EurActiv.com*, August 14, 2014. http://www.euractiv.com/sections/europes-east/slovakia-grumbles-eu-begins-crisis-russia-food-ban-talks-307795.
15. "Slovenian Exports to Ukraine, Russia Tumble," *Business Report Online*, September 4, 2014. http://www.iol.co.za/business/international/slovenian-exports-to-ukraine-russia-tumble-1.1746231.

19

Cyprus and Malta:
The Impact of Europeanization

Roderick Pace

CYPRUS AND MALTA ARE THE SMALLEST OF THE FOUR EUROPEAN
Union (EU) island states (the other two are Ireland and the UK). Located in
the Mediterranean region on the southern edge of the EU security zone,
these two nations have a checkered history stretching back millennia. They
share some parallel historical experiences, but differ in key respects. This
chapter focuses mainly on their experience in the EU, particularly since the
recent Eurozone crisis. For Cyprus the crisis has had a profound negative
effect leading to a decline in public support for the EU. Malta remained
largely unscathed by the crisis, which explains why Maltese citizens' support for the EU is still buoyant; nevertheless, since over a third of the population is neutral as to whether the EU is a good thing, Euro-skepticism might
be a sleeping giant, ready to wake up as soon as the island experiences a
major exogenous shock.[1]

Cyprus and Malta joined the EU for a number of reasons. The 2004 enlargement dynamics, comprising most of the newly independent states of
Central and Eastern Europe, exercised a "drag" effect on the Mediterranean
island states, who did not wish to be left behind. But "jumping onto the
moving train" was not the only motivating factor. Cyprus and Malta both
had association agreements with the EU dating back to the early 1970s. In
1987, Cyprus had concluded a customs union agreement with the European
Community. Cyprus and Malta had other important political objectives to
achieve through membership: Cyprus thought that membership would has-
ten the reunification of the island after its forcible division by Turkey in
1974, whereas for Malta, membership was a long-held objective of the
then-governing Nationalist Party, which, since independence in 1964, had
strived to berth the country in the secure harbors of the West. However,

both nations had a number of other motives, which are rooted in the politics and economics of small states.

Small State Literature

The end of the Cold War and the dismantling of communism in Central and Eastern Europe led to many small European states seeking integration with the EU and NATO. For this reason, scholarly interest shifted to small state security, the challenges they posed to the process of European integration, and their impact on EU governance and NATO.[2] Enlargement and the internal institutional rebalancing taking place within the Union led to a number of studies on individual small states, both those wanting to join and those wishing to stay out of the EU, as well as on the general theme of small states in the EU.[3] Other studies on small states in general focused on the economic performance and economic resilience of small states,[4] security and diplomacy,[5] and internal cohesion.

Following Iceland's financial crash (2008–2011), parallels began to be drawn between it and other small European states such as Cyprus, Ireland, Luxembourg, and Malta mainly due to the disproportionate size of their financial sectors compared to their gross domestic product (GDP) and the perceived risks of an Icelandic-style currency collapse. Analyzing Iceland's case, Baldur Thorhallsson laid special emphasis on the need of small states to seek "shelter" from the destructive forces of globalization and international relations when these overshadow their ability to cope with them, adding, "The EU not only provides access to the largest world market; it provides small states with shelter from economic downturns and a seat at the negotiating table."[6] Thorhallsson laments that Iceland was abandoned because it did not form part of the EU. However, as shall be discussed further, Cyprus as an Economic and Monetary Union (EMU) member state also felt abandoned when it had to accept a financial bailout and a "haircut" in 2013, following the collapse of its banking sector.

The economic rationale behind small states' decision to join a regional integration organization must begin by being cognizant of David Vital's argument that "short of outright military conflict, the weakest spot in the small power's armor is the economic one."[7] Michael Handel recognizes that some "weak" states can mitigate the negative effects of external economic pressure by diversifying their exports and markets, while cautioning that they should certainly avoid conducting their trade with only one state, "especially not with a great power."[8] This was one of the reasons that led Cyprus and Malta to join the EU.

EU membership provides small states with access to bigger markets and acts as their gateway to the global market. Traffic through the gate moves in both directions. Transfers from the EU budget for those small member states whose level of GDP per capita falls below the EU average is another advantage. However, the biggest advantage is that small states participate in the decisionmaking institutions and in shaping EU policies. Less tangible benefits include stronger consumer protection and easier travel for their citizens in Europe as a result of the adoption of the common currency by eighteen member states and the Schengen Agreement, which Malta (but not Cyprus) joined in 2007. Connections are very important for islands. As EU member states, they also gain more relevance in international and multilateral negotiations and can pursue their objectives through the collective power of the EU. One cannot imagine how Cyprus and Malta could safeguard their interests in world trade or climate change negotiations without pursuing them as part of an alliance of states, provided they can ensure their interests are taken on board by their allies.

EU membership has other important domestic political dimensions in small states. Public support for integration is crucial and relies on perceptions, which are formed by various forces, such as political parties, sectoral interest groups, lobbyists, and the media. Perceptions may be rooted in the small state's history, political culture, and often its physical geographical location. For example, the Baltic states' decision to join NATO, which was supported by their publics, is a product of their history and geographic location on the borders of Russia. Just because they are small, European small states are not free from the dichotomy that often troubles other member states between domestic politics and EU decisionmaking. There are sufficient examples of this, such as Denmark's rejection of the Treaty of Maastricht, Ireland's initial botching of the Treaties of Nice and Lisbon, Norway's European Economic Community and EU membership referenda, and the saga of Iceland's application as it follows the troughs and crests of the country's shifting public opinion on the issue. Malta would not have joined the EU had the 2003 membership referendum gone differently. Hence, the way that domestic political forces are lined up is very relevant in the EU, particularly since the Union is not a federation but a complex confederal union.

Last there is the issue of Europeanization. The Europeanization literature has grown extensively, but I limit myself to Claudio Radaelli's definition as "processes of (a) construction, (b) diffusion and (c) institutionalization of formal and informal rules, procedures, policy paradigms, styles, 'ways of doing things' and shared beliefs and norms which are first defined and consolidated in the making of EU decisions and then incorporated in the logic of domestic discourse, identities, political structures and public policies."[9] Radaelli and Theofanis Exadaktylos further differentiate between "Europeanization as a domestic impact of Europe" and "Europeanization as a creative usage of Europe"[10] and the related concepts of uploading and downloading. It is argued in this chapter that as EU member states, Cyprus and Malta were not only passively Europeanizing but also trying to upload their own objectives on to the EU.

A Changing EU

Since Cyprus and Malta joined the EU in 2004, the Union has been changing in many ways, and the two island states have had to adapt and navigate these new developments. The number of member states increased from twenty-five in 2004, to twenty-seven in 2007, and twenty-eight in 2014. The enlargement process is still ongoing though not with the same velocity that had characterized it in the period 1998–2003.[11] The Treaty Establishing a European Constitution was rejected in 2005, but most of its contents were salvaged by means of the Lisbon Treaty, which created two new treaties, the Treaty on European Union (TEU) and the Treaty on the Functioning of the European Union. Notwithstanding the financial crisis, the Eurozone has grown to eighteen member states following the inclusion of Slovenia (2007), Cyprus and Malta (2008), Slovakia (2009), Estonia (2011), and Latvia (2014).

The Lisbon Treaty, which came into effect on December 1, 2009, has expanded the powers of European Parliament but maintained its mostly consultative function in the Common Foreign and Security Policy. The newly created European External Action Service (EEAS) has been compared to a new powerful "institution" (not in the meaning of Article 9, TEU), which challenges the interinstitutional balance in the EU's external relations. Bart Van Vooren asks whether the EEAS is "a new institution, or indeed, a sui generis cog in the EU's institutional machinery."[12] He concludes that the functional autonomy of the EEAS gives it a lot of power to influence policy, but legally its autonomy is less than that of the European Central Bank (ECB) but more than that of the Committee of Permanent Representatives and the European Defense Agency.[13]

Public perceptions have also been affected by the euro crisis and the inability of the Union to handle it decisively. The emphasis placed on austerity to address the basic economic flaws in the southern states, such as burgeoning public debts and fiscal deficits, has exasperated unemployment rates and social hardships, which soured public support for the EU, except in Malta, which was not deeply affected by the recession.[14] It has led to the growth in support for extreme parties, particularly on the far right, as witnessed by the 2014 European elections.

Cyprus, Malta, and the Financial Crisis

All the member states that joined the EU in 2004 or later are obliged to join the EMU as well. Malta and Cyprus joined the EMU in 2008. Preparation for the changeover to the euro started in May 2005 when the two island states' currencies, the Cyprus pound and the Maltese lira, joined the European Exchange Rate Mechanism to satisfy one of the entry criteria, namely, exchange rate stability. In the following two years, the countries took steps to satisfy the other Maastricht economic convergence criteria (a fiscal deficit not exceeding 3 percent of GDP, a public debt of around 60 percent of GDP, and low inflation and long-term interest rates) and take other steps to ensure that the changeover would not lead to price inflation and would cause as little public backlash as possible. The changeover to the euro was successfully completed in both countries, and in a press release issued soon after, the European Commission quoting Flash Eurobarometer (public opinion survey) No. 222–223 announced "the vast majority of the population in Cyprus and in Malta, 95 percent and 90 percent respectively, consider the changeover to the euro in their country to have been smooth and efficient."[15]

Cyprus and Malta succeeded in achieving the prescribed macroeconomic targets. Indeed, in 2007 the Commission was able to announce a clean bill of health for the two EMU aspirants, highlighting that Malta had reduced its government deficit from nearly 10 percent of GDP in 2003 to 2.6 percent in 2006; likewise Cyprus had managed to reduce its own deficit from 6.3 percent in 2003 to 1.5 percent in 2006. In the case of public debt, in 2006 Malta's stood at 66.5 percent and was declining, whereas Cyprus's stood at 65.3 percent and was heading toward 61.5 percent by the end of 2007.[16] This progress helped raise optimism that the Growth and Stability Pact could restrain government spending, leading to stronger public finances, which in turn would strengthen the Eurozone countries' resilience to exogenous shock.[17] However, this did not happen. When the recession struck in 2008, and particularly the following year when its negative effects began to grow, the governments of Cyprus and Malta increased spending, and their fiscal deficits slipped their EMU moorings. There might have also been an ideological reason for this in the case of Cyprus, which for the first time in its history was led by a communist president, Demitris Christofias, who favored state intervention in the economy.

Six months after Cyprus and Malta introduced the euro, the global financial crisis struck. This found the Maltese banking system hardly exposed to bad debts, but the same could not be said of the Cypriot banks. The Icelandic currency collapse conjured images of a similar financial debacle occurring in Cyprus and Malta because of the size of their financial services sectors. In Iceland's case, three of the collapsing banks held assets that were eleven times the size of GDP, making it impossible for the Icelandic Central Bank to intervene as the banker of last resort. Developments in Cyprus between 2011 and 2013 were similar in many ways. Cypriot banks had accumulated huge deposits and large liabilities by holding Greek bonds. In May 2011, Cyprus was downgraded by many of the leading rating agencies, and the country was shut off from borrowing in the international money markets. The immediate cause of its insolvency was an EU decision, with which Cyprus had concurred, to write off billions of Greek sovereign debt and which led to a sudden increase of €4 billion in the Cypriot banks' liabilities, making it impossible for them to continue operating. On December 23, 2011, Russia agreed to loan Cyprus €2.5 billion to help it overcome its financial problems. In the next six months the magnitude of the problem grew. The Cypriot banks in trouble held an estimated €20 billion in Russian offshore deposits and the Nicosia authorities tried at first to reach agreement with Russia for more bailout loans. But Moscow was unwilling to provide Cyprus with the comfort it sought unless this was done in joint agreement with the EU. Realizing that Russia was not willing to bail it out, on June 25, 2012, Cyprus requested the EU to step in. The bailout was formally approved by the EU in May 2013, after Cyprus accepted a troika (the European Commission, the ECB, and the International Monetary Fund [IMF]) financial package of €10 billion for the period 2013–2016 with a number of accompanying austerity measures, including a wholesale pruning of bank deposits, metaphorically referred to as the "Cyprus haircut."[18]

The Cypriot financial crisis has also affected Cyprus's relations with Ukraine, which like Russia had substantive economic interests in Cyprus and were badly hit by the haircut. In 2012, Cyprus and Ukraine tried to revamp relations. However, when the Ukraine crisis unfolded in 2014, Nicosia was torn between allegiance to its long-term ally Russia, Ukraine, and the EU. On the Ukraine crisis, Cyprus consistently harped on the necessity of a political solution and that sanctions should be applied "in a cautious and reserved manner."[19] Thus Cyprus has sided with those EU member states with a less hawkish approach to Russia. But it has also applied most of the restrictions agreed by the EU Council.

In the meantime, following the presidential election of February 2013, a new president, the conservative Nicos Anastasiades, took office, and he had no choice but to face the dire situation handed down to him by his predecessor. The austerity measures included the restructuring of the Bank of Cyprus with the consequent laying off of around 2,500 employees; the complete closure of one of the main Cypriot banks, Laiki, which was absorbed by the Bank of Cyprus; cuts in civil service salaries and benefits; increases in taxation; a tax on deposits of over €100,000; the replacement of some deposits with bonds; huge losses of more than 40 percent on uninsured deposits; the strengthening of anti–money laundering measures; and a privatization program. As *The Economist* observed, the bailout made the Cypriot recession worse than previously forecasted.[20] In the same vein, Andreas Theophanous described the decisions as very harsh and destructive, further suggesting a temporary Cypriot exit from the Eurozone unless the EU was ready to change its approach to make it possible for Cyprus to recover without having to leave it.[21]

In the wake of the Cyprus banking and financial crisis, sections of the international press were ready to compare Malta and Luxembourg with Cyprus and Iceland on the grounds that the former countries' financial institutions also held deposits far in excess of their GDP.[22] The issue had two dimensions: the extent to which Malta's and Luxembourg's banks were exposed to bad debt and the liabilities that would devolve to the national authorities and deposit guarantee schemes in the event of a banking collapse.

In July 2013, the Malta Financial Services Authority said that although events in Europe (particularly Cyprus) had "heightened perceptions about the risks of hosting a large banking sector in a small country . . . these perceptions were closely analyzed by major global institutions and agencies, including the European Commission, the IMF, Standard & Poor's, Fitch, Bloomberg and Reuters, who agreed that the size of the Maltese banking sector presented no particular risk."[23] The authority quoted the IMF, which said, "In the case of Malta, these risks are contained because the large international banking segment has limited balance sheet exposures to the Maltese economy and negligible contingent claims on the deposit compensation scheme."[24] The Maltese banks were hardly exposed to Greek bonds.

The deterioration of Cyprus's financial solvency has several other facets. Reliable press reports claim that the Pikis Commission report[25] blamed the Cypriot government led by Christofias for the crisis due to his profligate public spending, which saw the national debt nearly double between 2008 and 2012, jumping from 48.9 percent of GDP to 86.6 percent. This spending effectively weakened the Nicosia authorities' capacity to deal with the crisis when it struck. However, an independent report by the Central Bank of Cyprus published around the time of the Pikis Commission report, not only confirmed most of the latter's findings but also emphasized the other source of trouble, namely, the deteriorating balance sheet of the private banks due to the lack of adequate supervision, a failure that was also blamed on the government.[26] In the words of the report,

> the banks engaged in imprudent lending both domestically and through their rapid expansion abroad, mainly in Greece and East Europe because of failures in their risk management systems and poor lending practices. This included taking on an inappropriate and ultimately fatal €5.7bn exposure to Greek Government Bonds (GGBs). . . . In 2012, private sector indebtedness in Cyprus reached 271 per cent of GDP, the highest level in the EU, with most of this secured on property that was declining in value.[27]

In the wake of the EU recession, the Cypriot and Maltese economies experienced a downturn in 2009, but the following year they bounced back, though the Cypriot economy did so with lower growth rates than the Maltese one. The Cypriot economy kept growing until the end of 2011, when it suddenly nosedived with GDP contracting by 2.4 percent and 5.4 percent in 2012 and 2013, respectively (see Table 19.1). The difference in the economic fortunes of the countries is stark but cannot be attributed to bad luck (or the lack of Machiavelli's "fortuna"). Just like Iceland, Cyprus and Malta being small would have been predicted as lacking the human capacity, knowledge, and information to adequately engage in the proper supervision of their international financial services sectors. However, Malta managed to set up adequate supervisory institutions, whereas Cyprus did not. In addition, the Maltese banking sector was divided into two distinct spheres: two large banks that borrowed and loaned locally and were thus exposed only to domestic liabilities, with negligible foreign ones, and foreign banks, which raised finance overseas and lent in the international markets and had limited liabilities in the domestic Maltese economy.

It is evident that membership of the EMU has not managed to restrain public spending in Cyprus and Malta, and both countries need to curb their national debt and government spending to prepare themselves for future economic crises. Being small, Cyprus and Malta have very open economies, which makes them more susceptible to international shocks. This means that they need to be more prudent in building up their economic resilience. The EU offers shelter to small states, but the Cypriot experience shows that this shelter is not unlimited. Small states need to have clear policies on how to employ membership as a shelter, and they must be ready to implement the appropriate national measures to make the best use of it. They must avoid risky policies.

EU Effect on Domestic and Foreign Policies

EU membership has had an effect on the domestic and foreign policies of Cyprus and Malta. The island states ratified the Treaty Establishing a Constitution for Europe in mid-2005 and the Lisbon Treaty, which succeeded it, in 2008. Malta joined the Schengen Agreement abolishing passport and other border controls at the end of 2007, and Cyprus is going through the Schengen evaluation to determine whether it can be allowed to join. Cyprus's main difficulty is that although it wishes to join and has no opt-out from the agreement, it is prevented from doing so by the central government's lack of control of the northern part of the island, which is under Turkish occupation.

Cyprus and Malta take their turns at the EU rotating presidency of the Council, which gives them the chance to influence EU developments. Cyprus held the presidency between July and December 2012, the period when it was grappling with its own economic crisis. Malta is preparing to take it on at the start of 2017. The Cypriot presidency also had to confront an additional problem provoked by Turkey, which froze its relations with the presidency of the Council for the whole of the Cypriot presidency. During this period, Turkey did not align itself with EU positions or statements in international forums. On December 9, 2011, just before the start of the Cypriot presidency, the European Council warned Turkey against such a drastic course of action.[28] Turkey's behavior is related to the unresolved Cyprus conflict and Ankara's determination to avoid anything that smacks of a direct or indirect recognition of the Republic of Cyprus.

Table 19.1 General Government Debt, Government Deficit, and GDP Growth of Cyprus and Malta

	2002	2003	2004	2005	2006	2007	2008	2009	2010	2011	2012	2013	2014
General Government Gross Debt as a percentage of GDP and in raw terms (millions of euro)													
Cyprus	65.1	69.7	70.9	69.4	64.7	58.8	48.9	58.5	61.3	71.5	86.6	111.7	
	7246.2	8093.3	8963.3	9490.7	9445.0	9307.3	8388.2	9864.5	10674.5	12778.4	15349.5	18442.2	
Malta	57.9	66.0	69.8	68.0	62.5	60.7	60.9	66.5	66.0	68.8	70.8	73.0	
	2632.6	3022.3	3211.9	3355.4	3253.6	3385.1	3632.5	3962.6	4257.7	4607.3	4871.2	5243.1	
General Government Deficit as percentage of GDP													
Cyprus	4.4	-6.6	-4.1	-2.4	-1.2	3.5	0.9	-6.1	-5.3	-6.3	-6.4	-5.4	
Malta	-5.7	-9.0	-4.6	-2.9	-2.7	-2.3	-4.6	-3.7	-3.5	-2.7	-3.3	-2.8	
Real GDP Growth rate in percentages													
Cyprus	2.1	1.9	4.2	3.9	4.1	5.1	3.6	-1.9	1.3	0.4	-2.4	-5.4	-2.3
Malta	2.4	0.7	-0.3	3.6	2.6	4.1	3.9	-2.8	4.2	1.5	0.8	2.6	3.5

Source: Eurostat - General Government Gross Debt as a percentage of GDP; General government deficit/surplus. At http://ec.europa.eu/eurostat/web/government-finance-statistics/data/main-tables (accessed April 16, 2015).

Previously a similar dispute, which is still unresolved, was provoked by Turkey on July 29, 2005, in the context of the signing of the protocol to extend the EU-Turkey Customs Union agreement to the new member states that joined the EU in 2004. Ankara issued a unilateral declaration stating that by signing the protocol it was not in any way recognizing the Republic of Cyprus.[29] Effectively this meant that Turkish ports and airports would remain closed to Cypriot ships and airplanes until a comprehensive settlement of the Cyprus problem could be reached. Turkey's stand went against the letter and spirit of the protocol, forcing the EU to issue a counter declaration on September 21, 2005, declaring Turkey's position to be illegal and calling on her to observe the protocol.[30]

Significantly, both Cyprus and Malta have joined the European Defense Agency. However, both experienced difficulties in participating in the "Berlin plus" arrangement establishing cooperation between NATO and the EU, allowing the latter to use NATO assets to mount its operations. This was mainly due to Turkey's objections since participation in the Berlin plus requires countries to be members of NATO or its Partnership for Peace (PfP). Malta had joined PfP in 1995, left it a year later, and reactivated its membership in 2008, following which it no longer faced problems in the Common Security and Defence Policy. Cyprus cannot join NATO or the PfP without overcoming Turkey's objections. Turkey's policy has paralyzed the Berlin plus and considerably restricted Cyprus's participation in EU operations.

The military assets of Cyprus and Malta are shown in Table 19.2. The Cypriot armed forces number more than seven times those of Malta, but the latter plays a bigger role in EU operations overseas. In fact, Malta participates in five EU peacekeeping operations—EU NAVFOR Op Atlanta operating off the Coast of Somalia, EU training Mission Somalia, EUFOR Libya, EUBAM Rafah, and EUMM Georgia. In addition the Armed Forces of Malta regularly

Table 19.2 Defense Data for Cyprus and Malta, 2012

	Cyprus	Malta
Total Defense Expenditure	€323 million	€39 million
Defense Expenditure as a Percentage of GDP	1.81%	0.58%
Defense Expenditure per Capita	€370	€93
Number of Military Personnel	11,932	1,510
Number of Civilian Personnel	711	97
Average Number of Troops Deployed	4	20
Average Number of Troops Deployed as Percentage of Total Number of Military Personnel	0.03%	1.3%
Deployable Land Forces	173	105

Source: European Defence Agency, Defence Data Portal at http://www.eda.europa.eu/info-hub /defence-data-partal/Malta/year/2012

post troops in Bosnia Herzegovina under the umbrella of the Organization for Security and Co-operation in Europe to monitor compliance with the Dayton Peace Accords. Under the UN flag Malta twice deployed personnel to the Interim Force in Lebanon. From 2008 onward, Malta has deployed an officer at the EU NAVFOR Operational Headquarters in Northwood, UK (Operation Atlanta). Twelve military personnel including two officers were deployed aboard the Dutch naval vessel *Johan de Witt* in April 2010, and further deployments were made each year up to the present. Three noncommissioned officers were deployed with three members of the Irish Defence Forces as part of EUTM Somalia (based in Uganda) to train members of the Somali army; five military personnel have been involved with EUFOR Libya including two at the force headquarters in Rome. Maltese armed forces officers were placed in readiness to participate in EUBAM Rafah, an EU mission to guard the Rafah crossing into Gaza; two personnel have been regularly deployed in the observer mission in Georgia.[31]

This Maltese activism in international EU-staffed peacekeeping operations is backed by government and opposition—in short, by cross-party consensus between the only two parties represented in the Maltese parliament—the governing Labor Party (LP) and the Opposition Nationalist Party (PN). The LP used to oppose such involvement, and at one point when it was still in opposition, also threatened to withdraw Malta from the European Defence Agency once elected to government. However, it later dropped its objections as it did to Malta's participation in the PfP. Up to 2008, the LP also took a rather doctrinaire approach to the interpretation of neutrality enshrined in the Maltese constitution. Today both parties agree on the need to change the neutrality clauses in the constitution although they have been unable to settle down to actually discussing any changes.[32]

Public Opinion and Support for the EU

The Eurozone crisis has had a predictable effect on Cyprus and Malta. Public opinion surveys carried out by Eurobarometer (summarized in Table 19.3) bring this out clearly. The main question asked is "In general, does the EU conjure up for you a very positive, fairly positive, neutral, fairly negative or very negative image?" The results show that since 2009 the positive sentiment toward the EU has shrunk by half in Cyprus, from 51 percent in 2009 to 26 percent in 2014. The positive sentiment sank to its lowest level in 2013, when the effect of the austerity measures began to be felt, and correspondingly the percentage of Cypriots with a negative image peaked at 54 percent and 59 percent that same year.

In the same period, Malta's public support for the EU hovered between 36 percent and 48 percent, while the negative sentiment ranged between 9 percent and 23 percent. In Malta's case, those holding a neutral position ranged between 30 percent and 45 percent. The decline in the positive sen-

Table 19.3 Public Opinion in Cyprus and Malta,ᵃ percentage

	Cyprus			Malta		
	Positive	Negative	Neutral	Positive	Negative	Neutral
EB82						
2014	24	38	35	47	8	44
EB81						
2014	26	38	35	43	9	45
EB80						
2013	17	54	29	41	14	43
EB79						
2013	17	59	24	45	15	37
EB78						
2012	25	44	31	37	23	36
EB77						
2012	29	36	34	36	22	39
EB76						
2011	39	21	39	36	19	41
EB75						
2011	42	20	38	36	20	39
EB74						
2010	33	25	42	43	16	35
EB73						
2010	37	26	36	48	17	30
EB72						
2009	51	32	16	46	18	32

Source: Eurobarometer, specific issues indicated wtih EB(volume number) above.

Notes: a. Responses to the question: "In general, does the EU conjure up for you a very positive, fairly positive, neutral, fairly negative, or very negative image?"

Positive and Negative columns include "very" positive/negative and "fairly" positive/negative, respectively, added to produce total positive and total negative.

timent between the second half of 2010 and the end of 2012 was mostly due to public concern about the future of the Eurozone. From the start of 2013, public opinion began to turn more positive while at the same time the negative sentiment declined.

The European Elections

On joining the EU, Cyprus was allocated six seats in the European Parliament (EP) and Malta five, despite the fact that its population was comparable to that of Luxembourg, which had six seats. Following the ratification of the Treaty of Lisbon, Malta's seats were increased to six. Given the legislative importance of the EP, particularly since the Treaty of Lisbon came into effect, the small number of seats allocated to Cyprus and Malta using the principle of "digressive proportionality" makes it difficult for them to participate in all the key EP committees. Cypriot members of the EP (MEPs) have given importance to the powerful Foreign Affairs Committee, where EU relations with Turkey feature regularly, and the EP Delegation for Relations with Turkey. Two Cypriot MEPs have participated in each of these bodies since 2004. The Maltese MEPs' interests have been more mixed, but three committees in particular, the budgets, petitions, and the committee on civil liberties, justice and home affairs, where migration issues are discussed, seem to have a special attraction for them.

Certain trends emerging from the first three European elections held in Cyprus and Malta (see Tables 19.4 and 19.5) are significant. Voter turnout is markedly below that of national elections (parliamentary and presidential in the case of Cyprus) and in decline. Turnout is declining faster in Cyprus than in Malta. In Cyprus it accelerated slightly between 2009 and 2014, probably due to the unpopularity of the EU after the financial crisis and the imposition of austerity. Both island states elected an all-male delegation of MEPs in the 2004 election, but while Cyprus elected three women MEPs in subsequent elections, Malta elected seven. Indeed, following the 2014 election the ratio of male to female Maltese MEPs is two to four. Since 2004, no Euro-skeptic party from Cyprus and Malta managed to secure representation in the EP, except two parties that previously opposed membership. The Cypriot Communist Party and the Maltese Labor Party, which radically opposed membership, have done well. The Cypriot Communist Party has managed to elect two MEPs in each of the three European elections. In Malta, the LP changed its policy on membership in 2004 and went on to elect more MEPs than the governing PN in 2004 and 2009. Following its 2013 national election victory by a wide margin of votes and a nine-seat parliamentary majority, the LP was expected to hang on to its MEP majority in the 2014 European election. However, it missed the fourth MEP seat by a whisker despite outpacing the PN by a margin of more than 13 percent and an overall difference of 33,000 votes. The six seats were shared equally between the LP and PN.

Participation in the EP has helped the two island states pursue some of their national priorities: migration in the case of Malta, the "Cyprus problem" in the case of Cyprus. The EP has been reluctant to involve itself concretely in the Cyprus conflict. Applying the same realpolitik approach adopted by the European Council, it has preferred to allow the parties involved—Cyprus, Greece, Turkey, and the UK—to negotiate under UN auspices. Criticism of Turkey on its human rights record and other serious failings such as its stubborn reluctance to fully implement the 2005 protocol on the customs union, have not gone beyond declaratory EP resolutions. The EP was very hostile toward Cyprus after the Greek Cypriots rejected the Annan plan for the reunification of the island in a referendum held just prior to membership in April 2004. Pat Cox, then EP president, had issued a statement deeply regretting the outcome of the referendum among the Greek Cypriot community, adding that "it is regrettable that the referendum did not produce a change of heart, despite the fact that the problem is not what it was

Table 19.4 Malta: European Elections and National Voter Turnout

		Turnout	LP MPs/ MEPs	LP % of Vote	PN MPs/ MEPs	PN % of Vote	Gender Male	Gender Female
2004	Europe	82.4	3	48.4	2	39.8	6	0
	National Parl.	95.7						
2009[a]	Europe	78.8	4	54.8	2	40.5	6	0
	National Parl.	93.3					3	3
2014	Europe	74.8	3	53.4	3	40.0	2	4
	National Parl.	93						

Source: EEP and Eurostat Election Databases and national agencies; Electoral Commission Malta
Notes: National Election in Malta took place in 2003, 2008, and 2013.
a. In 2009, three Maltese MEPs resigned after they were elected to the national parliament. In the by-elections, three women MEPs were elected.

thirty years ago."[33] This statement soothed Turkish disappointments but angered the Greek Cypriots. Since the forcible division of the island in 1974, an act that has been universally condemned, the Greek Cypriots have considered themselves to be the aggrieved party. However, the presence of Cypriot MEPs in the Parliament, particularly in the most influential political groups, has redressed the balance slightly in that institution.

The Maltese MEPs have mostly focused on the migration problem in the central Mediterranean. They have done so in conjunction with the efforts made by their government at the Council level. In the EP, the Maltese effort has involved a two-pronged initiative: one in the Budgets Committee to ensure that EU initiatives to tackle the migration problem, particularly the financing of the EU border agency Frontex, are well financed; the other was to seek revision of the so-called Dublin Two (EU) Regulation, which among other things places the responsibility for asylum seekers arriving at the EU's border on the member state concerned. A revision of this regulation would pave the way for a policy of sharing the "burden" or "responsibility" throughout the EU. The need for a common approach to migration has become more urgent in recent years following a surge in "boat people" crossing the Mediterranean on their way to Europe and the loss of human life associated with it. According to Tom Miles, in the first half of 2014, there was a 60 percent increase in the number of such migrants arriving on Europe's Mediterranean shores—100,000 people by the end of July. It is estimated that some 800 people went missing as a result of tragedies on the high seas.[34] An estimated 308 of these refugees landed in Malta. Most of them come from Syria, Eritrea, Libya, and other trouble spots in Africa. The United States and the EU operate resettlement schemes. In 2009, the European Council approved the EU's pilot project on intra-EU relocation from Malta (EUREMA), which

Table 19.5 Cyprus: European Elections and National Voter Turnout

	Turnout		DISY		DIKO		AKEL		EDEK[a]		Other		Gender	
			MPs/MEPs	% of Vote	MPs/MEPs	% of Vote	MPs/MEPs	% of Vote	MPs/MEPs	% of Vote	MPs/MEPs	% of Vote	Male	Female
2004	Europe	72.5	2	28.2	1	17.1	2	27.9	0	10.79	1[b]	10.8	6	0
	Presidency	90.5												
	National Leg.	91.8												
2009[a]	Europe	59.4	2	35.7	1	12.3	2	34.9	1	9.9	0	0	4	2
	Presidency	90.8												
	National Leg.	89.0												
2014	Europe	43.9	2	37.8	1	10.8	2	27	1	7.7	0	0	5	1
	Presidency	81.6												
	National Leg.	78.7												

Source: EEP and Eurostat Election Databases and national agencies

Notes: Presidential elections took place in 2003, 2008, and 2013. National Election took place in 2003, 2008, and 2013.

a. In the 2009 election, the Cypriot party EDEK joined the ALDE group in the EP; in 2014 they joined the S&D.

b. Party for Europe contested only once.

has been renewed periodically since then. Maltese efforts on the migration issue have also led to the establishment of the European Asylum Support Office in Malta.[35] The UN High Commissioner for Refugees (UNHCR) estimates that less than 30 percent of the estimated 19,000 refugees who arrived in Malta since 2002 remain on the island.[36] Around 2,500 refugees have been relocated since the start of the relocation schemes in 2005.[37]

Cyprus faces an equally daunting task. According to the UNHCR, between 2003 and 2013, Cyprus received some 48,000 applications for refugee status.[38] These applications started declining in 2009, but they may start increasing again as a result of the conflicts in Syria, Iraq, and Gaza. Both Cyprus and Malta keep applicants for refugee status in detention centers until their applications are processed. The conditions in these centers, which are financed largely from the EU budget, have raised the ire of several human rights groups.

Natural Gas and the Cyprus Problem

Before the 2004 enlargement, hopes were entertained of a solution to the Cyprus problem once it joined the Union. In April 2004, just before the date of accession, two referenda were organized in the Greek and Turkish parts of the island on the Annan plan negotiated under UN auspices which provided for a confederal unification of the island. While the plan was being negotiated, the citizens of Cyprus were practically kept in the dark on its contents. This explains the knee-jerk reaction of the Greek Cypriots when they rejected the plan. This rejection raised hostilities against Greek Cypriots in EU official circles, and the exclusion of the Turkish Cypriots led to a few initiatives in their favor, including the opening of several border crossings in the green line separating the two parts of Cyprus as well as EU budgetary aid. Efforts by President Christofias (2008–2013) to resolve the issue led nowhere. Christofias had first supported the Annan plan, then retracted his support just before the referendum.

The Cypriot economic crisis and the discovery of offshore gas reserves in Cyprus's Exclusive Economic Zone (EEZ) seemed to offer new conditions for a breakthrough, the assumption being that it would mellow the Republic of Cyprus's preconditions for a settlement. The exploitation of gas reserves was perceived not only as an answer to Cyprus's external energy dependence but also as a source of finance to help the island restore its economic balance. It would benefit gas-hungry Turkey and help diversify Europe's gas supplies at a time when such diversification was a priority due to the deteriorating relations with Russia. But any hopes that the existence of such wealth on the continental shelf would encourage a joint exploitation effort were dashed when Turkey threatened force to stop further exploration.

At the beginning of 2014, Turkish naval vessels intercepted and forced a Norwegian ship from prospecting in Cyprus's EEZ. Turkey is not a signatory to the UN Convention on the Law of the Sea, and the EU has repeatedly called on her to ratify it. Furthermore, the EU stresses "the sovereign rights of EU Member States which include, inter alia, entering into bilateral agreements, and to explore and exploit their natural resources in accordance with the EU *acquis* and international law, including the UN Convention on the Law of the Sea."[39] The international community, including the United States, upholds Cyprus's claims to its EEZ. Instead of incentivizing a solution to the Cyprus problem, the dispute over exploration rights in the EEZ has in the words of Cypriot foreign minister Ioannis Kasoulides (a former MEP) led to a throwback to the age of gunboat diplomacy.[40]

"Hope springs eternal" in the Cyprus problem. In February 2014, the president of the Republic, Nicos Anastasiades, and the leader of the Turkish Cypriot community, Derviş Eroğlu, made a joint declaration initiating "structured" negotiations under UN auspices. The momentum of this new round of talks is subdued, but the leaders of the two communities have pledged to put everything on the negotiating table and seek solutions, following which any agreement reached will be put to a referendum in the two communities.[41] Former EU Commission president José Manuel Barroso, who left his post, appointed Peter Van Nuffel as his personal envoy for Cyprus, but the new president, John-Claude Juncker, has not appointed his envoy.

The Influence of Cyprus and Malta on the EU

In the first decade of EU membership, Cyprus and Malta moved along the learning curve and busied themselves with implementing the EU *acquis*, a process that is broadly referred to in the academic literature as Europeanization. This adaptation process has required them to download a number of policies, structures, and practices, which are ingrained in the EU. However, they have found it difficult to upload their own policy objectives on to the EU except in rare cases, such as Malta's successful effort to engage the EU in the tackling its migration problem. Cyprus has been markedly less successful in pursuing a lasting solution to the Cyprus problem. It has also had to face a barrage of hostility from Turkey as in the case of the Berlin plus, the 2005 protocol extending the customs union, the closure of Turkish ports to Cypriot traffic, Ankara's boycott of Cyprus's EU presidency, and gunboat diplomacy in its EEZ.

In the EP the two island states have projected their influence. Cyprus has managed to claw back some of the support it lost in the aftermath of the 2004 Annan plan referenda. It had the opportunity to stamp its influence on the EU during its preparations for and the gestation of the rotating presidency in the second half of 2012. However, this opportunity was hampered by the financial crisis, which hit it in 2011. That year must surely be recorded in its history as an *annus horribilis*, considering also the explosion that devastated the Evangelos Florakis Naval Base and led to the destruction of a power station supplying half of Cyprus's electricity.

The two island states' integration in the EU has made them more economically and socially open. However, it is difficult to determine where the source of this greater openness lies—whether in the process of European integration or from globalization. Certainly the EU with its interconnections with the rest of the world acts as the islands' gateway to the global system. Openness has accelerated nascent processes within their societies, leading to some deep changes that would have otherwise taken a long time to mature. Malta introduced divorce in 2011, which for decades had been blocked by the Catholic Church.[42] On April 14, 2014, it legalized same-sex unions with the possibility of adoptions.[43] Cyprus has changed its laws to improve the respect of civil and human rights, but a bill granting more rights to the LGBT community is still languishing in Parliament, unable to make any progress due to the opposition of the Greek Orthodox Church. The EU has no power to enforce changes in the legal regime on such issues as LGBT rights, divorce, or in vitro fertilization because these competencies are the preserve of the member states. What the process of EU integration does is strengthen the milieu of knowledge and information in which the domestic political debate occurs, thus facilitating change.

The role of the media—local and international, the traditional and the newer social media—is also crucial. They shape outlooks and political discourse. Networks that are wholly or partly promoted by EU funding, such as those involving the exchange of teachers, students, and researchers; the promotion of language training; the growing ease of travel resulting from the strengthening of EU communications networks and infrastructure, including the freedom of the skies, which has made low-cost air travel easier; the consolidation of pan-European highways; the Internet; and the growth of tourism can have big impacts on changing insular societies, which is what has been happening in Cyprus and Malta since they joined the EU.

Conclusion

The analysis in this chapter has traced the contours of the EU experience of Cyprus and Malta to see whether the EU can indeed act as a shelter for small states and in what sense. The discussion establishes that membership satisfies the small state's main concerns of access to larger markets and allies with whom to protect itself in the global economy and world negotiations. However, this shelter is not unfettered, and unless a member state adopts the right kind of policies, it can find itself in trouble and lose effectiveness over other goals it wishes to achieve.

What is evident in the case of Cyprus and Malta is that they have managed to upload some of their national priorities on the EU, but progress on the Cyprus problem was not realized, as previously hoped, while the country felt badly treated when it faced its financial crisis. Cypriot backlash against the EU as shown by opinion polls is thus understandable. But the case of the Cypriot financial crisis also shows the cost of not adapting on time. Cyprus had long postponed reforms to strengthen supervision of the financial sector and discourage money laundering activities. This weakened its position considerably when it asked the EU for a financial rescue plan. The Cyprus haircut shows that the shelter the EU offers to small states is not unlimited, and it will not cover imprudent behavior.

Adopting the EU *acquis*, a process of Europeanization, has not raised insurmountable difficulties for the two states. Since 2008, Malta made a remarkable adaptation in its approach to the Common Security and Defence Policy by fully engaging in it, including in the EU's peacekeeping missions abroad.

Small size and lack of human capacity make it difficult for small states to understand many economic, social, and political trends and processes and where they are heading. At the same time, small states show a remarkable capacity to bounce back, and it is likely that if Cyprus eventually manages to exploit its considerable gas resources, it will definitely do so, as it did after the devastation caused by the 1974 Turkish invasion.

Participation in decisionmaking institutions provides small states with a voice in the decisionmaking process. Representation in the European Parliament gives them the opportunity to pursue their objectives in that institution as well, particularly since the Lisbon Treaty increased the EP's powers. But such participation, comprising also the European elections, can affect the internal equilibria in their own domestic politics. The European elections in Cyprus and Malta have smoothed the way for the integration of Euro-skeptical parties (AKEL and LP) in the European political mainstream. They have also led to the participation of more women in Cypriot and Maltese politics. The methods of the European Parliament are also having an effect on the two island states' national parliaments, which have gained new status as the guardians of the principle of subsidiarity since the Lisbon Treaty came into effect.

Appendix Table 19.A1 Main Political Events in Cyprus and Malta Since They Joined the EU

Year	Cyprus	Malta
2003	*16 February.* Presidential election; Tassos Papadopoulos elected president.	*8 March:* Membership referendum: 53.6% in favor, 46.4% against, turnout 91%. *12 April:* General election: Nationalist Party 51.8%, Labour Party 47.5%, turnout 96.9%.
2004	*24 April:* Separate referenda in the government controlled part of Cyprus and the northern part occupied by Turkey on the Annan Plan for the reunification of the islands. Result: Greek Cypriots: 24.17% vote in favor, 75.83% against; Turkish Cypriots: 64.90% in favor, 35.09% against. Turnout was 89% among Greek Cypriots and 87% among Turkish Cypriots. *1 May:* Joins the EU *13 June:* European election	*1 May:* Joins the EU *12 June:* European Election
2005	*30 June:* Cyprus becomes the eleventh member state to ratify the Treaty Establishing a Constitution for Europe	*6 July:* Malta becomes the twelfth member state to ratify the Treaty Establishing a Constitution for Europe
2006	*21 May:* House of Representatives elections	
2007		*21 December:* Joins the Schengen Agreement removing border controls on passenger travel within the area covered by the agreement
2008	*1 January:* Introduces the euro *17–24 February:* Presidential election; Dimitris Christofias elected president.	*1 January:* Introduces the euro *8 March:* General election; Nationalist Party returned to government by a narrow margin. *6 February:* Lisbon Treaty ratified
2009	*6 June:* European election	*6 June:* European election
2010		
2011	*22 May:* House of Representatives elections	*28 May:* Referendum on divorce
2012	*25 June:* Cyprus requests a bailout from the European Stability Mechanism *28 June:* Ratification of ESM Treaty *3 July:* Ratification of Article 136 *26 July:* Ratification if TSCG.	*19 July:* Ratification of ESM Treaty *2 October:* Ratification of Article 136
2013	*17–24 February:* Presidential election; Nicos Anastasiadis elected president *25 March:* €10 billion bailout for the country	*9 March:* General election; won by a nine seat majority by the LP *11 June:* TSCG ratified by parliament.
2014	*25 May:* European election	*24 May:* European election

Notes

1. For an account of Maltese euro, see Pace (2011).
2. See, for example, Bauwens et al. (1996), Goetschel (1998), Thorhallsson (2000), Pace (2000), Manners (2000), Bunse (2009), Steinmetz and Wivel (2010), and Panke (2010).
3. Stefanou (2005), Pace (2001), and Thorhallsson (2000, 2004).
4. Briguglio and Kisanga (2004), Briguglio et al. (2008).
5. Cooper and Shaw (2009), Archer and Nugent (2006), Archer, Bailes, and Wivel (2014).
6. Thorhallsson (2010), p. 209.
7. Vital (1972), p. 55.
8. Handel (1990), p. 235.
9. Radaelli (2003), p. 30.
10. Radaelli and Exadaktylos (2010).
11. Ibid.
12. Van Vooren (2010), p. 10.
13. Ibid., p. 21
14. Carammia and Pace (forthcoming).
15. European Commission, "Changeover to the Euro in Cyprus and Malta," press release IP/08/602, April 18, 2008. Available at http://europa.eu/rapid/press-release_IP -08-602_en.htm?locale=en (accessed August 5, 2014).
16. See European Commission website at http://europa.eu/legislation_summaries /economic_and_monetary_affairs/institutional_and_economic_framework/l25093_en. htm (accessed August 5, 2014).
17. Pace (2006).
18. Details of the rescue package can be found on the European Commission website at http://ec.europa.eu/economy_finance/assistance_eu_ms/cyprus/index_en.htm (accessed August 6, 2014).
19. Ministry of Foreign Affairs, Cyprus, "EU Restrictive Measures in Response to the Ukraine Crisis," press release, July 17, 2014.
20. "The Cypriot Economy: Through a Glass, Darkly," *The Economist*, April 27, 2013. Available at http://www.economist.com/news/finance-and-economics/21576666 -outlook-even-grimmer-it-was-time-bail-out-through.
21. Theophanous (2013), p. 17.
22. See, for example, Patrick Collinson, "The Bizarre Banking Loophole That Has Opened Up in Malta," *Guardian*, April 6, 2013, available at http://www.theguardian.com /money/blog/2013/apr/06/banking-loophole-malta (accessed April 6, 2013); Ian Traynor, "Cyprus's Banks Have Been Tamed—Are Malta and Luxembourg Next?," *Guardian*, March 25, 2013, available at http://www.theguardian.com/business/2013/mar/25/cyprus -banks-malta-luxembourg; Martin Santa, "Analysis: Malta Unlikely to Follow Cyprus into Crisis," Reuters, May 13, 2013, available at http://www.reuters.com/article/2013/05 /13/us-eurozone-malta-analysis-idUSBRE94C04H20130513.
23. Malta Financial Services Authority, "Economic and Market Overview," July 2013. Available at http://www.mfsa.com.mt/pages/publications.aspx?doc=eIMF (accessed August 8, 2014).
24. Ibid., quoting the IMF's "Malta—2013 Article IV Consultation Concluding Statement," May 15, 2013, pp. 7–8, available at www.imf.org/external/pubs/ft/scr/2013 /cr13203.pdf (accessed July 17, 2014).
25. Judge Georgios Pikis, a former Supreme Court president and member of the International Court of Justice in The Hague, chaired the three-member commission, set up on April 2, 2013. The other two members were Panayiotis Kallis and Yiannakis Constantinides, both former Supreme Court judges who later resigned and were replaced with Andreas Kramvi, a former Supreme Court judge, and Eliana Nicolaou, a former ombudswoman and judge. The (Greek) reference to the report seems to be the

following: Pikis, G. M., Kramvis, A., and Nicolaou, E., (2013), ς Επιτροπής για τη Διεξαγωγή Έρευνας Σχετικά με την Κατάσταση στην οποία Περιήλθε το Τραπεζικό Σύστημα καυπριακής Δημοκρατίας.But there is no Url address.

26. Central Bank of Cyprus, "Independent Commission on the Future of the Cyprus Banking Sector: Final Report and Recommendations," October 2013. Available at http://www.centralbank.gov.cy/nqcontent.cfm?a_id=12561&lang=en (accessed July 17, 2014).

27. Ibid., point 3.4.2, p. 22.

28. European Commission, "Turkey: 2013 Progress Report," Staff Working Document, Brussels, October 16, 2013, p. 4, available at http://ec.europa.eu/enlargement /countries/detailed-country-information/turkey/index_en.htm accessed August 6, 2014), referring to European Council (2011) Conclusions, point 14: "Recalling the Council conclusions of 5 December on enlargement, with regard to Turkish statements and threats, the European Council expresses serious concern and calls for full respect for the role of the Presidency of the Council, which is a fundamental institutional feature of the EU provided for in the Treaty."

29. Ministry of Foreign Affairs (Republic of Turkey), "Declaration by Turkey on Cyprus," July 29, 2005. Available at http://www.mfa.gov.tr/declaration-by-turkey-on -cyprus_-29-july-2005.en.mfa (accessed July 20, 2014).

30. European Union, "EU Enlargement: Turkey—Declaration by European Community and Member States," Brussels, September 21, 2005. Available at http://eu-un .europa.eu/articles/en/article_5045_en.htm (accessed July 17, 2014).

31. Details are available on the website of the Armed Forces of Malta at http://www .afm.gov.mt and Common Security and Defence Policy website at http://www.eeas.europa .eu/csdp/missions-and-operations/.

32. For a brief discussion of Maltese neutrality see Pace (2013).

33. "Statement by Pat Cox on the Referendum in Cyprus," press release by the president of the European Parliament, Brussels, April 24, 2004. Available at http://www.europarl.europa.eu/former_ep_presidents/president-cox/press/en/cp0110.htm (accessed September 3, 2014).

34. Tom Miles, "Mediterranean Boat People Numbers Soar to Near 100,000 This Year," Reuters, Geneva, July 24, 2014. Available at http://www.reuters.com/article /2014/07/24/us-europe-migrants-idUSKBN0FT1UK20140724 (accessed August 8, 2014). These figures are corroborated by the UN High Commissioner for Refugees, which in a midyear update states that 88,000 refugees were landed in Italy in the first half of 2014 as a result of the Italian rescue mission Mare Nostrum. See http://www .unhcr.org.mt/news-and-views/press-releases/753 (accessed August 10, 2014).

35. European Union (2010).

36. Ibid.

37. Ibid.

38. UNHCR Office in Cyprus, newsletter, January–April 2014. Available at http://www.unhcr.org.cy/ (accessed August 10, 2014).

39. European Commission (2013), p. 17.

40. Ambrose Evans-Pritchard, "Gas Bonanza for Cyprus Hostage to Strategic Battle with Turkey," *Telegraph*, February 18, 2014. Available at http://www .telegraph.co.uk/finance/newsbysector/energy/oilandgas/10647382/Gas-bonanza-for-Cyprus-hostage-to-strategic-battle-with-Turkey.html (accessed July 7, 2014).

41. Press and Information Office (Cyprus), "Joint Declaration of the Two Leaders on the Re-Launching of the Talks on the Cyprus Problem," Cyprus Government Press Office, February 11, 2014. Available at http://www.moi.gov.cy/moi/pio/pio.nsf /index_en/index_en?opendocument (accessed August 10, 2014).

42. Pace (2012).

43. Act IX, "An Act to Regulate Civil Unions and to Provide for Matters Connected Therewith or Ancillary Thereto," 2014.

20

Latvia, Lithuania, and Estonia: Successful Adaptation

Renee Buhr

THE BALTIC STATES OF LATVIA, LITHUANIA, AND ESTONIA ARE OFTEN included in the list of highly successful European Union (EU) accession states. According to Anders Åslund, the Baltics were particularly "clever" in their adoption of market and political reforms that led to systems he characterizes as "full-fledged market economies with limited public sectors and high economic growth . . . democracy and limited corruption."[1] In this chapter, these cases are used to examine three aspects of the interaction between domestic and EU politics. These aspects are (1) the role that the EU played in the transitions of these governments and their economies, (2) the interaction between domestic politics in EU member states and the EU itself, and (3) the potential for accession states and the EU to weather critical events such as the recent world economic crisis.

As will become evident, none of these interactions are as simple as they may appear at first glance. The economic policies adopted by the Baltics seem to be taken directly from the neoliberal economic playbook; however, scholars argue that this relationship is far more complex than a simple adoption of policies recommended by international organizations (IOs) such as the International Monetary Fund (IMF) or the EU. Likewise, the interaction between domestic politics and the EU is complicated and the powerful influence of the EU is addressed only sporadically in domestic political contests. In the following pages, these international and domestic factors will be examined in order to explain policies in the Baltic states and the relationship of those policies to EU membership. In short, Euro-skepticism and economic crises have had limited effects on the governments' commitments to neoliberal economic policies or voting behavior, and in this way the Baltics differ significantly from some of their fellow EU member states.

The Coincidence of EU/IO Policy Prescriptions and Policy Adoption in the Baltics

The economic characteristics praised by Åslund are hallmarks of the neoliberal economic thinking typical of international organizations such as the EU, IMF, and World Bank in the 1990s. Washington Consensus–based policy recommendations included fiscal discipline, tax reforms lowering marginal rates, trade liberalization, openness to foreign direct investment, and privatization.[2] Later, the Copenhagen criteria and the policies recommended to accession states by the EU included macroeconomic stability (price stability and attention to balance of payments), openness in trade, and "limited state influence on competitiveness."[3] Since the Baltic states desired the assistance of international organizations such as the IMF and future membership in the EU, the incentives to pursue policies in line with those suggested by these bodies appears obvious.

East European states looking to attract capital to assist in their transition to viable market economies were encouraged to keep their taxes low, their barriers to financial transactions minimal, and their currencies stable to attract capital investment in the form of foreign direct investment (FDI) and private investment.[4] The Baltic states adopted a formula of capital mobility and exchange rate stability (by pegging currencies to the euro and later working to join the Eurozone) and fueled the "miraculous" growth of their economies during the 1990s with the resultant capital flows from foreign banks.[5] These states also adopted business-friendly policies such as low tax rates, low levels of regulation, and relatively low wage rates while minimizing the social welfare system and unemployment expenditures.

From 1991 to 2008, the Baltics were dubbed "economic tigers" and from 2000 to 2007 saw average real GDP growth rates of 7.5 percent, 8.2 percent, and 8.6 percent for Lithuania, Estonia, and Latvia, respectively.[6] Although some of the growth was driven by liberalized trade, a great deal of it was the result of capital inflows in the form of FDI and private investment funded primarily by Scandinavian banks. The initial resulting economic growth was spectacular; however, this model of growth also makes a state "particularly prone to both debt-led growth during upswings and FDI reversals during downswings."[7]

When the economic crisis hit the Baltics, it hit them hard. Latvia experienced a −4.6 percent change in real GDP growth in 2008 and −17.7 percent in 2009. In the same years, Lithuania's numbers were 2.8 percent and −14.8 percent. Unemployment rates were abysmal, even when compared with a number of other EU member states outside the Eurozone, with Latvia experiencing 17.1 percent unemployment in 2009 and 18.7 percent in 2010, Lithuania at 13.7 percent in 2009 and 17.8 percent in 2010, and Estonia at 12 percent in 2010 and 14 percent in 2011. Inflation spiked in Estonia in 2008 to 10 percent; in Latvia and Lithuania it rose into double digits in 2007 and 2008 but was brought under control by 2010 as a result of the crisis and through "internal devaluation" policies that included wage, pension, and budget cuts.[8] Public expenditures remained below that of Eurozone states, so the tentative recoveries of these economies since 2011 have been fueled primarily by private borrowing and consumption.[9] Throughout this period of hardship, the Baltic governments maintained a commitment to austerity, and outsiders praised this commitment and the purported quiescence of the Baltic states' populations, in spite of evidence of economic policy debates and even protest in Latvia and Lithuania.

The level of protest has been muted compared with other EU member states. A number of explanations have been forwarded to explain this phenomenon: the relative weakness of labor unions, emigration as a means of escape from skyrocketing unemployment, long-term hardship that has left vulnerable populations hopeless and demotivated, and legal/administrative barriers to protest.[10] Likewise, few policy changes can be seen in the Baltics, even in the face of hardship and protest. Finally, the rapid rise in Euro-skeptic voting seen in other EU member states has not been echoed in the Baltics, in spite of the hardship and protest of austerity measures easily attributed to EU decisions. In the following section, the existing arguments for this EU-compliant behavior are addressed.

Scholarly Explanations for the Coincidence of Policies Adopted

The apparent similarities between EU-suggested policy and economic policies adopted by the Baltics could lead one to believe that EU and international economic organizations were able to strong-arm the Baltics into accepting their suggestions wholesale. It could even appear that domestic actors had no agency in the key economic and political decisions made during the postcommunist transition. Scholars dispute both of these assumptions, arguing that many factors—material, ideational, international, and domestic—led to the creation of the Baltic version of postcommunist transition.

Each author addressed herein aims to answer the question: what led certain postcommunist states to adopt liberal (political and economic) policies and institutions? They emphasize some particular mechanism or pathway, and these pathways can be crudely broken down into two main divides: rationalist versus constructivist and international versus domestic actors. The term *emphasize* should be noted here since most scholars integrate these pathways. Figure 20.1 depicts these pathways.

There are three pathways under the rubric of "rationalist." The first begins with a material desire for the benefits of EU membership, which leads domestic policymakers to adopt policies in compliance with EU conditionality. According to Judith Kelley, "states respond to incentives and sanctions imposed

Figure 20.1 Post-Soviet Transition of the Baltic States

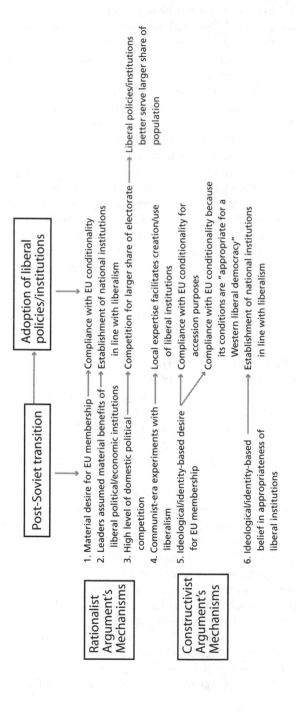

by international actors, thereby maximizing their payoffs."[11] Åslund's explanation appears to fit into pathways one and two, as he discusses the roles of the international community (EU and international economic organizations) and the elites in states such as Poland, who drew up plans for transition to the market economy.[12] Rachel Vanderhill and Milada Anna Vachudova discuss the intersection of pathways one, two, and three, explaining EU-compliant policy behaviors as the result of the material benefits of EU accession and the ways these interacted with domestic elites' own material (and electoral) interests.[13]

Communist-era experiments are cited in the works of Keith Darden and Lik Bennich-Björkman and Branka Likić-Brborić, as depicted in pathway four. Both explain the Estonian grassroots understanding and valuation of economic liberalism as a result of late-communist-era experiments. Given some leeway to experiment with reforms to the agricultural and service sectors, Estonia developed a homegrown cadre of liberal economists that was prepared to lead the restructuring of the economy when independence came.[14] This pathway is placed squarely between the rationalist and constructivist camps since material and ideational factors appear in these works.

Rawi Abdelal provides a useful example of pathway five, as he emphasizes the role of nationalists in the adoption of neoliberal policies. Nationalists in non-Russian post-Soviet states as a rule adopted a position in favor of reorientation away from Russia and toward Europe, as they viewed their dependence on Russia to be their greatest security threat. Where nationalists won over the former communists and the population (as in Lithuania) the postindependence government adopted neoliberal policies.[15] Rachel A. Epstein appears to integrate both pathways five and six, as she discusses the conditions that best favored the implementation of EU policy suggestions. These conditions fall within the broader constructivist literature and include a high level of policy uncertainty among domestic actors, the perceived status of the international organization making the suggestions, and the credibility of those suggestions.[16]

It is not the goal of this chapter to test these arguments against one another. Indeed, the authors cited often argue against such an endeavor and in favor of a synthesis of arguments. Rather, this literature is addressed here as a means of informing the reader of the existing arguments and drawing some broad conclusions about the influence of the EU in the Baltic states and the level of commitment the Baltics have to neoliberal policies. For example, if external influence (such as EU conditionality and material rewards) fully explains Baltic policy choices, then we might expect more volatility in policy behavior in the face of a crisis or Euro-skepticism. If, however, these neoliberal policy choices are the result of a belief in the utility or appropriateness of these policies, and domestic political elites largely agree on those beliefs, then we should expect less volatility in neoliberal policy positions even in the face of challenges from the EU and the global economy.

Domestic and EU Politics in the Baltics
Latvia: Right-Wing Coalitions and the "Penguin" Revolution

Domestic politics. There are a number of key characteristics found in Latvian politics in the post-Soviet era. First, the party cleavages and their relationship to ethnicity bear noting. The parties are divided primarily along the usual left–right socioeconomic dimension, but the left-right dimension has been ethnicized to some extent, with the right-wing parties considered "Latvian" and the left-wing parties associated with "Russians."[17] These party cleavages are highly consequential; the "Latvian" control of the right side of the political spectrum has meant that every government since independence has been a right-wing coalition. While some of the left-wing parties have improved their performance over the years since 1991, they have yet to gain control of the government.[18] (Detailed election results are provided in the appendix to this chapter.)

Second, the party system has been relatively volatile since independence. The volatility can be seen in the rapid turnover of Saeima (parliament) deputies, the rapid rise of new parties in several elections, high voter volatility, and party fragmentation.[19] Brand-new parties can perform well and even win the largest share of votes in some cases. Voters are not very likely to vote for the same party in two elections: for example, in the 2010 elections, only half of Latvian voters voted for the same party they had in 2006.[20]

Two issues have been the source of voter interest and, in some cases, protest—corruption and economic policy. In 2002, incoming President Vaira Vīķe-Freiberga established Latvia's anticorruption agency, the Corruption Prevention and Combating Bureau (KNAB) in response to reported campaign financing by oligarchs.[21] KNAB was at the center of the 2006 Umbrella Revolution, a protest movement that demonstrated opposition to the firing of the head of KNAB, Aleksejs Loskutovs, after he ordered the prime minister, Aigars Kalvītis (People's Party), to repay money that was overspent during the 2006 elections. Kalvītis's government fell in 2007. High-profile cases such as this one and the 2011 corruption investigation against Ainārs Šlesers of the Latvia's First Party/Latvian Way coalition (which led President Valdis Zatlers to call new Saiema elections) likely fuel voter perceptions of corruption in Latvia.

Since the economic crisis, the main focus of debates in political campaigns in 2010 and 2011 has been economics, welfare policy, taxes, pensions, and the national economy.[22] Popular frustration with economic conditions and domestically instituted austerity measures required by the IMF and the European Commission came to a head after a 2009 New Year's speech by then prime minister Ivars Godmanis (Latvia's First Party). Godmanis called on the Latvian people to "huddle together like penguins" to endure the crisis. This led to the so-called Penguin Revolution in early

2009, a series of mass protests against the government. Godmanis's government fell as a result of the protests and was replaced with a five-party coalition led by current prime minister Valdis Dombrovskis.[23]

European politics. The importance of economic policy in political debates and in triggering protests would seem to have obvious implications for the Latvian view of the EU and its calls for neoliberal economic policy and austerity. However, this connection between domestic policy and EU conditions has not yielded much impact on voting behavior, whether domestic or at the European Parliament level. The stability of domestic policy and voter habits may be the natural result of an electoral cleavage that always favors the political right and, as such, neoliberal policies. Alternatively, it could be the result of a pro-EU consensus among political elites and major political parties that leaves Euro-skeptic voters out in the cold.

Latvia and its Baltic neighbors engaged in "internal devaluation" as a means of maintaining the value of their currencies following the economic crisis. This set of policies imposed hardships on the population in the form of wage and budget cutbacks during a period of high unemployment. However, the strategy achieved a key goal: Latvia was accepted into the Eurozone on January 1, 2014.

The Latvian public has some potential for Euro-skepticism, as evidenced by the accession referendum vote and recent Eurobarometer survey results. In the accession referendum held in 2003, 66.9 percent of those who turned out voted "yes."[24] The main political parties favor Latvia's membership in the EU. Discussion of the EU is limited during campaigns (where domestic policy debates dominate), but when it is discussed the mainstream parties voice support for relevant aspects of the EU; parties on the left emphasize the benefits that may accrue from the EU's social welfare policy harmonization, whereas parties on the right emphasize access to EU markets and FDI. In short, there is a mainstream consensus in favor of the EU. The only viable party that has on occasion flirted with Euro-skepticism is the radical right For Fatherland and Freedom (TB/LNNK); this party began the independence period as a Euro-skeptic party but warmed toward the EU in the late 1990s and early 2000s so much that expert survey results placed them into the pro-EU area of the political opportunity space.[25]

This consensus behavior by political elites means that there is a wide opening in the Euro-skeptic political opportunity space.[26] The Eurobarometer data should give Latvian lawmakers some cause for concern. Increasing numbers of citizens are questioning the wisdom of EU membership in the wake of the economic crisis, as seen in Figures 20.2 and 20.3. The high number of respondents indicating that Latvian membership in the EU is neither good nor bad is intriguing; this is completely out of line with responses to this question in other member states.

Figure 20.2 Eurobarometer Results on Latvia's Membership in the EU

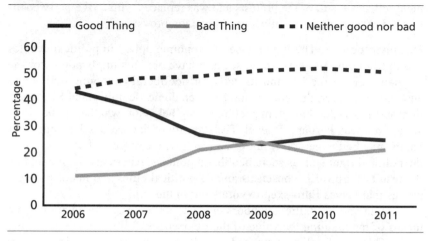

Figure 20.3 Eurobarometer Results on Benefits to Latvia from EU

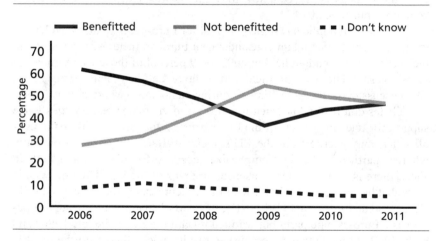

Recent EP elections. European Parliament results from 2009 and 2014 may give us an understanding of whether Euro-skeptic voting has increased as a result of the economic crisis. The choice of EP party group can be used as an indicator of a member of EP's (MEP) position on the EU.[27] For the purposes of this chapter, the following groups are considered pro-integration: Group of the European People's Party, Christian Democrats (EPP), Group of the Progressive Alliance of Socialists and Democrats in the European Parliament (S&D), and the Alliance of Liberals and Democrats for Europe (ALDE).

Some groups demonstrate particular critiques of the EU but appear to be generally pro-EU. These include the European United Left/Nordic Green Left group (GUE-NGL), which advocates for a "socially equitable European integration process" but is critical of the EU's market policies, and the more critical Greens/European Free Alliance (Greens/EFA), which voices concerns with the effects of market legislation on social and health services and the democratic deficit of the EU. The European Conservatives and Reformists (ECR) group puts forth a position they call "Euro-realism," which calls for an intergovernmentalist model of integration. Finally, the Europe of Freedom and Democracy Group (EFD) is the most Euro-skeptic—it includes parties such as Britain's UK Independent Party and Italy's Lega Nord.

Despite the pain that the economic crisis inflicted and Latvia's generally high level of Euro-skepticism, there was little change from the 2009 to 2014 EP elections. In 2009, six of the nine Latvian MEPs were in pro-EU groups: four in EPP, one in S&D, and one in ALDE. Three were in mildly Euro-skeptic groups: one each in GUE/NGL, Greens/EFA, and ECR. In 2014, the distribution was similar, with four MEPs in EPP, one in S&D, one in Greens/EFA, and one in ECR. The final member represents the Union of Greens and Farmers and has not yet been attributed to a party group. These results indicate that the Latvian electorate is still likely to vote for pro-EU MEPs. The Euro-skeptic voting that does appear hails from the left side of the political spectrum. In both elections a TB/LNNK candidate won a seat, but the choice to join the ECR group, rather than the more Euro-skeptic EFD group, is an important indicator of TB/LNNK's reluctance to throw in with the hard Euro-skeptic camp.

Debates about the EP were also derailed by concerns with Russia's recent actions in Crimea. Concerns about a resurgent Russia and accusations that Latvian Russians may be supportive of Russia's recent actions took center stage. One of the Latvian MEPs, Kārlis Šadurskis, went so far as to challenge another MEP, Tatjana Ždanoka of the Russian minority For Human Rights in a United Latvia party, of supporting Russian aggression in Crimea.[28] If it is indeed the norm for EP election debates to focus on domestic policy in lieu of EU issues, then this election cycle also had an additional distraction—Russian resurgence—to take time away from the discussion of the European Union.

Lithuania: The "Normal" Party System

Domestic politics. Lithuania has seen regular exchanges of power between the center-left and center-right since independence, and the party system is deemed relatively stable (despite a temporary stage of volatility in the early 2000s). (Detailed election results are provided in the appendix to this chapter.) The regular exchanges of power from the left to right side of the political spectrum are often explained as the result of late-communist-era dynamics.

The active reform of the Lithuanian Communist Party (LCP), first through internal policy debates and then in making a clean break with the Communist Party of the Soviet Union in 1989, allowed it to emerge in 1990 as the Lithuanian Democratic Labor Party (LDDP) and a viable left-wing party.[29] Likewise, the national movement that emerged at the same time, the Lietuvos Persitvarkymo Sajudis, emerged as a viable right-wing party known as the Homeland Union.[30] The LDDP avoided the label of "Russian" by embracing Lithuanian national identity early, thus minimizing the potential for the overlap of ethnic and right-left political cleavages that we see in Latvia.[31]

There are challenges, however. Voter turnout is relatively low—only 46 percent of eligible voters voted in the 2004 first-round elections for the Seimas, whereas in 2012, 52 percent of eligible voters turned out. Mindaugas Jurkynas attributes the low turnout to disenchantment with the government and its apparent inability to deal with real socioeconomic challenges. The public perception of government corruption likewise plays a role. In 2004, Prime Minister Rolandas Paksas (Liberal and Center Union) was impeached for corrupt behavior, and recent investigations have focused on the leader of the Labour Party, Viktor Uspaskich.[32]

Policy debates since independence have revolved around economic policy. The right-wing parties typically campaign on and enact low taxation levels, low budget deficits, and deflationary policies. In the wake of the 2009 economic crisis, the right-wing coalition government led by the Homeland Union/Lithuanian Christian Democrats adopted such policies.[33] The left-wing governments often adopt economic policies similar to those of the right, despite campaign promises to the contrary. Voters accuse the Social Democrats and their coalition partners of prioritizing the needs of business rather than addressing problems of unemployment, low salaries, and health care.[34] Since neither the right nor the left has proven able to deal with these socioeconomic concerns, it is common for voters to "punish" the coalition in office and bring in a coalition from the other side of the political spectrum with each election. The 2012 election is an example of this behavior, as the left-wing coalition led by the Social Democrats displaced the right-wing government that instituted many of the post-2009 austerity measures.

Protests revolve around these economic issues, especially the way the post-Soviet economy creates "haves" and "have-nots." The investigation and impeachment of Paksas triggered a series of protests; Paksas had campaigned as a defender of the have-nots and his supporters believed the corruption allegations to be a tool used by the dominant elites to overturn a free election. Likewise, in 2009 demonstrations were organized by trade union confederations in response to austerity measures adopted by the right-wing coalition government. After the trade union members dispersed, other protesters remained, eventually leading to riot police putting down the protest as they demanded entry to the Seimas.[35]

European politics. As in Latvia, economic issues are particularly salient, and the post-2009 years have been difficult. However, the saliency and popular critique of economic policies does not appear to have translated into Euroskepticism, either in the electorate or among political parties and elites. Battles surrounding economic policy and austerity measures appear to be waged on the national level—even EP debates focus on national issues rather than the EU explicitly. The political parties, including the Conservatives (Homeland Union), Liberal and Center Union, Social Democrats, and others are generally pro-EU. There have been very brief flirtations with Euro-skepticism in parties such as the Liberal Democratic Party (2004) and Agrarians (late 1990s), but even these flirtations have been deemed "soft" by scholars.[36]

In 2015 Lithuania joined the Eurozone. Prior to 2015, they used a currency board that tied the value of litas to the euro in the drive to maintain fiscal discipline and monetary stability, and thus encourage investment. During the crisis, this predictably meant that Lithuania had little economic policy leeway, and the adoption of internal devaluation policies was a logical, if painful, solution.

Unlike Latvia, the demand for a Euro-skeptic party appears small. In the 2003 accession referendum, Lithuanian voters posted one of the biggest "yes" votes in the accession states at 90 percent. However, those who stayed home from the referendum were more likely to be Euro-skeptic than those who voted, so there may be some limited Euro-skeptic potential.[37] Nonetheless, Eurobarometer data and EP election results appear to indicate that the Lithuanian population is relatively pro-EU. In Figures 20.4 and 20.5 this relatively positive attitude toward membership in and benefits derived from the EU was apparent even during the financial crisis.

EP elections. The 2014 EP election results differed little from the 2009 results. In the 2009 elections eight of Lithuania's eleven MEPs were in pro-EU groups, with four in EPP, three in S&D, and two in ALDE. One joined the ECR with its Euro-realist position, and two joined the strongly Euroskeptic EFD. The party group breakdown from the 2014 election seems to be similar, as seven of the MEPs will join EPP, S&D, and ALDE, and one that is currently unaffiliated (from the Lithuanian Peasants and Greens Union) has indicated an interest in EPP. Again, one MEP will sit with ECR and two will sit with EFD.

Considering how little Euro-skepticism is demonstrated in Lithuania, it is surprising that the very Euro-skeptic EFD has two MEPs from Lithuania. Regardless, the economic crisis did not change the pro-EU/Euro-skeptic breakdown of MEPs. As with Latvia, Lithuania's electorate appeared to be most focused on concerns with a resurgent Russia; this dominated discussion during recent Lithuanian presidential elections and likely redirected conversation from EU topics toward topics focused on the perceived threat from Russia.

Figure 20.4 Eurobarometer Results on Lithuanian Membership in EU

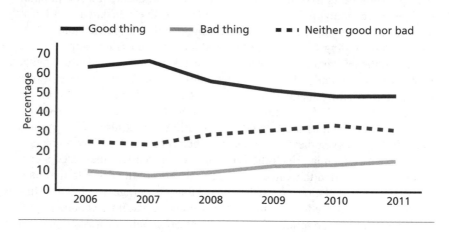

Figure 20.5 Eurobarometer Results on Benefits of Lithuanian Membership in EU

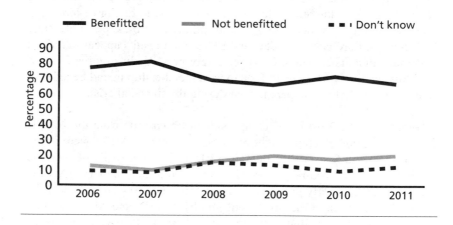

Estonia: Policy Debates Within Broad Governing Coalitions

Domestic politics. The composition of Estonian coalition governments since independence differs from both the Latvian and Lithuanian experience. Estonian governments have generally governed to the right, and this should probably be expected given the typical electoral cleavage in the country that favors right-wing parties over left-wing ones.[38] However, coalition governments have regularly included both right- and left-wing parties, leading one scholar to claim "there are currently very few inconceivable coalition combinations in Estonia."[39] (Detailed election data are included in the appendix to this chapter.)

Estonia's rapid transition to a market economy, with its attendant creation of a flat tax, abolishment of corporate taxes, privatization of industry, and balanced budgets may have been put forth by obvious right-wing leaders such as the Pro Patria Union party's Mart Laar (prime minister from 1992 to 1994 and again from 1999 to 2003), but he was joined in these efforts by MPs from center-left parties such as the Moderates (now the Social Democrats). In times of budget surplus, such as the mid-2000s, both right- and left-wing parties were able to reach compromises on their economic policy differences, as when the Reform Party implemented the tax cuts they desired while the Center Party (who favors a progressive tax system) got their preferred policy of raising pensions.[40] However, these economic policy differences have caused governments to fall on occasions when compromise was difficult, as was the case in the 2001, when the tax-cutting tendencies of the Reform Party bumped up against Moderates' demands for higher pay for teachers.[41] In other words, despite the apparent consistency of the neoliberal policy bent of the Estonian government since independence, coalition governments have included a variety of voices that include left and right political tendencies, and on occasion those policy differences have been consequential in breaking up coalition governments.

The Estonian-Russian ethnic divide in Estonia has expressed itself in different ways from Latvia. The parties established to appeal to the ethnic Russian minority in Estonia—the United People's Party and the Russian Party of Estonia—have fared poorly at the ballot box since the 1999 elections. Some scholars argue that this is the result of gradual integration of Russian voters into the Estonian parties.[42] Nonetheless, the ethnic Russian minority in Estonia is still sizable at 25 percent of the population,[43] and the salience of remaining ethnic tensions became apparent in the Bronze Soldier riots in 2007, when riots broke out as the result of the Estonian government's decision to move the statue of the Bronze Soldier from downtown Tallinn to a military cemetery.

The Bronze Soldier riots are the only riots noted in the recent scholarship on Estonia. Unlike Latvia and Lithuania, Estonia has not been the site of mobilized movements protesting either perceived corruption or austerity measures taken in light of the 2009 economic crisis. The muted popular response cannot be attributed to the severity of the economic crisis or government response to the same, since the economic numbers were similar for the three Baltic states and the Estonian government adopted stringent austerity measures to finalize their entry into the Eurozone and maintain access to EU structural funding. Rather, scholars have argued that the muted popular response may be attributable to the ways the crisis and protest were framed by the government. The crisis was characterized as exogenous in nature (minimizing the potential to blame the suffering on Estonian government policies), and protest was characterized as "unpatriotic," perhaps even thuggish and too similar to the behavior evinced during the Bronze Soldier riots.[44]

Estonian political campaigns have largely focused on socioeconomic concerns. Debates among candidates have focused on tax policy (the flat tax versus progressive taxation), family leave policy, and public sector/pensioner wages.[45] The electorate has continued to support the coalition parties even after the economic crisis; the center-right coalition government elected in 2007 and responsible for implementing much of the harsh medicine of austerity was successful in regaining control of the Riigikogu in 2011 elections. Austerity was enough to drive the Social Democrats from the coalition government, and they clearly increased their vote share in the 2011 elections, but the rightist Reform Party and Pro Patria and Res Publica Union nonetheless gained enough votes to make up the current coalition government.

European politics. In response to the recent crisis, the Estonian government implemented an internal devaluation policy similar to those in the other Baltic states: public sector wages were slashed, the pension age increased, taxes were raised, and access to benefits was limited in an attempt to maintain the value of the currency until a transition to the Eurozone could be completed. Austerity measures at home were complemented with drawing funds from the EU to speed recovery. All of this occurred in the face of a steep increase in unemployment. The government banked on entry into the Eurozone as the cure to the state's economic woes; the goal of entering the Eurozone was achieved on January 1, 2011.

The fact that these measures were implemented with little protest is interesting for a few reasons. Estonia is relatively Euro-skeptic by some scholars' accounts, and the results of the 2003 accession referendum may be indicative of this purported Euro-skepticism. The measure passed with a "yes" vote of 66.83 percent. Estonian political parties, while largely in favor of integration with the EU, have been sometimes "Euro-pragmatist" in their approach, believing that entry into the Union is necessary but with reservations about the EU itself. Viable parliamentary parties like the Centre Party and Res Publica on occasion have demonstrated some soft Euro-skeptic tendencies, and individual lawmakers within a number of viable Estonian parties have expressed Euro-skepticism even when their parties' official positions were pro-EU.[46] However, Eurobarometer results for Estonia do not demonstrate the kind of Euro-skepticism we see in Latvia. In Figures 20.6 and 20.7, we see an Estonian population that generally views membership in the EU as a good thing that benefits the country.

Figure 20.6 Eurobarometer Results on Estonian Membership in EU

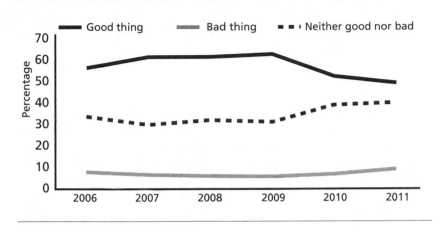

Figure 20.7 Eurobarometer Results on Benefits of EU Membership for Estonia

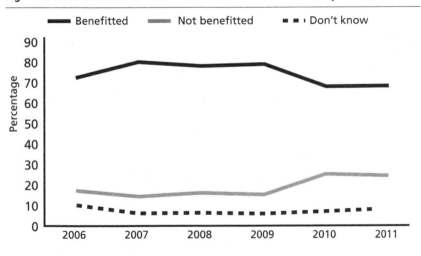

EP elections. The groups to which Estonian MEPs will belong in 2014 are identical to those they joined after the 2009 elections. In both cases, half of Estonia's six MEPs sit with ALDE. One sits with S&D, one with EPP, and one with the Greens/EFA. The Greens/EFA group shows some signs of Euro-skepticism. But with this mild exception, all of the other MEPs are with groups that are typically considered pro-EU.

As with the other cases already examined, there is no evidence that the economic crisis and EU-directed solutions to that crisis changed voters' behaviors in the recent EP elections. Estonia's voting population overwhelmingly chose candidates that would join with pro-EU parties in both the 2009 and 2014 elections.

Conclusion

The wave of Euro-skepticism that drew so much attention in the 2014 EP elections largely passed over the Baltics. Voting patterns for MEPs were generally stable in all three states, with the same share of MEPs of a pro-EU bent versus a Euro-skeptic bent being chosen in the 2009 and 2014 elections. The effects of popular critique of austerity policies in the wake of the economic crisis tend to be seen at the domestic rather than the EP level.

The state with the most potential for Euro-skepticism is Latvia, but EP voting behavior does not appear to reflect a persistent Euro-skepticism or the more immediate Euro-skepticism that the 2009 economic crisis may have engendered. Latvian voters elect MEPs that are largely pro-EU, and even those that are somewhat critical are in the soft Euro-skeptic groups. The existing Euro-skepticism could become a serious problem, however, if the reason for this voting behavior is because of a lack of supply of Euro-skeptic parties. If demand for such a party exists but is not being met by viable parties, then a minor party may be able to use this as a "wedge" issue with which to increase its significance in the party system.

Estonian voters demonstrated less Euro-skepticism overall, and five of the six incoming MEPs will sit with pro-EU groups. In Estonia, the main effects of Euro-skepticism (or at least criticism of austerity measures) play out in coalition dynamics, as parties such as the Social Democrats leave governing coalitions in protest of austerity measures.

Lithuania provides us with the most interesting evidence. The overall level of Euro-skepticism is lower than in the other Baltic states, yet the Lithuanian MEPs have among them the most Euro-skeptic MEPs from the Baltics. The presence of these Euro-skeptics is not attributable to the economic crisis alone, since the same number of Euro-skeptic MEPs were elected in 2009 as 2014. Based on the case study evidence presented here, it appears that Lithuanian voters, accustomed to regular economic policy debates and changes in government, may be willing to punish their elected officials at both the domestic and EU levels.

The introduction to this volume asks whether the member states would prefer a confederal or federal model of EU governance. It is difficult to say what level of integration the Baltic populations would prefer, given the case study evidence. On the one hand, the commitment of these states to EU-advocated neoliberal economic policies is obvious. On the other hand, the literature discussed and the case studies indicate that this apparent compliance with EU recommendations may be more instrumental, or even more coincidental, than it may seem at first glance.

For the right-wing political parties, either level of integration should serve their purposes of maintaining access to markets and finance in the EU space. If confederalism calls for lower levels of integration, historically this has meant that the free trade element of European cooperation was emphasized; for the right wing, this would be the ideal situation by maintaining access to markets but minimizing what some Estonian lawmakers have called the more "socialist" aspects of the Union.

For the left-wing political parties, a confederal structure may be problematic if this means abandoning the harmonization of welfare state policies. Since this is the Baltics' left-wing parties' primary means of supporting a pro-EU position, the loss of this potential benefit of EU membership could cause them to move to a more Euro-skeptic position. The fact that most of the Baltics' soft Euro-skeptic MEPs come from this side of the political spectrum lends some credibility to this concern. This problem would not be limited to the Baltics; throughout the EU space, the rapprochement of left-wing parties and the EU in the 1990s was based on the potential for the EU to even out welfare state policies as a counterbalance to the capitalist and free trade aspects of the Union. Without this goal, left-wing parties may have an incentive to pull back on their support. Thus a confederal model that maintained the neoliberal economic aspects of the Union but pulled back on the social welfare aspects may find its support diminishing from the left side of the spectrum in the Baltics and the wider EU space.

Appendix: Parliamentary Election Results

Table 20.A1 Latvia, 2006

Party Name	Translation	Party Position	Vote Share (%)
Tautas Parija	People's Party	Center-right	19.56
Zaļo un Zemnieku savienība	Union of Greens and Farmers	Center	16.71
Jaunais laiks	New Era	Center-right	16.38
Saskaņas Centrs	Harmony Center	Center-left	14.42
Latvijas Pirmās partijas/ partijas Latvijas Ceļš vēlēšanu apvienība	Latvia's First Party/ Latvia's Way	Center-right	8.58
Apvienība Tēvzemei un Brīvībai/ LNNK	For Fatherland and Freedom/LNNK	Radical right	6.94

Notes: Resultant coalition government: center-right led by People's Party. Party positions drawn from Pryce (2012), Bloom (2011), Millard (2011).

Table 20.A2 Latvia, 2010

Party Name	Translation	Party Position	Vote Share (%)
Vienotība (coalition of New Era, Civic Union, and Society for Other Politics)	Unity	Center-right	31.9
Saskaņas Centrs	Harmony Center	Center-left	26.61
Zaļo un Zemnieku savienība	Union of Greens and Farmers	Center	20.11
Apvienība Tēvzemei un Brīvībai/ LNNK	For Fatherland and Freedom/LNNK	Radical right	7.83
Par Labu Latviju (Coalition of Latvia's First Party/ Latvia's Way and People's Party)	For a Good Latvia	Center-right	7.82

Notes: Resultant coalition government: center-right led by People's Party. Party positions drawn from Pryce (2012), Bloom (2011), Millard (2011).

Table 20.A3 Latvia, 2011

Party Name	Translation	Party Position	Vote Share (%)
Saskaņas Centrs	Harmony Center	Center-left	28.43
Zatlerareformupartija	Zatler's Reform Party	Center-right	20.8
Vienotība	Unity	Center-right	18.8
Apvienība Tēvzemei un Brīvībai/ LNNK	For Fatherland and Freedom/LNNK	Radical right	13.86
Zaļo un Zemnieku savienība	Union of Greens and Farmers	Center	12.19

Notes: Resultant coalition government: center-right (Unity, Zatlers Reform Party and For Fatherland & Freedom).

Table 20.A4 Lithuania, 2004

Party Name	Translation	Party Position	Percentage of Seats
Darbo partija	Labor	Center (populist)	27.7
Tėvynės Sąjunga–Lietuvos krikščionys demokratai	Homeland Union–Lithuanian Christian Democrats	Conservative right	17.7
Lietuvos socialdemokratų partija	Social Democratic Party	Center-left	14.2
Lietuvos liberalų ir centro sąjunga	Liberal and Center Union	Center-right	12.8
Naujoji sajunga/Social-liberalai	New Union/ Social Liberals	Center-left	7.8
Liberalų demokratų partija	Liberal Democrats	Center-right (populist)	7.8

Notes: Resultant coalition government: center-left (Social Democrats, Labor, Social Liberals, Union of Peasants and New Democracy). Jurkynas (2005, 2009) used to determine party positions.

Table 20.A5 Lithuania, 2008

Party Name	Translation	Party Position	Percentage of Seats
Tėvynės Sąjunga–Lietuvos krikščionys demokratai	Homeland Union– Lithuanian Christian Democrats	Conservative right	32
Lietuvos socialdemokratų partija	Social Democratic Party	Center-left	17.7
Tautos prisikėlimo partija	National Resurrection Party	Indeterminate	12.8
Partija Tvarka ir teisingumas	Order and Justice Party	Center-right	10.6
Lietuvos Respublikos liberalų sąjūdis	Liberal Movement	Center-right	7.8
Darbo partija	Labour	Center-left (populist)	7.1

Notes: Resultant coalition government: center-right (Homeland Union, National Resurrection, Liberal Movement, Liberal, and Center Union).

Table 20.A6 Lithuania, 2012

Party Name	Translation	Party Position	Percentage of Seats
Lietuvos socialdemokratų partija	Social Democratic Party	Center-left	27
Tėvynės Sąjunga– Lietuvos krikščionys demokratai	Homeland Union– Lithuanian Christian Democrats	Conservative right	23.6
Darbo partija	Labour	Center-left (populist)	20.7
Partija Tvarka ir teisingumas	Order & Justice Party	Center	7.9
Lietuvos Respublikos liberalų sąjūdis	Liberal Movement	Center-right	7.1
Lietuvos lenkų rinkimų akcija	Electoral Action of Poles in Lithuania	Minority	5.7

Notes: Resultant coalition government: center-left (Social Democrats, Labour, Order and Justice, Electoral Action of Poles in Lithuania).

Table 20.A7 Estonia, 2003

Party Name	Translation	Party Position	Percentage of Seats
Eesti Keskerakond	Center Party	Center	25.4
Res Publica	Res Publica	Center-right	24.6
Eesti Reformierakond	Reform Party	Center-right	17.7
Eestimaa Rahvaliit	People's Union	Agrarian	13.0
Isamaaliit	Pro Patria Union	Conservative right	7.3
Sotsiaaldemokraatlik Erakond	Social Democrats (formerly Moderates)	Center-left	7.0

Notes: Resultant coalition government: center-left (Social Democrats, Labour, Order and Justice, Electoral Action of Poles in Lithuania).

Table 20.A8 Estonia, 2007

Party Name	Translation	Party Position	Percentage of Seats
Eesti Reformierakond	Reform Party	Center-right	27.8
Eesti Keskerakond	Center Party	Center	26.1
Isamaa ja Res Publica Liit	Pro Patria and Res Publica Union	Conservative right	17.9
Sotsiaaldemokraatlik Erakond	Social Democrats	Center-left	10.6
Eestimaa Rahvaliit	People's Union	Agrarian	7.1
Erakond Eestimaa Rohelised	Greens	Green	7.1

Notes: Resultant coalition government: center-right (Reform Party, Pro Patria and Res Publica Union, and Social Democrats).

Table 20.A9 Estonia, 2011

Party Name	Translation	Party Position	Percentage of Seats
Eesti Reformierakond	Reform Party	Center-right	28.6
Eesti Keskerakond	Center Party	Center	23.3
Isamaa ja Res Publica Liit	Pro Patria and Res Publica Union	Conservative right	20.5
Sotsiaaldemokraatlik Erakond	Social Democrats	Center-left	17.1
Erakond Eestimaa Rohelised	Greens	Green	3.8
Eestimaa Rahvaliit	People's Union	Agrarian	2.1

Notes: Resultant coalition government: center-right (Reform Party, Pro Patria and Res Pulica Union, and Social Democrats).

Notes

1. Åslund (2007), p. 3.
2. Williamson (2000).
3. For information on accession criteria, see http://ec.europa.eu/economy_finance /international/enlargement/criteria/index_en.htm.
4. Hübner (2011).
5. Vanags (2011).
6. Hübner (2011).
7. Thorhallsson and Kattel (2013), p. 91.
8. Juska and Woolfson (2012).
9. Connolly and Hartwell (2014).
10. Juska and Woolfson (2012).
11. Kelley (2004), p. 428.
12. Åslund (2007).
13. Vanderhill (2008), Vachudova (2005).
14. Darden (2009), Bennich-Björkman and Likić-Brborić (2012).

15. Abdelal (2001).
16. Epstein (2008).
17. Ikstens (2007).
18. Bloom (2011).
19. Kruezer and Pettai (2003).
20. Bloom (2011).
21. Galbreath (2008).
22. Organization for Security and Cooperation in Europe, "Latvia, Parliamentary Elections, 2 October 2010: Final Report," Warsaw, December 10, 2010, available at http://www.osce.org/odihr/elections/latvia/74785 (accessed February 2, 2014) and "Latvia, Parliamentary Elections, 17 September 2011: Final Report," Warsaw, December 19, 2011, available at http://www.osce.org/odihr/elections/86363 (accessed February 2, 2014).
23. Millard (2011).
24. Ikstens (2007).
25. See Muižnieks (2005), Marks et al. (2006).
26. Buhr (2012).
27. Links to the websites of these party groups can be found at http://www.europarl.europa.eu/aboutparliament/en/007f2537e0/Political-groups.html.
28. For more information, see Damien McGuinness, "'Russian Agent' Row Hits Latvia Election," BBC News, April 10, 2014. Available at http://www.bbc.com/news/blogs-eu-26972863.
29. The LDDP joined with the Social Democrats in 2000 and adopted the name of the Social Democratic Party.
30. See Abdelal (2001), Clark and Pranevičiūte (2008).
31. In any event, it is unlikely that a Lithuanian versus non-Lithuanian divide would be a particularly effective strategy. Lithuania was the least "Russified" of the former Soviet SocialistRepublics. Of all Soviet Socialist Republics in 1989, Lithuania had one of the lowest levels of linguistic Russification, with just 1.8 percent of those claiming Lithuanian identity speaking Russian as their primary language (Gorenburg 2006).
32. Jurkynas (2009, 2013).
33. Jurkynas (2009)
34. Jurkynas (2005).
35. Juska and Woolfson (2012).
36. Duvold and Jurkynas (2007).
37. Ibid.
38. Pettai (2003).
39. Sikk (2007).
40. Solvak and Pettai (2008).
41. Pettai (2003).
42. Ibid.
43. According to CIA World Factbook, see https://www.cia.gov/library/publications/the-world-factbook/geos/en.html.
44. Thorhallsson and Kattel (2013).
45. Pettai (2003).
46. See Sikk (2007), Solvak and Pettai (2008).

21

Romania and Bulgaria: From Laggards to Exceptional Cases

Natalia Cugleşan and Mihaela Herbel

ROMANIA AND BULGARIA SIGNED THE EUROPEAN UNION (EU) AC-
cession Treaty in 2005 but did not become full EU members until 2007.
There are opinions that economic and international pressure, rather than domestic issues, caused the 1989 events, yet the fall of communist regimes in
Romania and Bulgaria, as in all Central and Eastern European states, indicated that the national populations rejected the communist model.[1] Because
both countries had to overcome major barriers during the accession process[2] and faced large delays in structural reforms, they were decoupled
from the other ten member states who became EU members in 2004. Many
of these problems have persisted into the postaccession period.

"Laggard" as a Concept of Performance

In this context, one of the main questions would be why and how are Romania
and Bulgaria exceptional cases in the illiberal political landscape of the new
member states. To address this question, one has to analyze the preaccession
period. In this chapter we provide an in-depth account of transition, preaccession, and postaccession periods in Romania and Bulgaria to explain why they
experienced less significant political backsliding during the postaccession and
crisis periods than did other new member states in Eastern Europe. First, this
chapter looks at the evolution of the two countries since 1989 in historical perspective. Next, it assesses their political and economic performance during the
crisis; in the third section, it looks at citizens' attitudes since accession. The
conceptual lens of "laggard-ness" will be used to support the idea that because
the governments of the two countries have been perpetual laggards since 1989,
in comparison with their neighbors, electors put their trust in the European
project and in the European institutions and showed less support for Euro-
skeptic illiberal political attitudes and behavior.

The State of Democracy in the Postcommunist Period

The collapse of communist regimes in Central and Eastern Europe led to the rediscovery of democracy and included rebuilding the state based on rule of law and development of a multiparty system. Romania and Bulgaria approached this process differently and a few elements were definitive: the experience and quality of democracy in the interwar period, the scale and credibility of the political leaders who have reestablished the traditional political parties (overruled during the communist regime), and the political voting culture of the citizens.[3] Thus, it was not a surprise that postcommunist governments included former members of the Communist Party, the so-called second echelon or high-profile members during the old regime. Free and fair elections were organized in both countries, but they did not lead to a radical change of regimes or include a substantial participation of democratic parties. Elections were organized in the aftermath of the fall of communism, and the newly reestablished parties with a democratic orientation did not have sufficient time and were not encouraged to organize politically and have national representation. This explains why in Romania and Bulgaria unreformed left parties ruled by former communists won the 1990 general elections.

In Romania, the general and presidential elections on May 20, 1990, which led Ion Iliescu to power, revealed the importance of party infrastructure and adequate resources for winning elections when the National Salvation Front (NSF) gained enough votes to enable a comfortable governing majority of 66.3 percent.[4] After the adoption of the constitution in November 1991, new general elections took place in September 1992, and brought to power the Democratic National Salvation Front (FDSN), which emerged from the former NSF and was led by Iliescu. As a consequence, the pace of reforms slowed, and the democratization process came under the influence of pressures exerted by external actors like the United States and the European Union.[5] Already in 1996, as the first alternation in power took place, Romania was lagging behind other Central European states (Poland, Czech Republic, and Hungary) in consolidating its democratic institutions.

The reforms introduced by the coalition government represented a first step toward Europeanization, but it was a timid attempt, and as a result of the inefficient governance process, the Social Democracy Party of Romania returned to power in 2002, under the new name of FDSN. The Adrian Năstase government continued the EU accession negotiations, started by the Romanian Democratic Convention, after the Helsinki Summit in December 1999.

In Bulgaria, the transition from communism to democracy was performed through a "soft" change, which consisted of the replacement of Todor Zhivkov with Petar Mladenov on November 10, 1989. The results of the June 1990 general election maintained the Bulgarian Socialist Party (BSP) government in power, even though in January 1990 the Congress of the Bulgarian Communist Party (BCP) gave the green light to a multiparty system.

The shift produced when the BCP decided to change its name to BSP in April 1990 denounced the ideology of the dictatorship of the proletariat but did not actually represent a change of substance.[6] However, the initiation of democratization in Bulgaria, including removal of the BCP organizations in factories and institutions; organization of free and fair elections; depoliticization of the army, administration, police, and so on was achieved with the contribution of round-table talks launched in mid-January 1990.[7]

In Bulgaria, and more evident than in Romania, the alternation in power has been a continous shift between left and right, which negatively affected the democratization process. For instance, the June 1990 parliamentary elections witnessed the electoral victory of the BSP, which won the majority of seats and formed the government, but after the adoption of the new consitution, the 1991 general elections brought the coalition of the United Democratic Forces and the Movement for Rights and Freedoms to power.[8] The tensions between the coalition partners led to early elections in 1994, which were won by the Coalition for Bulgaria, formed by the BSP and other smaller parties. These frequent changes in political orientation handicapped the consolidation of a stable party system. Moreover, given the detiorating economic situation, the socialist government called early elections in 1997, leading to the victory of the United Democratic Forces.

The political instability of the 1990s continued even after EU accession, especially in the context of the crisis; the latest examples were the 2014 parliamentary elections, just one year after the 2013 elections, when Citizens for European Development of Bulgaria won the most votes but could not form the government. Instead, a coalition government led by BSP was formed but experienced a loss of credibility and had to accept early elections in October 2014. As a result, the BSP suffered a major defeat, losing almost half the seats obtained in the 2103 elections. Government reshuffles caused political instability, either by changing prime ministers and adopting new governing programs or as a result of breaking up coalition governments, followed by forming new coalition governments and more shifting of each new government's priorities and agendas.

In Romania, there were political events similiar to those experienced in Bulgaria. They started with the change of the Petre Roman government in September 1991 and its replacement by the Theodor Stolojan government, which did not necessarily put the reform package on hold but caused delays, resulting in the loss of opportunities to attract foreign investments. The change in power and the set-up of the coalition government in 1996 was also characterized by political instability: the resignation of Prime Minister Victor Ciorbea, replaced with Radu Vasile in 1998, then the resignation of Vasile, replaced with Mugur Isărescu in December 1999.

After EU accession, Romania experienced political instability in four successive stages. First was the National Liberal Party (PNL)–Democratic

Party (PD) coalition break-up in spring 2007, followed by the removal of the PD from the government coalition; the new government benefited from support in Parliament by the Social Democratic Party (SDP). Second was the PDL-SDP coalition break-up in 2009 for strategic reasons (the two parties wanted to designate their own candidates for the presidential election expected in November 2009). Third was the fall of the Mihai Răzvan Ungureanu government as a result of a censure motion filed by the opposition in April 2012. Fourth was the Social Liberal Union (USL) coalition break-up, through the withdrawal of the National Liberal Party in February 2014.

Another feature of political instablity in Romania was the existance of tense relations between two key institutions: the Presidency and Parliament. Members of the SDP and the Liberal Party tried to impeach President Traian Băsescu in 2007 and 2012 on the grounds that he violated the constitution. He was accused of exceeding his authority and meddling in government affairs, but without clearly demonstrating the violation of the fundamental law, the Constitutional Court did not support the charges against the president. Băsescu survived the referenda on both impeachment attempts, but his relations with Parliament were deeply affected by these events. This executive and legislative instability negatively influenced Romania's economic development.

The State of the Economy After 1990

The transition from a centralized economy to a market economy was a slow and painful process for both countries. Governed by left parties with consistent communist roots, Romania and Bulgaria avoided the mass privatization that resulted in stagnation and a decline of overall production due to the lack of distribution markets, especially after the dissolution of the Council for Mutual Economic Assistance. The slogan "we do not sell our country" condemned the economy to recession, followed by high rates of unemployment, inflation, and falling living standards. Privatization reforms were aimed at the service sector, while the industrial sector remained largely unchained and under state ownership as there were no domestic investors able to modernize the enterprises.

As the main form of privatization in the 1990s occurred though foreign direct investment (FDI), a comparative analysis of the 1991–1997 timeframe of FDI in Romania and Bulgaria and other states from Central and Eastern Europe is highly relevant.[9] Analysis reveals that between 1991 and 1994, the FDI in Romania and Bulgaria were comparable only to Estonia and Slovakia, although in terms of area and population Romania and Bulgaria are larger. In contrast to countries such as Hungary, Poland, and the Czech Republic, the amounts of FDI in these countries were greater.

Reforms and economic restructuring encountered increased resistance, particularly from the administrative leadership of the economic units, which were in agreement with the trade unions and feared losing the financial gains and influence of the companies' employees. The main consequences of the pseudo-reforms promoted by the socialist governments in Romania and Bulgaria were that the national currencies continued to depreciate, while industrial production decreased and unemployment rose.

In Romania, inflation often fluctuated, reaching 256.1 percent in 1992 and then dropping to 136.7 percent in 1994 and 32.3 percent in 1995 before rising again to 150 percent in 1998. The gross domestic product (GDP) decreased in the first years of the 1990s but started to slightly recover, beginning in 1993, just to drop again in 1997 when the economic restructuring process began. After 2000, the GDP rose continously until 2008, if at an uneven pace. The leu/US dollar exchange rate continuously dropped after 1990, reaching 7,167.94 leu for US$1. The rate stabilized with the introduction of the Romanian new leu. Unemployment increased from 3 percent in 1991 to 10.9 percent in 1994, and then decreased to 8.9 percent in 1995.

In Bulgaria, the 1996 economic and financial crisis was characterized by falling industrial production with an 8 percent increase in unemployment, an 11.7 percent currency depreciation (US$1 = 782 Bulgarian lev), and galloping inflation, approximately 1,080 percent,[10] in early 1997. To tackle these issues and to control the monetary exchange rate, the Currency Board System was introduced and tied the lev to the deutsche mark at a fixed parity, and later to the euro.[11]

Corruption was another issue that affected both countries; dubious privatizations (companies were deliberately bankrupted and sold at ridiculously low prices), influence peddling, or bribery were the realities of the privatization process. Also, illegal restitutions of land, forest, and estates occurred as a result of corrupt officials. For instance, in Romania, the influence of politicians, especially those who were members of Parliament but at the same time held positions in the general meetings of the shareholders of Romanian companies, have led to acts of corruption, in particular by giving and receiving bribery, influence peddling, tax evasion, or organized crime. A small fraction of these politicians have been investigated and brought to justice, either because the corruption files were not resolved or had been annulled by criminal liability or because of the lack of legal framework. Only after the establishment of the National Anticorruption Directorate in 2005 could elected members of the European Parliament (EP), ministers, deputies and senators, county council presidents, mayors, or magistrates be prosecuted. As a result, between 2010 and 2013, twelve members of the EP, six members of the government and former cabinet members, together with local officials, county council presidents, and mayors were sentenced to prison. In the efforts of combating organized crime in Bulgaria, the January 21, 2014, European Commission Monitoring Report, mentioned, "Bulgaria has made an important investment in the structures to fight organised crime, leading to the creation of specialised bodies at the level of the judiciary and police, as well as major steps to improve the legal framework for asset forfeiture."[12]

The Road Toward the EU

Romania and Bulgaria were invited to start accession negotiations with the EU during the Helsinki European Council meeting in December 1999. They were were not included in the first group with the other candidate states from Central and Eastern Europe because they had more difficulties fulfilling the Copenhagen criteria. For instance, in the case of minority rights, Romania made significant progress with its Hungarian minority who began to enjoy political representation in the Romanian Parliament and had their rights enshrined in the constitution (the right to native language education, media channels, etc.). Bulgaria, on the other hand, had to tackle the issue of its Turkish minority; Article 15 in the constitution, on minorities, was changed, and the Movement for Rights and Freedoms Party agreed to join the coalition government after the elections of 1991 and started to participate in political life.

The accession negotiations opened on February 15, 2000, and ended in fall 2004. In 2000, Romania provisionally closed six chapters, while Bulgaria closed eleven chapters by the parliamentary elections of June 2001. The new Bulgarian cabinet, led by Simeon Saxe-Coburg-Gotha, continued the negotiations successfully and managed to close another eleven chapters by the end of 2002. In Romania, between 2001 and 2004, the Năstase government continued the accession negotiations and managed to close the last two chapters (Competition and Justice and Home Affairs) during the accession conference on December 8, 2004. In the first three years (2000–2002) of the accession talks, all the chapters were open, and only sixteen were successfully closed during that period; the biggest problems encountered in Romania were in connection with the chapters on the Free Movement of Services, Competition, Agriculture, Regional Policy, Environment, and Justice and Home Affairs.[13] The 2004 Commission report mentioned the closing of the negotiations on all chapters as well as the progress and shortcomings that needed to be corrected by January 1, 2007, such as for the Justice and the Control of Corruption chapters. Taking into account the difficulties faced by the two countries in transposing EU legislation, transition periods were allowed for Energy, Agriculture, Transport, and Taxation. They required a more adequate institutional framework for regional and environmental policies to promote, implement, and monitor the requested measures.[14]

Both countries benefited from transition periods to enforce EU environmental law; the most important measures that had to be adopted related to air quality, waste management, water quality, industrial pollution, and risk management. In the case of water and waste directives, transition periods until 2018 applied, as they required important resources and a longer timeframe.[15] In addition, the difficulties faced in the accession negotiations in the transposition and implementation of EU legislation, in particular, Justice and Home Affairs and Competition, were reflected in the Accession Treaty (Articles 36–38) and led to the EU Council decision to apply the safeguard clause under Articles 38 and 39.

Therefore, the postaccession conditionality applied to Bulgaria and Romania is about the will and capacity of the two countries to fulfill the commitments they undertook during negotiations and when they signed the Accession Treaty.[16] The European Commission semester progress reports that the fulfillment of the provisions of the Accession Treaty were included within the Cooperation and Verification Mechanism (CVM) in two areas: judicial reform and the fight against corruption in the case of Romania, and judicial reform, fight against corruption, and organized crime in the case of Bulgaria.

For Bulgaria, the report emphasized the need for adopting constitutional amendments guaranteeing the independence of the judiciary, enforcing the Criminal Procedure Code, launching the Civil Procedure Code, as well as progress on judiciary reform. The monitoring reports from 2008 and 2009 continued to report progress but without signaling the weaknesses of the law enforcement process or the necessary conditions for the proper functioning of institutions responsible for judicial reform and the fight against high-level corruption—namely, the adoption of the Code of Procedure and civil law judicial systems and the creation of the State Agency for National Security to fight corruption and organized crime.

The Romanian government adopted new civil and criminal codes, but they could not be implemented until the parliamentary debates on the procedure codes ended. They finally entered into force in February 2014. In terms of combating high-level corruption, Parliament refused to waive/lift the immunity for elected officials at the request of the National Anticorruption Directorate. The 2009 monitoring progress report mentioned that Bulgaria made some improvements, but not enough to fight against organized crime and "fraud against EU interests." It also recorded serious delays in judicial proceedings.

The extension of the Mechanism for Cooperation and Verification (MCV) to be replaced with CVM, Cooperation and Verification mechanism after 2010, and the connection of the results of the monitoring reports with the Schengen file was interpreted as a purely political position of the EU Council, given that the Schengen *acquis* only stipulates the fulfillment of technical measures for the accession to the Schengen space.[17] On the other hand, the EU institutions had other measures to determine whether the two countries fulfilled their commitments with regard to justice and the fight against corruption.

The 2008 Crisis and the Governments' Responses
The Performance of the Two Governments
as a Response to the Financial Crisis

As member states of the EU, Romania and Bulgaria experienced the economic and financial crisis later than other members because their trade relations with other states were not affected by the crisis until the second half of 2008. The crisis became noticeable after 2009, although the authorities did not openly admit it because of their electoral interests: Bulgaria had scheduled parliamentary elections for July and Romania had planned presidential elections for late November. Still, Romania was more vulnerable to the crisis than Bulgaria, due to its flexible/floating exchange rate system, as opposed to the fixed Bulgarian one, which was tied to the euro. Moreover, by maintaining the same taxes, Bulgaria did not have to resort to loans, like Romania did. The crisis led to a higher unemployment rate (see Table 21.1) of over 10 percent in Bulgaria and 7.3–7.4 percent in Romania.

Another pressing problem was the recent banking crisis, caused by the increasing number of creditors not repaying loans to the banks. Numerous banks from the two nations were confronted by nonperforming loans, which increased the vulnerability of the banking system. The rate of the nonperforming loans rose to values three to four times higher than those in other Central and Eastern European states. According to the World Bank, in 2014 they reached 21.6 percent in Romania and 16.4 percent in Bulgaria, as compared with 5 percent in Poland and Slovakia.[18]

Table 21.1 Economic Indicators Before and During the Crisis

Indicators	2007	2008	2009	2010	2011	2012
GDP Growth Rate (%)						
Bulgaria	6.5	6.2	−5.5	0.4	1.7	1.0
Romania	6.3	7.4	−6.6	−1.7	2.5	0.6
Unemployment Rate (%)						
Bulgaria	6.9	5.6	6.8	10.3	11.3	12.3
Romania	6.4	5.8	6.9	7.3	7.4	7.0
GDP per Capita[a]						
Bulgaria	37	43	44	43	45	50
Romania	42	46	46	45	49	50
Trade Growth Ratio (%)						
Export						
Bulgaria	14.6	13.1	−22.5	33.3	24.75[b]	2.5
Romania	13.7	13.7	−13.5	28.1	18.87	−0.6
Import						
Bulgaria	41.9	15.9	−33.3	−5.2	15.64[b]	−4.7
Romania	25.1	9.6	−22.5	20.1	15.97	−0.5

Source: Eurostat.
Notes: a. PPS, EU-27=100. b. These data refer to imports and exports only; services are not included.

As a result, the economic and financial crisis represented a difficult test for the governments of Romania and Bulgaria in terms of their capacity to manage it. After the budget deficit in 2008, Romania was forced in 2009 to resort to using international financial institutions for support in combating the negative effects of the crisis (this explains the increase in the public debt from 13.4 percent in 2008 to 23.6 percent in 2009). This undertaking proved insufficient, as it was accompanied in 2010 by increased governmental austerity measures, especially by rationalizing public spending. The public sector was hit very hard, and wages were cut by 25 percent. Pensioners could not accumulate pensions with public sector wages in the new legal framework, and vulnerable groups experienced cuts in social welfare payments.

Romania began to recover from the economic crisis in the third quarter of 2011 (Table 21.1). Overall, macroeconomic stability was achieved by the Emil Boc government with relatively high costs: a €20 billion loan, austerity measures consisting of temporary reduction of wages by 25 percent beginning in July 2010, a value-added tax increase from 19 percent to 24 percent, and taxation on pensions (taxes and social insurance contributions for pensions higher than 1,000 leu or €226). Bulgaria and Romania were both hit by the economic crisis at the end of 2008 and beginning of 2009. Yet unlike Romania, Ireland, or Portugal, Bulgaria has not taken loans from the International Monetary Fund or the World Bank but was forced to adopt austerity measures: freezing wages and pensions until 2013, reducing the number of public sector employees by more than 10 percent, and introducing taxes on pensions and cuts in public spending of government ministries. One of the negative effects of the reduction of public sector employees was rising unemployment (Table 21.1). In both countries, the sectors most affected by the austerity measures were health and education. Not only were the wages of the medical staff frozen, but in 2011 the Romanian government decided to close more than sixty hospitals on the grounds of dysfunctional management.

The austerity measures caused the deepening of social inequalities in Bulgaria, which resulted not only in street protests but in the replacement of Prime Minister Boc in February 2012 with Boyko Borisov, and a new cabinet led by Ungureanu, former chief of the Foreign Intelligence Service. There were strong protests against the Borisov government because of falling living standards, and the result was another change of government in March 2013 when President Rosen Plevneliev nominated Marin Raykov, former deputy foreign minister, as interim prime minister until elections could take place in May 2013.

The Romanian and Bulgarian governments could have used more efficient instruments for attenuating the effects of the financial crisis like: judicious use of budgetary resources, stimulating FDI, and absorption of EU structural funds. In terms of budgetary resources, the low share of investments in the annual budgets diminished opportunities for major projects and the cofinancing capacity of the state to use EU structural funds. In Romania, for instance, even though the budget for 2014 provided a 0.5 percent increase in investments for raising the absorption rate through budgetary rectifications, the funds allocated for investments were further reduced. FDI also declined during the crisis, compared to the previous period (see Figure 21.1).

The reasoning behind these numbers are explained by the difficulties faced by investors and also by the inability of the Romanian and Bulgarian governments to attract more consistent FDI due to frequent legislative changes and underdeveloped infrastructures. Thus, the low share of FDI, coupled with the poor performance of the economies, including uneven territorial development, caused GDP per capita to decrease during the crisis, compared to the level reached in 2008 (see Figure 21.2). Despite the fact that the structural funds allocated to the two countries for 2007–2013 remained consistent, they could have been used more effectively during the times of austerity, as they had been in Poland. After joining the EU, the two countries had access to higher levels of structural and cohesion funds than they had during the preaccession period: €19.668 billion for Romania and €6.853 million for Bulgaria.

Romania and Bulgaria encountered major difficulties in absorbing the structural funds due to poor management. At the end of 2012, Romania succeeded in using only 12 percent of its structural funds, situating itself as one of the EU's laggard states. Bulgaria did better and managed to absorb 34 percent of its structural funds in the same period.[19] Although it has im-

Figure 21.1 Foreign Direct Investments in Bulgaria and Romania, 2003–2013, in millions of euros

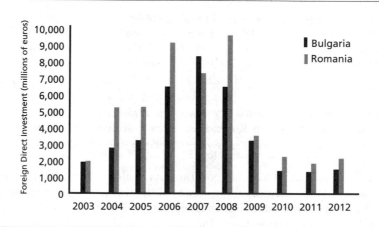

Source: Bulgarian National Bank and National Bank of Romania Reports.

proved its performance, according to the 2013 report from the Ministry of European Funds, Romania managed to absorb only 33.47 percent by the end of 2013. The Romanian government set targets to raise the absorption rate for 2014 and 2015, but the budgetary execution and the implementation of investment programs financed through European funds did not perform at the expected pace and only reached 48 percent according to the Ministry of European Funds (October 17, 2014). Major issues were the failure to meet EU regulations and corruption charges in the use of funds, which led to the suspension of payments for Romania's human resources development operational program (2012) and for Bulgaria's environment operational and regional development programs.

The absorption of EU funds would have produced better results if the ruling governments in the countries had promoted the transfer of competences to the regional and local levels. From the Commission's viewpoint, EU regional policy should lead to strong involvement of subnational authorities in the planning and implementation of regional development programs. Instead, Romania and Bulgaria have centralized the planning and elaboration process of the programs on the grounds that as unitary states, they are responsible for ensuring a balanced development of all regions. After accession to the EU, decentralization debates aimed at efficient public administration but have not resulted in the adoption of laws on regionalization or decentralization, mainly because the political elite and political parties could not reach consensus on a common project of regionalization, but

Figure 21.2 Gross Domestic Product per Capita of Bulgaria and Romania, 2004–2012, in US dollars

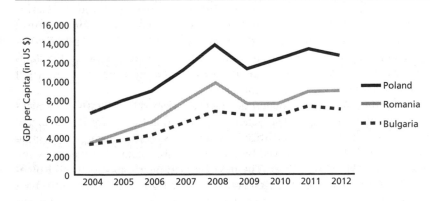

Source: World Bank

also due to resistance at the local level. As centralized unitary states, the national and local public authorities did not agree with the division of competences with private actors, and the culture of partnership was insuficiently developed to stimulate their cooperation in major projects.

Effects of Poor Performance

External. A possible explanation for the continued backwardness and incremental policymaking after 2007 is that before the EU accession, the Commission used conditionality as an instrument and lever to enforce necessary reforms in Bulgaria and Romania. After 2007 this possibility was dramatically reduced. The most relevant aspect in this direction is the laggard pace made toward strengthening the rule of law and eliminating of political involvement in justice. The political authorities from the two states exhibit what Venelin Ganev has defined in the literature as postaccession hooliganism.[20] Thus, the monitoring reports through the MCV continue to apply seven years after the Romanian and Bulgarian EU accessions due to the long list of unfulfilled commitments.

Difficulties and tensions have also arisen from Romania and Bulgaria's poor performance with Schengen and the euro. The nations were scheduled to enter the Schengen system together in 2011. In accordance with the Schengen evaluation procedure, Romania and Bulgaria received questionnaires from the member states; after these formalities were fulfilled, the assessment and verification visits were scheduled to occur. The visits were to determine how the Schengen *acquis* on data protection; visa policy; land, sea, and air border control; as well as the SIS/SIRENE systems were to be implemented. In April 2010, the EU Council determined that Romania and Bulgaria had fulfilled the conditions based on the analysis of the questionnaire responses. Moreover, the European Parliament, while debating the Council's decision in its meeting on June 16, 2010, approved the Carlos Coelho report with 525 votes in favor, 54 abstentions, and 18 votes against. This report confirmed "that both countries comply with data security requirements for connecting to the Schengen Information System, the database used by border control agents to exchange information in the fight against crime and illegal immigration."[21]

The June 29, 2010, Council decision confirmed that the two countries met the technical criteria. The Schengen Evaluation Report for Romania and Bulgaria (regarding the SIS/SIRENE system) was debated during the meeting in February 2011 and approved by the EU member states, but the accession deadline in 2011 was not met. The next Council decisions regarding Romania's accession into the Schengen area and the 2012 and 2013 reports did not bring any certainty regarding an accession date. Since there is no consensus for an accession vote, the topic was removed from the Council's agenda. The hope now is for accessing into the Schengen area in fall 2015 or spring 2016.

Regarding entry into the Eurozone, Romania set an initial obective for 2015, aiming to enter in the Exchange Rate Mechanism II (ERM II) by 2012. The financial crisis disrupted the adjustment process for the macroeconomic indicators, and Romania did not manage to enter the ERM II as initially planned. For the entire period of 2007–2012, Romania did not meet the nominal convergence criteria except for the debt to GDP ratio.

The convergence program for 2011–2014 (see Table 21.2) was prepared in accordance with the requirements set by the European Commission and by taking into account the 2010 European Council decision on the coordination of the policies and fiscal reforms to be coherent and integrated at the European level. Thus, the 2011–2014 convergence program envisaged a structural deficit below 2 percent for achieving a budget deficit below 3 percent to fulfill the 2015 obective. The 2012–2015 convergence plan maintained the goal of joining the euro in 2015 and established some targets for the budget deficit in the coming period: 2.8 percent in 2012, 2.2 percent in 2013, 1.2 percent in 2014, 0.9 percent in 2015.

In the new context, according to the most recent statements from President Băsescu and also supported by the government, Romania hopes to join the euro in 2019. Inflation and the budget deficit did not pose great difficulties; beginning in 2013, Romania escaped excessive deficits, and inflation fell below 2.0 percent in 2013.[22] In Bulgaria, the fulfillment of the convergence criteria could have been accomplished in more favorable

Table 21.2 Convergence Economic Indicators for Romania and Bulgaria

Maastricht Nominal Convergence Criteria	2007	2008	2009	2010	2011	2012
Inflation Rate (%)						
Romania	5.9	7.9	5.6	6.1	4.6	3.4
Bulgaria	9.4	12.0	2.5	3.0	3.4	2.4
Budget Deficit (%)						
Romania	− 2.5	−5.8	−8.3	−6.8	−5.2	−3.0
Bulgaria	3.4	3.2	3.2	−3.1	−2.1	−1.9
Debt to GDP Ratio (%)						
Romania	13.0	13.4	23.6	30.5	34.7	37.8
Bulgaria[a]	18.2	14.1	14.8	16.2	16.3	18.5
Exchange Rate to Euro (%)						
Romania	10.44	0.03	−15.1	0.7	−0.6	−4.56
Bulgaria	0.0	0.0	0.0	0.0	0.0	0.0
Long-Term Interest Rate (%)						
Romania	7.1	7.7	9.7	7.3	7.3	7.3
Bulgaria	4.7	5.4	7.2	6.0	5.4	5.3

Source: European Commission's Convergence Reports (2008–2012), Eurostat (2007–2012).

conditions, given the introduction of the Currency Board System in 1997. However, it has ensured the fulfillment of the exchange rate criterion against the euro to the Bulgarian lev (€1 = 1.95 lev). Compared to others, this system presents both advantages and disadvantages in terms of the convergence criteria.[23] The Currency Board System has the advantage of compliance with tax and financial discipline; from this perspective, Bulgaria was not in a position to ask for financial support from international financial institutions. This is also clear from the evolution of public debt in Bulgaria, for the period 2009–2011 (see Table 21.2): from 14.8 percent in 2009 to 16.2 percent in 2010 to 16.3 percent in 2011.

The 2009–2012 convergence plan was prepared in accordance with the 2010–2013 fiscal framework and envisaged to achieve a balanced budget (budget surplus of 0.5 percent), which was vital for reducing the public debt, within the Currency Board System. The package of structural reforms intended to ensure balanced economic growth in Bulgaria included the promotion of policies designed to increase productivity and restructure the economy by increasing the share of the sectors with higher added values. So far, Bulgaria has not anounced a deadline for joining the euro.

The Countries and the Citizens React to the Crisis

Results of the economic crisis. The economic crisis in Bulgaria and Romania led to less enthusiasm toward European integration and the European institutions. However, it has not shaken people's trust in them. One of the most interesting effects of the economic/financial crisis in Bulgaria and Romania with regard to the EU is that even though enthusiasm for the integration project has diminished, trust in European institutions is still high. The reasons enthusiasm has diminished are easy to identify. The first is a sort of normalization of EU integration, marked by accession in 2007. On the other hand, this "return to Europe" is simultaneous with the global economic crisis, as a result of which many Eastern European governments have introduced austerity measures. Also in this context political forces in the two countries have tried to blame the EU for the austerity measures. For example, the left-wing Romanian governments in power since 2012 have pushed the idea of a "detachment" from Europe by using slogans such as "Romania is not a Western colony" to gain electoral support on the austerity measures introduced by the (right-wing) governments before 2012. In Bulgaria as well, some rather marginal political forces, such as the extremist party Ataka, have used anti-EU messages in the 2014 campaign for the European elections to capitalize on the anti-EU feelings, but have failed to do so.[24]

The citizens of the two countries maintain their trust in the European institutions. For example, according to one Eurobarometer survey (80, 2013), the trust of the Romanian and Bulgarian citizens in the European institutions is among the highest in the EU: 76 percent in Romania and 75 percent in Bulgaria. The same source indicates that the values of the trust in EU institutions in Romania and Bulgaria are comparable to those in other states that have not been hit so hard by the crisis. Moreover, the positive representation about the EU was shared by over 40 percent of the population and only slightly less than 10 percent had a negative image of the EU.

The reasons that explain the high levels of trust in the European institutions vary. According to most observers, they revolve around the low levels of trust in the national institutions. Moreover, as illustrated by the waves of protests that took place since 2012 in both countries, citizens feel that only the European institutions can influence the national government to continue reforms in important sectors, such as justice and the rule of law. For example, waves of protests took place in Romania after the incumbent government limited the rights of Romanian citizens living abroad to vote in the presidential elections at the end of 2014, and reform of the justice system was an important issue of the protesters. This situation raised questions about the conclusion of Philip Levitz and Grigore Pop-Eleches, who explained the trust that Eastern European citizens had in EU institutions by the fact that they did not understand that EU leverage over national authorities ended with accession.[25] The protest demonstrated that important sectors of society, through their participation in protests, make an important contribution to preventing postaccession backsliding by national governments, and that those citizens feel empowered by the their countries' EU membership.

The crisis adds up to European integration on the list of the enabling factors for populism. There are reasons to believe that together with the global economic crisis, the EU accession has been a political game changer, since it empowered large categories of citizens (primarily youth), and thus created the domestic influence needed for successful Europeanization.[26] However, one question remains unanswered: why did the protests emerge after 2007 and not after 1989, since the economic conditions were similar? Four answers merit particular attention. First, the generations coming of age in 1989 and afterward were marked by the memory of repression, not only the communist one but also the postcommunist ones, as was the case of the famous "mineriads" in Romania in 1991. Second, as Peter Vanhuysse shows (for Hungary, Czechoslovakia, and Poland, but the argument can be extended to Romania and Bulgaria), the post-1989 social policies of giving pensions to large categories of factory workers were carefully designed not only to ensure the transition to market economies but also to contain the possible protests from the very well-organized trade unions.[27] Third, the large Romanian and Bulgarian economic diasporas throughout Western Europe emerged after EU accession and, since 2007, have become politically active. Fourth, as Ivan Krastev shows, the protest became possible in the postaccession years because of the global crisis of representative democracy, a crisis that has been marked by mass protests organized through social media.[28]

The protests in Romania and Bulgaria emerged for different reasons. Although, the protests ended up having the same demands and consequences. In Romania, citizens came out on the streets at the beginning of 2012 to protest against a new bill for privatization of health care services. Health Undersecretary Raed Arafat, former director of the public emergency service, publicly opposed the bill, which prompted President Băsescu to ask for his resignation on television. Arafat's resignation mobilized urban citizens in several large cities to take to the streets to defend him, and finally the bill was rejected. The second wave of protests broke out later in 2012 and gave birth to a civic movement. These protests were prompted by the powers given by several governments to a Canadian corporation for extracting gold in Roşia Montană using cyanides. The mine project dated back before accession and was the beginning of an environmental problem that soon became a political one because it exposed the corruption and lack of transparency of several Romanian cabinets. The last wave of protests took place after the first round of presidential elections in 2014, when thousands of Romanians living in the main European capitals were not able to vote because the Ministry of Foreign Affairs had organized the elections poorly. Soon this turned into a political protest against the Social Democrat Victor Ponta,[29] also a candidate in the elections, who was accused of deliberately preventing the diaspora vote. In the end, citizens in the main Romanian cities mobilized against the cabinet and Ponta lost the presidential elections to the liberal Klaus Iohannis.

In Bulgaria, the protests broke out as a result of high electricity bills in January 2013. By February, thousands of citizens were on the streets of major Bulgarian cities protesting the political system and asking for the resignation of the Borisov cabinet. After violent clashes between the protesters and the police, Borisov resigned at the end of February. By May 2013, the protests emerged again, but this time they had an environmental/political orientation and were prompted by the nominations made by the new Plamen Oresharski cabinet. In May, environmental activists started protesting against the nomination of a controversial figure for minister of investment planning. He eventually withdrew his candidacy. In June the young media mogul Delyan Peevski was appointed head of the national security agency, which prompted another series of protests. After Parliament revised this decision, the protests continued until July 2014, when the Oresharski cabinet finally resigned.

The outcomes of the Bulgarian and Romanian protests can be seen on three levels. First, the protests managed to change the domestic political scene. Second, they prompted change in the mainstream parties' political agendas and created new political players. Finally, the protests led to a rather interesting development for the extreme right nationalist parties in both countries: they started to lose electoral ground. There are several reasons for these changes.

The domestic political scenes changed. The first and most evident consequence of the protests in both countries was domestic change. In Romania, the protests against the gold mine in Roşia Montană not only managed to block the project but also became a test for the political class, on both the left and the right, during the last rounds of elections. In Bulgaria, the protests managed to reverse appointments in high-profile governmental positions, as was the case of Ivan Danov, an investment planning minister in the Bulgarian Oresharski cabinet and the case of Peevski, the head of the security agency. Ministerial positions were also kept or lost under the pressure created by the protests, as shown in the Romanian cases of Arafat and of the two ministers of foreign affairs who lost their jobs in November 2014 for poorly organizing the presidential elections abroad. The protests also led to two cabinets resigning in Bulgaria (those of Borisov and Oresharski) and one in Romania (the Boc cabinet, which resigned in early 2012). The protests were the major force behind the rather surprising victory of the liberal Iohannis over the Social Democrat Ponta, a victory the polls failed to predict and one that is important because it brought an ethnic German as a leader of a rather conservative orthodox country.

The second consequence of the protests was a change in the political agenda. The mainstream parties changed, and new political players emerged. As Spirova and Stefanova noted, being pro- or anti-European will tend to surpass other electoral cleavages.[30] During the protests, being pro-European became synonomous with being pro-justice and especially anticorruption, an agenda introduced and supported especially by the EU. The mainstream parties in both countries understood and had to adapt,[31] even though this meant breaking political arrangements for high-profile positions or even losing political comrades to judicial prosecution or prison for corruption. Moreover, the EU's penalties for anticorruption and the domestic demand for a cleaner political system created new political players. For example, in the last Romanian presidential elections, Monica Macovei, former minister of justice, a member of the European Parliament, and an icon of anticorruption in the country, managed to secure 4.5 percent of the votes in the first round, with 1 percent more than the traditionally strong Hungarian ethnic party UDMR (Democratic Alliance of Hungarians in Romania). The Bulgarian Protests Network, a citizen movement that emerged during the protests in 2013–2014 against the Oresharski cabinet, is a new political player that finally managed to make the government resign but did not organize itself politically.

The third consequence of Europeanization was probably the most important. The political scene in both countries changed, and the once-powerful extreme right parties lost considerable support. In Romania, the Greater Romania Party, whose leader Corneliu Vadim Tudor managed to get into the runoff of the 2000 presidential elections, lost parliamentary representation in the 2008 elections when it did not manage to reach the 5 percent threshold. In the European elections in 2009, the party managed to secure three seats, but in the 2014 elections, it did not qualify for the EP. In Bulgaria, the extreme right party Ataka, whose leader Volen Siderov qualified in the runoff in the 2006 presidential elections, also lost support in the following three rounds of parliamentary elections. In the 2007 and 2009 European legislatures, the party gained three, then two seats, yet at the 2014 European election the party did not manage to secure any representation. What could explain this interesting outcome in a regional political landscape marked by nationalist backsliding? Trying to explain election results where extreme right leaders such as Tudor or Siderov managed to get into the runoffs, Grigore Pop-Eleches convincingly shows that it is not the extreme right political agendas or the personal charisma of the leaders of "unorthodox parties" that attract voters but protest voting against the mainstream political groups.[32] Pop-Eleches's argument implies that what the EU's new political agendas, together with the global waves of protests, have done is enlarge the political market and options for protest voting. Therefore, the extreme right lost (electoral) ground in favor of new political players who emerged in the postaccession context.

Conclusions and Looking to the Future

In the early 2000s, Romania and Bulgaria were considered the laggards of Eastern Europe. Both countries were torn by corruption and were unhealthy economies and democracies. Today, they are rather exceptional cases in a regional political landscape where illiberal political behavior seems to be gaining ground. These countries seem exceptional because their postaccession political history has experienced much less democratic backsliding than that of some of their neighbors. This chapter has explored the reasons behind this rather curious outcome. It has found that economically and politically both still have a long way to go until they could be considered truly integrated. However, it has also found that what in the first decade of the 2000s seemed to be a great disadvantage—the low level of citizen trust in national institutions—in the long run has proved to be an advantage: the level of citizen trust in the European institutions has risen. In the postcrisis global context, the dissatisfaction with national institutions and the trust in the European agendas (especially anticorruption and modernization/Europeanization) have fed several rounds of protests, which in turn have led to a more accountable (or at least more fearful) political class and even unexpected electoral outcomes. Ivan Krastev is right to question whether "protest is a better instrument than elections for keeping elites accountable,"[33] and the question remains open, but it is clear that the recent protests in Bulgaria and Romania have done a lot for the consolidation of the two countries' civil societies.

Notes

1. Carmen González-Enríquez (2001).
2. Spendzharova (2003), Bideleux and Jeffries (2007).
3. Hibbing and Patterson (2004).
4. Pavel and Huiu (2003), Bideleux and Jeffries (2007).
5. Gallagher (2001).
6. Bideleux and Jeffries (2007), pp. 92–93), Giatzidis (2002), p. 54.
7. Spirova (2010), pp. 403–404.
8. Bideleux and Jeffries (2007), p. 103, Giatzidis (2002), p. 53.
9. Altomonte and Guagliano (2003), p. 225.
10. Dobrinsky (2000), pp. 597–598.
11. Avramov (1999).
12. "On Progress in Bulgaria Under the Co-Operation and Verification Mechanism," COM, 2014, 36 final, Zugriff, 2014.
13. European Commission "Communication from the Commission Monitoring Report on the State of Preparedness for EU Membership of Bulgaria and Romania, " COM (2006), 549 final, Zugriff, 2006.
14. Papadimitriou and Phinnemore (2004), Spendzharova and Vachudova (2012).
15. Cuglesan (2008), Scheinberg and Mol (2010).
16. Gateva (2010).
17. In this respect, see the statements of the presidents of Bulgaria and Romania from September 2010, concerning the postponement of accession to Schengen. http://www.mediafax.ro/politic/basescu-despre-aderarea-la-spatiul-schengen-romania-are-de-trecut-si-obstacole-de-ordin-politic-7356195.
18. Katy Barnato, "Bulgaria Bank Fail Flags Region's 'Achilles Heel,'" *CNBC*, June 30, 2014. Available at http://www.cnbc.com/id/101800155 (accessed August 30, 2014).
19. Paliova and Lybek (2014).
20. Ganev (2013).
21. Clive Leviev-Sawyer, "Bulgaria, Romania a Step Closer to Schengen Visa Zone," *Sofia Echo*, June 17, 2010. Available at http://sofiaecho.com/2010/06/17/918711_bulgaria-romania-a-step-closer-to-schengen-visa-zone (accessed January 17, 2014).
22. According to the INS (National Institute of Statistics), which is estimated at the end of 2013 to be 1.55 percent.
23. Galic (2012).
24. See Yasen Georgiev and Desislava Petrova, "Bulgaria," EU-28 Watch No. 10, Economic Policy Institute. Available at http://www.eu-28watch.org/?q=node/1219.
25. Levitz and Pop-Eleches (2010), p. 471.
26. Spendzharova and Vachudova (2012).
27. Vanhuysse (2006).

28. Krastev (2014b).

29. The Romanian Social Democratic Party is the offspring of the former Communist Party, and protesters accused Ponta of communist practices when organizing the vote in the diaspora.

30. Spirova and Stefanova (2012), p.77.

31. Vachudova (2014), p. 128.

32. Pop-Eleches (2010).

33. Krastev (2014b).

22

Croatia:
Challenges After EU Accession

Vuc Vuković and Luka Orešković

CROATIA IS THE NEWEST MEMBER OF THE EUROPEAN UNION, JOIN-ing in 2013. It is a small economy with a population of 4.3 million, and a gross domestic product (GDP) slightly below $60 billion. As a small open economy it tends to be rather sensitive to external macroeconomic shocks, which is why the recession that hit the country is still showing no signs of receding. Unlike the majority of Europe, Croatia only felt the effects of the recession in 2009. GDP growth declined for the final two quarters of 2008, but did not turn negative until the first quarter of 2009, when the total yearly decline was 7.4 percent (see Figure 22.1).[1] Growth has been nega-tive ever since, dragging the country through twenty-three consecutive quarters of recession,[2] with still no signs of a robust recovery. European Commission (EC) growth projections are 0.2 percent for 2015 and 1.1 per-cent for 2016, published by the European Commission (EC). Both num-bers still do not represent the robust recovery necessary to significantly decrease unemployment.[3] And while inflation is still low, borderline defla-tion, the public debt to GDP is expected to rise above 85 percent in 2015, a consequence of a still large budget deficit of 5.6 percent.[4] As a conse-quence, the country's credit rating status has been downgraded to "junk," and foreign direct investment (FDI) has hit its lowest level in decades.

This is why the new government, when it formally took office in 2011, set attracting foreign investments as its most important goal for achieving a quick recovery.[5] However the strategy has failed to produce any positive re-sults so far. In 2012 and 2013, FDI decreased even further. It recovered in 2014, mainly due to money attracted from EU structural funds. However, Croatia was not particularly successful in tapping these funds, falling short of high expectations that money from the EU would kick-start the recovery. According to the Ministry of Regional Development and EU Funds, in the

Figure 22.1 Croatian Annual GDP Growth, by Components, 1998–2014

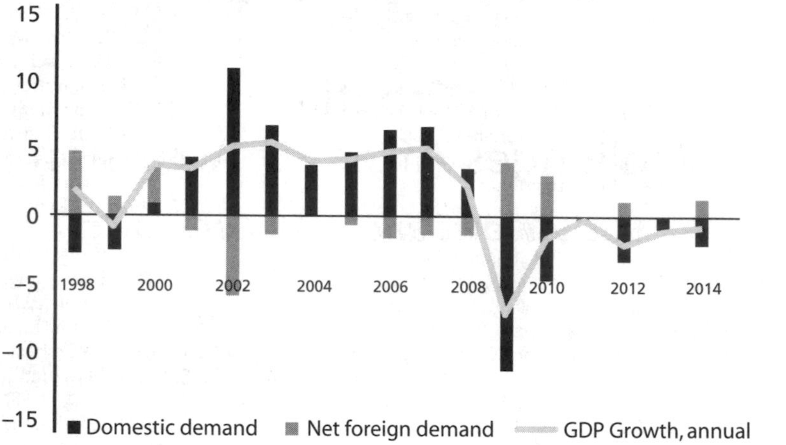

Source: Croatian Bureau of Statistics (DZS 2014a).

Note: Data for 2014 are official estimates of the Croatian Bureau of Statistics. Domestic demand includes consumption, government spending, and investments.

first year of membership Croatia only managed to attract 350 million kunas (€45 million) more than it paid in membership fees. It paid 4.1 billion kunas in fees and received 4.4 billion kunas from EU funds.[6] The largest problem for the government, however, is that 95 percent of Croatians say that their country is in a bad state, and 85 percent of them do not believe the situation will get any better over the next twelve months.[7]

The main reason for this pessimism is a high level of unemployment, which also started soaring in 2009, and currently stands around 17.7 percent.[8] Unemployment and an inflexible labor market were problems even before the crisis (see Figure 22.2), when total factor productivity growth was low (nominal wages grew much faster than productivity); job growth was sluggish (average 1.6 percent in the precrisis decade, compared with 4.4 percent average GDP growth), while activity rates were among the lowest in the EU (44 percent for those over age fifteen, and 57 percent for those age fifteen to sixty-five).[9] The shock of the crisis further worsened this situation, raising the poverty rate to 48 percent for an unemployed person. Naturally this gave rise to even more protection from the public sector labor unions, since finding oneself without a job during the recession significantly increased the risk of poverty, especially among a population overburdened with debt.

Youth unemployment is particularly worrisome, standing at 48.6 percent, the third highest in the EU, behind only Spain and Greece. The high

Figure 22.2 Croatian Unemployment Rates, 1996–2014

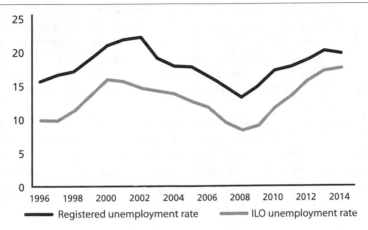

Source: HZZ, Croatian Employment Service, "Monthly Statistical Bulletin 11," Zagreb (2014).

Note: The registered unemployment rate constitutes those registered with the employment bureau, while the ILO rate constitutes of those surveyed periodically, according to the standard international methodology.

level of youth unemployment is the central reason for many young, university-educated people fleeing the country, thus worsening the sustainability of the pension system and adding to an overall bleak state of the economy. The aging of the population is rapid, net migration is negative, debt levels are at their historical highs, and the rising budget deficit keeps adding pressure on debt sustainability. It is therefore not at all surprising that the population is mostly pessimistic, both for the short term and on the long-term horizon.

Origins of the Crisis

The shock of the crisis spillover that hit Croatia in 2009 only exposed the pre-existing instabilities of a growth model fueled by debt. The reason for the delay can be traced on one hand to the relatively underdeveloped domestic financial system. Domestic banks were well capitalized before the crisis and, unlike their mother banks in Europe, were not exposed to mortgage risks nor were they holding peripheral government debt (at least not to the same extent). In fact, it was the domestic (albeit foreign-owned) banks that virtually bailed out the government in 2009 by opening more liquidity when sources of financing were scarce. This is in stark contrast to what happened across Europe at the time, where huge foreign debt and unsustainable deficit issues were triggered primarily due to large government bailouts of banks. In Croatia, luckily, it was the other way around. Even without government bailouts of banks or large stimulus packages, Croatia found itself in similar troubles as the rest of the so-called peripheral Eurozone. It too suffered from large current account deficits before the crisis (an average current account deficit was around 7 percent of GDP),[10] coupled with the highest levels of government and public debt in the region (see Figure 22.3), primarily due to large infrastructure spending on highways done from 2002 until 2007.

The debt accumulated in those years could not be repaid swiftly, so during the peak of the crisis years, in addition to budget problems due to rising unemployment, the debts made in the past due for payment. For the HDZ government at the time, this initiated a strategy of constant debt reprogramming where new debts were being made to service the old ones, at higher interest rates than before (on average 1.5 percentage points higher). In every new budget the majority of the deficit was attributed to interest payments, meaning that the burden of old debt remains the biggest constraint on the budget.[11] Because of this constraint, the Croatian public debt increased significantly during the crisis, from 58 percent in 2008 to a projected 85 percent in 2015, without a single bailout or stimulus package.

This clearly suggests that the country has found itself exposed to preexisting structural instabilities of the past, where the economy was creating a growth model based on debt (both government and private sector), and in which the current account deficits were used to fuel consumption, government spending, and housing bubbles instead of investment. This growth

Figure 22.3 Croatian Budget Deficit (Right Axis) and Public Debt Levels (Left Axis) as Percentage of GDP, 2002–2013

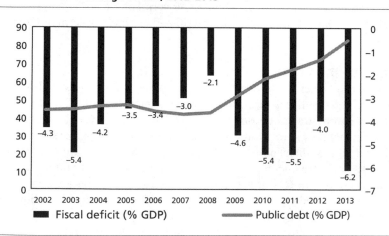

Source: HNB, Croatian National Bank, "Bilten 208," Zagreb (2014).

model is very similar to the one applied in most peripheral Eurozone countries. Croatia faced overexpenditures in large infrastructure projects, such as highways in 2003–2004, stadiums for the world handball championship in 2009, and for substantial mismanagement of its public services. Additional constraints were high levels of corruption and political vote buying, in which politicians in power used populist policies during favorable economic times to buy political support. Politicians seized the opportunity to use relatively cheap borrowing on the international market[12] to fund their electoral victories by broadening the welfare state and offering concessions to particular electoral groups. Votes were bought by increasing pensions, extending war veteran benefits, and hiring more public sector workers and increasing their wages to create a perception of higher employment. A famous example of vote buying in Croatia, which virtually wrecked the pension system, was a concession made by former prime minister Ivo Sanader (currently serving a prison sentence for corruption charges) to the pensioners to increase their pensions in 2007, as a compensation of what they lost due to the 2002 pension reform.[13]

Designing such a system based on debt and capital inflows from abroad made the country increasingly vulnerable to outside shocks. Once the credit flow stopped in 2009, a crisis of a structurally unsustainable system was inevitable. Most countries of the Eurozone periphery, Croatia among them, found themselves in a typical sudden credit stop,[14] usually a characteristic of emerging economies with pegged currencies (in most cases against the dollar). The credit stop made it difficult for countries like Croatia to borrow on international markets, and with the crisis making a dent in the domestic public finances, deficits quickly soared and debt started rising. One can conclude that the outside shock from the US financial crisis brought the domestic instabilities of Croatia and similar peripheral economies to the surface, thus creating a trigger for the upcoming sovereign debt crisis.

Even today, the Croatian economy cannot shake its dependency on income from abroad. Tourism consists of 16.5 percent of the country's GDP, around 3.3 percent of GDP is attributed to remittances from abroad,[15] and 5.2 percent was a precrisis average in FDI.[16] The postcrisis average for FDI is 2.2 percent, suggesting that the main source of decline in the country's GDP was precisely the loss of foreign investment (see Figure 22.4). This is partially why the government has decided to maximize efforts in attracting foreign investments.

Overall, close to a quarter of the country's GDP is dependent on money from abroad. The imbalance between average wages and average household consumption suggests that one part of this mismatch is balanced by money from abroad, such as remittances and income from tourism; however, the majority of it is due to high consumer debt. The large debt of the private sector is currently in the process of deleveraging, thus further constraining

Figure 22.4 Croatian FDI (Right Axis) and Current Account Balance (Left Axis), 2000–2013

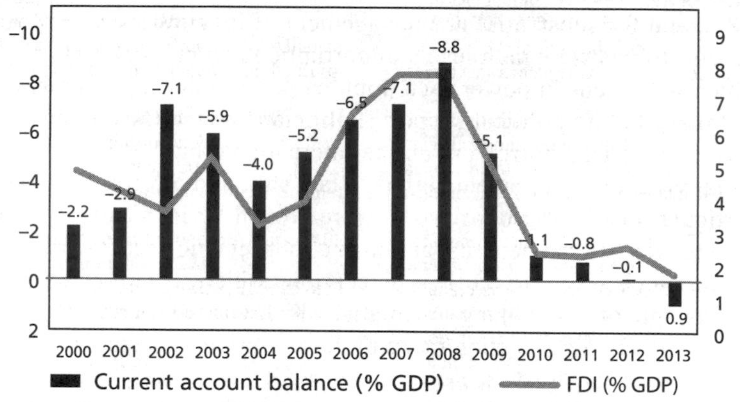

Source: HNB, Croatian National Bank, "Bilten 208," Zagreb (2014).

consumption, which has also failed to recover since the 2009 shock. Domestic aggregate demand, as the growth of GDP, has been negative ever since the crisis started (see Figure 22.1).

Negotiation Process and EU Accession

With economic instabilities and unbalanced public finances at the fore long before the 2009 crisis, Croatians saw the EU as a sign of new hope. EU accession was presented to the public as the end goal of the country's transition. After a gloomy first decade of Croatian independence characterized by a four-year war, unstable democratic consolidation, dubious privatization schemes, and a number of corruption scandals, the new decade underscored the European Union as the crucial foreign policy goal for a nation seeking international recognition and the end of economic and political hardship. Not surprisingly the created perception of the Union at the time induced an immediate 80 percent support in favor of membership.

Over the years, the support has dissipated. One of the reasons could be the length of the negotiation process during which the pendulum of EU support was swinging from as high as 80 percent in 2003 to as low as 40 percent in 2005.[17] Since then, it has been more or less stable around 50 percent until 2011, when, in the final few months of campaigning, the support for the EU went back up to over 60 percent. A whole range of factors influencing the vote can explain the shift of attitudes. The most important one triggering vast Euro-skepticism was the condition of full cooperation with the

International Criminal Tribunal for the former Yugoslavia in The Hague, whose negative opinions on Croatia's collaboration had postponed the start of negotiations a number of times, in 2003 and 2004. In the Eurobarometer survey at the time, citizens expressed their discontent that Croatia was being treated unfairly.[18] The consequence was a doubling of negative attitudes toward the EU to 48 percent in the middle of 2005. Other factors that could have contributed to the rising Euro-skepticism were disputes with neighboring EU member states Italy and Slovenia over border issues, a range of domestic corruption scandals that pushed the final entry date further away, and even negative opinions expressed by some member states. All of this created an animosity of some citizens toward the EU, which was no longer being perceived as Croatia's silver lining.

The country's two main political parties, SDP and HDZ, along with other smaller parties that were parts of coalition governments in the past ten years, fully supported EU membership from the beginning of the negotiation process. The only opposition came from nonparliamentary parties and various obscure public figures. Even as opinion surveys uncovered a rising discontent with EU membership in the middle of the decade, the main political parties decided to ignore this side of public opinion. The consequence was that there were never any real debates held about EU membership, with the political elites presenting the EU from a one-sided argument, rarely expressing the potential disadvantages to the public and using generic arguments against the critics. The information given to the public was never entirely truthful, which could have been one reason some voters never switched their opinion back in favor of membership.[19]

The lack of information resulted in 87 percent of the voters revealing they were not well enough informed about the EU in 2011.[20] The intensive pre-referendum campaign lasting for two months did decrease that number, but only 15 percent of the voters considered themselves to be well informed about the EU in 2012.[21] Several studies have recognized that the voters' poor knowledge and lack of understanding of the real consequences of EU entry were the true reasons behind Croatia's rising Euro-skepticism.[22] In addition, a serious lack of trust in domestic political institutions along with dissatisfaction over government performance further triggered negative attitudes toward the EU.[23] Issues relating to the loss of sovereignty, identity, and culture as well as issues revoking the potential exploitation of the country's wealth by foreigners gave further rise to Euro-skepticism.

The lack of clarity and information around the negotiation process was a main problem for Croatians[24] and further undermined the trust in political elites to protect domestic interests that had kept the divide of opinions over membership at a more or less constant level throughout the negotiation process. The uncertainty over what the political elites had negotiated fueled the perception that Croatia was not entirely ready for the EU. In combination with the Eurozone sovereign debt crisis, this has only intensified negative attitudes toward the EU, bringing the economy to the fore of public focus, which could have been one of the reasons people started to apply economic reasoning to a greater extent than before.

Relationship with the European Commission: Positive Pressures from Abroad

Croatia entered the EU on July 1, 2013, in the midst of a five-year recession and with high expectations of the government (and initially parts of the population) that EU entry would provide a boost to growth, primarily in terms of taking advantage of structural funds. In fact, one of the crucial pillars of the government's strategy to revitalize investments rested on hopes of realizing EU-funded investment projects. The government even created a new Ministry of Regional Development and EU Funds to serve this purpose. Unfortunately, during the first six months of membership not a lot of money was pulled from EU funds, which brought intensified criticism upon the government for its incompetence. A year and a half after membership, Croatia is receiving barely more money from the EU than it is paying in membership fees.[25]

When Croatia joined the EU, it was already under the burden of large macroeconomic and structural imbalances. It needed a commitment mechanism for engaging in structural reforms. In November 2013, it entered the procedure of the European Semester, during which the EU opened the Excessive Deficit Procedure (EDP) for Croatia in January 2014.[26] The EDP as the corrective arm of the Stability and Growth Pact makes sure that member states adopt the appropriate policies to reduce their fiscal deficits and public debts when they breach the 3 percent deficit to GDP limit and the 60 percent debt to GDP limit. Since Croatia entered the Union with over 5 percent deficit and over 70 percent debt to GDP, it was mandatory for the EDP to help steer the country into a painful fiscal consolidation process.

In April 2014, the Croatian government produced a national reform program to address the concerns expressed by the Commission.[27] Along with describing the measures taken so far, it has outlined measures to be taken from 2014 to 2017.[28] The key challenges for the government are to promote competitiveness and job growth, while simultaneously addressing the fiscal imbalances by cutting the budget deficit and lowering public debt.

After a diligent in-depth review of the Croatian economy,[29] in June 2014 the EU made a set of country-specific recommendations laying out the necessary reforms the country must apply.[30] The EU commended the government for initiating certain reforms such as increasing the flexibility of the labor market, streamlining the benefits system, taking measures aimed at reducing tax evasion and better tax collection, and taking certain steps to enhance the business environment.[31] However, it keeps emphasizing the worrisome fiscal imbalances and the necessity of further, deeper reforms, in part to successfully finish the fiscal consolidation process and in part to initiate economic recovery. The EU has given the government a clear direction on which areas to reform and how. Apart from fiscal consolidation, which is still the biggest issue, there is a series of other reforms the government should attend to. These include the cost effectiveness of the health care sector, pension reform, the second phase of labor market reforms (focused on wage setting and lowering youth and elderly unemployment), overhaul of governance in state-owned enterprises, reform of the judicial system, improving efficiency of public administration, development of a proper bankruptcy framework,[32] and better measures aimed to fight corruption, among other things, in public procurement and state-owned enterprises.[33]

However, recommending which reforms must be made and implementing these recommendations are proving to be two very different things. The government faces constant resistance from certain social groups, and constant criticism from others, including the European Commission itself. One reason for the government's slow responsiveness at this moment are the upcoming general elections in 2015, but more important is the resistance from public sector unions and a whole range of interest groups that are still successfully avoiding any demand for proper structural reform. From public sector unions to war veterans, pensioners, and most of all local politicians and their cronies, too many groups in society are dependent, directly or indirectly, on the government and its budget. It is only natural to expect such groups to vehemently oppose any attempts at reform and to protect their privileged status quo.

Another constraining factor in the country's development and one of the main contributors to the government's wastefulness and its irresponsible public finances is Croatia's central problem for decades: corruption. Croatia is one of the most corrupt EU member states, with only Greece, Spain, and Romania faring worse.[34] Public procurement is an area particularly prone to corruption, where 64 percent of domestic entrepreneurs state that corruption is extremely high in public procurement procedures, and 89 percent say it's impossible to get a contract with the government without "pulling strings."[35] Furthermore, on a local level, a quarter of public funds allocated to public procurement are corrupt monies.[36] There is an interdependent relationship between local quasi-entrepreneurs[37] and local political elites where politicians reward their cronies with rigged contracts, and they in turn provide the necessary political support.[38] It has been found that Croatian local politicians can actually increase their re-election chances with higher levels of corruption.[39]

In public companies, corruption is also rampant. In a series of arrests and anticorruption raids, many former CEOs of state-owned enterprises are facing trials or have already been convicted. One such famous case implicates the former prime minister, Ivo Sanader, who used his influence to extract vast amounts of money from public enterprises for personal use, in addition to procuring campaign financing of his political party, HDZ, in the same way. The trial ended in 2014,[40] with Sanader convicted and sentenced to nine years in prison, along with some of his associates who got lower punishments, and his political party, which was ordered to return the money it received illegally (approximately 30 million kunas; €4 million).[41] According to currently ongoing trials, other political parties might not be immune to this type of behavior. Such practices of pulling money from public enterprises for party financing are colloquially dubbed "black funds" of political parties.

In such an environment, the EU remains the most important factor of outside pressure on the Croatian government to undergo political action. It is possible to say that without EU pressure during the negotiation process, an indictment against a powerful prime minister such as Sanader might not have been possible. After all, one of the positive effects of EU integration for Croatia was precisely the outside pressure that forced governments to engage in anticorruption raids. Many are hoping it will be left to the EU once again to push for reforms and necessary budget cuts. Under the procedure of the European Semester, it will be harder for any government to keep sustaining a system of large deficits and wastefulness that in part supports corruption and in part unsustainable concessions for a whole range of interest groups.

Political Threats and Attitudes Toward the EU

The imposed austerity policies combined with an inability of both governments during the crisis period to revert the downward GDP growth trend have certainly affected their popularity. Much like all of Europe (apart from Germany), public trust in politicians has reached its lowest levels,[42] giving rise to various antiestablishment movements. However, in Croatia this trend has surfaced in the form of calling for referendums as a way to apply direct democracy. Citizens have lost faith in the political system and see the referendums as a viable tool to influence public policy, particularly after the success of the anti–gay marriage referendum in 2013, organized by a right-wing citizens' initiative with strong organizational support from the Croatian Catholic Church. Encouraged by the success of this ideologically driven referendum, three other efforts have arisen, two of which have failed and one that is still in procedure. All three efforts were made in 2014. First there was an ideological plea for a referendum on prohibiting the use of the Cyrillic alphabet in public buildings in minority areas, followed by a politically motivated referendum call for changing the parliamentary voting system to preferential voting. Both of these failed to collect the necessary amount of signatures, falling short by a marginal level.

The third call for a referendum was economically oriented. It was organized to prevent the government from assigning a private concession for domestic highways, an idea of the government to reduce some of the huge debt burden from highway construction (30 billion kunas of debt and guarantees). A large part of the civil sector rebelled against the idea, claiming that the highways are Croatian and should not be sold to foreigners, and they should therefore remain in public ownership. Led by the unions of the Croatian Highways, a public company, they successfully acquired the necessary amount of signatures and have filed for a referendum to be called on this decision by the government. If this referendum proves successful, it could give rise to a whole new strategy of political action in Croatia.

Rising Euro-skepticism can also be seen as manifesting itself in the recent run-off in the Croatian presidential elections of 2014, where in addition to the three established political candidates who represent the majority of parliamentary parties on the political spectrum, a fourth candidate has succeeded in gaining sufficient support to register his candidacy on a platform of anti-bank, quasi-anarchistic, and anti-EU policy. Ivan Sinčić, a twenty-four-year-old student representing a nongovernmental organization fighting forced evictions, has campaigned and qualified on a political platform advocating annulment of all citizen debt, expansive monetary policy, and arrests of a large segment of incumbent public officials and politicians for "treason," and the country's exit from the EU. Gaining support of 16.42 percent in the election's first round should not be ignored but carefully considered as a comprehensive indicator of citizens' attitudes toward the EU a year after entering the Union.[43] This context and successful referendums on topics such as the constitutional definition of marriage as only heterosexual, considered in the context of the progressive ruling of the European Court of Justice on same-sex marriage, can be taken as indicators of attitudes toward the EU and how certain sentiments persist despite formal integration and general support for membership. Persistence of Euro-skepticism in a part of the society can be interpreted in the context of rising skepticism toward the established national political institutions and politicians, which have all unanimously advocated EU membership. Having lost the public's trust in their ability to deliver on planned and promised policy goals and to reverse negative economic and social trends, the lack of trust toward national political organizations is spilling over from the national political arena and manifesting itself as Euro-skepticism. These sentiments are further perpetuated by a number of judicial proceedings—charging high-level officials, ministers, and even a prime minister with organized corruption and graft—that have recently been concluded with guilty verdicts, offering final evidence on the depth and extent of corruption in the political system, and consequently undermining trust in the national and, by extension, European political institutions.

An opposing framework of national identity must also be considered as working in favor of public support for the country's EU membership. The country spent almost a century in federations and unions with the countries of western Balkans, such as Serbia, Bosnia and Herzegovina, and Montenegro, with often negative public sentiment toward this part of Croatia's past, which stemmed from the violent break and independence war that resulted in high human casualties and economic wreckage. A considerable part of the population of Croatia has consistently sought to define themselves and the country within a framework that is "the opposite" (or at least different) from the western Balkan countries that make up a large part of Croatia's neighborhood. This becomes the idea of the country's EU membership as the opposite, better, alternative to its southeast European, western Balkan past affiliation.

Croatian Influence on the EU

For the European Union as a whole, Croatia's accession process has been marked by several key changes. The most important has to do with the conditionality principle for EU accession, where traditionally countries had to meet a set of conditions before starting the negotiation process for joining the Union. However, Croatia may be the last country to join the EU under such a conditionality principle. In the cases of Serbia and Kosovo, the improvement of their bilateral relations was not a precondition for Serbia's commencement of negotiations, instead making the normalization of relations a part of their negotiating framework for EU membership, thereby aiming to solve issues through the negotiation process.[44]

However, with entrance into the EU, Croatia has also taken on a new role within the region as an informal "front man" for EU candidate countries in the western Balkans, six of them currently in this status (Bosnia and Herzegovina, Montenegro, Serbia, Albania, Kosovo, and Macedonia), in their EU accession process. Taking on the role of representing, to an extent, the entirety of the EU toward the western Balkan countries has brought both positive and negative public sentiment. While politically hailed as a positive tool for improving the state of things in the neighboring Bosnia and Herzegovina—a country long troubled by political quagmire and economic stagnation and a significant number of ethnic Croatian citizens who have long struggled to realize political equality with other ethnic groups in the country—the public's attitudes toward other EU member candidates varies. Although there are a few negative public sentiments voiced on the topic of the EU membership of Albania, Macedonia, Kosovo, and Montenegro, Serbia's membership bid might prove a challenge in terms of reconciling public attitudes with EU and national policy. While the national policy of the Croatian government has so far been explicitly not to use the right of veto, it has done so on the EU accession process of its neighbors to solve bilateral issues. Recent public opinion polls indicate a significant rift between policy and public opinion. In a recent public opinion poll conducted by Alpheus Policy InSight and Ipsos Puls, 61.5 percent of Croatians believe

Croatia should use its veto power to make all of its bilateral issues with Serbia a condition for EU membership.[45]

Conclusions

Today's Croatia falls into the Eastern bloc of the EU: smaller, somewhat corrupt, badly in debt, with high unemployment and political instability. Although its banks are solid, they were still negatively affected by the financial crisis. However, Croatia is unique in its dependence on outside funding from tourism and remittances. The EU was supposed to be its solution, but has raised more issues to address. Croatia has a longer way to go than most of the other EU member states before the rigors of financial and political instability are behind it.

Notes

1. DZS (2014a).
2. There was a single period of above zero growth in the third quarter of 2011 (DZS 2012), however it was only 0.4 percent, after which the trajectory remained negative. This single quarter failed to change opinions of the population that the country is starting to recover. In fact, the majority of the population agrees that the country is by now in recession for six straight years (T-portal, "Od Sanaderove države u banani do šest godina recesije," November 29, 2014. Available at http://www.tportal.hr/biznis /politika-i-ekonomija/360669/Od-Sanaderove-drzave-u-banani-do-sest-godina -recesije.html).
3. European Commission (2014a).
4. EU estimates for 2014.
5. Kukuriku coalition, "Plan 21," Political and economic program of the Kukuriku coalition, 2011. http://www.kukuriku.org/files/plan21.pdf.
6. European Commission (2014c).
7. Eurobarometer (2014a).
8. HZZ—Croatian Employment Service, "Monthly Statistical Bulletin 11," Croatian Employment Service, Zagreb, 2014. http://www.hzz.hr/UserDocsImages/stat_bilten _11_2014.pdf
9. DZS (2014b).
10. HNB—Croatian National Bank, "Bilten 208," Zagreb, 2014. http://www.hnb.hr /publikac/bilten/arhiv/bilten-208/ebilt208.pdf.
11. Ministry of Finance (Croatia), "Obrazloženje državnog proračuna i financijskih planova izvanproračunskih korisnika za 2014. I projekcije za 2015. I 2016. Godinu," Budgetary documents, Republic of Croatia Ministry of Finance, Zagreb, 2014.
12. Rates were historically low for a country that in its short history of independence went through a war and a banking crisis in the end of the 1990s.
13. Index.hr, "Započinje predizborna isplata duga umirovljenicima," bulletin board comment, 2007. Available at http://www.index.hr/vijesti/clanak/zapocinje-predizborna -isplata-duga-umirovljenicima/365390.aspx (accessed November 19, 2007). Jutarnji list, "Sanader: Nisam dijelio packe: Isplata duga umirovljenika do kraja godine," May 16, 2007. Available at http://www.jutarnji.hr/template/article/article-print.jsp?id =174495. The objective of the 2002 pension reform was to stabilize the pension system

by lowering the gap between revenues raised from contributions and the size of pension expenditures in the pay-as-you-go system (contributions only covered roughly 60 percent of all pension expenditures). The idea was to gradually transform the pay-as-you-go system to a fully based individual contribution system by 2030, an idea that was successful in lowering the gap until 2007. Those who lost were pensioners who ended up in retirement after the reform took place, so to win over their votes, and thus get the support of a coalition partner (the Croatian Pensioner Party) Sanader made interventions into the system that almost completely nullified the positive effects of the reform and its expected effects on the stabilization of the pension system.

14. Reinhart and Rogoff (2009).

15. This is the official estimate, although it certainly underestimates these remittances' importance in the domestic economy, since a significant amount of funds enter the country via unofficial sources. A working paper from the European Central Bank estimates remittances to Croatia to be around 6 percent of GDP just before the crisis (Schiopu and Siegfried 2006).

16. HNB (2014).

17. Perkovic (2013).

18. Renata Franc and Vanja Medjugorac, "Support for EU Membership in Croatia Has Fallen Dramatically Since Accession Negotiations Began in 2003," *LSE European Politics and Policy* (blog), April 2, 2013. Available at http://blogs.lse.ac.uk/europpblog /2013/04/02/croatia-euroscepticism.

19. Ibid., Perkovic (2013).

20. Ipsos Puls, "Stavovi hrvatskih građana prema priključenju Europskoj Uniji," Survey for the Delegation of the European Union in Croatia, Ipsos Puls Public Affairs, Zagreb, 2011.

21. Ibid.

22. GONG, "Euroscepticism in Croatia at the Doorstep of the EU: Sources and Arguments," GONG Report, Zagreb, 2011. http://gong.hr/media/uploads/dokumenti /20110618.euroscepticismincroatiaathedoorstepoftheeu_en.pdf.

23. Štulhofer (2006).

24. Ipsos Puls (2011).

25. European Commission (2014c).

26. European Commission (2014c).

27. Croatian government (2014a). "National Reform Programme 2014." *Europe 2020 in Croatia*, European Commission, April 2014. http://ec.europa.eu/europe2020 /pdf/csr2014/nrp2014_croatia_en.pdf 28 Croatian government (2014b).

29. European Commission (2014d).

30. European Commission (2014e).

31. European Commission (2014d).

32. The EC welcomed the newly established prebankruptcy framework in their assessments, however what the Commission failed to realize about this procedure is its inherent vulnerability to misuse and corruption, since it only protects the debtors at the full expense of the creditors. The prebankruptcy framework has already raised much controversy in Croatia, where many entrepreneurs close to political elites have used it to legally write off their debts by presenting rigged financial statements and rigged claims. Several arrests have already been made because of it, with more to follow.

33. European Commission (2014e).

34. European Commission (2014f).

35. Ibid.

36. Vuković (2014).

37. The term *quasi-entrepreneurs* refers to those businesses that exist for the sole purpose of gaining public procurement contracts, with the value of contract often much higher than their capacities and net worth.

38. In accordance with the findings in Bueno De Mesquita et al. (2005).

39. Vuković (2014).

40. This is only one of the six major cases against Sanardi. Hina and Željko Petrušić, "Fimi Medija: Sanaderu Devet Godina Zatvora!," *Jutarnji*, March 11, 2014. Available at http://www.jutarnji.hr/fimi-media—sanaderu-devet-godina-zatvora/1172471/.

41. Ibid.

42. Trust for Parliament is down to 12 percent, trust in parties 8 percent, Eurobaromter (2013a).

43. DIP-Croatian Electoral Commission (2015) Final electoral results for the President of the Republic of Croatia. First round. Zagreb, January 2015. http://www.izbori.hr/106pre/rezult/1/rezultati.html.

44. Luka Orešković, Croatia and the EU: Revisiting the Conditionality Principle," March 18th 2014, *HuffingtonPost*.http://www.huffingtonpost.com/luka-oreskovic/croatia-and-the-eu-accession_b_4974793.html

45. Ipsos Puls and Alpheus Policy Insight (2014), "Citizens in favor of electoral system changes, placing requirements on Serbian EU accession" December 16, 2014. http://insight.alpheus.hr/m/articles/2014-12-16.htm.

23

The EU and the Member States: Concluding Thoughts

Eleanor E. Zeff and Ellen B. Pirro

WE HAVE ADDRESSED THREE MAJOR QUESTIONS IN THIS BOOK: what form will the future European Union (EU) take? How have the member states addressed recent economic, financial, and geopolitical crises? How do the member states interact with the EU?

Throughout the chapters, the authors have explored the question of the EU's future from their member states' perspectives. The most pressing and recent question, especially in light of the financial and economic crises in Europe, has been whether the euro will fail and, if it does, whether the EU can exist as a well-functioning union with federal aspirations without a common currency. How deep should European integration go, and in what ways can it offer its members the most benefits—with a deeper or wider type of integration? Would a federation last longer and lead to more effective policies, or would the prospect of losing too much sovereignty and facing too much centralized control scare off peripheral or potential members? In Chapter 2, John McCormick offers the idea that the EU should move toward a confederal union rather than "an ever closer union" on the federal model.[1] This idea is not exactly new, as the UK, Denmark, and Hungary, among other member states, have long advocated a looser union. The rise of Euro-skepticism in all the member states further indicates that many EU citizens might also prefer a "less-than-federal" union, or at least do not fully trust the EU, a necessary ingredient for a successful union.

Perhaps this is a good time to reconsider the idea of a confederal Europe, a union of independent states that rely on each other and work together in various overarching or supranational institutions for mutual benefits. Confederation, if that were the goal, would still bind the states together under cooperative and shared institutions but would allow each state to retain more sovereignty, and without fear of an ever-encroaching EU. In

2010, Eurobarometer findings indicated that 80 percent of Europeans approved of joint actions against terrorism, and around 70 percent wanted to join together on energy, research, and environmental affairs. Even states such as Ukraine see the benefits of joining and aspire to membership. As it appears that the EU is most likely to stay together in some form, it should now consider the benefits of confederation, but what should this confederation look like, and what problems does it face? In Chapter 6 on the Benelux countries, Karen M. Anderson suggests that "Belgium's multilingual federalism is often viewed as a model for what a (con-)federal Europe might look like."

Some of the member states' views on confederation versus federation shed light on the various ideas that are under consideration in discussions about "what future shape the EU will adopt?" For example, in the Baltic states, support for a confederal model of governance is dependent on the different political views expressed in the electorate. Right-wing parties that desire free trade but fewer socialist and state-directed policies would be more in favor of confederalism than would left-wing parties, supporting harmonizing member states' welfare and other types of social policies (see Chapter 20). Belgium and Luxembourg support the federal model of governance and are for continuing integration, but Euro-skepticism has been growing in the Netherlands, and the Dutch are less supportive of a strong federal union than they have been in the past, so much so that their views now approach the strong Euro-skepticism seen in Sweden, Austria, and the UK. The strongly Euro-skeptic states—and this group now includes Greece, Hungary, and the Czech Republic along with the UK, Sweden, and Austria—have never supported a "United States of Europe" type of federation model. Hungary even considers a confederal model to be too restrictive.

Many of the Eastern European states, which had formerly been dominated by the Soviet Union and the communist model of governance, were reluctant to join another union where they would have to give up their sovereignty again. Yet the benefits of joining the EU, with its free trade and monetary support to modernize, trumped their reservations, and currently eleven former Eastern bloc states are now members of the EU. Some, such as Latvia, Slovakia, Estonia, and Slovenia, have also become Eurozone members, signifying their belief in a closer union along federal lines. Spain and Portugal have different concerns. Early supporters of a strong EU, and both Eurozone members, they were significantly affected by the recent financial crisis. Both countries have a lot of diversity and are decentralizing; in Spain, Catalonia and the Basque territories are considering separation measures, and even Portugal is facing decentralization demands. With decentralization a concern within the countries themselves, there is little support for a federal EU at this time. Italy, one of the founding members of the EU and long considered a pro-Europe state, has become increasingly marginalized in recent years, so confederalism might be a good option.

Ireland is another country that has been pro-Europe and has benefited from its membership, but it also voted "no" to an EU constitution, became more Euro-skeptic after the adverse affects of the economic crisis on its economy, and has social policies and foreign policy issues that would not easily fit into a federal model of governance. Confederalism could be a good fit for Ireland. The citizens of Denmark, through their frequent referenda have consistently voted against a federal EU model. At this point, Greece is no longer a truly sovereign state because it is governed by EU and International Monetary Fund requirements necessitated by its several bailouts. Its "no" vote in the July 5, 2015, referendum could be seen as defiance to this loss of sovereignty. In Austria, the experience of the recent financial crises shocked the country, despite its own ability to come out unscathed, but has led to a rise of right-wing nationalist parties. The country remains pro-Europe, but a confederal model would better suit its non-central position in the EU. Sweden remains a primarily Euro-skeptic country and now Finland, formerly very prointegrationist, has become more Euro-skeptical as well. Many of the smaller countries, including some new members—Romania, Bulgaria, and Croatia as well as Malta, Cyprus, and the Baltic states—are witnessing growing Euro-skepticism in the aftermath of the economic and financial crises, but nevertheless see no other future for themselves outside of EU membership. Croatia and Bulgaria are especially worried about the loss of their young people to other member states in the EU. For them, on the periphery but needing the support of a union of other states, a confederal model of governance might be a good option. Germany is in favor of a stronger, more federal union and recently strongly supported EU-wide reductions in greenhouse gases as well as REACH, a comprehensive regulatory procedure, and other EU-wide environmental, social, and economic policies. It sees the future of Europe as united, although its citizens are tired of supporting countries such as Greece, which do not always (or even often) follow EU-wide directives and laws. France, with its "petit oui" (little yes) for the Treaty of Maastricht demonstrated that it is not so supportive of federalizing the EU, and it remains in the shadow of Germany. It has benefited from membership in the EU, but not as much as Germany has and so is always having to catch up. It supports a strong EU but with reservations and a great desire to keep as much of its sovereignty as possible. Poland weathered the economic crisis very well and has benefited greatly from its EU membership. The recent crisis in Ukraine, however, demonstrated to the country that it cannot entirely count on the EU for support against Russia, so it has begun to strengthen its military forces and reassert its sovereignty and independence from some EU policies. The Baltic states are also worried about Russian encroachment and are looking more toward NATO for support than to the EU, which they recognize as having limitations especially financially and in foreign affairs.

The terrible financial crisis of 2008 and subsequent recessions in many EU member states, especially Ireland, Greece, and Portugal, have shaken Europeans and made them question EU policies and the methods and effectiveness of integration. The British are thinking of calling a referendum on their EU membership, and the French are vocal about their pessimism for their future and their relationship with the EU. Yet, an interesting mentality has developed. Although movement toward deeper federation slowed, Croatia has joined and other applicant states are waiting to join. Many thought the euro was doomed and that the EU itself might have numbered days. Instead, there is a growing and expanding EU. Latvia has joined the euro, and other states are preparing their economies for euro membership as well. In response to the 2008 economic crisis, the EU started a program of quantitative easing and structural adjustments, so that even if Greece exits the common currency ("Grexit"), the euro is in better shape than before the crisis. If Greece were to exit, the ECB could focus more attention on strengthening euro problems in Portugal and Spain. Although recovery in many European states is slower than hoped, many, like Ireland, are recovering and are doing business as usual. The EU remains the wealthiest marketplace in the world despite the recent economic downturn.

The world watched the financial crisis unfold and the European experiment in integration falter. It has taken a long, slow process of creating new mechanisms to monitor budgets and allow the European Central Bank extensive powers to begin to emerge from the deep recession of 2008–2012. After coming out of recession briefly, 2014 ended with an overall EU back in recession and many countries shaky. It is true the fiscal crisis hit some countries particularly hard. The real estate bubble struck the UK, Spain, and France to some extent. This led to a EU-wide slowdown in trade, beginning with Germany at its center. Fiscal woes beset nations with major sovereign debt, especially Greece, Spain, Ireland, and Portugal. But it also seriously affected Cyprus, Italy, and Slovenia. Countries that were not in serious trouble through the worst of the financial downturn still suffered as trade lagged and their export-dependent economies declined. This was particularly true in Eastern Europe, affecting the Czech Republic, the Baltic states, Poland, Romania, Bulgaria, and to some extent Hungary. At the beginning of 2015, all the European member states are striving hard to put their economies back on a growth track, increase trade, and generally emerge from the recession-prone situation they have been mired in. All the projections are for slow but positive growth rates (only about 1.5 percent). Only Greece remains severely threatened and may yet need to pull out of the Eurozone or be ousted for failure to meet its commitments. In Spain, Prime Minister Mariano Rajoy stated that if Greece were to exit the euro, it would be a "negative message that euro membership is reversible." EU governments are closely monitoring development in Greece now that the possiblity of a Eurozone exit has been raised. The growth of Euro-skepticism in public opinion, the emergence of anti-EU right-wing parties, and the many threats that have arisen to the EU will challenge Brussels from all directions, and it remains to be seen how the European bureaucrats will cope.

Ukraine poses a wider challenge than the difficulties of one small, post-communist state. For much of the EU, the threat is to energy security. A great proportion of the EU gets its oil and gas from Russia via pipelines, which travel through Ukraine. Sanctions against Russia for its seizure of the Crimea and military involvement in Ukraine pose ongoing threats to supplies of gas and oil, and the EU is urgently exploring alternatives.

In Eastern Europe, Russia poses a security threat. The Baltic states feel they are on the front lines of a resurgent Russian empire, and their very independence is on the line. Poland and the other Visegrad states similarly believe Russia covets their return to a pro-Russian sphere. They are strengthening their ties to the EU and NATO and making security arrangements with a fearful eye eastward. Only Hungary, which is flirting with a pro-Russian stance, differs from this viewpoint. Hungary's position threatens EU unanimity and may need to be dealt with in the near future as the Russian situation continues to percolate and demand attention.

The Future?

It is very important to study the relations of the EU to its member states to better understand how the EU functions and what shape it will take in the future. Throughout the book, the authors have explored the various relations that the member states have with the EU and its bureaucracy. These relations are constantly changing, and the recent crises, both financial and foreign policy, are examples of how events, as well as history, culture, and existing structures, can influence how the member states feel about the EU and how they interact with it. How the EU has reacted to several recent crises and events has already had significant effects on the member states, and these changes will continue to affect relations between the members and the EU well into the future. It is important to note that no state has pulled out of the EU and others are eager to join, yet the findings here suggest that the EU will have to address the rise in Euro-skepticism. The Union continues despite crises and setbacks.

Note

1. Multilevel governance is another way to look at how the EU is functioning as a type of union. The problem with multilevel governance is that it has never been able to reach the level of a theory. It is also very obvious that the EU functions on many different levels, so the approach does not explain anything new, nor does it distinguish itself very clearly from federalism/confederalism. As an approach, it has been very useful, however, and has allowed researchers to explore the EU in its entirety rather than just by its institutions or its policies. This volume introduces the idea of confederalism, rather than multilevel governance, as an explanation for the relations between the member states and the EU and among the member states.

Acronyms

CAP	Common Agricultural Policy
CEE	Central and Eastern Europe
CFSP	Common Foreign and Security Policy
COREPER	Committee of Permanent Representatives
CSF	Community Support Framework (EU)
CVM	Cooperation and Verification Mechanism
EC	European Community
ECB	European Central Bank
ECOFIN	Council of Economic and Financial Ministers
ECOSOC	Economic and Social Committee
ECU	EC monetary unit prior to 1998
ECJ	European Court of Justice (the Court)
ECSC	European Coal and Steel Community
EDC	European Defense Community
EEC	European Economic Community (also, Common Market)
EEZ	Exclusive Economic Zone
EFSF	European Financial Stability Facility
EFTA	European Free Trade Association
EIB	European Investment Bank
EMS	European Monetary System
EMU	Economic and Monetary Union
ERDF	European Regional Development Fund
ERDP	European Regional Development Policy
ERM	Exchange Rate Mechanism
ESDP	European Security and Defence Policy

EUAC	EU Advisory Committee
EUHR	European Union High Representative
EUROPOL	European Police Office
FDI	foreign direct investment
GATT	General Agreement on Tariffs and Trade
GDP	gross domestic product
GNI	gross national income (EU)
GNP	gross national product
IC	Instruction Committee
IGC	Intergovernmental Conference
IM	Internal Market
JHA	Justice and Home Affairs
MEPs	members of the European Parliament
NATO	North Atlantic Treaty Organization
OECD	Organisation for Economic Cooperation and Development
PHARE	East European Countries Accession Program
PR	Permanent Representation
QMV	Qualified Majority Voting
R&D	research and development
SEA	Single European Act
SGCI	General Secretariat of the Interministerial Committee
SGP	Stability and Growth Pact
TEU	Treaty on European Union (aka, the Maastricht Treaty)
UKIE	Office of the Committee for European Integration
VAT	value-added tax
VER	Voluntary Export Restraints
WEU	Western European Union
WTO	World Trade Organization

Bibliography

Abdelal, Rawi. *National Purpose in the World Economy: Post-Soviet States in Comparative Perspective*. Ithaca, NY: Cornell University Press, 2001.

Adamczyk, Artur. "The Role of Poland in the Creation Process of the Eastern Partnership." *Yearbook of Polish European Studies* 13 (2010): 195–204.

Adler-Nissen, Rebecca. *Opting Out of the European Union*. Cambridge: Cambridge University Press, 2014.

Aichholzer, Julian, Sylvia Kritzinger, Markus Wagner, and Eva Zeglovits. "How Has Radical Right Support Transformed Established Political Conflicts? The Case of Austria." *West European Politics* 37, no. 1 (2014): 113–137.

Alapuro, Risto. "What Is Western and What Is Eastern in Finland?" *Thesis Eleven* 77, no. 1 (2004): 85–101.

Albonetti, Achille. *L'Italia, la politica estera e l'unità dell'Europa*. Rome: Edizioni Lavoro, 2005.

———. *Preistoria degli stati uniti d'Europa*. Milano: Giuffrè, 1960.

Alfieri, Alessandro. *La politica estera delle regioni*. Bologna: Il Mulino, 2004.

Allam, Miriam S., and Achim Goerres. "Economics, Politics or Identities? Explaining Individual Support for the Euro in New EU Member States in Central and Eastern Europe." *Europe-Asia Studies* 63, no. 8 (2011): 1399–1424.

Altomonte, Carlo, and Claudia Guagliano. "Comparative Study of FDI in Central and Eastern Europe and the Mediterranean." *Economic Systems* 27, no. 2 (2003): 223–246.

Amato, Giuliano. "Italy: The Rise and Decline of a System of Government." *Indiana International & Comparative Law Review* 4, no. 1994 (1994): 225–230.

Amnesty International. *Injustice Renamed: Discrimination in Education of Roma Persists in the Czech Republic*. London: Amnesty International, 2010.

Andersen, Svein S., and Kjell A. Eliassen. "The EC as a New Political System." In *Making Policy in Europe*, edited by Svein S. Andersen and Kjell A. Eliassen, 3–18. London: Sage, 1993a.

———. "Informal Processes: Lobbying, Actor Strategies, Coalitions and Dependencies." In *Making Policy in Europe*, 2nd ed., edited by Svein S. Andersen and Kjell A. Eliassen, 44–61. London: Sage, 2001a.

———, eds. *Making Policy in Europe: The Europeification of National Policy-Making*. London: Sage, 1993b.

————, eds. *Making Policy in Europe.* 2nd ed. London: Sage, 2001b.

Anderson, Karen M., Sanneke Kuipers, Isabelle Schulze, and Wendy van den Nouland. "Belgium: Linguistic Veto Players and Pension Reform." In *The Handbook of West European Pension Politics,* edited by Ellen M. Immergut, Karen M. Anderson, and Isabelle Schulze, 297–348. Oxford: Oxford University Press, 2007.

Anderson, Leif. *Beslutsfatterna.*Stockholm: PM Bäckström Förlag,1996.

Andreatta, Filippo. "La sfida dell'Unione Europea alla teoria delle relazioni internazionali." In *L'Europa sicura: Le politiche di sicurezza dell'Unione Europea,* edited by Serena Giusti and Andrea Locatelli, 13–29. Milano: Egea, 2008.

Antošová, Veronika, Dana Skálová, and Naďa Birčiaková. "Income Situation and Living Condition of Czech Households According to Statistics EU." *International Journal of Management Cases* 15, no. 4 (2013): 20–36.

Archer, Clive, Alyson J. K. Bailes, and Anders Wivel, eds. *Small States and International Security: Europe and Beyond.* London: Routledge, 2014.

Archer, Clive, and Neill Nugent. "The European Union's Member States: The Importance of Size." *Journal of European Integration, Special Issue* 28, no. 1 (2006): 3–6.

Arkestijn, Fred. *Nederlands bijdrage EU-begroting eenmalig lager.* Den Haag: Centraal Bureau voor de Statistiek, 2010.

Armstrong, 2013 (Lankowski, please supply)

Arter, David. "The EU Referendum in Finland on 16 October 1994: A Vote for the West, Not for Maastricht." *Journal of Common Market Studies* 33, no. 3 (1995): 361–387.

————. *Politics and Policy-Making in Finland: A Study of a Small Democracy in a West European Outpost.* Basingstoke: Palgrave Macmillan, 1987.

————. "Small State Influence within the EU: The Case of Finland's 'Northern Dimension Initiative.'" *Journal of Common Market Studies* 38, no. 5 (2000): 677–697.

Åslund, Anders. *How Capitalism Was Built: The Transformation of Central and Eastern Europe, Russia, and Central Asia.* Cambridge: Cambridge University Press, 2007.

Aspinwall, Mark, and Gerald Schneider,eds.*The Rules of Integration: Instituitonalist Approaches to the Study of Europe.*New York: Manchester University Press, 2001.

Auel, Katrin, and Tapio Raunio. "Debating the State of the Union? Comparing Parliamentary Debates on EU Issues in Finland, France, Germany and the United Kingdom." *Journal of Legislative Studies* 1, no. 1 (2014): 13–28.

Auel, Katrin, Oliver Rozenberg, and Angela Tacea. "To Scrutinise or Not to Scrutinise? Explaining Variation in EU-Related Activities in National Parliaments." *West European Politics* 38, no. 2 (2015): 282–304.

Auer, Stefan. "The Limits of Transnational Solidarity and the Eurozone Crisis in Germany, Ireland and Slovakia." *Perspectives on European Politics and Society* 15, no. 3 (2014): 322–334.

Avramov, Roumen. "The Role of a Currency Board in Financial Crises: The Case of Bulgaria." Discussion Paper6. Bulgarian National Bank, Sofia, Bulgaria, 1999.

Badiello, Lorenza. "Il ruolo delle rappresentanze regionali europee a Bruxelles."*EuropaEurope*9 no. 1 (2000): 166–171.

Bakker, Bas B., and Christoph Klingen. "Sheltered from the Storm." *Finance & Development* 49, no. 9 (2012): 44–47.

Balducci, Massimo. "Italy and the Ratification of the Maastricht Treaty." In *The Ratification of the Maastricht Treaty,* edited by Finn Laursen and Sophie Vanhoonacker, 195–201. Maastricht: Kluwer Law, 1993.

Bale, Tim, Seán Hanley, and Aleks Szczerbiak. "May Contain Nuts? The Reality Behind the Rhetoric Surrounding the British Conservatives' New Group in the European Parliament." *Political Quarterly* 81, no. 1 (2010): 85–98.

Bardi, Luciano, and Gianfranco Pasquino. *Euroministri: Il governo dell'Europa*. Milano: Il Saggiatore, 1994.

Baun, Michael, and Dan Marek. "The Implementation of EU Environmental Policy in the Czech Republic: Problems With Post-Accession Compliance?" *Europe-Asia Studies* 65, no. 10 (2013): 1877–1897.

Bauwens, Werner, Armand Clesse, and Olaf F. Knudsen. *Small States and the Security Challenge in the New Europe*. London: Brassey's, 1996.

Beneš, Vít, and Jan Karlas. "The Czech Presidency." *Journal of Common Market Studies* 48, Annual Review (2010): 69–80.

Bennich-Bjorkman, Li, and Branka Likic-Brboric. "Successful but Different: Deliberative Identity and the Consensus-Driven Transition to Capitalism in Estonia and Slovenia." *Journal of Baltic Studies* 43, no. 1 (2012): 47–73.

Bergh, Andreas, and Magnus Menrekson. *Varfor gar det bra for Sverige? Om sambanden mellan offentlig sektor, ekonomisk frihet, och ekonomisk utveckling*. Stockholm: FORES + IVRIG,2012.

Bergman, Torbjörn. "National Parliaments and EU Affairs Committees: Notes on Empirical Variation and Competing Explanations." *Journal of European Public Policy* 4, no. 3 (1997): 373–387.

Bergsten, C. Fred, and Jacob Funk Kirkegaard. "The Coming Resolution of the European Crisis: An Update." Policy Briefs in International EconomicsPB12-18, Peterson Institute for International Economics, Washington, DC, 2012. http://www.iie.com/publications/pb/pb12-18.pdf.

Beyers, Jan, and Guido Dierickx. "The Working Groups of the Council of the European Union: Supranational or Intergovernmental Negotiations?" *Journal of Common Market Studies* 36, no. 3 (1998): 289–317.

Bideleux, Robert, and Ian Jeffries. *Balkans: A Post-Communist History*. London: Taylor & Francis, 2007.

Bindi, Federiga. *Italy and the European Union*. Washington, DC: Brookings Institution Press, 2011.

Bindi, Federiga, and Luciano Bardi. "Italy: The Dominance of Domestic Politics." In *National Public and Private EC Lobbying*, edited by M.P.C.M.van Schendelen, 93–112. Dartmouth: Aldershot, 1993.

Bindi, Federiga, and Manuela Cisci. "Italy and Spain: A Tale of Contrasting Effectiveness in the EU." In *Member States of the European Union*, edited by Simon Bulmer and Christian Lequesne, 142–163. Oxford: Oxford University Press, 2005.

Bindi, Federiga, and Steffano Grassi. "The Italian Parliament: From Benevolent Observer to ActivePlayer." In *National Parliaments on Their Ways to Europe: Losers or Latecomers?* edited by Andreas Maurer and Wolfgang Wessels, 269–300. Schriften des Zentrum für Europäische Integrationsforschung: NOMOS Verlagsgesellschaft, 2001.

Birch, Anthony. "Approaches to the Study of Federalism." *Political Studies* 14, no. 1 (1966): 15–33.

Bischoff, C., and M. Wind, "Denmark." In *Routledge Handbook of European Elections*, edited by Donatella M. Viola, London: Routledge, 2015.

Blankart, Charles. "The European Union: Confederation, Federation or Association of Compound States?" *Constitutional Political Economy* 18, no. 2 (2007): 99–106.

Blondel, Jean. *The Organization of Governments: A Comparative Analysis of Governmental Structures.*London: Sage, 1982.

Blondel, Jean, and Ferdinand Müller-Rommel. *Governing Together: The Extent and Limits of Joint Decision-Making in Western European Cabinets.* New York: St. Martin's Press, 1993.

Blondel, Jean, and Jean-Louis Thiebault, eds. *The Profession of Government Ministerin Western Europe.* Houndmills: Macmillan, 1991.

Bloom, Stephen. "The 2010 Latvian Parliamentary Elections." *Electoral Studies* 30 (2011): 379–383.

———. "Does a Nationalist Card Make for a Weak Hand? Economic Decline and Shared Pain." *Political Research Quarterly* 65, no. 1 (2012): 166–178.

Bocci, V.E. "Il potere estero delle regioni: Il caso dell'ufficio di collegamento della Regione Toscana." *Le Istituzioni del federalismo* 1, no. 21 (2000): 63–88.

Bock-Schappelwein, Julia, Helmut Mahringer, and Eva Rückert. "Kurzarbeit in Deutschland und Österreich: Endbericht." Österreichisches Institut für Wirtschaftsforschung, 2014.

Bohle, Dorothee, and Dóra Husz. "Whose Europe Is It? Interest Group Action in Accession Negotiations : The Cases of Competition Policy and Labor Migration." *Politique européenne* 15, no. 1 (2005): 85–112.

Bolgherini, Silvia. *Come le regioni diventano europee: Stile di governo e sfide comunitarie nell'Europa mediterranea.* Bologna: Il Mulino, 2006.

Bomberg, Elizabeth, and Alexander Stubb. *The European Union: How Does it Work?* Oxford: Oxford University Press, 2012.

Bonvicini, Giani, and Alessandro Colombo. *L'italia e la politica internazionale.* Bologna: Il Mulino, 2009.

Bossaert, Danielle. "Luxembourg: Flexible and Pragmatic Adaptation." In *Fifteen into One? The European Union and its Member States*, edited by W. Wessels, A. Maurer, and J. Mittag, 298–314. Manchester: Manchester University Press, 2003.

Brenke, Karl, Ulf Rinne, and Klaus F. Zimmermann. "Short Time Work: The German Answer to the Great Recession." Institute for the Study of Labor Discussion Paper 5780, 2013. http://ftp.iza.org/dp5780.pdf.

Breuss, Fritz. "Effects of Austria's EU Membership." *Austrian Economic Quarterly* 2 (2013): 1–12.

Briguglio, Lino, Gordon Cordina, Nadia Farriugia, and Constance Vigilance, eds. *Small States and the Pillars of Economic Resilience.* Islands and Small States Institute, University of Malta and Commonwealth Secretariat, London, 2008.

Briguglio, Lino, and Eliawony Kisanga, eds. *Economic Vulnerability and Resilience of Small States.* Islands and Small States Institute, University of Malta and Commonwealth Secretariat, London, 2004.

Bříza, Petr. "The Czech Republic: The Constitutional Court on the Lisbon Treaty Decision of 26 November 2008." *European Constitutional Law Review* 5, no. 1 (2009): 143–164. doi:10.1017/S1574019609001436.

BuCar, Maja. "Involving Civil Society in the International Development Cooperation of 'New' EU Member States: The Case of Slovenia." *Perspectives on European Politics and Society* 13, no. 1 (2012): 83–99.

Bueno de Mesquita, Bruce, Alastair Smith, Randolph M. Siverson, and James D. Morrow. *The Logic of Politics Survival.* Cambridge, MA: MIT Press, 2005.

Buhr, Renee. "Seizing the Opportunity: Euroscepticism and Extremist Party Success in the Post-Maastricht Era." *Government and Opposition* 41, no. 1 (2012): 544–573.

Bulmer, Simon. "Domestic Politics and Economic Community Policy-Making." *Journal of Common Market Studies* 21, no. 4 (1983): 349–564.

Bulmer, Simon, and Christian Lequesne. *The Member States of the European Union*. Oxford: Oxford University Press, 2005.

Bunse, Simone. *Small States and EU Governance: Leadership Through the Council Presidency*. New York: Palgrave Macmillan, 2009.

Buonanno, Laurie, and Neill Nugent. *Policies and Policy Processes of the European Union*. Basingstoke: Palgrave Macmillan, 2013.

Burgess, Michael. *Comparative Federalism: Theory and Practice*. London: Routledge, 2006.

Calavita, Kitty. *Immigrants at the Margins*. New York: Cambridge University Press, 2005.

Cananea, Giacinto della. "Italy." In *The National Coordination of EU Policy: The European Level*, edited by Hussein Kassim, Anand Menon, B. Guy Peters, and Vincent Wright, 129–146. Oxford: Oxford University Press, 2001.

Caporaso, James. "Toward a Normal Science of Regional Integration." *Journal of European Public Policy* 6, no. 1(1998): 160–164.

Carammia, Marcello, and Roderick Pace. "The Giant Is Still Sleeping: The Third European Election in Malta." *Journal of South European Society and Politics*, forthcoming.

Caretti, Paolo. "La nuova disciplina della partecipazione dell'Italia al processo normativo comunitario e delle procedure di esecuzione degli obblighi comunitari, dettata dalla legge n. 86 del 1989 alla prova: La prima legge comunitaria." *Rivista italiana di diritto pubblico comunitario*, no. 1 (1990): 330–350.

Cartabia, Marta, and Joseph H. H. Weiler. *L'Italia in Europa: Profili istituzionali e costituzionali*. Bologna: Il Mulino, 2000.

Cartwright, Andrew, and Agnes Batory. "Monitoring Committees in Cohesion Policy: Overseeing the Distribution of Structural Funds in Hungary and Slovakia." *Journal of European Integration* 34, no. 4 (2012): 323–340.

Cassese, Antonio. *Parliamentary Foreign Affairs Committees: The National Setting*. Padova: CEDAM, 1982.

Castles, Stephen, and Mark J. Miller. *The Age of Migration: International Population Movements in the Modern World*. New York: Guilford Press, 1993.

CBOS Public Opinion Research Center. "Concerns related to the introduction of the euro." Available at http://www.cbos.pl/EN/publications/reports/2014/151_14.pdf.

Chagnollaud, Dominique, and Jean-Louis Quermonne. *Le gouvernement de la France sous la Ve République*. Paris: Fayard, 1996.

Chelini, Michel-Pierre. "Le plan de stabilisation Pinay-Rueff, 1958." *Révue d'histoire moderne et contemporaine* 48, no.4 (2001): 102–123.

Christodoulou, Nikos, and George Christodoulou. "Financial Crises: Impact on Mental Health and Suggested Responses." *Journal of Physcotheraphy and Psycosomatics* 82, no. 5 (2013): 279–284.

Chubb, Basil. *The Government and Politics of Ireland*, 3rd ed. Abingdon: Routledge, 1992.

Churchill, Winston. "A Speech at Zurich University." In *Sinews of Peace*, edited by Randolph S. Churchill, 199–201. Boston: Houghton Mifflin, 1949.

CIPI. *Le lobby d'Italia a Bruxelles*. Brussels: Centro Italiano di Prospettiva Internazionale, 2006.

Ciriolo, Antonio. *Il dipartimento per il coordinamento delle politiche comunitarie*. Lecce: Milella, 1991.

Clark, Terry D., and Jovita Pranevičiūte. "Perspectives on Communist Successor Parties: The Case of Lithuania." *Communist and Post-Communist Studies* 41, no. 4 (2008): 443–464.

Coakley, John. "Irish Public Opinion and the New Europe." In *Ireland and the European Union*, edited by Michael Holmes, 100–110. Manchester: Manchester University Press, 2005.

Connolly, Richard, and Christopher A. Hartwell. "Developments in the Economies of Member States Outside the Eurozone." *Journal of Common Market Studies* 52 (2014) (Suppl. S1): 202–218.

Conti, Nicolò, and Luca Verzichelli. "La dimensione europea del discorso politico: Un'analisi diacronica del caso italiano (1950–2001)." In *L'Europa in Italia*, edited by Maurizio Cotta, Pierangelo Isernia, and Luca Verzichelli, 61–116. Bologna: Il Mulino, 2005.

Cooper, Andrew F., and Timothy M. Shaw, eds. *The Diplomacies of Small States: Between Vulnerability and Resilience*. Basingstoke: Palgrave Macmillan, 2009.

Copeland, Paul. "Central and Eastern Europe: Negotiating Influence in an Enlarged European Union." *Europe-Asia Studies* 66, no. 3 (2014): 467–487.

Corporate Excellence—Centre for Reputation Leadership. "How the Reputation of a Country Can Either Help or Hinder the Internationalisation of a Company's Reputation." Insights Strategy Document 126, 2012.

Cotta, Maurizio. "The Centrality of Parliament in a Protracted Democratic Consolidation: The Italian Case." In *Parliament and Democratic Consolidation in Southern Europe*, edited by Ulrike Liebert and Maurizio Cotta, 55–91. London: Pinter,1990.

———. "Il parlamento nella prima repubblica." In *La politica italiana*, edited by Pierangelo Isernia and Luca Verzichelli, 79–91. Bari: Laterza, 1996.

Cotta, Maurizio, Pierangelo Iserina, and Luca Verzichelli. *L'Europa in Italia: Elite, opinione pubblica e decisioni*. Bologna: Il Mulino, 2005.

Cowles, Maria Green, James A. Caporaso, and Thomas Risse-Kappen. *Transforming Europe: Europeanization and Domestic Change*. Ithaca, NY: Cornell University Press, 2001.

Cowley, Philip, and Mark Stuart. "The Cambusters: The Conservative European Union Referendum Rebellion of October 2011." *Political Quarterly* 83, no. 2 (2012a): 402–406.

Cramér, Per. *Neutralitet och Europeisk integration*. Stockholm: Norstedts, 1998.

Craveri, Piero, and Gaetano Quagliariello. *Atlantismo ed europeismo*. Rubbettino: Soveria Mannelli (Catanzaro), 2003.

Crouch, Colin, and Franz Traxler. *Organised Industrial Relations in Europe: What Future?* London: Sage, 1995.

Cuglesan, Natalia. "Implementarea legislatiei comunitare de mediu si noile responsabilitati ale autoritatilor publice din Romania." In *Tehnologii pentru protectia mediului: legislatie, teorie si aplicatii*, edited by Roman Morar, 49–80. Cluj-Napoca: Dacia, 2008.

Darden, Keith. *Economic Liberalism and Its Rivals: The Formation of International Institutions among the Post-Soviet States*. Cambridge: Cambridge University Press, 2009.

D'Atena, Antonio, and Eugenio Lanzillotta, eds.*Da Omero alla Costituzione europea: Costituzionalismo antico e moderno*. Tivoli: TORED, 2003.

De Giovanni, Biagio. "La funzione pubblica europea: Una proposta." *EuropaEurope, Nuova serie* 7, no. 4–5 (1998): 15–19.

De Grauwe, Paul. "Design Failures in the Eurozone: Can They Be Fixed?" LSE Europe in Question Series Discussion Paper 57, London School of Economics and Political Science,2013.

Dekker, Paul, and Josje den Ridder. "Burgerperspectieven 2013/3." *Kwartaalbericht van het Continu Onderzoek Burgerperspectieven.* Sociaal en Cultureel Planbureau, 2013.

Della Porta, Donatella, and Manuela Caiani. *Quale Europa? Europeizzazione, identità e conflitti.* Bologna: Il Mulino, 2006.

Dellepiane, Sebastian, and Niamh Hardiman. "Governing the Irish Economy: A Triple Crisis." Geary Institute Working Paper WP2011/03, University College Dublin, February 21, 2011.

Deloy, Corinne. "The Civic Platform (PO) Won the Polish General Elections." *European Elections Monitor*, October 10, 2011. http://www.robert-schuman.eu/en /eem/1175-the-civic-platform-po-won-the-polish-general-elections.

De Micheli, Chiara, and Luca Verzichelli. *Il Parlamento.* Bologna: Il Mulino, 2004.

DePorte, Antonie. *Europe Between the Superpowers: The Enduring Balance.* New Haven, CT: Yale University Press, 1980.

De Santis, Roberto. "The Euro Area Sovereign Debt Crisis: Safe Haven, Credit Rating Agencies, and the Spread of the Fever From Greece, Ireland, Portugal." European Central Bank Working Paper 1419, Frankfurt, 2012.

Deubner, Christian. "The French 'No' in the 2005 Referendum (November 8, 2005)." UCLA Center for European and Eurasian Studies, 2005.

———. "Saving the Euro—My Way: Competing French and German Visions for Euro Governance." *IP Journal*, German Council on Foreign Relations, May 20, 2011. https://ip-journal.dgap.org/en/ip-journal/topics/saving-euro-my-way.

Di Palma, Giuseppe. *Surviving Without Governing:The Italian Parties in Parliament.* Berkeley: University of California Press, 1977.

Di Palma, Giuseppe, Sergio Fabbrini, and Giorgio Freddi, eds. *Condannata al successo? L'Italia nell'Europa integrata.* Bologna: Il Mulino, 2003.

Dichiarazione N. 13. "Sul ruolo dei Parlamenti Nazionali nell'Unione Europea." *Unione Europea, raccolta dei Trattati* 1, no. 1 (1993).

Dichiarazione N. 14. "Sulla conferenza dei parlamenti."*Unione Europea, raccolta dei Trattati*, 1, no. 1 (1993).

Didier, Michel, and Gilles Koléda. *Compétitivité France-Allemagne:Le grand écart.* Paris: Economica, 2011.

Dinan, Desmond. *Ever Closer Union*, 2nd ed. Boulder, CO: Lynne Rienner Publishers, 1999.

———. *Ever Closer Union*, 4th ed. Boulder, CO: Lynne Rienner Publishers, 2010.

Dobrinsky, Rumen. "The Transition Crisis in Bulgaria." *Cambridge Journal of Economics* 24, no. 5 (2000): 581–602.

Dolezal, Martin, and Eva Zeglovits. "Almost an Earthquake: The Austrian Parliamentary Election of 2013." *West European Politics* 37, no. 1 (2014): 1–9.

Dohse, Dirk, Christiane Krieger-Boden, and Rüdiger Soltwedel. "EMU Calls for Comprehensive Labor Market Reform." *Intereconomics* 34, no. 2 (1999): 55–63.

Dörfer, Ingemar. "Sixty Years of Solitude: Sweden Returns to Europe." *Scandinavian Studies* 64, no. 4 (1992): 594–606.

Down, Ian, and Carole J. Wilson. "Opinion Polarization and Inter-Party Competition on Europe." *European Union Politics* 11, no. 62 (2010): 61–87.

Duffy, Bobby, and Tom Frere-Smith. "Perceptions of Reality: Public Attitudes Towards Immigration." Ipsos Mori Social ResearchReport, January 2014.

Duroselle, Jean-Baptiste. *Storia diplomatica dal 1945 ai nostri giorni*.Milano: LED Edizioni Universitarie, 1998.

Duvold, Kjetil, and Mindaugas Jurkynas. "Europeanization Without Party Involvement: The Case of Lithuania." In *European Union and Party Politics in Central and Eastern Europe*, edited by Paul Lewis and Zdenka Mansfeldová, 107–127. Houndmills: Palgrave Macmillan, 2007.

Dworkin, Ronald. *Freedom's Law: The Moral Reading of the American Constitution*. Cambridge, MA: Harvard University Press, 1996.

Dyson, Kenneth. "The Evolving Timescapes of European Economic Governanace: Contesting and Using Time." *Journal of European Public Policy* 16, no. 2 (2009): 286–306.

DZS—Croatian Bureau of Statistics. "Annual Gross Domestic Product, 1995–2012 (ESA 2010)." First Release, Croatian Bureau of Statistics, Number 12.1.5, 2014a (accessed September 10, 2014a).

———. "Employment and Wages, 2013." Statistical Reports 1526, Croatian Bureau of Statistics. Zagreb, 2014b.

———. "Statistical Information 2012." Croatian Bureau of Statistics. Zagreb, 2012.

Economist Intelligence Unit. "Austria: Country Report." *The Economist*, 2011.

———. "Democracy Index 2011: Democracy Under Stress." *The Economist*, 2012. http://www.eiu.com/public/topical_report.aspx?campaignid=Democracy Index2011.

———. "Democracy Index 2012, Democracy At a Standstill." *The Economist*, 2013. http://pages.eiu.com/rs/eiu2/images/Democracy-Index-2012.pdf.

Economou, Marina, Michael Madianos, Lilly Peppou, Athanaios Patelakis, and Costas Stefanis. "Major Depression in the Era of Economic Crisis: A Replecation of a Cross-Sectional Study Across Greece." *Journal of Affective Disorders* 145, no. 3 (2013): 308–314.

Egan, Michelle, Neill Nugent, and William E. Paterson. *Research Agendas in EU Studies: Stalking the Elephant*. Basingstoke: Palgrave Macmillan, 2010.

Einhorn, Eric, and Jessica Erfer. "Denmark: Euro-Pragmatism in Practice." In *The European Union and the Member States*, 2nd ed., edited by Eleanor E. Zeff and Ellen B. Pirro, 173–190. Boulder, CO: Lynne Rienner, 2006.

Elazar, Daniel. *Constitutionalizing Globalization: The Postmodern Revival of Confederal Arrangements*. Lanham, MD: Rowman & Littlefield, 1998.

Elmér, Heidi, Gabriela Guibour, David Kjellberg, and Marianne Nessén. "Riksbankens penningpolitiska åtgärder under finanskrisen—utvärdering och lärdomar" *Penning—Och Valutapolitik*3 (2012). http://www.riksbank.se/Documents /Rapporter/POV/2012/rap_pov_artikel_1_121017_sve.pdf.

Encarnación, Omar Guillermo. *Spanish Politics: Democracy After Dictatorship*. New York: Polity, 2008.

Enderlein, Henrik, Jacques Delors, Helmut Schmidt, Peter Bofinger, Laurence Boone, Paul De Grauwe, Jean-Claude Piris, Jean Pisani-Ferry, Maria João Rodrigues, André Sapir, and António Vitorino. "Completing the Euro: A Road Map Towards Fiscal Union in Europe." Report of the Tommaso Padoa-Schioppa Group. Paris: Notre-Europe—Jacques Delors Institute,2012.

Engbersen, Godfried, Marek Okólski, Richard Black, and Cristina Panţîru. "Introduction: Working Out a Way from East to West: EU Enlargement and Labour Migration From Central and Eastern Europe." In *A Continent Moving West? EU Enlargement and Labour Migration From Central and Eastern Europe*, edited by Richard Black, Godfried Enghersen, Marek Okólski, and Cristina Panţîru, 7–22. Amsterdam: Amsterdam University Press, 2010.

Epstein, Rachel A. *In Pursuit of Liberalism: International Institutions in Postcommunist Europe.* Baltimore: Johns Hopkins University Press, 2008.
———. "When Do Foreign Banks 'Cut and Run'? Evidence from West European Bailouts and East European Markets." *Review of International Political Economy* 21, no. 4 (2014): 847–877.
European Bank for Reconstruction and Development. "Transition Report 2012." European Bank for Reconstruction and Development, London, 2013.
European Bank for Reconstruction and Development, European Investment Bank and World Bank Group."Final Report on the Joint IFI Action Plan." London: European Bank for Reconstruction and Development, 2011.
European Commission. "Assessment of the 2014 National Reform Programme and Convergence Programme for Croatia." Commission Staff Working Document SWD(2014) 412 final, Brussels, July2014b.
———. "Assessment of the 2014 National Reform Programme and Convergence Programme for the Czech Republic." Commission Staff Working Document-COM(2014) 404 final. Brussels, 2014d.
———. "Council Recommendation on the National Reform Programme of Croatia and Delivering a Council Opinion the Convergence Programme of Croatia." *Official Journal of the European Union* 57, no. 247 (2014c): 50–56.
———. "Economic Review of the Financial Regulation Agenda." Commission Staff Working Document SWD(2014) 158 final.Brussels, 2014.
———. "EU Anti-Corruption Report." Report from the Commission to the Council and the European Parliament. Brussels, 2014.
———. "EU Budget 2013 Financial Report." Luxembourg: Publications Office of the European Union, 2014a.
———. "The European Constitution: Post-Referendum Survey in the Netherlands." Flash Eurobarometer, June 2005.
———. "European Economic Forecast: Autumn 2014." European EconomyReport 7/2014. Brussels, 2014. Accessed November 7, 2014.
———. "European Economic Forecast: Winter 2014." European Economy Report 2/2014. Brussels, 2014.
———. "First Report on Economic and Social Cohesion 1996." EU Commission Working Document, Luxembourg: Office for Official Publications of the European Communities, 1999.
———. "Macroeconomic Imbalances: France 2013."European Economy Occasional Papers 136. Brussels, April 2013.
———. "The Recapitalization of Financial Institutions in the Current Financial Crisis: Limitation of Aid to the Minimum Necessary and Safeguards Against Undue Distortions of Competition." Brussels: European Commission, 2008.
———. "Standard Eurobarometer 80: National Report Croatia." Autumn2013a.
———. "Standard Eurobarometer 80:Public Opinion in the European Union, First Results." Autumn 2013b.
———. "Standard Eurobarometer 81: National Report Croatia." Spring 2014.
European Council. "European Council 24/25 March 2011 Conclusions." EUCO 10/1/11 REV 1. Brussels, April 2011. http://www.consilium.europa.eu/uedocs /cms_data/docs/pressdata/en/ec/120296.pdf.
———. "European Council 9 December 2011 Conclusions." EUCO 139/1/11 REV 1. Brussels, December 9, 2011. Accessed August 6, 2014. http://data.consilium .europa.eu/doc/document/ST-139-2011-REV-1/en/pdf.
Eurobarometer."Nationaler Bericht: Österreich." Standard Eurobarometer (80). Brussels: Eurobarometer, 2013.

European Union. "Regulation (EU) No 439/2010 of the European Parliament and of the Council of 19 May Establishing a European Asylum Support Office." *Official Journal of the European Union* L132 (2010): 11–28.

Evans, Jocelyn, and Gilles Ivaldi."The Shock of Sunday's French Municipal Elections Was the Socialist Defeat not a Front National Victory." LSE Comment, London School of Economics, April 1, 2014. http://blogs.lse.ac.uk/europpblog /2014/04/01/the-Shock-of-sundays-french-municipal-elections-was-the -socialist-defeat-not-a-front-national-victory/ (accessed April 13, 2014).

Evans, Peter, Harold K. Jacobson, and Robert D. Putnam. *Double-Edged Diplomacy: International Bargaining and Domestic Politics.* Berkeley: University of California Press, 1993.

Evans, Stephen. "Reluctant Coalitionists: The Conservative Party and the Establishment of the Coalition Government in May 2010." *Political Quarterly* 83, no. 3 (2012): 478–486.

Fabbrini, Sergio. *Compound Democracies: The Growing Similarities Between the U.S. and Europe.* Oxford: Oxford University Press, 2007.

———. *L'europeizzazione dell'Italia: L'Impatto dell'Unione Europea sulle istituzioni e le politiche italiane.* Roma: GLF editori Laterza, 2003.

Fabbrini, Sergio, and Simona Piattoni. *Italy in the European Union: Redefining National Interest in a Compound Polity.* Lanham, MD: Rowman & Littlefield, 2008.

Falkner, Gerda. "The EU14's 'Sanctions' Against Austria: Sense and Nonsense." *ECSA Review: Journal of the European Community Studies Association* 14, no. 1 (2001): 14–20.

———. "Institutional Performance and Compliance with EU Law: Czech Republic, Hungary, Slovakia and Slovenia." *Journal of Public Policy* 30, no. 1 (2010): 101–116.

Falkner, G., and L. Hunt. "Austria: Frictions and Mixed Feelings." In *The European Union and the Member States,* edited by E. B. Pirro and E. Zeff, 237–252. Boulder: Lynne Rienner Publishers, 2006.

Falkner, Gerda, Oliver Treib, Miriam Hartlapp, and Simone Leiber. *Complying with Europe? EU Harmonization and Soft Law in the Member States.* Cambridge: Cambridge University Press, 2005.

Fargion, Valeria, Leonardo Morlino, and Stefania Profeti. *Europeizzazione e rappresentanza territoriale: Il caso italiano.* Bologna: Il Mulino, 2006.

Featherstone, Kevin. "The Greek Sovereign Debt Crisis and the EMU: A Failing State in a Skewed Regime." *Journal of Common Market Studies* 49, no. 2 (2011): 193–217.

Featherstone, Kevin, and Claudio M. Radaelli. *The Politics of Europeanization.* Oxford: Oxford University Press, 2003.

Fernandes, Sofia, and Kristina Maslauskaite. "Deepening the EMU: How to Maintain and Developthe European Social Model?A Study for the Federal Chancellery of Austria."Notre-Europe—Jacques Delors Institute Report, Paris,2013.

Fernández Guerrero, Ismael, Agustin González, and Celestino Suárez Burguet. "Spanish External Trade and EEC Preferences." In *European Integration and the Iberian Economies,* edited by George N. Yannopoulos, 144–168. New York: St. Martin's Press, 1989.

Ferraris, Luigi Vittorio. *Manuale di politica estera italiana (1947–1993).* Bari: Laterza, 1996.

Fink-Hafner, Danica. "Post-Accession Politicization of National EU Policy Coordination: The Case of Slovenia." *Public Administration* 92, no. 1 (2014): 39–54.

Finnegan, Richard B., and James L. Wiles. "The Invisible Hand or Hands Across the Water." *Eire-Ireland* 30, no. 2 (1995): 50–55.

Fischer, Karin, Rauf Gönenç, and Robert W. Price. "Austria: Public Sector Inefficiencies Have Become Less Affordable." OECD Economics Department Working Papers 897, OECD Publishing, Paris, 2011.

FitzGerald, Garret. "Ireland and the European Union." *Radharc* 3(2002): 123–135.

———. *Reflections on the Irish State.* Dublin: Irish Academic Press, 2003.

Fitzgibbon, John. "Citizens Against Europe? Civil Society and Eurosceptic Protest in Ireland, the United Kingdom and Denmark." *Journal of Common Market Studies* 51, no. 1 (2013): 105–121.

Forsyth, Murray. *Unions of States: The Theory and Practice of Confederation.* Leicester: Leicester University Press, 1981.

France Stratégie. "Quelle France dans 10 ans?" Paris: Commissariat général à la stratégie et à la prospective (CGSP), 2014.

Franck, C., H. Leclerq, and C. Vandevievere. "Belgium: Europeanization and Belgian Federalism." In *Fifteen into One? The European Union and Its Member States*, edited by W. Wessels, A. Maurer, and J. Mittag, 69–91. Manchester: Manchester University Press, 2003.

Francioni, Francisco. *Italy and EC Membership Evaluated.* London: Pinter, 1992.

Freddi, Giorgio, ed. *Scienza dell'amministrazione e politiche pubbliche.* Rome: Carocci, 1989.

Frognier, André Paul. "Elite Circulation in Cabinet Government." In *The Profession of Government Ministerin Western Europe*, edited by Jean Blondel and Jean-Louis Thiebault, 119–135. Houndmills: Macmillan, 1991.

Furlong, Paul. "The Italian Parliament and European Integration: Responsibilities, Failures and Successes." In *National Parliaments and European Union*, edited by Philip Norton, 35–45. London: Routledge, 1996.

Galbreath, David. "Still 'Treading Air'? Looking at the Post-Enlargement Challenges to Democracy in the Baltic States." *Demokratizatsiya* 16, no. 1 (2008): 87–96.

Galic, Jelena. "Does the Currency Board Regime Provide an Exit Strategy: Example of the Transition Economy in the Process of EU/EMU Accession." *Journal of Central Banking Theory and Practice* 1 (2012): 59–75.

Gallagher, Tom. "Building Democracy in Romania: Internal Shortcomings and External Neglect." In *Democratic Consolidation in Eastern Europe: Vol. 2: International and Transnational Factors*, edited by Alex Pravda and Jan Zielonk, 383–412. Oxford: Oxford University Press, 2001.

Gamble, Andrew. "Better Off Out? Britain and Europe." *Political Quarterly* 83, no. 3 (2012): 468–477.

Ganev, Venelin I. "Post-Accession Hooliganism: Democratic Governance in Bulgaria and Romania after 2007." *East European Politics & Societies* 27, no. 1 (2013): 26–44.

Gateva, Eli. "Post-Accession Conditionality: Support Instrument for Continuous Pressure?" KFG Working Paper 18, Zugriff, 2010.

Gattermann, Katjana. "News about the European Parliament: Patterns and External Drivers of Broadsheet Coverage." *European Union Politics* 14, no. 3 (2013): 436–457. doi:10.1177/1465116513476146.

Gebert, Konstanty. "Reinventing Europe: Poland and the Euro Crisis." ECFR Paper, February 7, 2012. http://www.ecfr.eu/content/entry/commentary_reinventing _europe_poland_and_the_euro_crisis.

George, Stephen. *An Awkward Partner: Britain in the European Community.* Oxford: Oxford University Press, 1990.
———. *Politics and Policy in the European Union*, 3rd ed. Oxford: Oxford University Press, 1996.
Gerbet, Pierre. *La construction de l'Europe.* Paris: Imprimerie Nationale, 1983.
Giatzidis, Emil. *An Introduction to Post-Communist Bulgaria: Political, Economic, and Social Transformations.* Manchester: Manchester University Press, 2002.
Gibson, Heather, Stephan Hall, and George Tavlas. "The Greek Financial Crisis: Growing Imbalance and Sovereign Spreads." Bank of Greece Working Paper 124, Athens,2011.
Ginsberg, Roy H. *Demystifying the European Union*, 2nd ed. Lanham, MD: Rowman and Littlefield, 2010.
Ginsborg, Paul. *History of Contemporary Italy: Society and Politics: 1943–1988.* London: Penguin, 1990.
Goetschel, Laurent, ed. *Small States Inside and Outside the European Union: Interests and Policies.* Alphen aan den Rijn, Netherlands: Kluwer Academic, 1998.
Goetz, Klaus H. "European Integration and National Executives: A Cause in Search of an Effect?" *West European Politics* 23, no. 4 (2000): 211–231.
Goldstein, Leslie Friedman. *Continuing Federal Sovereignty: The European Union in Comparative Context.* Baltimore: Johns Hopkins University Press, 2001.
Golias, Peter, and Eugen Jurzya. "Solutions to the Debt Crisis in the EU From the Slovak Perspective." INEKO Institute Published Series, 2013.
González-Enríquez, Carmen. "De-Communization and Political Justice in Central and Eastern Europe." In *The Politics of Memory: Transnational Justice in Democratizing Societies*, edited by Alexandra Barahona Brito, Carmen González-Enríquez, and Paloma Aguilar, 218–246. Oxford: Oxford University Press, 2001.
Gorenburg, Dmitry. "Soviet Nationalities Policy and Assimilation." In *Rebounding Identities: The Politics of Identity in Russia and Ukraine*, edited by Dominique Arel and Blair Ruble, 278–303. Baltimore: Johns Hopkins University Press, 2006.
Gorton, Matthew, Philip Lowe, and Anett Zellei. "Pre-Accession Europeanisation: The Strategic Realignment of the Environmental Policy Systems of Lithuania, Poland and Slovakia Towards Agricultural Pollution in Preparation for EU Membership." *Sociologia Ruralis* 45, no. 3 (2005): 202–223.
Gower, Jackie, and John Redmond, eds. *Enlarging the European Union: The Way Forward.* Aldershot: Ashgate, 2000.
Graziano, Paolo, and Maarten P. Vink, eds. *Europeanization: New Research Agendas.* Basingstoke: Palgrave Macmillan, 2007.
Grunberg, Gérard. "The Crisis of Mainstream Parties in France."*Policy Network*, May 29, 2014. http://www.policy-network.net/pno_detail.aspx?ID=4663&title =The+crisis+of+mainstream+parties+in+France.
Grzymala-Busse, Anna, and Abby Innes. "Great Expectations: The EU and Domestic Political Competition in East Central Europe." *East European Politics & Societies* 17, no. 1 (2003): 64–73.
Guillén, Mauro. *The Rise of Spanish Multinationals.* New York: Cambridge University Press, 2005.
Guizzi, Vincenzo. "Italy: A Consideration of the Position of the National Parliaments in the European Union." In *The Changing Role of Parliaments in the European Union*, edited by Finn Laursen and Spyros A. Pappas, 151–164. Maastricht: Kluwer Law, 1996.
———. "La legge La Pergola, 86/89: Una impostazione nuova del circuito decisionale e operativo Italia-Comunità." *Rivista di diritto europeo* 30, no. 1 (1990): 3–16.

Gundle, Stephen, and Simon Parker. *The New Italian Republic: From the Fall of the Berlin Wall to Berlusconi*. London: Routledge, 1996.

Gunther, Richard, and José Ramón Montero. *The Politics of Spain*. New York: Cambridge University Press, 2009.

Guzzetta, Giovanni, and Francesco S. Marini. *Diritto pubblico Italiano e Europeo*. Torino: G. Giappichelli Editore, 2006.

Haas, Ernst B. "Technocracy, Pluralism and the New Europe." In *A New Europe*, edited by Stephen A. Graubard, 62–88. Boston: Houghton Mifflin, 1964.

———. *The Uniting of Europe. Political, Social and Economical Forces 1950–1957*. London: Stevens & Sons, 1958.

Habdank-Kolaczowska, Sylvana. "Nations in Transit 2013: Authoritarian Aggression and the Pressures of Austerity." Freedom House Report, 2013. http://www.freedomhouse.org/sites/default/files/NIT%202013%20Booklet%20-%20Report%20Findings.pdf.

Hakhverdian, Armen, Erika van Elsas, Wouter van der Brug, and Theresa Kuhn. "Euroscepticism and Education: A Longitudinal Study of 12 EU Member States, 1973–2010." *European Union Politics* 14, no. 4 (2013): 522–541.

Hallerberg, 2011 (Lankowski, please supply)

Halje, Lovisa. "Hur stor del av vår lagstiftning härrör från EU?" In *Arvet från Oxenstierrna: reflektioner kring den svenska förvaltningsmodellen och EU*, edited by Thomas Bull, Lovisa Halje, Maria Bergstrøm, Jane Reichel, and Joakim Nergelius, 20–38. Stockholm: Svenska Institutet för Europapolitiska Studier, 2012.

Hamilton, Daniel. "The Changing Nature of the Transatlantic Link: US Approaches and Implications for Central and Eastern Europe." *Communist and Post-Communist Studies* 46, no. 3 (2013): 303–313.

Hämynen, Laura. "Suomen vaikuttaminen Euroopan Unionin lainvalmisteluun ja direktiivien kansallinen täytäntöönpano." Oikeuspoliittisen tutkimuslaitoksen tutkimustiedonantoja 108, Helsinki, 2011.

Handel, Michael. *Weak States in the International System*. London: Psychology Press, 1990.

Hanley, Seán. "Dynamika utváření nových stran v České republice v letech 1996–2010: hledání možných příčin politického zemětřesení."*Sociologický časopis* 47, no. 1 (2011): 115–136.

———. "Embracing Europe, Opposing EU-rope? Party-Based Euroscepticism in the Czech Republic." *Opposing Europe? The Comparative Party Politics of Euroskepticism*,vol.1,*Case Studies and Country Surveys*, edited by Aleks Szczerbiak and Paul Taggart, 243–262. Oxford: Oxford University Press, 2008a.

———. "A Nation of Sceptics? The Czech EU Accession Referendum of 13–14 June 2003." *West European Politics* 27, no. 4 (2004): 691–715.

———. *The New Right in the New Europe: Czech Transformation and Right-Wing Politics 1989–2006*. London: Routledge, 2008b.

Hardiman, Niamh, ed. *Irish Governance in Crisis*. Manchester: Manchester University Press, 2012.

Haughton, Tim. "For Business, for Pleasure or for Necessity? The Czech Republic's Choices for Europe." *Europe-Asia Studies* 61, no. 8 (2009): 1371–1392.

———. "Money, Margins and the Motors of Politics: The EU and the Development of Party Politics in Central and Eastern Europe." *Journal of Common Market Studies* 52, no. 1 (2014): 71–87.

Haughton, Tim, Tereza Novotná, and Kevin Deegan-Krause. "The 2010 Czech and Slovak Parliamentary Elections: Red Cards to the 'Winners.'" *West European Politics* 34, no. 2 (2011): 394–402.

Havlík, Vlastimil, Milan Hrubeš, and Marek Peccina. "For Rule of Law, Political Plurality, and a Just Society: Use of the Legislative Veto by President Václav Havel." *East European Politics and Societies* 28, no. 2 (2014): 440–460.

Hayward, Jack, and Anand Menon. *Governing Europe*. Oxford: Oxford University Press, 2003.

Hefftler, Claudia, Christine Neuhold, Olivier Rozenberg, and Julie Smith. *Palgrave Handbook of National Parliaments and the European Union*. Basingstoke: Palgrave Macmillan, 2015.

Heipertz, Martin, and Amy Verdun. *Ruling Europe*. Cambridge: Cambridge University Press, 2010.

Herman, Valentine, and Rinus Van Schendelen, eds. *The European Parliament and the National Parliaments*. Farnborough: Saxon House, 1979.

Hey, Jeanne A. K. *Small States in World Politics: Explaining Foreign Policy Behavior*. Boulder: Lynne Rienner, 2003.

Hibbing, John R., and Samuel C. Patterson. "The Emergence of Democratic Parliaments in Central and Eastern Europe." In *Parliaments in the Modern World*, edited by Gary W. Copeland and Samuel C. Patterson, 129–150. Ann Arbor: University of Michigan Press, 1994.

Hills, John. "Safeguarding Equity During Fiscal Consolidation: Which Tax Bases to Use." In *The Role of Tax Policy in Times of Fiscal Consolidation: Economic Papers (502)*, edited by Savina Princen and Gilles Mourre, 80–93. Brussels: European Commission, 2013.

Hina and Željko Petrušić. "Fimi Medija: Sanaderu Devet Godina Zatvora!" *Jutarnji*, March 11, 2014. http://www.jutarnji.hr/fimi-media—sanaderu-devet-godina -zatvora/1172471/.

Hix, Simon. "The Study of the European Community: The Challenge to Comparative Politics." *West European Politics* 17, no. 1 (1994): 1–30.

Hix, Simon, and Bjørn Høyland. *The Political System of the European Union*, 3rd ed. Basingstoke: Palgrave Macmillan, 2011.

Hloušek, Vít, and Petr Kaniok. "Europe and the 2013 Czech Parliamentary Election, October 25–26 2013." EPERN Election Briefing 74, March 6, 2014.

Hloušek, Vít, and Lubomír Kopeček."Caretaker Governments in Czech Politics: What to Do about a Government Crisis." *Europe-Asia Studies* 66, no. 8 (2014): 1323–1349.

HM Treasury. "Spending Review 2010." Stationery Office CM 7942. London, 2010.

Hobolt, Sara B. "Citizen Satisfaction with Democracy in the European Union." *Journal of Common Market Studies* 50, Supplement S1 (2012): 88–105.

Hoffmann, Stanley. "Obstinate or Obsolete: The Fate of National State and the Case of Western Europe." *Daedalus* 95, no. 3 (1966): 862–915.

Holborn, Hajo. *The Political Collapse of Europe*. New York: Knopf, 1951.

Hollanders, Hugo, and Nordine Es-Sadki. "Innovation Union Scoreboard 2014." European Commission. 2014. http://ec.europa.eu/enterprise/policies/innovation /files/ius/ius-2014_en.pdf.

Holmberg, Sören. "ETTFall for EU." SIEPS Europapolitisk Analys Paper 8,2013. http://www.sieps.se/sites/default/files/2013_8epa.pdf.

———. "Nu har en majoritet svenskar mentalt gatt med i EU." SIEPS Europapolitisk AnalysPaper 5,2010. http://www.sieps.se/sites/default/files/639-2010_5epa _final.pdf.

———. "Swedish Opinion on the Swedish Membership in the European Union." SOM-Institutet Report 5,2012.http://www.som.gu.se/digitalAssets/1374/1374095 _swedish-opinion-on-the-eu-membership-2011—v2-.pdf.

Holmberg, Sören, and Klara Sommerstein. "Svenska folkets bedömning av offentliga myndigheters verksamhet." SOM-InstitutetReport 8, 2013. http://www.som.gu.se/digitalAssets/1455/1455170_sv-bed—mning-av-off-verksamhet-2012.pdf.

Holmberg, Sören, and Frida Vernersdotter. "Åsikter om att införa euron som valuta i sverige." SOM-Institutet Report 15, 2013. http://www.som.gu.se/digitalAssets/1452/1452702_euroopinion-som-rapport-2013-15.pdf.

Holmberg, Sören, Lennert Weibull, and Henric Oscarsson. "Venska Trender 1986–2010." SOM-Institutet, 2010. http://www.som.gu.se/digitalAssets/1457/1457395_1342667_svenska-trender-1986-2010.pdf.

Holmqvist, Anette. "Finns inget folkligt tryck mot EU-medlemskape." *Aftonbladet*, January 23, 2013. http://www.aftonbladet.se/nyheter/article16115718.ab.

Hooghe, Liesbet. "Belgium: Hollowing the Center." In *Federalism and Territorial Cleavages*, edited by Ugo M. Amoretti and Nancy Bermeo, 335–386. Baltimore: Johns Hopkins University Press, 2004.

Hooghe, Liesbet, and Gary Marks. *Multi-Level Governance and European Integration.* Lanham, MD: Rowman & Littlefield, 2001.

Hoops, Joshua, Ryan Thomas, Jolanta Drzewiecka, and Susan Ross. "Polish Plumber as a Pawn in the British Newspaper Discourse on Polish Post-EU Enlargement Immigration to the UK." Paper presented at the Annual Meeting of the International Communication Association, Suntec Singapore International Convention & Exhibition Centre, Suntec City, Singapore, 2010.

Hoskyns, Catherine. "Gender Perspectives." In *European Integration Theory*, edited byAntje Wiener and Thomas Dietz, 217–236. New York: Oxford University Press, 2004.

Hosli, Madeleine O., Mikko Mattila, and Marc Uriot. "Voting in the Council of the European Union After the 2004 Enlargement: A Comparison of Old and New Member States." *Journal of Common Market Studies* 49, no. 6 (2011): 1249–1270.

Huber, Peter, and Doris Anita Oberdabernig. "Decomposing Welfare Wedges: An Analysis of Welfare Dependence of Immigrants and Natives in Europe." WIFO Working Papers 459. Austrian Institute of Economic Research,Vienna, 2014.

Hübner, Kurt. "Baltic Tigers: The Limits of Unfettered Liberalization." *Journal of Baltic Studies* 42, no. 1 (2011): 81–90.

Hyvärinen, Anna. "Suomen mahdollisuudet vaikuttaa valmisteilla olevaan EU-lainsäädäntöön." Oikeuspoliittisen tutkimuslaitoksen tutkimuksia 241. Helsinki, 2009.

Hyvärinen, Anna, and Tapio Raunio. "Who Decides What EU Issues Ministers Talk About? Explaining Governmental EU Policy Co-ordination in Finland." *Journal of Common Market Studies* 52, no. 5 (2014): 1019–1034.

Ikstens, Jānis. "Does EUrope matter? The EU and Latvia's Political Parties."In *European Union and Party Politics in Central and Eastern Europe*, edited by Paul Lewis and Zdenka Mansfeldová, 86–106. Houndmills: Palgrave Macmillan, 2007.

Ingebritsen, Christine. "Coming Out of the Cold: Nordic Response to European Union." In *Europe's Ambiguous Unity: Conflict and Consensus in the Post-Maastricht Era*, edited by Alan Cafruny and Carl Lankowski, 239–256. Boulder: Lynne Rienner Publishers, 1997.

Innes, Abby. "The Political Economy of State Capture in Central Europe." *Journal of Common Market Studies* 52, no. 1 (2014): 88–104.

International Monetary Fund. "Greece: Ex Post Evaluation of Exceptional Access Under the 2010 Stand-By Arrangement." Country Report 13/156, Washington, DC, 2013a.

————. "Greece: Request for Extended Arrangement under the Extended Fund Facility." Country Report 12/57, Washington, DC, 2012.

————. "Greece: Staff Report on Request for Stand-By Agreement." Country Report 10/110, Washington, DC, 2010.

————. "Republic of Poland." Country Report 13/219, 2013b

Irish Department of Foreign Affairs. *Challenges and Opportunities Abroad*. White Paper, 1996.

Jääskinen, Niilo. "Eduskunta: aktiivinen sopeutuja." In *EU ja Suomi: Unionijäsenyyden vaikutukset suomalaiseen yhteiskuntaan*, edited by Tapio Raunio and Matti Wiberg, 114–134. Helsinki: Edita, 2000.

Jacoby, Wade. "The EU Factor in Fat Times and in Lean: Did the EU Amplify the Boom and Soften the Bust?" *Journal of Common Market Studies* 52, no. 1 (2014): 52–70.

Jagelka, Tomáš. "Bilateral Trade and the Eurozone: Evidence from New Member Countries." *World Economy* 36, no. 1 (2013): 48–63.

Jedlicka, Jan, and Katarzyna Rzentarzewska. "Cohesion Policy and Other EU Assistance Programmes in 2014–2020." Ceska Sporitelna EU OfficeSpecial Analysis, Prague, March 2014.

Jenssen, Anders Todal, Pertti Pesonen, and Mikael Gilljam. *To Join or Not to Join: Three Nordic Referendums on Membership in the European Union*. Oslo: Scandinavian University Press, 1998.

Jerneck, Magnus. "Sveriges inflytande iEU efter krisen."SIEPS Europapolitisk Analys Paper 10, 2013. http://www.sieps.se/sv/publikationer/sveriges-inflytande-i-eu-efter-krisen-201310epa.

Johansson, Karl Magnus, and Tapio Raunio. "Organizing the Core Executive for European Union Affairs: Comparing Finland and Sweden." *Public Administration* 88, no. 3 (2010): 649–664.

Johansson, Karl Magnus, and Jonas Tallberg. "Explaining Chief Executive Empowerment: EU Summitry and Domestic Institutional Change." *West European Politics* 33, no. 2 (2010): 208–236.

Join, Arjen, and Paul Hart. "Public Leadership in Times of Crisis: Mission Impossible?" *Public Administration Review* 63, no. 5 (2003): 544–553.

Jokela, Juha. *Europeanization and Foreign Policy: State Identity in Finland and Britain*. London: Routledge, 2011.

Jones, Erik. "The Benelux Countries: Identity and Self-Interest." In *Member States and the European Union*, edited bySimon Bulmer and Christian Luquesne, 164–184. Oxford: Oxford University Press, 2005.

————. "Merkel's Folly." *Survival* 52, no. 3 (2010): 21–38.

Joyce, Michael, Matthew Tong, and Robert Woods. "The United Kingdom's Quantitative Easing Policy: Design, Operation and Impact." *Bank of England Quarterly Bulletin* 51, no. 3 (2011): 200–212.

Jurkynas, Mindaugas. "The 2004 Presidential and Parliamentary Elections in Lithuania." *Electoral Studies* 24, no. 4 (2005): 770–777.

————. "The Parliamentary Election in Lithuania, October 2008." *Electoral Studies* 28, no. 2 (2009): 329–333.

————. "The Parliamentary Election in Lithuania, October 2012." *Electoral Studies* 34 (2013): 334–338.

Juska, Arunas, and Charles Woolfson. "Policing Political Protest in Lithuania." *Crime, Law and Social Change* 57, no. 4 (2012): 403–424.

Kaczyński, Piotr Maciej. "Polish Council Presidency 2011 Ambitions and Limitations." SIEPS Europapolitisk Analys Paper 3, 2011.

Kałan, Dariusz. "A Beautiful Future for Central Europe: Hungary's Regional Policy in the Period 2010–2013." *PISM Policy Papers* 28, no. 76 (2013): 1–11.

Kaniok, Petr, and Vít Hloušek. "Shaping of Czech Debate on the Euro: Position of Václav Klaus in 1999–2002 Period." *Romanian Journal of European Affairs* 14, no. 2 (2014): 42–62.

Karlas, Jan. "National Parliamentary Control of EU Affairs: Institutional Design After Enlargement." *West European Politics* 35, no. 5 (2012): 1095–1113.

Kassim, Hussein. "The European Administration: Between Europeanization and Domestication." In *Governing Europe*, edited by Jack Hayward and Anand Menon, 139–161. Oxford: Oxford University Press, 2003.

Kassim, Hussein, B. Guy Peters, and Vincent Wright, eds. *The National Coordination of EU Policy: The Domestic Level*. Oxford: Oxford University Press, 2000.

Katzenstein, Peter J. *Small States in World Markets*. Ithaca, NY: Cornell University Press, 1985.

Katzenstein, 1998 (Lankowski, please supply)

Kawecka-Wyrzykowska, Elżbieta. "Poland's Public Finance Convergence with the Euro Area." *Central European Business Review* 2, no. 2 (2013): 51–60.

Keatinge, Patrick. "Security Policy." In *Ireland and EC Membership Evaluated*, edited by P. Keatinge.London: Pinter, 1990.

Keatinge, Patrick, and Brigid Laffan. "Ireland: A Small Open Polity." In *Politics in the Republic of Ireland*, 3rd ed., edited by John Coakley and Michael Gallagher, 320–349. London: Routledge, 1999.

Kelley, Judith. "International Actors on the Domestic Scene: Membership Conditionality and Socialization by International Institutions." *International Organization* 58, no. 3 (2004): 425–457.

Kelstrup, Morten. "Denmark's Relation to the European Union: A History of Dualism and Pragmatism," In *Denmark and the European Union*, edited by Lee Miles and Anders Wivel, 14–29. London: Routledge, 2014.

Kelstrup, Morten, Dorte Sindbjerg Martinsen, and Marlene Wind. *Europa i forandring: En grundbog om eu's politiske og retlige system*, 2nd ed. Copenhagen: Hans Reitzels Forlag, 2012.

Kennan, George (under pseudonym "X"). "The Sources of Soviet Conduct." *Foreign Affairs*, July 1947.

Keohane, Robert Owen, and Stanley Hoffmann. "Conclusions: Community Politics and Institutional Change." In *The Dynamics of European Integration*, edited by William Wallace, 276–300. London: Pinter, 1990.

Keohane, Robert Owen, and Joseph S. Nye. "Interdependence and Integration." In *Handbook of Political Science*, vol. 8, edited by Fred I. Greenstein and Nelson W. Polsby, 363–414. London: Addison-Wesley, 1975.

Kingdom, John. *Government and Politics in Britain*, 4th ed. Cambridge: Polity Press, 2014.

Kingdon, John W. *Agendas, Alternatives, and Public Policies*. New York: Harper Collins, 1995.

Kinnunen, Jussi. "Managing Europe from Home: The Europeanisation of the Finnish Core Executive." *Dublin: Organising for EU Enlargement Project*, OEUE Phase 1, Occasional Paper 3.1–09.03, University of Helsinki, 2003.

Klamert, Marcus. *The Principle of Loyalty in EU Law*. Oxford: Oxford University Press, 2014.

Klarič, Matej, and Miroslav Stanjojevič."The Impact of Socio-Economic Shocks on Collective Bargaining and Social Dialogue in Slovenia." CELSI Discussion Paper No. 11 (2013).

Knutelská, Viera. "Working Practices Winning Out over Formal Rules: Parliamentary Scrutiny of EU Matters in the Czech Republic, Poland and Slovakia." *Perspectives on European Politics and Society* 12, no. 3 (2011): 320–339.

Kolodko, Grzegorz W. "A Two-Thirds Rate of Success: Polish Transformation and Economic Development, 1989–2008." UNU-WIDER Research Paper 2009/14, 2009.

Komárek, Jan. "The Czech Constitutional Court's Second Decision on the Lisbon Treaty of 3 November 2009." *European Constitutional Law Review* 5, no. 3 (2009): 345–352.

Kopeček, Lubomír. *Fenomén Václav Klaus: Politická biografie.* Prague: Barrister & Principal, 2012.

Krastev, Ivan. *Democracy Disrupted: The Global Politics of Protest.* Philadelphia: University of Pennsylvania Press, 2014a.

———. "The Global Politics of Protest." *IWM Post* 113 (2014b): 3–4.

Kratochvíl, Petr. "The Qualified Majority Voting and the Interests of the Czech Republic." In *Central Europe Beyond Double Enlargement,* edited by Algimantas Jankauskas and Ramūnas Vilpišauskas,143–164. Vilnius: Vilnius University Press, 2004.

Kratochvíl, Petr, Jurij Fjodorov, Lucia Najšlová, and Karel Svoboda. "Ukrajinská krize: Dopady a rizika pro Českou republiku." Ústav mezinárodních vztahů Policy Paper, Prague, 2014.

Kritzinger, Sylvia. "Austria: What Contributed to the FPÖ's Protest Vote?" *Policy Network,* May 27, 2014, 1–6.

Krotz, Ulrich, and Joachim Schild. *Shaping Europe: France, Germany, and Embedded Bilateralism From the Elysée Treaty to Twenty-First Century Politics.* Oxford: Oxford University Press, 2013.

Kruezer, Marcus, and Vello Pettai. "Patterns of Political Instability: Affiliation Patterns of Politicians and Voters in Post-Communist Estonia, Latvia and Lithuania." *Studies in Comparative International Development* 39, no. 2 (2003): 76–98.

Krupavicius, Algis. "Lithuania." *European Journal of Political Research* 50, no. 7–8 (2011): 1045–1057.

Kudrna, Zdenek. "Cross-Border Resolution of Failed Banks in the European Union After the Crisis: Business as Usual." *Journal of Common Market Studies* 50, no. 2 (2012): 283–299.

———. "The Future of the Euro: Agreements to Disagree and Prospective Scenarios from the 2014 Vienna Debate." University of Vienna, EIF Working Paper 3, 2014.

Kudrna, Zdenek, and Daniela Gabor. "The Return of Political Risk: Foreign-Owned Banks in Emerging Europe." *Europe-Asia Studies* 65, no. 3 (2013): 548–566.

Labohm, Hans. "Evaluation of the Netherlands EU Presidency." Institute of International Relations Working Paper, 2004.

Lach, Jiří, James T. Laplant, Jim Peterson, and David Hill. "The Party Isn't Over: An Analysis of the Communist Party in the Czech Republic." *Journal of Communist Studies and Transition Politics* 26, no. 3 (2010): 363–388.

Ladrech, Robert. "The Europeanization of Domestic Politics and Institutions: The Case of France." *Journal of Common Market Studies* 32, no. 1 (1994): 69–88.

Laffan, Brigid. "Managing Europe from Home in Dublin, Athens and Helsinki: A Comparative Analysis." *West European Politics* 29, no. 4 (2006): 687–708.

Laffan, Brigid, and Sonia Mazey, "European Integration: The European Union—Reaching an Equilibrium?" In *European Union: Power and Policy-Making,* 3rd ed., edited by Jeremy Richardson, 31–54. New York: Routledge, 2006.

Laffan, Brigid, and Rory O'Donnell. "Ireland and the Growth of International Governance." In *Ireland and the Politics of Change*, edited by William J. Crotty and David E. Schmitt, 156–177. London: Longman, 1998.

Laffan, Brigid, and Jane O'Mahony. *Ireland and the European Union*. Basingstoke: Palgrave Macmillan, 2008.

Lampinen, Risto, Olli Rehn, and Petri Uusikylä. *EU-asioiden valmistelu Suomessa*. Helsinki: Eduskunnan kanslian, 1998.

La Palombara, Joseph. *Interest Groups in Italian Politics*. Princeton, NJ: Princeton University Press, 1964.

Laqueur, Walter. *Europe in Our Time: A History 1945–1992*. New York: Viking Penguin, 1992.

Lee, Simon. "No Plan B: The Coalition's Agenda for the Economy." In *The Cameron-Clegg Government: Coalition Politics in an Age of Austerity*, edited by Simon Lee and Matt Beech, 59–72. Basingstoke: Palgrave Macmillan, 2011.

Leonardi, Robert, and Raffaella Y. Nanetti. *Le regioni e l'integrazione Europea: Il caso Emilia-Romagna*. Milano: Franco Angeli, 1991.

Leuffen, Dirk, Berthold Rittberger, and Frank Schimmelfennig. *Differentiated Integration: Explaining Variation in the European Union*. Basingstoke: Palgrave Macmillan, 2012.

Levitz, Philip, and Grigore Pop-Eleches. "Monitoring, Money and Migrants: Countering Post-Accession Backsliding in Bulgaria and Romania." *Europe-Asia Studies* 62, no. 3 (2010): 461–479.

Lewis, Paul, and Zdenka Manfeldova. *The European Union and Party Politics in Central and Eastern Europe*. Basingstoke: Palgrave, 2007.

Lijphart, Arend. *Democracies: Patterns of Majoritarian and Consensus Government in Twenty-One Countries*. New Haven, CT: Yale University Press, 1984.

Lindberg, Leon N. *The Political Dynamics of European Economic Integration*. Stanford, CA: Stanford University Press, 1963.

Lindberg, Leon N., and Stuart Scheingold. *Europe's Would-Be Polity; Patterns of Change in the European Community*. Englewood Cliffs, NJ: PrenticeHall, 1970.

Lister, Frederick K. *The European Union, the United Nations, and the Revival of Confederal Governance*. Westport, CT: Greenwood Press, 1996.

Liu, Zuoku. "The Root Causes and Influences of Slovenian Banking Crisis." Working Paper Series on European Studies, Institute of European Studies, Chinese Academy of Social Sciences 7, no. 5, 2013.

Lowi, Theodore J. "Four Systems of Policy, Politics and Choice." *Public Administration Review* 32, no. 4 (1972): 298–310.

Lynch, David J. *When the Luck of the Irish Ran Out*. Basingstoke: Palgrave Macmillan, 2010.

Lyons, Pat. "'It's the Economy, Stupid': Popular Support for EU Accession in the Czech Republic." *Sociologický časopis* 43, no. 3 (2007): 523–560.

Magone, Jorge. *Contemporary Spanish Politics*. New York: Routledge, 2008.

Mair, Peter. "The Election in Context." In *How Ireland Voted*, edited by Michael Gallagher and Michael Marsh, 283–297. Basingstoke: Palgrave Macmillan, 2011.

Majone, Giandomenico. "Federation, Confederation, and Mixed Government: An EU-US Comparison." In *Comparative Federalism: The European Union and the United States in Comparative Perspectives*, edited by Anand Menon and Martin Schain, 121–147. Oxford: Oxford University Press, 2006.

———. *Regulating Europe*. New York: Routledge, 1996.

Manners, Ian. "Small States and the Internal Balance of the European Union: Institutional Issues." In *Enlarging the European Union: The Way Forward*, edited by Jackie Gower and John Redmond, 123–135. Aldershot: Ashgate, 2000.

Manolopoulos, Jason. *Greece's "Odious" Debt: The Looting of the Hellenic Republic by the Euro, the Political Elite and the Investment Community*. London: Anthem Press, 2011.

Mansfeldová, Zdenka. "Central European Parliaments over Two Decades—Diminishing Stability? Parliaments in Czech Republic, Hungary, Poland, and Slovenia." *Journal of Legislative Studies* 17, no. 2 (2011): 128–146.

Markou, Christos, George Nakos, and Nikolaos Zaharisdis. "Greece: A Most Enthusiastic, Reluctant European." In *The European Union and the Member States*, 2nd ed., edited by Eleanor E. Zeff and Ellen B. Pirro, 193–210. Boulder: Lynne Rienner Publishers, 2006.

Marks, Gary, Liesbet Hooghe, Moira Nelson, and Erica Edwards. "Party Competition and European Integration in the East and West: Different Structure, Same Causality." *Comparative Political Studies* 39, no. 2 (2006): 155–175.

Martinez-Mongay, Carlos, and Luis AngelMaza Lasierra. "Competitiveness and Growth in the EU." European Economy Economic Papers 355. January 2009.

Matějková, Jolana. *Děda se taky nebál: Rozhovor s Alexandrem Vondrou*. Prague: Paseka, 2012.

Mattern, Frank, Eckart Windhagen, Markus Habbel, Jörg Mußhoff, Hans-Helmut Kotz, and Wilhelm Rall. "The Future of the Euro: An Economic Perspective on the Eurozone Crisis." McKinsey & Company Research Report, 2012.

Mattila, Mikko. "Roll Call Analysis of Voting in the European Union Council of Ministers After the 2004 Enlargement." *European Journal of Political Research* 48, no. 6 (2009): 840–857.

Mattila, Mikko, and Tapio Raunio. "Drifting Further Apart: National Parties and Their Electorates on the EU Dimension." *West European Politics* 35, no. 3 (2012): 589–606.

———. "Kuka edustaa EU: n vastustajia? Euroopan parlamentin vaalit 2004." *Politiikka* 47, no. 1 (2005): 28–41.

Maurer, Andreas, and Wolfgang Wessels, eds. *National Parliaments on Their Ways to Europe: Losers or Latecomers*. Baden Baden: Nomos, 2001.

Mayer, Gerit, Torben Andersen, and Michael Muller. "Employment Restructuring and Flexibility in Austrian and Danish Banking." *European Journal of Industrial Relations* 7, no. 1 (2001): 71–87.

Mazzoni Honorati, Maria Luisa. "La 'partecipazione' parlamentare al processo normativo europeo." *Rivista Italiana di Diritto Pubblico Comunitario* 5, no. 1 (1995): 27–40.

McCormick, John. *European Union Politics*. New York: Palgrave Macmillan, 2011.

———. *Why Europe Matters*. New York: Palgrave Macmillan, 2013.

McKay, David. *Designing Europe: Comparative Lessons from the Federal Experience*. Oxford: Oxford University Press, 2001.

Mény, Yves, Pierre Muller, and Jean-Louis Quermonne, eds. *Adjusting to Europe: The Impact of European Integration on National Institutions and Policies*. London: Routledge, 1996.

Middlemas, Keith. *Orchestrating Europe: The Informal Politics of the European Union, 1973–95*. London: Fontana Press, 1995.

Miles, Lee, and Anders Wivel, eds. *Denmark and the European Union*. London: Routledge, 2014.

Millard, Frances. "Electoral System Change in Latvia and the Elections of 2010." *Communist and Post-Communist Studies* 44 (2011): 309–318.

Miller, Vaughne. "How Much Legislation Comes from Europe?" Commons Library Research Paper 10/62, 2010.

Milward, Alan S. *The European Rescue of the Nation State.* London: Routledge, 1992.

Milward, Alan S., Federico Romero, and George Brennan. *The European Rescue of the Nation-State,* 2nd ed. London: Routledge, 2000.

Ministry for Infrastructure and Development of the Republic of Poland. *Biuletyn informacyjny fundusze Europejskie w Polsce,* no. 34, 2014.

Monnet, Jean. *Mémoires.* Paris: Fayard, 1976.

Moravcsik, Andrew. *The Choice for Europe: Social Purpose and State Power from Messina to Maastricht.* Ithaca, NY: Cornell University Press, 1998.

———. "The European Constitutional Settlement." In *Making History: European Integration and Institutional Change at Fifty,* edited by Sophie Meunier and Kathleen McNamara, 23–50. Oxford: Oxford University Press, 2007.

———. "Federalism in the European Union: Rhetoric and Reality." In *The Federal Vision: Legitimacy and Levels of Governance in the United States and the European Union,* edited by Kalypso Nicolaidis and Robert Howse, 161–190. Oxford: Oxford University Press, 2001.

———. "Negotiating the Single European Act." In *The New European Community: Decisionmaking and Institutional Change,* edited by Robert O. Keohane and Stanley Hoffman, 41–84. Boulder, CO: Westview Press, 1991.

Morgan, Roger, and Clare Tame, eds. *Parliament and Parties: The European Parliament in the Political Life of Europe.* Basingstoke: Macmillan, 1996.

Morlino, Leonardo. *Democracy Between Consolidation and Crises: Parties, Groups, and Citizens in Southern Europe.* Oxford: Oxford University Press, 1998.

Morviducci, Claudia. *Il parlamento italiano e le comunità europee.* Milano: Giuffré, 1979.

Muiznieks, Nils. "Latvia." In *Racist Extremism in Central and Eastern Europe,* edited by Cas Mudde, 101–128. New York: Routledge, 2005.

Müller, Jan-Werner. "Eastern Europe Goes South: Disappearing Democracy in the EU's Newest Members." *Foreign Affairs,* March/April 2014. http://www.foreignaffairs.com/articles/140736/jan-werner-mueller/eastern-europe-goes-south.

Müller-Brandeck-Bocquet, Gisela. *Frankreichs Europapolitik.* Wiesbaden: VS Verlag für Sozialwissenschaften, 2004.

Muñoz, Jordi, Mariano Torcal, and Eduard Bonet. "Institutional Trust and Multilevel Government in the European Union: Congruence or Compensation?" *European Union Politics* 12, no. 4 (2011): 551–574.

Naurin, Daniel and Rutger Lindahl, "Out in the Cold? Flexible Integration and the Political Status of Euro Opt-Outs" *European Union Politics* 11, no. 4 (2010)

Nedergaard, Peter. "The Internal Market and the Common Agricultural Policy: The Normalization of EU Policy Making in Denmark." In *Denmark and the European Union,* edited by Lee Miles and Anders Wivel, 30–46. London: Routledge, 2014.

Niemann, Arne, and Philippe Schmitter. "Neofunctionalism." In *European Integration Theory,* edited by Antje Wiener and Thomas Diez, 45–66. Oxford: Oxford University Press, 2004.

Niskanen, Maarit. "Asavallan presidentin ulko- ja turvallisuuspoliittinen päätösvalta Suomen valtiosäännössä." PhD diss., University of Lapland, 2009.

———. "Onko sotilaallinen kriisinhallintalaki ulkopolitiikan johtamista vai EU-Asia?" *Lakimies* 104, no. 2 (2006): 244–256.

Norton, Philip, ed. *National Parliaments and the European Union*. London: Routledge, 1996.

Nousiainen, Jaakko. "From Semi-Presidentialism to Parliamentary Government: Political and Constitutional Developments in Finland." *Scandinavian Political Studies* 24, no. 2 (2001): 95–109.

Nowotny, Ewald. "The Austrian Social Partnership and Democracy." Department of Economics Working Paper 93-1, University of Vienna, 1993.

Nugent, Neill. *The Government and Politics of the European Union*. Basingstoke: Palgrave Macmillan, 1994.

Nygaard, Christian, Adam Pasierbek, and Ellie Francis-Brophy. "Bulgarian and Romanian Migration to the South East and UK: Profile of A2 Migrants and Their Distribution." Report Prepared for the South East Strategic Partnership for Migration, University of Reading, 2013.

O'Donnell, Rory. *Ireland in Europe: The Economic Dimension*. Institute for International and European Affairs, 2002.

Oesterreichische Nationalbank. "The Austrian Financial Markets: A Survey of Austria's Capital Markets." Vienna, 2004.

Olsen, Johan. P. "European Challenges to the Nation State." In *Political Institutions and Public Policy*, edited by Bernard Steunenberg and Frans van Vucht, 157–188. Amsterdam: Kluwer Academic, 1997.

O'Mahony, Jane. "Ireland and the European Union: A Less Certain Relationship," In *Political Issues in Ireland Today*, edited by Neil Collins and Terry Cradden, 15–33. Manchester: Manchester University Press, 2004.

Orenstein, Mitchell A. "Six Markets to Watch: Poland, from Tragedy to Triumph." *Foreign Affairs*, January/February 2014.

OECD. "France—Redresser la Compétitivité," Série Politiques Meilleures, November, 2013. http://www.oecd.org/fr/apropos/editionsocde/2013-11-Rapport-OCDE-sur -la-competitivite-en-France.pdf. (Accessed July 15, 2014).

———. "OECD Economic Survey of Austria." Organisation for Economic Cooperation and Development, Paris, 2013.

———. "Sickness, Disability and Work: Breaking the Barriers. Sweden: Will the Recent Reforms Make It?" Directorate for Employment, Labour and Social Affairs, Paris, 2009.

Orlowski, Witold M. "Accelerate Change: Higher Saving Is the Key to Higher Growth for New EU Members." *Finance & Development* 41, no. 2 (2004): 34–35.

Orzoff, Andrea. *The Battle for the Castle: The Myth of Czechoslovakia in Europe, 1914–1948*. Oxford: Oxford University Press, 2009.

Ostrom, Elinor. *Governing the Commons: The Evolution of Institutions for Collective Action*. Cambridge: Cambridge University Press, 1990.

O'Toole, Fintan. *Ship of Fools: How Stupidity and Corruption Sank the Tiger*. London: Faber & Faber, 2010.

Pace, Roderick. "Euroscepticism in a Polarized Polity." *South European Society and Politics* 16, no. 1 (2011): 133–157.

———. "Growing Secularization in a Catholic Society: The Divorce Referendum of 28 May 2011 in Malta." *South European Society and Politics* 17, no. 4 (2012): 573–589.

———. "Malta." In *Strategic Cultures in Europe: Security and Defence Policies Across the Continent*, Vol. 13. *Schriftenreihe des Zentrums für Militärgeschichte und Sozialwissenschaften der Bundeswehr*, edited by Heiko Biehl, Bastian Giegerich, and Alexandra Jonas, 243–254. Wiesbaden: Springer, 2013.

————. "Malta and EU Membership: Overcoming 'Vulnerabilities,' Strengthening 'Resilience.'" *European Integration* 28, no. 1 (2006): 33–49.

————. *Microstate Security in the Global System: EU-Malta Relations.* Malta: Midsea Books, 2001.

————. "Small States and the Internal Balance of the European Union: The Perspective of Small States." In *Enlarging the European Union: The Way Forward*, edited by Jackie Gower and John Redmond. Aldershot: Ashgate, 2000.

Page, Edward C. "Europeanization and the Persistence of Administrative Systems." In *Governing Europe*, edited by Jack Hayward and Anand Menon, 162–178. Oxford: Oxford University Press, 2003.

Paliova, Iana, and Tonny Lybek. "Bulgaria's EU Funds Absorption: Maximizing the Potential!" IMF Working Paper, Zugriff, 2014.

Paloheimo, Heikki. "The Rising Power of the Prime Minister in Finland." *Scandinavian Political Studies* 26, no. 3 (2003): 219–243.

Palosaari, Teemu. *The Art of Adaptation: A Study on the Europeanization of Finland's Foreign and Security Policy.* Tampere: TAPRI Studies in Peace and Conflict Research 96, 2011.

Panke, Diana. *Small States in the European Union: Coping with Structural Disadvantages.* Farnham: Ashgate, 2010.

Papadimitriou, Dimitris, and David Phinnemore. "Europeanization, Conditionality and Domestic Change: The Twinning Exercise and Administrative Reform in Romania." *Journal of Common Market Studies* 42, no. 3 (2004): 619–639.

Pappas, Spyros. *National Administrative Procedures for the Preparation and Implementation of Community Decisions.* Maastricht: European Institute of Public Administration, 1995.

Pavel, Dan, and Julia Huiu. *Nu putem reuşi decît împreună: O istorie analitică a Convenţiei Democratice, 1989–2000.* Iaşi: Polirom, 2003.

Pechova, Andrea. "Legitimising Discourses in the Framework of European Integration: The Politics of Euro Adoption in the Czech Republic and Slovakia." *Review of International Political Economy* 19, no. 5 (2012): 779–807.

Pedersen, Rasmus B. "Denmark and the Council of Ministers." In *Denmark and the European Union*, edited by Lee Miles and Anders Wivel, 95–108. Oxford: Routledge, 2014.

Perkovic, Jese. "National Heroes vs. EU Benefits: Croatia and the EU Conditionality." *CEU Political Science Journal* 8, no. 2 (2013): 177–201.

Pesonen, Pertti, ed. *Suomen EU-kansanäänestys 1994: Raportti äänestäjien kannanotoista.* Helsinki: Ulkoasiainministeriö, Eurooppatiedotus ja Painatuskeskus, 1994.

Peters, B. Guy. "Bureaucratic Politics and the Institutions of the European Community." In *Euro-Politics: Institutions and Policymaking in the "New" European Community*, edited by Alberta Sbragia, 75–122. Washington DC: Brookings Institution, 1992.

Peters, B. Guy, and Jon Pierre. "Multi-Level Governance and Democracy: A Faustian Bargain?" In *Multi-Level Goverance*, edited by Ian Bache and Matthew Flinders, 79–92. Oxford: Oxford University Press, 2004.

Petersen, Thieß, and Michael Bohmer. "20 Years of the European Single Market: Growth Effects of European Integration." Bertelsmann-Stiftung Policy Brief 2, 2014.

Petersen, Thieß, Michael Bohmer, and Johannes Weisser. "20 Jahre Binnenmarkt: Wachstumseffekte der zu-nehmenden EU-Integration." BertelsmannStiftung Policy Brief 2,2014.

Peterson, John, Elizabeth Bomberg, and Richard Corbett. "Conclusion." In *The European Union: How Does it Work?*, 3rd ed., edited by Elizabeth Bomberg, John Peterson, and Richard Corbett, 224–237. Oxford: Oxford University Press, 2012.

Pettai, Vello. "The Parliamentary Elections in Estonia, March 2003." *Electoral Studies* 23, no. 3 (2003): 828–834.

Piris, Jean-Claude. *The Future of Europe: Towards a Two-Speed EU?* Cambridge: Cambridge University Press, 2012.

Pistelli, Lapo, and Fiore Guelfo. *Semestre nero: Berlusconi e la politica estera.* Roma: Fazi Editore, 2004.

Pistone, Sergio. *L'Italia e l'unità europea.* Torino: Loescher, 1982.

Pollack, Mark A. *The Engines of European Integration: Delegation, Agency and Agenda Setting in the EU.* New York: Oxford University Press, 2003.

———. "Theorizing EU Policy-Making." In *Policy-Making in the European Union*, 6th ed., edited by Helen Wallace, Mark A. Pollack, and Alasdair Young, 14–43. Oxford: Oxford University Press, 2010.

Pop-Eleches, Grigore. "Throwing Out the Bums: Protest Voting and Unorthodox Parties after Communism." *World Politics* 62, no. 2 (2010): 221–260.

Posen, Adam, Ajai Chopra, Angel Ubide, Paolo Mauro, Jacob Funk Kirkegaard, and Nicolas Veron. "Rebuilding Europe's Common Future: Combining Growth and Reform in the Euro Area." Peterson Institute for International Economics Briefing 14-5, December2014. http://www.iie.com/publications/interstitial.cfm?ResearchID=2724.

Posner, Paul, and Jón Blöndal. "Democracies and Deficits: Prospects for Fiscal Responsibility in Democratic Nations." *Governance* 25, no. 1 (2012): 11–34.

Pou Serradell, Victor. *España y la europe comunitaria* [Spain and the European Community]. Navarra: EUNSA,1973.

Pridham, Geoffrey. "The EU's Political Conditionality and Post-Accession Tendencies: Comparisons From Slovakia and Latvia." *Journal of Common Market Studies* 46, no. 2 (2008): 365–387.

Provveditorato generale dello Stato. *Gli organi dello Stato: Guida agli Uffici degli Organi costituzionali, giurisdizionali e amministrativi dello Stato 1998.* Roma: Istituto Poligrafico e Zecca dello Stato, Libreria dello Stato, 1998.

Pryce, Paul. "The 2011 Parliamentary Election in Latvia." *Electoral Studies* 31, no. 3 (2012): 613–639.

Pšeničnik, Dušan, and Michal Kotlarik. "European Foundation:An Opportunity at the Local Level." *Lex localis: Revija za lokalno samoupra* 11, no. 3 (2013): 709–727.

Puchala, Donald. "Domestic Politics and Regional Harmonization in the European Communities." *World Politics* 27, no. 4 (1975): 496–520.

Puchalska, Bogusia."The Charter of Fundamental Rights of the European Union: Central European Opt-Outs and the Politics of Power." *Europe-Asia Studies* 66, no. 3 (2014): 488–506.

Puetter, Uwe. "Europe's Deliberative Intergovernmentalism: The Role of the Council and European Council in EU Economic Governance." *Journal of European Public Policy* 19, no. 2 (2012): 161–178.

Putnam, Robert D. "Diplomacy and Domestic Politics: The Logic of Two-Levels Games." *International Organizations* 42, no. 3 (1988): 427–460.

Radaelli Claudio M., "The Europeanization of Public Policy" in *The Politics of Europeanization*, edited by Kevin Featherstone and Claudio M. Radaelli. Oxford: Oxford University Press, 2003.

Radaelli, Claudio M., and Theofanis Exadaktylos. "New Directions in Europeanizatiou Research." In *Research Agendas in EU Studies: Stalking the Elephant*, edited by Michelle Egan, Neill Nugent, and William E. Paterson, 189–215. Basingstoke: Palgrave Macmillan, 2010.

Rakušanová, Petra. "The Constitutional Debate: A One Man Show? Václav Klaus and the Constitutional Discourse in the Czech Republic." *Perspectives on European Politics and Society* 8, no. 3 (2007): 342–373.

Ram, Melanie H. "Legacies of EU Conditionality: Explaining Post-Accession Adherence to Pre-Accession Rules on Roma." *Europe-Asia Studies* 64, no. 7 (2012): 1191–1218.

Raunio, Tapio. "Finland: Moving in the Opposite Direction." In *The Madisonian Turn: Political Parties and Parliamentary Democracy in Nordic Europe*, edited by Torbjörn Bergman and Kaare Strøm, 112–157. Ann Arbor: University of Michigan Press, 2011.

———. "The Finnish Eduskunta and the European Union: The Strengths and Weaknesses of a Mandating System." In *The Palgrave Handbook of National Parliaments and the European Union*, edited by Claudia Hefftler, Christine Neuhold, Olivier Rozenberg, and Julie Smith, 406–424. Basingstoke: Palgrave Macmillan, 2015.

———. "Hesitant Voters, Committed Elite: Explaining the Lack of Eurosceptic Parties in Finland." *Journal of European Integration* 27, no. 4 (2005): 381–395.

———. "Parlamentaarinen vastuu ulkopolitiikkaan: Suomen ulkopolitiikan johtajuus uuden perustuslain aikana." *Politiikka* 50, no. 4 (2008): 250–265.

———. "Semi-Presidentialism and European Integration: Lessons from Finland for Constitutional Design." *Journal of European Public Policy* 19, no. 4 (2012): 567–584.

———. "Whenever the EU Is Involved, You Get Problems: Explaining the European Policy of the (True) Finns." Sussex European Institute Working Paper 127, 2012.

Raunio, Tapio, and Simon Hix. "Backbenchers Learn to Fight Back: European Integration and Parliamentary Government." In *Europeanised Politics? European Integration and National Systems*, edited by Klaus H. Goetz and Simon Hix, 142–168. London: Frank Cass, 2001.

Raunio, Tapio, and Teija Tiilikainen. *Finland in the European Union*. London: Frank Cass, 2013.

Raunio, Tapio, and Matti Wiberg. "How to Measure the Europeanisation of a National Legislature?" *Scandinavian Political Studies* 33, no. 1 (2010): 74–92.

Reid, T.R. *The United States of Europe: The New Superpower and the End of American Supremacy*. London: Penguin, 2004.

Reinhart, Carmen M., and Kenneth S. Rogoff. *This Time Is Different: Eight Centuries of Financial Folly*. Princeton, NJ: Princeton University Press, 2009.

Richardson, Jeremy, ed. *European Union: Power and Policy-Making*, 3rd ed. New York: Routledge, 2006.

———. "Policy-Making in the EU: Interests, Ideas and Garbage Cans of Primeval Soup." In *European Union: Power and Policy-Making*, 3rd ed., edited by Jeremy Richardson, 1–21. New York: Routledge, 2006.

Risse, Thomas. "A European Identity? Europeanization and the Evolution of Nation State Identities." In *Transforming Europe: Europeanization and Domestic Change*, edited by Maria Green Cowles, James Caporaso, and Thomas Risse, 198–216. Ithaca, NY: Cornell University Press, 2001.

Roberts, Andrew. "How Stable and Reasonable is Postcommunist Public Opinion? The Case of the Czech Republic." *Europe-Asia Studies* 66, no. 6 (2014): 925–944.

Rometsch, Dietrich, and Wolfgang Wessels. *The European Union and Member States: Towards Institutional Fusion.* Manchester: Manchester University Press, 1996.

Rose, Richard. "The End of Consensus in Austria and Switzerland." *Journal of Democracy* 11, no. 2 (2000): 26–40.

Roy, Joaquin, and Aimee Kanner. "Spain and Portugal: Betting on Europe."In *The European Union and the Member States*, edited by Eleanor E. Zeff and Ellen B. Pirro, 235–266. Boulder: Lynne Rienner Publishers, 2001.

Royo, Sebastián. "The 2004 Enlargement: Iberian Lessons for Post-Communist Europe"*South European Society & Politics* 8, nos. 1–2(2003): 287–313.

———. *From Social Democracy to Neoliberalism.* New York: Martin's Press, 2000.

———. "Institutional Degeneration and the Economic Crisis in Spain." *American Behavioral Scientist* 58, no. 12 (2014): 1568–1591.

———. *Lessons from the Economic Crisis in Spain.* New York: Palgrave, 2013a.

———. "The Limits of Convergence: Portugal in the European Union." *South European Society & Politics* 18, no. 2 (2013b): 197–216.

———. "Portugal and Spain in the EU: Paths of Economic Divergence (2000–2007)." *Análise Social* 45, no. 195 (2010): 209–254.

———. *Varieties of Capitalism in Spain: Remaking the Spanish Economy for the New Century.* New York: Palgrave, 2008.

Royo, Sebastián, and Paul Christopher Manuel, eds. *Spain and Portugal in the European Union: The First Fifteen Years.* London: Frank Cass, 2003.

Rutkowski, Aleksander. "Ceilings and Anchors: Fiscal Rules for Poland." *ECFIN Country Focus* 4, no. 4 (2007): 1–6.

Salmon, Trevor C., and William Nicoll. *Building the European Union: A Documentary History and Analysis.* Manchester: Manchester University Press, 1997.

Sartori, Giovanni. *Ingegneria costituzionale comparata.* Bologna: Il Mulino, 1994.

———. *Una occasione mancata.* Roma: Laterza, 1998.

Scharpf, Fritz W. "The Asymmetry of European Integration, or Why the EU Cannot Be a 'Social Market Economy.'" *Socio-Economic Review* 8, no. 2 (2010): 211–250.

———. "A Game-Theoretical Interpretation of Inflation and Unemployment in Western Europe." *Journal of Public Policy* 7, no. 3 (1987): 227–257.

———. "Monetary Union, Fiscal Crisis and the Preemption of Democracy." MPIfG Discussion Paper 11/11, Max Planck Institute for the Study of Societies, Cologne, 2011.

Scheinberg, Anne, and Arthur Mol. "Multiple Modernities: Transitional Bulgaria and the Ecological Modernisation of Solid Waste Management." *Environment and Planning C: Government and Policy* 28, no. 1 (2010): 18–36.

Schiopu, Ioana, and Nikolaus Siegfried. "Determinants of Workers' Remittances: Evidence from the European Neighboring Region." European Central Bank Worker 688, 2006.

Schmidt, Vivien A. *Democracy in Europe: The EU and National Polities.* New York: Oxford University Press, 2006.

Schmitter, Philippe C. "Some Alternative Futures for the European Polity and Their Implications for European Public Policy." In *Adjusting to Europe: The Impact of the European Union on National Institutions and Policies*, edited by Yves Mény, Pierre Muller, and Jean-Louis Quermonne, 25–40. London: Routledge, 1996.

Schneider, Jan David. "Financial Transaction Tax (FTT): Why the EU Needs the FTT But the FTT Does Not Need the EU." European Policy Centre Policy Brief, 2014.

Sekce pro evropské záležitosti Úřadu vlády České republiky. "Ekonomické Dopady Asociační Dohody Eu S Ukrajino." SEZ Policy Brief 1,2014.

Sikk, Allan. "From 'Sexy Men' to 'Socialists Gone Nuts': The European Union and Estonian Party Politics." In *European Union and Party Politics in Central and Eastern Europe*, edited by Paul Lewis and Zdenka Mansfeldová, 40–63. Houndmills: Palgrave Macmillan, 2007.

Slany, Krystyna, and Brygida Solga. "Społeczne skutki poakcesyjnych migracji ludności polski." Komitet Badan nad Migracjami PAN, Warsaw, 2014.

Slaughter, Anne-Marie, Alec Stone Sweet, and Joseph H. H. Weiler. *European Courts and National Courts: Doctrine and Jurisprudence*. Oxford: Hart, 1998.

Šlosarčík, Ivo. "The Czech Republic: Impacts of and Experience with EU Membership." *Eastern Journal of European Studies* 2, no. 2 (2011): 21–30.

———. "Good, Bad or Boring? Three Views of the Czech Presidency." *International Issues & Slovak Foreign Policy Affairs* 18, no. 3 (2009a): 3–11.

———. "The Treaty of Lisbon & the Czech Constitutional Court: Act II." CEPS Policy Brief 197, 2009b.

Soddu, Paolo. *Ugo La Malfa: Il riformista moderno*. Roma: Carocci, 2008.

Solana, Javier. *A Secure Europe for a Better World*. Thessaloniki: European Council 26/06, 2003.

Solvak, Mikhel, and Vello Pettai. "The Parliamentary Elections in Estonia, March 2007." *Electoral Studies* 27, no. 3 (2008): 574–577.

Spence, David. "The Co-Ordination of European Policy by Member States." In *The Council of the European Union*, edited by Martin Westlake, 353–372. London: Cartermill, 1995.

Spendzharova, Aneta Borislavova. "Bringing Europe in? The Impact of EU Conditionality on Bulgarian and Romanian Politics." *Southeast European Politics* 4, no. 2–3 (2003): 141–156.

Spendzharova, Aneta Borislavova, and Milada Anna Vachudova. "Catching Up? Consolidating Liberal Democracy in Bulgaria and Romania After EU Accession." *West European Politics* 35, no. 1 (2012): 39–58.

Spiegel, Peter. "Inside Europe's Plan Z." *Financial Times*, May 14, 2014. http://www.ft.com/intl/cms/s/0/0ac1306e-d508-11e3-9187-00144feabdc0.html.

Spinelli, Altiero. *Diario europeo*, Vol. 3, *1976–1986*, edited by Paolini Edmondo. Bologna: Il Mulino, 1992.

———. *Ilmanifesto di ventotene*. Bologna: Il Mulino, 1991.

Spirova, Maria. "Bulgaria Since 1989." In *Central and Southeast European Politics Since 1989*, edited by Sabrina P. Ramet, 401–420. Cambridge: Cambridge University Press, 2010.

Spirova, Maria, and Boyka Stefanova. "The European Dimension of Minority Political Representation: Bulgaria and Romania Compared." *East European Politics & Societies* 26, no. 1 (2012): 75–92.

Stefanou, Constantin. *Cyprus and the EU: The Road to Accession*. Aldershot: Ashgate, 2005.

Steinmetz, Robert, and Anders Wivel, eds. *Small States in Europe: Challenges and Opportunities*. Farnham: Ashgate, 2010.

Stevenson, David. *Cataclysm: The First World War as Political Tragedy*. New York: Basic Books, 2004.

Stokes, Bruce. "Key Takeaways from the European Union Survey." Pew Research Center, May 12, 2014. http://www.pewresearch.org/fact-tank/2014/05/12/5-key-takeaways-from-the-European-Union-Survey.

Stubb, Alexander, Helen Wallace, and John Peterson. "The Policy-Making Process."In *The European Union: How Does it Work?* edited by Elizabeth Bomberg and Alexander Stubb, 136–155. Oxford: Oxford University Press, 2003.

Štulhofer, Aleksandar. "Euroscepticism in Croatia: On the Far Side of Rationality?" In *Croatian Accession to the European Union*, vol. 4, *The Challenges of Participation*, edited by Katarina Ott, 141–160. Zagreb: Institute of Public Finance and Friedrich Ebert Stiftung, 2006.

Svensson, Palle. "Five Danish Referendums on the European Community and the European Union: A Critical Assessment of the Franklin Thesis." *European Journal of Political Research* 41, no. 6 (2002): 733–750.

Szczerbiak, Aleks. *Poland Within the European Union: New Awkward Partner or New Heart of Europe?* Abingdon: Routledge, 2012.

Tamames, Ramon. *Guía del Mercado Común Europeo: España en la Europe de los doce* [Guide of the European Common Market: Spain in the Europe of the Twelve]. Madrid: Alianza Editorial,1986.

Tanasoiu, Cosmina. "Europeanization Post-Accession: Rule Adoption and National Political Elites in Romania and Bulgaria." *Southeast European and Black Sea Studies* 12, no. 1 (2012): 173–193.

Telò, Mario. "L'Italia nel processo di costruzione europea." In *Storia Dell'Italia repubblicana*, vol. 3, 131–253. Torino: Einaudi, 1996.

Thatcher, Margaret. *The Downing Street Years*. London: Harper Collins, 1993.

Theophanous, Andreas. "The Way Out of the Cyprus Economic Crisis." Notre-Europe —Jacques Delors Institute Policy Paper 96, Paris, September 2013. http://www.notre-europe.eu/media/thewayoutofthecypruscrisistheophanous -ne-jdisept2013.pdf.

Thorhallsson, Baldur. *Iceland and European Integration: On the Edge*. Aldershot: Ashgate, 2004.

———. "The Icelandic Crash and its Consequences: A Small State Without Economic and Political Shelter." In *Small States in Europe: Challenges and Opportunities*, edited by R. Steinmetz and A. Wivel, 199–214. Aldershot: Ashgate, 2010.

———. *The Role of Small States in the European Union*. Aldershot: Ashgate, 2000.

Thorhallsson, Baldur, and Rainer Kattel. "Neoliberal Small States and Economic Crisis: Lessons for Democratic Corporatism." *Journal of Baltic Studies* 44, no. 1 (2013): 83–103.

Thulesius, Hans O., and Birgitta E. Grahn. "Reincentivizing—ANew Theory of Work and Work Absence." *BMC Health Services Research* 7, no. 100 (2007). doi:10.1186/1472-6963-7-100.

Tiilikainen, Teija. *Europe and Finland: Defining the Political Identity of Finland in Western Europe*. Aldershot: Ashgate, 1998.

———. "Finland—An EU Member with a Small State Identity." *Journal of European Integration* 28, no. 1 (2006): 73–87.

———. "Suomen ulkopoliittinen johtamisjärjestelmä uuden perustuslain mukaan." *Politiikka* 45, no. 3 (2003): 212–222.

Tomšík, Karel. "Changes of the Czech Agriculture After Accessing to the EU." *Advances in Agriculture & Botanics: International Journal of the Bioflux Society* 2, no. 2 (2010): 111–120.

Traxler, Franz. "Austria: Still the Country of Corporatism." In *Changing Industrial Relations in Europe*, edited by Anthony Ferner and Richard Hyman, 239–261. Oxford: Blackwell, 1998.

Treib, Oliver. "The Voter Says No, But Nobody Listens: Causes and Consequences of the Eurosceptic Vote in the 2014 European Elections." *Journal of European Public Policy* 21, no. 10 (2014): 1541–1554.

Tweede Kamer der Staten-Generaal. "Vaststelling van de begrotingsstaten van het Ministerie van Economische Zaken (XIII) voor het jaar 2014." *Vergaderjaar 2013–2014*, 33 750 xiii, no. 2. The Hague, 2013.

UK Parliament. "European Union, Audit of Benefits and Costs of UK Membership) Bill."(2010) http://services.parliament.uk/bills/2010-12/europeanunionaudit ofbenefitsandcostsofukmembership.html accessed 12.04.15

———. "United Kingdom, Withdrawal from the European Union Bill." (2013). http://services.parliament.uk/bills/2013-14/unitedkingdomwithdrawalfrom theeuropeanunion.html (Accessed December 4, 2015).

———. UK Referendum Bill (2014): http://services.parliament.uk/bills/2014-15 /europeanunionreferendum.html. (Accessed October 22, 2014).

Urbániková, Marína, and Jaromír Volek. "Between Europeanization and De-Europeanization: A Comparative Content Analysis of the Pre-Election Presentation of the EU Agenda in the Czech Quality Press." *Communications* 39, no. 4 (2014): 457–481.

Vachudova, Milada Anna. "EU Leverage and National Interests in the Balkans: The Puzzles of Enlargement Ten Years On." *Journal of Common Market Studies* 51, no. 1 (2014): 122–138.

———. *Europe Undivided: Democracy, Leverage, and Integration After Communism.* Oxford: Oxford University Press, 2005.

Vanags, Alf. "Economic Integration and Cohesion in the Baltic Sea Region: A Critical Perspective from the Baltic States." *Journal of Baltic Studies* 42, no. 1 (2011): 91–102.

Vanderhill, Rachel. "The EU and Non-Accession States: The Cases of Belarus and Ukraine." *Perspectives* 16, no. 2 (2008): 53–76.

Vanhuysse, Pieter. *Divide and Pacify: Strategic Social Policies and Political Protests in Post-Communist Democracies.* Budapest: Central European University Press, 2006.

Van Kessel, Stijn, and Saskia Hollander. "Europe and the Dutch Parliamentary Election." EPERN Election Briefing 71, September 2012.

Van Vooren, Bart. "A Legal-Institutional Perspective on the European External Action Service." Centre for the Law of EU External Relations,Working Paper No. 124 2010/7, The Hague, 2010.

Varsori, Antonio. *L'Italia nelle relazioni internazionali dal 1943 al 1992.* Roma: Laterza, 1998.

Väyrynen, Raimo. "Finland and the European Community: Changing Elite Bargains." *Cooperation and Conflict* 28, no. 1 (1993): 31–46.

Vital, David. *The Inequality of States.* Westport, CT: Greenwood Press, 1972.

Vuković, Vuk. "Korupcija u javnim nabavama i posljedice na politički reizbor: Primjer lokalne samouprave u Hrvatskoj." Hrvatska Udruga Banaka Working Paper, September 2014.

Waever, Ole. "Explaining Europe by Decoding Discourses." In *Explaining European Integration,* edited by Anders Wivel, 100–146. Copenhagen: Political Studies Press, 1998.

Wallace, William. "Europe as a Confederation: The Community and the Nation State," *Journal of Common Market Studies* 21, no. 1(1982): 57–68.

Watts, Ronald L. *Comparing Federal Systems.* Montreal: Institute of Intergovernmental Relations, 2008.

Wendel, Mattias. "Lisbon Before the Courts: Comparative Perspectives." *European Constitutional Law Review* 7, no. 1 (2011): 96–137.

Wessels, Wolfgang, Andreas Maurer, and Jurgen Mittag, eds. *Fifteen into One? The European Union and Its Member States.* Manchester: Manchester University Press, 2003.

Westlake, Martin. *The Council of the European Union.* London: Cartemill, 1996.

Wiener, Antje, and Thomas Dietz, eds.*European Integration Theory.* New York: Oxford University Press, 2004.

Wiles, James L., and Richard B. Finnegan. *Aspirations and Realities: A Documentary History of Economic Development Policy Since 1922.* Westport, CT: Greenwood Press, 1993.

Williamson, John. "What Should the World Bank Think About the Washington Consensus?" *World Bank Research Observer* 41, no. 2 (2000): 251–264.

Wind, Marlene. "The Blind, the Deaf and the Dumb! How Domestic Politics Turned the Danish Schengen Controversy into a Foreign Policy Crisis." In *Danish Foreign Policy Yearbook 2012*, edited by Nanna Hvidt and Hans Moritzen, 131–156. Copenhagen: Danish Institute For International Studies, 2012.

———. "The European Rights Revolution." In *Denmark and the European Union*, edited by Lee Miles and Anders Wivel, 159–174. London: Routledge 2014.

———. "The European Union as a Polycentric Polity: Returning to a Neo-Medieval Europa?" In *European Consitutionalism Beyond the State*, edited by Marlene Wind and Joseph H. H. Weiler, 103–135. Cambridge: Cambridge University Press, 2003.

———. "The Nordics, the EU and the Reluctance Towards Supranational Judicial Review." *Journal of Common Market Studies* 48, no. 4 (2010): 1039–1063.

———. "When Parliament Comes First: The Danish Concept of Democracy Meets the European Union." *Nordic Journal of Human Rights* 27, no. 2 (2009): 272–288.

Winzen, Thomas. "European Integration and National Parliamentary Oversight Institutions." *European Union Politics* 14, no. 2 (2013): 297–323.

Wright, Vincent. "The National Coordination of European Policy-Making: Negotiating the Quagmire." In *European Union: Power and Policy-Making*, edited by Jeremy Richardson, 148–169. New York: Routledge, 1996.

Wyplosz, Charles. "Europe's Quest for Fiscal Discipline."European Economy Economic Papers 498,April2013.http://ec.europa.eu/economy_finance/publications/economic_paper/2013/ecp498_en.pdf. (Accessed February 8, 2014).

Zahariadis, Nikolaos. "Complexity, Coupling, and Policy Effectiveness: The European Response to the Greek Sovereign Debt Crisis." *Journal of Public Policy* 32, no. 2 (2012): 99–116.

———. "National Fiscal Profligacy and European Institutional Adolescence: The Greek Trigger to Europe's Sovereign Debt Crisis." *Government & Opposition* 48, no. 1 (2013): 33–54.

———. "The Politics of Risk-Sharing: Fiscal Federalism and the Greek Debt Crisis." *Journal of European Integration* 35, no. 3 (2013): 271–285.

Zeff, Eleanor E., and Ellen Pirro, eds. *The European Union and the Member States*, 2nd ed. Boulder: Lynne Rienner Publishers, 2006.

Zubek, Radoslaw, and Katarina Staronovo. "Organizing for EU Implementation: The Europeanization of Government Ministries in Estonia, Poland, and Slovenia." *Public Administration* 90, no. 4 (2012): 937–956.

Zupančič, Rok, and Miha Hribernik. "Small States as 'Contributing Nations' to the EU's Normative Power: The Case of Slovenia." *Romanian Journal of European Affairs* 11, no. 4 (2011): 34–49.

Zweifel, Thomas D. *International Organizations and Democracy: Accountability, Politics and Power.* Boulder: Lynne Rienner Publishers, 2005.

The Contributors

Eleanor E. Zeff: Associate Professor of Political Science, Drake University, Des Moines, Iowa

Ellen B. Pirro: Professor of Political Science, Iowa State University, Ames, Iowa

Karen M. Anderson, Associate Professor, Political Science, University of Southampton UK.

Federiga Bindi, Jean Monnet Chair, University of Rome Tor Vergata, Rome, Italy & Sr. Fellow SAIS John Hopkins, Washington DC

Renee Buhr, Associate Professor, Department of Political Science, University of St. Thomas, St. Paul, Minnesota.

Natalia Cuglesan: Lecturer, Altiero Spinelli Center for the Study of European Governance, Babeş-Bolyai University, Cluj-Napoca, Romania

Christian Deubner, (Dr.habil.), FEPS Scientific Council, Brussels, Leiter Europagruppe SWP Berlin A.D.

Leif Johan Eliasson, Associate Professor of Political Science, East Stroudsburg University, PA.

Richard Finnegan, Professor Emeritus, Stonehill College, Easton, MA.

Artur Gruszak, Associate Professor of International Relations, Jagiellonian University in Krakow, Poland

Mihaela Herbel, Researcher, Department of International Studies and Contemporary History, Babeş-Bolyai University, Cluj-Napoca, Romania

Zdenek Kudrna, Austrian Academy of Sciences, Institute for European Integration, Vienna, Austria

Carl Lankowski, Deputy Director of Area Studies at the Foreign Service Institute, U.S. Department of State.

Peter Loedel, Professor, Department of Political Science, West Chester University, UK

Janet Mather, Principal Lecturer in Politics, Department of History, Politics and Philosophy, Manchester Metropolitan University, UK.

John McCormick, Professor, Department of Poitical Science, Indiana University and Perdue University at Indianapolis (IUPUI), Indiana

Tamás Novák, Austrian Marshall Plan Foundation Fellow in Central European Studies at the Center for Transatlantic Relations, Johns Hopkins University, and Deputy Director of the Institute of World Economics, Hungarian Academy of Sciences.

Luka Oreškovi , Co-Chair, Emerging Europe Business and Government Study Group, Harvard University Center for European Studies, Cambridge, MA.

Roderick Pace, Professor, Institute for European Studies, University of Malta, Malta

Tapio Raunio, Professor of Political Science, School of Management, University of Tampere, Finland,

Sebastian Royo, Professor of Government and Vice Provost. Suffolk University, MA.

Vuk Vukovic, London School of Economics, Lecturer; and Department of Economics, Zagreb School of Economics and Management, Great Britain

Kieran Williams, Visiting Professor, Political Science, Drake University, Des Moines, Iowa

Marlene Wind, Professor, Law Colleges at both University of Copenhagen, Denmark and University of Oslo, Norway.

Nikolaos Zahariadis, Professor, University of Alabama at Birmingham.

Index

About the Book

CAN THE EUROPEAN UNION SURVIVE REPEATED ECONOMIC CRISES? If it survives, will it stay as it is or take on a new form? This new edition of *The European Union and the Member States*, fully revised and updated, addresses these questions as it explores the complex relationship between the EU and each of its now twenty-eight members.

The country chapters follow a common format, considering: How and in what areas does EU policy affect, and how is it affected by, the member states? What mechanisms do the member states use to implement EU policy? What is each state's compliance record? Covering the full range of political, economic, and social issues, the authors offer an insightful discussion of the interplay of EU initiatives with strong, existing national policies and traditions.

Eleanor E. Zeff is associate professor of political science at Drake University. **Ellen B. Pirro** is lecturer in political science at Iowa State University.